The practical management of the

developmentally disabled child

The practical management of the
developmentally disabled child.

ALBERT P. SCHEINER, M.D., F.A.A.P.

Co-Director, Child Development Service;
Professor of Pediatrics,
University of Massachusetts Medical School,
Worcester, Massachusetts

ISRAEL F. ABROMS, M.D., F.A.A.P.

Chief of Pediatric Neurology;
Professor of Pediatrics and Neurology,
University of Massachusetts Medical School,
Worcester, Massachusetts

with 155 *illustrations and 1 color plate*

The C. V. Mosby Company

ST. LOUIS • TORONTO • LONDON   1980

WS
350.6
S 35 p
1980

LIBRARY
CORNELL UNIVERSITY
MEDICAL COLLEGE
NEW YORK CITY

AUG 2 1980

Copyright © 1980 by The C. V. Mosby Company

All rights reserved. No part of this book may be reproduced
in any manner without written permission of the publisher.

Printed in the United States of America

The C. V. Mosby Company
11830 Westline Industrial Drive, St. Louis, Missouri 63141

Library of Congress Cataloging in Publication Data

Scheiner, Albert P   1928-
    The practical management of the developmentally dis-
abled child.

    Bibliography: p.
    Includes index.
    1. Developmentally disabled children. 2. Child
development deviations. I. Abroms, Israel F., 1933-
joint author. II. Title. [DNLM: 1. Child development deviations.   WS350.6 P895]
RJ135.S36   618.92   80-13725
ISBN 0-8016-0061-8

GW/CB/B 9 8 7 6 5 4 3 2 1   02/A/250

Contributors

ISRAEL F. ABROMS, M.D., F.A.A.P.

Chief of Pediatric Neurology;
Professor of Pediatrics and Neurology,
University of Massachusetts Medical School,
Worcester, Massachusetts

CARLTON AKINS, M.D.

Associate Professor, Department of Orthopedics,
University of Massachusetts Medical School,
Worcester, Massachusetts

LOUIS E. BARTOSHESKY, M.D., M.P.H.

Assistant Professor of Pediatrics,
Center for Birth Defect Evaluation and
Genetic Counseling, Tufts–New England
Medical Center Hospital, Boston, Massachusetts

ANTHONY BASHIR, Ph.D.

Lecturer in Pediatric Medicine,
Harvard Medical School;
Division of Hearing and Speech,
Children's Hospital Medical Center,
Boston, Massachusetts

CONSTANCE U. BATTLE, M.D., F.A.A.P.

Professor, Child Health and Development,
George Washington University
School of Medicine and Health Sciences;
Medical Director and Chief Executive Officer,
The Hospital for Sick Children, Washington, D.C.

ROBIN DAVIDSON, M.D.

Associate Professor, Department of Neurosurgery,
University of Massachusetts Medical School,
Worcester, Massachusetts

CAROL M. DONOVAN, M.A., R.P.T.

Instructor in Pediatrics,
University of Massachusetts Medical School,
Worcester, Massachusetts

PAUL H. DWORKIN, M.D.

Assistant Professor of Pediatrics,
West Virginia University School of Medicine,
Morgantown, West Virginia

F. EDWARD GALLAGHER, D.M.D.

Director of Training for Dentistry for the
Developmental Evaluation Clinic,
Children's Hospital Medical Center,
Boston, Massachusetts

TIMOTHY HOPKINS, M.D.

Instructor in Urology, Department of Surgery,
University of Massachusetts Medical School;
Attending Urologist, Memorial Hospital,
Worcester, Massachusetts

BURTON F. JAFFE, M.D.

Otolaryngologist, Beth Israel Hospital,
Children's Hospital Medical Center,
Boston, Massachusetts;
Brookline Hospital, Brookline, Massachusetts;
Cambridge City Hospital, Cambridge, Massachusetts;
Newton-Wellesley Hospital,
Newton, Massachusetts

MELVIN D. LEVINE, M.D.

Associate Professor of Pediatrics;
Chief, Division of Ambulatory Pediatrics,
Children's Hospital Medical Center,
Boston, Massachusetts

DAVID M. LUTERMAN, D.Ed.

Professor of Communication Disorders;
Director of Thayer Linsley Nursery,
Department of Communication Disorders,
Emerson College, Boston, Massachusetts

NEAL A. McNABB, M.D.

Clinical Associate Professor,
University of Rochester Department of Pediatrics;
Director of Pediatrics,
Genessee Hospital, Rochester, New York

PANOS G. PANAGAKOS, M.D.

Assistant Professor of Orthopedic Surgery,
University of Massachusetts Medical School,
Worcester, Massachusetts;
Chief of Orthopedics, St. Joseph's Hospital,
Lowell, Massachusetts;
Consultant in Orthopedic Surgery,
Handicapped Children's Services,
Commonwealth of Massachusetts

I. B. PLESS, M.D.

Professor of Pediatrics,
Epidemiology and Health, McGill University;
Director, Community Pediatric Research Program,
Montreal Children's Hospital, Montreal,
Quebec, Canada

RICHARD M. ROBB, M.D.

Associate Professor of Ophthalmology,
Harvard Medical School;
Ophthalmologist-in-Chief,
Children's Hospital Medical Center,
Boston, Massachusetts

ALBERT P. SCHEINER, M.D., F.A.A.P.

Co-Director, Child Development Service;
Professor of Pediatrics,
University of Massachusetts Medical School,
Worcester, Massachusetts

HOWARD C. SHANE, Ph.D.

Division of Hearing and Speech and
Developmental Evaluation Clinic,
Children's Hospital Medical Center,
Boston, Massachusetts

EDWIN A. SUMPTER, M.D.

Associate Professor of Pediatrics,
Department of Pediatrics,
University of Massachusetts Medical School,
Worcester, Massachusetts

To
our loving wives
Barbie and Elva
for their friendship, support, and
constructive criticism

Foreword

There is only one phrase adequate to describe the kind of change that has occurred in the last decade regarding the care and training of the child with a developmental disability — a social revolution. This revolution and the new humanism are providing handicapped children and adults with a restoration to full citizenship, a change in public perception, reinforcing legislation, and a highly informed consumer activist force. In professional areas the improvement has engendered the formation of supporting interdisciplinary teams, who now operate with a fresh and zealous determination. Pediatricians and allied professionals of the past labored steadily and credibly, but without complete fulfillment. They now find themselves on the "front line" as enhanced service resolves are being formed on all sides. The current changes in the world of the child with special needs have been created with only limited leadership from physicians, but a very significant opportunity exists for restitution of this potential. Pediatricians and family physicians have critical and basic contributions and can provide a mature and stabilizing role in the revolution. This book gives substance to the facets of continuing care responsibility, which rests with the physician, and offers viable guidelines for the empathetic physician.

Three action areas thus characterize the work of the "new" pediatrician, all well discussed in this text. First is *participation in team activities*. For the child with multiple problems there are inevitably multiple factors in the required support system. Physicians, who have historically been accustomed to definitive problem solving in their own offices, are now learning that they can effectively share program decisions with other child care experts in the setting of an egalitarian conference. It is characteristic to discover that the truly interdisciplinary system is enormously rewarding, especially regarding the potential for reaching ultimate single-discipline goals.

The second element is *availability of program monitoring or coordination of responsibilities*. Present services for handicapped children often focus on immediate or short-term objectives and lack personal assignment for program management or continuity during life passages. The pediatrician with special involvement in the child and the family can, on a continuing basis, offer a special relevance as programs evolve. Here again, the responsibility exists for establishing communication systems with the multiple components of child care. Participation by the earnest pediatrician will usually be deeply appreciated.

The third issue is *special advocacy for the needs and special features of children with developmental disabilities*. Articulate vigilance is required even though human rights on the behalf of children and the handicapped population are now technically guaranteed. Physicians have a leadership potential for public education and community guidance. This has been traditionally granted by society, and this legacy should be positively utilized.

These three roles all carry a real excitement regarding professional fulfillment for the pediatrician. They represent areas in which they can participate in a special way in the revolution. Beyond this, it is implicit that inspired medical care activities are the core of the relationship with the child and family. The primary physician can bring special insight to help management for the handicapped child. The physician working in community programs and clinics can provide particular guidance for the child with special needs. The pediatrician in the referral center can offer definitive study of and support for this troubled population. All can learn extensively from experiences of these remarkable parents and from their fellow workers in the child care world. Pediatricians can, at the same time, provide special insight, counsel, coordination, and leadership in the best traditions of stewardship, which is intrinsic to their guild.

This book provides a rich resource of information and programatic ideas for the modern pediatrician and family physician, consonant with the concepts of the evolution/revolution mentioned earlier. The editors and the contributors are to be commended for an adventurous outreach.

Allen C. Crocker

Associate Professor of Pediatrics,
Harvard Medical School;
Director of the Developmental Evaluation Clinic,
Children's Hospital Medical Center,
Boston, Massachusetts

The work of the pediatrician is tending away from being predominantly concerned with acute illness and increasingly toward the care of children with continuing disorders.*

Ronald C. Mac Keith
(1908-1977)

Preface

Services to developmentally disabled children and their families challenge the most capable and caring primary care physician.†‡ Epidemiologic studies§‖ indicate that the prevalence of chronic illness ranges from 5% to 20% of all children, depending on the definition of chronic illness and methods used for the identification of these youngsters. If learning disabled, mentally retarded, and behaviorally disturbed children are all included, the prevalence easily accounts for one third of all youngsters served by the primary care physician.

The response of the service system to the time-consuming and complex care of these children has been a proliferation of clinics, agencies, schools, and mental health services, which has resulted in the erosion of the role of the pediatrician and family physician. The increase in the number of specialized services dissects the child into several functional parts and tends to increase the burden on the family in terms of money, time, and energy. Studies*† that have reviewed the roles of the primary care physician and the specialty clinic indicate that although specialty clinics function reasonably well in the medical management of the youngsters, there is a striking lack of involvement of the primary care physician. A large percentage of the children receive primary care from the specialty care source, and a surprising number of parents cannot identify any primary care source whatever. One cannot help but conclude that many parents are confused as to who is responsible for their child's health care and that they need an overall director for their child's rehabilitation program.

Pless‡ states, "Clearly, there is not one challenge but many. What is at stake is nothing less than pediatrics' ability to provide effective care to a group of children who more than any other have first claim on it." Pless' proposal for advocacy includes children with learning disabilities, mental retardation, behavioral difficulties, epilepsy, cerebral palsy, spina bifida, and other chronic illnesses. Although there are obvious differences among diabetes, learning disabilities, spina bifida, and arthritis,

*Mac Keith, R. C.: Contributions to the journal, Dev. Med. Child Neurol. **20**:14, 1978.

†Mattsson, A.: Long-term physical illness in childhood—a challenge to psychosocial adaptation, Pediatrics **50**:801, 1972.

‡Pless, I. B., Saterwhite, B., Van Vechten, D.: Division, duplication, and neglect: patterns of care for children with chronic disorders, Child Care Health Dev. **4**:55, 1978.

§Haggerty, R. J., Roghmann, K. J., and Pless, I. B.: Child health and the community, New York, 1975, John Wiley & Sons, Inc.

‖Pless, I. B., and Douglas, J. N. B.: Chronic illness in childhood, J. Pediatr. **47**:405, 1971.

*Kanthor, H., et al.: Areas of responsibility in the health care of the multiply handicapped child, Pediatrics **54**:779, 1974.

†Pless, I. B., Saterwhite, B., Van Vechten, D.: Division, duplication, and neglect: patterns of care for children with chronic disorders, Child Care Health Dev. **4**:55, 1978.

‡Pless, I. B.: The challenge of chronic illness, Am. J. Dis. Child. **126**:741, 1973.

many of the management concepts are similar.

We have chosen to focus on the children with learning disabilities, sensory deficits, mental retardation, behavioral difficulties, epilepsy, cerebral palsy, and spina bifida because we believe that services to these children share a common body of knowledge in management skills, neurodevelopmental evaluation, and cognitive assessment techniques. We believe that the time-consuming care and complex nature of these children's disabilities has in many instances expelled them from the mainstream of primary care. This exclusion has resulted in further disruption of the family as it attempts to cope with daily living and struggles to obtain comprehensive services.

The object of this book is to provide primary care physicians, medical students, nurses, occupational and physical therapists, speech pathologists, social workers, psychologists, and educators with a guide to the practical skills necessary to screen, diagnose, evaluate, and develop treatment plans for developmentally disabled children. The manner in which the professional should serve the developmentally disabled child and family is suggested. We include the genetic aspects of some of these disorders and their implication for the family as well as methods for the identification of the infant who is at high risk for developmental sequelae. Support mechanisms that we have found helpful for families are suggested. Techniques for neurodevelopmental office screening and assessment are described for early identification of the child with cerebral palsy, a developmental delay, or a learning disability. The management of children with spina bifida, seizure disorders, behavior disorders, and developmental delays is discussed along with the individual contributions of the pediatric neurologist, orthopedist, otolaryngologist, developmental center personnel, and myelodysplasia clinic staff. Practical aspects such as methods of record keeping are described. The rehabilitation and intervention processes for these youngsters are presented along with the impact that these disabilities have on families. Assessment of audiological, visual, and speech difficulties is included because of the frequent association of these conditions with developmental disabilities and the problems they present, even in the absence of multiple handicaps.

Our overall goal is to present a functional conceptual approach for physicians and allied professionals that is applicable to the busy clinic or office. The complexity of individual disabilities requires a consistent, methodical approach plus the professionals' interest and willingness to give of themselves in terms of time and energy. Many of the diagnostic and assessment techniques can be performed by allied professionals. The decision as to which method or model should be used would be determined by prevailing circumstances, the individual primary care physician, or the interdisciplinary team. The decision to seek consultation from other professionals should also be made with the existing circumstances and the individual needs of the child and family in mind. The contributors have all had extensive experience in primary care or in the direction of services to developmentally disabled children. They integrate theoretical concepts of care with practical application to provide continuous, comprehensive, community care to developmentally disabled children and their families.

• • •

The scholars, teachers, friends, and relatives who have influenced our careers, thoughts, and writing are numerous. Major contributors to our professional ethos and actions may have been unconsciously omitted, but to all we owe our motivation for the writing of and many ideas presented in *The Practical Management of the Developmentally Disabled Child.*

We are especially indebted to Margaret Baber, Charles Barlow, William Berenberg, William Bradford, Berry Brazelton, Randolph Byers, Stewart Clifford, William Cochran, Cecil Drillien, Gilbert Forbes, Bernard Freedman, Barry Hanshaw, Sam Javett, Cesare Lombroso, Jim MacWhinney, Donald Matson, David Pyke, Jack Tizard, and Keasley Welch.

We thank our children—Caryn, Stephen, and David Abroms; Laurie, Cathy, and Martha Scheiner; and Tod Gulick—for providing us with a meaningful understanding of child development and our hope for the future.

Albert P. Scheiner
Israel F. Abroms

Contents

The practical management of the

developmentally disabled child

The doctor who cares for children is more highly qualified to care for a child who has a chronic illness than he often recognizes. In a chronic illness the child and family need professional allies on whom they can depend to be their vigorous advocate, to enlist the best help available, to communicate closely with other professionals, and to coordinate or be aware of all that is going on.

M. Green and R. J. Haggerty[50]

1

The role of the primary care physician

Constance U. Battle

For decades most developmentally disabled children have been inextricably trapped like "the man without a country" in the world of primary care. Delivery of the multiple services required has been fragmented, uncoordinated, and competitive. As a result the primary care physician's role has been eroded. The few pedi-atricians who were strongly interested believed themselves to be vastly underprepared to take on the multiple problems of the developmentally disabled child and his family. These problems are neither exciting nor easily solved. What is a pediatrician to do? Even with concerted effort, the end result can be discouraging. On the other hand, helping a child and his family achieve equilibrium and even *some* of the satisfaction, achievements, and pleasures of life easily attainable by the normal child can be one of the deeply satisfying and ongoing joys of a pediatrician's professional life.

A significant number of developmentally disabled children will always require services. They are our responsibility as pediatricians. The practice of medicine and pediatrics is changing and expanding. Nutritional disorders have nearly disappeared, infectious diseases are disappearing, and there may be increased survival among markedly impaired children. However, certain disabilities in childhood, for example, those due to accidents, will never disappear. In addition to a reduced need for traditional care, there is increased awareness, sensitivity, and ability to detect developmental delay. With a prevalence of between 10% and 30%, depending on which diagnostic categories are included and on how the population is assessed, children with developmental disabilities are clearly part of America's hope for the future.

Among a significant portion of the 7000 re-

1

cent graduates of pediatric residency programs surveyed by the Task Force on Pediatric Education, there seems to be an incipient awareness that their residencies had not provided sufficient experience in the following areas[105]:

- Longitudinal rather than episodical care of well children (50%)
- Care of patients with chronic diseases such as diabetes, cystic fibrosis, and rheumatoid arthritis (18%)
- Care of patients with various manifestations of chronic cerebral dysfunction (40%)
- Care of patients with psychosocial and/or behavioral problems (54%)
- Ambulatory care in the community and within the medical school or hospital (56%)
- Preparation for involvement in child advocacy (e.g., learning about the special problems of poor children, children of racial minorities, children in single-parent homes, abused children, and handicapped children) (51%)
- Community programs affecting children (custodial institutions, nursery schools, juvenile courts, and programs for exceptional children) (73%)

If training in each of these identified areas had been adequate, the pediatrician would be able to leave the training period equipped with a critical basis for competence as well as comfortable in the provision of pediatric primary care for the developmentally disabled child.

Of the fellows who responded to a survey by the Pediatric Manpower Committee of the American Academy of Pediatric (AAP),[26] 1600 indicated the following subspecialty interests that they currently emphasize or would like to emphasize:

- Behavioral and emotional problems
- Cerebral palsy
- Child psychiatry
- Chronic diseases
- Parent counselling
- Developmental delay and/or child development
- Developmental disabilities
- Habilitation and teratology of handicapped children
- Mental retardation
- Rehabilitation

In summary, approximately one-fifth of the areas of emphasis concern aspects of delivery of care to the developmentally disabled child.

The recent collection of data and analyses by the Pediatric Task Force on Education and the Pediatric Manpower Committee[26] are extremely helpful for future planning on an individual as well as a group basis. Consideration and discussion of lacunae and recommendations for pediatric education and practice are not new, however, and have occurred over the past two decades.[18,54,56,88] In the late 1960s Brent and Morse[23] indicated that the residency program should simulate the practice situation more closely and that the role of the practitioner must be elevated within pediatric departments. This could be accomplished by establishing faculty positions for deliverers of primary pediatric care who have a legitimate academic role, namely, the delivery of responsible health care and research in the areas of pediatric education and delivery of care. Programs for training the pediatrician in private pediatricians' offices have come in and out of vogue for many years, but currently an organized movement is revealing more interest and personal investment in teaching by private pediatricians.[3]

An AAP survey indicating that only 11% of those fellows surveyed noted an increase in the demand for chronic illness services[26] appears incomprehensible to those pediatricians whose exclusive work is with developmentally disabled children. About 20% noted a significant decrease, whereas 60% noted no change. However, two other findings are readily understandable—an increase in demand for services regarding school problems noted by 60% of the pediatricians and a decrease in demand for care of sick patients in the hospital. The finding by the Pediatric Manpower Survey can be explained by combining the number of pediatricians who noted a significant increase in demand for counselling services (38%) with those who noted an increase in demand for chronic illness services specifically (11%). Thus nearly half of the pediatricians (49%) perceive an increase in demand for nontraditional services for which they were not trained.

Hansen and Aradine,[59] in 1974, reviewed the changes occurring in the delivery of pediatric primary health care and the increased participation in the process by patients and families. Believing that such sharing of responsibility could make pediatrics more effective and satisfactory, they summarized the essential goals of primary care: competence, efficiency, and accessibility. Secondary goals of primary care include comprehensiveness, continuity of care, and coordination in resource utilization within the medical, social, and educational systems. Two other goals for primary care debated at the time of the Hansen-Oradine article but well recognized today characterize the issues of a changing professional-patient relationship: primary care must be patient and family centered; primary care serves a multiprofessional interdisciplinary function.

Parents repeatedly seek the recommendation of a physician in their community who will care for the child with a major, or even minor, developmental delay. Kanthor, Pless, and Satterwhite[69] found that in a study of mothers with children suffering from spina bifida primary physicians were perceived as contributing little to the rehabilitative and coordinative care for these children. Most said that no single physician was responsible for providing overall direction to their child's care.

In conclusion, developmentally disabled children exist and require multiple, complex, and coordinated services within and without the traditional structure of medicine. The future of all child health care, especially that of the child with a developmental disability, is linked to the future role of the primary care pediatrician. Forces already in motion will inevitably reduce the pediatrician's traditional work load.[56] This chapter will provide the primary care pediatrician with an overall approach to the practical management of children with developmental disabilities.

PRIMARY CARE
Definition of primary care

In a statement on primary care in pediatrics, the American Academy of Pediatrics indicated the fundamental attributes, or anchor points, of primary care and phrased them in terms of pediatric services as follows[4]:
- Acceptance of continuing or longitudinal

responsibility for the whole child in health and disease from conception to young adulthood is the characteristic patient care approach of the pediatrician.
- Accessible first contact medical care to children for any health or disease problem, including all forms of preventive care, is the common task of the pediatrician.
- Coordination of required medical services beyond the basic level of care is part of the primary care provided by the pediatrician. (Pediatricians also provide other specialists with most medical services at a secondary level and many at the tertiary level, by necessity making referrals.)
- Primary care functions of the pediatrician also include organization and provision of diagnostic and treatment services on a community-wide basis, including screening, health education, outreach, and follow-up when appropriate to ensure that prevention and other health needs of all children are met.

Current trends toward primary care

A solid trend reflective of current interest in primary care has emerged in recent years among medical students in America who use the National Intern and Resident Matching Program.[47] The trend toward primary care careers continues to escalate, with approximately 66% of the graduates selecting pediatrics, family practice, internal medicine, or obstetrics and gynecology residencies. In 1977 2600 more positions in primary care were filled than in 1974, an increase of more than 40%. Previously, 8% of medical students have pursued pediatric training; in 1977 10% pursued a pediatric career. In that specialty 84% of the 1652 positions offered through the matching program were filled, a percentage second only to that in internal medicine.[86,109]

The setting of primary care: the office

Most Americans receive their health care in the physician's office. The most recently published statistics collected in 1975 concerning ambulatory medical care rendered in pediatricians' offices indicated an estimated 46.7 million visits.[38,39] In terms of total office visits, the

46,684,000 visits to pediatricians ranked fourth among all physician specialties. The number of visits decreased as the age of patients increased. There were more examinations of children under 2 years of age than in any other age group, thus reflecting the most frequently stated reason for visiting a pediatrician—the well-baby examination.

Fourteen problems, complaints, or symptoms accounted for about 67% of all pediatric visits, revealing a relatively narrow clinical range for pediatricians as compared with general and family practitioners. Nearly two and a half times as many problems would be required to account for a comparable 67% of the visits to general and family practitioners. A nonsymptomatic problem, usually an examination, was the reason for approximately a third of all pediatric visits. In terms of the extent of impairment that might result if no care was obtained only 10% of the visits were, by the pediatrician's judgment, "serious" or "very serious." A sizable proportion (60%) was categorized as "nonserious." The percentage of new problems presented to pediatricians (51%) exceeded that for all physicians (35%).

Routine histories and examinations (either limited or general) were the most common diagnostic services provided. The proportion of visits at which histories or examinations were performed was generally higher for pediatricians than for all physicians. The percentage of pediatric visits at which medical counselling was a significant part of the office visit also exceeded the percentage for all physicians. The average encounter time between pediatricians and their patients was approximately 12 minutes, compared to an average time duration of 15 minutes per visit for all physicians.

Finally, data on disposition reveal that pediatricians, when compared to all physicians, were more likely to have a telephone follow-up and less likely to schedule a return visit, thus indicating acute, self-limiting problems characteristic of children. No follow-up was planned after 24% of the visits, which reflects the large amount of well-child care occurring at ambulatory pediatric office visits.

These data, which describe some of the characteristics of pediatric practice, have certain implications. The data indicate that pediatricians spend considerable time with children who are not ill. Therefore it appears reasonable for a primary care physician to be oriented to the delivery of care to children who are not ill but who have special chronic conditions. Office mechanisms that would enable the practitioner to initiate this change are suggested in Chapter 17.

Congress has established a policy that places major responsibility for the nation's health care with primary care deliverers—the pediatricians, family practitioners, and internists. The Health Professions Educational Assistance Act of 1976 (PL 94-484) was designed to alter the balance between specialty and primary care physicians by requiring that an eventual 50% of all resident training slots be in primary care specialties. Mental health training has been mandated for primary care residents to help them appreciate the special skills of core mental health practitioners.[116] Under the new law, primary health care providers are now required not only to treat patients with clearly defined mental disorders, but also to give support and guidance to patients with a wide range of emotionally related "problems of living." Finally, the trend toward deinstitutionalization will require that persons returning to the community rely on primary care physicians for general medical treatment, psychotropic drug therapy, and counselling.[116]

Current status of training programs for primary care

Recognition by pediatric health service providers that many of the important health needs of infants, children, and adolescents were not being met as effectively and as fully as necessary led to the formation of the Task Force on Pediatric Education. The task force met from 1976 to 1978 to identify those health needs and point out the educational strategies required to prepare future pediatricians to meet them.[109]

Following are six issues that were found to be at the core of current problems in pediatric education[109]:

1. Biosocial and developmental problems, such as early family adjustment difficulties and school failure, adversely affect

the health of many children and adolescents. These problems are serious and very widespread. All pediatricians should have the skills to cope with them.

2. The health needs of adolescents are being inadequately met. Pediatrics should now take full responsibility for improving health care for and research regarding this segment of the American population.

3. The care provided children with chronic handicapping conditions continues to be grossly inadequate. Although pediatricians are uniquely qualified to provide this care, too many residency programs underemphasize this aspect of pediatrics.

4. Pediatric research is essentially office-based primary care, whereas pediatric education often centers around tertiary patient care experiences. Provision of excellent ambulatory care experiences during the pediatric residency should be emphasized and augmented.

5. Pediatric education is financed largely by revenues generated from hospital patient care. It is difficult to obtain adequate financial support for the education of residents in ambulatory settings. An increased understanding of this problem and major revisions of reimbursement formulas are urgently required.

6. Fee-for-service reimbursement policies currently encourage pediatricians to treat as many patients per day as possible and discourage the time-consuming counselling essential in effective diagnosis and treatment of biosocial and developmental problems. To meet these needs pediatricians must spend more time with fewer patients. Fair reimbursement mechanisms for time spent, not for numbers seen, must be developed now.

Four issues (1, 3, 4, and 6) address either inadequacies or deficiencies, which leave the newly (and supposedly best-) trained graduate ill-equipped in providing primary care to children in general and developmentally disabled children in particular. Other issues (2 and 5) have significant impact on the delivery of care to the developmentally disabled population.

Remediation and implementation will require a commitment of talent, space, and money.

Recommendations of the task force

As a result of the extensive survey and scrutiny of pediatric training today, the task force made 11 recommendations.[109] These recommendations (p. 6) should be carefully considered by every pediatrician as well as by those who influence pediatric undergraduate, graduate, and continuing medical education. Each of these recommendations has special pertinence for pediatricians or allied health care providers who wish to assess their potential to care for the developmentally disabled and to remedy any deficiencies. Suggestions regarding the steps an individual pediatrician may take to correct some of the deficiencies follow later in this chapter.

DEFINITION AND SCOPE OF DEVELOPMENTAL DISABILITIES

Many conditions and diseases of children have either entirely or nearly disappeared. Those conditions which have come to be called developmental disabilities have not disappeared, however. In fact, some conditions seem to be more prevalent, perhaps due to better overall detection of developmental disabilities earlier than in the past, increasing sophistication in detection of milder developmental disabilities, and the use of increasingly complex technology.

Exhorting pediatricians to redouble their efforts to solve a problem they have created, Gruenberg[53] goes so far as to designate the problem as a "man-made epidemic" of developmental disabilities. Mortality of handicapped infants has declined due to better obstetrical and perinatal care. Other advances have brought mortality for handicapped children into line with rates for normal children. For certain handicapped individuals, 30 years have been added to life expectancy at birth. It is likely that there are more children with developmental disabilities now than in the past.

It can be challenging to recognize handicapping conditions that affect various systems of the body, such as congenital heart defects or diabetes. While not absolutely more difficult, it

RECOMMENDATIONS OF THE 1978 TASK FORCE ON PEDIATRIC EDUCATION*

1. A national policy should be formulated which would require a periodic assessment of the health status and needs of children and adolescents. This policy must recognize regional differences, but evolve from a national commitment to our youth. This assessment should include all children and adolescents while specially identifying those with societally disadvantaged racial, ethnic, and socioeconomic origins; those with unusual vulnerabilities; and those living in hazardous and non-nurturing environments.
2. Pediatric education must be based on what is best for children. Pediatric education, manpower planning, and service delivery systems should be more responsive to the health needs of children and adolescents. Among other needs are the need to be valued, to have comprehensive health care, and to be reared in stable families.
3. All medical students should have a clinical experience of approximately equal length in pediatrics and internal medicine. Pediatric experience should emphasize the processes of human growth and development and their relationship to health and disease.
4. The minimum duration of the residency in general pediatrics should be 36 months. Learning time should be apportioned upon the criterion of the need for competence in both the biomedical and biosocial aspects of pediatrics. The health needs of children and adolescents should be explicitly considered in planning the educational program. There should be increased emphasis on the biosocial aspects of pediatrics and adolescent health.
5. Residency training programs should be flexible and provide for increasing levels of supervisory responsibility as the resident's medical judgment matures. Education should take place in a variety of environments, including ambulatory, community, and in-patient settings.
6. In the future, pediatrics will increasingly be practiced in groups which emphasize the health team concept. Therefore, pediatricians should be prepared to serve as members, as leaders, and as consultants in such health teams. Contact with nurses, allied health personnel, and other potential team members should be designed into pediatric residency programs.
7. Pediatricians must accept responsibility for developing a plan of personal continuing education. However, department chairpersons and program directors must recognize the responsibility of the teaching institution to provide continuing education opportunities suited to each pediatrician's needs.
8. Vigorous support for programs in academic pediatrics should continue in all generic areas of study and increase significantly in those involving biosocial concerns. Educational guidelines should be developed for all programs in which prospective academicians are trained.
9. Pediatricians should collaborate with family physicians, as well as with non-physician health care providers, in training personnel and in planning to meet the health care needs of children and adolescents. In the three-year family practice training program, there should be a minimum of six months of training under the supervision of the pediatric department. This training should focus on the primary care needs of children.
10. In order to meet standards of excellence in the health care of all children and adolescents, at least the present number of graduates from pediatric residencies should be maintained. This is an even more critical issue if the currently unmet needs of children and adolescents are to be satisfactorily addressed. Further, we recommend the development of a singular and cohesive national plan, albeit represented by a pluralism in programs, to assure access to excellent pediatric health services in all underserved areas of this nation.
11. Our society has an obligation to muster all those services required to meet the health needs of all our children. This obligation necessitates the development by the federal government of a coherent policy which provides realistic support for child health services; the implementation by regional and local government of specific regional responses to child health needs based on their more limited resources and selected requirements; and the adoption by insurers of realistic reimbursement formulas for ambulatory care, community services, biosocial pediatrics, and health maintenance. The future of pediatric education can no longer be dependent on antiquated in-hospital reimbursement mechanisms.

*Task Force on Pediatric Education: The future of pediatric education, report, Evanston, Ill., 1978, American Academy of Pediatrics, copyright American Academy of Pediatrics 1978.

can be equally, if not more, challenging to identify and treat handicapping conditions that are directly related to abnormal brain structure and/or function or malnutrition. A developmental disability falls into the latter category. It can be defined as an abnormality beginning in fetal life or early childhood, which precludes or significantly impedes normal physical and/or mental development. Included in this definition are mental retardation, cerebral palsy, and other neurologically handicapping conditions; deafness; speech disorders; blindness; mental illness; autism; and disorders of comprehension or effective use of language. Johnston and Magrab[68] define the developmentally handicapped child as one who has failed to progress at a normal rate in acquiring certain developmental skills in motor, adaptive, communicative, and social spheres. This is discussed in detail in Chapters 4 and 8. Following is a legal definition of developmental disability:

The term "developmental disability" means a disability attributable to mental retardation, cerebral palsy, epilepsy, or another neurological condition of an individual found to be closely related to mental retardation or to require treatment similar to that required for mentally retarded individuals, which disability originates before such individual attains age 18, which has continued or can be expected to continue indefinitely, and which constitutes a substantial handicap to such individual.[57]

It is interesting to review the legislative history of the developmental disability concept, which evolved in the early 1970s. Gradually it became recognized that mental retardation, cerebral palsy, and epilepsy (autism was later added) were major causes of substantial handicaps to adults disabled in childhood, that these three conditions may overlap clinically, and finally that all three of these disorders implied multiple handicaps requiring special and similar services throughout childhood and adult life. As a result, the developmental disability legislation combines a functional definition as well as categorical groups.

There still remains some philosophical dispute about the designation "developmental disabilities." Is it a "laundry list" of disabling conditions or categories grouped together because they share such characteristics as severity

and age of onset? Is developmental disability a description of the function limitations of an individual with lifelong service needs regardless of any medical or diagnostic label? Whatever the resolution of this difference, developmental disability legislation has as its underlying philosophy and clear intent a functional, noncategorical approach to severe disability originating in childhood. Children with these major handicaps are viewed as a special group on the basis of service needs rather than systems or status.

Considerable methodological and descriptive difficulties in obtaining estimates of overall prevalence of developmental disability have been encountered. Ambiguous conditions and definitions of those conditions abound. In addition to controversies in diagnosis, difficulties exist in identifying appropriate care because of continued ignorance and social stigma. In many conditions there is considerable clinical overlap. Pless[87] suggests that chronic disorders in children represent a relatively homogenous group, since they differ in several fundamental aspects from the more common, episodical illnesses of childhood. He has described and evaluated some of the problems involved in those studies which suggest that the total cumulative prevalence of chronic conditions in children under 18 years of age is between 10% and 20%.[87,89-91] A long-term prospective study of children and adolescents under age 16 who were residents of Erie County, New York, demonstrated a cumulative prevalence rate of 1313.2 cases per 100,000 children. One out of every 76 children under age 16 had been diagnosed as having one of the long-term diseases being reviewed.[106] The total numbers increase if the estimates suggesting there are 8.7 million children and adolescents who are considered developmentally disabled are included.[64] Siantz[100] suggests that if families of the developmentally disabled individuals are also counted, more than 20 million persons are affected by a developmental disability.

A reliable and thorough health surveillance report is published by the Health Surveillance Registry of the Division of Vital Statistics, Community Health Program, Ministry of Health, Province of British Columbia.[31] This annual report, providing both statistical data and discussion, is helpful in appreciating the difficulty of assessing how many children exist who have handicapping conditions.

United States statistics are available in a recently published review of surveys on the health status of children (1963 to 1972) by the Department of Health, Education, and Welfare.[62] In these surveys, chronic illnesses were classified by the degree of limitation imposed on the activities of affected children. The absolute number of children with limiting chronic conditions had increased from 1,120,000 in 1959 to 1,791,000 in 1961. These numbers exclude the children with illnesses that do not restrict activity and children who are so severely disabled as to require institutionalization or residential treatment. In the most recent survey year (1970) more chronically ill noninstitutionalized children were able to carry on their major activity — play for the younger, school for the older — than in 1959 to 1961. At both times the prevalence of limiting chronic conditions increased with age and was greater among boys than girls. Asthma, with or without hay fever, was by far the foremost cause of activity limitation among children and youths. Pless,[91] in a review of data from a regional survey, examined the patterns of care provided to children with chronic physical illness by primary care physicians. The study indicated that on the average, 7.4% of all children seen annually have one or more chronic conditions.[91]

Although such data as that discussed earlier, may obfuscate rather than clarify the situation for the practitioner, it is important to be aware of the data available on the prevalence of developmental disability. However the pediatrician interprets these data, it is certain that disabled children will exist and require service. To be able to assess what to do, the pediatrician should consider prevalence before determining, in broader terms, the expected outcome of therapeutic interventions.[47]

THE ROLE OF A PEDIATRICIAN CARING FOR CHILDREN WITH DEVELOPMENTAL DISABILITIES

The pediatrician or family practitioner is the logical physician to care for children with developmental disabilities and the optimal physician to serve as ombudsman for a child who does not progress or progresses slowly through the normal developmental stages of childhood.

Several of the ensuing chapters describe the variety of insults that can occur at different stages of brain development. As Pless indicates in Chapter 17, only rarely does the child with a developmental disability have a single problem requiring services from only one professional. A wide range of professional input is usually required for definitive diagnosis, problem identification, and treatment planning. The pediatrician, however, is the key person to identify, plan for, and manage the treatment of the developmentally disabled child. The organization of treatment, and indeed of everyday living, for such a child and family has such numerous and complex ramifications that it demands continuous coordination of services for the child and his family. The primary care physician's goal is to help the family achieve the best adjustment possible in a particular circumstance.[15,82] The evaluation of the disability is important to plan for substantive function, but the aim is a status for the child that enables him to function in an appropriate niche of society.

Unless the primary care physician organizes, interprets, and integrates the total medical care, the child's care and ultimately the child himself may become fragmented and lost among the various medical and allied health specialties evaluating and treating him. By accepting this responsibility, the physician rightfully assumes a primary position in the life of a developmentally disabled child.[12,13]

OBJECTIONS OF PHYSICIANS TO PROVIDING PRIMARY CARE FOR DEVELOPMENTALLY DISABLED CHILDREN

The more common problems the physician encounters in attempting to provide primary care for the developmentally disabled child are of two major categories: deficiencies in training and experience and little or no third-party compensation for diagnosis and management of developmental disabilities in children. Quotations that pediatricians have proffered in group discussions conducted by the author throughout the country over the past decade are found below: These quotations illustrate their resistance to providing care themselves to developmentally disabled children in the office setting.

Pediatricians attest to deficiencies in training and experience in at least nine areas:

- Coordination or management of complex or multiple conditions, even with subspecialist assistance
- Longitudinal observations
- Developmental and psychological assessment of the child
- Psychosocial implications of developmental disability, handicapping conditions, or chronic illness for the child, parents, and family
- Utilization of and communication with a consultant
- Interviewing and counselling
- Multidisciplinary teamwork
- Roles and boundaries of other disciplines, for example, physical therapy
- Psychological burden to the physician in providing care to many children with multiple problems

In October 1978, the Committee on Children with Handicaps of the American Academy of Pediatrics[32] issued a position paper stating that physicians must receive third-party compensation for coordination, staffing, and follow-up efforts on behalf of the developmentally disabled. In addition, it was pointed out that they should be compensated for counselling and school visits on behalf of these patients. The justification is that such activities are all appropriate extensions of the physician's primary care role in the diagnosis and management of developmental disability in children. All pediatricians will have to do their part to promulgate

---

IS THERE A ROLE FOR THE PRIMARY CARE PHYSICIAN IN THE CARE OF THE DEVELOPMENTALLY DISABLED?

Quotations—"Primary responsibility should be with a multidisciplinary team of pediatric subspecialists"

Deficiencies in training and experience

Complexity or multiple facets of condition	"I feel uneasy in handling all the complex medical aspects of a child with meningomyelocele—just keep the patient stable."
	"I usually refer chronic problems in older children to the internist or to the teaching hospital."
	"While I'd like to manage children with a handicapping condition, mental retardation, or a complex chronic disease, I recognize that I have never had the opportunity during my pediatric training for longitudinal observations of chronic conditions."
Psychological knowledge and skills	"I think I can manage such patients medically, but how am I to find out about the psychological implications of chronic physical disease?"
	"I feel helpless when treating a 16-year-old male dwarf."
	"You know, I've never actually had the benefit of a basic course in child development."
Teamwork and interdisciplinary work	"I find it difficult, if not impossible, to work on a team. It's hard for me to communicate with a physical therapist."
	"I can never reach the pertinent specialist in times of emergency or crisis. He's only available on Wednesday afternoons in the muscular dystrophy clinic, for example."

Compensation problems

Time constraints and/or reimbursement	"Assuming I can learn something about the psychological implications, how can I schedule enough time to discuss feelings and attitudes with the child and his family?"
	"The economic necessity of spending short periods of time with large numbers of patients discourages the time commitment that for me is essential for effective management of the child with a chronic illness."
	"How can I arrange for the time financially?"
	"I'm too busy with well-child care and acute care to expand the scope of this practice."

this position in their local jurisdictions so that they can be relieved of the pressures for a high-volume, superficial involvement, spend the time required for the developmentally disabled, and be adequately compensated for that time.

DIFFERENCES BETWEEN CARE OF ACUTELY ILL AND DEVELOPMENTALLY DISABLED CHILDREN

Many differences exist between the care of acutely ill and developmentally disabled children. These difficulties are clearly presented in Table 1-1. Any physician providing primary care in time develops the ability to shift gears automatically between these different types of patients. New physicians need to make themselves aware of these differences so that they will perform in synchrony with the circumstances.

AREAS OF KNOWLEDGE AND SKILLS NECESSARY FOR THE PRIMARY CARE OF DEVELOPMENTALLY DISABLED CHILDREN AND THEIR FAMILIES

To prepare to serve as a primary care physician for the child with developmental disabilities, the pediatrician-in-training needs to acquire knowledge and skills in the seven areas discussed in Fig. 1-1. It is equally important for the pediatrician already in practice to acquire this knowledge and skill. A review of the literature on various primary care and development curricula under consideration is further revealing to a physician traditionally trained in pediatrics.[2] The recommendations of the Task

Table 1-1. Differences between care of the acutely ill and the developmentally disabled child

Factors	Acutely ill child	Developmentally disabled child
What child needs	Patient and family need immediate assessment and diagnosis	Patient and family require multiple assessments over long period of time
		Patient and family needs to know long-term prognosis
	Patient needs immediate treatment; may need follow-up	Patient requires long-term therapy
		Patient needs follow-up
	Patient needs routine and acute illness care	Patient needs routine, acute illness care, long-term care, and crisis intervention care
	Patient may require counselling	Patient and family may require on-going or intermittent counselling
What physician provides	Physician usually names a diagnosis	Physician may or may not be able to diagnose developmental disability
	Physician usually knows cause	Physician may or may not know cause
	Physician can discuss short-term prognosis and duration in general terms	Physician may or may not know prognosis
How physician provides	Usually cares for child independently	Will need to have a commitment to team; will need to work at times with a team, or with subspecialist, allied health worker, or educational specialist
Physician-patient relationship	Physician tells patient (parent) what to do; patient obeys; "curing"	Physician helps patient and family to help himself and themselves; patient and family use expert help; "caring"
Physician-patient model	Guidance-cooperation	Mutual participation
Involvement with parents	Intense, short-lived	Usually not intense; of long duration
Characteristics of condition	Patient: limited, circumscribed, reversible, usually no residual disability	Patient: on-going; may be life long, irreversible
	Physician: challenging to medical acumen	Physician: anxiety-producing; depressing; may be fulfilling or satisfying
Duration	Short: days, weeks	Long: weeks, months, years
Orientation	Disease	Health and/or equilibrium
Setting	Office or hospital	Usually office
Outcome	Diagnosis and cure	Management

Patient focus

Core medical knowledge: child development and rehabilitation

Acute illness
Chronic illness
Health
Growth
Developmental assessment
Motor
Cognitive
Language
Social
Emotional

Behavior
Early screening
Rehabilitation or habilitation,
   treatment methods, and adaptive
   equipment
Patient and parent education

Psychological issues

Psychological assessment
Psychological disturbance
Behavioral problems
Ability to interview
Ability to hold conference with
   parents and with representatives
   of nonmedical agencies
Ability to counsel

Ability to manage anxiety
Ability to manage depression
Ability to manage deterioration
Ability to manage death
Ability to manage hopelessness
Attention to vulnerabilities,
   strengths, resources of child
   and family

Sociological issues

Sociology and culture of family
Specific culture and socioeconomic characteristics of the child
Social problems, for example, substance abuse, child abuse, spouse abuse
Knowledge of the community: characteristics and resources
Ability to aid families in dealing with professionals on behalf
   of their child

Physician focus

Self-awareness

Awareness of strengths, resources, vulnerabilities, and problems
Awareness of professional and personal characteristics and objectives
Awareness of burn-out syndrome and how to reduce its impact
Recognition of boundaries of competence
Ability to set limits on demands made on physician
Awareness of danger of overidentification with parents
Awareness of physician's own separateness from the family
Awareness of necessity for ability to tolerate uncertainty

Management skills

Ability to develop life care plan
Ability to establish and run an effective and financially sound office
Ability to obtain effective consultation
Ability to develop treatment plan for child and family
Working knowledge of child health services
Managing time
Record keeping

Team relationships

Respect for other health care workers
Awareness of necessity for team in care of developmentally disabled child
Awareness of team dynamics
Awareness of role function of team members
Ability to provide range of role functions
Ability to give feedback to team
Awareness of complexities of leadership in case management
Ability to act as leader-facilitator, if necessary
Ability to act as case manager

Patient and physician focus

Physician-patient relationships

Awareness of models of physician-patient relationships
Awareness of professional/friendship boundaries
Awareness that primary relationship is physician-child not physician-parents
Awareness of danger in creating undue dependency in patient and/or parents
Ability to recognize and deal with lack of congruity between physician's and
   child's and/or parents' assessment of needs

Fig. 1-1. Areas of knowledge and skills necessary for the primary care pediatrician to deliver care to the developmentally disabled.

Force on Pediatric Education[109] are also helpful to pediatricians interested in closing some of the gaps in their knowledge and experience.

The suggestions that follow build on the basic traditional aspects of pediatric education and training experience. They are intended to help physicians develop their skills in delivery of primary care to developmentally disabled children.

Core medical knowledge: child development and rehabilitation

It should not be suprising that to obtain a thorough medical knowledge for care of the developmentally disabled population (normal and abnormal), the pediatrician must systematically study child and adolescent development. There is no substitute for this study. In addition, the pediatrician needs to learn how to appropriately assess a child's development and how other disciplines such as psychology and occupational therapy evaluate developmental status. The price in time and effort is high, but the payoff is invaluable to the pediatrician in planning for and managing the child who is developmentally delayed.

A distinction has been drawn between developmental assessment (screening), which is an important part of the evaluation of the young child, and evaluation, which requires a clinician with additional specialized skills—a synthesis of knowledge from pediatrics, genetics, neurology, developmental psychology, and psychiatry.[92] The identification and evaluation process of the child who is at high risk or is developmentally delayed is described in Chapters 2, 3, and 8. Such evaluations can be performed by a generalist who has the knowledge to recognize the existence of a problem and can collect data on which to base the necessary judgments of whether or not to seek consultation and further study. Shonkoff and co-workers[96] and Smith[102] have reviewed the assessment of developmental problems in pediatric practice. Province[92] has suggested a helpful tool, the *Interview for One Day,* which enables the clinician not only to gather developmental data, but also to gain impressions about what goes on between the child and his family.

Although one should be cautioned not to assign labels too early inasmuch as predictions about future function are tentative at best, the importance of early diagnosis cannot be overemphasized. Minimizing a developmental disability depends on early detection. Many excellent guides to development assessment are available.*

The primary care physician should become involved in the child's rehabilitation, even if only as an observer. This will provide an opportunity to learn about prognosis in an unfamiliar context and about the availability of complex and creative adaptive equipment. A spoon with the bowl perpendicular to the shaft, a tub seat, or a motorized wheelchair may itself significantly enhance the quality of life for a child and his family. It is also important to establish a relationship between the primary care physician and the rehabilitation team, who can be consulted as problems arise. A national network of courses is offered each year under the auspices of the American Academy for Cerebral Palsy and Developmental Medicine, which deals with habilitation or rehabilitation of children with chronic disorders in general and with specific conditions. Another useful source of information is the journal *Developmental Medicine and Child Neurology,* the official journal of the American Academy for Cerebral Palsy and Developmental Medicine, which treats all aspects of care for the developmentally disabled: mental, rehabilitational, and psychosocial.

In considering rehabilitation, what immediately comes to the pediatrician's mind is motor handicap. The effect of a child's disability, however, extends beyond the impairment of motor function, since motor dysfunction is usually part of the multiple handicap. Focussing professional attention and parental anxiety on this dysfunction initiates a cycle that profoundly alters the normal course of child development and family dynamics as well as the mutual intervention of these processes.[35,60,81]

Despite the controversy about the efficacy of health education, there is little doubt that children and families are interested in health

---

*See references 5, 9, 27, 45, 61, 65-68, 72, 84, 85, 92, 99-101, 111, and 112.

information and that the physician has a responsibility to use newly developed, effective methods for imparting this information.[55]

Psychological issues

The psychological issues are numerous and largely unfamiliar to the traditionally trained physician. To acquire knowledge about psychological assessment and issues, the pediatrician must enter into a dialogue with child psychiatrists and pscyhologists.[73,115] The physician must first learn to analyze the child's external appearance, behavior, and performance; second, observe parent-child interaction; and third, become skillful in eliciting historical material that will be helpful in differential diagnosis. Sharpening parent interview and counselling techniques is best done under the tutelage of an experienced social worker or psychologist in regularly scheduled conferences.[80] Once a level of sophistication in interviewing is achieved, physicians can periodically examine their own interviewing techniques and enlist an objective critic, perhaps by joining a professional group to evaluate and sharpen skills.[15,20,48]

The pediatrician needs to study some of the comprehensive texts for nonpsychiatrists that treat basic child and adolescent care concepts such as stress and coping.* Other texts include behavioral pediatrics[43,71,101] and the management of the mentally retarded child, along with concepts such as behavior modification, normalization, and deinstitutionalization.[22,29,80,113] Several available guides treat the medical management of chronic illness and the necessary practice arrangements.[7,28,34] Finally, the issues surrounding the death of a child are also important.[10,98]

A small but helpful body of literature is available on the feelings, reactions, and behaviors of a child and his family as they are affected by developmental disability.† Many of these are noted later in this text. A review of normal parent-child relationships is also important.[33,104] One such clear and cogently presented review is an account of the sociopsychological impact

*See references 6, 72, 83, 94, 103, and 114.
†See references 1, 15, 19, 24, 58, 83, 105, and 106.

of a serious illness (polio) on 14 children and their families.[35] Such a study, along with individual anecdotal accounts such as *Journey*,[78] the story of a hemophilic boy, is invaluable to the pediatrician who treats developmentally disabled children. Both sophisticated and anecdotal studies have great value in illustrating familial coping mechanisms. There are no easy ways of exposing oneself to this type of literature. One can only organize one's life to keep up with pertinent literature that is not precisely "medical."

Sociological issues

The sociological literature is equally important. The physician needs to know about the following:

- Children in America's first 200 years[52]
- The current cultural and sociological changes,[21] which will be reflected in the next generation of Americans[25]
- New roles of parents in the changing institution of the family[70,107,110]
- The trend toward normalization of the deviant[113] and the deinstitutionalization of the disabled individual[22,29]
- Analysis of child-rearing and family life patterns associated with poverty[30,63,67]
- Single-parent families[16]
- Child care services[93]
- How parents can change the system[36]
- Social policy issues in improving child health services[97]

These are but some of the broader areas with which the pediatrician must be familiar to be effective. The values and views of society direct and influence the socialization process of a child, as does disability. The latter not only affects the socialization of the child who is developmentally disabled, but also all of the important people in his life as well as those with whom he interacts socially.[1]

Self-awareness of the physician

Physicians, like all persons, need to devote some time to themselves: to know themselves and their needs, goals, strengths, and weaknesses. Unless they take time to review these areas they cannot be optimally helpful to others in an enduring and significant manner. The strengths and resources of physicians, as well as their vulnerabilities and problems, have been reviewed by concerned pediatricians, who in their discussion keep in mind the child and his caregiver.[44,51]

Burn-out syndrome, or "primary care physician, heal thyself." A consequence of neglecting oneself is burn-out syndrome. A lengthy discussion of burn-out syndrome follows because of its extraordinary impact on the physician's effectiveness. Burn-out syndrome has been rarely mentioned in the pediatric literature. If physicians allow burn-out to occur, their potential for affecting the quality of life of both the developmentally disabled child and his family may never be achieved.

Although this discussion is directed at the physician, it has implications for all human service personnel. As indicated earlier, primary care physicians must become aware of feelings, reactions, and behaviors, not only of children with developmental disabilities and their parents, but also, equally important, of their own feelings, reactions, and behaviors. Awareness of the likelihood of burn-out syndrome and how to recognize it before it occurs can prevent it or reduce its impact. In many ways the reactions of health care professionals who treat children with developmental disabilities and their families are similar to those of the parents. The intensity experienced by the health care professionals is not as great as that of the parents, but the multiplicity of major problems for which they are responsible is a significant factor. Physicians experience burn-out syndrome as a result of continuous, intense, and intimate work with a large number of people with major problems.

What is burn-out syndrome? Physicians are often required to work intensely and intimately with children and their parents on a continuous basis. They learn about these persons' psychological, social, and/or physical problems and are expected to provide aid or treatment. This type of professional interaction creates strong feelings of emotion and personal stress, which often can be disruptive and incapacitating.

Primary care physicians may defend themselves against these strong emotions through techniques of detachment. If they treat patients in a more remote, objective way, it becomes easier to perform the necessary tasks without suffering psychological discomfort. This difficult (and almost paradoxical) process of distancing oneself from people to help or cure them has been called "detached concern."[74] No explicit training in such techniques occurs, although the importance of detachment processes in client-patient interactions is clearly recognized in medical professions. The lack of preparation for coping with the unique emotional stresses of their work makes many physicians unable to maintain the caring and commitment that they initially brought to the job, thus precipitating burn-out. Maslach[75] describes the evolution of this constellation of characteristics from the 1960s, indicating that it had been a taboo subject, which the helping professions shunned. Maslach presented survey studies of various health care professionals from the early 1970s, and Freudenberger[74-76] had described experiences of staff members in free clinics and residential group homes.[37-39]

Burn-out syndrome involves the loss of concern for the people with whom one is working. In addition to physical exhaustion (and sometimes even illness) burn-out syndrome is characterized by an emotional exhaustion in which the professional no longer has any positive feelings, sympathy, or respect for clients or patients. A very clinical and dehumanized perception of patients may develop, in which they are labeled in derogatory ways and treated accordingly. The patients and their parents are viewed as somehow deserving of their problems and are blamed for their own victimization.[8,95] A deterioration in the quality of care or services that they receive ensues. The professional who experiences burn-out syndrome is unable to deal successfully with the overwhelming emotional stress of the job. Failure to cope can be manifested in a number of ways, ranging from impaired performance and absenteeism to various types of personal problems such as alcohol and drug abuse, marital conflict, and mental illness.

How to recognize burn-out syndrome. Various verbal and nonverbal techniques are used by helping professionals to reduce the amount of personal stress in their interactions with patients. In different ways each of these techniques enables the professional to see the patient less personally, to view the relationship with the patient in objective analytical terms, and to reduce the intensity and scope of the emotional arousal experienced.

Most of these techniques allow physicians to distance themselves from the patients while maintaining a genuine concern for their well-being. Since some techniques preclude any continued caring, however, they can result in the same total detachment and dehumanization found in burn-out syndrome. In these instances the helping professional's psychological self-protection is achieved at the expense of the child and his family. Some of the common stress-reducing techniques used by pediatricians are semantics of detachment, intellectualization, situational compartmentalization, and psychological withdrawal.[76] Each of these techniques is described in detail to facilitate their detection before they become ingrained in the physician-patient relationship.

If one uses *semantics of detachment* to describe children, they can be made to appear more inaminate and consequently less human. Some of these terms are derogatory labels, whereas others are abstract terms referring to large and undifferentiated units ("the retarded"). Another form of objective language is labelling patients in terms of the functional relationship the physician has with them (e.g., "the patient load"). In some cases patients are not referred to by name but rather by their immediate problem ("the Down child"). Also, the inclusion of professional jargon in interviews with patients often distances the physician from someone who is emotionally upsetting.

With a related technique, *intellectualization,* the situation is recast in more theoretical and less personal terms. By dealing with the abstract qualities of people (rather than the more human ones) the helping professional can "objectify" the situation and react in a less emotional way. In dealing with an agitated adolescent who is being verbally abusive, for example, the helping professional may stand back and look at the patient's problems analytically, thinking "he's acting out," and thus not become personally upset.

Helping professionals often make a sharp distinction between their job and their personal life, thereby achieving *situational compartmentalization.* They rarely discuss their family or personal affairs with their co-workers, and they often have explicit agreements with their spouses and friends not to "talk shop."

Another technique for reducing emotional arousal is psychological withdrawal; one minimizes psychological involvement in stressful interactions with other people in a number of ways. One obvious approach is to distance oneself physically from the other person, while continuing a minimal interaction (by standing farther away, avoiding eye contact, keeping one's hand on the door knob, or hurrying through the physical examination of a developmentally disabled child). Psychological withdrawal is also evidenced by professionals who communicate with the patient in impersonal ways, such as greeting the family with superficial generalities or utilizing form letters. In some cases the professionals simply spend less time with a patient, either by deliberately cutting down the length of the formal interview or by spending more of their time talking and socializing with other patients.

Significant factors in coping. Maslach's[76,77] research findings thus far point to five variables that influence whether or not professionals will experience burn-out syndrome. Following are some of the factors found significant in a study of child care workers:

- High patient-staff ratio
- Number of hours in direct personal contact with patients—little patient variety
- Lack of social-professional support systems
- Lack of training in interpersonal skills
- Inability to articulate personal feelings

How physicians can protect themself from burn-out syndrome. Some of the helpful recommendations made by Freudenberger[41] for the child care worker can be modified minimally and applied equally well to the physician.

Physicians conducting periodic self-examinations have an awareness of their motivation for delivering pediatric primary care to the developmentally disabled. It is sensible and even necessary for survival, not to mention success in providing good care, to understand that dedication without self-awareness can lead to overexertion, fatigue, and eventual poor performance.

Physicians will need to balance their energy investment in work with their personal lives and then schedule time for outside activities. The usefulness of physical exercise in replenishing mental and emotional energy expended cannot be underestimated.

In setting a work schedule, the physician must be aware that the number of hours any one individual can work and still be productive is limited. It is important to reduce the number of hours spent in direct contact with the patients and to schedule shorter work shifts. It is also important to vary one's schedule between interaction with patients and other work, between stressful types of patients and those who are not stressful, and between crisis intervention and more relaxed interaction with patients.

Physicians need to develop some mechanism to share the doubts as well as successes of the care they provide. The pediatric office staff should engender a mutually caring environment.

It is essential for primary care physicians to pay closer attention to their own internalized structure and character makeup, since these areas are often neglected. If physicians recognize a lack of inner organized structure in themselves, they can overcome it. If, on the other hand, they continue to be defensive and rationalize this lack, they, in fact, will be promoting burn-out syndrome in themselves.

Freudenberger notes that "not seeing our own loneliness, deprivation, or personality flaws is a tragic form of pride and unconscious narcissism. It is tragic because it hurts the child and it deprives us of the pleasure of seeing a little bit better who we are at this point in our lives, why we work and do what we do, and what we could become if we were more authentic."[42]

Pediatricians who work with developmentally disabled children and their parents need to be sensitive to the potential importance of burn-out syndrome in themselves; they must recognize its symptoms, how it occurs, and what they can do to minimize its eventual effects on themselves and their patients.

Physician's management skills

Pediatricians can obtain management skills in a number of educational ways; short, long, and on-going courses are widely available. A time management course is sine qua non for every physician. The secret may be to list what one wishes to accomplish, prioritize the list, and then act on that list. There is time to do what has been set as a priority.

An excellent text published in 1977 (and its predecessor from 1968) offers useful management information regarding the health care of children within the office setting.[49,50] Texts that treat the style and management of a pediatric practice are available as well.[11]

To develop a wide knowledge of community agencies, pediatricians may purchase, read, and use directories. More important, they need to visit the more prominent agencies to establish personal contact. Formulating a life plan for patients and their families is discussed elsewhere.[14] This management tool is one of the most important aspects of patient care if physicians wish to care well for a developmentally disabled child. The life plan is for both the family and the physician as primary provider of medical and emotional care.

Team relationships

In the acute care hospital setting, the physician has very little opportunity to interact within a team. On the other hand, in the care of a developmentally disabled child teamwork is absolutely necessary to look at the whole child in a comprehensive manner, assess, plan for the intervention, and manage and coordinate all the complex ramifications. It is necessary to appreciate the interdisciplinary process, well described by Johnston and Magrab[68] and others.[28] Not only do the physician and each member of the team need to be professionally competent, but they also need to understand each other's professional function. In addition, there are less concrete factors that contribute to the team function and to the decisions made. These include the emotional climate of the team, its dynamics, and the style of leadership. The function of the team is described more fully in Chapter 4.

The leadership role greatly affects the quality of work accomplished by an interdisciplinary team. There are two types of leadership—the first type is required for taking primary responsibility in the on-going management of a particular child and his family; the second type, team leader facilitation, is better accomplished by a person trained in managing group interaction. The first type of leadership may be provided by the physician who will consistently follow the child through his childhood.

Physician-patient relationships

The final area about which the physician needs to be knowledgeable concerns the interaction between the physician and the patient (child and/or parents).[44,51] Physicians should be careful to remember their primary responsibility as children's physicians. They must honestly face differences between their perceptions of the child's needs and the perceptions of the child and parents.

Physicians must tread the fine line between "caring" and some degree of detachment to provide objective management of the child's and family's problems. Physicians also need to note and reflect on the outcry of consumers, which has developed from patient frustration and lack of understanding of their own and the physician's respective roles.[17] Finally, a review of models of physician-patient relationships is helpful to keep a perspective of the interaction.[108]

CONCLUSION

The purpose of this chapter has been to provide background, general guidance, and specific issues for the pediatrician and the allied health worker in training or in practice to consider in the care of the developmentally disabled child and to prepare the way for providing such care.

REFERENCES

1. Albrecht, G. L., editor: The sociology of physical disability and rehabilitation, Pittsburgh, 1976, University of Pittsburgh Press.
2. Alpert, J. J.: Curricula: the variety of strategies. The training of the primary care physician. In Berwick, D. M., editor: The roles of family practice, internal medicine, obstetrics and gynecology and pediatrics in providing primary care. Report of the Seventy-third Ross Conference on Pediatric Research, Columbus, Ohio, 1977, Ross Laboratories, p. 38.
3. Ambulatory training in office is being revived, Pediatr. News, vol. 12, Sept. 1978, p. 1.
4. American Academy of Pediatrics: Statement on primary care pediatrics, Evanston, Ill. Oct. 30, 1975.
5. Apley, J., editor: Care of the handicapped child, a Festschrift for Ronald MacKeith, Philadelphia, 1978, J. B. Lippincott Co.
6. Arnold, L. E., editor: Helping parents help their children, New York, 1978, Brunner/Mazel, Inc.
7. Bain, H. W., editor: Chronic disease in children, Pediatr. Clin. North Am. **21:** entire issue, Nov. 1974.
8. Bandura, A., Underwood, B., and Fromson, M. E.: Disinhibition of aggression through diffusion of responsibility and dehumanization of victims, J. Res. Personality **9:** 253, 1975.
9. Barnard, K. E., and Erickson, M. L.: Teaching children with developmental problems: a family care approach, ed. 2., St. Louis, 1976, The C. V. Mosby Co.
10. Barnebey, N., and Ruppert, E.: Parents of chronically ill or physically handicapped children. In Arnold, L. E., editor: Helping parents help their children, New York, 1978, Brunner/Mazel, Inc., p. 174.
11. Bass, L. W., and Woffson, J. H.: The style and management of a pediatric practice, Pittsburgh, 1977, University of Pittsburgh Press.
12. Battle, C. U.: The role of the pediatrician as ombudsman in the health care of the young handicapped child, Pediatrics **50:** 916, 1972.
13. Battle, C. U.: Care of the child with multiple handicaps. In The care of children with chronic illness. Report of the Sixty-seventh Ross Conference on Pediatric Research, June 9 to 11, 1974, Columbus, Ohio, Ross Laboratories.
14. Battle, C. U.: Formulating a life plan for parents of children with congenital and acquired spinal cord injury, No. 4, Continuing education in the treatment of spinal cord injuries series. In Proceedings of Dissemination of Research in Treatment of Spinal Cord Injuries, Washington, D.C., Aug. 8 and 9, 1974.
15. Battle, C. U.: Chronic physical disease: behavioral aspects, Pediatr. Clin. North Am. **22:**525, 1975.
16. Bel Geddes, J.: How to parent alone—a guide for single parents, New York, 1974, Seabury Press, Inc.
17. Belsky, M. S., and Gross, L.: Beyond the medical mystique: how to choose and use your doctor, New York, 1975, Arbor House Publishing Co., Inc.

18. Bergman, A. B.: Pediatric manpower problems are solvable, Pediatr. Clin. North Am. **19**:281, 1972.

19. Bergsma, D., and Pulver, A. E., editors: Developmental disabilities: psychologic and social implications, Birth Defects **12**(4): entire issue, 1976.

20. Bernstein, L., Bernstein, R. S., and Dana, R.: Interviewing: a guide for health professionals, ed. 2, New York, 1973, Appleton-Century-Crofts.

21. Boocock, S. S.: Children and society. Presented at the annual meeting, American Association for the Advancement of Science, New York, Jan. 1975.

22. Braddock, D.: Opening closed doors: the deinstitutionalization of disabled individuals, Reston, Va., 1977, Council for Exceptional Children.

23. Brent, R. L., and Morse, H. B.: Not in our own image: educating the pediatrician for practice, Pediatr. Clin. North Am. **16**:793, 1969.

24. Brightman, A.: Like me, Boston, 1976, Little, Brown & Co.

25. Bronfenbrenner, U.: Who cares for America's children. In Vaughan, V. C., and Brazelton, T. B., editors: The family: can it be saved? Chicago, 1976, Year Book Medical Publishers, Inc.

26. Burnett, R. D., and Bell, L. S.: Projecting pediatric practice patterns, Report of survey by Pediatric Manpower Committee, part 2, Pediatrics, **62**(suppl.):625, 1978.

27. Capute, A. J., and Biehl, R. F.: Functional developmental evaluation: prerequisite to habilitation, Pediatr. Clin. North Am. **20**:3, 1973.

28. The care of children with chronic illness. Report of the Sixty-seventh Ross Conference on Pediatric Research, Columbus, Ohio, 1975, Ross Laboratories.

29. Cherington, C., and Dybwad, G.: New neighbors: the retarded citizen in quest of a home, DHEW publ. no. (OHD)74-21004, Washington, D.C., 1974, Department of Health, Education and Welfare.

30. Chilman, C. S.: Growing up poor, SRS publ. No. 109, (reprinted), 1969, Washington, D.C., Department of Health, Education and Welfare, Social and Rehabilitation Service, Office of Research, Demonstrations, and Training.

31. Chronic disabilities, congenital anomalies, genetic defects. Health Surveillance Registry Annual Report—1976, HSR publ. no. 2, Victoria, B.C., Canada, 1978, Division of Vital Statistics, Community Health Programs, Province of British Columbia Ministry of Health.

32. Committee on Children with Handicaps: Financial compensation for evaluation and therapy of children with developmental disabilities, Pediatrics **62**:602, 1978.

33. Committee on Infant and Preschool Child, American Academy of Pediatrics, and the National Center on Child Abuse and Neglect: Parenting—An annotated bibliography, DHEW publ. no. (OHDS)78-30134, Washington, D.C., 1978, Department of Health, Education and Welfare, Children's Bureau/Administration for Children, Youth and Families, Office of Human Development Services.

34. Committee on Standards of Child Health Care: Standards of child health care, ed. 3, Evanston, Ill., 1977, American Academy of Pediatrics.

35. Davis, F.: Passage through crisis: polio victims and their families, Indianapolis, 1963, Bobbs-Merrill Co., Inc.

36. DesJardine, C.: How to organize an effective parent group and move bureaucracies for parents of handicapped children and their families, Chicago, 1971, Coordinating Council for Handicapped Children.

37. Downey, J. A., and Low, N. L., editors: The child with disabling illness: principles of rehabilitation, Philadelphia, 1974, W. B. Saunders Co.

38. Ezzati, T. M.: Ambulatory medical care rendered in pediatricians' offices during 1975, advance data, vital and health statistics, DHEW publ. no. 13, Washington, D.C., Oct. 13, 1977, National Center for Health Statistics.

39. Ezzati, T. M.: Ambulatory care utilization patterns of children and young adults, data from the National Health Survey, vital and health statistics, series 13, no. 39, DHEW publ. no. (PHS) 78-1790, Washington, D.C., 1978, National Center for Health Statistics.

40. Freudenberger, H. J.: Staff burn-out, J. Soc. Issues, **30**:159, 1974.

41. Freudenberger, H. J.: The staff burn-out syndrome, Washington, D.C., 1975, Drug Abuse Council, Inc.

42. Freudenberger, H. J.: Burn-out: occupational hazard of the child care worker, Child Care Q. **6**:90, 1977.

43. Friedman, S. B., editor: Behavioral pediatrics, Pediatr. Clin. North Am. **22**: entire issue, Aug. 1975.

44. Garrard, S. D., and Richmond, J. B.: Psychological aspects of the management of chronic diseases and handicapping conditions in childhood. In Lief, H. I., Lief, V. F., and Lief, N. R., editors: The psychological basis of medical practice, New York, 1963, Harper & Row, Publishers.

45. Gesell, A., and Amatruda, C. S.: Developmental diagnosis normal and abnormal child development, ed. 2, New York, 1947, Harper & Row, Publishers.

46. Graettinger, J. S.: Results of the NIRMP for 1977, J. Med. Educ. **53**:83, 1978.

47. Grave, G. D., and Pless, I. B., editors: Chronic childhood illness: assessment of outcome. Report of the conference sponsored by the John E. Fogarty International Center for Advanced Study, May 1 to 5, 1974. In The health sciences and National Institute of Child Health and Human Development, third in the series Teaching of preventive medicine, DHEW publ. no. (NIH)76-877, Bethesda, 1974, National Institutes of Health.

48. Green, M.: Interviewing. In Green, M., and Haggerty, R. J., editors: Ambulatory pediatrics II: personal health care of children in the office, Philadelphia, 1977, W. B. Saunders Co., p. 441.

49. Green, M., and Haggerty, R. J., editors: Ambulatory pediatrics, Philadelphia, 1968, W. B. Saunders Co.

50. Green, M., and Haggerty, R. J., editors: Ambulatory

pediatrics II: personal health care of children in the office, Philadelphia, 1977, W. B. Saunders Co.

51. Green, M., and Haggerty, R. J.: The clinician's job. In Green, M., and Haggerty, R. J., editors: Ambulatory pediatrics II: personal health care of children in the office, Philadelphia, 1977, W. B. Saunders Co., p. 434.

52. Grotberg, E. H., editor: 200 years of children, DHEW Publ. No. (OHD) 77-30103, Washington, D.C., 1977, Department of Health, Education and Welfare, Office of Human Development, Office of Child Development.

53. Gruenberg: Focus on solving "man-made epidemic" of disabled children, Pediatr. News, **12:**5, Oct. 1978.

54. Haggerty, R. J.: Commentaries. Do we really need more pediatricians? Pediatrics **50:**681, 1972.

55. Haggerty, R. J.: Patient and parent education. In Green, M., and Haggerty, R. J., editors: Ambulatory pediatrics II: personal health care of children in the office, Philadelphia, 1977, W. B. Saunders Co., p. 423.

56. Haggerty, R. J., Roghmann, K. J., and Pless, I. B.: Child health and the community, New York, 1975, J. Wiley & Sons, Inc.

57. Hammer, P., and Richman, G.: Developmental disabilities: the orientation notebook, developmental disabilities/technical assistance system, ed. 3, Chapel Hill, N.C., Summer, 1977, The Frank Porter Graham Child Development Center, The University of North Carolina at Chapel Hill.

58. Hannam, C.: Parents and mentally handicapped children, West Drayton, England, 1975, Penguin Books Ltd.

59. Hansen, M. F., and Aradine, C. R.: The changing face of primary pediatrics. Review and commentary, Pediatr. Clin. North Am. **21:**245, 1974.

60. Haslam, R. H. A., editor: Habilitation of the handicapped child, Pediatr. Clin. North Am. **20:** entire issue, Feb. 1973.

61. Haynes, U.: A developmental approach to case finding with special reference to cerebral palsy, mental retardation, and related disorders, DHEW publ. no. 2017, Rockville, Md., 1969, Department of Health, Education and Welfare, Public Health Service.

62. Health status of children: a review of surveys 1963-1972, DHEW publ. no. (HSA) 78-5744, Rockville, Md., 1978, Department of Health, Education and Welfare, Public Health Service, Health Services Administration, Bureau of Community Health Services.

63. Herzog, E., and Lewis, H.: Children in poor families: myths and realities, Am. J. Orthopsychiatry **40:**375, 1970.

64. Hobbs, N.: The futures of children: categories, labels and their consequences, San Francisco, 1975, Jossey-Bass, Inc., Publishers, p. 83.

65. Illingworth, R. S.: The development of the infant and young child, ed. 5, Edinburgh, 1974, Churchill Livingston.

66. Illingworth, R. S.: Basic developmental screening

0-2 years, ed. 2, Oxford, 1977, Blackwell Scientific Publications Ltd.

67. Irelan, L. M., editor: Low-income life styles, DHEW publ. no. SRS-ORD-175, Washington, D.C., 1971, Department of Health, Education and Welfare, Social and Rehabilitation Service, Office of Research and Demonstration.

68. Johnston, R. B., and Magrab, P. R.: Developmental disorders: assessment, treatment, education, Baltimore, 1976, University Park Press.

69. Kanthor, H., Pless, B., and Satterwhite, B.: Areas of responsibility in the health care of multiply handicapped children, Pediatrics **54:**779, 1974.

70. Keniston, K., and The Carnegie Council on Children: All our children: the American family under pressure, New York, 1977, Harcourt Brace Jovanovich, Inc.

71. Kenny, T. J., and Clemmens, R. L.: Behavioral pediatrics and child development: a clinical handbook, Baltimore, 1975, The Williams & Wilkins Co.

72. Lewis, M.: Clinical aspects of child development, Philadelphia, 1973, Lea & Febiger.

73. Lewis, M.: Child psychiatric consultation in pediatrics, Pediatrics **62:**359, 1978.

74. Lief, H. I., and Fox, R. C.: Training for "detached concern" in medical students. In Lief, H. I., Lief, V. F., and Lief, N. R., editors: The psychological basis of medical practice, New York, 1963, Harper & Row, Publishers.

75. Maslach, C.: Burned-out, Hum. Behav. **5:**16, 1976.

76. Maslach, C.: Burn-out: a social psychological analysis. Presented at the American Psychological Association, San Francisco, 1977.

77. Maslach, C., and Pines, A.: The burn-out syndrome in the day care setting, Child Care. Q. **6:**100, 1977.

78. Massie, R., and Massie, S.: Journey, New York, 1975, Alfred A. Knopf, Inc.

79. McKay, R. J., Jr.: Where are we now: a current cross-section. The status of pediatrics. In Berwick, D. M., editor: The roles of family practice, internal medicine, obstetrics and gynecology and pediatrics in providing primary care. Report of the Seventy-third Ross Conference on Pediatric Research, Columbus, Ohio, 1977, Ross Laboratories, p. 32.

80. Menolascino, F. J., editor: Psychiatric approaches to mental retardation, New York, 1970, Basic Books, Inc., p. 654.

81. Molnar, G. E., and Taft, L. T.: Pediatric rehabilitation. Part I: cerebral palsy and spinal cord injuries, Curr. Probl. Pediatr. **7**(3):3, 1977.

82. Molnar, G. E., and Taft, L. T.: Pediatric rehabilitation. Part II: spina bifida and limb deficiencies, Curr. Probl. Pediatr. **7**(4):3, 1977.

83. Murphy, L. B., and Moriarty, A. E.: Vulnerability, coping and growth from infancy to adolescence, New Haven, Conn., 1976, Yale University Press.

84. Mussen, P. H., Conger, J. J., and Kagan, J.: Child development and personality, ed. 4, New York, 1974, Harper & Row, Publishers.

85. Neubauer, P., editor: The process of child develop-

ment, New York, 1976, New American Library, Inc.

86. Pediatrics is holding its own at all levels, Pediatr. News **12**(7):1, 1978.

87. Pless, I. B.: Epidemiology of chronic disease. In Green, M., and Haggerty, R., editors: Ambulatory pediatrics, Philadelphia, 1968, W. B. Saunders Co., p. 760.

88. Pless, I. B.: The changing face of primary pediatrics, Pediatr. Clin. North Am. **21**:223, 1974.

89. Pless, I. B., and Roghmann, K. J.: Chronic illness and its consequences: observations based on three epidemiologic surveys, J. Pediatr. **79**:351, 1971.

90. Pless, I. B., and Satterwhite, B. B.: Chronic illness. In Haggerty, R. J., Roghmann, K. J., and Pless, I. B., editors: Child health and the community, New York, 1975, John Wiley & Sons, Inc., p. 78.

91. Pless, I. B., Satterwhite, B. B., and VanVechten, D.: Chronic illness in childhood: a regional survey of care, Pediatrics **58**:37, 1976.

92. Province, S.: Developmental assessment. In Green, M., and Haggerty, R. J., editors: Ambulatory pediatrics II: personal health care of children in the office, Philadelphia, 1977, W. B. Saunders Co., p. 374.

93. Roby, P., editor: Child care—who cares? Foreign and domestic infant and early childhood development policies, New York, 1975, Basic Books, Inc., Publishers.

94. Rowlands, P.: Children apart, New York, 1973, Pantheon Books, Inc.

95. Ryan, W.: Blaming the victim, ed. 2, New York, 1976, Vintage Books.

96. Schonkoff, J., et al.: Assessment and management of developmental problems in pediatric practice. Presented at Ambulatory Pediatric Association Meeting, New York, April 25, 1978.

97. Schorr, L. B.: Social policy issues in improving child health services: a child advocate's view, Pediatrics **62**:370, 1978.

98. Shneidman, E. S.: Death: current perspectives, Palo Alto, Calif. 1975, Mayfield Publishing Co.

99. Siantz, M. L. de L., editor: Proceedings of the Symposium on Infant Development, sponsored by University Affiliated Program for Child Development, Georgetown University. Continuing Education, Nursing, Washington, D.C., 1976, Georgetown University.

100. Siantz, M. L. de L., editor: The nurse and the developmentally disabled adolescent, Baltimore, 1977, University Park Press.

101. Simons, R. C., and Pardes, H., editors: Understanding human behavior in health and illness, Baltimore, 1977, The Williams & Wilkins Co.

102. Smith, R. D.: The use of developmental screening by primary-care pediatricians, J. Pediatr. **93**:524, 1978.

103. Steinhauer, P. D., and Rae-Grant, Q., editors: Psychological problems of the child and his family, Toronto, Ont., Canada, 1977, The Macmillan Co. of Canada, Ltd.

104. Stevens, J. H., and Mathews, M., editors: Mother/child, father/child relationships, Washington, D.C., 1978, National Association for the Education of Young Children.

105. Strauss, A. L.: Chronic illness and the quality of life, St. Louis, 1975, The C. V. Mosby Co.

106. Sultz, H. A., et al.: Long-term childhood illness, Pittsburgh, 1972, University of Pittsburgh Press.

107. Susser, M. W., and Watson, W.: Sociology in medicine, ed. 2, New York, 1971, Oxford University Press.

108. Szasz, T., and Hollender, M.: A contribution to the philosophy of medicine: the basic models of the doctor-patient relationship, Arch. Intern. Med. **97**:585, 1956.

109. Task Force on Pediatric Education: The future of pediatric education, report, Evanston, Ill. 1978, American Academy of Pediatrics.

110. Vaughan, V. C., and Brazelton, T. B., editors: The family—can it be saved? Chicago, 1976, Year Book Medical Publishers, Inc.

111. Weiner, I. B., and Elkind, D.: Child development: a core approach, New York, 1972, John Wiley & Sons, Inc.

112. Whipple, D. V.: Dynamics of development: euthenic pediatrics, New York, 1965, McGraw-Hill Book Co.

113. Wolfensberger, W.: The principle of normalization in human services, National Institute on Mental Retardation, Toronto, Ont., Canada, 1972, Leonard Crainford.

114. Wolff, S.: Children under stress, West Drayton, England, 1969, Penguin Books Ltd.

115. Wrate, R. M., and Kolvin, I.: A child psychiatry consultation service to pediatricians, Dev. Med. Child. Neurol. **20**:347, 1978.

116. Wright, L.: Primary health care physicians to assume expanded role. In Feelings and their significance, vol. 20, no. 1, Columbus, Ohio, 1978, Ross Laboratories.

What project could possibly be more worthwhile or important for any country than one which concentrates its efforts and energies upon the reproduction of the healthiest possible citizens for the future?

Sir John Peel[68]

2

The high-risk mother and infant

Albert P. Scheiner

BACKGROUND INFORMATION

The perinatal and early postnatal periods form the watershed of life for the developing infant and his family. At this time the primary care physician is afforded the greatest opportunity to affect the subsequent quality of life of the infant and the family. The opportunities at the very least include the early identification and comprehensive care of the high-risk infant and health education and family planning for the mother.

Studies indicate that 7% to 13% of all pregnancies result in an infant who weighs less than 2500 g.[62] The incidence of mental retardation and neurological disorders in this population range from 30% in infants below 1000 to 13% in infants who are appropriate for gestational age and weigh between 1700 and 2000 g.[28,65] The incidence of learning disabilities has been less accurately defined but is undoubtedly in excess of the number of children who are subsequently identified as being mentally retarded.[28] Autism, child abuse, and failure to thrive have all been more frequently reported in infants who experienced perinatal difficulties.[28,51,53]

The involvement of the primary care physician in the follow-up of these *at-risk* and *high-risk* neonates is exceedingly important. Participation by the primary care physician in the follow-up process can substantially decrease the rapidly growing numbers of clinics that are being established for the early identification, evaluation, and care of infants with potential developmental disabilities. The primary care physician could also be very helpful in gathering needed information that relates the developmental outcome of the infant to the neonatal treatment regimen used in individual intensive care nurseries. The follow-up of these infants in the office setting would be less costly and relieve much of the anxiety that families must experience when attending a special clinic in a large, impersonal medical center.

Concepts of risk

Tjossem[85] has defined three types of potential developmental risk categories for infants and children, as follows:

1. Established risk—children with identified developmental disabilities that may have associated congenital syndromes or malformations such as Down syndrome
2. Environmental risk—infants born to families of lower socioeconomic status, parents who are emotionally disturbed, or caregivers who for other reasons interact poorly with their offspring and provide a poor caretaking milieu
3. Biological risk—children who have experienced such untoward perinatal events as congenital viral infections, prematurity, or hypoxia or have had plumbism, meningitis, or trauma during the postnatal period

The infants who are at established risk are discussed in Chapter 8 under the topic of mental retardation. This chapter focuses primarily on infants who are at biological risk and who often find themselves in precarious positions because they are the offspring of a mother who lives in a less-than-optimal environment. Although a child is never solely at biological or environmental risk, it is necessary to focus on a particular risk category to provide more extensive information about a more manageable group of infants. A suggested plan in which the vast majority of infants who are subsequently developmentally delayed come from the high-risk group is described in Fig. 2-1.

Rogers[72] indicated that the broad concept of "at risk" used in screening and early identification of developmentally disabled infants results in the establishment of risk categories that may include up to 80% of all live infants. Although this results in the identification of 70% of all children with handicapping conditions, the number requiring intensive observation is too large to be manageable. This inefficient, exhaustive effort requires the definition to be narrowed to serve small populations with a greater degree of accuracy. Rogers describes a group that consists of only 5% to 10% of infants at *high* risk rather than those merely at risk. These infants contribute approximately 25% of all subsequent handicaps. Following are factors that place an infant *at risk* and may warrant admission to the neonatal intensive care unit:

- Respiratory distress
- Asphyxia—Apgar score of less than 6 at 5 minutes
- Less than 33 weeks gestational age
- Weight of less than 1800 g
- Cyanosis or suspected cardiovascular disease
- Major congenital malformations requiring surgery or cardiac catheterization
- Convulsions, sepsis, hemorrhagic diathesis, or shock
- Meconium aspiration
- Abnormal behavioral characteristics of longer than 24 hours duration suggestive of central nervous system disturbance

When the following criteria were used to follow infants born in a regional neonatal intensive care unit, 25% of the infants had severe handicapping conditions:

- Weight of 1500 g or less; born to a mother of lower socioeconomic status or adolescent mother increases risk
- Mother with known alcoholism, drug addiction, hydantoin use, schizophrenia, or chronic depression
- Small for gestational age, that is, below the 10th percentile for weight and head circumference and born to a mother of lower socioeconomic status or adolescent mother
- Known or suspected central nervous system disease such as severe asphyxia, neonatal seizures, microcephaly, or hydrocephalus
- Infants with congenital rubella, cytomegalovirus infection, toxoplasmosis, or syphilis
- Identifiable developmental disability, for example, myelodysplasia, chromosomal abnormalities, or sensory impairment
- Insulin-dependent diabetic mother who experienced a difficult perinatal course

Utilizing this high-risk classification rather than the at-risk concept requires less effort to identify a large number of children who will be developmentally disabled. This select group of high-risk infants is more manageable for the primary care physician and less[18] likely to include

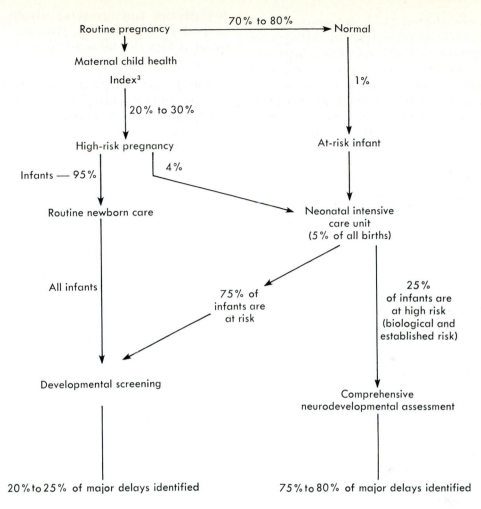

Fig. 2-1. Using a maternal-child health index, 20% of all pregnancies will be identified as being high risk. About 5% of all newborns will enter a neonatal intensive care unit (NICU). About 80% of NICU newborns will come from the high-risk pregnancy group, the remaining 20% from the normal pregnancy group. About 25% of all infants entering the NICU will be at high risk for subsequent developmental disabilities and will contribute to the majority of *severely* (DQ <50) developmentally disabled youngsters.

conditions that relate primarily to sociocultural factors. This latter group may be more appropriately identified through screening programs during the preschool period. The problems of these children appear to be sociopolitical in nature and may be more expeditiously dealt with by politicians, educators, and social service agencies. The physician should provide primary medical support to and advocacy for this group. Studies suggest that intervention with this population has generally been unsuccessful unless a massive ecologically oriented program is developed.[44]

On the other hand, the high-risk biological category listed on p. 22 is the primary purview of the physician. With regionalization, most, if not all, of these high-risk babies will have or should have been involved in a neonatal intensive care unit. Prior to discharge, a primary care physician should be identified for follow-up and on-going health supervision.

Screening versus comprehensive assessment

The number of youngsters requring an intensive assessment in the primary care setting will vary, depending on the socioeconomic status of the patient population served and whether or not the high-risk or at-risk definition is used. The socioeconomic level of the patient is important because prematurity is one and a half times as frequent in families of lower socioeconomic status than in middle-class or upper-class families (13% versus 7%).[63] The early identification of developmentally disabled infants requires comprehensive developmental evaluation. Such assessment techniques as the Michigan Profile,[23] Knobloch's Adaptation of the Gesell Behavioral Assessment,[52] or the Bayley Scales[7] are used for this purpose. All these tests and the neuromaturational examination by Prechtl[70] or Milani-Comparetti[59] are described in Chapter 4. The infant who is *at risk* or who has no history of an untoward perinatal event can be evaluated using such screening techniques as the Knobloch and Pasamanick[52] Developmental Screening Inventory or Frankenburg's Developmental Screening Test[32] and an adequate neurological examination.

The sensitivity of a particular developmental screening test can be enhanced by the use of a more extensive and comprehensive examination; however, the addition of more standardized test items, while increasing clinical reliability, simultaneously decreases the capability of screening large numbers of children. Therefore in an effort to increase clinical reliability the choice of the primary care physician should be to intensively observe and assess a relatively small number of high-risk infants and use developmental screening techniques for the vast majority of other pediatric patients.

As will be discussed in the Chapters 3 and 4, these efforts can only be worthwhile if a positive outcome can be related directly to the early age at which treatment and family support are initiated. The cost of early detection and early treatment must then be balanced against the human waste and suffering that may occur in the absence of such programs. As Rogers[72] indicates, screening programs require longitudinal observations and transfer the initiative from the parents or patients to the professionals. This not only increases cost but also creates a level of anxiety in the families of normal as well as abnormal children that is usually not present in the routine health maintenance program.

Reproductive and caretaking casualty as it relates to factors that place an infant at high risk for subsequent developmental disabilities

If the primary care physician is to be alert to the perinatal factors that place an infant at high risk for subsequent developmental disabilities, the transaction between reproductive and caretaking casualty must be understood. Studies by Hanshaw and co-workers[40], Graham and associates[35], Drillien[26] and Bacola and colleagues[5] in the long-term follow-up of children who suffer congenital infection, hypoxia, and respiratory distress or who have a low birth weight suggest that the outcome of untoward perinatal events is closely related to the socioeconomic status of the family. This selective morbidity among lower socioeconomic children as compared to the middle-class and upper-class children can only be interpreted when one studies the physical, biological, and social environment, the family genetics, and the transactional state that occurs between the perinatal complications and these children. The potential for a positive developmental outcome for the newborn appears to be related to an interaction between the severity of the initial injury, the infant's inherent capabilities for recovery, and such environmental factors as the nutritional status of the mother and infant, subsequent exposure to disease, and the facilitation of the cognitive and affective process by the caregiver. The unidimensional concept of cause and effect, as described in Fig. 2-2, is no longer applicable. What is now observed is the result of a transaction between the multiple variables just described, which changes over time and includes appropriate intervention (Fig. 2-3).

Attempts to measure outcome based on such single variables as Apgar scores,[29] duration of apnea, hypoxia, and birth weight have been appropriately replaced by research models utilizing multifactoral analysis, including socioeconomic status and measures of caretaking capability. The continuum of reproductive casuality, as presented by Lilienfeld and Parkhurst[55] and further studies by Pasamanick and Knobloch,[68] implies a direct relationship between the degree of neonatal injury and the long-term neurological, affective, and cognitive outcome of the youngster. It is apparent that

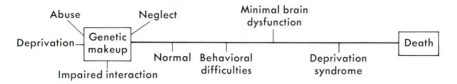

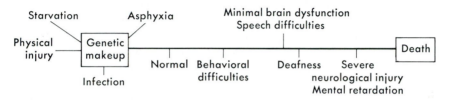

Fig. 2-2. The continua of caretaking and reproductive casualty each imply direct and separate relationships among perinatal events, childrearing practices, and outcome.

$(v^1 + t^1) \ (v^2 + t^2) \ (v^3 + t^3)$ △ Dynamic state in constant flux

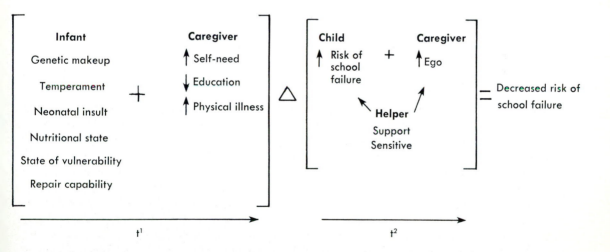

v = variable

t = time

Δ = changing state

Fig. 2-3. There is a transaction between factors that affect the infant and the characteristics of the caregiver. These determine school performance. Intervention models provide helpers that attempt to impact on child-rearing practices by improving the ego and performance of the caregiver. The caregiver in turn facilitates the cognitive growth of the infant or child, which results in a decreased risk of school failure and illness.

a profound neonatal insult may lead to severe intellectual and neurological dysfunction; however, even in those instances in which there is a severe hypoxic episode, the outcome may be variable. In the more mildly affected infant and the infant without apparent perinatal injury or infection, the outcome may be determined by such variables as the infants' genetic threshold to withstand injury, their repair capability, the state of nutrition, and subsequently their interaction with parents or their participation in a preschool experience.

Psychiatric risk studies[3] and studies of offspring of schizophrenic parents have emphasized the interaction of these multiple variables. Sameroff and Chandler[75] reviewed the long-term follow-up studies by Graham[35] and revealed a waning of minor neurological signs and developmental delays as the youngster approaches school age. These studies suggest an incredible capability for repair by the infant and child. The study by Sameroff and Zax[76] of schizophrenic mothers whose infants experienced perinatal difficulties indicated that these infants did not fare as well as similar infants of nonschizophrenic mothers. The less-than-optimal behavioral qualities in both infants and caregivers led them to predict the less-than-favorable cognitive and affective outcome for these infants. They postulated a transactional state created as a result of the interaction of the infant and the caregiver and presented the concept of continuum caretaking casualty.

The study by Hanshaw and co-workers[40] of children with inapparent congenital cytomegalovirus infection emphasized the selective morbidity among infants of lower socioeconomic status and the vulnerability of the unwed teen-aged mother. The number of pregnant, unwed teen-aged mothers from lower socioeconomic groups who had infection was greater than the number of middle-class or upper-class mothers with infection, although the mothers of lower socioeconomic status made up a smaller percentage of the total pregnant women studied. There was a significant IQ difference among the congenitally infected infants and the matched and random controls (Fig. 2-4, *A*). The significance of the effect of the socioeconomic status of the youngsters is emphasized when the in-

fected, matched, and random groups are distributed according to socioeconomic class. The middle-and upper-class groups showed no significant IQ difference among the infected, matched, and random groups (Fig. 2-4, *B*), whereas 30% of the children of lower socioeconomic status were predicted to experience school failure on the basis of a low IQ.

It is apparent that a profound neonatal insult may lead to severe intellectual and neurological dysfunction, but as Bacola and co-workers[5] and Drillien[26] indicated, the untoward environmental conditions that are associated with the lower socioeconomic status of the high-risk infant compound the perinatal factors that may result in ultimate intellectual impairment. The evaluation of the high-risk infant, therefore, requires study of the following:

- The medical and psychiatric status of the mother who is at risk of having a high-risk infant
- The perinatal events that lead to subsequent intellectual difficulties
- The caregiver on which the infant depends for help and fulfillment of developmental needs and the environment in which the infant develops

THE HIGH-RISK MOTHER

Depending on the socioeconomic class of the mother, Aubrey and Pennington[4] noted that 20% to 30% of all pregnancies can be identified as being at high risk for potential complications that may jeopardize the health and survival of the mother and infant. The mothers who were identified as being at high risk gave birth to 70% to 80% of the infants with low birth weights, respiratory distress syndrome, or apnea—all of which have high rates for potential mortality and morbidity. The mothers who were not previously identified as being at high risk unexpectedly contributed to the remaining 20% to 30% at-risk infants (a strong case against home deliveries) (Fig. 2-1).

The pathological, epidemiological, and socioeconomic factors that increase maternal and infant mortality and morbidity include these four categories:

1. The general demographic and physical characteristics of the mother, such as so-

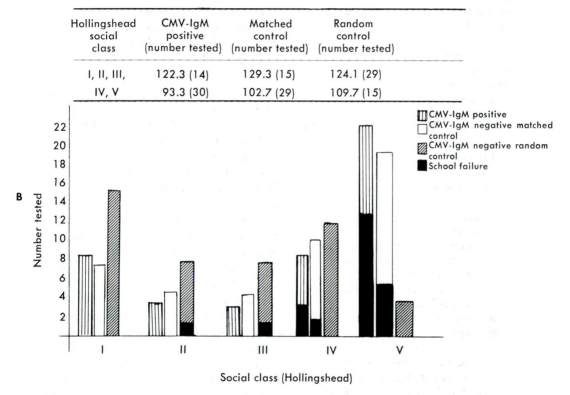

	Number tested	Mean IQ
CMV-IgM positive	44	102.5
A CMV-IgM negative (matched controls)	44	111.7
CMV-IgM negative (random controls)	44	119.2

Hollingshead social class	CMV-IgM positive (number tested)	Matched control (number tested)	Random control (number tested)
I, II, III,	122.3 (14)	129.3 (15)	124.1 (29)
IV, V	93.3 (30)	102.7 (29)	109.7 (15)

Fig. 2-4. A, The relationship of IQ with inapparent congenital cytomegalovirus (CMV) infection (CMV-IgM positive). The interreaction between inapparent infection and socioeconomic status is demonstrated in **B. B,** Relationship between school failure, cord CMV-IgM antibody, and social class. (From Hanshaw, J. B., et al.: CNS sequelae of congenital cytomegalovirus. In Krugman, S., and Gershon, A. A., editors: Infections of the fetus and the newborn infant, New York, 1975, Alan R. Liss, Inc.)

cioeconomic status, educational achievement, age, height, and weight

2. Coexisting medical conditions such as diabetes, use of medication, and toxemia as well as psychiatric disorders
3. The mother's past reproductive history
4. Any complications of the current pregnancy

Obviously, the last category markedly increases the predictability of potential difficulties in the newborn period. Following is an expanded list of the factors that increase mortality and morbidity:

A. Demographic and physical characteristics
   1. Maternal age of 15 years or less or 35 years or more
   2. Massive obesity
   3. Lower socioeconomic status
B. Maternal obstetrical history
   1. Genital tract anomalies such as incompetent

cervix, cervical malformation, or uterine malformation
2. Any previous abortions
3. Previous stillborn or premature infant
4. Macrosomia of greater than 4000 g in two infants
5. Maternal malignancy, leiomyoma, or ovarian mass
6. Parity of 5 or more
7. Previous infants with isoimmunization
8. History of eclampsia
9. Previously known genetic congenital or familial disorder
10. Previous delivery of high-risk infant
11. Medical need for termination of previous pregnancy

C. Maternal medical history
1. Chronic hypertension—moderate to severe
2. Severe renal disease
3. Severe heart disease with congestive failure or cyanotic heart disease
4. Diabetes—classes B through F
5. Drug addiction or alcoholism
6. Chronic pulmonary, liver, or gastrointestinal disease
7. Malignancy
8. Severe anemia
9. Hydantoin therapy related to seizure disorder

D. Early or late pregnancy—related factors
1. Failure of uterine growth
2. Exposure to such teratogens as radiation infection or chemicals
3. Pregnancy complicated by isoimmunization
4. Severe preeclampsia or eclampsia
5. Potential breech delivery
6. Placenta previa or abruptio placentae
7. Polyhydramnios or oligohydramnios
8. Greater than 42 weeks gestation or premature labor at less than 37 weeks gestation
9. Premature rupture of membranes (less than 37 weeks)
10. Multiple gestations
11. Abnormal oxytocin challenge test results or falling estriol levels

Demographic and physical characteristics that correlate with increased perinatal risk

Socioeconomic status[16] is the most important correlate with increased perinatal mortality and morbidity. Abruptio placentae, placenta previa, placental insufficiency, and toxemia are all predisposing factors for small for gestational age and premature infants and are more common in mothers of lower socioeconomic status. The fact that birth weight correlates directly with perinatal mortality and morbidity is well established.[55] This direct correlation between infant mortality and low birth weight is not only true in developing third-world countries but is also true in industrialized nations. The difference between the birth weights of infants from various socioeconomic classes in itself accounts for the difference in perinatal mortality between the rich and the poor.[74]

Studies[12,16,71] from such industrialized nations as Great Britain support the direct relationship between adequacy of nutrition and infant mortality. Maternal weight gain during pregnancy correlates directly with the birth weight of the infant and consequently with infant mortality. On the basis of these studies several clinics in the United States and Canada have initiated nutritional therapy during pregnancy, resulting in a decrease in infant morbidity and mortality and an associated increase in the birth weight of the infant. The National Academy of Science[71] supports a weight gain of at least 9 to 11 kg in a previously well-nourished woman.

Maternal age also has a direct bearing on perinatal risk, the risk being greatest in the teen-aged mother under 17 years of age and a mother over 35 years of age.[16] In 1975,[60] although the number of infants born decreased in all groups, births to young teenagers increased by 21% over the number born in 1966. From 1966 to 1975, the total births to women over 30 years of age decreased from 23.3% to 16.5%, which is an important shift in light of the fact that the incidence of low birth weight and congenital anomalies among infants rises steeply with increasing age and parity. During this same period (1966 to 1975) the overall out-of-wedlock pregnancy rate increased along with the previously noted increase in early teenage (less than age 18 years) pregnancies. The incidence of low birth weight infants and perinatal mortality in infants born to out-of-wedlock mothers are almost double that of infants born to married women.

Half the pregnancies of young teen-aged

mothers and a third of the pregnancies of older teen-aged mothers (18 to 19 years of age) were out of wedlock. The incidence of out-of-wedlock conception is even greater when one considers that a third of the married teenagers delivered within 6 months of being married. The teen-aged mother frequently terminates her education and does not seek prenatal care until late in her pregnancy. Although there is a substantially greater number of out-of-wedlock teen-aged pregnancies among black youngsters as compared to white youngsters, the numbers of pregnancies in the white youngsters is increasingly significant.[60] The involvement of the white teenager may relate to the sudden interest in the teen-aged pregnancy problem.

New York's Nassau County,[17] which had the second highest medium income in the country in 1976, had a 12% increase in teen-aged pregnancies, whereas pregnancies in persons over 20 years of age decreased by 9%. About 76% of the 29,000 sexually active teenagers in that county had no assistance with family planning. In 1975[71] 13% of births to mothers 15 years of age resulted in infants weighing 2500 g or less at birth, as compared to 9% of births to 19-year-old mothers, 7.1% of births to women 20 to 24 years of age, and 6% of births to women 25 to 29 years of age. The reason for the high incidence of low birth weight infants among young teenagers is not clear. There is an increased incidence of anemia, preeclampsia, and urinary tract infections in this population, and in general teenagers only seek prenatal care late in their pregnancy. The speculation that the teenager is not sufficiently mature sexually to sustain a full-term pregnancy was not confirmed by studies that compared prematurity and perinatal mortality rates in women under and over 14 years of age.[19]

Coexisting medical and obstetrical conditions

Toxemia. Following are conditions that are commonly associated with and are known to have a major effect on the production of low birth weight and congenital anomalies in infancy.

- Maternal age—15 years of age or less or greater than 35 years of age

- Incompetent cervix or other uterine or genital anomalies
- Parity of 5 or more
- Preeclampsia and eclampsia
- Chronic illness, especially diabetes, hypertension, renal disease, severe heart disease, severe anemia
- Drug addiction, hydantoin therapy, alcoholism
- Placenta previa or abruptio placentae
- Multiple gestations

Toxemia, hemorrhage, and sepsis continue to be responsible for the vast majority of cases of prematurity, fetal wastage, and maternal death.[47] The cause of toxemia still remains obscured, despite an estimated incidence of 5% to 7% and associated perinatal mortality of 8.1% with severe preeclampsia. In the vast majority of cases fetal mortality with severe toxemia is associated with prematurity. The decrease in the blood flow to the uterus may result in malnutrition with as much as a 400 to 700 g decrease in fetal weight. Good prenatal care and management help to decrease both maternal and infant mortality and morbidity.

Cardiovascular disease. Cardiovascular disease due to rheumatic fever was at one time the most common organic maternal cardiac lesion. With the advent of adequate diagnosis and treatment of group A β-hemolytic *Streptococcus,* cyanotic heart disease is now the most common cardiac lesion among mothers and results in the decreased birth weight of the infant.[81] There is also increased incidence of cardiac anomalies in infants of women with cyanotic heart disease. Women with congenital heart disease contemplating pregnancy should be thoroughly evaluated, and surgical correction should be accomplished prior to conception when indicated. Collagen diseases, in general, do not markedly affect fetal or neonatal outcome; however, scleredema and systemic lupus erythematosus have a major impact on perinatal mortality when associated with hypertension and renal disease.[20,30]

Diabetes. Maternal diabetes is linked with increased risk of premature birth, associated hypoglycemia, congenital anomalies, and stillbirth. Gellis and Hsia[33] reported a maternal death rate of 15% and a fetal wastage of 59%

among diabetic mothers chosen at random. Perinatal mortality varies between 8% and 30%, depending on the adequacy of management and the association of such preexisting diabetic complications as vascular disease, renal involvement, and retinopathy. No relationship between transient or gestational diabetes, which appears during pregnancy, and perinatal mortality has been proved. The meticulous control of the diabetic mother is of utmost importance. Poor diabetic control is associated with increased perinatal mortality, macrosomia, and subsequent lower IQ scores compared to infants of well-controlled diabetic mothers.[18] The incidence of congenital anomalies in infants of diabetic mothers is 6.4% in contrast to 2.4% in offspring of nondiabetic controls. The relationship between diabetic control and subsequent anomalies has not been established.

Alcoholism. The offspring of the mother with chronic alcoholism has been reported to have a recognizable pattern of multiple congenital anomalies such as microcephaly, micrognathia, blephrophimosis, microphthalmia, cardiac defects, intrauterine growth retardation, and developmental delay.[41,48] These infants have also been reported to have increased perinatal mortality. A recent prospective study by Ouellette and co-workers[64] indicated that the frequency of all abnormalities was twice as great in the offsprings of heavy drinkers, but the fetal alcohol syndrome that had been previously reported was not noted. It is not known if alcohol itself acts as a direct toxin or whether other factors must be present to produce abnormalities. It is suggested that heavy drinking during the first trimester had the greatest effect on fetal maldevelopment, whereas alcohol excess near term may have greater effect on fetal nutrition and size. There is little question that there is a definite increased risk to the fetus of the mother who drinks excessively during pregnancy. The Federal Drug Administration[32] has recently suggested that not more than 2 ounces of alcohol per week or two drinks per day be consumed by a woman who is pregnant. I have seen one youngster with many of the stigmata of the fetal alcohol syndrome born to parents who were alcoholics but reportedly had not been drinking for 2 years prior to the mother's pregnancy. This would seem to suggest irreparable damage to the germ plasm rather than a direct teratogenic effect on the fertilized ovum.

Seizure disorders and the hydantoin syndrome. Data presented by the American Academy of Pediatrics indicated that 3 out of every 1000 women received hydantoin (phenytoin, mephenytoin, and ethotoin) therapy during their pregnancy.[2] Hanson and co-workers[42] suggested that approximately 11% of their offspring would display enough features to be classified as having the fetal hydantoin syndrome. This syndrome consists of mental deficiency, prenatal and postnatal growth failure, microcephaly, craniofacial abnormalities, nail and distal phalangeal hypoplasia, and associated cardiac defects. The facts that approximately 6000 infants will have had an intrauterine exposure to hydantoin-containing drugs and that a significant number will have mental retardation along with congenital malformations indicate the need for adequate genetic counselling and possible alternate means of seizure control prior to pregnancy. The mechanism for the production of these abnormalities is unclear.

Smoking. In a review regarding the effects of smoking on the fetus and newborn child, Holsclaw and Topham[46] indicated that smoking causes the following:

• Changes in fetal cardiorespiratory physiology
• Decreased birth weight and size by as much as 400 g and a decrease in length by 1.3 cm
• Increased perinatal mortality and congenital malformations
• Possible relationship with sudden infant death and respiratory disease

These are all preventable conditions; unfortunately smoking is supported by major advertising efforts, poor adult models, and few deterrents by the federal government.

Psychiatric illness and emotional stress. The relationship of psychiatric illness during pregnancy with perinatal difficulties and subsequent abnormalities of offsprings has been extensively studied.[58,75] The review by Sameroff and Chandler[75] indicated that such broad categories as depression and schizophrenia are not sufficient to identify the potentially high-risk mother. They do emphasize that the chronicity and severity of the mother's illness along with the number of her previous pregnancies, age, and socioeducational status are all important variables in predicting prenatal difficulties. McDonald's[58] review of the literature in terms of potential prematurity, low birth weight, and congenital anomalies identified shortcomings of many of these studies. From the better studies he concluded that such factors as maternal anxiety along with dependency, sexual immaturity, and the mother's poor attitude toward her pregnancy had an impact on the variables that contribute to prematurity, abortion, and other obstetrical complications. Evaluation of the emotional status and the prenatal and perinatal history of the mother has been consolidated into questionnaires[4] that identify the high-risk mother.

Methods of monitoring the high-risk pregnancy

Intrapartum electronic and biochemical monitoring and measures of fetal-placental-maternal integrity continue to provide the greatest information in regard to potential risk to the infant and mother. Following are intrapartum factors that place an infant at high risk:

- Severe preeclampsia or eclampsia
- Polyhydramnios or oligohydramnios
- Amnionitis
- Membranes prematurely ruptured for over 24 hours
- Placenta previa
- Abruptio placentae
- Meconium staining of amniotic fluid
- Abnormal presentation
- Multiple gestation
- Fetal weight of less than 1500 g or more than 4000 g
- Persistant fetal bradycardia—less than 120 and unchanged by maternal position and loss of variability
- Fetal tachycardia—greater than 170
- Prolapsed cord
- Fetal acidosis—pH of 7.25 or less prior to second stage of labor
- Evidence of maternal distress, that is, hypotension or hypoxia
- Abnormal oxytocin challenge test results; falling urinary or low plasma estriol determination

- Immature or intermediate lecithin/sphingomyelin (L/S) ratio or an abnormal rapid surfactant test

The primary care physician should be aware of the measures and techniques used in the identification of the potentially high-risk neonate. These can be used as guidelines in predicting subsequent developmental sequelae, and their use in managing the pregnancy is also a measure of the competence of the obstetrician. The primary care physician is in a position to judge the adequacy of the obstetrical care of the mother. The physician may want to suggest that the mother seek an alternate source of care if it appears that she is being, or has been in the past, inadequately managed during pregnancy. The high-risk mother should be encouraged to continue her primary medical care after the completion of her pregnancy. Adequate health maintenance may help prevent the birth of another high-risk infant.

Current techniques for the management and identification of the high-risk pregnancy consist primarily of monitoring the following:

- Plasma and urinary estriol determinations
- Biparietal diameter using ultrasound
- Amniotic fluid L/S ratio examination
- Fetal heart rate
- Blood gases and pH through the fetal scalp

Maiscels and co-workers[57] addressed the need for careful assessment of the maturity of the infant when elective delivery is being considered. They point out that 15% to 33% of cases of hyaline membrane disease can be avoided using ultrasound in conjunction with the L/S ratio to accurately determine the length of gestation.

A decrease in the urinary estriol level after 8 weeks generally represents a compromise in fetal well-being. It is important to monitor the urinary estriol levels in states such as diabetes, preeclampsia, and essential hypertension.

Ultrasound is a noninvasive procedure that uses pulsed high-frequency sound waves to determine the fetal head size, the location of the placenta, and the number of fetuses present. The serial measurement of fetal head size is important to determine the gestational age of the fetus. This can best be accomplished between 18 and 22 weeks, when readings are most accurate. Other indications for the use of ultrasound are the questions of hydrocephalus, anencephaly, and spina bifida. It should always be used to locate the placenta and the fetus prior to amniocentesis.

Analysis of amniotic fluid obtained through amniocentesis not only provides information in regard to chromosomal disorders and congenital metabolic abnormalities (Chapter 9) but also provides information about the maturity of the fetus. It has been demonstrated that the essential surface-active agent for pulmonary maturity is a phospholipid, lecithin. The lecithin level in the amniotic fluid rises sharply at 33 weeks, whereas the sphingomyelin level remains constant. In maternal diabetes the L/S ratio may give false-positive evidence of fetal pulmonary maturity. In most instances it is a reliable measure for prognosticating the potential risk for the respiratory distress syndrome.

The monitoring of the fetal heart rate in conjunction with fetal scalp and capillary blood samples is a reliable measure of intrauterine asphyxia and hypoxia.[8] The combined use of both techniques correlates better with the clinical state of the infant than either one alone. A fetal scalp pH of less than 7.2 when combined with late decelerations of the fetal heart rate and/or decreased beat-to-beat variability shows a high correlation with a subsequent decreased Apgar score.

Other measures of fetal-maternal well-being include the ratio of urea nitrogen to total nitrogen as a measure of maternal nutrition and tachodynamometry as a measure of maternal uterine contractions. The latter is used in conjunction with fetal heart monitoring to identify the relationship of the fetal heart beat to the uterine contractions. As mentioned previously, these special techniques are especially important to the high-risk mother. The presence of a 20% intrapartum obstetrical risk even in the mother presumably with minimal risk supports the use of fetal heart monitoring for all women at the time of delivery. In those instances in which the mother is at potential risk for intrapartum difficulty, an oxytocin stress test, which induces mild contractions, may be very helpful in further predicting the potential problems for the mother and infant. The effects of the contractions on the fetal heart rate are monitored in a manner similar to the actual labor monitoring.

In summary, just as new methods in neonatal care have had a major impact on neonatal morbidity and mortality, there appears to be little question that the combined current knowledge of obstetrics and neonatology could further decrease perinatal mortality and morbidity by 40%.[56]

THE HIGH-RISK INFANT

Studies that predict developmental outcome become rapidly obsolete with changing patterns of care; however, factors that consistently contribute to increased neonatal mortality and morbidity remain unchanged (p. 28). Low socioeconomic status, gestational age, and weight continue to be directly related to increased perinatal mortality and morbidity.

The rapid obsolescence of treatment regimens and the heterogenous groupings of subjects studied contribute to the confusion and the interpretation of studies that correlate outcome with perinatal events and infant characteristics. The appropriate for gestational age premature infant with a benign neonatal course is often pooled with small for gestational age infants of similar weight who have experienced a great deal of neonatal difficulty. A mixture of such subjects in a single study provides little help in predicting developmental outcome for the individual infant. A suggested approach to the study of perinatal events and factors that affect subsequent developmental risk would be the classification of infants according to the following:

1. Gestational weight and age
2. The presence or absence of specific perinatal disorders such as hemolytic disease, asphyxia, respiratory distress syndrome, and central nervous system hemorrhage
3. Treatment regimens, such as mechanical ventilation, CPAP, and exchange transfusions, as they relate to perinatal disease state
4. Overall miscellaneous factors, which include laboratory findings that are generally secondary to categories 1 and 2

Disease states and untoward perinatal events should be very specifically defined, not only in terms of duration and intensity but also in terms of the extent of damage to the infant as they relate to individual repair capability and resistance to stress. These latter qualities may be reflected in the behavioral and clinical state of the infant as measured by Apgar score, tone, awareness, seizures, gastrointestinal symptoms, and neurological state. The behavioral and physical characteristics paired with laboratory data are far more meaningful than any single category.

The infant could then be homogenously grouped according to specific weight, gestational age, perinatal events, behavioral and physical state, laboratory studies, and treatment regimens. Interstudy comparisons would then be possible. In the absence of research that studies neonates in a prescribed, orderly fashion and provides the natural history of these specific categories, the provision of accurate information to parents in regard to ultimate outcome is exceedingly difficult.

The low birth weight and small for gestational age infant

The small for gestational age infant is at greater risk for perinatal and subsequent developmental disabilities than the infant appropriate for gestational age. Fig. 2-5 describes common conditions associated with deviations in intrauterine growth. The careful determination of the expected date of confinement by maternal history and assessment of the gestational age of the infant using the Dubowitz method[29] or examining the anterior vascular capsule of the lens[45] have important prognostic implications.

Winick and co-workers[89,90] make the distinction between the contributions of intrinsic and extrinsic fetal growth retardation factors (Fig. 2-6). Intrinsic factors are related to genetic and established defects, whereas extrinsic factors relate to abnormalities within the fetal environment, such as vascular compromise secondary to preeclampsia or deficient maternal nutrition. Causal relationships of extrinsic factors producing general malformations and abnormalities should also be recognized. The extrinsic group is divided into type 1 and type 2 infants. The growth retardation of type 1 infants is related to maternal vascular disease and associated with asymmetrical growth failure with

sparing of the brain and decrease in liver size and associated depletion of glycogen stores. The type 2 infants experience overall growth retardation related to maternal malnutrition and are seen more commonly in developing countries. The potential for overlap is present in both groups, with symmetrical growth failure being present in those infants who are exposed to a less-than-optimal intrauterine environment for the full 9 months. Many of the studies that relate maternal nutrition to prematurity of the infant may, in fact, be studies of underweight, small for gestational age infants.[82]

Infants in Drillien's[27] recent study of low birth weight infants born in Edinburgh between 1966 and 1971 are classified according to the following:
1. Infants with developmental abnormalities due to adverse factors early in pregnancy
2. Infants with low birth weight due to severe complications later in the pregnancy
3. The pure premature who does not appear to have been affected by any adverse prenatal conditions and is presumably constitutionally normal at birth

The infants in Drillien's category 1 have associated developmental abnormalities with one major or more than three minor congenital abnormalities; the infants in group 2 were born to women with preeclampsia or chronic disease. She further categorizes the small for gestational age infant into the group of *very* small infants who fall below the 3rd percentile and the small for gestational age infants who are between the 3rd and 10th percentile but are not optimal in growth and weight. The infants who were *very* small for gestational age secondary to adverse factors in early pregnancy have the greatest mortality and morbidity. The lower the birth weight, the greater the potential for acute and subsequent problems. Those infants with the greatest degree of growth retardation were more likely to have associated developmental abnormalities.

The low birth weight infant appropriate for gestational age

The overall outlook for the low birth weight infant whose weight is appropriate for gestational age has improved markedly. Stewart and co-workers[83] attribute the improved prognosis

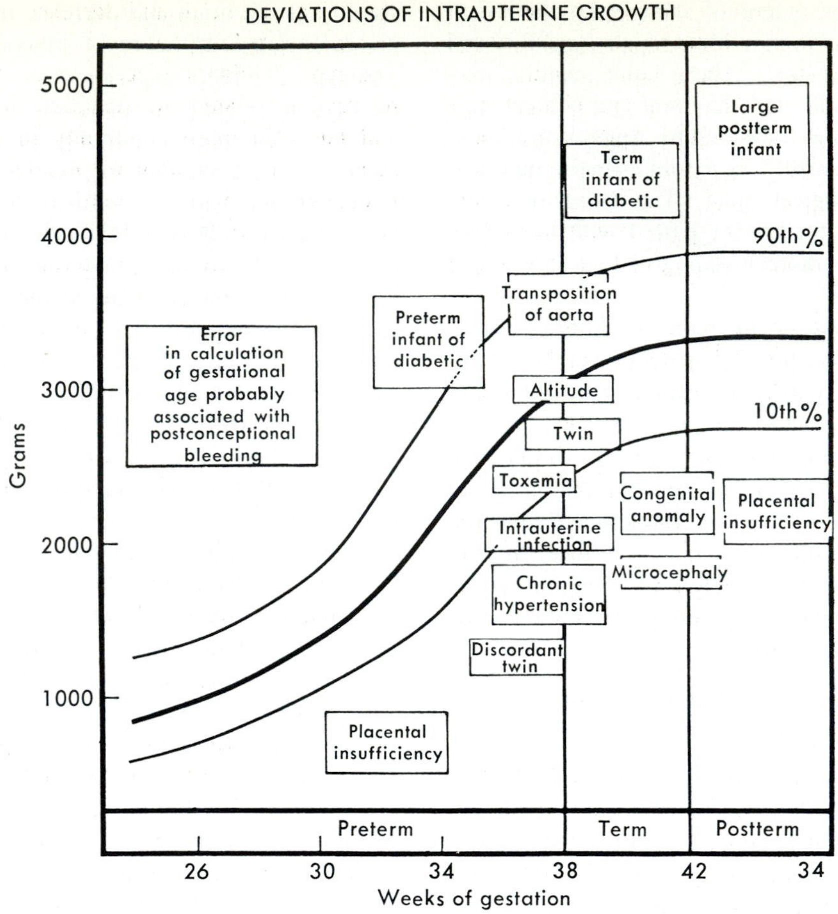

DEVIATIONS OF INTRAUTERINE GROWTH

Fig. 2-5. Conditions associated with deviations of intrauterine growth, which may be associated with significant morbidity, represented graphically to indicate the approximate birth weight and gestational age at which the condition is likely to occur. (From Jonxis, J. H. P., Visser, H. K. A., and Troelstra, J. A.: Aspects of prematurity and dysmaturity. Presented at Nutrician Symposium, Groningen, Netherlands, 1967, Leiden, Netherlands, 1968, Stenfert Kroese, N.V.)

of infants of 1000 g or less born after 1970 to the introduction of the following:

- Regionalization of intensive care with new transportation equipment
- L/S ratio determinations
- Continuous positive airway pressure
- Mechanical ventilation techniques with simultaneous improvement of gas monitoring measures
- Improved partial and total parenteral nutrition

The survival of the less than 1000 g infant was 13% from 1965 through 1970 as compared to 32% from 1966 through 1975. About 68% of the total study population of infants under 1000 g were subsequently described as being normal.[83] Between 1966 and 1975 Stewart compares a 41% survival rate of infants weighing between 751 and 1000 g with an 8% survival rate of infants weighing below 750 g. About 78% of all these infants were subsequently described as being normal. Drillien[27] reported that only 9.6% of 283 Edinburgh infants born between 1966 and 1971 and weighing less than 2000 g were severely handicapped when assessed between the ages of 1 and 3 years. The figure for those less than 1500 g was only 13.7% and for those 1501 to 2000 g, 7.1%.

Contrary to the often-stated belief that we

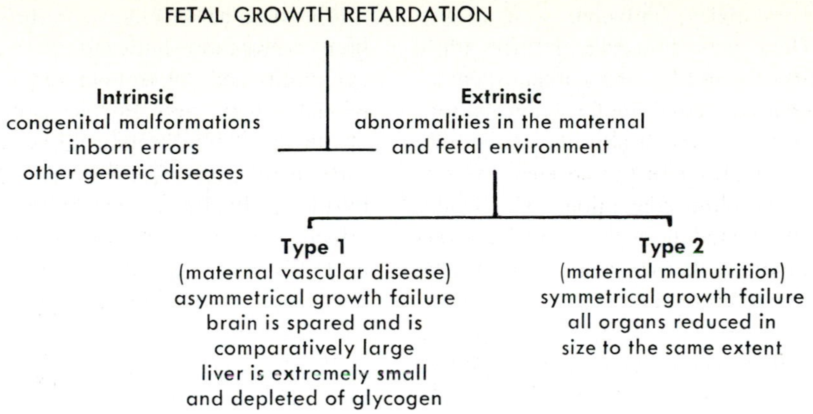

FETAL GROWTH RETARDATION

Fig. 2-6. The distinction between intrinsic and extrinsic factors in intrauterine growth retardation. (From Winick, M.: Maternal nutrition. In Brent, R. L., and Harris, M. I., editors: Prevention of embryonic fetal and perinatal disease, HEW publ. no. (NIH) 76853, Washington, D.C., Department of Health, Education and Welfare.)

Table 2-1. Spastic diplegia in survivors of very low birth weight*

Authors	Year of birth	Birth weight (g)	Sample number	Spastic diplegia (%)
Lubchenco et al. (1972)	1947 to 1950	<1500	133	32
Drillien (1964)	1948 to 1960	<1360	91	20
McDonald (1967)	1951 to 1953	<1580	560	7
Wright et al. (1972)	1952 to 1956	<1500	65	9
Davies and Tizard (1975)	1961 to 1964	<1500	58	10
Davies and Tizard (1975)	1965 to 1970	<1500	107	0

*From Davies. P. A., and Tizard, J. P. M.: Dev. Med. Child Neurol. **17:**317, 1975.

have improved the survival of infants at the expense of quality of life, studies by Stewart and co-workers,[83] Hagberg and colleagues, [38] and Davies and Tizard[22] (Table 2-1) suggest that both have been improved with current methods of prenatal care. Dargassies[21] studied a large group of premature infants from birth to school age, and some for as long as 18 years. She found severe neurological sequelae in only 21% of the population. The sequelae were related directly to the degree of prematurity. About 31% of the infants demonstrated developmental sequelae at 28 weeks as compared to 9% at 37 weeks.

As one would suspect, the quality of postnatal care and subsequent untoward postnatal events also have a direct relationship to the long-term developmental outcome of the infant.

Once again those factors which predispose an infant to intracranial hemorrhage, hypoxia, hypoglycemia, and respiratory distress would seem to relate directly to the developmental outcome of the infant. Davies and Tizard,[22] in their study of very low birth weight and subsequent neurological defects in infants under 1500, suggested that spastic diplegia may be related to hypothermia on the first day of life, which is associated with intraventricular hemorrhage.

Untoward perinatal events

Hemolytic disease. A recent study of the neurological and psychological outcome in fetal erythroblastosis by Sederholm[80] indicated that kernicterus has all but been eliminated. Only 2 children out of 71 showed evidence of spastic cerebral palsy, and none were clearly athetotic. There was, however, a surprisingly high incidence of mild hearing impairment as well as impaired visual motor coordination, speech disturbance, and strabismus. The study is difficult to interpret in the absence of controls and double-blind precautions. The sequelae noted were related more closely to the severity of the hemolytic disease as measured by the level of hemoglobin than by the level of bilirubin. As in other studies, there does appear to be some minor neurological and cognitive sequelae in the areas of muscle tone, speech, language, and visual motor coordination.

The proper management of the Rh-negative mother is more appropriately covered in a text focusing on neonatal and perinatal care. In addition to the adequate management of the infant with hemolytic disease, physicians are also obligated to adequately manage the Rh-negative mother. The prevention of Rh sensitization is now possible with the use of Rh immunoglobulins. This should be given to all Rh-negative women who deliver Rh-positive infants and are not sensitized as a result of the pregnancy. The medication should be given within 72 hours of delivery. The Rh immunoglobulins should also be used in Rh-negative women undergoing spontaneous therapeutic abortions. There is some question whether this should also be given to Rh-negative neonates who are born to Rh-positive mothers in an effort to avoid future sensitization from the birth of their offspring.

Hypoglycemia. The confusion regarding the long-term effects of hypoglycemia in the newborn relates to the definition of hypoglycemia and its frequent association with other potentially damaging neonatal events such as asphyxia, prematurity, small for gestational age, and polycythemia. Dodson[24] indicates that a blood glucose concentration of 40 mg/ml in the full-term infant or 30 mg/ml or less in a premature infant is 3 standard deviations below the mean values of healthy newborn infants. He suggests that these levels, even in the absence of seizures, may in themselves be significant. Some investigators define hypoglycemia as blood concentration of less than 30 and 20 mg/ml in term and premature infants, respectively. The

use of these lower glucose values relates to the high correlation between the occurrence of symptoms and subsequent sequelae; however, neonates with high glucose concentration that are in the hypoglycemic range may also have subsequent neurological dysfunction or injury. Further difficulty in interpreting the long-term effects of hypoglycemia in the newborn relates to its frequent association with congenital malformations of the brain, potentially damaging neonatal events such as asphyxia, placental insufficiency, preeclampsia, sepsis, erythroblastosis, polycythemia, and respiratory distress, which in themselves may be damaging.

Dodson describes two general conditions that are associated with neonatal hypoglycemia: decreased substrate availability and abnormal substrate utilization. In the latter category are infants of diabetic mothers who have an excessive insulin release in response to maternal carbohydrates and infants with sepsis who have an increased sensitivity to insulin when compared with the normal insulin response.

In the presence of hypoxia and hypotension, there is a cellular deficiency of glucose as a result of decreased blood flow, and with seizures there is an increased glucose consumption. These factors suggest that the absolute blood glucose level may not be the sole determinant of carbohydrate need and utilization and that neurological sequelae may be present in the absence of symptoms. There is little question that the neurological sequelae of hypoglycemia are more common in the presence of symptoms. Less than 33% of symptomatic newborns are normal on long-term follow-up, and infants who are treated early and do not have seizures are normal in 75% of instances.[24] The hypoglycemic infant of the diabetic mother seems to be resistant to adverse effects of hypoglycemia and have a better prognosis than the other symptomatic groups. Infants who do not respond to glucose therapy in the presence of hypoglycemia suggest the presence of associated central nervous system damage, possibly related to the preexisting hypoxia.

Hypocalcemia. The infant with uncomplicated neonatal tetany due to hypocalcemia has an excellent prognosis for normal development. The sequelae of hypocalcemic tetany that oc-

Table 2-2. Prognosis of neonatal
seizures—relation to neurological disease*

Neurologic disease†	Normal development‡ %
Hypoxic-ischemic encephalopathy	10 to 20
Primary subarachnoid hemorrhage	90
Intraventricular hemorrhage	<5
Hypocalcemia	
Early onset	50
Later onset	80 to 100
Hypoglycemia	50
Bacterial meningitis	20 to 50
Developmental defect	0

*From Volpe, J. J.: Clin. Perinatol. **4**:43, 1977.
†Includes cases accompanied by seizures.
‡In general, periods of follow-up do not extend to school age.

cur on the first or second day and that are associated with hyperbilirubinemia, respiratory distress, prematurity, or asphyxia relate directly to the primary disorder rather than the hypocalcemia itself (Table 2-2).[86]

Congenital nonbacterial infections. Nonbacterial infection of the newborn infant places him at high risk for subsequent neurological difficulties. Hanshaw and Dudgeon[39] present an excellent review of this topic. Herpesvirus, unlike cytomegalovirus, *Toxoplasma,* and the rubella virus, is the only member of the TORCH* group that does not produce inapparent infection.[38] It is a disease of the newborn that is acquired during the birth process. About 85% of the herpes cases are attributable to type II and are more frequently associated with chorioretinitis than type I. The clinical symptoms of the disease are variable consisting of lesions of the eyes, mouth, pharynx, or genitalia. About 50% of the cases that have central nervous system involvement have serious long-term neurological complications.

Congenital cytomegalovirus infection is the most common congenital infection and occurs in 0.6% to 1% of all live births. Even in the presence of inapparent infection, it has a high morbidity. Hanshaw and co-workers[40] demonstrated a 30% incidence of school failure as a

*Toxoplasma, the rubella virus, cytomegalovirus, and herpesvirus.

result of associated symptoms such as mental retardation, severe deafness, and high-frequency hearing losses. Congenital rubella infection during the first 8 weeks of gestation carries a 10% to 35% risk of mental retardation.[46] Sensory neurological loss is the most common clinical manifestation of the disease; however, central auditory perceptual deficits can also be present. The incidence of the triad of cataracts, deafness, and heart disease has been markedly decreased by rubella immunization.

Congenital toxoplasmosis is similar to congenital cytomegalovirus in that only a relatively small number of infants manifest the severe form of the disease with chorioretinitis, hepatosplenomegaly, jaundice, anemia, thrombocytopenia, pneumonia, rash, and central nervous system calcification. About 70% of the infants with toxoplasmosis have inapparent infections,[9] which may also be associated with such sequelae as mental retardation, motor dysfunction, and a high incidence of visual impairment.

Congenital syphilis should also be considered in the differentiation of the infant with a rash, purulent sniffles, hemorrhagic rhinitis, and rhagades. The neurological sequelae, optic atrophy, chorioretinitis, tabes dorsalis, mental paresis, and dementia, manifest themselves in adolescence and even later in life.

Asphyxia. Asphyxia of the fetus and newborn accounts for a major portion of total fetal loss and fetal brain injury and therefore warrants extensive discussion. About 90% of infants with cerebral palsy are thought to have sustained injury during the perinatal period, whereas only 10% sustained insults during the postnatal period.[9] An understanding of the terminology and pathological physiology of asphyxia is necessary for the interpretation of existing studies and clinical findings.

Neonatal asphyxia is defined as the impairment of respiratory gas exchange, either between the mother and fetus or within the lungs of the newborn infant. This impaired gas exchange results in a decrease in pH, an elevated P_{CO_2}, and a depression of P_{O_2}. The ability of the fetus to withstand untoward effects of oxygen deprivation appears to be related to the ability to maintain cerebral blood flow through adequate blood pressure. The human fetus and full-term newborn are unique in that they have cardiac glycogen stores. The amount of these stores is directly related to the gestational age of the infant. These stores can be drawn on for anaerobic support of cardiac output, which maintains adequate blood flow and pressure. Factors that decrease glycogen stores such as malnutrition and chronic intrauterine anoxia make the fetus and newborn more vulnerable to perinatal oxygen deprivation. However, their capability for anaerobic metabolism, decreased energy requirements, and ability to use ketones result in a relatively less damaging effect during periods of hypoxia.

Acute fetal asphyxia is produced by the interruption of blood supply or total airway occlusion in the neonate. Predisposing mechanical factors that are associated with an increased incidence of asphyxia include cord accidents, multiple pregnancies, cephalopelvic disproportion, and infant malposition and subsequent shoulder dystocia. Maternal factors that contribute to fetal asphyxia include hemorrhage, placenta previa, abruptio placentae, preeclampsia, diabetes, prolonged labor, hypertension, severe anemia, and cardiorespiratory disease. Obviously, overuse of maternal analgesia and anesthesia as well as the use of antihypertensive agents can cause depression and asphyxia in the newborn. The characteristics of the fetus that are associated with neonatal asphyxia include prematurity with associated pulmonary immaturity, congenital malformations, hemolytic disease, intrauterine infection, and intrauterine growth retardation. The hallmarks of intrapartum asphyxia are meconium passage, loss of beat-to-beat variability with subsequent fetal tachycardia or bradycardia (less than 120, greater than 170), late deceleration, or an unchanging irregular heartbeat. Hypoxia not only causes direct cellular damage and necrosis but also has been implicated as a major pathogenic factor in neonatal intercranial hemorrhage.[87]

The follow-up studies of infants with asphyxia are beleaguered with the same inconsistency noted previously in the study of sequelae of the preterm and small for gestational age infant. Inconsistencies in the definition of asphyxia, the method of selection (resulting in the study of heterogenous populations), the variety of risk factors considered, the methods of data collection and the variety of professionals making observations account for many of these discrepancies.

The definition of asphyxia in infants varies from having an Apgar score of less than 3 at 1 minute and less than 5 at 5 minutes to having an Apgar score of 0 or not being able to establish respiration at 20 minutes. Sources of data vary from direct observations by midwives and primary care physicians to review of records by research assistants. Methods of assessing cognitive capability also range from use of screening tests such as the Denver Developmental Screening Test to traditional IQ test and developmental assessment techniques such as the Bayley, Stanford-Binet, and Wechsler Intelligence Scale for Children — Revised (WISC-R). Few, if any, studies include caretaker interaction; the quality of the acquisition of cognitive skills; consistent prenatal, neonatal, and postnatal clinic observations; and sequential electroencephalographic studies of the infant.

A notable exception is Graham and co-workers,[34] who, in 1957, provided an excellent model for the study of asphyxiated infants. Although their measures of the behavioral state of the infant have been replaced by the Brazelton Behavioral Scale and their measure of asphyxia by the Apgar score, their method has major merit. They considered four separate categories of information in the study of asphyxiated infants. They were the signs of fetal anoxia, the signs of intrapartum fetal anoxia, the signs of anoxia at birth and the subsequent behavior state of the infant, and the postnatal signs of central nervous system injury or repair capability.

The relationship of developmental outcome to the severity of hypoxia was demonstrated by Neligan and colleagues[62] when they studied two groups of infants. The community group consisted of infants who experienced a delay of 1 to 4 minutes in establishing respiration; another group consisted of infants who experienced a delay of greater than 5 minutes. The community group, in contrast to the hospital group, was made up of infants with severe perinatal asphyxia, many of them taking more than 20 minutes to establish regular respirations. The community-based group on follow-up, like the infants in Graham's study, did reasonably well with little or no sequelae. This result was in contrast to the hospital group, which experienced developmental sequelae in 30% of the cases. Werner,[88] in an ambitious study of children on Kauai, also demonstrated that 30% to 50% of infants who were identified as experiencing moderate to severe perinatal complications subsequently had questionable or below normal development. Rose and Lambruoso,[73] their 1970 study of asphyxiated full-term infants who had experienced neonatal seizures, found a 70% morbidity. In 1976, Scott[79] reported a morbidity of 25% in infants who did not establish regular respiration for 20 minutes. His study is a testimonial to the sophistication of current methods of resuscitation; 7 of the 15 infants with Apgar scores of 0 survived. His study further stressed that not only is the presence of asphyxia as measured by Apgar scores, important, but also of equal importance is the duration of asphyxia as well as the chronicity of stress. As Graham and associates[34] indicated, the evaluation of the role of asphyxia as a contributing factor in neurological and developmental sequelae must include consideration of the prenatal and intrapartum history, the degree of asphyxia at birth, clinical and behavioral states of the infant, and associated laboratory correlates.

The obstetrical complication scale developed by Parmelee, Sigman, and Kopp[66] to assess infants at risk covers the historical events of the prenatal and natal periods as well as the onset of respiration and the Apgar score. It is the impression of Parmelee and co-workers that acute intrapartum events may be highly associated with neonatal events and are more likely related to long-term developmental morbidity. Their scale utilizes the scoring process developed by Prechtl,[69] who states that a single event such as maternal age may not be significant; however, when coupled with intrapartum complications such as abruptio placentae or maternal hypertension, a hazardous series of events occur that may be predictive of perinatal infant morbidity and mortality.

The use of the Apgar scores in the assessment of the degree of asphyxia and subsequent neurological sequelae has been well established. Drage and co-workers[25] indicated that the lower the 5-minute score, the higher the mortality and the greater the neurological sequelae. It is clear, however, that the Apgar score in itself is not sufficient, and the consideration of prenatal and intrapartum history as well as serial observation, behavior, and the clinical state of the infant adds to the prognostic capability of the clinician. All observers stress the need for sequential observation of the neonate if one is to assess the consequences of asphyxia.

A single or serial blood pH, P_{CO_2}, or P_{O_2} test, when considered alone, has not been shown to be of major prognostic value in determining the subsequent developmental status. Brown, Purvis, and Forfar[11] demonstrated that the same low PO_2 values were equally compatible with death as well as with normal development. As a result of their study of the neurological aspects of perinatal asphyxia, they noted that certain behavioral characteristics could identify those infants who would have subsequent neurological deficits. They used the symptoms feeding difficulties, apnea, apathy, convulsions, hypothermia, cerebral cry, and persistent vomiting to predict ultimate outcome. They defined asphyxia in terms of specific antepartum disorders, fetal distress, abnormal Apgar scores, abnormal gas levels, and the need for ventilation or severe postnatal distress.

Several authors have identified characteristic neurological patterns associated with asphyxia. Brown, Purvis, and Forfar[11] described the following patterns of muscular tone as being associated with asphyxia: hypotonia, transition from hypotonia to extensor hypertonus, extensor hypertonus, and normal flexor tone commensurate with gestational age. Volpe and Pasternak,[87] in their discussion of hypoxic-ischemic encephalopathy in the full-term infant, described the characteristic pattern of weakness in the proximal limbs, with greater involvement of the upper rather than the lower extremities. They also described three clinical states ranging from hypotonia during the first 12 hours, progressing to increased tone and siezures in the next 12 to 24 hours (potential progression depending on the severity of the hypoxia), to increased stupor and brain stem ocular motor abnormalities at 72 hours. If the infant progresses to this final stage, death more than likely will occur.

The neurological characteristics described by Brown, Purvis, and Forfar[11] and Volpe and Pasternak[87] are similar to those described by Sarnat and Sarnat.[77] In 1976 they identified three stages of neonatal encephalopathy following fetal distress. It was their contention that signs of ischemia and hypoxia are difficult to separate clinically, but when observed sequentially in conjunction with encephalographic changes, they are prognostic of subsequent sequelae. Rose[73] correlated unifocal, multifocal, periodic, and flat electroencephalograms with the follow-up status of the infants he studied. He found that infants in whom periodic, multifocal, and flat electroencephalograms persisted proved to have the poorest prognosis, whereas the unifocal and normal electroencephalograms were predictors of a more positive outcome.

The criteria used for clinically significant asphyxia in the Worcester Memorial Hospital Neonatal Intensive Care Unit in Worcester, Massachusetts, require that an infant have at a minimum one major criterion in conjunction with one or more minor criteria. Following are the major criteria:

A. An Apgar score of less than 3 at 1 minute and less than 6 at 5 minutes, or an Apgar score of less than 3 at 1 minute with assisted ventilation utilizing oxygen by mask or by endotracheal intubation
B. Neonatal seizures or other neurological signs or behaviors as described by Sarnat and Sarnat[77]

Following are the minor criteria:

A. Severe intrapartum difficulty
   1. Maternal hypovolemic shock requiring transfusion
   2. Maternal cardiac arrest
   3. Severe intrapartum hemorrhage
   4. Abruptio placentae
   5. Placenta previa
   6. Cord tied tightly around the neck
   7. Prolapse of the cord
B. Abnormal fetal monitoring
   1. Late deceleration without beat-to-beat variability
   2. Heart rate below 120 or above 170 with decreased beat-to-beat variability
C. Abnormal acid-base and blood gas status from fetal scalp monitoring or neonatal blood samples
D. Postnatal difficulties
   1. Severe respiratory distress syndrome with periods of severe apnea
   2. Electroencephalographic abnormality, including multifocal, continuous activity, periodic patterns with isopotential phases, or total isopotential electroencephalogram

Using these criteria, 59 infants from birth to 2 years of age were identified and followed (Fig. 2-7). The mean age of the population was 14 months. The follow-up mechanism consisted of careful observation of the infants in the neonatal intensive care unit and follow-up at the adjusted chronological ages of 4, 9, 15, and 24 months. The assessment tool used was a Piagetian instrument that incorporated the neurodevelopmental assessment of Milani-Comparetti[59] (Chapter 4). In addition, the infants had routine physical examinations, including audiological and ophthalmological evaluations. Subsequent seizures, cerebral palsy, hydrocephalus, microcephaly, or a developmental delay in gross motor, language, cognitive, or fine motor skills of greater than 30% is considered a significant developmental sequela. A delay of less than 30% is considered suspect. In keeping with previous studies,[35,75,88] it was anticipated that the developmental delay in the suspect group would diminish or be eliminated over time. Twenty-five infants had electroencephalograms with greater than class II abnormalities. Fourteen (23.7%) showed evidence of significant neurodevelopmental sequelae. Developmental abnormalities in those infants with asphyxia associated with neonatal seizures and abnormal electroencephalograms were greater than those for infants who experienced asphyxia alone (33% versus 8.6%). Those infants who were postmature (greater than 42 weeks) and who experienced asphyxia with seizures were most vulnerable to developmental sequelae. About 50% of these infants (three out of six) showed significant developmental abnormalities. The overall incidence of sequelae in the population studied is far less than that described by Volpe[86] and Rose and Lombroso.[73] This may be related to current vigorous

A

WEIGHT (g)	NUMBER	GESTATIONAL STATUS	ABNORMAL EEG	SEQUELAE
<1000	3	SGA	Not done	1 suspect
>1000 to <1500	2	SGA	Not done	1 suspect
>1501 to <2500	5	SGA	1 abnormal	1 suspect
Subtotal	**10**	**SGA**	**1 abnormal**	**3 suspect**
1000 to 1500	6	AGA	1 abnormal	1 CP, 2 suspect
>1501 to <2500	3	AGA	1 abnormal	1 CP, 1 suspect
>2500	4	AGA	1 abnormal	1 suspect
Subtotal	**13**	**AGA**	**3 abnormal**	**2 seq, 4 suspect**
Total	23	AGA, SGA	4 abn	2 seq (8.6%) 7 sus (30%)

B

WEIGHT (g)	NUMBER	GESTATIONAL STATUS	ABNORMAL EEG	SEQUELAE
<1500	4	SGA	2	2 CP, 2 suspect
>1501 to <2000	1	SGA	Not done	Suspect
>2001 to <2500	2	SGA	2	1 developmental delay 1 myoclonic seizure
Subtotal	**7**	**SGA**	**4**	**4 seq, 3 suspect**
<1500	4	AGA	2	1 CP
>1501 to <2000	5	AGA	1	1 delayed 1 CP, 1 suspect
>2001 to <2500	3	AGA	1	1 CP
>2501	11	AGA	8	1 delayed, 1 suspect
Subtotal	**23**	**AGA**	**12**	**5 seq, 2 suspect**
3400 to 3700	6	>42 weeks	5	3 seizures, 2 suspect
Total	36	AGA, SGA >42 weeks	21	12 seq (33%)
Overall total	**59**	**AGA, SGA**	**25**	**14 seq 23.7%**

Fig. 2-7. A, Developmental sequelae following significant clinical asphyxia in the absence of neonatal seizures is 8.6%. **B,** In the presence of neonatal seizures the sequelae increased to 33% (3.8 times). The postmature infant is especially vulnerable to sequelae in the presence of clinically significant asphyxia associated with seizures.

methods of resuscitation and subsequent management. Six of these infants had a 1-minute Apgar of 0, and only one has thus far shown sequelae. The short-term nature of the follow-up makes it difficult to predict whether or not some of the infants who are described as normal or suspect will go on to have subsequent school problems.

In conclusion, significant asphyxia can best be identified by using a combination of the major and minor criteria noted previously. The ability to predict developmental outcome depends on the perinatal history and the sequential observation of the infant, including Apgar scores, behavioral and neurological status, repeated electroencephalographic studies, and subsequent caretaking qualities.

CARETAKING CASUALTY

The biologically high-risk infant appears to be especially vulnerable to an adverse caretaking environment. Beset with problems, the neonate is not infrequently born to a mother of lower socioeconomic status, who may be limited in her physical, intellectual, or emotional resources. The importance of the relationship between maternal, physical, and mental well-being, the health and temperament of the infant, and the subsequent quality of the interaction between the caregiver and the infant has been well established.

Kemp[50] suggests that the optimal time for identifying the potentially poor maternal-infant couple is during pregnancy or immediately following the birth of the infant. Careful observation of the mental health status of the mother, her anxieties in regard to the infant and pregnancy, information regarding her own upbringing, and her expectations for the infant all seem to be helpful in identifying the potentially neglectful and abusive parent. The infant's acute medical needs, which often require immediate physical separation and subsequent interactional deprivation, may make the situation worse.[6,49] The maternal attachment may be further complicated by a need to prepare for the possibility of her infant dying or, in the event of survival, to prepare to deal with the special needs that the infant's physical condition may dictate. Kaplan and Mason[49] add to the mother's list of chores the need to overcome the feeling of maternal failure at not delivering a full-term infant.

As noted previously, Sameroff and Chandler[75] present a comprehensive discussion of the transaction between the high-risk infant and the caregiver. They stress the multivariable nature of the effects of the untoward perinatal events and subsequent behavior and development of the infant. The difficult temperament of the small for gestational age infant when contrasted to the appropriate for gestational age infant has been noted by Drillien[28] and Als and co-workers.[1] Drillien describes the small for gestational age infant as dystonic and irritable. Als and colleagues stress the importance of making parents aware of the inherent temperament of the infant rather than having them interpret this difficulty as a defect in their caregiving capability. Thomas and Chess[84] discuss in the New York Longitudinal Study the importance of the infant's temperament as it relates to parent-child interaction. The infant who is dysrhythmic and of high intensity needs to be matched with a caregiver with special qualities to guard against an unfavorable behavioral outcome. The infant with perinatal difficulties may be dysrhythmic or of high intensity and consequently is placed in double jeopardy for potential behavioral and developmental failure. In 1970 Carey[14] developed a simplified version of the temperament scale used by the New York Longitudinal Study. His questionnaire, which is adaptable to office practice when completed by the parents, gives results comparable to the time-consuming procedure used by Thomas and Chess.

The methods of measuring the interaction between infant and caregiver are, at best, difficult. The Caldwell Home Inventory[13] attempts to measure those specific characteristics which are conducive to the "optimal" cognitive development of infants. Bromwich's[8] Maternal Behavior Progression attempts to measure more specifically the caregiver-infant interaction. The measure consists of six levels. The first several levels of the assessment address the maternal-infant attachment, and the upper levels demonstrate the mother's increasing capability of providing growth-promoting experiences for the infant. Some of the very premature infants who have retrolental fibroplasia, cerebral palsy, or disorders such as bronchopulmonary dysplasia are, unfortunately, born to overwhelmed, frightened, teen-aged parents. Despite all efforts at support and intervention, some parents are unable to provide an adequate caregiving environment.

The incidence of child abuse and neglect is greater in the high-risk infant. This would appear to be due to an interactional effect of a needy infant born to parents who themselves have limited resources and great needs. As noted earlier, the situation may be compounded by the events surrounding the birth of the infant that interfere with maternal attachment. Kennell, Voos, and Klaus[51] present a very strong case for early bonding during the first hours of life, reporting a high incidence of abuse and neglect among infants of parents deprived of early bonding experiences. Green and Solnit[36] described the vulnerable child syndrome with long-term effects on childrearing practices as a parental response to such life-threatening illnesses as prematurity.

The role of the primary care physician in this area is clear. First, the physician must advocate the humanization of the perinatal experience for the parents and the infant. The body of literature that supports the concept of critical periods of attachment cannot be ignored. Second, programs that offer support to families who have biologically high-risk infants must be encouraged. Finally, the physician must be knowledgeable and alert to signs and symptoms of child abuse and neglect.

CONCLUSION

In conclusion, regional perinatal and neonatal intensive care units working in conjunction with primary care physicians are recognized as the major mechanism for finding cases of infants and children who are at established, biological, or environmental risk for developmental disabilities. In a major effort to provide comprehensive care to this population, the neonatal intensive care units in conjunction with primary care physicians should provide or identify resources for the high-risk infant and his family that will do the following:

- Offer follow-up assessment, early identification, comprehensive evaluation, and on-going intervention in the areas of health maintenance and neurodevelopment
- Provide appropriate support and counselling to families of infants with developmental disabilities
- Make every effort to prevent the recurrence of a high-risk pregnancy by adequate sex education, family planning, medical follow-up, and early prenatal care

Only through such intensive efforts can physicians fulfill their professional commitment to provide for ''the reproduction of the healthiest citizens for the future.''[68]

REFERENCES

1. Als, A., et al.: The behavior of the full-term but underweight newborn infant, Dev. Med. Child Neuro **18:** 590, 1976.
2. American Academy of Pediatrics committee on drugs: Anticonvulsants and pregnancy, Pediatrics **63:**331, 1979.
3. Anthony, J. E., and Koupernik, C.: The child and his family—children at psychiatric risk, New York, 1974, John Wiley & Sons, Inc.
4. Aubrey, R. H., and Pennington, J. C.: Identification and evaluation of the high-risk pregnancy: a perinatal concept, Clin. Obstet. Gynecol. **163:**27, 1973.
5. Bacola, E., et al.: Perinatal and environmental factors

in late neurological sequelae, Am. J. Dis. Child **112:** 359, 1966.
6. Barrett, C., et al.: Neonatal separation: the maternal side of interactional deprivation, Pediatrics **45:**197, 1970.
7. Bayley, N.: Bayley scales of infant development, New York, 1969, Psychological Corp.
8. Bowe, E. T., et al.: Reliability of fetal blood sampling, Am. J. Obstet. Gynecol. **107:**279, 1970.
9. Brann, A. W., and Dykes, F. D.: The effects of intrauterine asphyxia on the full-term neonate, Clin. Perinatol. **4:**149, 1977.
10. Bromwich, R.: Focus on maternal behavior and infant intervention, Am. J. Orthopsychiatry **46:**439, 1976.
11. Brown, J. K., Purvis, R. J., and Forfar, J. O.: Neurological aspects of perinatal asphyxia, Dev. Med. Child Neuro. **16:**567, 1974.
12. Butler, N.: Late postnatal consequences of fetal malnutrition. In Winick, M., editor: Current concepts of nutrition—nutrition and fetal development, vol 2, New York, 1974, John Wiley & Sons, Inc., p. 173.
13. Caldwell, B.: The Caldwell inventory of home stimulation, Little Rock, Ark., 1976, University of Arkansas Press.
14. Carey, W. B.: A simplified method of measuring infant temperament, J. Pediatr. **77:**188, 1970.
15. Carey, W. B., and McDevitt, S. C.: Revision of the infant temperament questionnaire, Pediatrics **61:**735, 1978.
16. Chez, R. A., et al.: High-risk pregnancies: obstetrical and perinatal factors. In Brent, R. L., and Harris, M. I., editors: Prevention of embryonic, fetal, and perinatal diseases, publ. no. NIH76-853, Bethesda, Md., 1975, Michelin Institute of Health, Department of Health, Education and Welfare.
17. Children bearing children, Med. News p. 11, Nov. 7, 1977.
18. Churchill, J. H., Bersudes, H. W., and Nemor, E. J.: Neuropsychological deficits in children of diabetic mothers—a report for the collaborative study of cerebral palsy, Am. J. Obstet. Gynecol. **105:**527, 1969.
19. Coates, J. B.: Obstetrics in the very young adolescent, Am. J. Obstet. Gynecol. **108:**68, 1970.
20. Cox, J. B.: Disseminated lupus erythematosus in pregnancy, Obstet. Gynecol. **26:**511, 1965.
21. Dargassies, S.: Long-term neurological follow-up study of 286 truly premature infants, Dev. Med. Child Neuro. **19:**462, 1977.
22. Davies, R. A., and Tizard, J. P. M.: Very low birth weight infants and subsequent neurological deficits, Dev. Med. Child Neuro. **17:**317, 1975.
23. D'Eugenio, D. B., and Rogers, S. J.: Assessment and application. In Schafer, S. D., and Moersch, M. S., editors: Developmental programming for infants and young children, vol. 1, Ann Arbor, Mich., 1977, University of Michigan Press.
24. Dodson, E. W.: Neonatal metabolic encephalopathies,

hypoglycemia, hypocalcemia, hypomagnesemia, and hyperbilirubinemia, Clin. Perinatol. **4:**131, 1977.

25. Drage, J. S., et al.: The Apgar score as an index of infant morbidity, Dev. Med. Child Neuro. **8:**141, 1966.

26. Drillien, C. M.: The growth and development of the prematurely born infant, Baltimore, 1964, The Williams & Wilkins Co.

27. Drillien, C. M.: Etiology and outcome of low birth weight infants, Dev. Med. Child Neuro. **14:**563, 1972.

28. Drillien, C. M.: Abnormal neurological signs in the first year of life in low birth weight infants: possible prognostic significance, Dev. Med. Child Neuro. **14:**575, 1972.

29. Dubowitz, L. M. S., Dubowitz, V., and Goldberg, C.: Clinical assessment of the gestational age in the newborn infant, J. Pediatr. **77:**1, 1970.

30. Fear, R. E.: Eclampsia superimposed on renal scleraderma—a rare disease of mankind and fetal mortality, Obstet. Gynecol. **31:**69, 1968.

31. Fetal alcohol syndrome, FDA Drug Bulletin. **7:**18, 1977.

32. Frankenberg, W. K., and Dodds, J. B.: The Denver developmental screening test, J. Pediatr. **71:**181, 1967.

33. Gellis, S. S., and Hsia, D. Y.: The infant of the diabetic mother, Am. J. Dis. Child. **97:**1, 1959.

34. Graham, F. K., et al.: Relationships between clinical status and behavior test performance in a newborn group with histories suggesting anoxia, J. Pediatr. **50:**177, 1957.

35. Graham, F. K., et al.: Development three years after perinatal anoxia and other potentially damaging newborn experiences, Psychol. Monogr. **76:**3, 1962.

36. Green, M., and Solnit, A.: The reactions to the threat and loss of a child—a vulnerable child syndrome, Pediatrics **34:**58, 1964.

37. Griffith, J. F.: Nonbacterial infections of the fetus and newborn, Clin. Perinatol. **4:**117, 1977.

38. Hagberg, B., Hagberg, G., and Olow, I.: The changing patterns of cerebral palsy in Sweden, 1954-1970, Acta Paediatr. Scand. **64:**187, 1975.

39. Hanshaw, J. B., and Dudgeon, J. A.: Viral diseases of the fetus and newborn, Philadelphia, 1978, W. B. Saunders Co.

40. Hanshaw, J. B., et al.: School failure and deafness after silent congenital cytomegalovirus infection, N. Engl. J. Med. **295:**468, 1976.

41. Hanson, J. W., Jones, K. L., and Smith, D. W.: Fetal alcohol syndrome, J.A.M.A. **235:**1458, 1976.

42. Hanson, J. W., et al.: Risks to the offspring of women treated with hydantoin anticonvulsants with emphasis on the fetal hydantoin syndrome, J. Pediatr. **89:**662, 1976.

43. Haskins, R., Finkelstein, N. W., and Steadman, D. J.: Infant stimulation programs and their effects, Pediatr. Ann. **7:**99, 1978.

44. Hittner, H. M., Hirsch, M. J., and Rudolf, A. J.: Assessment of gestational age by examination of the anterior vascular capsule of the lens, J. Pediatr. **91:**455, 1977.

45. Hooper, L. Z.: Congenital rubella in the United States. In Krugman, S., and Gershon, A., editors: Infections of the fetus and newborn, New York, 1975, Allan R. Liss, Inc.

46. Holsclaw, D. S., Jr., and Topham, A. L.: The effects of smoking on fetal neonatal and child development, Pediatr. Ann. **7:**105, 1978.

47. Jaffe, R. B., et al.: High-risk pregnancies: maternal medical disorders. In Brent, R. L., and Harris, M. I., editors: Prevention of embryonic, fetal, and perinatal disease, publ. no. NIH76-853, Bethesda, Md., 1975, Michelin Institute of Health, Department of Health, Education and Welfare, p. 27.

48. Jones, K. L., and Smith, D. W.: Recognition of fetal alcohol syndrome in early infancy, Lancet **2:**999, 1973.

49. Kaplan, D., and Mason, E.: Maternal reactions to premature birth viewed as an acute emotional disorder, Am. J. Orthpsychiatry **30:**539, 1960.

50. Kemp, C. H.: Approaches to preventing child abuse. A home visitors concept, Am. J. Dis. Child. **130:**941, 1976.

51. Kennell, J., Voos, D., and Klaus, M.: Parent-infant bonding. In Helfer, R. E., and Kemp, C. H., editors: Child abuse and neglect, Cambridge, Mass., 1976, Ballinger Publishing Co.

52. Knobloch, H., and Pasamanick, B.: Gesell and Amatruda's developmental diagnosis, ed. 3, Hagerstown, Md., 1974, Harper & Row, Publishers.

53. Knobloch, H., and Pasamanick, B.: Some etiologic and prognostic factors in early infantile autism and psychosis, Pediatrics **55:**182, 1975.

54. Lilienfeld, A. M., and Parkhurst, E.: A study of the association of factors of pregnancy and parturition with the development of cerebral palsy: a preliminary report, J. Hyg. **53:**262, 1951.

55. Lubchenco, L. O.: The high-risk infant—intrauterine growth and neonatal morbidity and mortality, Philadelphia, 1976, W. B. Saunders Co.

56. MacKeith, R.: Save a baby, editorial, Dev. Med. Child Neuro. **19:**717, 1977.

57. Maisels, M. J., et al.: Elective delivery of the term fetus, J.A.M.A. **238:**2036, 1977.

58. McDonald, A. L.: Role of the emotional factors in obstetrical complication, a review, Psychosom. Med. **30:**222, 1968.

59. Milani-Comparetti, G.: Routine developmental evaluation in normal and retarded children, Dev. Med. Child Neuro. **9:**631,1967.

60. National Center for Health Statistics: Vital statistics report, teenage childbearing, U.S., 1966-75, vol. 26, no. 5, Hyattsville, Md., 1977, Department of Health, Education and Welfare.

61. Neligan, G., Prudham, D., and Steiner, H.: The formative years: birth, family, and development, Oxford, 1974, Oxford University Press.

62. Niswander, K. R., and Gordon, M.: Women and their pregnancies, Philadelphia, 1972, W. B. Saunders Co.

63. Osofsky, H. J., and Kendall, N.: Poverty as a criterion of risk. In Schwartz, J. L., and Schwartz, L. H., edi-

tors: Vulnerable infants, New York, 1977, McGraw-Hill Book Co.

64. Ouellette, E. M., et al.: Adverse effects on offspring of maternal alcohol abuse during pregnancy, N. Engl. J. Med. **297**:528, 1977.

65. Pape, K. E., et al.: The status at two years of low–birth weight infants born in 1974 with birth weights of less than 1001 gm, J. Pediatr. **92**:253, 1978.

66. Parmelee, A. H., Sigman, M., and Kopp, C. M.: Selection of developmental assessment techniques for infants at risk, Merrill-Palmer Q. **22**:177, 1976.

67. Pasamanick, B., and Knobloch, H.: Prospective studies on the epidemiology of reproductive casualty methods, findings, and some implications, Merrill-Palmer Q. **12**:27, 1966.

68. Peel, J.: Introduction. In Butler, N. R., and Abelman, E. D., editors: Perinatal problems, Edinburgh, 1969, E. S. Livingstone, Ltd.

69. Prechtl, H. R. F.: Neurological sequelae of prenatal and perinatal complications, Br. Med. J. **4**:763, 1967.

70. Prechtl, H. R. F., and Beintema, D.: The neurological examination of the full-term infant; a manuel for clinical use from the department of experimental neurology, University of Grogingen, London, 1964, Spastics Society Medical Education and Information Unit.

71. Proceedings from the Workshop on Nutritional Supplementation and Outcome of Pregnancy, Sagamore Beach, Mass. 1971, Washington, D. C., 1973, National Academy of Science.

72. Rogers, M. G. H.: Early recognition of handicapping disorders of childhood, Dev. Med. Child Neuro. **13**:88, 1971.

73. Rose, A. L., and Lombroso, C. T.: Neonatal seizure state, Pediatrics **45**:404, 1970.

74. Rush, D., et al.: The prenatal project: the first 20 months of operation. In Winick, M., editor: Current concepts of nutrition—nutrition and fetal development, vol. 2, New York, 1974, John Wiley & Sons., Inc.

75. Sameroff, A. J., and Chandler, M. J.: Reproductive risk and the continuum of caretaking casuality. In Horowitz, F. D., et al., editors: Review of research, vol. 4, Chicago, 1977, University of Chicago Press.

76. Sameroff, A. J., and Zax, M.: Perinatal factors of the offspring of schizophrenic women, J. Newborn Ment. Dis. **157**:191, 1973.

77. Sarnat, H. B., and Sarnat, M. S.: Neonatal encephalopathy following fetal distress, Arch. Neurol. **33**:696, 1976.

78. Saxon, S. A., et al.: Intellectual deficits in children born with subclinical congenital toxoplasmosis: a preliminary report, J. Pediatr. **82**:792, 1973.

79. Scott, H.: Outcome of very severe birth asphyxia, Arch. Dis. Child. **51**:712, 1976.

80. Sederholm, T.: Neurological and psychological outcome of fetal erythoblastosis. In Bossart, H., et al.: Perinatal medicine, Zurich, 1973, Hans Huber Medical Publisher.

81. Shaeffer, G., Arditili, L. I., and Salomon, H. A.: Congenital heart disease and pregnancy, Clin. Obstet. Gynecol. **11**:1048, 1968.

82. Smith, C. A.: Affect of maternal malnutrition upon the newborn infant in Holland, ꞌ 1944-45, Pediatr. **30**:229, 1947.

83. Stewart, A. L., et al.: Prognosis for infants weighing 1000 grams or less at birth, Arch. Dis. Child. **52**:97, 1977.

84. Thomas, A., and Chess, S.: Temperament and development, New York, 1977, Brunner Mazel, Inc.

85. Tjossem, T. D.: Intervention strategies for high risk infants and young children, NCHD Mental Retardation Research Centers Series, Baltimore, 1976, University Park Press.

86. Volpe, J. J.: Neonatal seizures, Clin. Perinatol. **4**:43, 1977.

87. Volpe, J. J., and Pasternak, J. F.: Parasagittal cerebral injury in neonatal hypoxic-ischemic encephalopathy—clinical and neurological features, J. Pediatr. **91**:492, 1977.

88. Werner, E. E.: Final report—the Kauai study: follow-up of adolescence, publ. no. PHS MC-R-060 22 0 01-02, Davis, Calif., 1976, University of California, Davis, pp. 39-49.

89. Winick, M.: Study of the growth of the human placenta. No. 3, intrauterine growth failure, J. Pediatr. **71**:390, 1967.

90. Winick, M., Brasel, J. A., and Belasco, E. G.: Effect of prenatal nutrition upon pregnancy risks, Clin. Obstet. Gynecol. **16**:184, 1973.

3

Neurodevelopmental assessment

Carol M. Donovan
Israel F. Abroms

THE ROLE OF THE PRIMARY CARE PHYSICIAN

The current direction of medicine is a health-maintenance focus rather than a disease-oriented viewpoint. One must consider health maintenance in terms of a holistic framework that includes promotion of health, nutrition, and development. To do this, professionals, such as the primary care physician, public health nurse, or pediatric nurse practitioner, who have routine contact with infants and children, will need to enhance their skills in the developmental area. This includes an increased knowledge of normal growth and development, which would serve a twofold purpose:

- Provide parents of infants and young children with anticipatory guidance concerning developmental issues, which would increase the parents' understanding of their children's current and emerging stages of development; and help parents to formulate realistic expectations for their children, and thus facilitate better parent-child interaction, including general management and discipline techniques.

- Develop a more efficient screening system for all children so that appropriate referrals could be made for those infants and children with developmental disabilities. Such referrals would allow more appropriate intervention and permit the professional to develop standards that would reflect a minimum of false-positive cases and at the same time identify the child who would benefit from some type of intervention.

At the present time there is no one profession that provides all the skills to developmentally assess young children with developmental disabilities. However, there are a number of groups of professionals who, because of their training and exposure to other disciplines, have begun to develop transdisciplinary skills for the comprehensive evaluation of young infants and children.

Ideally, professionals who see large numbers of children in well-baby care should identify one person within their group to do developmental screening and assessment. An alternative in a larger organization is to recruit a "developmentalist," who would be responsible for assessing all infants and young children identified as being at high risk (Chapter 2). The results of such testing would be discussed with the primary care physician and the parents, and a plan formulated for intervention if needed. The developmentalist could then be responsible for the necessary follow-up and referrals.

It has been suggested that all high-risk infants and children need ongoing routine developmental assessment in a primary care setting or in a developmental clinic. At the same time all children should have some type of *screening* to idenitify those youngsters who are in need of service but do not meet the initial high-risk criteria.

PROCEDURES FOR A FORMAL DEVELOPMENTAL ASSESSMENT
Evaluation setting

For very young infants, the usual examining room is an appropriate place for developmental screening. After the age of 4 months, the infant has begun to discriminate strangers and is developing attachment behaviors. A part of this process is the association of the stranger in the white coat with unpleasant memories. Therefore a room other than the examining room may be used. A room that is not overly large and filled with distractions is obviously most conducive to a comfortable test setting. A carpeted floor would be ideal. A vinyl-covered foam mat, approximately 2 m square, which also folds in half for storage, is useful for infants up to the age of 18 months. After that age it is usually easier to test the child by having him sit in a small chair at a table that is an appropriate size and height.

Parent participation

Parents can provide an invaluable resource for gathering information about the child, as well as assisting in administering the test. Some infants and young children will not vocalize or talk in strange situations, whereas they will at home. The examiner can obtain desired information from the parents by asking them an open question such as, "What kind of sounds does your baby make?" If they are uncertain, one can provide them with a number of choices, such as, "Have you ever heard the baby use any consonant sounds, such as 'baba,' 'dada,' or 'gaga,'" or does he mainly use a variety of vowel sounds, such as 'ahh,' 'ooo,' or 'eee'?" By offering a choice and not indicating that one answer is better than the other, the examiner will find that the parents can usually provide an accurate report, such as that the baby does make vowel sounds but they have not, as yet, heard consonant sounds. Using this as a method of teaching development, the examiner can explain to the parents that vowel sounds are very appropriate in the beginning of speech and the next sounds will be more consonant-type sounds. It is important to recognize that "mama" and "dada" are emotionally laden and may be inaccurately interpreted as words. One way to avoid this is to ask if the child has any words other than "mama" or "dada" and not to count the latter as actual words unless the examiner hears their appropriate use as real words within the test situation.

Prior to the test, it is well to explain to the parents that to accurately establish the child's level of functioning the examiner will administer items until the child reaches a ceiling. In the process of reaching a ceiling, there will be any number of items in which skills are emerging and the child will have some successes and some failures. This type of performance is normal, and it is important to note that the examiner will be administering items that one would not expect the child to successfully perform. This explanation usually makes parents feel better when the examiner enters the phase of testing in which the youngster is no longer successful. However, it will be useful for the examiner to point out to the parents some of the actions that the child has taken which indicate those skills are indeed emerging. It is preferable to end the test situation with an item that the examiner is reasonably certain that the child can pass. This helps both child and parents feel more positive about the child's accomplishments.

In addition to gathering information from the parents, it is very appropriate to use them to administer a number of test items. This is particularly helpful in an infant who is slow to warm up to the examiner. Successful testing usually involves having the child or infant sit with the parents while the examiner interviews the parents and gathers baseline data. If the infant is not yet sitting on his own, the examiner can administer some of the test items with the infant seated on the parent's lap; then the child can be placed on the mat and continue to have the parent seated slightly behind him. Depending on how much rapport has developed between the examiner and the child, the test can be administered directly or the parents can continue to be involved. If the examiner is not successful in administering a test item, it is wise to ask the parents whether they think they can get the child to perform the task. As suggested before, it is the parents who are usually most successful in getting the child to vocalize or play a special game such as pat-a-cake or peekaboo. All families have their own ways of playing these games and use their own individual words or gestures. It has been our experience that the parents will recognize clearly when a child is unable to successfully complete an item but by giving him an opportunity to try, they believe the child has been given the best opportunity to perform.

In the case in which the parents believe the child may do better without their presence, this is an option. If the evaluation is a formal assessment, it would be particularly appropriate to have the parents view the evaluation via a two-way mirror or remote video setup. In this way, if decisions are made about a definite delay in the child, the parents would still believe they have observed what the child can and cannot do. This diminishes the fears that develop in a situation in which someone takes the child away and returns with the diagnosis of retardation. Depending on the age and the cooperation of the child, the parents may be present in the room and the meaning of each test item can be explained. If the examiner believes this process will be too disruptive to the child, the types of items that will be administered and how they test such concepts as causality, imitation, ability to find a hidden object, or motor skills can be explained prior to the test. After the testing is completed, the examiner should explain the results to the parents, being certain to ask them if they have any additional questions.

Selection of test instrument

The decision as to which test instrument should be used is based on a thorough understanding of test construction, type of population to be tested, training and experience of the examiner, and purpose of the testing. The latter may be the most important because the reason for the test and what information the test is expected to yield will ultimately determine the choice.

To evaluate[18] the merits of a test, one should explore whether certain factors were considered in constructing the test. Standardization refers to the fact that a set procedure, apparatus, and criteria for scoring have been established. Some standardized tests include age norms, which determine where items are placed on the scale. Age norms are usually established by testing a sample of children of various ages and determining at which point a certain percentage (usually 50% or more)[4] of the children in that age bracket passed certain items. This is the norm for when that particular skill is achieved. For a test to be appropriately normed, the population used should be representative of the United States population, having a representative distribution of males and females, races, and social classes. The Bayley Scales of Infant Development[4] is noted for being the most well-standardized infant test currently available. Standardization and norms were based on a far more representative sampling of infants and young children of today's culture than the two older tests, the Gesell[32] and the Cattell[15] (Table 3-1). Other factors are reliability and validity.

Test reliability and validity. The problem of reliability is essentially one of determining the degree of consistency present in any observation or measurement. This problem refers to the fact that the test should provide enough criteria that the examiner may determine whether the child successfully passed the item. The infor-

Table 3-1. Developmental assessments and screening tests

Test	Author	Age range	Areas evaluated	Comments	Source
Developmental assessments					
Bayley Scales of Infant Development	Bayley (1969)	2 to 30 months	Mental (problem solving, fine motor, language, social)—163 items Motor (gross, fine)—81 items Behavior checklist (social behavior, activity level, attention span, persistence, endurance)	Raw scores change to Mental Development Index and Psychomotor Development Index 1262 children, good cross sample of U.S. population, race, sex, education of head of household Score pass-fail based on criteria in manual Score indicates infant's current developmental status in relation to peers, not necessarily predictive of later IQ	Manual and test kit, The Psychological Corp., New York, N.Y.
Cattell Infant Intelligence Scale	Cattell	2 to 30 months	Social, adaptive, language	Downward extension of Stanford-Binet 5 items/month, 2 to 12 months 5 items/2 months, 12 to 24 months	Psychological Corp., New York. N.Y.
Early Intervention Developmental Profile	Rogers, et al. (1976)	Birth to 3 years	Perceptual/fine motor, cognitive, language, social, self-care, gross motor	Concurrent validity Piagetian approach to cognitive assessment Neurodevelopmental reflexes 274 items Used by team or person trained in transdisciplinary approach	University of Michigan Press, Ann Arbor, Mich.
Gesell Developmental Schedules	Gesell and Armatruda (1940)	4 weeks to 6 years	Adaptive (eye-hand coordination, manipulation), gross motor, fine motor, language, personal-social	Standardized on white middle-class population, 1925 to 1940; may not represent current U.S. population fairly Yields developmental quotient Items good description of developmental sequence if not accurate reflection of current age norms for attainment	Gesell, A., and Armatruda, C.: Developmental diagnosis, ed. 3 (Knobloch, H., and Pasamanick, B., editors), New York, 1974, Harper and Row, Publishers.

Continued.

Table 3-1. Developmental assessments and screening tests—cont'd

Test	Author	Age range	Areas evaluated	Comments	Source
Screening tests					
Denver Developmental Screening Inventory	Dodds and Frankenberg (1967)	2 weeks to 6 years	Personal-social, fine motor adaptive, language, gross motor, 105 items	Test-retest and reliability done on small sample; Standardized on 1036 children; this population may be over-representative of middle class; Designed to be used by professional and paraprofessional via observation and parent question; Should be used to screen; It is not a diagnostic tool; Better screen over 30 months of age; Manual accompanies	J. Pediatr. **71**:181, 1967. LADOCA, E. 51st. Avenue and Lincoln Street, Denver, Colo.
Developmental Screening Inventory	Knobloch and Pasamanick (1966)	1 to 18 months	Adaptive, gross motor, fine motor, language, personal-social; History—observations of behavior and parents' questionnaire	Based on Gesell norms	Pediatrics **38**:1095, 1966. Department of Pediatrics, Albany Medical College, Albany, N.Y.
Guide to Normal Milestones of Development	Haynes and Haynes (1966)	1 to 36 months	Gross motor, adaptive/fine motor, language, social; Eight primitive reflexes	Plastic wheel; No score sheet; Simple equipment	A developmental approach to case-finding, HEW Publ. No. HSA 75-5403, Washington, D.C., 1975, Department of Health, Education and Welfare.

mation must be clear enough that another observer would make the same judgment (interobserver reliability). Test-retest reliability indicates if further tests will be consistent within the same time frame if the same child is seen on different days. However, in testing infants and children remember that their behavior will change over time because their growth is so rapid.

Validity refers to the extent the test correlates to some criterion external to itself. Predictive validity refers to how well the results of a particular test answer the question, "What will happen in the future?" that is, do developmental scores predict how well a child will do on a later test of intelligence? There is much discussion of the fact that infant tests are not to be used in this fashion because they may not be valid in predicting future functioning in the child. It is obvious that one cannot take the test result as a sweeping assumption, but rather one must look at how old the infant was at the time of testing—4 months versus 18 months would make a difference in how well the test is able to predict the future. A poor performance in a child over 18 months would be a better predictor of the future than a poor performance in an infant of 4 months, but does not necessarily predict how the child will function at school age.

Concurrent validity refers to how well a test correlates with other measures that test similar skills in the same age range. Tests that have not been normed on their own such as the Early Intervention Developmental Profile[78] (EIDP) are considered to have concurrent validity with other infant tests, such as the Bayley[4] and Gesell[32] because the age norms that are used on the EIDP are the same as those derived for the aforementioned tests. Preliminary tests[77] done on a small number of children using the EIDP and the Bayley indicate that the tests are highly correlated.

Some assessment tools, because of their complex nature, should only be used by people who have the appropriate training and background. The Bayley Scales of Infant Development[4] were designed to be used by professionals with a background in psychology or child development who are thoroughly trained in the testing procedures by another experienced examiner. Milani-Comparetti and Gidoni's[61] Developmental Evaluation is most correctly used by professionals with a training in neurodevelopment, such as physical therapists, neurologists, and pediatricians. Others, such as the Denver Development Screening Test,[31] were designed expressly to be used by either paraprofessionals or professionals. Thus for all practical purposes, if a nurse is the designated developmentalist, it may be more appropriate to choose an instrument like the Gesell,[32,47] which is somewhat easier to administer, or have the nurse trained by examiners experienced in the Bayley Scales.[4]

Type of population. If the population to be tested is "normal," screening should be used to detect any aberrations in normal growth and development. Based on the age of the child, there are a number of screening tests from which one could choose (Table 3-1). However, if one has selected a population that meets certain high-risk criteria, the instrument should provide great sensitivity and specificity to detect any abnormalities in hearing and vision as well as deviations of development in the perceptual/fine motor, cognitive, language, social, gross motor, and self-care areas.

Infants and young children with specific handicaps, such as visual impairment, hearing impairment, or extreme motor involvement, may need tests that are specifically adapted for them to adequately assess their true abilities.

The Hiskey Nebraska[38] (normed on hearing-impaired as well as normal children) and the Leiter Scales of International Performance[52] were specifically designed for hearing-impaired and nonverbal children. Both of these tests are appropriate for children who are developmentally 2 years old. The Maxfield-Bucholz Scale of Social Maturity,[58] an adaptation of Doll's Vineland Scale of Social Maturity,[21] is used with blind infants. There have been no widely distributed tests designed to test motorically involved children. There have been attempts to adapt some of the Piagetian tasks involved in the Uzgiris-Hunt Scales[88] and the Early Intervention Developmental Profile[78] to test such infants. In dealing with these children, positioning of the child is critical to allow for adequate control of any voluntary movement, which will facilitate better performance.

Desired results. The purpose of developmental screening is to identify infants or young children who will require more extensive evaluation if they fail the screening examination. However, it is important *not* to use a screening test to do a comprehensive developmental assessment. Some of the negative impressions associated with such screening tests as the Denver Developmental Screening Inventory[31] have been generated because it has been misused. When one is testing to determine a developmental quotient (DQ) because it is important for school placement or because one wishes to compare longitudinal data, a test that yields a valid and reliable DQ would be the most appropriate. In this case, the Bayley Scales of Infant Development[4] might be the instrument of choice. However, if one is testing to get necessary developmental data for diagnostic purposes and programming, such tests as the Gesell [32,47] and the Early Intervention Developmental Profile[78] (which look at distinct yet interrelated areas of development) would be more useful. If a child is identified as having difficulty in a specific area, follow-up assessment using specialized instruments should be done. One such test is the Receptive-Expressive Emergent Language (REEL)[12] scale for speech and language or the Pre-Speech Assessment Scale[63] for oral-motor and feeding assessment. The Milani-Comparetti Developmental Evaluation[61] can be used for gross motor and reflex development. The next step would be to clearly delineate how one would plan for intervention.

In following up extremely high-risk infants, the Early Intervention Developmental Profile[78] has been useful. Although it was initially designed to be a programming tool, it is composed of a number of developmental milestones that provide a very good descriptive assessment. In all of the traditional developmental evaluations (i.e., Bayley,[4] Gesell,[47] and Catell[21]), cognitive functioning is looked at in terms of language, fine motor, adaptive, and social skills and some problem-solving ability. Problem solving, causality, object permanence, and spatiality tasks as well as vocal and gestural imitation are most clearly indications of early cognitive functioning. This concept is particu-

larly useful in infants who have some motor impairment because of the adaptability of the EIDP. The infant can indicate his understanding of certain concepts through directed eye movements and other means. Another area that the Early Intervention Developmental Profile includes is neurodevelopmental reflexes. The integration of primitive reflexes, as well as the emergence of higher level protective, righting, and equilibrium reactions, are essential to normal motor development. These reflexes are included in the self-care sections of the profile, as well as in the fine and gross motor sections. The unique features of this test have made it the most useful for our purposes. It can be supplemented by the Bayley Scales of Infant Development[4] or Stanford-Binet[83] when it is necessary to determine a DQ. The Early Intervention Developmental Profile results can determine at which age level a particular child is functioning and give a profile of individual strengths and weaknesses in the perceptual/fine motor, cognitive, language, self-care, and gross motor areas. One can also determine rates of development over time, which can be linked with the American Association of Mental Deficiency (AAMD) classifications as follows[35]:

Profound delay	Developmental rate less than one fifth the normal rate
Severe delay	Between one fifth and one third the normal rate
Moderate delay	Between one third and half the normal rate
Mild delay	Between half and two thirds the normal rate
Borderline delay	Between two thirds and four fifths the normal rate
Normal range	Between four fifths and greater than the normal rate

"It is recognized that five of these categories have been defined as levels of retardation by the A.A.M.D. Although the classification into the A.A.M.D. categories would depend on deviation I.Q. scores, and adaptive behavior measures. It was decided to use those categories to classify the index of developmental rate."[77] It is thus useful to determine the child's level of developmental functioning in specific areas and establish at what rate they had been developing up until that point in time and then observe for changes in developmental rate over time. For example, a child 12 months of age functioning at a 6-month level would indicate a moderate developmental delay because the child was developing at 50% the normal rate. If that rate persisted, one would expect the child at 18 months to perform at a 9-month level. However, if the child makes rapid gains, he may test at a 12-month level. The child's rate would then be said to have increased. One would need tests at future points in time to determine if that new rate will persist or if the child will regress to a slower rate.

Interpretation of test results. The test instrument used is only as good as the examiner, who, through experience and clinical judgment, can make appropriate interpretations of the test items. There has been much discussion and literature to the effect that an infant's DQ will not be predictive of later intellectual functioning. There is, however, a general consensus that if an infant functions in the lower ranges of capability, it is more significant and predictive of mental retardation. Illingworth[44] noted that a mild to moderate delay combined with the history and medical and neurological examinations will stand up over time. Wachs[91] stated that using an instrument such as the Uzgiris-Hunt Scales,[88] which is reported to test cognitive functioning without becoming contaminated with social and adaptive skills, may also be more reliably predictive.

CONCEPTS OF COGNITIVE AND NEUROLOGICAL MATURATION
Piagetian concepts of cognitive development

Piaget[21a,25,33,71,72] viewed cognitive development as a continuous process of organization and reorganization, or structures. Piaget's term for these structures is "schema." These schemata form the framework on which incoming sensory data can fit, but it is a framework that is continually changing. Each new organization integrates the previous schema into itself by adding more information to expand it (assimilation) or correcting and changing existing schema (accommodation). Although this process is invarient and continuous, Piaget broke the process into distinct periods: sensorimotor, preoperational, concrete operational, and formal operational. This is a stage theory in which each new period is marked by entirely new ways of thinking, interacting, and understanding. There is a hierarchy of behavior, but within any period there will always remain some earlier behaviors.

Development occurs because there is a drive to master the world or to understand and explain the unknown. All persons develop in the same sequence and in the same way but do not necessarily move at the same rate. Mentally retarded individuals will never reach formal operations or, in the case of the profoundly retarded, concrete operations.

During the sensorimotor period (from birth to approximately age 2), the infant learns to attach meaning to the sensory information— what the infant sees, hears, smells, tastes, touches, and manipulates. The infant must interact with the environment to learn. For this to occur, the infant must be exposed to a variety of experiences with objects and people. At first the neonate sees himself as one with his mother, but after the first several months of life the infant has differentiated himself as a separate being but still sees himself as the center of the universe, an all-powerful being who controls everything around him. The task of the infant during the sensorimotor period is to begin to put his abilities into focus. As meaning and understanding grow, the infant's behavior becomes more purposeful and goal directed. During this time the adult supplies the child with the words to describe the world. The young child also has started to communicate with the adult through gestures, vocalizations, and, finally, words. The child begins to remember past events and starts to formulate concepts of how the world operates. At this point, approximately 2 years of age, the child enters the preoperational phase of concrete operations, in which learning continues on a more conceptual and symbolic level. The infant understands more abstractions and continues to learn new ways of ordering his world. Tasks to be mastered during the sensorimotor period are those which deal with causality, imitation, object permanence, play, and spatiality.

Causality. The awareness of cause-and-effect relationships develops as the infant begins to differentiate himself from an object. In the early stages the infant sees himself as the

Table 3-2. Cognition—object permanence

Age (months)	Characteristics
Newborn	Focuses briefly on object
2	Displays prolonged gaze; object or person Follows moving objects
3 to 4	Watches place where moving object disappeared
6	Attains partially hidden object
7	Looks to floor when something falls
8 to 9	Attains completely hidden object (single visible displacement)
10 to 12	Repeatedly finds toy hidden under one of several covers (multiple visible displacement)
18	Displays single invisible displacement
18 to 21	Searches systematically for object hidden in a successive invisible displacement

Table 3-3. Cognition—play and exploration of objects

Age (months)	Characteristics
Newborn	Focuses briefly on object brought into line of vision Becomes still or active in response to sound
1 to 4	Deliberately focuses vision on objects Brings objects to mouth
5 to 8	Mouthes Is capable of prolonged visual regard Shakes Bangs
9 to 12	Notices details of objects; turns objects over to view all sides Pokes at objects Throws Empties containers Imitates new action, for example, pulls switch on busy box Places one item in container Uses tools to bang, mark, etc.
13 to 15	Shows objects to adult Gives objects to adult; wants objects back Fills containers completely Attempts to replace lids on pans and boxes Uses toy car appropriately
16 to 18	Initiates ball play Feeds doll bottle (combines two objects in play) Names object or asks, "What that?"
18 to 24	Acts out familiar sequences—going to store, taking care of baby Is capable of pretend play without props

cause of all events, and he lacks true goal-directed behavior. After an effect has occurred by accident, he repeats actions to produce the same effect. This develops to the point at which the infant initiates a behavior by choosing a means to achieve a desired end. He begins to experiment with new means in an intentional way and learns that other people and things cause events to happen.

Imitation. The repetition of a movement or sound is imitation. In the first stages the infant can only repeat gestures and sounds with which he is familiar. He progresses to a stage of imitating new and more complex actions and sounds and these become more precise. Imitation is an example of accommodation. The infant changes his action to mirror the environment. This process can result in qualitative changes in the schema.

Object permanence (Table 3-2). The awareness that objects do not cease to exist when they are not in sight is object permanence. The infant maintains a mental image of the object and is able to systematically search for it in its absence.

Play (Table 3-3). Pursuit of a means for its own sake is play. This is repetition of pleasurable actions, which later develops into acting out of previous experiences, or pretending. Play is an example of pure assimilation. The infant

has total control over making new information fit into existing structures, resulting in quantitative changes in the schema.

Spatiality. Understanding that objects occupy space and have certain physical properties, although they may vary in their relationship to the child and to each other, is spatiality.

Motor and reflexive maturation

Motor development can also be regarded as a series of schemata in which new motor and reflexive advances integrate previous patterns of motor and reflexive behavior. The gross motor milestones of major importance appear in Table 3-4. The orderly progression of fine motor function in the upper limbs through the first year is given in Table 3-5.

Table 3-4. Major gross motor developmental milestones

Age (months)	Characteristics
Newborn	Turns head to either side when in prone position
	Holds head erect for 2 or more seconds when upright
2	Raises and maintains head at 45-degree angle for 20 seconds when in prone position
	Bobs head but keeps it erect when upright
4	Can maintain head and chest up at 90-degree angle (puppy position)
	Rolls to supine position when in prone position
5	Can pull to sit; has no head lag when in supine position
6	Rolls to prone position when in supine position
	Extends legs; takes large fraction of weight when upright
	Sits with support
	Sits alone for few seconds
7	Assumes quadruped position when in prone positon
	Sits alone for 20 to 30 seconds
8	Assists in pull to stand; sits unsupported for 3 to 5 minutes when upright
9	Creeps on all fours
	Sits alone and steady
10	Assumes sitting position alone
	Pulls to stand using furniture
	Cruises
12	Stands alone
	Walks with one hand held
15	Walks alone well
18	Climbs stairs with one hand held
24	Jumps in place
	Climbs stairs alone

Table 3-5. Major hand function and reaching milestones

Age (months)	Characteristics
Newborn	Opens hands randomly
	Displays grasp reflex
	Shows some hand-to-mouth, midline activity
2	Closes fingers reflexively on object for 3 to 5 seconds
3	Looks at hands
	Activates arms on sight of desired object
	Brings hands directly to mouth
4	Displays ulnar-palmar prehension
	Reaches when hand and object in view
	Fingers own hands in play at midline
5	Shows radial-palmar prehension
	Displays visually directed reach (bilateral)
	Integrates grasp reflex
	Transfers toys from hand to hand
6 to 7	Displays unilateral reach
	Holds one cube and reaches and attains second cube
	Rakes or scoops up raisin
	Has complete thumb opposition on cube
8	Displays inferior pincer grasp with raisin
9	Pokes with isolated index finger
	Begins active release
10	Displays neat pincer grasp
12	Shows mature grasp and smooth release

In the first 2 years of life, the infant changes from an "apedal" newborn to a "quadrupedal" infant at 6 to 9 months and becomes a "bipedal" infant between 1 and 2 years of age. The study of reflex activity in this evolution of motor development was considerably accelerated by the work of Magnus.[55a] Major contributions in understanding neonatal and early infancy reflexive behavior were made by Peiper[69a] in Germany, Andre-Thomas[2a] in France, and Illingsworth[44] in Great Britain. Recent workers in this field include Prechtl and Beintema,[73] Wolff,[92a] Lipsett,[53a] Milani-Comparetti and Gidoni[60,61] and Brazelton.[7]

In general, the newborn is thought to have reflex activity mainly at the spinal and brain stem levels and this activity becomes integrated and elaborated on at the diencephalic and cortical levels during the period of infancy and beyond. At the structural level the brain has its full complement of neurons in place by 20 to 24 weeks of gestation. Neurons will grow, develop elaborate dendritic processes with spines, and form more complex synaptic connections with other neurons in the cortex, diencephalon, brain stem, and spinal cord.[45,52,74,80] Neuroglial cells continue to proliferate in subependymal germinal matrix areas in the hemispheres and the outer layers of the cerebellum until about 2 months and 9 months of age, respectively.

Myelinization of central axons by oligodendroglial cells commences at the end of the second intrauterine trimester and becomes accelerated during the first 6 months after birth. This process attenuates by 5 or 6 years and ceases by the end of the second decade of life.[90]

The brain of the newborn weighs about 300 to 350 g; by 2 years, 1000 g, and by sixteen years it reaches its adult maximum of 1300 to 1400 g. Thus within 2 years of birth the weight of the brain has tripled—a remarkable feat.

Clinically, during this time we see marked cognitive, motor, and reflexive development.[67] In assessing developmental maturation of an infant, the elaboration and eventual integration of reflexes is important.

The evolution of reflexes in infancy[5,28]

Spinal level. Spinal level reflexes are phasic responses to designated stimuli, which result in stereotypical patterns of movement. Examples of spinal level reflexes are flexor withdrawal, extensor thrust, crossed extension, crossed abduction, and stepping (Fig. 3-1, *A*). They are among the primitive reflexes found in the normal neonate, which should become integrated within the first 2 months of life. (See pp. 67 and 68 for instructions on how to test these reflexes.)

Brain stem level. "Brain stem reflexes are static postural reflexes and affect changes in distribution of muscle tone throughout the body, either in response to change of the position of the head and body in space (by stimulation of the labyrinths), or in the head in relation to the body (by stimulation of proprioceptors of the neck muscles)."[28] These brain stem reflexes are also considered a part of the primitive reflex pattern of neonates and young infants. These reflexes usually become integrated within the first 4 to 6 months of life. Persistence beyond this age indicates delayed maturation of the central nervous system. The significance of the delay relates to whether the higher level reflexes have emerged and to the nature and character of the primitive responses. These primitive responses, even in the early months of life, should never be obligatory but rather a momentary attitude from which an infant can easily move. Examples of brain stem reflexes are the asymmetrical tonic neck reflex (ATNR), symmetrical tonic neck reflex (STNR), tonic labyrinthine reflex (TLR), associated reactions,

and positive and negative support reactions.

Asymmetrical tonic neck reflex. Testing for the ATNR (Fig. 3-1, *B*) is done both by watching the spontaneous movements of the infant as well as by passively turning the infant's head and observing for the reaction in the extremities (extension of the arm and leg on the face side and/or the flexion of the arm and leg on the skull side) or palpating for changes in tone. As the infant grows older he may not demonstrate the reflex in a supine position, but once he is stressed by being placed in an upright position, one can observe the reflex in the child's movements.

In an older child, the test for the ATNR is known as the Schilder test. The child stands with his eyes closed and arms in front of him while his head is passively turned and extremities watched for the response just discussed. The response can also be tested in a quadruped position.

Symmetrical tonic neck reflex. The STNR is elicited by passively moving the head in complete extension—the upper extremities extend while the lower extremities move into a flexion pattern. The converse is also true—when the head is flexed, the upper extremities flex and the lower extremities extend. This posture is seen in many quadruped animals such as the cat; it would be unusual to see such clear responses in a normal full-term baby. One might feel the changes in muscle tone by palpation rather than see overt movement in the extremities as in the ATNR. However, it is believed that the STNR does inhibit the infant from assuming a stable quadruped position, which would allow mobility (i.e., creeping). Until the STNR is integrated between 6 to 8 months of age creeping is not possible. The obvious changes in the extremities due to the position of the head is seen in children with overt central nervous system (CNS) damage, that is, cerebral palsy. One would test for the STNR by placing the child prone over the examiner's knee and lifting the head into extension and observing for changes in the extremities, either movement or muscle tone. The same procedure could be repeated by flexing the child's head as well as observing the active movements of the child.

Tonic labyrinthine reflex. The TLR is evoked by the position of the head in space, which

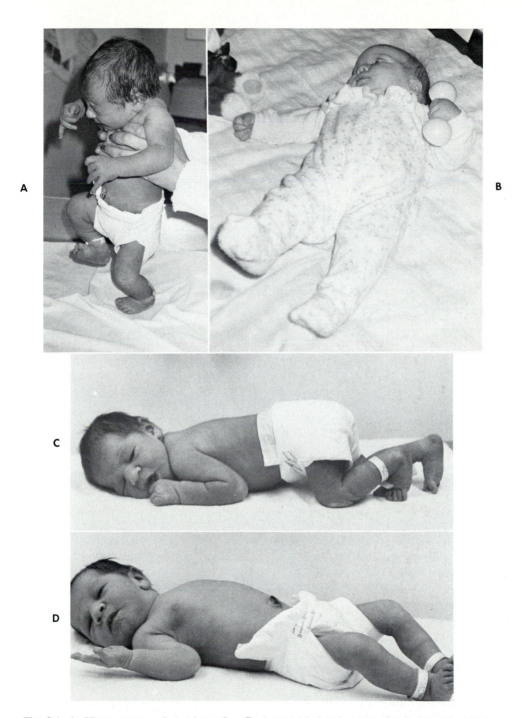

Fig. 3-1. A, Vigorous neonatal stepping reflex. **B,** Asymmetrical tonic neck reflex in 2-month-old infant. **C,** Influence of the tonic labyrinthine reflex in the neonate causes infant to assume flexed position when prone. **D,** Extension and abduction at the hips and shoulders in the supine position.

Continued.

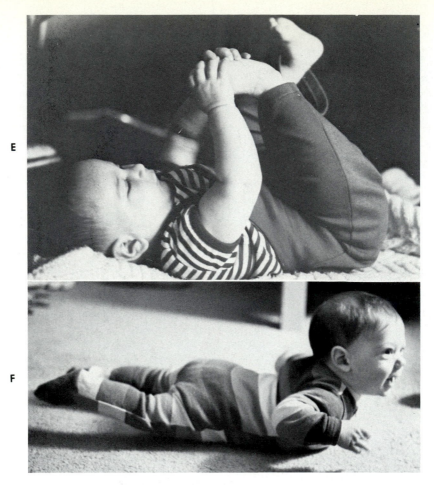

Fig. 3-1, cont'd. E, Flexion in supine position indicates integration of tonic labyrinthine reflex in 6-month-old child. **F,** Pivot prone position indicates integration of tonic labyrinthine reflex in 6-month-old child.

Continued.

affects the labyrinths and thus causes a change in overall tone in the body. This change in tone is sustained as long as the head's position remains unchanged. The body responds to being in the supine position with increased extensor tone and in the prone position with increased flexor tone. Although flexion dominates in the normal neonate, it is usually increased in the prone position, whereas in the supine position one can observe more extension in the extremities. This reflex should be integrated at between 4 and 6 months of age, thus at 6 months the infant spontaneously assumes a pivot prone position, indicating complete extension and integration of the TLR in the prone position. In the supine position he can assume a total flexion pattern, lifting the head and legs at the same time. In the young infant one usually has to observe his spontaneous activity to see these positions, which would indicate integration of the TLR. Besides watching for the spontaneous motions of the infant, one can also passively move him into the desired position and determine if there is resistance to movement by palpating for increased tone (Fig. 3-1, *C* to *F*).

These positions are used in older children in the Kraus-Weber test, which was originally designed to assess strength and flexibility in the abdominal muscles and back extensors. However, it does allow the examiner to observe for the presence of primitive reflexes. Ayres[3] has developed her theory around children who demonstrate this apparent lack of integration of

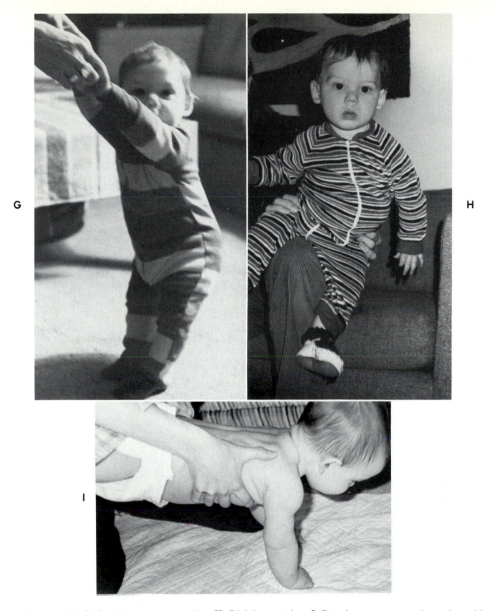

Fig. 3-1, cont'd. G, Positive support reaction. **H,** Righting reaction. **I,** Parachute response at 6 months, with extension of arms when infant is thrust forward and down. *Continued.*

primitive reflexes. In the child who has more overt disorders, one would observe the influence of this reflex in more dramatic opisthotonic posturing, which is the increased extension in the supine position.

Associate reactions. These reactions may be seen in a very young infant, particularly when he attempts to use his upper extremities. While using one arm for reaching and grasping, the contralateral side shows a similar pattern. However, by 6 months of age the infant has developed unilateral reach and can hold onto one cube as he reaches for a second without showing any ''overflow'' of extension, causing him to drop the first cube. The examiner, however, should be aware of any of these reac-

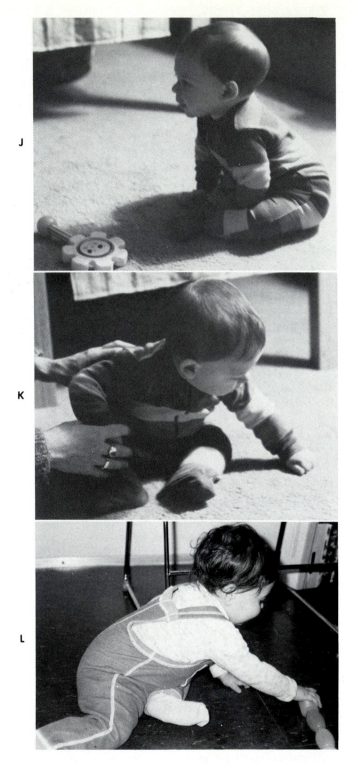

Fig. 3-1, cont'd. J and **K,** Propping reaction. **L,** Body-on-body rotation at 9 months; upper trunk twists in opposite direction of lower trunk at 9 months.

tions when observing a child perform a skilled movement with his preferred hand, such as picking up a small pellet and releasing it into a bottle. It would be considered pathological if the opposite hand was fisted. This pattern of associated reactions is also seen when a child attempts to walk; both arms come up in a flexed posture pattern. Although this bilateral "high guard" is acceptable in early walkers, within a few months after the child starts to walk the arms should come down to his sides. A child who shows a unilateral pattern should be examined carefully for other signs of hemiparesis.

Positive support reactions. After the phasic stepping and placing reactions become integrated, the tonic reactions take over. When the balls of the infant's feet come into contact with a supporting surface it is an exteroceptive and proprioceptive stimulus, which results in extension in the lower limbs. A positive support reaction (Fig. 3-1, *G*) differs from the crossed extension pattern in that it is a tonic reflex and the tone is maintained while there is contact with the supporting surface. Positive support reactions are seen in normal infants from 3 to 8 months of age, at which time they have developed the balance to maintain themselves upright without relying on tonic patterns. Early pathological patterns may be indicated by the infant who will not only hold his lower extremities in extension to an extreme degree, but will also show inward rotation and adduction of the hips (scissoring) as well as remaining up on his toes. Positive support reaction in normal infants usually allows them to maintain their weight with a flat foot and show negative support reactions.

Negative support reactions. Negative support reactions are the converse reactions, which allow the infant to relax the extremity when it is no longer in contact with the supporting surface. At 8 or 9 months of age this phenomenon allows the infant to lift his leg to take a step forward. Children who display CNS difficulties remain in the pathological positive support reaction and are unable to show a relaxed posture.

Midbrain level. "Righting reactions interact with each other and work towards establishment of normal head and body relationship in space as well as in relation to each other."[28]

Labyrinthine and optical righting. The head responds to input from the labyrinths as well as optical cues (after 2 months of age) (Fig. 3-1, *H*). This response makes the body automatically position the head vertically with the eyes horizontally. It is first seen at 6 to 8 weeks in the prone position, by 4 months in lateral tilt (head only), and by 6 months in supine position and full lateral tilt of the body. The infant who is held in these positions will automatically move his head and trunk to assume the neutral position. Once the righting reaction is activated, it continues through life and can only be inhibited through voluntary control, as seen in the difficulty in keeping the head lowered in a diving maneuver or in a golf swing.

In the infant with severe visual impairment, one would assume that it is only labyrinthine righting that is keeping his head oriented in space. These infants have a tendency to keep their heads tilted downward, indicating that the labyrinthine righting alone may not be sufficient to keep the head in the correct position without optical cues. The child with impairment of the eighth cranial nerve, that is, with sensory neural hearing loss, may have associated balance difficulties because of the impairment of the labyrinthine mechanism.

Body on body righting. For the first 6 months of life, neck righting predominates, so when the head turns, the body follows as a whole, not segmentally. However, at 6 months of age segmental rotation of the trunk should allow the infant to initiate a roll with either the lower extremities or the upper extremities, and the rest of the body should follow. This tendency for the infant's body to follow other segments will allow him to roll over, sit up, and assume a quadruped position. The ability to perform segmental maneuvers will be absent in the child with increased tone due to CNS difficulty. It is important to observe whether the infant develops trunk rotation, which indicates appropriate tone in the body, as well as making an assessment of the tone in his extremities.

Automatic movement reactions. Automatic movement reflexes are observed in "infants and young children and are not strictly righting reflexes but are reactions produced by changes in the position of the head and, hypothetically, involve either the semicircular canals or labyrinths of neck proprioceptors.''[28] An example of this is the Moro reflex, which is described on p. 67. More advanced reflexes seen in older infants are the Landau and protective reactions.

LANDAU REACTION. The Landau position is similar to the pivot prone position except that when the infant is held in a suspended prone position, he responds by extending the head, trunk, and lower extremities. If the head is flexed, the infant relaxes into the flexed position. Infants who are still at a brain stem level are unable to perform this maneuver. Positive reaction is normal from 5 months to 2 or 2½ years.

PARACHUTE REACTION. Parachute reaction is the protective reaction of the upper extremities in response to a quick change in position (Fig. 3-1, *I*). This reaction is elicited by lowering the infant in a head first position toward the floor. The arms come out into abduction and extension to protect the head. In eliciting the parachute, one should observe for the symmetrical response of the arms and watch the hands, which should open to take the weight. This reflex should be easily elicited by 6 to 7 months, and its absence with a concurrent demonstration of the primitive pattern, that is ATNR, would bear careful watching. This response remains throughout life.

PROPPING REACTION. In the sitting position one should be able to elicit an anterior prop, so when the infant loses his balance forward, his arms come out in a protective response (Figs. 3-1, *J* and *K*). This is followed at 7 months with a similar reaction when the infant is tilted laterally, and posterior reaction should develop between 9 to 12 months of age. Protective reactions also last throughout life, as seen in the automatic response when an older child or adult falls, which may result in a Colles fracture of the forearm.

Cortical level. Cortical responses are the highest level of reflexes; they are a result of interaction among the cortex, the basal ganglia, and the cerebellum. It is not possible to elicit appropriate equilibrium reaction unless the lower level reflexes at the brain stem have been integrated. Equilibrium reactions become apparent from 6 months of age. These can be tested in prone and supine positions between 6 and 7 months of age by placing the infant on a tiltboard and observing for the appropriate response. An equilibrium response is seen when the head is maintained at midline and the body responds to the shift in the center of gravity by curving the spine and allowing the arm and leg on the raised side to extend while the limbs on the lower side show a protective response. One can elicit the responses at 6 to 7 months of age in prone or supine positions, but it may not be necessary to test for them if the infant is showing signs of appropriate motor development, that is, body on body righting and the ability to maintain himself in an upright seated position for a few minutes. In infants who have delays in these motor milestones, one may wish to test for development of equilibrium reactions in the prone and supine positions. However, equilibrium responses should be tested in the older infant in a seated position and again when he is standing. This can be done by placing the child on a tiltboard and tipping the supporting surface or by applying pressure to the trunk of the child in an attempt to disrupt his balance. A summary of maturation of reflexive behaviors is seen in Table 3-6.

Maturation in other areas

Visual maturation. Delayed visual development or congenital blindness is usually seen with other developmental disabilities in the multiply handicapped child but can occur as an isolated deficit (Table 3-7). With blindness, constant roving eye movements are invariable; if the deficit is unilateral, a strabismus of the affected eye is common (Chapter 11).

Hearing development. Normal milestones in hearing are summarized in Table 3-8. Pathological conditions are covered in Chapter 10. In practice it is often very difficult to be sure of a partial hearing loss in an infant until 6 to 8 months of age. Repeated clinical testing and expert audiometry must be performed until a definitive answer can be obtained.

Language development. Table 3-9 outlines the normal sequence of development of expressive and receptive language skills acquired during infancy. Delay of language skills may reflect global retardation and/or hearing loss,

Table 3-6. Maturation of reflexive behaviors

Reflex	Appearance	Integration
Root	24 to 28 weeks* with reinforcement 32 weeks—good	3 to 5 months
Suck	28 weeks—suck-swallow 34 weeks—coordinated	
Moro	28 weeks—exhaustible 32 weeks—complete	4 months
Palmar grasp	28 weeks—fair 32 weeks—solid	4 to 5 months
Plantar grasp	28 weeks 32 weeks—solid	9 months
Neck righting	32 to 34 weeks	5 to 6 months
Stepping	34 weeks—minimal 37 weeks—solid	2 to 4 months
Placing	37 weeks	2 to 4 months
Tonic labyrinthine	Newborn	5 to 6 months
Asymmetrical tonic neck	Newborn to 1 month	4 to 5 months
Prone righting, optic labyrinthine	1½ to 2 months	Persists
Supine righting	5 to 6 months	Persists
Lateral righting (head)	4 to 5 months	Persists
Lateral righting (trunk)	6 months	Persists
Parachute	6 to 7 months	Persists
Protective reaction (anterior)	5 to 6 months	Persists
Protective reaction (lateral)	6 to 7 months	Persists
Protective reaction (posterior)	9 to 10 months	Persists
Equilibrium reactions		
Prone	6 months	Persists
Supine	7 months	Persists
Sitting	9 months	Persists
Standing	18 months	Persists

*Weeks refer to gestational age.

Table 3-7. Major visual milestones

Age	Characteristics	Age	Characteristics
Newborn	Blinks at bright light Turns head and eyes to diffuse light Fixes and follows briefly at 8 to 12 inches through 20-degree angle on either side of vertical meridian	4 to 5 months	Reaches accurately for a toy with either hand
2 weeks	Watches mother's face during feeding	6 to 7 months and onwards	Can be tested with rolling balls test and Sheridan-Stycar test
1 month	Smiles responsively Cries or blinks at a looming object	8 to 9 months	Fixes on and accurately pokes at or picks up a raisin
2 months	Watches an adult walking across room Follows a slowly moving object attentively through a 90-degree horizontal arc		Can be tested uniocularly, with mother covering one eye with her hand
		19 to 23 months	Anticipates trajectory of a moving object
3 months	Turns head toward an object and fixes and follows in all directions	3 years	Can be tested for visual acuity with small pictures
		5 years	Can be tested with letters

Table 3-8. Major auditory milestones[65]

Age (months)	Characteristics
Newborn	Displays alerting response Startles, blinks, and displays body movement Varies respirations and sucking in response to sound (may increase or decrease)
1	Stills to voice or soft noise Startles to loud noise
2	Becomes alert, eyes may search for sound
3 to 4	Shifts eyes to lateral sound, especially voice
4 to 5	Turns head to side of noise
7 to 9	Turns head to side and indirectly below
9 to 13	Turns head to side and below
13 to 16	Turns head to side, below, and indirectly above
15 to 21	Turns head directly to all signals—side, below, and above

which should be screened for through parental history, clinical examination, and special tests. However, delay of expressive language in a child should not lead to a diagnosis of retardation without careful cognitive testing.

NEURODEVELOPMENTAL ASSESSMENT AT DIFFERENT AGES
Newborn assessment

To adequately interpret the findings of a neonatal assessment, the examiner must review the pertinent history, the pregnancy, labor, and delivery (Chapter 2). Those factors such as the health status of the mother prior to labor and delivery, the delivery itself, drugs used to sedate the mother, the type of delivery, and the neonate's immediate response to intrapartum events as evidenced by Apgar scores may have a significant bearing on how the infant responds to neonatal behavioral and neurological examinations. The infant's weight and gestational age as determined by the Dubowitz scale[25] will have a direct bearing on his performance and behavior. In the preterm infant the conceptual age

Table 3-9. Major language milestones

Age (months)	Characteristics	
	Expression	Reception
Newborn	Cries Makes reflexive throaty sounds	Startles to loud noise Brightens to voice
2	Begins open-vowel sounds (coos) Makes differentiated cries	Shifts eyes to voice
4	Coos two or more syllables (begins to babble) Vocalizes emotions other than by cry	Turns head to voice
5	Laughs and squeals	Responds to voice inflections and tone
6	Makes bisyllabic repetitions	Responds to name
9	Displays intonation patterns of native language Says one word	Understands verbal command Recognizes names of a few common objects
12	Jargons Says three or four words	Responds with word to say "bye-bye"
15	Says four to six words Uses gestures to communicate	Points on request to common objects Points to five body parts Follows simple commands
18	Says 10 or more words Combines two words Names common objects	Points to named pictures
24	Begins use of pronouns Makes two to three word sentences Has 200-word vocabulary Names pictures	Follows 2 or 3 related directions

would need to be known at the time of evaluation, as well as any medication that the infant had been receiving. In evaluating a high-risk population one must realize that many of these newborns are treated with drugs such as aminophylline to control apnea and bradycardia. This alters their behavioral patterns and makes them more irritable and less responsive to social stimuli. Infants on seizure medication such as phenobarbital and phenytoin have decreased responsiveness. It is best to evaluate an infant half way between feedings or closer to the next feeding, when the infant is more likely to be alert for testing. The room used for testing should be warm enough to allow the infant to be undressed and remain comfortable and as free from distractions and noise as possible.

When the infant is first approached, it will be necessary to determine the state of the infant. Brazelton, in the *Neonatal Behavioral Assessment Scale,*[7] has defined six behavioral states (i.e., state I, quiet sleep; state II, active or rapid eye movement (REM) sleep; state III, drowsiness; state IV, quiet alertness; state V, active wakefulness; and state VI, crying). The five states previously described by Prechtl and Beintema[73] and others omitted the "drowsy" state included in the Brazelton scale. Before disturbing the infant, an assessment should be made of the infant's posture, activity level, pattern of respiration, and color. In addition to the routine newborn assessment it is useful to look at the following qualities and activities, which Brazelton[7] describes in *Neonatal Behavioral Assessment Scale.*

Habituation. Response decrement or habituation tests require a sleeping infant to stop responding to the repeated presentation of a bright light, bell, or pinprick. The infant should ideally habituate in three or four trials. This ability to shut out meaningless stimuli is purported to be an early measure of attention, which is an important prerequisite for cognitive processing.

State control. Brazelton has described six behavioral states, ranging from deep sleep to crying. The examiner should record these qualities of the child's state. How difficult was it to wake the child from a sleep state and bring him into a quiet alert state so that he could interact with his environment? Many preterm infants who are otherwise within normal limits

seem harder to rouse than full-term infants, although lethargy can be a sign of CNS difficulty. For those infants who are hard to arouse it is helpful to undress them and provide vestibular stimulation by moving them quickly from a supine to an upright position. Once the infant is in an alert state, note whether he is able to maintain that state or if he needs constant stimulation to keep him awake. The opposite extreme is when an infant goes from a sleep state to a crying awake state and appears irritable and difficult to soothe. At the end of the examination judgments should be made on the infant's ability to maintain an alert state, what it takes to elicit crying from the infant, and how easily consoled he is once he starts to cry. These early behaviors may be some indication of the later temperament of the infant.

Response to environment

Vision screening. An initial visual screening is done by noting the infant's response to light in the sleep state just described, in which the infant should initially blink when light is shown in his eyes, as well as his ability to focus and follow both inanimate and animate stimuli while awake. This task is usually most successfully done in a dimly lit room, which encourages the infant to open his eyes and focus on the stimulus.

By 32 weeks of gestation, the infant will display an ipsilateral and consensual pupillary response. At 36 weeks conceptual age, the preterm infant does have the ability to momentarily focus on a visual target or the examiner's face and shows some ability to visually track through an arc of 10 to 20 degrees. The full-term newborn should turn his head and eyes towards a diffuse source of light and can focus and follow a slowly moving stimulus horizontally for at least a 30-degree arc. The object, for example, yarn ball, penlight, or the examiner's face, should be approximately 20 to 30 cm away from the infant's eyes for him to focus. At this age it is usually easier for him to follow the object from the midline out rather than across the midline. The examiner should watch for conjugate eye movements; sustained nystagmus or wandering eye movements without focussing could denote impaired vision.

Hearing screening. Northern and Downs[65]

believe the best response to a sound stimulus is obtained when the neonate is in state II sleep. As in the habituation test, a bell produces blinking or movement or the infant will awaken. The auditory stimulus is then repeated when the infant is in an alert state. The examiner watches for change in the infant's activity level or respiratory pattern; it may increase or decrease. In this quiet state, the sound of a bell or voice may produce a blink or startle response or an alerting response with widening of the eyes. An infant held up and facing to the side should turn his eyes toward a voice. The difficulty with hearing screening at this age is the significant number of false-positive results. These infants should be carefully monitored for hearing impairment in the ensuing weeks.

Tone and movement patterns. Tone and movement patterns are important aspects of the neonatal neurological examination. The movements of the limbs must be judged as to the amount, speed, and quality of movement. The latter should be analyzed for symmetry, range, smoothness, and the presence of tremors. A full-term healthy infant in the awake state shows smooth movements with approximately 60-degree arcs of movement and a reciprocal kicking pattern of the lower limbs. A preterm infant, even at term, who is able to move one limb at a time still seems to have jerky, overshooting limb movements. In particular, this is seen in the arms as they move out into an abduction pattern. Tremulousness is also often observed in the preterm infant and may be seen in otherwise normal full-term infants.

Posture is assessed by looking at the overall position of the trunk and limbs. The full-term infant assumes a symmetrical flexion pattern with the arms held close to the body in adduction and the elbows, hips, and knees flexed. Abnormal postures in the supine position would include opisthotonus, retracted shoulders, or legs in hyperextension.

The preterm infant of less than 32 weeks gestation will display diminished tone and extension postures in the upper and lower extremities. As the infant approaches term, flexion posturing appears in a caudocephalad sequence. By 36 weeks there is a somewhat froglike position, with the hips abducted and flexed. When infants born at 28 to 32 weeks are seen at

term, hypotonia remains, and they appear to have shoulder-girdle weakness.[43]

In the prone position the influence of the tonic labyrinthine reflex is seen in the normal increase in flexor tone. The infant's hands are fisted and his knees are drawn up under his abdomen in the fetal position. The healthy, full-term baby can easily lift his head up from side to side, suggesting early integration of the tonic labyrinthine reflex.

When the infant is supported in the upright position, he should take some weight on his feet, and his righting reactions cause the trunk to straighten out, bringing the head in line with the body. If leaned forward, the infant makes automatic stepping movements. This righting reaction may not be as easily elicited in the preterm infant who, as described earlier, displays decreased truncal tone.

Primitive reflexes*

Sucking reflex. One can observe the suck of the infant by placing a finger into the infant's mouth. The stimulus should produce rhythmical sucking movements. The suck reflex is present as early as 28 weeks,† but it is not until 34 weeks that the suck is coordinated with the swallow reflex so that the infant can take his nourishment by mouth. If the infant does not start to suck immediately when the finger is placed in the mouth, sucking may be elicited by moving the finger in and out of the mouth and stimulating the hard palate at the same time. A poor suck after 36 weeks may indicate general depression of the CNS. The suck must be evaluated in terms of strength, duration, rhythm, and coordination of the ingestion of liquid with breathing and swallowing.

Rooting reflex. To evaluate rooting, the examiner should stroke the corners of the mouth, upper lip, and lower lip in turn with the finger, taking care to include the oral mucosa. After stimulation the infant should turn his head in the direction of the stimulus and attempt to suck the stimulating finger. The reflex will be hard to elicit in an infant who has just been fed.

Oculovestibular reflex. The oculovestibular reflex is tested by supporting the baby behind the neck and trunk, then holding him at arm's

*See references, 2, 4, 8, 49, 68, 73, 82, and 86.
†Weeks refer to gestationa-conceptual age.

length away from the examiner and rotating in one direction. One should observe the infant's eye movements, which should move in the direction of the spin. On cessation a brief period of nystagmus should be seen with the slow component being in the direction opposite the spin. The procedure should be repeated, rotating the infant in the opposite direction.

Asymmetrical tonic neck reflex. The examiner can observe the infant's spontaneous motor activities and check the ATNR by noting whether a turn of the head to either side will produce a response in the extremities. One can formally test the reflex by passively turning the head to one side and watching for extension of the extremities on the face side and flexion of the extremities on the occiput side. Tone changes in the extremities may be evident in the newborn period only with passive movements of the limbs with the head turned to one or other side. At any age, this response should never be obligatory, so the infant cannot flex the extended arm or leg.

Neck righting reflex. To test for neck righting, one can turn the infant's head to one side with the infant in a supine position and the head in midline. The infant's shoulders follow the direction of the head, with the trunk turning as a whole. This reflex appears between 34 and 37 weeks gestation.

Moro reflex. The Moro reflex can be tested by holding the infant over the crib in a suspended, supine position, supporting the trunk and head. One should quickly release the hand that supports the infant's head, allowing it to drop back 20 to 30 degrees, then observe the response in the infant's extremities. A complete Moro response in a full-term infant consists of abduction of the shoulders and extension of the elbows, wrists, and fingers, followed by a recovery phase of flexion and adduction. The Moro response may be elicited as early as 28 weeks, but flexion will be absent. The response is weak and is easily exhaustible. From 32 to 36 weeks the extension-abduction component of the Moro response will become more vigorous, and thereafter the flexion component becomes more evident.

Traction response. To test traction response, one should grasp the infant's wrists and slowly pull him into the sitting position. The full-term infant should respond with contraction of the shoulder and elbow muscles. The preterm infant of 34 to 37 weeks will have some shoulder participation in this reflex, but none is seen before 34 weeks. The normal full-term infant will usually display some initial head lag with the traction response, but the head and shoulder tone has increased to an extent that by the time the body is raised about 60 degrees from the supporting surface the head will align with the body and remains in line for at least 2 or more seconds once the infant is completely upright. If the head bobs forward, the infant tries to pick it up again and keep the head erect. If the infant should display complete head lag, it can indicate either a weakness of the anterior neck muscles or an extensor thrust pattern, indicating hypertonicity of the neck extensors.

Palmar grasp. One should place the infant in a supine position, taking care to keep his head in a midline or neutral position to eliminate the influence of the asymmetrical tonic neck reflex, when testing palmar grasp. The grasp reflex is elicited by placing the examiner's index finger into the infant's palm from the ulnar side and applying pressure against the palm. The infant's fingers should curl around the examiner's finger and sustain the grasp for up to 10 seconds. An asymmetrical response may indicate a lower brachial plexus injury or Klumpke paralysis. In the preterm infant the grasp reflex is present but weak at 28 weeks, but becomes stronger by 34 weeks, and is maintained for 4 to 5 seconds by 37 weeks.

Galant reflex (trunk incurvation). To evaluate the Galant reflex, the examiner must place the infant in the suspended prone position, and stroke the area from the lower rib cage to the sacrum 2 cm from the vertebral column. The infant should respond by curving the trunk and elevating the hips with a concavity on the stimulated side. The test should be repeated on the opposite side. A well-developed response will show complete incurvation of the whole spinal column. It is present in the preterm infant after 32 weeks but the movement is less developed. In infants with a transverse lesion of the cervical or thoracic spinal cord the response will be absent.

Stepping reflex. One can test stepping by holding the baby upright, well supported around his trunk, and allowing the soles of the feet to come into contact with a firm surface. The examiner should lean the infant forward and observe the movement of his legs. A full-term infant will take high stepping movements. This reflex is not usually seen before 36 weeks.

Placing reflex. The infant should be cradled against the examiner's body and one foot restrained to test the placing reflex. One should then lift the infant so that the dorsal part of the foot is stimulated by the edge of the table. The infant should respond by a movement that looks like he is stepping up onto the table. The test should be repeated on the opposite side. This reflex is not present until 35 weeks gestation and is less vigorous in the preterm infant.

Ankle clonus reflex. One can test the ankle clonus reflex by applying quick pressure to the ball of the foot, producing rapid dorsiflexion. This procedure should not elicit any response from the infant. If clonus is present, ascertain whether this is sustained for eight to ten beats. The test should be repeated on the other side.

Crossed extensor reflex. The examiner should place the infant in the supine position with one leg flexed and the other extended to test the crossed extensor reflex. The examiner should then apply a brisk scratch of the thumbnail to the foot of the extended leg and observe the response in the opposite leg. This leg should extend and adduct in the full-term infant. In the preterm infant the response would be one of flexor withdrawal, similar to the stimulated leg, followed by some extension with no adduction component.

Plantar grasp. To test plantar grasp, one should place the infant in the supine position with the head in the midline and touch the base of the toes without touching the dorsum of the foot. The infant should respond by flexing all his toes.

Two-month assessment

During the first 2 months of life, rapid neurological development is taking place in the infant, as indicated by his increased response to his environment, patterns of sleep and wakefulness, and by the appearance of sleep spindles in the EEG pattern.[46] The infant is becoming more tuned in to external stimuli; in the first weeks he has mainly responded to internal stimuli. He is born with a set of reflexes that allows him to come into contact with the world (suck, grasp, orientation to sound and light, vocalization, and movement). During the first month, these reflexes undergo definite modifications as a consequence of environmental stimuli. When the infant is hungry, he only sucks on a nipple that produces milk and learns to reject a pacifier. He is beginning to use his senses to maintain contact with the environment and to explore it.

Visual assessment. The infant will now focus for longer periods of time on interesting objects or a face. There is a clear preference for new and interesting shapes, and research has demonstrated his ability to discriminate size and shape.[55] He will begin to scan his environment and is able to focus and follow a moving person who is approximately 1m away in a 180-degree arc. His eyes will follow vertically or in a circle. The 4-week-old infant will blink at the approach of a looming object perceived as a threat.

Hearing assessment. At this age the infant should not only show a startle response to a loud noise, but he should also alert to sound by eye widening, stilling, quieting his respiratory pattern, or sucking more slowly. When a sound is presented, the infant's eyes should begin to shift toward the source of the sound especially if the sound is the human voice.

Social assessment. Now the infant will not only maintain eye contact for longer periods of time, but he will also respond with a smile to a person who is talking and smiling at him. If the adult chooses to use infantlike sounds (described below), the infant shows vocal contagion by vocalizing back to the talking adult.

Language assessment. The infant has learned that his cry is a way of communicating his needs to a caregiver. The infant has developed a repertoire of different cries to indicate whether he is hungry, in pain, or frightened. By 2 months he can begin to vocalize sounds. These are usually soft, cooing, pleasure sounds or open vowel sounds such as "ah," "ooh," or "ee." Receptively, he is beginning to respond and become aware when a voice speaks to him by quieting and adopting a listening pose, watching the speaker's face intently.

Cognition assessment. At 8 weeks of age the infant has already entered what is considered

Piaget's stage II, primary circular reactions, which spans the age period from approximately 1 to 4 months. Primary circular reactions refer to the continual repetition of a new experience. If you place a rattle in the infant's hand and shake it, the infant will continue to move his arm in a way to repeat the effect of making a sound, yet without it being an intentional shake. This circular reaction is also seen when the infant opens his hand to feel the blanket or mother's face or hair and the hand continues to open and close to repeat the sensation of feeling the texture. Another primary circular reaction noted in the area of social responsiveness is vocal contagion. If the adult responds by vocalizing back to him sounds similar to those he has already made, the infant continues without realizing someone else has made those sounds.

Self-care/feeding assessment. At 2 months of age the infant uses a suckling pattern,[62] which is characterized by protraction and retraction of the tongue. The liquid is obtained through a rhythmical licking compression action of the tongue on the nipple combined with jaw opening and closing, involving activity of the entire sucking organ. The lips are loosely approximated, so liquid may dribble out of the corners of the mouth. The infant should have no difficulty initiating the suck or coordinating the suck with swallowing and breathing. If a bite reflex is elicited, it should be easily relaxed, since a strong tonic reaction would be considered abnormal. A rooting response is still present.

Perceptual/fine motor assessment. The infant's hands are open and he will show some midline play and hand-to-mouth coordination as he attempts to stick his finger or fist into his mouth to suck on it. He still must use the remnants of the grasp reflex to hold objects, but he can maintain his grasp for a few seconds. All his fingers act together to reflexively hold the object, but the thumb does not participate. An object presented overhead may cause him to become alert and excited, so his arms move, but there is no attempt to reach with the hand and aim for the object.

Gross motor assessment. When observed in the supine position, the 2-month-old infant usually appears to have more asymmetrical movements than the neonate. This is due to the influence of the ATNR, which causes the extremities on the face side to extend and the extremities on the skull side to flex when the head is turned. This pose seems to help bring the hands to the infant's attention; within the next month hand-watching activity is seen in most infants. This pose, however, should never be an obligatory posture, but rather an attitude that the infant moves in and out of at will. The head control and the pull-to-sit maneuver have further improved, so once the infant is brought into the upright position, the head is maintained fairly steadily with only occasional loss of head control in a bobbing movement.

In the prone position, the infant's neck and trunk extensors are gaining in strength, so he is able to lift his head and chest off the table to a 45-degree angle, which he can maintain without difficulty for at least 20 seconds. He may drop his head to rest but quickly lifts it again. This degree of head control shows that the extensor muscle group, or antigravity muscles, are overcoming the flexed posture characteristic of the newborn. The infant who has good head and neck control may surprise himself by rolling over. Once he gets his head up, if he turns it to one side, his body will follow due to the influence of the neck righting response. In the upright position the infant continues to show the trunk righting reaction, and the neonatal stepping and placing reactions may persist.

As the infant gains head control, a primitive Moro response should begin to show signs of integration. The TLR is seen, just as in the newborn period, with some flexion in the extremities, but it is beginning to become integrated as evidenced by the neck and trunk extension as well as the extension and external rotation of the hips.

Four-month assessment

The 4-month-old infant is becoming increasingly aware that the environment is something apart from himself and that it holds many interesting things to look at, listen to, taste, and touch. He is also on the threshold of mastering developmental tasks so that he can act directly on the environment at will. His increasing visual acuity allows him to focus on objects 1.5 to 2.5 m away, and the improved head control in the prone and supine positions enables him to pursue an interesting visual spectacle with his head and eyes for longer periods of time. In the motor realm he can direct his upper extremities with more coordination, so for the first time he can reach out toward an interesting object and bring it to his mouth.

Visual assessment. An infant's vision can be further screened at this age by presenting objects or people at a variety of focal lengths to see at which point he is able to respond to the stimulus. By this age the infant should begin to pick out familiar people who approach silently 1.5 to 2.5 m away. The infant will bring his hands into view and have periods of hand-watching behavior. Also at this chronological age his visually directed reach is beginning to develop. At an earlier age the arms may have waved in excitement at the sight of an object. Batting movements then occur and later more skillful, whole-handed reaching. Thus the infant's visual acuity can be tested by offering him objects of different sizes, shapes, and colors.

Hearing assessment. Hearing can best be tested at this time using a variety of calibrated noisemakers such as a low-pitched clicker, a higher pitched bell, and a voice presented at the side of the infant. The head and eyes should begin to turn to localize the sound when it is presented on either side.

Social assessment. During the preceding months the infant's smile was readily given to any smiling adult. At about 4 months of age the infant has a tendency to smile more preferentially, in that he will smile more readily at his mother or a familiar caregiver. This smiling behavior is greatly influenced by the infant's temperament; an easy-going, well-tempered infant may never stop smiling at adults, whereas it may always be difficult to coax a smile from the "slow to warm up"[84] or irritable infant. At about 4 to 5 months the infant will start to actively engage an adult in some form of interaction. This behavior is seen when the infant is presented with a still-faced adult and he attempts to attract the adult's attention with smiles and vocalizations.

Language assessment. The infant is now increasing his repertoire of sounds. He will coo and gurgle to announce his pleasure, as well as make more scolding or fretting noises. Con-

sonant sounds are beginning to be heard often, such as back of the throat sounds, like "ga," or bilabial sounds, like "ba" or "m." He can communicate his needs to a receptive caregiver by his differentiated cries. The infant will attend more and more to speech and will respond to the speaker's tone of voice.

Cognition assessment. In the area of cognition the infant is beginning to perform the secondary circular reactions characteristic of Piaget's stage III (Fig. 3-2, A). The schematic repertoire of the last 4 months has consisted mainly of looking at objects and some mouthing to explore the objects. Now he is able to more purposefully combine a number of these schemas, in that when he sees an object, he will be able to directly reach for it and then bring it to his mouth. He will turn his head to pursue an object across the midline. He may fix momentarily on the spot where the object disappears. When a ball is rolled behind an opaque cover, he will quickly lose interest in it and as yet has no concept that it will reappear on the other side. The object, at this time, is lost to him. The random "primary circular" movements such as shaking an object are becoming more purposeful. Thus shaking is added to his capabilities for exploring objects, in addition to visual regard and mouthing.

Self-care/feeding assessment.[62] The automatic rooting and sucking of the younger infant has now been replaced by voluntary searching for the nipple and initiation of feeding. The infant anticipates the approach of a nipple or spoon by opening his mouth and slightly protruding his tongue. The 4-month-old infant still uses the suckling pattern but uses slightly more lip pressure in ingesting fluids and in spoon feeding.

Perceptual/fine motor assessment. The 4-month-old supine infant attempts to reach for objects by moving his whole arm in the direction of the object when he can see his arm and the object at the same time. The sight of a toy may cause him to move both arms in excitement, so one or both are eventually brought close enough to the object for him to try to direct his hand to grasp it. The reflexive grasp of the earlier age is becoming integrated, so when the infant sees a rattle or cube, he can initiate a voluntary ulnar palmar grasp by extending his

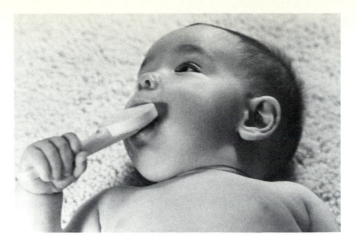

Fig. 3-2. Mathew at 4 months—mouthing.

fingers to apprehend it. The object is then raised to the midline, held over the head to be looked at, or mouthed. Within 3 to 4 weeks the infant will also start to practice transferring the items from hand to hand using an active grasp but a crude release pattern. At this age the thumb does not participate in the grasp of a cube and is held in loose adduction. It is never normal for an infant's thumb to remain in the palm of the hand.

Gross motor assessment. In the supine position the influence of the asymmetrical tonic neck reflex should no longer be evident, and the infant should spend most of his time with his head in the midposition, thrusting arms and legs in play, extending his knees so that he can see his feet (this will entice him to start reaching for them), and bringing them toward his mouth. The infant can roll from back to side but does not have enough body rotation to complete the turn. In a pull-to-sit maneuver there should be no head lag and the infant can now assist in pulling up to sit; the infant's legs should be flexed. When the infant is seated and supported about the hips, he can maintain his neck and upper trunk in an extended position, but the lumbar region remains rounded. If pulled into or placed in a standing position, the infant will start to actively take some weight on his feet. The hips may remain flexed, but the knees are strongly hyperextended. He has developed better control of the head and trunk in the prone position because the neck and back extensors

have become stronger. The head and chest are raised to 90-degree angle with forearm support, and the infant is beginning to push up on extended forearms. This "puppy" position is easily maintained for long periods of time. His hips are now fully extended, and the infant may be able to initiate a roll from the prone to supine positions by turning his head and eliciting a neck righting response. In prone suspension the infant lifts his head and chest in such a way that the spine arches and the beginning of hip extension can be seen (beginning Landau).

Although the infant's spontaneous activities will give a clue to the integration of the primitive reflexes, the ATNR and neck righting, Moro, stepping, and placing reflexes should be tested at this state of integration.

Six-month assessment

The 6-month-old infant has a new perspective on the world; he can remain upright for prolonged periods of time when he is supported in the seated position. This position allows him to use his hands so sufficiently that no object is safe from his attempts to grab it, mouth it, shake it, or bang it. The infant will also actively seek to engage his parents in social interactions through positive means of smiling, vocalizations, or reaching out to touch their faces as he actively commands their attention.

Visual assessment. The visual assessment for age 6 months is the same as the 4-month assessment.

Hearing assessment. Age 6 months seems to be a landmark at which the quality and quantity of vocalizations by a hearing impaired infant will seriously drop off. Up until that age hearing impaired infants will vocalize in a manner similar to infants whose hearing is intact. Careful questioning of the parents may reveal that this has decreased and should alert one to pay particular attention to the infant's hearing responses. Lateralization to different sound sources should be tested as at 4 months using a variety of noisemakers with different frequencies and decibel levels.

Social assessment. The 6-month-old infant will show clear preferences for his mother, and he is beginning to experiment with the image of his mother and himself as two distinct individuals. When held by the mother, the infant will pull back to examine the mother's face and hair in an effort to distinguish the parts of mother that are different from him. Infants will play with their hands and feet, coming to the realization that those body parts are a part of them. Although influenced by individual temperament, now is the time when true laughter is heard in response to pleasurable activities or physical play that the infant enjoys. The infant will also seek to gain an adult's attention by his loud vocalizations, reach out to touch the adult's face if he is close enough, and use his social smile in an effort to engage the adult in some form of pleasurable interaction.

Language assessment. At 6 months the infant should begin to recognize his own name when it is called and start to respond differently to various words that are coupled with consistent intonation patterns in the voice such as "no" or consistent gestures such as "come here" with the adult offering open hands. Expressively, the infant is chaining more and more syllables together and his babbling becomes more complex as he experiments with a variety of vowel and consonant combinations.

Cognition assessment. At age 6 months the infant is well into stage III, secondary circular reactions, which spans the age period of 4 to 8 months. During this stage the infant has an intense interest in sounds and actions. Activities are performed for the environmental effect, as well as the propriokinesthetic feedback. During

stage III the infant begins to engage in some goal-directed behavior. He tries to repreat unusual events but the goals are established after the behavior has begun. This is the beginning of the infant's understanding of causality, but at this time the infants remains egocentric. He still sees himself as the cause of all behaviors. He will perform ritualistic acts to have a pleasurable experience repeated, but he does not make the connection between the real cause and effect. This activity is seen when an adult plays a bouncing game with the infant. The infant will continue the motion of bouncing up and down or waving his arms in an attempt to make the activity happen again. When presented with a Busy Surprise Box (a toy that has an animal figure pop through an open door once an appropriate gadget has been worked) and shown how to work it, the infant will continue to bang on the toy to make it happen again. The infant lacks the fine motor skills to accurately work some of the gadgets but he desires a repetition of the figure popping out.

Imitation may occur if the adult interjects a familiar sound that is within the infant's repertoire once the infant has started to babble some other sounds. The infant may begin to switch and make his vocalizations match the model presented by the adult. This skill emerges at 6 months and becomes more strongly consolidated by the end of this stage.

Object permanence is seen when the infant can remove a cover from a partially hidden toy, thus maintaining the image of the whole toy although he can only see part of it (Fig. 3-3, A). He will, however, remove a diaper from his face, which blocks his total perception of the world, with a deliberate hand motion.

At this period of time play consists of shaking, banging, mouthing, and swiping at everything (Fig. 3-3, B). There is no differentiation between objects or interest in their novelty. However, the infant does continue to visually explore his toys by gazing at them for increasingly long periods of time. The secondary circular reaction for which this period is named is seen in the deliberate action on a toy the minute he grabs for it. He immediately will start to shake it or bang it. It is this deliberate action that differentiates the secondary circular reac-

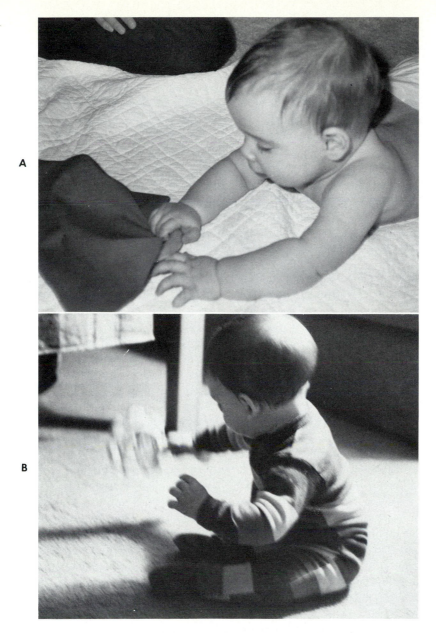

Fig. 3-3. A, Mathew at 6 months—uncovering a partially hidden object. **B,** Eric at 6 months—shaking and banging.

tion characteristics of a stage III infant from the more random movements of a stage II infant.

Spatiality concepts are demonstrated when an infant immediately looks to the floor when a object falls, without needing to track it. This is the beginning of the appreciation of gravity, as well as the elements of object permanence. These combined elements are also seen in the

search with his hands for a missing toy once it is dropped out of sight. The stage III infant is just beginning to represent or hold an image of objects no matter what position the objects are in. If presented with a bottle that is upright, the infant can rotate the bottle 90 degrees to guide the nipple into his mouth.

Self-care/feeding assessment.[62] The suckling pattern of the first 6 months is beginning to change to a true suck. The intrinsic muscles of the tongue work to make the tongue tip elevate as it grasps the nipple, move up toward the hard palate, and subsequently drop; this, in combination with the greater lip approximation, causes the buildup of negative pressure, and fluid is drawn into the mouth. This sucking pattern requires less work than the more infantile suckling pattern, and the jaw stays relatively quiet. The infant may switch back and forth at will between a suckling and sucking pattern, but the pattern of sucking or suckling, swallowing, and breathing still remains rhythmical, so the infant should display no difficulty with any form of liquid.

At the same time that he is showing maturity in his sucking pattern, he is also able to accept pureed foods from a spoon. Previously he had reached forward with his tongue to meet the spoon and used a suckling pattern to remove the food; now the infant can keep his tongue quiet in his mouth and wait for the loaded spoon to approach. The infant's tongue at this age will assume a characteristic U-shape pattern. The top lip comes down to clean the food off the spoon; negative pressure is built up in the mouth and the food is sucked off the spoon. The tongue tip is elevated and the bolus of food is worked back in the mouth until the infant swallows it. Swallow is accompanied by greater lip approximation. Some gagging and coughing at this age is normal until the infant becomes more proficient at handling the rougher food consistency.

With increased texture added to his diet, an infant at about 5 to 6 months of age will show a munching pattern. Munching can be described as the "flattening and spreading of the tongue, combined with an up and down motion of the jaw. The body of the tongue may elevate slightly and make contact with the hard palate, but the tongue makes no lateral movement to transfer food onto teeth. The food is mashed or pulverized against the hard palate."[62]

Munching develops from the phasic bite reflex and sucking pattern and is the precursor to chewing. The bite reflex should be completely integrated as an involuntary automatic reaction at this time. The infant may bite in a playful

mood once his hunger has been satiated. One characteristic commonly seen in infants with neurological difficulties is the inability to tolerate solids and increased texture in their diet. Such an infant will not allow the spoon to enter his mouth and, instead, will bunch up his tongue, which pushes the spoon away in what is known as a "tongue-thrust pattern." This pathological pattern would be present at any time the caregiver attempts to introduce the nipple or spoon into the mouth, even when the infant is obviously hungry.

Perceptual/fine motor assessment. Reaching now becomes a more direct unilateral approach of one hand toward the object. The movement is controlled from the shoulder, and the infant reaches with the forearm in pronation and the elbow partially extended. The mass grasp of the younger infant is becoming more refined with greater participation of the radial side of the hand and thumb. Some thumb opposition toward the index finger will be seen when the infant holds a 1-inch cube. When presented with a very small item, the infant is not able to use his thumb and forefinger in opposition but rather reverts to the more gross motion of raking, extending all four fingers and flexing as he closes over the object. An alternative to this is the scooping motion, in which the infant uses the ulnar or hypothenar eminence to enclose the object and pick it up. At this stage he can more deftly transfer a small item from hand to hand. The infant can inhibit the overflow, which previously caused him to drop the cube and so he can now hold onto one cube and touch and grasp a second cube.

Gross motor assessment. The infant has gained enough extensor strength that he can lift his head and trunk up and support himself on extended elbows in the prone position. He can shift his weight and reach for an object in the prone position and maintain stability. Without the use of his arms, he will also assume the pivot prone position, in which the total body shows the complete extension pattern with only the stomach remaining in contact with the table. This activity would indicate the complete integration of the tonic labyrinthine reflex in the prone position. In the suspended prone position this position is known as the Landau reflex.

In the supine position the infant is gaining greater strength in his neck and trunk flexors, which is coupled with the activation of the supine righting reaction, so when an adult's hand is offered to the infant, the infant will lift his head and actively pull himself to the preferred seated position. If he remains on his back the legs are easily brought up, so his feet may be fingered or brought to his mouth. Being able to assume this flexed position while supine indicates the integration of the tonic labyrinthine reflex.

In the upright or seated position the infant will be able to maintain the upright posture for a few seconds when placed with his hands in front of him. If he falls forward, he can use his arms to push back up and begins to experiment with letting go so that he can use his hands in play activities instead of for balance. His legs are held in front of him, his hips are in abduction and external rotation, and his knees are flexed (ring sitting), which offer a wide base of support. If offered support around the hips, he can sit with a straight back. When fully supported in a high chair, he can sit for prolonged periods of time. Infants at this age also prefer to stand if given the opportunity. They will take full weight on their feet but depend on the adult for balance in the totally upright position. Their legs will remain stiff in a positive support reaction.

Higher level reflexes, that is, body on body reflexes, are seen for the first time when the infant is able to initiate a roll from his back to his stomach using a segmental rolling pattern with either the arm or hip leading. Righting reactions should be well established, so if the infant is tilted, he will quickly move his body to position the head in such a way that the eyes remain horizontal. This righting reaction had been observed by the eighth week in the prone position, but it takes until 6 to 7 months of age for it to be as well established in the supine or lateral tilt position. Equilibrium reactions, in which the body shows postural adjustments in response to a shifting base of support, can be observed if the infant is tested on a tiltboard in the prone and supine positions. The infant will adjust his body to the tilt by abducting his limbs on the high side, curving his spine in such a way that the concavity will be on the high side, while keeping his head in midline. Limbs on the low side stiffen in a protective reaction.

Nine-month assessment

The 9-month-old infant has developed some efficient means of locomotion, usually creeping on all fours, which allow him to explore wider segments of his world, as well as practice separating from his mother. The infant's new cognitive and fine motor skills interact, so the infant not only notices the novel details of an object, but he also has the fine motor skills, that is, isolation of the index finger, to provide the manual dexterity to explore the object further. This interest in and ability to explore the environment allows for further interaction with his surroundings and facilitates learning about them.

Visual assessment. In the eighth month the infant should have developed the ability to use conjugate binocular vision, so he can see an object and focus on it at a variety of distances. His visual acuity becomes so developed that he can easily see a very small item such as a raisin up to 1.5 m or more away. The infant should either reach for the object if he is close enough or creep over to get it. The examiner can experiment with moving small items out of the infant's reach and watch for his response. One should be aware of the need for contrast between the object and the background to rule out figure-ground difficulty. The examiner should observe the infant tracking a moving object, watching for any hint of strabismus, nystagmus, or head tilt, which would indicate visual dysfunction. Also, if a child is not successful at the expected age level, observation of how vision is used in other developmental tasks such as eye-hand coordination may give an indication of visual dysfunction as opposed to motor incoordination.

Hearing assessment. It is suggested that the examiner continue to use a variety of noisemakers that can be calibrated according to their frequency levels. Rustling paper near each ear from behind the infant is a good clinical test of high-frequency hearing perception. At the 9-month level, the infant will most reliably respond to the human voice, particularly when his name is called. He should turn to seek out the speaker. The volume of the voice can be raised or lowered to further check hearing responses in this informal setting. In addition, the infant should be starting to respond to verbal directions as well as beginning to imitate speech and nonspeech sounds. This highlights the necessity of a total developmental assessment to distinguish between infants with hearing impairment and those with global cognitive and/or language delay.

Social assessment. By 8 months the infant has moved into the peak attachment phase and will show strong attachment behaviors when left by the mother. The infant practices separation as he develops locomotion via crawling or creeping, but will do so only when he can remain in contact with the mother by keeping her in his visual field and can check back with her at will. The infant's increased language and imitation skills allow him to participate more fully in the so-called social games, such as pat-a-cake, peekaboo, and so-big, performing the actions on verbal cue.

Language assessment. Receptively, the infant begins to respond to specific content of speech instead of just to the rhythm and tone of voice. Certain often repeated words that represent familiar situations will produce a response in the infant; he either looks at the named object or person or performs the requested action, such as playing pat-a-cake or waving bye-bye. As described on p. 70, the infant who is reinforced for particular sounds within his repertoire begins to repeat those sounds at the appropriate time. He is learning new models of speech and may start to reproduce other sounds as real words, such as ''hi'' or ''bye.'' The examiner is cautioned to be somewhat skeptical of reports of the words ''mama'' or ''dada'' because the infant may be going through the transitional period of using those sounds in relation to the typical caregiving activities of those parents— ''mama'' being a comforting sound that the infant uses to express his need for some tender loving care, whereas ''dada'' can connote generalized excitement. The sounds are used in proximity to the parents but may not have become truly specific verbalizations at this age.

Cognition assessment. At 9 months the infant should have begun to show the characteristics of an infant who has entered Piaget's stage IV integration of previous schema (9 to 12 months). At this stage the infant's problem-solving abilities have developed, so one can observe the beginnings of intelligent thought. It is during this stage that the infant begins to respond to the novelty of objects and through careful visual examination notices details. For example, when handed a toy car, he would turn the object over and over in his hands and view it from all sides. At the same time the infant can use his isolated index finger to poke at the wheels and discover that the car has four moving parts, or wheels. His concept of causality has developed to the point at which he can select an end point or goal and an appropriate action or means to achieve the desired effects, for example, he will deliberately pull a string to pull a toy closer to him. This is a good example of the infant applying known means to new problems. In an earlier stage he might have discovered that shaking a string caused the toy at the end to come closer to him; thus, the mean's end relationship was discovered quite by accident. At this age, when presented with a busy box, the infant will begin to play appropriately with it (Fig. 3-4, *A*). This indicates that the aforementioned causality concept and awareness of the novelty of objects has matured. Parallel to these concepts, fine motor skills now allow the infant to perform appropriate actions of dialing a dial or pulling a light switch. In a social sphere the infant has begun to experiment with separation and individuation as he starts to perceive himself as a separate individual. Cognitively, he also begins to see he is not the cause of all things. During this period the infants starts to look for things and persons outside of himself that cause events to happen. Imitation skills are developing (Fig. 3-4, *B*), so the infant will imitate actions in his repertoire of movements, such as patting the floor or clapping hands and waving, as well as new movements, such as crumpling paper or sliding it on the floor. The infant will now also perform gestures that he cannot see himself perform. These include a variety of facial expressions, such as wrinkling his nose, sticking his tongue out, and speech and nonspeech sounds. The common

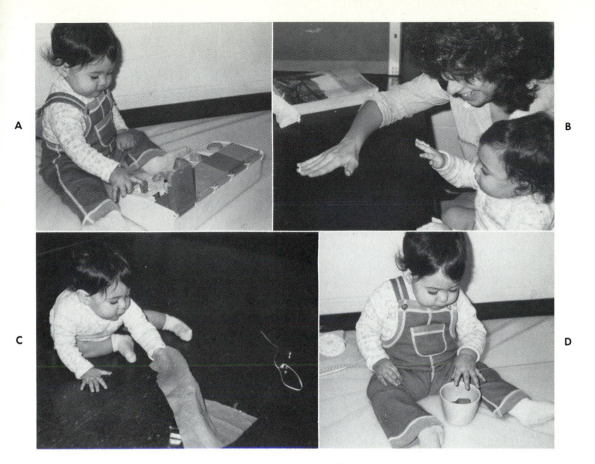

Fig. 3-4. A, Rachel at 9 months—imitating new motions by pulling switch on busy box with isolated index finger. **B,** Rachel at 9 months—imitating gestures in response to another person. **C,** Rachel at 9 months—successfully finding a hidden object. **D,** Rachel at 9 months—placing blocks deliberately in cup.

vocalizations that the infant has been babbling, such as "dadada" or "mamamama," are rapidly reinforced by parents and shaped into true verbal representation. The infant's object permanence skills allow him to maintain the image of an object that he sees hidden long enough to remove the covering from it (Fig. 3-4, C).

Play of the 9-month-old has become more sophisticated because of the concurrent development of cognitive concepts and fine motor skills. His play reflects his understanding of the relationship of objects to each other and what they represent in themselves. A cup may be brought immediately to the mouth in motor recognition of that item, whereas mouthing is not used to explore other objects. A box or can containing blocks is at first something that the infant dumps objects out of; then he becomes

aware of the spatial concept of containers, so he can practice active release and place one or two blocks into the can (Fig. 3-4, D). This activity holds the infant's interest and is repeated endlessly (putting one block in, taking it out). A new game develops around active release or throwing. The infant has developed the concept that releasing an object means it will fall to the ground because of gravity. The game develops when the infant figures out that he can involve the parent; the adult retrieves the dropped object. The adult has been noted to tire of this game much earlier than the infant, whereas the infant could continue indefinitely. Spatiality concepts, in addition to the one just described, are facilitated by the infant's ability to use more efficient locomotion to explore his environment, thus experimenting with distances, near-far relationships, and how to deal with barriers. The infant can not only move an object in relationship to himself, as seen when he completely rotates his bottle to insert the nipple in his mouth when it is presented bottom end first, but can also move himself in relationship to objects, which allows him to develop ideas of constancy of form and shape.

Self-care/feeding assessment.[62] The infant should develop the ability to handle increasingly textured foods, such as regular applesauce, cottage cheese, and mashed potatoes. Besides using his lips to remove food from the spoon, he will also use his upper lip and gum ridge to clean the food off the lower lip. A piece of toast or cracker is something that the infant can easily pick up and bite off with his newly erupted teeth or his gum ridge. The munching pattern of the earlier months is beginning to be replaced by the more mature chewing pattern. Chewing occurs on a vertical plane when the food is placed between the gum ridges, in the side of the mouth, or where the tongue starts to lateralize. When a cup is offered to a child of this age, the liquid is ingested if the child allows small amounts to be poured into his mouth or he attempts to use a sucking procedure to pull the liquid into his mouth. When he attempts to use this latter maneuver, one can observe the jaw moving up and down or possibly backward and forward in a fairly wide excursion. With this pattern, liquid is lost; fairly poor, inconsistent lip activity is common and the infant generally uses a combination of suckling and sucking. At this time the infant may start to hold the cup when it is brought to his mouth but will need assistance in monitoring the flow of the liquid and putting the cup down. Although the infant can finger feed himself, a spoon is still more of a toy to be banged than a tool for conveying food into his mouth.

Perceptual/fine motor assessment. The 9-month-old infant is now developing greater manual dexterity. In the preceding months his thumb became more active in adduction against the index finger as he attempts to pick up a small pellet. At 9 months he begins to isolate his index finger while he flexes his other fingers and brings his thumb around in opposition to it, so he displays a neat pincer grasp in picking up small items. His eye-hand coordination is sufficiently developed that once he notices a small item, such as a piece of cereal or lint, he can move to pick it up without any overshooting. Development of active release is just beginning to happen in a controlled manner. The infant usually needs to stabilize the forearm on the edge of the container before he can extend his fingers and thumb to let go of the item. Active release is first achieved with larger objects, and he will need to practice this phenomenon in the next few months to achieve precise release with smaller objects, such as a cube or a pellet.

Gross motor assessment. The infant will now prefer to be in an upright position when he is awake. He can now sit indefinitely, assuming a sitting position by rolling over to his stomache and then rotating his hips and pushing up with his hands or by moving into that position from an all-fours position when he has been creeping. Once seated he can freely move his center of gravity to reach for toys on either side and over his head, showing good equilibrium responses and body on body rotation. Balance is mostly maintained through equilibrium responses but should the force be great enough, the infant will show protective responses by propping anteriorly and to the sides, and at around 9 months he is begining to show posterior protective responses. When offered the adult's hand, he insists on helping to pull to an upright position. Once upright, he no longer needs to use his legs as stiff pillars of support, so the infants begins to relax his hip extensors and experiment with bouncing and weight shifting in an upright position. This skill in weight shifting will eventually lead to cruising in the next month or so.

Creeping or reciprocally moving in an quadruped position requires that the STNR be well integrated. Although a majority of infants creep before they walk, some infants develop other means of locomotion, such as hitching in a seated position. Many infants with mild to moderate cerebral palsy develop a "bunny hop," moving both lower extremities together in an all-fours position because of the residual influence of the STNR, whereas others learn to scoot along on their backs.

At this age the forward parachute response is active. Arms are extended as the infant is tilted forward while being held about the trunk. Observations of the infant's activity (as noted earlier) will give the examiner a great deal of information about the reflex development in the infant. In any infant with a questionable neurodevelopmental history or performance, each reflex should be tested separately to ascertain the integration of primitive reflexes and the appearance of higher level reflexes. This would include the ATNR, the TLR, and the righting, protective, and equilibrium responses.

Twelve-month assessment

The 12-month-old glories in being a bipedal animal. There is an intense interest in walking—so much so that gains in other areas may not be as rapid or noticeable until he masters the art of independent gait.

Visual assessment. Testing of vision is done in the same way as at 9 months.

Hearing assessment. Repeated sound localization should be performed laterally and below the child. Further hearing assessment can be done using a variety of simple verbal commands given at various levels of loudness.

Social assessment. The 12-month-old infant is finishing the practicing phase of separation and individuation. He is more confident in his abilities to handle separation initiated by himself, so he will creep or cruise wider distances away from the mother. At this point his attachment is still strong; if the mother initiates the separation, the child will be distressed.

Language assessment. A 12-month-old infant is very intent on expressing himself and communicating with the important adults around him. The infant should have three or four words in his repertoire and will consistently use these words, but he relies on gestures such as pointing to objects or pushing them away coupled with vocalizations that can be described as jargoning to indicate most of his needs. Jargoning is speech sounds that are linked together in a way that reflects the infant's intent by his inflection pattern. It can clearly be understood whether the infant is making a statement, asking a question, or giving a command. Receptively, the infant can respond to more of the content of a sentence, so he can follow simple commands that might involve two simple concepts, such as "go find Daddy" or "give

baby a kiss." The infant can respond to a verbal request to say a specific word.

Cognition assessment. A 12-month-old infant is in transition from stage IV to stage V (12 to 18 months), tertiary circular reactions. In stage V the infant attains the higher level of operations at which he begins to form new schema to solve problems instead of relying on previous ways of acting on objects. The infant finds new solutions by active experimentation and, through trial and error, achieves new success. The 12-month-old infant who is just beginning to enter this stage shows a willingness to persist in solving a problem that was not seen earlier. He is beginning to respond to new models but does not grasp some of the more sophisticated concepts that the child in late stage V (15 to 18 months) will display.

The 12-month-old infant will show some persistence in trying to activate a toy such as a music box and solving the problem of how to make it go by attempting to turn the knob. Since he does not have the strength or coordination to actually make music start, he is then willing to look for the cause outside of himself and turn the toy over to an adult for help. When introduced to a new object for the first time, he will take in the novelty of the situation, but unless he is given a new model of action, he most often reverts to the stage III behaviors of shaking and banging to make the object work. However, the 12-month-old infant will be ready to respond immediately to a model of a new action, such as squeezing a toy to make it squeak or pushing a toy car to make it go. His imitation may not be precise, but when given a model, he will try to make his actions conform to the model. The same is true in his imitation of new words. If an object is taken and hidden, he will go immediately to the correct hiding place on the first trial and on each succeeding trial. A younger infant has the tendency to go back to the place where he first found the object hidden, even though he clearly had seen the object hidden under a different covering. The younger infant does not have the persistence to keep on looking after he has been unsuccessful. His play is becoming more social in nature and the infant is more intent on getting adults involved in his play. The infant both shows a toy to an adult and plays the game of give and take. He is aware of the adult's reactions and the infant begins to find more joy in repeating an action that has brought pleasure and a favorable response, such as laughter, touching, and smiling from the adult. For the first time, a 12-month-old will completely fill a small container with objects instead of persisting in placing only one or two objects into the container. The infant's knowledge of supporting surfaces developed, so blocks will be piled beyond the confines of the container with the assurance that they will stay secure. The infant becomes aware of the relationship between items (besides a container and its contents), for example, how a stick can be used to bang on a drum or xylophone, how crayons make marks, and how a spoon is a tool to convey food to the mouth. Previously, those objects were played with, independent of their associated use.

Self-care/feeding assessment (dressing assessment).[62] Since the infant is now cognitively aware that the spoon can be used as a tool to convey food to his mouth, independent spoon feeding may be taken up and used as the primary way to feed himself unless, of course, the infant realizes a spoon is not as efficient as using his fingers to accomplish the same task. The infant of this age should be able to handle most mashed table foods, taking foods of most textures and chewing them well, using lateral tongue movements. Chewy beef may present a problem but luncheon meat, chicken, and fish that are chopped well should pose no difficulty for the infant.

A child of this age will attempt to cooperate in dressing activities or removing simple articles of clothing such as his hat, socks, shoes, and mittens when requested to do so. He will continue to cooperate in diapering and dressing activities by moving his limbs to push them through openings or to pull them out. In pulling a shirt over his head, he will assist by either pulling it down or off, to clear his face.

Perceptual/fine motor assessment. The infant now reaches precisely with a wrist that is slightly extended and shows ulnar deviation so as to orient the fingers toward objects to be picked up. The infant has gained increased manual dexterity, so he is able to turn the pages of a cardboard book and remove a cover from a cardboard box and has enough eye-hand co-

ordination to pick up a small pellet and release it into a half-inch opening of a vial or small bottle without forearm support. He will grasp a crayon by holding it in his fist with the point projecting out of the radial aspect. He then pronates his arm, thumb down, and attempts to mark with it. Refinement of the pencil grasp takes a full 2 years to develop. Increased strength in the infant's fingers allows him to squeeze a squeaky toy and produce a sound. The examiner is cautioned to be sure that the infant can isolate his index finger and use a neat pincer grasp. Many infants will develop some of the above mentioned functional skills (e.g., turning pages), albeit somewhat clumsily, without developing a pincer grasp.

Gross motor assessment. The 12-month-old infant's increased neurological maturation as well as his awareness of his environment and his desire to imitate adult behavior encourages him to let go, stand independently, and take a few independent steps. The infant's gait pattern at this time reflects his somewhat immature nervous system, in that he reverts to more primitive patterns of movement, particularly in the upper extremities when his body is stressed by the demands of maintaining a totally upright position. This is seen in the early walker's high guard position, in which the arms are held in a Moro-like abduction pattern. He compensates for his weak abdominal muscles by throwing his shoulders back to maintain his center of gravity as he moves forward, so his walk resembles more a stiff run than the controlled walk of the older child. His legs will be abducted and externally rotated in an effort to broaden his base of support. It has been suggested that the position of the arms is more for protection of the infant than for balance.[37] Because of frequent falls, the infant may revert to creeping to move swiftly from one place to another.

Fifteen-month assessment

If walking is well established, the 15-month-old can turn his attention to learning about the world in a new perspective. He uses this skill along with climbing, so nothing is safe from his explorations. At this point he is quite sure of himself, longs for the freedom to explore, but does not yet know the inherent dangers in many situations. The 15-month-old will also start to imitate more words and actions that are a part of his daily routine. This is seen in his play, as well as his attempts to master various self-care activities.

Visual assessment. See 9-month assessment.

Hearing assessment. See 9-month assessment and 12-month assessment.

Social assessment. The child at this age continues the trend set when he was 12 months old of feeling very confident of his ability to strike out on his own. This is enhanced by his more developed gross motor skills, in that he can usually walk well, which aids him in his explorations. He ''is exhilarated by his own abilities, continually delighted by the discoveries he makes in his expanding world, and quasi-enamored with the world and his own grandeur and omnipotence.''[56] This is the peak of the darting-off behavior of the child who fearlessly strikes out on his own. However, 15 months is also the beginning of the rapprochement period, when the child begins to relate to the mother as someone other than a comfort station that provides food, drink, and tender loving care. She becomes an individual with whom the toddler wishes to share his discoveries about the world. New objects are found and brought to the mother for her approval. The child would expect the mother to respond with delight equal to his own at his discoveries and be interested in participating in his activities. The child now more actively seeks to engage his parents in some form of games, whether it is the ''I'll go away and you'll have to catch me'' or any game of give and take, such as ball play.

Language assessment. By this age the child has gained the use of five or six more words, which he uses on a consistent basis. Some of these may appear to be phrases such as ''all gone'' or ''what's that'' but actually are holophrastic phrases because they essentially deal with one concept rather than combining two concepts, as the 18-month-old child would do, for example ''Mommy milk.'' Receptively, he is able to respond to more requests and can usually show a number of body parts, familiar items of clothing such as shoes, and familiar objects (ball, baby, cup). This identification of objects can also be translated to two-dimensional pictures if they are fairly realistic.

Cognition assessment. The 15-month-old infant is now well into stage V, so he is showing increasing sophistication in his problem-solving ability. If given a clear plastic vial with a raisin in it, he will try a number of behaviors to get it out. Some children at this age, responding to the shape of the vial, relate it to their experience with drinking and try to drink the raisin out of the vial, whereas others will stick their index finger in and attempt to poke and lift it out. When these attempts are not successful, reversion to the stage III shaking behavior is most often observed, with the child being successful in getting the raisin out in this manner. Occasionally, in their experimentation they come across the idea that if the vial is tipped over, gravity will assist them, or if the examiner gives them the model, the child attempts to copy the adult model. However, if given the vial again, the child may not remember the practical solution and will revert to the trial-and-error approach.

The example just given of the child attempting to drink the raisin out of the vial shows how the stage V child is beginning to group objects based on broad categories. This thought process is reflected by the child's actions: the vial, cups, and glasses are things to drink from. If the child is presented with a new item, such as a crayon, and a model of its use, he retains the causality concept that the crayon and items similar to it produce marks. When presented with some other form of writing utensil, the child will spontaneously scribble. It is not until later that he will gain use of appropriate verbal labels and begin to appreciate the true differences between such things as crayons, pencils, or pens. His play reflects his understanding of what the object is, for example, the baby doll is fed with a play bottle, the car is pushed, the blocks are stacked, and the toy phone is dialed and the receiver held next to the ear. The child may say ''hi'' but does not have the verbal or cognitive skills to elaborate on this or any of the play situations just mentioned.

Self-care/feeding assessment. Assessment of self-care and feeding can be done using the 12-month assessment.

Perceptual/fine motor assessment. By this age the child should approach an object that is close to him by anticipating the size of the object and adjusting his fingers accordingly. Objects placed out of reach will cause the young child to display the more immature grasp with all his fingers extended and abducted. Skills that are tested in this area of development reflect the concurrent development of certain cognitive and perceptual concepts that the child is now able to combine with his motor skills. An example of this is his ability to stack 1-inch cubes. At this age he should be able to stack two and may attempt to stack a third. If the child has difficulty with this task, one must distinguish whether he understands the cognitive concept of supporting surfaces or if motor difficulty is due to poor eye-hand coordination or grasp release pattern problems.

The child should also be able to orient a peg correctly and place it in a pegboard. Stacking cubes and positioning a peg indicate a child's awareness of vertical direction, which develops before his concept of the horizontal. He is also beginning to discriminate shapes and place a round form into a formboard. When presented with the other shapes, he is not yet able to match up the square and triangle, but may resort to stacking them on top of the round form or make some attempt to put one form into each insert. When the forms do not fit, he is not yet able to correct himself by either switching the forms or rotating the forms so that they do fit into the hole.

Gross motor assessment. By 15 months those infants who have been walking for several months will have become adept enough that they walk as their chief means of locomotion. The child now can come to a standing position independently in the center of the room. He does this by rolling over onto his stomach and pushing up to a hand-knee position and then up to his feet. His base of support is narrower and his arms should be at waist level. He is able to control his gait, so he can stop and start at will as well as change directions and turn corners. This demonstrates early motor planning abilities. He walks both sideways and backward. Children who have been provided the opportunity to learn how to deal with stairs will creep up and down the steps. The child can climb into and out of an adult-sized chair, and children have been known to explore tabletops and counters if not carefully watched. The child's

ball-handling skills consist of raising his arms over his head and bringing his arms forward as his fingers release the ball, so there is a slight cast to it. The child should be tested for this skill when standing if he is an independent walker to ascertain balance under those conditions. However, for children not yet walking this activity can be evaluated when sitting. The examine is still urged to watch for the presence of any primitive reflexes in the child's spontaneous activities. Sometimes under the stress of being totally upright, the child will demonstrate some posturing, that is, hands up in high guard and fisted combined with persistent toe walking. Their significance at this time is still questionable but it would be a soft neurological find worthy of noting.

Eighteen-month assessment

The 18-month-old child is often seen as entering the period known as the "terrible twos." As his skill in locomotion has grown, opening wider areas for exploration, he has become more aware of the things he cannot do because of his size, age, and inability to clearly communicate his needs to others. This so-called Ericksonian battle of autonomy versus shame and doubt is now on in full force, so the child is some one of amazing contrasts, at times fiercely independent and refusing all offers of adult assistance, while later clinging and demanding the adult's attention.

Visual assessment. Assessment of vision can be done using the 9-month assessment.

Hearing assessment. For informal auditory screening at this age, one can add auditory localization above and slightly to the right or left of the child's head. He should be able to immediately localize. In addition, he should be understanding and gaining more words, so responses to auditory commands given at different loudnesses as well as the child's language development should give a clue to the hearing status.

Social assessment. As noted earlier, the 18-month-old child's behavior is characterized by his inner turmoil when he wishes independence to perform chosen activities. Negativism may hit a peak and "No" or "Me do" becomes his favorite word. He becomes more aware of his possessions and defends his ownership by declaring "mine." His inability to get his own way or frustration at being unable to do something may result in a sobbing child who feels defeated or one who responds to the situation with anger and temper tantrums. The same period of time in which he is having flights of independence is also the beginning of the rapprochement, which sees the child again turning to the parent for solace and comfort. At times he becomes clinging, and incessantly demanding of the adult's time and attention to help him and to participate with him in all of his activities. This ambivalence, although trying at times for parents, is part of the social maturation of the child.

Language assessment. As the child becomes increasingly adept at imitating new words, his vocabulary increases and his memory improves, so he will retain words he has heard but not necessarily repeated constantly for longer periods of time. Linguists[51] have developed a taxonomy of words that are most commonly part of a first lexicon. These words have to do with the following:[51]

Category	Example
Labels	Baby, bottle, daddy
Rejection	No
Nonexistence or disappearance	All gone
Cessation of action	No, stop
Reoccurence of object and actions	More, again, another
Action on objects	Give, throw, do
Actions involved in locating objects or self	Up, down, sit, fall, go
Adjectives or descriptions of objects	Big, hot, dirty, pretty
Persons associated with objects (as in possession)	Person's name, Mommy's, mine

To qualify as using a two-word phrase, the child must express two distinct concepts, which Brown[8] describes as an agent action, for example, Daddy go; or an action object, for example, throw ball; or an agent object, for example, Mommy cup.

Cognition assessment. 18 months begins stage VI, the transitional period between sensorimotor intelligence and more symbolic reasoning. Piaget called this stage representational (18 to 24 months) because at this point the child

can think. He will now mentally run through a number of solutions rather than rely on active experimentation. This is the "ah-hah" experience. The child wants a cookie on the counter, looks around, and then pulls a chair to climb up and reach for it. The child is solving problems through reasoning. He can find a cause if he observes an effect. If something moves unexpectedly or makes a noise, the child will search for the cause.

Imitation is becoming more immediate and precise, it is particularly a time of growing vocabulary and for the first time the child begins to combine two words. His recognition of pictures is another emerging skill that is developing due to the child's increased understanding of the permanence of objects, coupled with the understanding that absent objects can be represented by two-dimensional forms. This concept is an example of the more conceptual thinking that will take place in the next periods of development.

The play skills of an 18-month-old are becoming more symbolic as he begins to act out familiar events, using his toys as props and in relationship to each other (Fig. 3-5, A). An example of this is using a tea set to cook for a doll and then feeding the doll. He will also shadow the adult's activities and try to mimic domestic scenes, such as helping to wash the dishes, dust, and vacuum. His play with a toy is an example of delayed imitation; he no longer needs the adult's model. At the same time he carries out activity on his own. The mimicking of domestic events shows his attempts to become involved in his parents' activities and to involve the parents in his.

The child also develops a systematic way of searching for an object that he does not directly see hidden (invisible displacement). The toy is hidden under a cup and then the cup and toy are passed under a cloth, leaving the toy under the cloth. When the cup is removed from under the cloth, the child will search for the absent toy, first under the cup and then make the mental deduction necessary to go on and search for it under the cloth. A younger child will only look as far as the cup and then believe the toy is lost, not making the transition from cup to cloth.

When the child is able to imitate the use of a

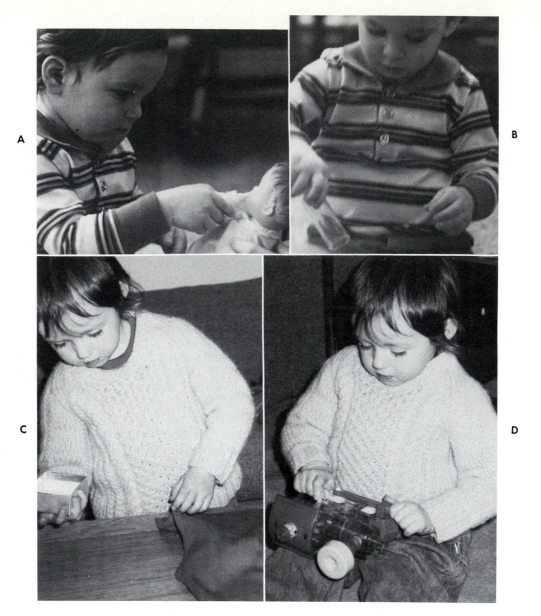

Fig. 3-5. A, Christopher at 18 months—combining two objects in play (feeds a doll a bottle). **B,** Christopher at 18 months—deliberately dumping vial to retrieve raisin. **C,** Anna at 18 months—searching in box and then under cloth to find toy (single invisible displacement). **D,** Anna at 18 months—looking for mechanism to activate train and attempting to wind it herself.

stick to retrieve an item out of reach, it shows not only growth in his imitation skills, but also in his spatial understanding the use of a stick as a tool to extend his grasp. The younger child does not respond to this demonstration, but rather bangs the stick while he attempts to move his body to reach the object. He also uses gravity to assist him in emptying a container (Fig. 3-5, *B*). The child who has entered stage VI is also beginning to show greater understanding of the differences in forms, in that he works puzzles with more accuracy and less trial-and-error approach. This demonstrates his ability to visualize the form as fitting into the inset, rather than having to try it manually.

Self-care/feeding assessment (dressing as-

sessment).[62] At 18 months of age the young child should be able to use his spoon independently to feed himself an entire meal. He may, of course, have difficulty with spoon feeding liquids such as soup, but most other foods should be easily conveyed to his mouth. Chewing[62] is now accomplished using more mature rotary patterns. "Rotary motion involves smooth interaction of the muscles which open and close the mouth with those that pull the jaw in a lateral or diagonal direction. By the age of a year and a half, everything the child needs for feeding has developed with the exception of refined rotary jaw movements."[62] A child of this age should also begin to handle a cup more independently, picking it up and putting it down. He will use his lower jaw to stabilize the cup by biting on the edge of the cup. "The child does not yet have the co-contraction for jaw opening and closing, so he provides the stabilization by biting down on the edge of the cup. Lip function is improved and there is much less liquid lost."[62]

The young child is more interested in imitating simple grooming action, such as attempting to brush his hair or teeth or using a washcloth. Although interested in the activities, the child is not yet skilled enough to truly accomplish the task.

Perceptual/fine motor assessment. At 18 months of age the child's eye-hand coordination as well as his grasp and release pattern should allow him to build a three-cube tower. Those children who still have difficulty with precise release may build a tower that is a bit shaking but nonetheless three cubes high. More adept children may be successful at adding more cubes. When presented with a formboard, there should be no hesitation in placing the round block, although the square and triangle are usually placed through trial and error. At this age trials by some children work, so all three forms are placed correctly, whereas other children have the idea of placing one form in each space but may mix up the square and the triangle or be unable to rotate either of those forms if they are slightly out of kilter. Although the child's release pattern has matured over the past 3 months, his release has not yet developed to the point that he can do it with the ease of an older child or adult. This is seen in the fact that he uses more pressure than is necessary when releasing the items, causing his towers to fall when he attempts to place a fourth or fifth block, or using excessive pressure in placing the forms into the formboard. However, his manual dexterity is becoming more efficient when he places pegs into a pegboard; now the norm is to be able to place all six pegs within 42 seconds.[4] When holding a crayon, the 18-month-old will start to extend his index and middle fingers in an attempt to guide it, although his hand is held pronated with the end of the crayon still in his palm. This is part of the sequence of moving toward the more mature tripod grasp seen in the 30-month-old child. The child has gained sufficient control over the scribbling that he will imitate strokes once given a demonstration.

Gross motor assessment. The 18-month-old child's balance has greatly improved; his gait becomes less wide based and his arms no longer hold a high or midguard position but rather are down at his sides, unless he is carrying something. His improved one-foot standing balance allows him to walk up and down stairs, which necessitates standing on one foot alone with a minimal support for balance. His improved balance also assists him when he seats himself in a small chair or squats in play by allowing him to carefully lower his center of gravity. He has now developed equilibrium reactions in standing, which are tested by having the child stand while the examiner grasps the child around his shoulders and tries to move him slightly off balance. The child should move his feet to maintain his balance in an upright position. The alternative would be to use a tiltboard. His "run" is still a fast walk, if run is defined in the true sense of the word, which means that at one period of time both feet have left the ground. However, the 18-month-old child can still move very quickly in a fast walk.

CONCLUSIONS

Following are some conclusions to bear in mind when performing neurodevelopmental assessments:

- Primary care physicians need to have a thorough knowledge of infant and child development and be able to perform assessments or work with allied professionals in the periodic neuromaturational assessments of their patients in the first few years.

• Delayed development can be in one or more of the following areas: cognitive, motor and reflexive, visual, auditory, language, and social.

• Screening and neuromaturational assessment of the newborn and through the first 2 years of life, whether for clinical or research purposes, should include evaluations in all six major areas of development as just outlined.

• The primary care physician is in the ideal position, knowing the child and family so well, to judge neuromaturation, give anticipatory guidance, and when necessary call in intervention assistance for the child.

REFERENCES

1. American Psychological Association: Standards for educational and psychological tests, Washington, D.C., 1974, American Psychological Association.
2. Amiel-Tison, C.: Evaluation of the neuromuscular system of the infant. In Rudolf, A., editor: Pediatrics, New York, 1977, Appleton-Century-Crofts.
2a. André-Thomas, Chesni, C. Y., and Saint Anne Dargassies, S.: Neurological examination of the infant, Clin. Dev. Med. no. 1, 1960.
2b. Arthur, G.: Arthur adaption of the Leiter international performance scale, Chicago, 1952, Stoelting Co.
3. Ayers, J.: Sensory integration and learning disorders, Los Angeles, 1972, Western Psychological Services.
4. Bayley, N.: The Bayley scales of infant development, New York, 1969, Psychological Corp.
5. Bobath, B.: Abnormal postural reflex activity caused by brain lesions, London, 1965, William Heinemann Medical Books Ltd.
6. Bower, T. G. R.: A primer of infant development, San Francisco, 1977, W. H. Freeman & Co., Publishers.
7. Brazelton, T. B.: Neonatal behavioral assessment scale, Clin. Dev. Med. vol. 50, 1973.
8. Brown, R.: A first language/the early stages, Cambridge, Mass., 1973, Harvard University Press.
9. Bruner, J., Jolly, A., and Sylva, K.: Play—its role in development and evolution, New York, 1976, Basic Books Inc., Publishers.
10. Buros, O. K.: The sixth mental measurement yearbook, Highland Park, N.J., 1965, Gryphon Press.
11. Buros, O. K.: The seventh mental measurement yearbook, vols. 1 and 2, Highland Park, N.J., 1972, Gryphon Press.
12. Bzoch, K., and League, E.: The receptive-expressive emergent language scale for the measurement of language skill in infancy, Baltimore, 1978, University Park Press.
13. Cairns, G., and Butterfield, E.: Assessing infants' auditory functioning. In Friedlander, B., Sterritt, G., and Kirk, G., editors: The exceptional infant, vol. III, New York, 1975, Brunner/Mazel, Inc.
14. Caplan, E.: The first twelve months of life, New York, 1973, Grosset & Dunlap, Inc.
15. Cattell, P.: Infant intelligence scale, New York, 1940, Psychological Corp.
16. Church, J.: Techniques for differential study of cognition in early childhood, Cognitive Studies **1:**1, 1970.
17. Cratty, B.: Perceptual and motor development in infants and children, New York, 1970, The Macmillan Co.
18. Cronbach, L. J.: Essentials of psychological testing, ed. 3, New York, 1970, Harper & Row, Publishers.
19. DiLeo, J.: Developmental evaluation of very young infants. In Hellmuth, J., editor: The exceptional infant. Vol. I, The normal infant, New York, 1967, Brunner/Mazel, Inc.
20. Dinno, N. D.: Early recognition of infants at risk for developmental retardation, Pediatr. Clin. North Am. **24:**633, 1977.
21. Doll, E. A.: Measurement of social competence: a manual for the Vineland social maturity scale, Minneapolis, 1953, American Guidance Service.
21a. Donovan, C.: The early intervention developmental profile: application in a transdisciplinary approach for families with handicapped children. Paper presented to the American Physical Therapy Association, New Orleans, 1976.
22. Drillien, C. M.: Abnormal neurologic signs in first year of life in low-birthweight infants: possible prognostic significance, Dev. Med. Child Neurol. **14:**575, 1972.
23. Drillien, C. M., and Drummond, M. B.: Neurodevelopmental problems in early childhood. Assessment and management, Philadelphia, 1977, J. B. Lippincott Co.
24. Dubose, R. F.: Predictive value of infant intelligence scales and multiply handicapped children, Am. J. Ment. Defic. **81:**388, 1976.
25. Dubowitz, L. M. S., Dubowitz, V., and Goldberg, C.: Clinical assessment of gestational age in the newborn infant, J. Pediatr. **77:**1, 1970.
26. Erickson, M.: Assessment and management of developmental changes in children, St. Louis, 1976, The C. V. Mosby Co.
27. Espenschade, A., and Eckert, H.: Motor development, Columbus, Ohio, 1967, Charles E. Merrill Publishing Co.
28. Fiorentino, M.: Reflex testing methods for evaluating C.N.S. development, Springfield, Ill., 1972, Charles C Thomas, Publisher.
29. Flavell, J. H.: The developmental psychology of Jean Piaget, New York, 1963, D. Van Nostrand Co.
30. Fraiberg, S.: The magic years, New York, 1959, Charles Scribner's Sons.
31. Frankenburg, W. K., and Dodds, J. B.: The Denver developmental screening test, J. Pediatr. **71:**181, 1967.
32. Gesell, A., et al.: The first five years of life, New York, 1940, Harper & Row, Publishers.

33. Ginsburg, H., and Opper, S.: Piaget's theory of intellectual development, ed. 2, Englewood Cliffs, N.J., 1979, Prentice-Hall, Inc.

34. Gratch, G., and Landers, W. F.: Stage IV of Piaget's theory of infant's object concepts: a longitudinal study, Child Dev. **42:**359, 1971.

35. Grossman, H.: Manual on terminology and classification in mental retardation, Washington, D.C., 1973, American Association on Mental Deficiency.

36. Haynes, U.: A developmental approach to casefinding, publ. no. 2017, Washington, D.C., 1969, U.S. Public Health Service.

37. Henderson, A., and Coryell, J.: The body senses and perceptual deficit. Proceeding of Occupational Therapy Symposium on Somato Sensory Aspects of Perceptual Deficit, Boston, 1972, Boston University.

38. Hiskey, M.: Hiskey-Nebraska test of learning aptitude, Lincoln, Neb., 1966, Union College Press.

39. Hogan, G., and Ryan, N.: Neurological evaluation of newborn, Clin. Perinatol. **4:**31, 1977.

40. Holle, B.: Motor development in children, normal and retarded, Oxford, England, 1976, Blackwell Scientific Publ.

41. Honzik, M.: Value and limitations of infant tests: an overview. In Lewis, M., editor: Origins of intelligence—infancy and early childhood, New York, 1976, Plenum Publishing Corp.

42. Hoskins, T. A., and Squires, J. E.: Developmental assessment: a test for gross motor and reflex development, Phys. Ther. **53:**117, 1973.

43. Howard, J., et al.: A neurological comparison of preterm and full term infants at term conceptional age, J. Pediatr. **88:**995, 1976.

44. Illingworth, R. S.: The development of the infant and young child: normal and abnormal, Baltimore, 1970, The Williams & Wilkins Co.

44a. Ingram, T. T. S.: Muscle tone and posture in infancy, Cerebral Palsy Bull. **5:**6, 1959.

44b. Ingram, T. T. S.: Clinical significance of the infantile feeding reflexes, Dev. Med. Child Neurol. **4:**159, 1962.

45. Jacobson, M.: Developmental neurobiology, New York, 1970, Holt, Rinehart & Winston, Inc.

46. Johnson, T., Moore, W., and Jeffries, J.: Children are different. Developmental physiology, ed. 2, Columbus, Ohio, 1978, Ross Laboratories.

47. Knobloch, H., and Pasamanick, B.: Gesell and Amatruda's developmental diagnosis, ed. 3, New York, 1974, Harper & Row, Publishers.

48. Knobloch, H., Pasamanick, B., and Sherard, E.: A developmental screening inventory for infants, Pediatrics **38:**1095, 1966.

49. Koenigsberge, M. R., and Driscoll, J.: Neurological examination of neonates. In Rudolf, A., editor: Pediatrics, New York, 1977, Appleton-Century-Crofts.

50. Kopp, C. B.: Fine motor abilities of infants. Dev. Med. Child Neurol. **16:**629, 1974.

51. Lahey, M., and Bloom, L.: Planning a first lexicon, which words to teach first, J. Speech Hear. Disord. **42:**340, 1977.

52. Leiter, R.: The Leiter international performance scale, Chicago, 1969, Stoelting Co.

53. Lemire, R. J., et al.: Normal and abnormal development of the human nervous system, New York, 1975, Harper & Row, Publishers.

53a. Lipsitt, L. P.: The study of sensory and learning processes of the newborn, Clin. Perinatol. **4:**163, 1977.

54. Litchtenberg, P., and Norton, D.: Cognitive and mental development in the first five years of life, Bethesda, Md., 1972, National Institute of Mental Health.

55. Lowrey, G. H.: Growth and development of children, ed. 7, Chicago, 1978, Year Book Medical Publishers.

55a. Magnus, R.: Körperstellung (body posture), Berlin, 1924.

56. Mahler, M., Pine, F., and Bergman, A.: The psychological birth of the human infant, New York, 1975, Basic Books, Inc., Publishers.

57. Matheny, A. P., Jr.: Assessment of infant mental development: Tetchy and wayward approaches, Clin. Perinatol. **4:**187, 1977.

58. Maxfield, K., and Bucholz, S.: A social maturity scale for blind preschool children, New York, 1957, American Foundation for the Blind.

59. Meier, J.: Screening and assessment of young children at developmental risk, HEW publ. no. (05) 43-90, Washington, D.C., March 1970, Department of Health, Education and Welfare.

60. Milani-Comparetti, A., and Gidoni, E. A.: Pattern analysis of motor development and its disorders, Dev. Med. Child Neurol. **9:**625, 1967.

61. Milani-Comparetti, A., and Gidoni, E. A.: Routine developmental examination in normal and retarded children, Dev. Med. Child Neurol. **9:**631, 1967.

62. Morris, S. E.: Oral-motor development: normal and abnormal. In Wilson, J., editor: Oral-motor function and dysfunction in children, Chapel Hill, N.C., 1978, Division of Physical Therapy.

63. Morris, S. E.: Pre-speech assessment scale. In Wilson, J., editor: Oral-motor function and dysfunction in children, Chapel Hills, N.C., 1978, Division of Physical Therapy.

64. Nicolosi, L., Harryman, E., and Kieshek, J.: Terminology of communication disorders, Baltimore, 1978, The Williams & Wilkins Co.

65. Northern, J., and Downs, M. P.: Hearing in children, Baltimore, 1974, The Williams & Wilkins Co.

66. Ostwald, P., and Peltzman, P.: The cry of the human infant, Sci. Am. **230:**84, March 1974.

67. Paine, R. S., and Oppe, T. E.: Neurological examination of children, Clin. Dev. Med. vols. 20 and 21, 1966.

68. Parmelee, A., and Michaelis, R.: Neurological examination of the newborn. In Hellmuth, J., editor: The exceptional infant. Vol. II, Studies in abnormalities, New York, 1971, Brunner/Mazel, Inc.

69. Pearson, P., and Williams, C.: Physical therapy services in the developmental disabilities, Springfield, Ill., 1972, Charles C Thomas Publisher.

69a. Peiper, A.: Cerebral function in infancy and childhood. New York, 1963, Consultants Bureau, pp. 167-307.

70. Phibbs, R.: Evaluation of the newborn. In Rudolf, A., editor: Pediatrics, New York, 1977, Appleton-Century-Crofts.

71. Phillips, J.: The origins of intellect, Piaget's theory, San Francisco, 1969, W. H. Freeman & Co., Publishers.

72. Piaget, J.: The origins of intelligence in children, New York, 1952, International Universities Press.

73. Prechtl, H., and Beintema, D.: The neurological examination of the full term newborn infant, Clin. Dev. Med. vol. 12, 1975.

74. Purpura, D. P.: Normal and aberrant neuronal development in the cerebral cortex of human fetus and young infant. In Buchwald, N. A., and Brazier, M. A. B., editors: Brain mechanisms in mental retardation, New York, 1975, Academic Press, Inc., pp. 141-170.

75. Rosenblatt, D.: Developmental trends in infant play. In Tizard, B., and Harvey, D., editors: Biology of a play, Clin. Dev. Med. 62:33, 1975.

76. Rogers, M. G. H.: The early recognition of handicapping disorders in childhood, Dev. Med. Child Neurol. 13:88, 1971.

77. Rogers, S.: Evaluation. In Moersh, M., and Wilson, T., editors: Early intervention project for handicapped infants and young children, Ann Arbor, Mich., 1976, University of Michigan Press.

78. Rogers, S., et al.: The early intervention developmental profile, Ann Arbor, Mich., 1975, University of Michigan Press.

79. Shirley, M.: The first two years: a study of twenty-five babies. Vol. 1, Postural locomotor development, Minneapolis, 1931, University of Minnesota Press.

80. Sidman, R. L., and Rakic, P.: Neuronal migration with special reference to developing human brain: a review, Brain Res. 62:1, 1973.

81. Sukiennicki, D.: Neuromotor development. In Banus, B., editor: The developmental therapist, Thorofare, N.J., 1971, Charles B. Slack, Inc.

82. Taft, L., and Cohen, H.: Neonatal and infant reflexology. In Hellmuth, J., editor: The exceptional infant. Vol. I, The normal infant, New York, 1967, Brunner/Mazel, Inc.

83. Terman, L. M., and Merrill, M. A.: Stanford-Binet intelligence scale, New York, 1967, Psychological Corp.

84. Thomas, A., and Chess, S.: Temperment and development, New York, 1977, Brunner/Mazel, Inc.

85. Tronick, E., and Brazelton, T. B.: Clinical uses of the Brazelton neonatal behavioral assessment. In Hellmuth, J., editor: The exceptional infant. Vol. III, Assessment and intervention, New York, 1975, Brunner/Mazel, Inc.

86. Turkewitz, G., and Birch, H.: Neurobehavioral organization of the human newborn. In Hellmuth, J., editor: The exceptional infant. Vol. II, Studies in abnormalities, New York, 1971, Brunner/Mazel, Inc.

87. Twitchell, T. E.: The automatic grasping responses of infants, Neuropsychologia 3:247, 1965.

88. Uzgiris, I., and Hunt, J.: Assessment of infancy. Ordinal scales of psychological development, Urbana, Ill., 1975, University of Illinois Press.

89. Vetter, H., and Howell, R.: Theories of language acquisition, J. Psycholinguist. Res. 1:31, 1971.

90. Volpe, J. J.: Normal and abnormal human brain development, Clin. Perinatol. 4:3, 1977.

91. Wachs, T. D.: Relation of infant performance on Piaget's scales between 12 and 24 months and their Stanford-Binet performance at 31 months, Child Dev. 46:929, 1975.

92. White, B., Castle, P., and Held, R.: Observations on the development of visually-directed reaching, Child Dev. 35:349, 1964.

92a. Wolff, P. H.: The serial organization of sucking in the young infant, Pediatrics 42:943, 1965.

93. Wood, B. S.: Children and communication, verbal and nonverbal language development, Englewood Cliffs, N.J., 1976, Prentice-Hall, Inc.

4

Early intervention

Carol M. Donovan
Albert P. Scheiner

CONCEPTS OF EARLY INTERVENTION

The catchwords of the 1960s were the "war on poverty" and "early intervention." Social scientists began to document that preschool children as early as age 3 showed consistent differences in cognitive skills, motivation for learning, and social competencies based on social class. Programs such as Head Start were implemented, and "compensatory education" became the way of the future. Investigators began to delve into infancy to find clues as to what shaped children's cognitive development and social competencies. White,[74] stated that infants as early as 10 months of age show differences that were directly related to the competencies of their caregivers. There was a popular view that individual differences seen in children were the result of deficits or abnormalities in the children. Intervention was aimed at changing these deficits and bringing children into the mainstream of what was considered normal, more desirable behavior. These children were described as being from "culturally deprived" homes. Overlapping this view is that of Jensen,[37] who had hypothesized that genetic differences among various segments of the population of the United States can account for differential performances among children. This view is supported by the high incidence of "cultural-familial" retardation in individuals who have no overt pathology but are found clustered in low-income groups.[34] A more enlightened view is that these children are culturally disadvantaged in a society rife with institutional racism and a vicious poverty cycle.

Major disabilities are distributed equally among all classes, but there is a higher incidence of biological risk factors such as prematurity, perinatal asphyxia, malnutrition, lead poisoning, and untreated childhood diseases among lower socioeconomic families.[56] This combination of factors reinforces Sameroff and Chandler's[64] model of the continuum of reproductive risk and caretaking casualty. Biological at-risk factors are compounded by environmental factors.

The results of compensatory education programs have been described as disappointing, but one cannot condemn the concept of early intervention based on a generalized overview of

89

compensatory education programs. Bronfenbrenner,[11] in his 1974 report to the Department of Health, Education and Welfare, reviewed how these programs had been evaluated. Programs that were the most successful were those like Levenstein's Toy Demonstrators.[46] She emphasized the parents as the primary individuals who would intervene with their children.

Bronfenbrenner cites Heber and Garber's Milwaukee Project[34] as a "radical solution" in terms of an ecological approach to early intervention. This project took black infants born to retarded mothers out of their homes and placed them in an intensive cognitively structured program. At age 5½ these experimental children showed a 30-point difference in their IQ from the control group. This difference continued to a lesser degree when the children entered school. Positive elements of this program included the curriculum in the day care program as well as the vocational training that the parents received. However, this approach can be seriously questioned in regard to the advisability of removing infants from their own ecosystems and placing them in an environment that is dominated by white middle-class values. It is particularly troublesome that the care of the infants was turned over to parent surrogates rather than trying to enhance the parents' own skills in dealing with their children. To make an impact on these families, it becomes obvious that the whole sociopolitical system, which allows inadequate health care, nutrition, and housing and underemployment, must be dealt with rather than just providing early intervention for young children. The parents themselves must be bolstered to become adequate primary caregivers and sources of support for their children within the context of their own culture.

Bronfenbrenner[11] outlines the following long-range plan that includes five uninterrupted stages:

1. Preparation for parenthood—child care, nutrition, and medical training
2. Before children come—adequate housing, economic security;
3. The first three years of life—establishment of child parent relationships of reciprocol interaction centered around activities that are chal-

lenging to the child, to establish the parent as the primary agent of intervention: home visits and group meetings;
4. Ages 4 through 6—exposure to cognitively oriented preschool program along with a continuum of parent intervention;
5. Ages 6 through 12—parent support of the child's educational activities at home and at school; parent remains primary figure responsible for the child's development as a person.

The evaluation of the success of programs involving early intervention looked primarily at IQ gains on standard psychometric tests. Some programs like Head Start also included health supervision and parent education. Looking at gains in areas besides IQ is especially important when judging the efficacy of intervention for handicapped children.

In the 1970s an awareness of children born with specific handicaps or considered medically at risk evolved. At the same time professionals in the field of mental retardation were introducing the concepts of deinstitutionalization and normalization. Federal legislation (PL 94-142) to provide equal access to public education for all children was also passed. The Bureau of Education for the Handicapped (BEH) under the Department of Health, Education and Welfare began to fund the First Chance Network in response to the Early Education Assistance Act (PL 91-230); these were innovative projects designed to demonstrate models of service delivery to handicapped children and their families. The Portage Project, directed by Shearer and Shearer,[67] provided home teachers in a precision teaching model to enrolled families in rural Wisconsin. Hayden and Dmitriev's[32] center-based Multidisciplinary Preschool Program for Down Syndrome Children was developed in Seattle. All these programs were pioneering efforts in the field of early intervention with handicapped preschoolers. These researchers employed a traditional staffing pattern using educators as the main interventionists and tried innovative ways of involving parents in the program. Like those who developed the Head Start program, they measured success in IQ gains or ability to pass developmental objectives. These researchers recognized the important concept that infants at established or biological risk are in as much need of attention as infants born into poverty and who are environmentally at risk.

Although programs to meet the needs of very young developmentally disabled children blossomed, it had become increasingly clear that there was a need for programs that enhanced the parents' capacity to care for their children in a therapeutic manner. Programs were needed to encourage parents' competence as caregivers as well as knowledgeable advocates for their children so that the parents could successfully interact with the medical, educational, and social systems. In addition, programs to foster the strengths of the family unit by placing the needs of the handicapped child in proper perspective and thereby enabling other members of that family to thrive were needed. This ecological approach of supporting the strengths of the family system was just as applicable to the infant who was at biological or established risk.

Based on these concepts, some early intervention programs began to look at the family systems approach. To develop a credible model, professionals had to examine the relationship of parents with their newborns, the normal growth and development of young children, and how that process was altered by the special needs of some children.

THEORETICAL OVERVIEW OF THE ATTACHMENT PROCESS

Prenatal and pre-prenatal development (health and nutritional status of a potential mother) have an important and lasting effect on the child. The interaction between an infant and its caregiver also has a profound effect on the ultimate affective and cognitive development of an individual. Bowlby[7] views "the child's first human relationship as the foundation stone of his personality, but there is no agreement on the nature or origin of that relationship."

The normal, full-term infant comes into the world with a set of reflexes and sensory abilities that put him in touch with the world. The infant has the ability to respond to sound, focus on an interesting visual stimulus such as a face, make eye contact, visually track, express his

needs through his cries, and be comforted by his caregiver through feeding or holding. These responses in the neonate suggest that the infant has an inherent set of characteristics that contribute to the attachment process. Bowlby[7] believes that these behavior systems are activated in the infant as a result of interactions with his environment, especially with a principal figure such as his mother. Support is given to this theory by the work of Lorenz, who described critical periods in the phenomenon of imprinting in birds, and Harlow's[29] naturalistic observation and experimentation with rhesus monkeys. Those researchers who have studied attachment behavior in infants on a cross-cultural basis add support to this viewpoint. Schaffer and Emerson,[65] in a study of 60 Scot infants, and Ainsworth,[1] in a study of 27 infants in Ghana, Africa, described developmental patterns that were remarkably similar. Universally, attachment behaviors have as their goal the maintenance of physical or perceptual contact with a mother figure.

In contrast to the theory that the infant is born with a set of intrinsic behaviors that facilitate the attachment process is the object relations theory. Freud's theory of oral gratification indicates that sucking not only reduced hunger but is also pleasurable in itself. A breast or nipple is regarded as the object that produces this feeling, and the infant learns that associated with this object is a mother, who then becomes the desired object. There is thus a secondary drive for the presence of the mother, which takes place because of social learning that promotes emotional dependency on this caregiver.

Mahler, Pine, and Bergman[51] in *The Psychological Birth of the Human Infant,* has given us a useful framework for looking at the development of attachment. Their object relations theory grew out of a psychoanalytic viewpoint. They also encompass some of Bowlby's theory by recognizing that the infant is contributing to this union with his own unique behavioral characteristics.

Mahler, Pine, and Bergman describe the neonate as being "in a normal autistic phase," in that physiological rather than psychological processes dominate; the infant is more "tuned in" to his own system than his environment.

During the first week of life the infant is not yet aware that a mother agent is present. Although the neonate is, for the most part, egocentric, he is capable of responding to external stimuli. This has been demonstrated by Fantz,[25] who showed the infant's ability to visually discriminate among a variety of simple to complex figures, by Eisenberg[23] in his experiment with auditory discrimination, and by Brazelton's[8] emphasis on the neonate's ability to be socially responsive (Fig. 4-1). Wolff[77] described various behavioral states of the newborn, which included alert inactivity that put the infant in touch with his environment.

Thus normal infants are not passive participants from birth but rather actively begin to seek contact with the caregiver, initially through such postural adjustments as cuddling when held or through eye contact. The latter activity continues to develop into prolonged gazing at the adult's face and following the adult's movements visually as well as vocalization and the social smile. The origins of the smile have been traced from the neonate's somewhat fleeting smile, which involves only the mouth in response to some type of stimuli (internal or external), to the early smiling at 1 month of age in response to a familiar voice (usually female), followed by a full-blown social smile involving the entire face and body in response to a smiling face (at approximately 8 weeks of age).[77]

Bonds of attachment are built between the caregiver and the infant as a result of a series of positive interactions with both the parent and the infant reinforcing each other. When the infant cries and the mother bestows care and affection, which is successful in soothing the infant, the whole sequence is likely to reoccur. A smiling baby gets more smiles. The infant who vocalizes frequently is responded to with more verbalizations. The infant in a sense can be seen to shape parental behavior. Together they build a mutually rewarding relationship.

During this early period the infant's greatest drive is for need satisfaction. Throughout the first month "mother" provides this service to the infant; through his increasing sensory awareness the infant becomes alert to the fact that mother exists as a need-satisfying object.

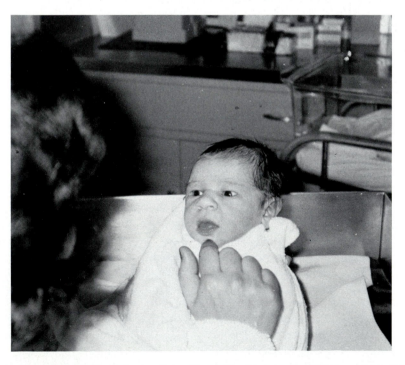

Fig. 4-1. Neonate in "normal autistic phase" is still capable of being engaged with mother, evidenced by eye contact and visual scanning of her face.

It is the beginning of what Mahler terms a "normal symbiotic phase." The infant is aware that his need satisfaction cannot come from within but rather comes from someone outside of himself. The infant will show an indiscriminate attachment to anyone who meets his needs during this period. The infant's needs for a mother or substitute is absolute. The mother's need for the infant is relative. As the young infant's needs are met by the mother, her ministrations are reinforced, and this leads to a social symbiosis on her part (Fig. 4-2).

At approximately 4 to 5 months of age, the peak of symbiosis is reached. The infant has now built up various schemes based on visual, auditory, and propriokinesthetic inputs, so he is now able to discriminate his mother from others. The ready social smile of the past few months becomes more selective. This preferential smiling in response to the mother is a crucial sign that a specific bond between the mother and the baby has been forged (Fig. 4-3). It is at this point that "differentiation," the first subphase of separation and individuation, begins. During the symbiotic phase, the "I" and the "not I" are still merged. However, at 5 to 6 months of age the infant has started to test out certain actions to differentiate himself from his caregiver (Fig. 4-4). When the infant is held, he will pull back to more easily visually examine his mother's face, and he will start to reach for her mouth, hair, glasses, or earrings, instead of "simply molding into mother when held." It is at approximately 7 months of age that the infant demonstrates his strongest attachment to a specific person. Besides prefer-

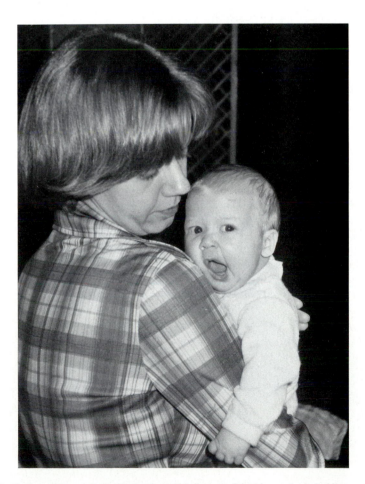

Fig. 4-2. Beginning of "normal symbiotic phase." Infant comforted by mother's holding and cuddling.

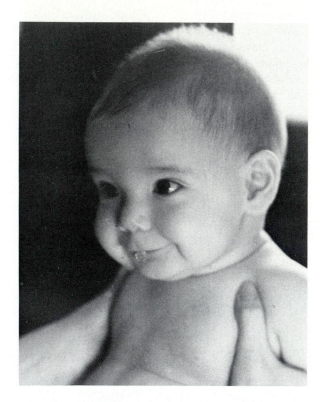

Fig. 4-3. Differential smile for mother only.

Fig. 4-4. ''Differentiation.'' Infant reaches out to explore mother's face.

ential smiling, the infant now uses forms of protest and crying when put down and left by the mother and will also seek to maintain contact with her by reaching out for her, clinging, etc. Infants have been observed using differential greeting patterns, such as smiling, crowing, and general excitement, when their mothers return.[1]

At 8 months of age a new phenomenon occurs, which is described as "stranger anxiety" or "stranger fear." It is distinct from the behavior revolving around the specific attachment. The infant, even with a parent present, reacts to the appearance of a nonfamiliar person. This reaction can be quite intense and is modulated by the infant's individual temperament and experience with strangers. This response lasts for a few months and gradually subsides if handled in a supportive fashion by the parents.

Mahler, Pine, and Bergman point out that in the same period, the second subphase of separation and individuation, one can observe the emergence of a practicing separation and checking back pattern. At 8 months of age the infant has started to develop locomotor skills, which presents a conflict. He can pull to stand and is also beginning to creep. He is torn between striking out on his own and needing to make visual or physical contact to ensure that his mother is still present. Once he moves away he will need to scurry back to play at her feet to emotionally refuel and to reassure himself of his mother's presence (Fig. 4-5). The infant has now begun to work in earnest on two developmental tasks: separation and individuation. Separation deals with "differentiation, distancing, boundary formation, and disengagement from the mother." Individuation is "evolution of the intrapsychic autonomy, perception, memory, and cognition and reality testing," which leads to the infant building on his own individual differences and becoming a unique individual.

The infant's first motoric exploration helps him to explore wider segments of his world and also learn to recognize and enjoy his mother from a distance. By the time the child has established independent locomotion through walking at 12 to 15 months of age, trust of, as Erickson[24] describes it, or attachment to at least one

significant other should be well established. The child may have established attachment to other significant individuals that play a consistent part of his life (father, siblings, or other caregivers). The child is aware that his basic biological needs (hunger, thirst, pain) can be reduced by another individual.

Now the child believes himself to be king of the mountain. He can do anything and everything because enough trust has been built that he believes his mother will rescue him from situations he should not get into. He practices separation and other tasks of exploration through increased cognitive and motoric capabilities and works toward the mastery of new skills. The infant actively initiates and participates in peekaboo games to reassure himself of some control over bringing his mother back. He also runs off to confirm that his mother will swoop down to pick him up. His earlier life had been one of total dependency. Now the child is struggling to establish autonomy.

At approximately 15 to 18 months the child is able to seek out and initiate more social contact through his mobility and increased ability to communicate through words and gestures. However, he also seems to revert to an earlier, more dependent period. He anticipates certain events from familiar signs and becomes very anxious and at times very clingy at an impending separation. Mahler, Pine, and Bergman label this third subphase "rapprochement." This is the phase of separation reaction, anxiety, and increased ambivalence and unpredictable behavior on the part of the child. At one time he wants to be cuddled and at another he pushes away and strikes out on his own, asserting his autonomy and beginning to say, "No." The child is beginning to come to grips with his own limitations as to what he can and cannot master. He is more interested in involving his mother in his actions, bringing her object, and pulling her to show her things; he demands more time and attention than during the preceding 6 months. He is aware of his separate status and tries to undo it. This can be an extremely trying period for both the mother and the child.

The stress of this period is eased around 21 months as his cognitive concept of object per-

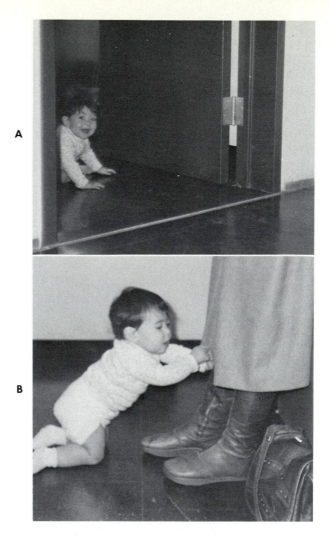

Fig. 4-5. A, Practicing separation. **B,** Checking back for "refueling."

manence becomes well established. Person permanence[5] is seen prior to full-scale object permanence if the relationship between the mother and child is harmonious. When the child is given the chance to experience brief separations and reunions, he will start to maintain an internal image of his mother and know that she will return. The child learns to substitute other individuals, that is, babysitter or teacher for comfort when the mother is not present. The way this crisis is resolved results in pattern and personality characteristics that the child carries onto the fourth subphase: the consolidation of the individuation. At this age Mahler, Pine, and Bergman believe the patterns of the individuation process are not phase specific but become more individualized. In the next few years the child establishes gender identity as well as sex role. This period builds on the infant's individual physical, cognitive, and temperament characteristics and how the environment both nurtures and challenges his ability to expand his horizons. Table 4-1 describes the relationship of the stages of attachment to emotional and cognitive development and infant behaviors.

THE ROLE OF THE PARENT IN EARLY INTERVENTION

The early attachment period coincides to Piaget's sensorimotor phase of intelligence building. Infants can and do seek out activities

Table 4-1. Relationship of stages of emotional, cognitive, and attachment
development to infant behaviors

Age	Emotional (Erickson)	Cognitive (Piaget)	Attachment (Mahler)	Infant behaviors
Newborn	Trust versus mistrust	Stage I— reflexive	Normal autistic phase	Responds primarily to physiological state Alerts, focuses, and tracks visual stimulus Blinks, stills, and alerts to voice
1 month		Stage II— primary circular reactions	Normal symbiotic phase	Is more responsive to environment Gives first social smile Follows moving person with eyes Is aware of strange environment
4 to 5 months		Stage III— secondary circular reactions	Peak of symbiosis Separation and individuation begins First subphase— differentiation	Smiles preferentially Repeats actions for environmental effects, for example, shakes, bangs Reaches out to explore mother's face
7 months			Second subphase— early practicing phase	Crawls, cruises—locomotion Experiments with separation he initiates Clings to mother (7 months) Protests separation (7 months)
8 to 9 months		Stage IV— coordination of existing scheme	Practicing phase	Has stranger anxiety (8 months) Finds hidden object (8 months)
12 months	Autonomy versus shame and doubt	Stage V— tertiary circular reactions		Walk independently Easily separates Conducts trial and error experimentation Speaks first words Communicates with gestures Shows and gives objects to adult Initiates games with adult
15 months			Third subphase— rapprochement	Says, "No" Tries to feed and dress self
18 months		Stage VI— representational period		Ambivalent behaviors—clings to or pushes adult away Uses adult to activate toys Has separation anxiety
21 months			Fourth subphase— consolidation of the individual	Object permanence well established Communicates with words and short sentences
24 months		Preoperational period		

that have brought them pleasure in the past, but they are also attracted to novelty, which facilitates their learning process. It is the infant's parents who are most often responsible for the variety and extent of external stimuli to which the child is exposed. The availability of objects provided by the parent facilitates the behaviors visual regard, swiping, reaching, and finally manipulation. White and Held's[76] studies of institutionalized infants indicated that visual motor coordination was accelerated by 6 weeks if appropriate stimuli were presented. The parents in essence help teach the infant about his world as they go about the normal routine of caring for and interacting with him.

White,[75] in his study of infants and preschoolers, defined the competent mother as one who has learned to enjoy her child and employs very little structured teaching. However, she is able to design the environment and encourage interaction that is initiated by both the child and herself, since maturational advances often depend on self-generated activity by the child. White believes that effective parenting can make the difference in producing a cognitively, socially, well-adapted child. He stresses that the quality of the interaction is more important than the amount of interaction. He had estimated that the most successful "supermother" seldom gives her child her undivided attention for more than 1 or 2 hours per day, nor does she do much deliberate teaching.

IMPLICATIONS FOR PROGRAMMING

In the past the mother and child relationship within the family was seen as a strong dyadic relationship that functioned as a separate entity and was identified as the model to be studied. Social scientists have since come to view the family as a system in which all members interact and participate with each other. Within the small interdependent family system, there are smaller links (mother-child, husband-wife, brother-sister). Each family builds up unique sets of interactions and ways its members function as individuals and as a family unit in interfacing other systems, that is, the extended family, church, and neighborhood as well as the more complex social, educational, and medical systems. In this era of women's rights, the father's role in the family may be expanded from a breadwinner to a more active caregiving parent. The feelings and concerns of the siblings of the newborn infant must also be considered.

One unifying theme keeps emerging: to have a harmonious parent-child relationship, there must be experiences that are pleasurable and reinforcing to both the parent and the child. A handicapping condition or major illness can distort this parent-infant relationship, forming a dependent attachment and ultimately limiting the child's ability to strike out on his own. Motorically involved, spastic children can be extremely hard to hold, feed, or dress, let alone cuddle. Children with sensory impairments are not receiving the necessary cues from their environment to build schemata for optimal emotional and cognitive growth. As a result the attachment process is altered and the parent and child must learn a different system for responding to each other's cues.

In the absence of positive reinforcement and because of continued caregiving responsibilities, parents may need respite so that they do not experience an emotional "burnout" and give up. They may also need help in determining the child's developmental age versus his chronological age so that the child is neither a victim of infantilism or pushed beyond his capability. Some children may grow cognitively and socially but may not possess the necessary motoric skills to strike out on their own and will remain nonambulatory and dependent for their care. This may produce a frustrated child who is denied autonomy because of his disability. In an effort to seek autonomy the youngster may then refuse to cooperate and set up endless conflicts between the parents and himself. This family will need assistance in allowing that child to make some choices to establish a sense of independence. The maintenance of the cognitive, emotional, and physical growth of the infant is a major goal of early intervention. Few parents are educated for the responsibilities of parenthood, and even fewer are ready for the demands placed on them by a child with a disability.

THE EARLY INTERVENTION AND FAMILY SUPPORT PROGRAM (EIFSP)—A SUGGESTED MODEL

The Early Intervention and Family Support Program (EIFSP) at the University of Massachusetts Medical Center (UMMC) is based on the philosophies of the Early Intervention Project for Handicapped Infants and Young Children at Ann Arbor, Michigan, a First Chance Project that was part of the BEH network of projects to demonstrate how to provide early intervention services to very young disabled children. The program was based on the following tenets:

- Early intervention in the lives of handicapped children is important for the development of the basic skills of walking, talking, and self-care and the sensorimotor exploration of their environment. These are the skills that are normally developed in children within a supportive home environment. When the process is altered by the presence of a disability, early intervention aims at habilitation that is appropriate for the developmental level of that youngster.
- Programming for this group can be most effectively accomplished by combining a center-based component with home visits and on-going parent groups. These services support the parents and facilitate their understanding and acceptance of their child's handicap.
- A team must be formed that has knowledge in the areas of motor, cognitive, self-help, language, and socioemotional development as well as a knowledge of family dynamics, physical health, and nutrition. The disciplines included are occupational therapists, physical therapists, speech and language pathologists, child development specialists, psychologists, and social workers. Such a team should function in a close alliance with a nutritionist, pediatrician, audiologist, ophthalmologist and other pediatric subspecialists.
- Most importantly, *parents* are the prime deliverers of service and the staff is expected to educate and train the parents in the skills necessary to provide a thera-

peutic environment within the context of the routine care of their handicapped infant or young child.

From January 1977 to June 1978 EIFSP served 118 families and their children. Their disorders include chromosomal abnormalities, cerebral palsy, seizure disorders, deafness, hearing impairment, visual impairment, autism, and a general developmental delay with no specific cause. The majority of the children have two or more major areas of developmental delay.

Diagnosis and evaluation

Children referred to the EIFSP are seen first in a diagnostic clinic. Referrals are accepted from the child's parents, community personnel, or the child's primary care physician. About 80% of the total referrals received are from primary care physicians. Our high physician referral rate has been attributed to the presence of a comprehensive diagnostic and treatment team, which includes a pediatrician. The team is supported by medical specialists in areas such as neurology, cardiology, ophthalmology, and orthopedics. Allied professionals include physical and occupational therapists, social workers, speech pathologists, audiologists, and educators. Particular attention has been given to communicating with the child's primary care physician. This establishes continuity of care, a sense of goodwill, and provides a mechanism for the ongoing education of the primary care physician. The clinic does not provide routine health care.

A child who lives within the area served by the EIFSP is assigned an intake worker, and an initial home visit is arranged to explain the format of the program. Initial home visits provide an opportunity to observe the child in the natural setting of the home. The parents can discuss their questions or concerns and their reasons for participating in the program. Developmental assessment, using the Early Intervention Developmental Profile or other appropriate instrument, is also performed in a setting conducive to the child's best performance. The information gathered is recorded in an intake summary that includes the reason for referral, social history, current developmental status of the child, and a plan for evaluation. This system enables the worker to schedule as many consultations as necessary on the day of the initial hospital evaluation. An effort is made to have both parents attend the clinic.

The clinical evaluation consists of observation of a free play episode, parent-child interaction, the completion of the developmental assessment, and an extensive pediatric examination. Pediatric history and examination include a thorough developmental and medical history and physical and neurodevelopmental examination of the child. The height, weight, and head circumference are used to assess the longitudinal growth of the child and the nutritional adequacy of the diet.

Time is spent ascertaining the parents' understanding of their child's development. A working diagnosis is formulated in a staffing conference along with a plan for completing the evaluation. The need for additional consultation and laboratory studies is determined. This is offered to the parents as the beginning of the management plan. On completion of all test procedures, a more formal information-sharing conference ("parent sharing") is held, with both parents present. If community personnel are involved, they are also included in the diagnostic information and planning. Diagnostic information and the prognosis for the child's development are shared with the parents. Families are almost always referred to the genetic clinic for comprehensive genetic counselling.

At the parent sharing, the parents are encouraged to ask questions and to share their thoughts about the diagnosis and treatment plan for their child. As a result of the developmental assessment and information gained, a master plan is developed. The goals include plans to teach the parents developmental techniques to facilitate their child's development. This is accomplished by providing them with information and reading material about their child's disability as well as informing them of other community resources. If the plan is to include enrollment in the EIFSP, home visits are started immediately and the family is informed of the availability of weekly center-based group sessions.

Program planning for most children is stated in the form of behavioral objectives for the next 3 or 4 months. These objectives break

---

SAMPLE OBJECTIVES

Child's name: Stephen
Chronological age: 18 months

Developmental age: 6 to 8 months
Dx: Mental/psychomotor retardation

Profile scale	Objectives
Cognitive	Uncover a hidden object Imitate three or more seen motor movements, such as clapping hands, banging and waving
Gross motor	Sit unsupported for 5 minutes Pivot on stomach 180 degrees Show a parachute reaction
Perceptual fine motor	Use an inferior pincer grasp to pick up a small piece of cereal Manipulate at least one gadget on busy box
Self-care	Hold a two-handled cup independently Pull arms out of shirt and pull shirt over head Finger feed a cracker
Language	Consistently imitate sounds in his repertoire Respond to verbal cue with learned motor movement (bye-bye, peekaboo) Consistently respond to name
Social	Participate actively in games like so big and pat-a-cake

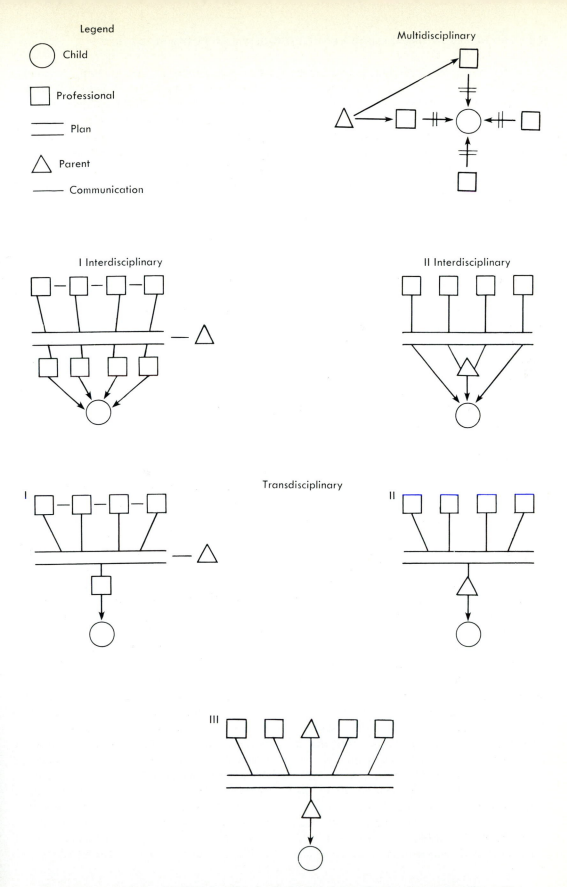

Fig. 4-6. Types of teams. (Modified from Schafer, D. S.: Early intervention developmental profile: application in a transdiscipiinary program. In Moersh, M., and Wilson, T., editors: Early intervention project for handicapped infants and young children, final report, 1973-1976, Ann Arbor, Mich., 1976, University of Michigan Press.)

down the stages of development into small, sequential steps. This teaches the parents to form reasonable expectations regarding their child's performance.

The objectives are then supplemented with an individualized program for each child (Chapter 11). The occupational therapist develops a plan that would facilitate oral motor development and alter abnormal feeding patterns. The child development specialist formulates some of the cognitive and language activities, and the physical therapist develops the gross motor plan. They develop a comprehensive plan with shared goals utilizing the interdisciplinary model rather than a multidisciplinary approach. As the individual professionals work on the team, they become more skilled in their colleagues' areas of expertise and the team becomes transdisciplinary (Fig. 4-6).

Time must be devoted to building the team concept as well as providing service for children and their families. Professionals on the team develop personal and professional respect for their colleagues, with the ultimate goal being to include the parent as a full team member.

Program implementation

Home visiting. Activities to facilitate the child's development are taught to the parents or primary caregiver. Each family is visited biweekly by their case coordinator or home visitor, who is assigned based on the disciplinary skills required to meet that child's major needs. During the home visits the therapist or teacher models, or demonstrates activities, and instructs the parents on specific skills needed to care for the child. Programming focuses on building the child's strengths as well as intervening in the area of greatest difficulty.

The home visits have unique advantages. They provide the home visitor with a sense of what the family can realistically accomplish with their child, given the economic or emotional limitations that may exist in the home or family. They provide an opportunity for the father, siblings, and extended family to be involved. The visits can be used to teach skills within the child's established routine (Fig. 4-7).

Center-based component. Developmental objectives are also addressed during the weekly center-based group sessions. During these sessions children are grouped by developmental level and a staff member suggests or models an activity or treatment technique for the parents. The group sessions provide the following three advantages:

1. They allow all members of the team to contribute their own disciplinary skills to the child, which can subsequently be implemented by the child's home visitor.
2. They provide the parents with an opportunity to spontaneously share experiences they have found useful with other parents.
3. They provide an opportunity for the parents to give emotional support to each other.

During these visits the parents have an additional option of attending a parents' group without their children. These groups provide a forum for discussion of such specific areas as dealing with relatives or medical and educational systems. They provide an opportunity for parents to share their feelings and give support to each other in coping with their children's disabilities. An ideal group has co-leaders, one of whom has skills in counselling and group dynamics, while the other is familiar with normal development and how a particular disorder can alter the developmental process.

All parents are offered the option of being linked with a resource parent from Parent Sharing. This is a community-based group of parents of children with a variety of disabilities. Individuals from this group are willing to act as supportive, empathic listeners with the advantage of having also been through similar situations. This referral can be made at the time of initial diagnosis.

Stages of parental reactions. There are a number of models that have been proposed to explain the reactions of parents to the handicap or illness in their child. These are described in Chapter 8. Kubler-Ross'[27a] model on death and dying has been adapted to this situation and can be useful. Another model[68] that can be used to explain the process of adjustment is the three crises described by Wolfensberger—novelty-shock, religious-emotional, and reality.

There is no set timetable for how long par-

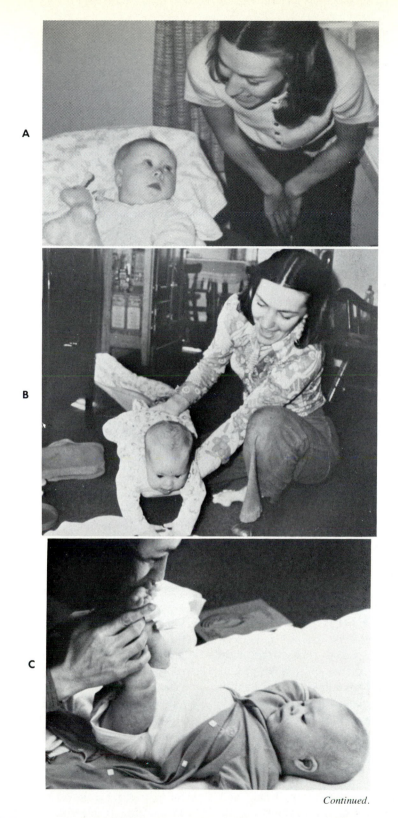

Continued.

Fig. 4-7. Home visitor helps parent realize that worthwhile intervention takes place during normal caring for infant. **A,** Talking. **B,** Changing positions. **C,** Diapering. **D,** Feeding.

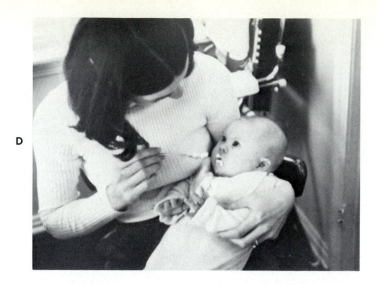

D

Fig. 4-7, cont'd. For legend see p. 103.

ents take to go through the process. Some parents stop at an early stage and never move on to the final reality crisis. The process of mourning and resolving does not happen just once, but rather may be repeated at various stages in the child's life. The first is at the time of birth or initial diagnosis; the second may be at age 3 or 5, when the child goes off to school. Another crisis may appear at the time of adolescence and again at approaching adulthood. These all will be times of rethinking and readjusting and times when the parents require maximal support from their primary care physician and other professionals. Rekindling of these feelings may occur around the child's birthday. It is a painful reminder that their 2-year-old is different from the norm.

Parents of disabled children have been described as leading a life of chronic sorrow.[55] Although one would hope that this is not entirely true, parents would confess that they never stop wishing that it did not happen to them, but because it has happened, their family has learned to live with this major life crisis.

Members of early intervention teams play a supportive role with the family during these difficult times; however, the primary care physician should provide the most consistent thread of continuity and support to the parents.

High-risk infants. Studies by Klaus and Kennell[41] have focused our attention on the importance of the period immediately following birth. Their studies indicate that mothers who deliver normal, healthy infants and are permitted to remain with their infant display a significant difference in maternal behavior from those who are separated from their infants. Their research may be criticized because of the relatively small numbers of mothers and infants involved and the lack of control over intervening variables; however, there is little question that they have made a major impact on effort to make the birth process less emotionally traumatic for both the infant and the family. Their emphasis on the critical nature of the first few hours after birth and what has become known as the "bonding process" has altered birthing practices in many obstetrical centers.

Despite efforts to humanize the birthing process, the need for intensive medical management for the low birth weight infant requires that the infant be separated from the mother (Fig. 4-8). Unfortunately, those neonates who are biologically at high risk for developmental disability also experience the initial disruption of the parent-infant interaction that may result in an increased chance for battering and neglect.[41]

The high-risk component of the EIFSP addresses this and other issues related to the developmental outcome of the high-risk infant.

In an effort to identify the infants in maxi-

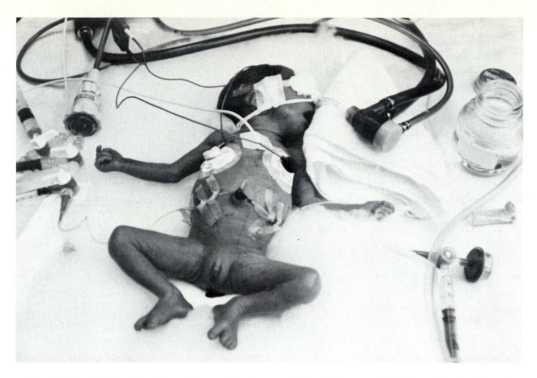

Fig. 4-8. Low birth weight infant with arterial and venous "lines" being mechanically ventilated and monitored. A parent's nightmare.

mal need of services, the criteria presented in Chapter 2 were established; they consider only very high perinatal and biological risk factors.

On identification of the infant, the team's social worker or program coordinator explains the program to the parents. The infant is then assessed and evaluated using a modified Brazelton Neonatal Behavioral Assessment.[8] This is done prior to discharge at 36 to 40 weeks conceptual age, as soon as the infant is considered well enough to undergo assessment. The infant's primary care physician is then consulted, and permission is obtained for continued follow-up. A meeting with the parents allows them to ask questions and voice concerns regarding their baby's development. We point out that the purpose of the program is to identify any problems that may appear as a result of the infant's high-risk history.

The families of babies who die are of special concern. They are frequently neglected by both the obstetrician and pediatrician. Kennell Slyter, and Klaus[42] have shown that mothers develop affectional ties with their infant regardless of the duration of their survival and regardless of whether or not they were viable. Rowe,[62] in a follow-up study of families who had experienced the perinatal death of an infant, stressed the importance of discussing the death of their infant with the family. Her study indicated that over 50% of the parents did not receive subsequent information regarding their infant's death. She also found that the duration of grieving could be decreased by half by discussing with the parents the nature and cause of their infant's death. Benfield's[6] study stressed the importance of working through the grief process with the family and the need to "unburden their lingering concerns and begin to look toward the future." The process parents experience is not unlike that experienced with the birth of a defective infant. They are plagued with anger, guilt, and disbelief that is often nurtured by misinformation and societal myths.

Weekly groups for parents with babies in the nursery are conducted by the clinical nurse specialist, social worker, and program coordinator. The goals of these sessions are to facilitate communication between the parents and the nursery staff and more importantly to use the parents as sources of information and support for each other.

Studies by Kaplan and Mason[39] indicate that parents of premature infants go through a complex process of adjustment, which includes an initial anticipation of grief and ends with the anxiety and the challenge of caring for the premature infant at home.

The psychological tasks that the mother of a preterm infant must master include:

1. Establishing an anticipatory grief reaction to prepare for the possible death of the infant
2. Dealing with guilt concerning her inability to carry and deliver a full-term infant
3. Accepting the realization that the infant will survive and the mother will be required to be a competent caregiver.
4. Overcoming the anxiety of caring for a medically vulnerable infant

The primary care nurse who is assigned to the infant and family assists the parents in gathering information about their infant's condition and provides consistent support. Visiting is unrestricted in the intensive care unit, and parents are encouraged to participate in as much of the care of their infant as possible.

The ongoing educational program attempts to transfer the care of the infant to the parent. The parents are assured that the special needs of the infant are only temporary and in time normal patterns of care will ensue. The parents' task is to provide an appropriate level of care to the infant while simultaneously enjoying the pleasures of having a new baby.

Prior to the infant's discharge, a conference is held in which the social worker, head nurse, and neonatologist plan for the infant's discharge. Appropriate referral is made to the Visiting Nurses Association, public health nurse, or a home visitor.

Clinic follow-up. Studies of low birth weight infants showed that a significant number of children at school age have major neurological deficits, such as mental retardation, motor handicaps, sensory impairment, or minor neurological dysfunction.[19-22] These studies concern infants born a number of years ago, prior to

major improvements in care for low birth weight and high-risk infants. The new morbidity of these infants is still unknown. Important components of our program are the early identification of potential problems and/or the assurance that an infant is developing normally.

The infants are seen in follow-up at the medical center after their discharge from the nursery. As noted previously, the clinic is staffed by an interdisciplinary team. If there are special concerns about an infant, he may be seen more often, but most infants are seen routinely at 4, 9, 15, 24, and 36 months of age. The following evaluation procedure is carried out:

1. Parent interview
2. Hearing and vision screening
3. Physical and neurological examination
4. Height, weight, and head circumference measurement
5. Developmental and behavioral assessment

Parent interview. During the first clinic visit the parents are asked to relate their understanding of the infant's course in the nursery. The time at the clinic is less stressful than the time actually spent with the baby in the nursery, so the parents are in a better position to really hear and understand what had occurred in the nursery. It is a goal of the clinic staff that the parents understand their infant's development as well as potential sequelae. This is also important in terms of future pregnancies. Since many of our high-risk infants are products of high-risk mothers, these women are often referred to a perinatologist for consultation regarding their subsequent pregnancies.

Parents give important information about their baby, and careful questioning provides diagnostic information as well as realistic descriptions of their infant's activities. Although parents do not understand the "why," they frequently and accurately describe a behavior that is significant, for example, undiagnosed seizures.

Hearing and vision screening. Established risk and high-risk infants have a high incidence of hearing impairment. Causes of sensory neural deafness include congenital viral infections such as rubella and cytomegalovirus. Perinatal and postnatal causes of deafness include hypoxia, traumatic delivery, preterm delivery, bacterial and viral meningoencephalitis, and ototoxic drugs used in the treatment of bacterial infections. Drugs such as kanamycin and gentamycin or diuretic drugs can injure or destroy the hair cells of the cochlea.[54] Kernicterus has in the past accounted for many athetoid, hearing impaired, cerebral palsied children. With the use of Rh_0 immunoglobulin (RhoGAM) and exchange transfusion, the contribution of hyperbilirubinemia to sensory neural losses has been negligible. The presence of multiple factors contributing to hearing loss in the newborn necessitates a careful monitoring of the hearing status of these infants. Their hearing should be evaluated by competent audiologists, even though hearing loss is not apparent. Massachusetts provides a hearing assessment to all high-risk children at no cost to the family. The main categories of infants that are eligible for such assessment include the following:

Birth weight under 1.8 kg

Exchange transfusion or severe jaundice of over 20 mg/100 ml

Apgar score below 7 at 5 minutes

Unusual skull shape or cleft palate

Family history of hearing loss in childhood

Neonatal meningitis

Use of ototoxic drugs gentamycin or kanamycin

Congenital infection, for example, rubella, CMV infection

These are similar to the recommendations of the Conference on Newborn Screening of 1971.[54]

Vision is also of major concern in this population. Preterm infants are at risk for retrolental fibroplasia.[28] The incidence of retrolental fibroplasia is inversely proportional to birth weight. All infants who receive oxygen therapy are seen by an ophthalmologist prior to discharge. It is important that these infants have ongoing evaluation of their visual status. The changes associated with retrolental fibroplasia can progress for a period of up to 6 months after treatment with oxygen has been discontinued. In the clinic observations are made regarding the coordinated, conjugated eye movements, prolonged focussing, and adequacy of visual function of the infant. Significant signs of visual impairment include poor visual tracking, meaningless wandering eye movements, objects held close for inspection, as well as apparent loss of peripheral vision. Infants who have questionable funduscopic examination results are referred back to the ophthalmologist.

Physical and neurological examination. A review of the infant's neonatal intensive care unit record is made to be certain that medical problems that arose in the nursery receive ongoing attention and follow-up. Such sequelae as anemia, bronchopulmonary dysplasia, retrolental fibroplasia, and hypertension and a previous history of necrotizing enterocolitis should all be extensively monitored. The head circumference is carefully measured to detect microcephaly, early hydrocephalus, or catch-up growth. The distinction between catch-up growth and early hydrocephalus is often difficult to detect even with the diagnostic use of a computerized axial tomography (CAT scan).

An obvious area of major concern is the diagnosis of cerebral palsy. Cerebral palsy is most often associated with preterm, very low birth weight infants (under 1500 g) or infants who have suffered severe perinatal difficulties. The early symptoms of cerebral palsy may be confused with dystonia. This sign was first described by Drillien in 1972.[21] In a study of 300 infants of birth weights of less than 2000 g, 6% of her sample developed overt cerebral palsy that was diagnosed at or before 1 year. About 23% exhibited moderate or severe dystonia during the first year that subsequently cleared. About 17% had mild signs of dystonia. Drillien has defined the phenomenon of increased tone and persistent primitive reflexes as "transient dystonia." By the very nature of the definition, the condition resolves itself. Some of these youngsters were diagnosed as neurologically normal at 1 year and in other instances the abnormal neurological signs reappeared after the child started to walk and were interpreted as soft neurological signs indicative of minimal brain dysfunction. A third of the children who exhibited abnormal neurological findings in the first year were identified during the second and third year as hyperactive and restless. Drillien's[22] earlier work suggested that those children who displayed soft neurological signs may go on to have learning disabilities. The follow-up study at age 7 of low birth weight infants (under 1500 g) who were previously neurologically abnormal demonstrated that they were significantly different from their neurologically normal peers. Less than one third were considered problem free, and nearly one fourth were having serious problems in a regular school setting.

As indicated previously, dystonia can be transient, and labelling these infants at an early age as being cerebral palsied is not appropriate. We have chosen to closely monitor these infants and provide parents with techniques for handling and positioning their infants in an effort to reduce their overall tone. This dystonia, or neural maturational delay, makes them difficult to hold or cuddle and inhibits the infant's initial reaching and grasping skills. The parents are encouraged to hold their infant in a flexion pattern, which seems to make the baby easier to handle. The vast majority of the children who displayed dystonia have subsequently resolved their increased tone. The cohort of infants we have followed are 18 months of age, thus it is too early to predict whether these infants will go on to show evidence of minimal brain dysfunction.

In addition to the physical and neurological examinations, the high-risk clinic provides an opportunity to discuss health maintenance issues such as good dental care for young children and safety issues such as use of car seats. This reinforces the efforts of primary care physicians in these areas.

Height, weight, and head circumference measurement. In addition to following the head circumference, the infant's height and weight are recorded and plotted on appropriate charts, for example, the Babson chart for preterm infants (Fig. 8-9, *A*). A careful nutritional history is obtained, with special attention paid to an adequate caloric intake for optimal growth. It is important to remember that the caloric intake must be adequate for the projected mean weight rather than the existing weight of the infant. A common problem has been poor weight gain and difficulty in feeding. These infants are referred to the child's primary care physician and, in conjunction with a nutritionist, a diet is suggested. The nutritionist may

recommend increased calories using carbohydrates or medium-chain triglyceride supplements. The difficulties related to the infant's feeding pattern are met with the services of an occupational and/or physical therapist.

Developmental and behavioral assessment. Infants up to 24 months of age are assessed using the Early Intervention Developmental Profile[61] discussed in Chapter 3. In the case of the preterm baby, the infant's age is adjusted by subtracting from the chronological age the difference between the gestational age, as judged by the Dubowitz,[22a] and 40 weeks (term). Therefore, when an infant is seen at a chronological age of 6 months, his adjusted age would be 4 months if he was born at 32 weeks of gestation. The ages selected for follow-up represent times at which many major developmental milestones should occur (Chapter 3).

At 24 months the Bayley Scales of Infant Development[3] are used to obtain a standardized score. Formal testing may be repeated as the child nears his third birthday if he has any developmental problem.

Infants who had suffered severe perinatal insults or are very premature (less than 30 weeks gestation) and of low birth weight take a long time to catch up developmentally. This delay is especially apparent during the early months of life. Any number of infants we have seen at an adjusted age of 8 weeks with a chronological age closer to 4 or 5 months present with major delays. Many do not smile, are not visually attentive, give poor hearing responses, and have limited head control. They are generally hypotonic and do not interact well with their environment. The period during which the infants are nonresponsive can be very trying for the parents. The social responsiveness of the infant does seem to improve by the time the infant is at 4 months adjusted age and chronologically 6 to 7 months old. For this group of parents there is a long waiting period for the first social smile.

There are few reports that provide detailed, longitudinal information regarding the status of the infant which can be used to prognosticate ultimate outcome. Well-known studies neatly summarize a large number of youngsters at school age but do not describe in detail early developmental milestones or the quality of their performance.

In our clinic population there appear to be certain developmental trends that are consistent with certain groups of infants. At this point these patterns are merely the impressions of the clinic staff and remain to be proved. However, as reported earlier, when preterm infants born before 32 weeks of gestation are seen at term, they do not resemble full-term infants. The developmental trend for these infants is for their social skills to begin to catch up first, followed by early cognitive and motor skills. In keeping with Drillien[19] study, our preterm infants also appeared to show the most consistent delay in the speech and language area. We have ruled out a hearing impairment in all of our older infants and have concentrated on encouraging the parents to use appropriate speech and language activities. Referral to a speech and language pathologist is made prior to age 2 for those children with moderate speech delay or language disorder.

Some of our full-term infants who have experienced severe asphyxia do extremely well initially, but at their 15-month visit some of these infants appear to have delays in performing some of the fine and perceptual motor tasks and display language delays similar to those of the preterm infant. Although it is believed that some of these difficulties will resolve, caution is used in discussing this with parents, especially when the infant is demonstrating an associated decreasing head growth. Given these facts, it is important to continue to monitor development in all areas rather than dismiss any infant from follow-up on the basis of early motor and cognitive development. It is important to remember that cognitive skills measured in infancy are very different from the problem-solving skills of the school-aged child. This situation also points out the need for professionals involved in the follow-up of such infants to document developmental patterns. This would not only add to the data regarding these infants but parents would also find it helpful to have this follow-up information. If a definite sensory deficit or a neuromuscular problem such as cerebral palsy is identified, the infant is enrolled in a more intensive program.

Evaluation and early identification of the infant with a developmental disability is a major goal of our program, but of far more importance is the human affective element of assisting a family in adapting to the birth of an extremely small infant who has had a life-threatening experience. The method of coping with the effects of these events on the parent-infant interaction is described to the family when discussing the discharge of the infant from the neonatal intensive care unit. However, the vulnerable child syndrome, which was described by Green and Solint,[27] is an ongoing issue. Their study indicated that this vulnerability was the result of a parent being told that their child was in danger of dying. They describe the symptoms as difficulty in separation, infantalism, bodily overconcern, and school underachievement. When appropriate, every effort is made to assure the parents of their youngster's well-being. This assurance is followed by helping the family to understand that their attitude toward the youngster relates to the initial life-threatening situation. They are then helped with setting behavioral limits, discipline, providing independence for the child, and breaking the cycle of mutual anxiety.

The life of the infant itself may be threatened. A recent study indicated that the postneonatal mortality among infants admitted to a neonatal intensive care unit was 44 per 1000 neonatal survivors during the first year of life.[44] Realistic anxiety must be addressed by the staff of the follow-up clinic but more importantly by the primary care physician. Many of the infants who meet our high-risk criteria have very special needs. Neurological problems such as hydrocephalus and seizure disorders are not uncommon.

The parents are justifiably concerned because no one can assure them during the early period that their infant will indeed grow and develop normally. It is important for parents to remain realistic and yet optimistic that their infant will indeed do well. Low expectations and the tendency to overprotect their infant would impede the child's progress.

Home visitor. Occupational and physical therapists, speech pathologists, and educators on the Early Intervention and Family Support

Program team also serve as home visitors for the families of high-risk infants. The home visitor is not only interested in the infant but also identifies the parents as the major focus of intervention. Mothers have stated that so much energy and concern has been directed at the baby that they feel neglected. Many of them describe emotions that prevent them from developing a close relationship with their infant. Some are able to ask for support from the infant's father and have an excellent relationship with him. Others feel the stress concerning the baby added to the strain in the relationship with the baby's father, and the mother feels very must alone. Simultaneously, fathers feel neglected and rejected. Therefore the home visitor's chief roles are that of an empathic listener and a source of information and support. Mothers appreciate someone who can reassure them that they are doing a good job and look forward to a helping person who can emphasize the normal aspects of the baby despite many of the existing problems. Several mothers have described their distress in response to their infant's behavior. The small for gestational age infant and the baby with apnea and bradycardia who is treated with theophylline are often irritable and difficult to manage. It is helpful for the mother to know that this is "normal" behavior and not related to her parenting techniques. In addition to being a source of support, the home visitor reinforces the efforts of the family to interact with their infant. Some parents are instinctively capable of picking up their infants' cues and providing them with appropriate interaction. Others are less sure of their capability, and ask the home visitor for guidance. The goal is for the parents to feel successful as parents, to develop appropriate developmental expectations for their infant, and feel pride in the infant's developmental success.

The home visitor is also responsible for assessing the adequacy of the environment and the parent-infant interaction. The Caldwell Home Inventory,[15] and the Bromwich Scale for Parent-Infant Interaction[9] are helpful in making objective judgments in these two important areas. Family planning is also discussed, and the parents are referred for appropriate counseling. The mother is encouraged to maintain her personal health, and such medical problems as gestational diabetes, kidney infection, and hypertension are pursued. It is important to remember that the quality of subsequent pregnancies are determined by the adequacy of the interim health and nutrition of the mother.

For the first 6 to 8 weeks after discharge the home visitor is in weekly contact with the family. At 8 weeks of age a developmental assessment is performed by the home visitor at home or in the follow-up clinic. If there are no major concerns regarding the infant or the family, the frequency of visits is lessened and there are more frequent phone contacts to reinforce the point that things are going well. As the infant matures, the home visitor continues to help the parents choose toys and activities to challenge him and avoid frustration or boredom so that the parent-child interaction remains successful. Discipline and behavior management become more at issue as the child gets older and are the two areas that can be observed most practically in the child's natural environment; assistance is given when needed. Kempe[40] has used the home visitor concept as a method to decrease child abuse in the high-risk family. Our program has been operational for approximately 2 years and there has been only one case of neglect in the infants we have followed.

EFFECTIVENESS OF EARLY INTERVENTION IN DEVELOPMENTALLY DISABLED CHILDREN

There are few published studies on the effects of early intervention for the high-risk or handicapped infant. In an overall evaluation[13,30] of the BEH program completed in 1976, 32 of the projects were selected for comprehensive evaluation. The children were assessed in the areas of motor, cognitive, communication, personal, social, and adaptive behaviors. The results of this study indicated:

...that the projects were accurately diagnosing the handicapping condition, and the broad range of services provided were appropriate to the needs of the children. The projects' effect on the children were generally positive, greatest in the area of personal/ social behavior, and least effective in the area of motor development, with the effects of intervention differing somewhat as the function of a handicapping condition. . . . home programs had a positive effect in all but the area of motor development, and center programs had a positive effect only on personal and social development. . . .

In sum, it appears that programs for the biologically impaired can prevent some ancillary problems from occurring and can reduce the effects of other ancillary problems. If intervention is to be effective, it should be undertaken as early in life as possible. Therefore, services may have to be provided for children who are only suspected of having impairments, as well as for those who have been definitely diagnosed.[13]

This philosophy nicely supports our current efforts to provide services to high-risk infants and their family using the high-risk criteria described in Chapter 2. In a period of 18 months between January 1977, and June 1978, 15 infants who were considered to be at established risk were born at or transported to the Worcester Memorial Hospital. This number included three with Down syndrome, four with meningomyelocele, two with other chromosomal abnormalities, and six with other multiple congenital malformations. These families were immediately made aware of such community service as Parent Sharing, Services for Handicapped Children, and the Early Intervention and Family Support team so that the crisis of having an infant with a serious problem could be somewhat alleviated by this network of resources. In addition, follow-up data on the 99 infants considered to be at high risk biologically revealed that 25% had definite sequelae, including cerebral palsy, microcephaly, myoclonic seizures, and/or visual impairment due to retrolental fibroplasia. An additional 20% were developmentally suspect, primarily for language delay. The most vulnerable groups were the asphyxiated infants with seizures, 35% of whom were developmentally abnormal, and those infants weighing between 640 and 1000 g, 60% of whom demonstrated sequelae. Other follow-up studies[17a] indicated that many infants we now call suspect may do well by the age of 5 or 6. However, in the meantime every effort is made to help the child make developmental gains and apply intervention when needed.

Data from the University of Michigan's Early Intervention Project for Handicapped Infants and Young Children[60] suggest that gains children make should be looked at in terms of function and not just in terms of IQ. Severely involved infants were shown to become more socially responsive as well as easier to feed and handle. Serving as their own controls, many of the 40 children involved in the program did not significantly increase their rate of development, but all of the children were able to maintain rates previously established.

The group as a whole showed no significant positive development rate change after treatment was initiated; however, 25% of the treated group demonstrated positive gains in motor and cognitive rate and better than 45% demonstrated significant gains in rate of language acquisition. It was believed that this increase in language skills reflected the parents' increased ease at reading their infants' cues. They geared their expectations to a more appropriate developmental level and this facilitated communication.

In addition to looking at formal assessment data, the rate of success at passing individual objectives was also measured. It was discovered that all children, no matter how profoundly retarded, were able to make progress on objectives that were written appropriately and geared to their own developmental rate. Overall, it was seen that there was a 76% success rate on objectives, indicating progress by the most retarded and the least retarded children. This finding was attributed to the staff's ability to work with the parents to appropriately plan treatment goals that allowed for progression, however slow.

Measurements were taken regarding the parents' attitudes toward having a handicapped child in the family. Another aspect of the program considered successful was that the parents believed there were more developmental activities that could be done at home for their child. They were also able to describe their child more negatively as well as positively. The parents in essence had become more realistic, were able to adjust their expectations for their child, and to put his needs into proper perspective. This resulted in all members of the family getting appropriate attention.

Another measure of success was the amount of appropriate parent-child interaction. This was measured by time samples during group sessions. Time sampling of behavior often substantiated the increased rate of development in a child's language ability. The most reliable predictor of the child's success was the mother's score on positive interaction—verbal, facial, and physical.

Consumer satisfaction. Our concern that we were creating undue anxieties in our families and not contributing to the care of their infants led us to examine how parents perceived the high-risk clinic. In 1978 we conducted a consumer satisfaction survey of the parents who had brought their children to the high-risk follow-up clinic. In this survey 77 out of 94 parents who had used the clinic were contacted and interviewed by phone or mail questionnaire.

The parents rated the advice and information they received about their infant's health and development from a number of sources. Primary care physicians and the University of Massachusetts Medical Center Clinic received ratings of good to excellent by 88% and 92%, respectively.

When this information was analyzed, it was found that the primary care physician usually gave global responses such as "healthy and beautiful" or specific medical information but neglected giving developmental information. The clinic, in contrast, gave both specific developmental and medical information.

About 87% of the families surveyed felt positive about the clinic experience, although 40% felt apprehensive before coming to the clinic. They felt relieved after the visit. This feeling of relief was attributed to the fact that the majority of the infants had done well and for the minority who did not, attention was being paid to early detection and habilitation. About 92% of the parents felt it was a good idea to assess infants systematically while young rather than waiting a few years.

CONCLUSIONS

The primary care physician can be exceedingly helpful in providing empathetic, consistent health maintenance. A significant adjunct to this health maintenance is the identification of the family support system, which would provide emotional support, education for the family regarding the child's disability, and habilitation for the youngster. It is therefore necessary for the primary care physician to be aware of the principles of intervention and how they can be used to effectively serve young patients and their families. The general goals of such programs are the maintenance of the emotional integrity of the family unit, the maximal development of the child, and the ultimate assurance that the parents would be competent, knowledgeable advocates for their children in the complex developmental disabilities service system.

The effectiveness of early intervention programming for developmentally disabled children and their families is difficult to interpret. Those children with auditory and visual handicaps clearly benefit from early identification and appropriate programming. At a minimum, intervention for the mentally retarded and physically handicapped child avoids developmental regression and decreases the disruption, anxieties, and confusion experienced by families with disabled children. Finally, well thought out programs offer guidance and a sense of hope that is embodied in an active habilitation program. There is little question that disabled children interact differently with their parents or caregivers than other children. Families need assistance in the interpretation of these behaviors and the implementation of activities that support optimal growth and development. They need this assistance for all their children, but especially for those children who display different patterns of development.

We, however, must be aware of our limitations. One usually finds enthusiastic, hopeful, and optimistic professionals in the field of early intervention. Despite the massive efforts of many people, not all children progress at an increased rate. This is a concept that both the parents and professionals must be aware of. As helping professionals we are all trained to make things better, to cure, and to make hardships go away. Unfortunately, this cannot be done in all instances, and we are neither being fair to ourselves nor to the families we serve if this is the picture we present. This not only has the potential of producing a sense of guilt and failure in the families we serve, but also creates a sense of failure for the professionals. As helping professionals we must be aware of the power that we possess and our ability to encourage independence versus dependence, calm versus disruption, and support versus judgment.

The intervention paradigm itself must be continuously questioned. The professional team has to share in the knowledge and the individual personal strength of each member. The family and primary care physician are intergral parts of that team. Physicians must seek the knowledge and skills that will enable them to relate adequately to their allied professional colleagues. If early intervention and family support programs are not available, physicians must advocate from their position of strength in the community for appropriate resources. They must be aware of the needs of the families they serve and optimally utilize community programs. The family is by far the most important member of the team. Parents of other handicapped children are also invaluable assets. All must be included as members.

Parents must be recognized as major contributors of information and primary decision makers for their children. With parents, professionals share the sorrows and frustrations as well as the joys and successes. They derive mutual satisfaction in the small gains as well as major developmental breakthroughs such as the first step or the first word. They must therefore assure the rights of the parents. Buscaglia[14] lists the basic rights of a family in his book, *The Disabled and Their Parents—A Counseling Challenge*. These are as follows[14,p.102]:

1. The right to sound medical knowledge regarding their child's physical or mental problem
2. The right to some form of continual reevaluation of their child at definite periodic intervals and a thorough, lucid explanation of the results of the findings
3. The right to some helpful, relevant, and specific information as to their role in meeting their child's specific physical and emotional needs
4. The right to some knowledge of the educational opportunities for a child such as theirs and what will be required for later admission for additional formal schooling

5. The right to a knowledge of the community resources available for assistance in meeting the family needs, intellectual, emotional, and financial
6. The right to knowledge of the rehabilitation services in the community and the resources available through them
7. The right to some hope, reassurance, and human consideration as they meet the challenge of raising a child with special needs
8. The right to some help in seeing their child's potentials instead of forever concentrating upon his imperfections
9. The right to good reading material to help them acquire as much relevant information as possible
10. The right to some interaction with other parents who have children with disabilities
11. The right to actualize their personal rights as growing, unique individuals, apart from their children

REFERENCES

1. Ainsworth, M.: The development of infant-mother attachment. In Caldwell, B. M., and Ricciuti, H. N., editors: Review of child development research, vol. 3. Child development and social policy, Chicago, 1974, University of Chicago Press, pp. 1 to 94.
2. Babson, G. S.: Growth record for infants in relation to gestational age and fetal and infant norms (combined sexes), 1970.
3. Bayley, N.: Bayley scales of infant development, New York, 1969, Psychological Corp.
4. Bell, R. Q.: Contribution of human infants to caregiving and social interaction. In Lewis, M., and Rosenblum, L. A., editors: The effects of the infant on its caregiver, New York, 1974, John Wiley and Sons, Inc., 1 to 20.
5. Bell, S. M.: The development of the concept of objects as related to infant-mother attachment, Child Dev. **41:**291, 1970.
6. Benfield, G. D., Leib, S. A., and Vollman, J. H.: Grief response of parents to neonatal death and parent participation in deciding care, Pediatrics **62:**171, 1978.
7. Bowlby, J.: Attachment, vol. 1, New York, 1969, Basic Books, Inc., Publishers.
8. Brazelton, T. B.: Neonatal behavioral assessment scale, Clin. Dev. Med. vol. 50, no. 8, 1973.
9. Bromwich, R.: Parent behavior progression, Los Angeles, 1976, University of California Press.
10. Bromwich, R.: Stimulation in the first year of life? A perspective on infant development, Young Child., Jan. 1977, pp. 71 to 82.
11. Bronfenbrenner, U.: Is early intervention effective? HEW publ. no. 74-25, Washington, D. C., 1974, Department of Health, Education and Welfare, Office of Child Development.
12. Brown, S. L., and Moersh, M., editors: Parents on

the team, Ann Arbor, Mich., 1978, The University of Michigan Press.
13. Bureau of Education for the Handicapped: A summary of services to preschool handicapped children through the Handicapped Children's Early Education Program, July 1, 1975 to June 30, 1976. Report submitted to Bureau of Education for the Handicapped, Department of Health, Education and Welfare, Chapel Hill, N.C., 1977, University of North Carolina Press.
14. Buscaglia, L.: The disabled and their parents—a counseling challenge, Thorofare, N.J., 1975, Charles B. Slack, Inc.
15. Caldwell, B.: Home observation for measurement of the environment, Little Rock, Ark., 1976, University of Arkansas Press.
16. Caplan, G., Mason, E. A. and Kaplan, D. M.: Four studies of crisis in parents of prematures, Ment. Health J. **1**:149, 1965.
17. Clarke, A., and Clarke, A. M.: Prospects for prevention and amelioration of mental retardation: a guest editorial, Am. J. Ment. Defic. **81**:523, 1977.
17a. Corah, N. L., et al.: Effects of perinatal anoxia after seven years, Psychol. Monogr. **79**:596, 1965.
18. Dinno, N.: Early recognition of infants at risk for developmental retardation, Pediatr. Clin. North Am. **24**:633, 1977.
19. Drillien, C.: A longitudinal study of the growth and development of prematurely and maturely born children, Arch. Dis. Child. **36**:283, 1961.
20. Drillien, C.: Aetiology and outcome in low-birthweight infants, Dev. Med. Child. Neurol. **14**:563, 1972.
21. Drillien, C.: Abnormal neurologic signs in the first year of life in low birthweight infants—possible prognostic significance, Dev. Med. Child. Neurol. **14**:575, 1972.
22. Drillien, C.: A longitudinal study of low-birthweight infants. Presentation at symposium at University of Massachusetts Medical School, May 1978.
22a. Dubowitz, L. M., Dubowitz, V., Goldberg, C.: Clinical assessment of gestational age in the newborn infant, J. Pediatr. **77**:1, 1970.
23. Eisenberg, R. B.: Auditory behavior in the human neonate: functional properties of sound and their ontogenetic implications, Int. Audiol. **8**:34, 1969.
24. Erickson, E. H.: Childhood and society, New York, 1950, W. W. Norton & Co., Inc.
25. Fantz, R.: Pattern vision in newborn infants, Science **140**:296, 1963.
26. Friedlander, B. Z., Sterrit, G. M., and Kirk, G., editors: Exceptional infant, vol. 3, New York, 1975, Brunner/Mazel, Inc.
27. Green, M., and Solint, A. J.: Reactions to the threatened loss of a child: a vulnerable child syndrome. Pediatric management of the dying child, part III, Pediatrics **34**:58, 1964.
27a. Kübler-Ross, E.: On death and dying, New York, 1969, The MacMillan Co.
28. Harley, R. D.: Pediatric ophthalmology, Philadelphia, 1975, W. B. Saunders Co.
29. Harlow, H. F.: The development of affectional patterns in infant monkeys. In Foss, B. M., editor: Determinants of infant behavior, vol. 1, New York, 1961, John Wiley & Sons, Inc.
30. Haskins, R., Finkelstein, N., and Stedman, O.: Infant stimulation programs and their effects, Pediatr. Ann. **7**:2, 1978.
31. Hayden, A., and Dmitriev, V.: The multidisciplinary preschool program for Down's syndrome children at the University of Washington Model Preschool Center. In Friedlander, B. Z., Sterrit, G. M., and Kirk, G., editors: Exceptional infant, vol. 3, New York, 1975, Brunner/Mazel, Inc.
32. Hayden, A., and Haring, N.: Early intervention for high risk infants and young children: programs for Down's syndrome children. In Tjossem, T., editor: Intervention strategies for high risk infant and young children, Baltimore, 1976, University Park Press.
33. Haynes, U.: The national collaborative infant project. In Tjossen, T., editor: Intervention strategies for high risk infants and young children, Baltimore, 1976, University Park Press.
34. Heber, R., and Garber, H.: The Milwaukee Project: a study of the use of family intervention to prevent cultural—familial retardation. In Friedlander, B. Z., Sterritt, G. M., and Kirk, G., editors: Exceptional infant, vol. 3, New York, 1975, Brunner/Mazel, Inc.
35. Hess, S.: Early experience and the socialization of cognitive modes in children, Child Dev. **36**:869, 1965.
36. Hunt, J. M.: Intelligence and experience, New York, 1961, The Ronald Press Co.
37. Jensen, A.: How much can we boost IQ and scholastic achievements? Harvard Educ. Rev. **39**:1, 1969.
38. Johnson, O.: The education of mentally retarded children. In Cruickshank, W., and Johnson, O., editors: Education of exceptional children and youth, ed. 2, Englewood Cliffs, N.J., 1967, Prentice-Hall, Inc.
39. Kaplan, D., and Mason, E.: Maternal reaction to premature birth viewed as an acute emotional disorder, Am. J. Orthopsychiatry, **30**:539, 1960.
40. Kempe, H. C.: Approaches to preventing child abuse: the health visitor's concept, Am. J. Dis. Child. **130**:941, 1976.
41. Klaus, M., and Kennell, J.: Maternal-infant bonding: the impact of early separation or loss on family development, St. Louis, 1976, The C. V. Mosby Co.
42. Kennell, J. H., Slyter, H., and Klaus, M. H.: The mourning response of parents to the death of a newborn infant, N. Engl. J. Med. **283**:344, 1970.
43. Kogan, K. L., Tyler, N., and Turner, P.: The process of interpersonal adaptation between mothers and their cerebral palsied children, Dev. Med. Child. Neurol. **16**:518, 1974.
44. Kulkarni, P., et al.: Postneonatal infant mortality in infants admitted to a neonatal intensive care unit, Pediatrics **62**:178, 1978.
45. Lambie, D., Bond, J. T., and Weikart, D.: Framework for infant education. In Friedlander, B. Z., Sterrit, G. M., and Kirk, G., editors: Exceptional

infant, vol. 3, New York, 1975, Brunner/Mazel, Inc.

46. Levenstein, P.: Cognitive growth in preschoolers through stimulation of verbal interaction with mothers, Am. J. Orthopsychiatry **40:**426, 1970.

47. Lewis, M., editor: Origins of intelligence; infancy and early childhood, New York, 1976, Plenum Publishing Corp.

48. Lewis, M., and Rosenblum, L. A., editors: The effect of the infant on its caregiver, New York, 1974, John Wiley & Sons, Inc.

49. Lubchenco, L.: Development of premature infants of low birth weight: evaluation at ten years of age, Am. J. Dis. Child. **102:**952, 1961.

50. Lubchenco, L., et al.: Sequelae of premature birth, Am. J. Dis. Child. **106:**101, 1963.

51. Mahler, M., Pine, F., and Bergman, A.: The psychological birth of the human infant, New York, 1975, Basic Books, Inc., Publishers.

52. Meier, J. H.: Early intervention in the prevention of mental retardation. In Milunskey, A., editor: The prevention of mental retardation and genetic disease, Philadelphia, 1975, W. B. Saunders Co.

53. National Institutes of Health: Perspectives on human deprivation: biological, psychological and sociological, Washington, D.C., 1968, Department of Health, Education and Welfare.

54. Northern, J., and Downs, M.: Hearing in children, Baltimore, 1974, The Williams & Wilkins Co.

55. Olshansky, S.: Chronic sorrow: a response to having a mentally defective child, Social Casework, April 1972.

56. Pasamanick, B., and Knobloch, H.: Epidemiologic studies on the complications of pregnancy and birth process. In Caplan, C., editor: Prevention of mental disorders in children, New York, 1961, Basic Books, Inc., Publishers.

57. Pines, M.: Why some three year olds get A's and some get C's, New York Times Magazine, July 6, 1979.

58. Rexford, E., Sander, L., and Shapiro, T., editors: Infant psychiatry: a new synthesis, New Haven, Conn., 1976, Yale University Press.

59. Rheingold, H. L.: The effect of environmental stimulation upon social and exploratory behaviors in the human infant. In Foss, B. M., editor: Determinants of infant behavior, vol. 1, New York, 1961, John Wiley & Sons, Inc., pp. 143-171.

60. Rogers, S.: Evaluation. In Moersh, M., and Wilson, T., editors: Early intervention project for handicapped infants and young children. Final report, 1973 to 1976, Ann Arbor, Mich., 1976, University of Michigan Press.

61. Rogers, S., et al.: The early intervention developmental profile, Ann Arbor, Mich., 1975, University of Michigan Press.

62. Rowe, J., et al.: Follow-up of families who experience a perinatal death, Pediatrics **62:**166, 1978.

63. Salapatek, P.: Visual scanning of geometric figures by human newborn, J. Comp. Physiol. Psychol. **8:**173, 1969.

64. Sameroff, A., and Chandler, M.: Infant casuality and the continuum of infant caretaking. In Horowitz, F. D., et al., editors: Review of child development research, vol. 4, Chicago, 1975, University of Chicago Press.

64a. Schafer, D. S.: Early intervention developmental profile: application in a transdisciplinary program. In Moersh, M., and Wilson, T., editors: Early intervention project for handicapped infants and young children, final report, 1973-1976, Ann Arbor, Mich., 1976, University of Michigan Press.

65. Schaffer, H., and Emerson, P. E.: The development of social attachment in infancy, Mongr. Soc. Res. Child Dev. **29:**1, 1964.

66. Schwartz, J., and Schwartz, L.: Vulnerable infants: a psychosocial dilemma, New York, 1977, McGraw-Hill Book Co.

67. Shearer, D., and Shearer, M.: The protage project: a model for early childhood intervention. In Tjossem, T., editor: Intervention strategies for high risk infants, Baltimore, 1976, University Park Press.

68. Smith, R. L.: An introduction to mental retardation, New York, 1971, McGraw-Hill Book Co.

69. Stone, L., Smith, H., Murphy, L., editors: The competent infant; research and commentary, New York, 1973, Basic Books, Inc., Publishers.

70. Tjossem, T., editor: Intervention strategies for high risk infants and young children, Baltimore, 1976, University Park Press.

71. Tjossem, T.: Early intervention: issues and approaches. In Tjossem, T., editor: Intervention strategies for high risk infants and young children, Baltimore, 1976, University Park Press.

72. Tulkin, S., and Kagan, J.: Mother-child interaction in the first year of life, Child Dev. **43:**31, 1972.

73. Uzgiri, I.: Patterns of vocal and gestural imitation in infants. In Stone, L. J., Smith, H., and Murphy, L., editors: The competent infant; research and commentary, New York, 1973, Basic Books, Inc., Publishers.

74. White, B. L.: Human infants: experience and psychological development, Englewood Cliffs, N.J., 1971, Prentice-Hall, Inc.

75. White, B. L.: The first three years of life, Englewood Cliffs, N.J., 1975, Prentice-Hall, Inc.

76. White, B. L., and Held, R.: Plasticity of sensorimotor development in the human infant. In Jellmuth, J., editor: Exceptional infant, vol. 1, New York, 1967, Brunner/Mazel, Inc.

77. Wolff, P.: Observations on the early development of smiling. In Foss, B. M., editor: Determinants of infant behavior II, New York, 1963, John Wiley & Sons, Inc., pp. 113 to 138.

78. Yarrow, L.: Separation from parents during early childhood. In Hoffman, M. L., and Hoffman, L. N. W., editors: Review of child development research, vol. 1, New York, 1964, Russell Sage Foundation.

79. Zelle, R.: Early intervention: a panacea or an experiment? M. C. N. **1:**343, 1976.

5

The child with myelodysplasia

Carlton Akins
Robin Davidson
Timothy Hopkins

Myelodysplasia is one of the most physically, psychologically, and economically devastating congenital illnesses facing the physician today. Innovations in surgical, pharmacological, and rehabilitative technology have enabled many infants with myelodysplasia to achieve a level of physical function unattainable two decades ago. The unique health care needs of myelodysplastic children are best served in a setting in which the patient can be evaluated by a pediatrician, a neurosurgeon, a urologist, an orthopedist, a nurse, a therapist, and a social worker during the same visit. Interdisciplinary myelodysplasia clinics offer the singular advantage of ready communication among a diverse group of physicians and other professionals who are responsible for the child's care. This enables the family and the child afflicted with multiple, ongoing problems to be managed by professionals of several different disciplines, who would be kept informed of all the other aspects of that individual's care. Communication, however, must not be just among the members of the myelodysplasia team. The patient and family must be made aware of the team's findings and plans. The primary care physician should both contribute to and receive from the team the information necessary for the day-to-day management of the youngster. For the child to function at his maximal level in the community, the school and other community professionals must also be involved and kept informed of the team's efforts to achieve the treatment goal. Only with the coordinated contributions of all these individuals can that goal be achieved.

Myelodysplasia is a systemic dysgenesis that begins before the twenty-seventh day of gestation as a failure of segmental neurulation. This failure most commonly occurs at the posterior neuropore and results in a myeloschisis, the most dramatic clinical presentation of myelodysplasia. The dysgenesis also includes failure of normal development of other neuroectodermal, mesodermal, and sclerotomal structures. This results in the frequent association of the Arnold-Chiari malformation as well as vertebral and other structural anomalies.

The incidence of myelodysplasia varies with the location of populations studied, ethnic background, sex, year, and parity, and possibly with socioeconomic status. There is no correlation with season or maternal age,[1] but there is a slightly increased incidence in females and a lower incidence in black and Jewish populations.[1] This suggests that environmental factors play a role in eliciting the expression of an underlying hereditary predisposition to this syndrome.[90] The incidence in the United States three decades ago was recorded at 2.53 per 1000 total births.[56] More recently, the incidence in the eastern United States was 1 per 1000 total births.[37] The inheritance pattern is clearly multifactorial. The incidence of central nervous system (CNS) malformation in children born after the first affected propositus with myelodysplasia was 6.6% in Great Britain[56] and 1.8% in the United States.[35,37]

Predictive data on pregnant women with a history of offspring with anencephaly and spina bifida may be obtained by amniocentesis at 16 weeks of gestation. An increase in alpha fetoprotein, an alpha 1 globulin synthesized by normal embryonal liver cells, yolk sac, and gastrointestinal tract, may indicate the presence of a fetus with anencephaly or myelodysplasia.[6,7] Antenatal diagnosis may be established by a combination of amniocentesis, B-mode ultrasonography and abdominal computed tomography. Maternal serum alpha fetoprotein may be elevated at 16 weeks in fetuses with open anencephalic or myelodysplastic deformities, and checking the serum alpha-fetoprotein level may be a reasonable screening procedure in primigravidas. Abnormal levels of alpha fetoprotein may also be present in premature infants and infants with congenital nephrosis, esophageal and duodenal atresia, omphalocele, and hepatocellular injury. Elevation of maternal serum levels may indicate a need for diagnostic amniocentesis.[7]

The cause of myelodysplasia is unknown. Neurulation, the first phase of neural tube development, begins at a gestational age of 21 days. The process then proceeds in a cephalocaudal direction, with posterior neuropore closure occurring at roughly the twenty-seventh day of gestation, when there are 21 to 29 somites.[47] Failure of posterior neuropore closure, resulting in the continuance of a neural plate in the lumbosacral area, or failure of neural tube formation at any point in the developing cord can then present as an open neural placode with associated failure of normal cephalad migration of the conus. As an initial embryogenic process, failure of neurulation in any area of the spinal cord would seem to prevent induction of normal surrounding mesodermal, sclerotomal, and ectodermal structures.

Myelodysplasia is included in the following classification of spina bifida and can form a useful framework on which to orient the spectrum of problems related to this disease:

A. Spina bifida occulta—associated anomalies
  1. Sinus tract
  2. Cutaneous hemangioma
  3. Hairy nevus
  4. Intraspinal epidermoid
  5. Intraspinal lipoma
  6. Hemivertebrae
  7. Diastematomyelia
  8. Intraspinal meningocele
B. Spina bifida cystica (operta)
  1. Meningocele
  2. Myelodysplasia
    a. Myelomeningocele
    b. Lipomyelomeningocele
    c. Myeloschisis
    d. Myelocystocele

This outline is not based on anomalous development of the stages of vertebral and neural tube growth, but rather is an attempt to supply a clinically oriented schema that crosses the phases of normal neural tube and vertebral development. The terms used are commonly seen and frequently used interchangeably, with some resulting confusion. The term myelodysplasia as used here implies the involvement of neural elements, either neural placode or roots or both, in the anomaly.

A developmentally oriented classification would place each lesion within one of the three phases of neural tube embryogenesis, implying that failure of normal development at a particular phase was responsible for the anomaly. Phase I of neural tube development, neurulation, would be associated with myeloschisis and myelomeningocele. Phase II, canalization of the caudal cell mass, would be associated with myelocystocele, and failures of phase III, retrogressive differentiation, would include meningocele and lipomyelomeningocele.[47]

CLINICAL PRESENTATION AND MANAGEMENT IN NEWBORNS
The lesion

The primary lesion represents a spectrum of clinical deficits, which at its most benign may present as a well-epithelialized sac associated with a localized radiculopathy (myelomeningocele) (Fig. 5-1). The most severe form, in which a neural placode with associated paraspinal musculature is completely exposed (myeloschisis), is frequently associated with a total lower motor neuron paralysis. The degree of the motorsensory polyradiculopathy, however, is independent of the clinical appearance of the lesion on the back; a well-covered myelomeningocele may be associated with an almost complete lumbosacral polyradiculopathy or a large thoracolumbar myeloschisis may occur with the preservation of significant function of roots afferent from and efferent to bowel, bladder, and lower extremity skin and musculature.

Associated neurosurgical problems

Hydrocephalus may present at birth in myelodysplastic infants or present clinically later in life. The cause of 80% of hydrocephalus cases (which occurs in approximately 80% of myelodysplastic infants) is occlusion of the fourth ventricular outflow foramina in association with the Chiari type II malformation (which is present in essentially all children with myelodysplasia). In the remaining 20% of hydrocephalic children with myelodysplasia the problem is secondary to aqueductal occlusion.[60]

Encephaloceles and other anomalies rarely occur in association with myelodysplasia but may preclude a surgical approach to the myelomeningocele. Poikilothermy, neurogenic hyperthermia, and inability to suck and swallow have been observed. Grand mal and other seizure patterns occur commonly.

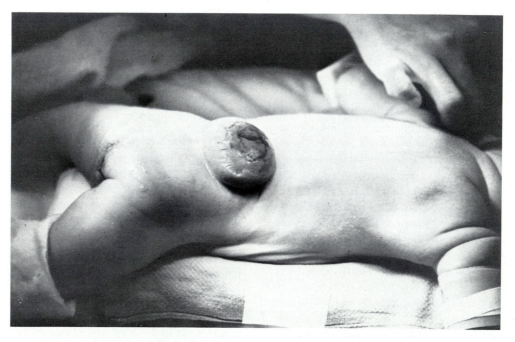

Fig. 5-1. Newborn with myelomeningocele.

Lückenschädl, in which extensive areas of ovoid thinning appear on the skull x-ray film of infants with myelodysplasia, is believed by some to carry a poor prognosis for normal intellectual development.[87] Rib fusion anomalies occurring in the right upper rib cage are present in about 20% of myelodysplastic infants and are usually asymptomatic.[62]

Inspiratory stridor and apnea may occur as a result of vagal dysfunction[5,26]; the latter is usually corrected when the increased intracranial pressure of hydrocephalus is reduced.

Decision to operate

Matson,[60] Lorber,[52,53] and others[74] have recorded clear criteria that remain appropriate indices for withholding surgical intervention in the neonate with myelodysplasia. These include the presence of a large thoracic or high lumbar myeloschisis associated with complete paralysis and overt hydrocephalus (clinically obvious macrocephaly). The decision to operate ultimately becomes the responsibility of the neurosurgeon. Patient and repeated counselling of both parents is undertaken to describe the host of problems that may afflict the affected child. However, the urgency for primary closure of the defect within the first 24 hours of life, which thereby commits the child and his family to an ongoing surgical and medical therapeutic program for life, makes the concept of truly informed consent at best a nebulous one. The description of the overwhelming nature of the disease presented in detail to parents who may already be psychologically and physically spent from the labor and birth process alone seems to preclude a completely rational decision on the parents' part.

The neonate with a large thoracic myeloschisis with an associated total caudal motor and sensory deficit and overt hydrocephalus is not a candidate for surgical closure. A medical and ethical problem, however, is raised with those children for whom a full therapeutic program is not elected. Approximately 30% of children thus approached will not die, which is the implied outcome of nonsurgical treatment.[31] These infants may not develop meningitis, severe increased intracranial pressure, or renal failure with or without sepsis (all

common modes of death in the untreated myelodysplastic infant). The myelodysplastic lesion may scar and epithelialize spontaneously, the hydrocephalus may eventually cease to advance, and the hydronephrosis may progress slowly. Such a child may or may not be cared for by his parents. In either case the ability to communicate may develop in the afflicted child, and the physician is then presented with a paraplegic patient with severe untreated orthopedic, urological, and neurosurgical problems (all of which make personal care, alimentation, and hygiene massive undertakings) who is aware of and may speak of his own plight. We offer no solution to this problem and have presented it only to advise physicians that a decision not to close a large myeloschisis or perform a shunt on an infant with massive hydrocephalus does not inevitably end in the child's death or lack of environmental awareness. Also, the decision not to operate does not conclude the physician's responsibility to the patient and family. The preceding discussion is not a valid argument for euthanasia in infants who fulfill Matson's and Lorber's criteria or for surgically treating all infants but rather is a plea for flexibility in making decisions and for ongoing evaluation of a child who is not initially subjected to a full surgical and medical treatment program following birth.

Neurosurgical management

The primary lesion is closed by excision of the parchmentlike portion of the covered sac, mobilization and closure of a pseudodura over neural elements, and extensive undermining and primary closure in the long axis of the lesion. Bipedicle grafts, bone removal, or specialized plastic surgical techniques may be required to effect a tension-free closure.[60,82] A well-epithelialized meningocele or myelomeningocele may be resected and closed on an elective basis later in infancy.

The child is kept immobilized in a sling for a period of several days postoperatively and fed intravenously. Sutures are usually removed 10 days after surgery.[31]

Hydrocephalus, which may develop at any time in children with myelodysplasia, most commonly presents within the first 3 weeks of life. It is suspected when the rate of head growth begins to accelerate beyond the normal growth curve for age and can be confirmed by computed tomographic scanning or ventriculography. If hydrocephalus is confirmed, treatment is effected ultimately by ventriculoperitoneal shunting, a modality that generally carries a decreased risk of death and further illness when compared to vascular shunts. Revision is required for growth and malfunction. The latter is suspected in children under 2 years of age when the head growth curve, which is monitored every 3 months following surgery, begins to accelerate or when such symptoms as lethargy, irritability or unexplained vomiting occur. Such symptoms may be insidious or appear very acutely. In older children symptoms of increased intracranial pressure such as headaches, somnolence, diplopia, and emesis may also present acutely and necessitate emergency revision of the shunt. When shunt malfunction is suspected, tests for patency and/or the site of obstruction are performed. These may include simple digital palpation and compression of the valve or reservoir; plain x-ray film examination of the skull, chest, and abdomen to determine whether all components are connected and that the distal catheter is in normal position; aspiration of the reservoir, if present; isotope ventriculography via the reservoir with measurement of clearance rates; and computed tomography of the brain.

Complications of both the closure of the myelomeningocele and of the shunt may occur. Breakdown of the primary closure may be associated with meningitis and necessitates an extended period of wound care and occasionally secondary grafting. Shunt malfunction may occur at the ventricular catheter, valve, or runoff catheter, and the signs and symptoms reviewed in the preceding discussion are the same for atrial and peritoneal shunt systems. Complications unique to atrial systems include catheter embolization, superior vena cava thrombosis, pulmonary hypertension, septicemia and glomerulonephritis.[27] Complications unique to peritoneal systems include viscus perforation, peritonitis, ascites, pseudocyst formation, hydrocele, and hernia.[17]

Urological management

Management of the urological problems of the child with spina bifida has assumed added significance with the development of improved neurosurgical procedures for the repair of myelomeningocele and the control of hydrocephalus. More children are surviving the first year of life and are at risk of developing urological problems. After the age of 2 the major cause of death in these children is renal insufficiency.[16,84]

The most frequent urinary problems are incontinence and/or urinary tract infections.[14,69] Only about 10% of children with spina bifida will be normally continent.[21,69,84,89] This has become very important socially because nearly half of these children will attend normal schools.[21] From 50% to 90% will eventually develop a urinary tract infection.[12,84,89] Most (87%) have normal intravenous pyelogram (IVP) results as newborns.[57] However, renal tract deformities, as discovered in autopsies of neonates with spina bifida, are four times more common than in normal newborns.[91] Up to 24% initially have vesicoureteral reflux.[49,57] Renal deterioration is nearly always secondary to abnormal lower urinary tract function. The pathophysiology involves abnormal innervation of the bladder and urinary sphincter. This may cause abnormal bladder emptying and its sequelae of infection, reflux, or increased bladder and urethral emptying pressure. These problems in turn may lead to hydroureter, hydronephrosis, pyelonephritis, and renal cortical loss.[14,16]

To achieve the urological goals of preservation of renal function and urinary continence, various treatment methods have been developed. Most of these are aimed at improving lower tract function and preventing urinary tract infection. Perhaps the greatest recent change in urological management has been the shift from urinary tract diversion to clean, intermittent urinary catheterization. Other urological advances include cystometric and sphincterometric evaluation, pharmacological manipulation of lower urinary tract function, Credé maneuver (manual expression of the urine by suprapubic pressure), operative procedures to decrease outlet resistance, use of the artificial urinary sphincter, and, rarely, urinary diversion.

The initial urological evaluation includes close observation of the neonate's voiding pattern in the first few days. A careful physical examination should include examining peripheral neurological function as well as noting rectal tone, testing the bulbocavernosus reflex (note anal contraction on the rectal examining finger upon squeezing the glans penis or clitoris) and examining for a distended bladder. A clean-voided specimen for urinalysis and culture should be obtained on the second or third day. This can be obtained by using a sterile bag method or by using the Credé maneuver and catching a midstream specimen. If the culture is positive (greater than 10^5 organisms/ml), the result should be confirmed by a second specimen obtained by suprapubic aspiration or urethral catheterization. One positive, properly collected midstream specimen is only 80% to 85% reliable, but two positive cultures of the same organism are about 95% reliable.[41] On the fourth or fifth day a serum creatinine should be measured. Any earlier evaluation may just reflect the renal function of the mother. A normal creatinine level in an infant is less than 0.5 mg/100 ml. At about 1 week of age an IVP should be performed using 2 mg of contrast medium/0.45 kg of body weight. The child must not be dehydrated. By waiting a week the common technically unsatisfactory pyelogram secondary to the neonate's low glomerular filtration rate and limited concentrating ability will usually be avoided.[45,77] If these studies are normal, a voiding cystourethrogram (VCUG) is not routinely done.

If a distended bladder is noted, the Credé maneuver is used on the infant. This is done by supporting the back of the pelvis with one hand (being careful to avoid the neurosurgical closure) and compressing backward and downward with the first two fingers of the other hand just above the symphysis pubis (Fig. 5-2). This is also done during the IVP if the infant does not void. An x-ray examination is done after use of the Credé maneuver to check the adequacy of emptying and to observe any possible ureteral dilation, possibly secondary to reflux.

In addition to inadequate emptying, several other problems may occur in infants with spina bifida. They include hydronephrosis, ureteral reflux, and urinary tract infection. The first procedure to be considered in children with urological deterioration is usually extensive dilation of the urethra and continuous antibiotic coverage. This has met with moderate success, especially if there is some evidence of external sphincter spasm on VCUG.[15,54] Duckett[20] has managed many of these children with vesicostomy. About 55% of his patients were operated on before age 1½. His results show 54% had sterile urine with normal or improved IVP and only 17% had infected urine but a normal or improved IVP. He had an 18% failure rate, and these infants went on to ileal conduit diversion. Other successful techniques have included resection of the external sphincter,[92] transureteroureterostomy,[58] and ureteral reimplantation.[38] Occasionally, as a last resort one is forced to perform an upper urinary tract diversion either by loop cutaneous ureterostomy, pyelostomy, or bowel conduit diversion.[14,84]

Neonatal reflux may occur in the infant with myelodysplasia and is probably on the same developmental basis as in neurologically normal children. Later, however, reflux may be found in 38% to 60% of spina bifida patients, probably secondary to neurological dysfunction and recurrent infection.[12,49,84] Whether this reflux will improve over a period of time with maintenance of sterile urine, as it often does in neurologically normal bladders, remains to be determined. Jeffs and co-workers[38] have reported success in 33 of 37 ureteral reimplantations into neurogenic bladders. The criterion for a successful outcome seems to be selecting bladders with large capacity and minimal trabeculations. Some researchers believe that use of the Credé maneuver is contraindicated with reflux, fearing that the ''water-hammer effect'' may lead to progressive renal damage.[71] On the other hand, it is doubtful whether sterile reflux leads to permanent upper tract damage. The pressure generated by use of the Credé maneuver is no greater than normal bladder con-

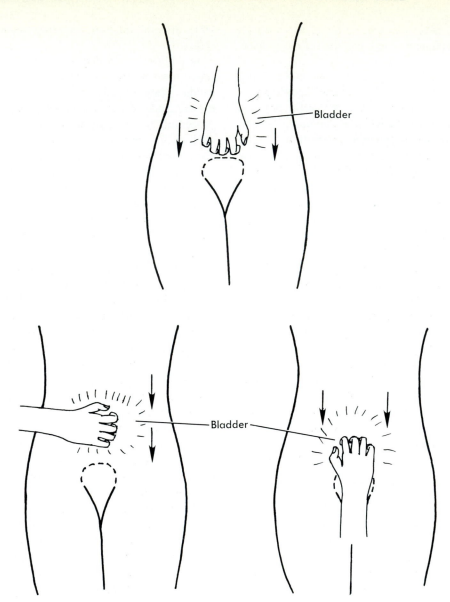

Fig. 5-2. Technique of bladder Credé maneuver. Position of hand can vary. Pressure should be toward the top of the bladder and downward toward the coccyx.

traction pressure as long as there is no outlet obstruction. It is imperative to keep those children with reflux who are managed without surgery on antibiotic suppression to decrease the incidence of recurrent infection and possible subsequent renal damage.[30]

Circumcision should not be performed because, if the child becomes incontinent, the foreskin may protect the meatus from dermatitis and meatal stenosis.

Orthopedic management

The initial orthopedic evaluation should be done very early in life, preferably before the neurosurgical closure and certainly within the first few days. Many of the deformities that are encountered can best be managed by prompt and aggressive conservative treatment, including proper positioning and stretching and holding devices. The orthopedic assessment should be thorough and include both upper and lower extremities as well as the axial skeleton. Any deformities of the upper extremities assume added importance for a child who may have to rely on his arms for support and motion.

Spinal deformity, aside from the obvious myelomeningocele, is not commonly present at birth. A severe kyphosis at the level of the myelomeningocele is the most important initial orthopedic problem and may require bony resection at the time of the primary neurosurgical repair to effect closure of the defect. Scoliosis is not usually seen in the newborn, but if it is present, it may be due to other associated congenital spinal anomalies such as hemivertebrae. Initial spinal x-ray examination should be done, since it is often helpful in determining the size and location of the posterior defect, as well as in defining other congenital anomalies.

Most of the deformities in the lower extremities of a newborn with a thoracic, lumbar, or sacral myelomeningocele are due to either muscular imbalance or intrauterine malposition.[80] The muscular asymmetry is related to the lower motor neuron defect and is part of the primary nerve root lesion. The intrauterine posture may be aggravated by the lack of normally functioning and balancing muscles.

Each joint in the lower extremities should be carefully examined to define any fixed deformity, to assess its range of motion in all planes, and to evaluate the muscles and nerves that control its motion. Muscle examinations in the newborn are difficult to perform and to interpret but should be done (p. 125). They often provide the explanation for joint deformity and are the baseline for all subsequent testing.

Hip dislocation or subluxation should be diagnosed and treated early. The management of children with these problems is not very different from that of otherwise normal children with the same problem.[50] The hips can usually be easily reduced by gentle traction and manipulation, and the reduction maintained by positioning the hips in flexion and abduction. This can be done by placing a soft wedge between the legs or by the use of a pillow splint. Some motion of the hips is usually possible in this position and is encouraged.

Knee deformities may be either flexion or more rarely extension, again usually due to muscular imbalance between the quadriceps and the hamstrings. These should be managed by gentle stretching on a regular basis to correct the contractures and then to maintain full motion. Too vigorous therapy may result in displacement of the distal femoral growth plate or fracture of the proximal tibia and should obviously be avoided. The correction achieved by stretching may require external splinting to prevent recurrence.

Ankle and foot deformities are the most common deformities seen in the newborn period and are a consequence of the fact that the muscles of the ankle and foot are innervated by the lowest spinal motor levels. The most common deformity is an equinovarus foot, secondary to intrauterine malposition and activity of the tibialis anterior and tibialis posterior without the balancing muscles. This, as well as most other foot deformities, should be aggressively treated in the neonate by vigorous stretching exercises supplemented by carefully padded and applied plaster casts. Because of the associated sensory loss, casts must be used only as holding devices and never to gain correction beyond that achieved by manipulation. Furthermore, casts should be changed often and should never be wedged to gain additional correction.

Surgical management of any of these problems is rarely indicated in the first several months of life. Much can be accomplished by positioning, stretching, and cautious use of holding devices, both in correcting deformity and maintaining motion. Special care must be taken in the infant with a high level of paralysis, who will like to lie with the hips flexed, abducted and externally rotated, the knees flexed, and the ankles in equinus.

In addition to the obvious benefit of a careful orthopedic assessment and early treatment to the newborn, the parents can also benefit from early contact with the orthopedist and physical therapist. Often one of the first questions the parents of a newborn with a myelomeningocele have is, "Will he walk?" Since the orthopedist and therapist are those members of the team most involved with standing and walking, their evaluation should be able to provide at least preliminary information about that aspect of the child's future. Several recent long-term studies of large series of patients with myelodysplasia have demonstrated the correlation between the spinal level of muscular paralysis and the likely ultimate level of ambulatory function (p. 125).[18,34,36] The child's sensory level frequently does not correlate well with the motor level of function. Patients with good motor function of the quadriceps and of all muscles above that level (which is usually the case) are likely to be at least domestic ambulators, albeit perhaps with braces. Obviously, those patients with lower spinal lesions are far more likely to walk, even without any external support devices, than are those with very high lumbar or thoracic lesions, who require major external support devices just to stand and are much less likely to have any independent walking ability. Regardless of the ultimate level of function, however, nearly all patients should be able to be upright as children and adolescents, with whatever external devices are necessary to achieve this position. This is strongly recommended because of the physiological and psychological advantages of the upright position in a child's developing years.

A corollary of this approach is that the legs, pelvis, and trunk must be able to achieve alignments that will permit whatever bracing may be necessary for the patient to stand. Furthermore, the stretching, splinting, and positioning that make this possible are the combined responsibility of the parents, the orthopedist, the therapist, and the orthotist. These latter three should provide the necessary help and guidance so that the parents are competent in and comfortable with the therapy and devices. Many of the leg deformities in the neonatal period can be corrected by early and vigorous nonoperative treatment, and the parents must be involved in this as early as possible.

MANAGEMENT IN CHILDHOOD
Neurosurgical management

Hydrocephalus may present after the neonatal period. An accelerated rate of head growth is a clinical hallmark, and scalp vein "dila-tion," sutural diastasis, a bulging and tense anterior fontanelle, the setting-sun sign, lower extremity spasticity, and irritability may all be clinical findings. Hydrocephalus, although presenting most commonly within the first 6 months of life, may be an initial clinical problem as late as the early teens. Poor school performance; deterioration in gait, memory, or handwriting; and headaches may be early symptoms of clinical hydrocephalus in a child who was previously compensated. Clinical "arrest" of hydrocephalus (but with persistent ventriculomegaly) occurs more commonly in hydrocephalus associated with myelodysplasia than with other forms of congenital hydrocephalus. Although this "arrest" may be suspected clinically for a variety of reasons, the shunt is not usually removed; however, elective lengthening may not be pursued.

An increase in head size is still a common clinical presentation of hydrocephalus in patients under 2 years of age, but in childhood it may be coupled with the symptoms and signs of increased intracranial pressure. The head circumference should be followed and an assessment of motor and developmental skills should be made regularly. The treatment of hydrocephalus in the older infant and child is the same as that for neonates. If shunt complications negate the use of the peritoneal cavity or either internal jugular veins as sites for the secondary absorption of spinal fluid, the isolated ureter, the right atrium, and the pleural cavities offer alternatives. Management of the shunt in infancy and childhood includes evaluation of valve function (as described on p. 120), neurological screening examination, and head circumference measurement at 3-month intervals in the first 2 years of life and every 6 months thereafter. Suspected poor function dictates more frequent assessment.

Other associated clinical problems may occur. Overt retardation and learning disabilities may become more apparent in the myelodysplastic child. Approximately 30% of these children are of low-normal or below normal intelligence. Seizures may continue to present a management problem or even surface initially in childhood.

MUSCLE TESTING OF INFANTS WITH MENINGOMYELOCELES*

Name _____

Date and time of birth _____ Date and time of examination _____

Condition of infant _____ Head circumference _____ Percentile _____

Other abnormalities _____

Motor examination: G—good   F—fair   P—poor   0—none   R—reflex

Joint	Movement	Main muscle	Level of innervation	Right	Left
Hip	Flexion	Psoas	$L_1 - L_3$		
	Extension	Gluteus maximus	$L_5 - S_1$		
	Abduction	Gluteus medius	$L_4 - S_1$		
	Adduction	Adductors	$L_2 - L_4$		
Knee	Flexors	Hamstrings medius	$L_4 - S_1$		
		Hamstrings lateral	$L_5 - S_2$		
	Extensors	Quadriceps	$L_2 - L_4$		
Ankle	Plantarflex	Gastrocnemius and soleus	$L_5 - S_2$		
	Dorsiflex	Tibia anterior	$L_4 - L_5$		
Subtalar	Inversion	Tibia posterior	$L_4 - L_5$		
	Eversion	Peroneal	$L_5 - S_1$		
Toes	Flexion	Long flexors	$S_1 - S_2$		
		Short flexors	$S_2 - S_3$		
	Extension	Common extensors	$L_5 - S_1$		
		Short extensors	$S_2 - S_3$		

Motor level _____

*From Freeman, J. M., editor: Practical management of meningomyelocele, Baltimore, 1974, University Park Press.

Urological management

In the well child without evidence of urological deterioration the IVP is repeated at 6 months of age, yearly until about age 5, and then every other year until puberty. Renal growth is measured and plotted on a renal growth chart as an added index of normal renal development. A failure of renal growth indicates a need for further evaluation.[46] With each IVP the number of films should be limited to decrease the cumulative radiation exposure. Preparation for the IVP is limited to overnight dehydration and a Fleet enema. Quantitative urine cultures are done every 3 months in the first 2 years, then every 6 months until age 5, and then yearly if they have been negative. A urinalysis is inadequate, since the correlation between pyuria and bacteriuria is only 50%.[72]

Therefore, if one relies on urinalysis alone, many infections will be missed. Urinary infections are often not clinically apparent and one must depend on laboratory detection. In the older child blood pressure should be routinely measured because there is an alarming incidence of hypertension.[73]

Evaluation of urinary control is usually made at age 4 or 5. This is done after adequate time has determined whether a child can be toilet trained and prior to entering school. If the child has several episodes of dryness, intermittent voiding, or the sensation of voiding, the outlook is hopeful.

At this stage urodynamic evaluation may be carried out. Several authors[84,92] believe that this is not especially useful or necessarily valid, since function may change from time to time. However, as techniques have improved and the understanding of bladder and sphincter function has increased, many have found urodynamic evaluation to have wider applicability.[4,73] This usually includes cystometry, in which carbon dioxide or water is instilled into the bladder via a catheter and simultaneous bladder pressure tracings are recorded. Electromyography of the urethral sphincter is also done either via an anal plug electrode, urethral surface electrode, perineal patch electrode, or by placement of a small wire electrode directly into the external sphincter. A rectal balloon to monitor changes in abdominal pressure, urethral pressure profilometry, and flowmetry may also be useful. Bethanechol (Urecholine) or propantheline (Pro-Banthine) can also be given parenterally to help evaluate denervation. Two main types of bladder disorders can usually be defined by these tests. The most common is the hypotonic or flaccid bladder, but approximately a third of the children will have a hypertonic or spastic bladder. Correlations between bladder contractions and sphincter action determine whether there is synergy or dyssynergy. Increased sphincter activity during a detrusor contraction is labelled detrusor sphincter dyssynergy. Various cystometric patterns are seen in these children because the neurological lesions are frequently incomplete (Fig. 5-3). There is poor correlation between the level of the neurological lesion and the type of bladder function.

Radiographic evaluation of the bladder and sphincter is done via the voiding cystourethrogram. Rough estimates of the type of bladder, coordination of voiding, and relaxation of the bladder neck and external sphincter may be determined. By combining the clinically observed voiding pattern, neurological examination, cystometric studies, and radiographic evaluation, a scientific approach to the management of the lower urinary tract in these children is possible.

Newer concepts of autonomic bladder innervation and control have influenced our use of pharmacological agents. Alpha-adrenergic receptors predominate in the bladder base, outlet, and urethra, where they cause contractions. Beta-adrenergic receptors are predominant in the bladder dome, where they cause relaxation. There is a predominance of cholinergic receptors throughout the bladder, and these are responsible for detrusor contraction during urination. Therefore it is believed that alpha receptors are responsible for bladder continence, beta receptors for bladder relaxation and facilitation of bladder filling, and cholinergic receptors for bladder emptying. The interaction between the adrenergic and cholinergic systems explains the active outlet and urethral opening during voiding.[39,75]

We can functionally separate the neurogenic bladder into a failure of bladder emptying and a failure of urine storage. Therapy may be directed at improving bladder emptying by increasing intravesicle pressure by the use of the Credé maneuver, by cholinergic stimulation, or by decreasing outlet resistance. Outlet resistance may be decreased by pharmacological means, urethral dilation, internal urethrotomy, or YV plasty of the bladder neck. Urine storage may be facilitated by bladder inhibition or by increasing resistance at the bladder outlet.[73]

Drugs causing alpha-adrenergic response (ephedrine, phenylephrine, imipramine or propranolol) increase outlet and urethral pressures and therefore may lead to a competent bladder neck and urinary continence. Alpha-adrenergic blockade with phenoxybenzamine has been

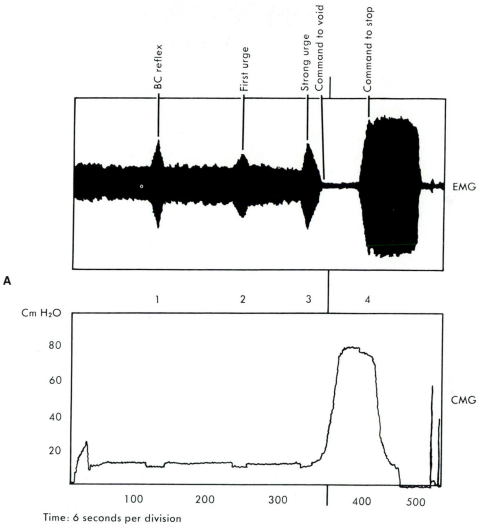

Fig. 5-3. Urodynamic evaluation. **A,** Normal. Cystometrogram and simultaneous electromyogram.

Continued.

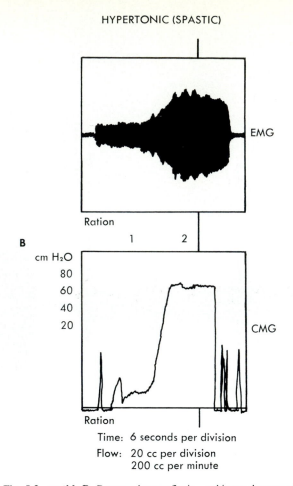

Fig. 5-3, cont'd. B, Detrusor hyperreflexia — sphincter dyssynergia.

Continued.

used to decrease bladder neck spasm and allow more complete emptying. Cholinergic stimulation with bethanecol (Urecholine) may lead to bladder contraction and in some complete emptying. Cholinergic inhibition with propantheline (Pro-Banthine) or oxybutynin (Ditropan) may block uninhibited contractions and increase bladder capacity.[39] These pharmacological agents are often used in combination (Fig. 5-4).

It is important that urine cultures be obtained as clean-voided midstream samples after preparation of the meatus (Fig. 5-5). They can also be obtained by catching the midstream sample after use of the Credé maneuver or by catheterization. If the culture is positive, it is important that the culture be confirmed by a second positive culture. Perhaps 20% of infections will have mixed species. This should be confirmed by a catheterized specimen or suprapubic tap. A urinary infection is diagnosed only if there is 10^5 organisms/ml of urine of the voided specimen. As few as 10^3 organisms/ml of urine of a catheterized specimen or suprapubic tap specimen is probably a significant finding. However, if a positive culture is confirmed, another culture must be taken 5 days after the patient is begun on therapy to verify that urinary sterilization has been obtained. Antibiotic treatment is usually continued for 10 days. Two weeks after stopping the course of treatment another culture is obtained to ensure that the urine remains sterile. In addition, patients can use nitrite dipsticks to check their own urine

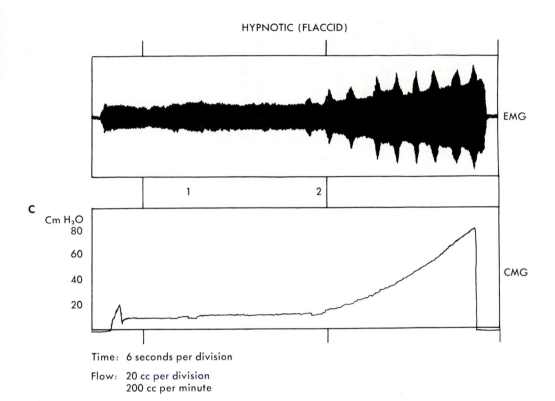

Fig. 5-3, cont'd. C, Detrusor areflexia—detrusor sphincter dyssynergia.

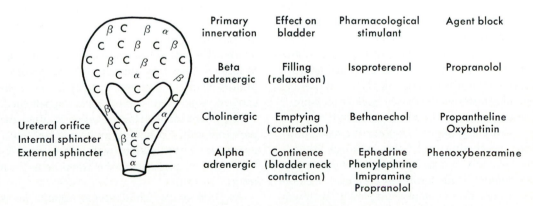

Fig. 5-4. Innervation of and effect on bladder by pharmacological agents used in bladder manipulation.

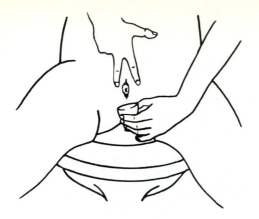

Fig. 5-5. Technique of midstream urine collection. Cup is held so it does not touch the body, and sample is only obtained while the subject is urinating with the labia held apart.

for infection. Patients with ileal loops must also undergo catheterization of their ileal loop via double-loop catheter technique every 6 months. Again, 10^5 organisms/ml is a presumptive diagnosis of infection. We strive to keep our ileal loops free of infection. The culture must not be taken from the bag. A double-catheter technique in which one catheter is cut off and a feeding tube is placed through this catheter into the inside of the loop reduces contamination and spurious results (Fig. 5-6).

No single development has influenced the management of urinary tract problems in children with neurogenic bladder as greatly as has intermittent catheterization. In 1972, Lapidus and associates[42,44] presented their experience in women with neurogenic bladders who were able to achieve continence and freedom from infections using clean intermittent catheterization. There have been several reports of the successful use of this technique in children.[12,39,54,73] It is believed that the key to prevention of urinary tract infection is maintenance of a good bladder blood supply by preventing overdistention and increased bladder pressure.[43] Children are maintained in diapers until age 4 to 6, when this program is begun. We have, however, successfully used this approach in children as early as age 3 months. Indications for intermittent catheterization include incontinence, inability to empty completely, recurrent urinary infections, high outflow resistance, and

upper tract changes secondary to lower tract dysfunction. The bladder should be of reasonable capacity without uninhibited contractions and with adequate urethral resistance. These criteria often must be achieved by pharmacological manipulation. The ideal subject is the child with a trabeculated bladder, sphincter spasm, and greater than 100 ml residual. This is also the child that faces the greatest risk of upper tract damage if untreated.[54] Long-term upper tract deterioration seldom occurs in children on this regimen.[42]

The method of self-catheterization is usually taught by a myelodysplasia clinic nurse. The basic principles are discussed, with the major emphasis placed on frequent catheterizations rather than on sterility. After discussion with the parents and demonstration of the anatomy and the technique, the parents and child are assisted with this procedure. When they have mastered it, usually in one short clinic visit, they are given an instruction sheet reiterating the principles and methods involved (pp. 132 and 133).

A 12 Fr metal or clear plastic catheter usually works satisfactorily in girls and an 8 Fr pediatric feeding tube or 12 Fr latex catheter in boys. A perineal urethrostomy is seldom necessary in boys. Girls do not generally need to use lubrication on the catheter, but boys often do. The catheter is washed inside and out after catheterization and may be stored in a clean covered container of any sort.

Lyon, Scott, and Marshall[54] found that 50% of incontinent girls became continent with intermittent catheterization. Lapidus and co-workers[42] found that only 9% of their patients had sterile urine before instituting intermittent catheterization but that 48% had sterile urine afterwards. They noted no incidence of renal deterioration and only one episode of pyelonephritis; 9 of 33 patients with hydronephrosis showed improved radiographic appearance. Clean intermittent catheterization is often the preferred initial form of treatment for lower urinary tract dysfunction, with urinary tract diversion now relegated to the status of a "last resort" measure.

As soon as the child seems capable he is taught self-catheterization. This usually can be

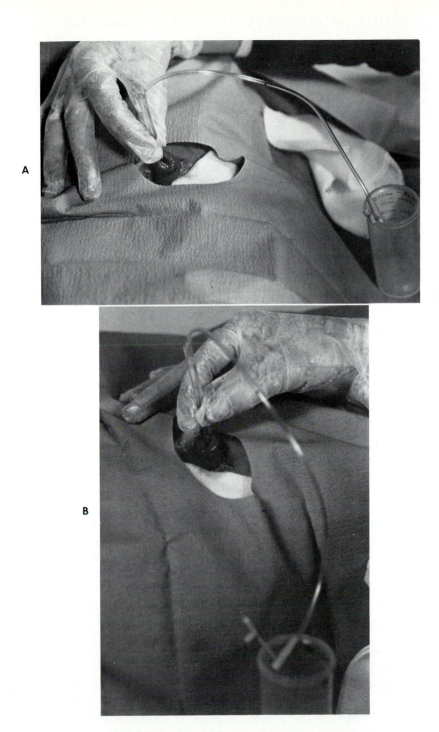

Fig. 5-6. Technique of double-catheter urine collection.

FEMALE INTERMITTENT CATHETERIZATION PROCEDURE
(clean technique)

Intermittent catheterization is the process of periodically emptying the bladder through the use of a catheter (small tube). This is done when there is a lack of control of bladder function. The procedure is done several times a day at regularly scheduled intervals that have been adjusted to your child's needs. The goals are two-fold: to prevent urinary tract infections that may be caused by urine left in the bladder and to attempt to keep your child dry during the day. When the procedure has been implemented successfully, your child may adjust more readily to activities such as school. If you have any questions, please contact: _____

Supplies you will need for this procedure are as follows:

Catheter	Clean washcloth
Container to catch urine	Lubricant (if necessary, use water-soluble lubricant such as K-Y jelly—
Basin of warm water	*no* petroleum jelly)
Soap	Clean, covered container to store catheter in after use

Procedure

1. Arrange supplies within easy reach.
2. Wash catheter with soap and water and rinse with clean water.
3. Place child on back with legs in frog position on flat surface such as table or bed. It is easier to reach the child if surface is about waist high. Stand on right side of child if you are right-handed, opposite side if you are left-handed.
4. Wash hands well with soap and water.
5. Separate labia with left hand. With soapy washcloth in right hand, wash around the urethra three times, moving from top to bottom and using a clean area of the washcloth each time.
6. Still separating labia with left hand, pick up catheter about 3 inches from the top with right hand. Place end of catheter in container to catch urine.
7. Gently insert the catheter into the urethra, pushing it in an upward and backward direction for approximately 1 to 1½ inches.
8. Allow urine to flow into container. When urine ceases to flow, use the Credé method to make sure the bladder is completely empty. Pinch off the catheter and remove it slowly.
9. Clean the area around the urethra, and dress the child.
10. Wash catheter with soap and water and rinse with clear water.
11. Store catheter in clean, covered container.

learned by 6 to 8 years of age but does vary with maturity and coordination. Until that time, the school nurse must often be closely involved in this endeavor. As promising as this procedure seems, it is not always successful. Child and parental motivation and compliance are necessary, and the procedure cannot succeed without them. Complications such as epididymitis, urethral stricture, or urethral injury have been rare. We have found it useful to have a parent test the urine with a nitrite dipstick monthly for unsuspected urinary tract infection.[29]

Other means of relatively conservative therapy have not been so successful. Prolonged catheter drainage can lead to urinary infection, bladder contraction, stone formation, and stricture formation. However, it is useful over a

short period of time, particularly in girls, to keep body casts from becoming soiled following orthopedic procedures. Boys can often be maintained with a condom catheter in that situation.

It is often difficult to keep a urinary incontinence appliance in place in a boy before puberty, especially if he has a small penis or is very active. In addition, the adverse psychological effects of spina bifida may be compounded by the wearing of a penile appliance. Penile clamps may lead to ulceration and stricture, especially in the child with an anesthetic penis. A satisfactory collection device has never been developed for girls.

Urethral plication, pudendal neurectomy, and perineal and bladder stimulation have not been very successful.[66] Resection of the urethral

---

MALE INTERMITTENT CATHETERIZATION PROCEDURE
(clean technique)

Intermittent catheterization is the process of periodically emptying the bladder through the use of a catheter (small tube). This is done when there is a lack of control of bladder function. The procedure is done several times a day at regularly scheduled intervals that have been adjusted to your child's needs. The goals are two-fold: to prevent urinary tract infections that may be caused by urine left in the bladder and to attempt to keep your child dry during the day. When the procedure has been implemented successfully, your child may adjust more readily to activities such as school. If you have any questions, please contact: _____

Supplies you will need for this procedure are as follows:

Catheter	Clean washcloth or cotton balls
Container to catch urine	Lubricant (use water-soluble lubricant such as K-Y jelly—*no* petroleum
Soap	jelly)
Basin of warm water	Clean, covered container to store catheter in after use

Procedure

1. Arrange supplies within easy reach.
2. Wash hands well with soap and water.
3. Wash catheter with soap and water and rinse with clean water.
4. Place child on back on flat surface. Stand on right side if you are right-handed, opposite side if you are left-handed.
5. Lubricate tip of catheter.
6. Hold penis erect on sides so as not to pinch off the urethra. Retract foreskin if not circumcised.
7. Wash head of penis with soap and water. Rinse with clear water.
8. Insert catheter gently into penis until urine begins to flow, then insert it 1 to 2 inches further, depending on the development of the child.
9. When urine ceases to flow, use the Credé method to make sure the bladder is completely empty.
10. Pinch off the catheter and gently remove it.
11. Wash catheter with soap and water and rinse with clear water.
12. Store catheter in clean, covered container.

---

sphincter has been used to decrease voiding resistance and decrease residual urine in the already incontinent patient. It is frequently used to reduce residual urine prior to implantation of an artificial sphincter.

When simpler methods of achieving urinary continence have failed, the use of the Scott prosthetic urinary sphincter has enabled many carefully selected children to avoid urinary diversion (Fig. 5-7). This is a totally implantable Silastic prosthesis. It consists of an inflatable cuff that surrounds the urethra, a reservoir, and a deflate-inflate mechanism. When the inflate bulb is squeezed, fluid is pumped from the reservoir into the periurethral cuff, compressing the urethra much like the normal sphincter. When the deflate bulb is squeezed, fluid flows back into the reservoir and the patient voids.

Any children who are considered as candidates for the artificial sphincter must be carefully evaluated. They must have normal or stable upper tracts, no uninhibited contractions that cannot be completely blocked with medication, and they must be able to empty the bladder completely.[14,76] No large series of children has yet been reported. However, four of nine children with spina bifida in Scott's series failed.[76] In combined series there has been a 30% to 60% rate of significant complications.[14,19] In addition, the sphincter has only been implanted since 1972 and has undergone several modifications since that time. Therefore it is still not a panacea for the incontinent child but seems to be an ever-brightening ray of hope.

Urinary diversion has been delegated by most urologists as nearly the last consideration in management of children with spina bifida. Indications are usually upper tract deterioration

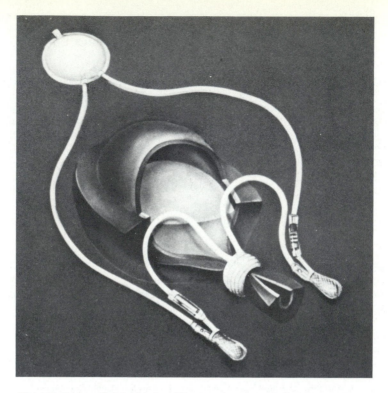

Fig. 5-7. Scott artificial sphincter. (Courtesy American Medical Systems, Inc.)

not reversible by lower tract manipulation, uncontrollable infection, persistent incontinence, with all management attempts failing, and persistent vesicoureteral reflux. Reflux has been successfully managed by transureteroureterostomy and/or reimplantation. Early temporary vesicostomy has been discussed earlier. Ureterostomy has been complicated by stomal stenosis, upper tract deterioration, and difficulty fitting appliances.[13,92] It has been successful with grossly dilated ureters and as a temporizing procedure.

There seems to be an increased incidence of progressive upper tract changes as the child grows older. The higher the neurological lesion, the greater seems to be the chance of upper tract change. Mebust and co-workers[63] found IVP deterioration by age 6 in 18% of males and 41% of females. The majority of IVP changes seem to occur in the first 4 years.[12,84] With this high incidence of upper tract deterioration, several researchers have favored urinary diversion at an early age, before upper tract deterioration has taken place.[12,13,25,84] Smith[83]

reported that 95% of IVPs remain normal if diversion is done before deterioration occurs, but if there is already deterioration, only 15% are improved by diversion. Shapiro and colleagues[78] found 76% of renal units improved or remained stable after diversion. The longer children with ileal loops are followed the greater the complication rate.[67,78] Two thirds of ileal loops subsequently require operative revision[78] (Figs. 5-8 and 5-9). Middleton and Hendren[67] found renal deterioration in 77% of children with ileal loops and a complication rate of 51% to 60%. Because of this high complication rate and renal deterioration, many have switched to making nonrefluxing colon conduits.[67,92] This seems to protect the kidney, but long-term follow-up has not been as extensively reported as it has for ileal loops (Fig. 5-10). Ileal loops or colon conduits must be followed by yearly IVPs for the rest of the patient's life.[78] A loopogram is useful only to help define the cause and location of deterioration. Loop urine cultures should be taken every 3 to 6 months and infection treated ap-

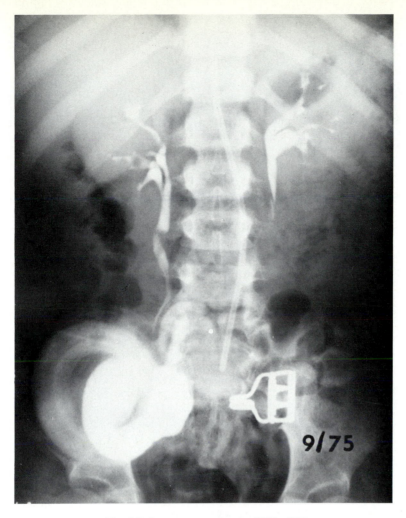

Fig. 5-8. Intravenous pyelogram (IVP), 1975.

propriately. The residual urine should be measured, and any increase over the normal 5 ml should be cause for further investigation. The culture must not be obtained from the bag. The culture is best obtained by a double-loop catheter technique.[85] The stoma should be prepped and draped as for urethral catheterization. A 14 or 16 Fr red rubber catheter is cut off and the proximal portion inserted just into the stoma. Through this a 5 or 8 Fr pediatric feeding tube is advanced into the loop and urine is obtained. Commercially prepared double-lumen catheters are available. This method has decreased the number of false-positive cultures by more than 20%.

Children who have undergone diversion oc-

casionally develop a purulent bladder discharge with or without fever. This may occur in up to 20% and is usually treated by daily bladder irrigations with 0.5% neomycin solution for 1 week.

Nearly one third of the children with ileal loops have had diversion only because of urinary incontinence.[12,14] In some of these children it may be possible to restore continence with pharmacological agents, intermittent catheterization, or the artificial sphincter. There have been several encouraging reports on undiversion.[14,33] It is imperative that these children have extensive reevaluation of their bladder function and that continence be established prior to undiversion.

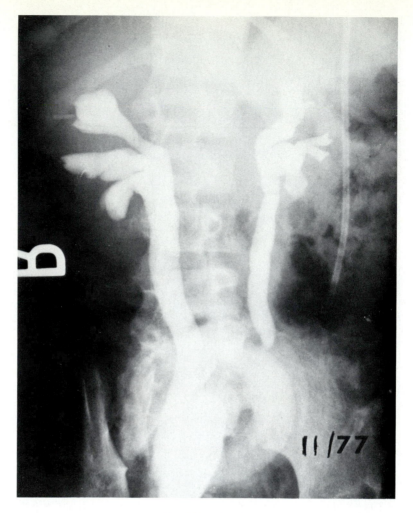

Fig. 5-9. IVP, 1977.

Bowel management

Control of the myelodysplastic child's bow-
els assumes increasing importance as he approaches school age. Surprisingly little has been
written about bowel management in these children.[92] Our goal is to establish fecal continence;
free from soiling, but with relatively regular
bowel evacuation. The urinary and rectal
sphincter have a common innervation (S2,S3,
S4), and therefore abnormalities in one are usually reflected in the other. Often sensation is
diminished or absent if rectal tone is lax. We
try to establish a management program relatively early. In the infant who retains stool
the bowel may often be evacuated with use of
bladder Credé maneuver, manual expression,

or by flexing the hips and compressing the
abdomen. At about age 2 to 2½ we attempt
to establish a regular program of bowel emptying. This should occur about the same time
every day and be compatible with the daily
activities of the child and his family. In general,
we begin by placing a glycerin suppository
against the rectal mucosa about 20 minutes after
dinner. About 30 minutes later we have the
child sit on the toilet, bear down, and try to
evacuate. If this is unsuccessful we may go to
half a Dulcolax suppository or even a pediatric
Fleet enema until a routine is established. Oral
agents are generally less predictable and less
satisfactory.

With the aid of a dietician the stool consis-

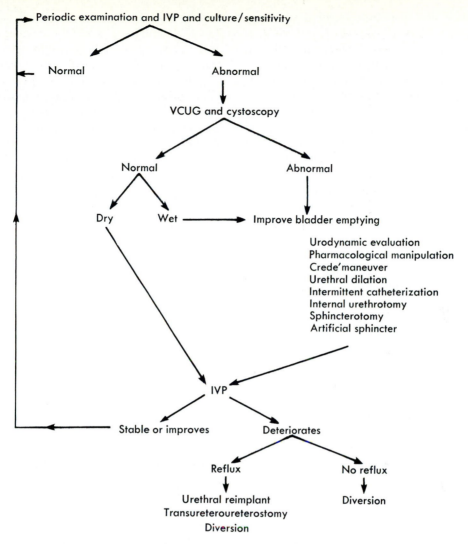

Fig. 5-10. Urological evaluation and management.

tency is changed by diet to keep it bulky but not hard. Brans, cereals, and fresh vegetables have been most useful. Usually we are able to establish an individual program that works to keep the child from soiling yet evacuating adequately.

Some mention should also be made of the problem of *obesity* in children with myelodysplasia. Too often there is a gradual excessive weight gain contributed to by relative inactivity that is not balanced by a reduction in calories. Coordination of total caloric needs with foods that help control stool consistency can result in appropriate weight and bowel control.

Orthopedic management

The second stage in orthopedic management begins with the second 6 months of the child's life. As noted previously, the initial neonatal and early infancy management is primarily nonoperative, with stretching and splinting used to improve and maintain skeletal alignment and flexibility. The second stage is that in which any additional measures are added to make it possible for the child to propel himself from place to place and to enable him to achieve the upright position. Sitting is the first step in this sequence, and most children will acquire some independent sitting balance by 6 to 9 months of age. For those children with very high levels of paralysis, which include their trunk musculature, modifications may have to be made. Some external adaptation in their sitting chairs and wheelchairs or other devices to help prop them up may be necessary.

By the end of the second 6 months, or near their first year, some prone mobility is a great advantage that enables the child to move about the floor and extend his environment. There are several prone mobility devices on wheels that enable the child to move about using his arms.[40] This is preferable to having the child just pull his legs along by his arms, since friction on anesthetic knees and feet may result in troublesome skin breakdown and ulceration.

The next major effort is to achieve the full upright or standing position. This may require what appears to some to be unnecessarily heroic measures in children who may not ultimately be community ambulators, but the advantages to the child of a new perspective with the potential to decrease urinary stasis and reduce bone atrophy far outweigh the effort involved. A successful standing program may require major external support for the child, with the specific measures individualized to the child.[48] Those children with high levels of paralysis are usually fitted with a standing frame, which provides stabilization of feet, ankles, knees, hips, pelvis, and trunk. Those with a lower level of deficit may be able to stand with lesser devices, but if there is any question about the ability to stabilize an area, it is preferable to "overbrace" rather than to provide insufficient external support. This is especially true in these children, who often have an impairment in proprioception and decreased feedback from their lower extremities, increasing the problems of balance. The external support must be rigid enough to enable the child to stand without having to use his hands for balance or support, since an important objective is freeing the arms and hands for other activities.

When head control has developed and standing is the immediate goal, consideration must be given to the specific bracing requirements of the individual child. Those with high levels of paralysis and without control of their trunk musculature will need an external trunk support. This is either a fixed part of the standing device or occasionally a removable rigid outer jacket that in turn can be secured to the frame. This may be necessary in those children with an early spinal deformity such as scoliosis, who use the jacket not only when they are standing. These measures should make it possible to provide a stable trunk over the pelvis.

Some pelvic stability is also often necessary and can be provided by a pelvic band attached to the leg portion of braces or the lower part of a standing frame. It should be possible to get the hips to a neutral position in all planes, that is no flexion deformity, no abduction or adduction contracture, and neutral rotations, so that the brace can then hold the hips in the "normal" standing position. If passive stretching, positioning, and splinting have not succeeded in obtaining this position in the first year of life, it may be necessary to do muscle or tendon release, lengthenings, or transfer at this time to make bracing possible.[65] One common problem is an imbalance between the stronger hip flexors and adductors and the weaker hip extensors and abductors.[79] This may result in a paralytic dislocation of the hip, secondary to the muscular imbalance. It may be necessary to release or transfer[51] the adductors as well as release or transfer the iliopsoas, the strongest hip flexor, to the greater trochanter.[79] There is some question as to whether the hips have to be located at this time, or whether it is more important to be sure that they are supple and symmetrical, even if they are dislocated.[3,24,50] There is no question, however, that a supple, painless hip is preferable to one which is stiff in extension, thereby making sitting difficult or impossible.[81]

The lowest portion of the standing device is the part most commonly used. It usually includes some means of holding the knees in extension and the feet and ankles in a stable plantigrade position. It must be possible to get the knees into virtually complete extension for bracing to be feasible. This can usually be accomplished by passive stretching, but may require surgical release at this time. The feet may also have to be operated on to achieve a plantigrade position, enabling the supported body weight to be born on as broad a surface as possible.

During the stage of fitting a brace and its initial application and use, it is particularly important that the parents and therapists observe the skin carefully and repeatedly to ensure that no skin breakdown or irritation develops in anesthetic areas. There should be a graduated protocol for brace use, increasing the time in the brace by small increments. No brace should be left on for more than 15 to 20 minutes the first time it is applied.

There are currently available a large number of different standing devices used to support the myelodysplastic child.[48,70] They share common features of a broad base and stabilizing components for whatever joints are paralyzed and require support. The specific brace used is less important than that the physician, therapist, and orthotist are familiar with its indications, fabrication, and application and can effectively instruct the family in its use.

Later, as tolerance and balance develop, the addition of hinges makes it possible to sit with the brace on, and later still, the leg portions can be released to make ambulation possible. Obviously those children with low levels of paralysis and strong functioning muscles around the hips and knees will require much less bracing, and those with good control of ankles and feet may not require any at all.

We try to have all our children standing by 18 to 24 months of age. The period from 9 to 18 months can therefore be a busy one with hospitalizations to surgically correct any deformities that have not been passively corrected by this time. Generally we try to minimize the period of immobilization after orthopedic procedures and to accomplish as much as possible with one operation. The difficulties of anesthetic skin and osteoporotic, easily fractured bones preclude long periods in casts and repeated, staged surgical procedures.

There is a wide variety of orthopedic surgical procedures available for these children. Each child must be considered individually in planning and carrying out the operations, since each child has specific deformities and needs.

Many good texts are now available about orthopedic management, and the reader is encouraged to consult them for more detailed information.*

Some general guidelines do exist, however, when considering surgical management. Balanced control of a supple joint is the ideal, and many procedures are designed to achieve this goal. The removal or transfer of deforming forces is a common denominator of many operations, as are soft tissue releases to achieve an increased arc of joint motion or to make possible a plantigrade foot. Joint fusions are not generally recommended to correct deformity, but corrective bone osteotomies are often advised.[55]

Fractures, unfortunately, are a common problem in children with myelodysplasia. These can occur with a minimum of trauma, are often seen when children come out of casts, and may be unrecognized if they occur in an anesthetic area. The common clinical presentation of localized warmth and swelling, systemic fever, and leucocytosis may make the differentiation between bone infection and fracture difficult, but the x-ray results are usually diagnostic. To prevent recurrence, a minimal period of immobilization after fracture is recommended, with the least possible external fixation device. If the alignment of the fracture can be easily maintained, it may even be possible to use the braces that the child already has rather than making a plaster cast. Most fractures will heal relatively quickly, and the early resumption of weight-bearing is encouraged as soon as fracture stability has been achieved.

Spinal deformities—scoliosis, kyphosis, lordosis, or a combination—are some of the most difficult management problems in myelodysplasia and are all too common. They may be secondary to the basic posterior bony defect, to an associated congenital anomaly, to muscular imbalance, or to other causes. Some deformities, especially kyphosis, may be apparent at birth and require immediate surgical correction at the time of closure of the defect. Others develop as the child grows and require treat-

---

*See references 2, 8, 11, 28, 61, 64, and 86.

ment then. Repeated clinical and x-ray examinations are necessary to detect the deformity early and to institute treatment. Bracing of the spine is much more difficult in myelodysplastic children than it is in others because of anesthetic skin and lack of voluntary muscle control, but can usually be accomplished successfully.[9] Plastic body jackets are used more often than other devices and require a skilled orthotist and compulsive parents. These should be considered holding devices, whose use can prevent the development of significant curves, rather than correcting devices, whose use can return the spine to a normal alignment.[10] Regular clinical and roentgenographic assessment of the spine must be made to follow the progress of the spinal deformities. If significant worsening occurs and the external supports are no longer successful in holding the curvature, then consideration must be given to spinal fusion. This should best be delayed as long as possible to permit continuing growth of the spine to occur, but may be necessary before skeletal maturity if the deformity is not manageable by nonoperative means.

The goal of surgical management of the myelodysplastic spine is to have a vertical trunk that is stable over a level pelvis. This can be complex and difficult surgery, with many potential intraoperative and postoperative complications. If there is a major defect in the bony elements of the posterior spine because of the myelomeningocele, it may not be possible to do a standard posterior fusion. The responsible surgeon must be able to perform whatever procedure or combination of procedures that is necessary to maximally correct the deformity and to maintain the correction. This may require an anterior as well as a posterior fusion, with or without internal stabilizing instrumentation.[10] The postoperative management is also very important and ideally permits the child to return to his preoperative level of activity as soon as possible.

MANAGEMENT IN ADOLESCENCE
Neurosurgical management

In the absence of any acute problems that necessitate emergency evaluation and management, yearly neurosurgical assessment is made.

Shunt management is the same as that described for childhood, and elective revision for growth is usually not necessary after age 12. There are, however, several specific conditions that may develop and require treatment. Decompensation related to the Arnold-Chiari malformation may occur. In late childhood and adolescence further constriction of hindbrain elements and/or progressive hydromyelia may superimpose a progressive spasticity of legs on the flaccid lower motor neuron paraparesis of the primary spinal lesion, or a lower motor neuron weakness of the upper extremities may develop.[32] Another potential problem is delayed onset of hydrocephalus, which is rare in adolescence but may develop and be manifest as disturbances in school performance, gait, or handwriting and chronic headache as the symptoms, with papilledema the only clinical sign.

An additional set of problems may develop associated with a slow decompensation of function of the cauda equina. Tethering of the conus may occur with spina bifida occulta or meningocele and may be associated with the adolescent onset of scoliosis or a lumbosacral radiculopathy. A lipoma of the cauda equina may occur with spina bifida occulta and present with a delayed polyradiculopathy. A lipomyelomeningocele usually does not increase in size (other than relatively) with advancing age. The outer third can be removed for cosmetic reasons without much risk of severing the nerve radicles that course through the lipoma, but extensive resection, even with the use of an operating microscope, does run this risk. Some decompensation in lumbar or sacral root function is not unusual in adolescents with lipomyelomeningocele. However, patients with resected and closed myeloschisis or myelocele usually do not develop neural decompensation in late childhood or adolescence.

Urological management

Most of the specifics of urological management defined in the section for childhood (pp. 125 to 135) pertain to the adolescent as well. Regular urological reevaluations are made on an annual basis in the absence of acute problems. In a stable situation urine is cultured annually and the IVP repeated every 2 years. Blood pressure is measured at each visit because of the incidence of hypertension described earlier.

One other area of concern that develops in late childhood and adolescence has heretofore received little attention. This is the question of sexual function in the patient with a myelomeningocele. With the increased longevity of these patients, sexuality is a subject that is going to be approached more frequently. Since the innervation of the genitalia is the same as that of the bladder and sphincters, sexual function in the patient with neurogenic bladder is usually abnormal.[92] Erection may be partial, and in some cases not sustained. Orgasm resulting from emotional stimuli may be possible, although, because of the lack of genital sensation, excitation and orgasm by direct stimulation may not be possible. With orgasm there may be failure of ejaculation due to abnormal sympathetic innervation or retrograde ejaculation due to an open bladder neck. Women may undergo normal labor and delivery, and caesarean section should be reserved for the usual obstetrical indications.[23]

It is the responsibility of some member of the team caring for the patient with a myelomeningocele to be knowledgeable, approachable, and sympathetic to the sexual needs of these patients. This responsibility usually is that of the urologist, and there are currently available several references to assist in the management of this aspect of their care.[15,68,88]

Orthopedic management

Management of the orthopedic aspects of the care of a myelomeningocele patient is the same continuum as that described for the neurosurgical and urological aspects. Periodic evaluation of the functional capacity and specific motion and muscular control of the joints in the legs is mandatory to detect and correct any problems that may arise. This is particularly true for spinal deformities.

With the completion of skeletal growth, it may be necessary to perform corrective surgery for any deformities that have developed during childhood. These can be due to any of the causes noted earlier, with persistent muscular imbalance and postural asymmetry being the usual causes. Bony procedures are more often performed during this period to provide a "final" correction, with growth now no longer a factor in recurrent deformity. Angular and rotational osteotomies as well as spine fusions fall within this group of surgical options.

Another aspect of the stability that occurs with skeletal maturity is that of final brace determination. If the initial prescription has a tendency to "overbrace" as described earlier and the patient has a clearly established ability to be functional without all components of the bracing, at this time it is reasonable to remove or modify any components that are clearly no longer necessary. Deterioration in specific muscular function during late childhood and adolescence is unusual, and should it occur a careful search for those entities described in the neurosurgical section (pp. 124 and 140) must be made.

One additional change that may occur in early adolescence also relates to the maturity of this period. A number of children who have previously been household or exercise ambulators will become wheelchair ambulators about age 13. This change has been well described[40] and probably relates to the increased energy necessary for walking because of the increased height and weight as well as the increasing acceptability of a wheelchair by the adolescent's peers. This change, especially among those with high levels of nerve involvement, should not, however, be interpreted as a condemnation of the earlier efforts to achieve the standing and walking positions, with all that they may require. The advantages of a maximum effort have already been described and clearly outweigh the expenditure it involves.

THE ROLE OF THE PRIMARY CARE PHYSICIAN

The child with myelodysplasia presents a series of complex problems in management from the day of birth through childhood and adolescence to adulthood. Recent advances in the specific areas of management—neurosurgical, urological, orthopedic, and orthotic—have succeeded in extending and improving the lives of these children, the majority of whom should now become functional in society.

The responsibility for ensuring that a maximal level of function is achieved must be shared by many. The family is of obvious importance, and they must have an understanding of the problems and a willingness to participate in the daily aspects of care. We believe that this understanding and guidance for the family can come from a coordinated, comprehensive multidisciplinary clinic, both directly and through the close involvement of the child's primary physician.

The complexity of the treatment process and the developmental needs of the youngster with myelodysplasia requires ongoing coordination of care by the primary care physician. Although the multispeciality clinic offers effective, comprehensive medical care, it cannot deal with the day-to-day problems and routine illnesses that confront families of children with complex disabilities. This concept is repeatedly presented throughout the text (Chapters 1, 8, and 17; however, few disabilities involve as many organ systems that require such intensive ongoing medical supervision and simultaneously require ethical decisions, everchanging rehabilitative program, and emotional support.

If the primary care physician is to function as a coordinator and serve as a resource for decision making in counselling, the physician should have the following:

- A willingness to provide traditional health care to the child
- A basic knowledge concerning the care and rehabilitation of the youngster with myelodysplasia, including the nature of the disability and its functional implications, the signs and symptoms associated with neurological, urological, and orthopedic complications, and the emotional and ethical issues which involve the child and the family
- An awareness of community resources that provide intervention for the child and support and education for the parents
- A knowledge of the developmental issues that impact on the education and vocational capabilities of the youngster

Community, school, and parents' groups are important resources and must be included in the total care plan. The complementary efforts of all these individuals and groups are necessary to continue the progress that has been made during the past two decades in the care of the myelodysplastic child.

REFERENCES

1. Alter, M.: Anencephalus, hydrocephalus and spina bifida, Arch. Neurol. **7:**411, 1962.
2. American Academy of Orthopaedic Surgeons: Symposium on myelomeningocele, St. Louis, 1972, The C. V. Mosby Co.
3. Barden, G. A., Meyer, L. C., and Stelling, F. H., III: Myelodysplastics—fate of those followed for twenty years or more, J. Bone Joint Surg. **57A:**643, 1975.
4. Bauer, S. B., et al.: Urodynamic evaluation of boy with myelodysplasia and incontinence, Urology **10:**354, 1977.
5. Bluestone, C. D., Delerme, A. N., and Samuelson, G. S.: Airway obstruction due to vocal cord paralysis in infants with hydrocephalus and meningomyelocele, Ann. Otol. Rhinol. Laryngol. **81:**778, 1972.
6. Brock, D. J. H., and Sutcliffe, R. G.: Alpha-fetoprotein in the antenatal diagnosis of anencephaly and spina bifida, Lancet **2:**197, 1972.
7. Brock, D. J. H., Bolton, A. E., and Monaghan, J. M.: Prenatal diagnosis of anencephaly through serum alpha-fetoprotein measurement, Lancet **2:**923, 1973.
8. Brocklehurst, G., editor: Spina bifida for the clinician, Clin. Dev. Med. **57:**0, 1976.
9. Bunch, W. H.: The Milwaukee brace in paralytic scoliosis, Clin. Orthop. **110:**63, 1975.
10. Bunch, W. H.: Myelomeningocele. In Lovell, W. W. and Winter. R. B., editors: Pediatric orthopaedics, 1978, J. B. Lippincott Co., p. 395.
11. Bunch, W. H., et al: Modern management of myelomeningocele, St. Louis, 1972, Warren H. Green, Inc.
12. Cass, A. S.: Urinary tract complications in myelomeningocele patients, J. Urol. **115:**102, 1976.
13. Cass, A. S.: Urinary diversion for neurogenic bladder in children, J. Urol. **115:**314, 1976.
14. Colodny, A. H.: Evaluation and management of infants and children with neurogenic bladder, Radiol. Clin. North Am. **15:**71, 1977.
15. Comarr, A. E.: Neurological disturbances of sexual function among patients with myelodysplasia. In McLaurin, R. L., editor: Myelomeningocele. New York, 1977, Grune & Stratton, Inc., p. 797.
16. Culp, D. A., Khrab, A., and Flocks, R. H.: Urologic management of the meningocele patient, J.A.M.A. **213:**753, 1970.
17. Davidson, R. I.: Peritoneal bypass in the treatment of hydrocephalus: historical review and abdominal complications, J. Neurol. Neurosurg. Psychiatry **39:**640, 1976.
18. DeSouza, L. J., and Carroll, N.: Ambulation of the braced myelomeningocele patient, J. Bone Joint Surg. **58A:**112, 1976.

19. Diokno, A. C., and Taub, M. E.: Experience with the artificial urinary sphincter at Michigan, J. Urol. **116:**496,1976.

20. Duckett, J. W.: Cutaneous vesicostomy in childhood, Urol. Clin. North Am. **1:**485, 1974.

21. Eckstein, H. B., and MacNab, G. H.: Myelomeningocele and hydrocephalus: the importance of moderate treatment, Lancet, p. 842, April 16, 1966.

22. Edvardson, P., and Setakleiv, J.: Distribution of adronergic receptors in the urinary bladder of cats, rabbits and guinea pigs, Acta Pharmacol. Toxicol. **26:**437, 1968.

23. Ellison, F. V.: Term pregnancy in a patient with myelomeningocele, uretero-iliostomy and partial paraparesis, Am. J. Obstet. Gynecol. **143:**33, 1975.

24. Feiwell, E.: Conservative treatment of hip dislocation in myelomeningocele. In McLaurin, R. L., editor: Myelomeningocele, New York, 1977, Grune & Stratton, Inc., p. 513.

25. Ferguson, D. E., and Geist, R. W.: Pre-school urinary tract diversion for children with neurogenic bladder from myelomeningocele, J. Urol. **105:**133, 1971.

26. Fitzsimmons, J. S.: Laryngeal stridor and respiratory obstruction associated with myelomeningocele, Dev. Med. Child Neurol. **15:**533, 1973.

27. Forrest, D. M., et al.: Complications of ventriculoatrial shunts. A review of 455 cases, J. Neurosurg. **29:**506, 1969.

28. Freeman, J. M., editor: Practical management of meningomyelocele, Baltimore, 1974, University Park Press.

29. Gillenwater, J. Y., et al.: Home urine cultures by the Dip-strip method: results in 289 cultures, Pediatrics **58:**508, 1976.

30. Goven, W. F., et al.: Management of Children with urinary tract infections, Urology **6:**273, 1975.

31. Guthkelch, A. N.: The indications and contraindications for early operation in myelomeningocele. In Morley, T. P., editor: Current controversies in neurosurgery, Philadelphia, 1976, W. B. Saunders Co.

32. Hall. P. V., Campbell, R. L., and Kalsbeck, J. E.: Meningomyelocele and progressive hydromyelia, J. Neurosurg. **43:**457, 1975.

33. Hendren, W. H.: Urinary tract refunctionalization after prior diversion in children, Ann. Surg. **180:**494, 1974.

34. Hoffer, M. M., et al.: Functional ambulation in patients with myelomeningocele, J. Bone Joint Surg. **55A:**137, 1973.

35. Holmes, L. B., Driscoll, S. G., and Atkins, L.: Etiologic heterogeneity of neural tube defects, N. Engl. J. Med. **294:**365, 1976.

36. Huff, C. W., and Ramsey, P. L.: Myelodysplasia. The influence of the quadriceps and hip abductor muscles on ambulatory function and stability of the hip, J. Bone Joint Surg. **60A:**432, 1978.

37. Janerich, D. T., and Piper, J.: Shifting genetic patterns in anencephaly and spina bifida, J. Med. Genet. **15:**101, 1978.

38. Jeffs, R. D., Jonas, P., and Schillinger, J. F.: Surgical correction of vesicoureteral reflux in children with neurogenic bladder, J. Urol. **115:**449, 1976.

39. Khanna, O. P.: Disorders of micturition, Urology **8:**316, 1976.

40. Kopits, S. E.: Orthopedic aspects of meningomyeloceles. In Freeman, J. M., editor: Practical management of meningomyelocele, Baltimore, 1974, University Park Press.

41. Kunin, C. M. Detection, prevention, and management of urinary tract infection, Philadelphia, 1972, Lea and Febiger.

42. Lapides, J., et al.: Clean intermittent self-catheterization in the treatment of urinary tract disease, J. Urol. **107:108:**458, 1972.

43. Lapides, J., et al.: Follow-up on unsterile intermittent self-catheterization, J. Urol. **111:**184, 1974.

44. Lapides, J. et al.: Further observations on self-catheterization, J. Urol. **116:**169, 1976.

45. Lebowitz, R. L., and Colodny, A. H.: Comments on urology section on myelomeningocele, Pediatrics **58:** 297, 1976.

46. Lebowitz, R. L., Hopkins, T., and Colodny, A. H. Measuring the kidneys using a renal growth and hypertrophy chart, Pediatr. Radiol. **4:**37, 1975.

47. Lemire, R. J., et al: Normal and abnormal development of the human nervous system, chapters 1 to 5, 1975, New York, Harper & Row, Publishers.

48. Letts, R. M., Fulford, R., and Hobson, D. A.: Mobility aids for the paraplegic child, J. Bone Joint Surg. **58A:**38, 1976.

49. Levitt, S. B., and Sandler, H. J.: The absence of vesicoureteral reflux in the neonate with myelodysplasia, J. Urol. **114:**118, 1975.

50. Lindseth, R. E.: Treatment of the lower extremity in children paralyzed by myelomeningocele. In AAOS instructional course lectures vol. XXV, St. Louis, 1976, The C. V. Mosby Co.

51. London, J. T., and Nichols, O.: Paralytic dislocation of the hip in myelodysplasia, J. Bone Joint Surg. **57A:**501, 1975.

52. Lorber, J.: Results of treatment of myelomeningocele, Dev. Med. Child Neurol. **13:279,** 1971.

53. Lorber, J.: Spina bifida cystica: results of treatment of 270 consecutive cases with criteria for selection for the future, Arch. Dis. Child. **47:**845, 1972.

54. Lyon, R. P., Scott, M. P., and Marshall, S.: Intermittent catheterization rather than urinary diversion in children with meningomyelocele, J. Urol. **113:** 409, 1975.

55. MacEwen, G. S., and Connally, T. F.: The lower extremity in myelomeningocele. In American Academy of Orthopedic Surgeons: Symposium on myelomeningocele, St. Louis, 1972, The C. V. Mosby Co., p. 174.

56. MacMahon, B., Pugh, T. F., and Ingalls, T. H.: Anencephalus, spina bifida and hydrocephalus. Incidence related to sex, race and season of birth, and incidence in siblings, Br. J. Prev. Soc. Med. **7:**211, 1953.

57. Magnus, R. V.: Vesicoureteral reflux in babies with myelomeningocele, J. Urol. **114:**122, 1975.
58. Malkin, R. B., Schellhammer, P. F., and Hackler, R. H.: Experience with transureteroureterostomy in the paraplegic patient with irreversible vesicoureteral reflux, J. Urol. **112:**181, 1974.
59. Matson, D. D.: Surgical treatment of myelomeningocele, Pediatrics **42:**225, 1968,
60. Matson, D. D.: Neurosurgery of infancy and childhood, part I, chapter 1, Springfield, Ill., 1969, Charles C Thomas, Publisher.
61. McLaurin, R. L.: Myelomeningocele, New York, 1977, Grune & Stratton, Inc.
62. McLennan, J. E.: Rib anomalies in myelodysplasia—an approach to embryogenic inference, Biol. Neonate **29:**129, 1976.
63. Mebust, W. K., Foret, J. D., and Valk, W. L.: Fifteen years of experience with urinary diversion in myelomeningocele patient, J. Urol. **101:**177, 1969.
64. Menalaus, M. B.: The Orthopaedic management of spina bifida cystica, London, 1971, E. & S. Livingstone.
65. Menalaus, M. B.: The hip in myelomeningocele, J. Bone Joint Surg. **58B:**448, 1976.
66. Merrill, D. B.: Clinical experience with the Mentor bladder stimulator for myelomeningocele patients. J. Urol. **112:**823, 1974.
67. Middleton, A. W., and Hendren, W. H.: Ileal conduits in children at the Massachusetts General Hospital from 1955-1970, J. Urol. **115:**591, 1976.
68. Mondi, T. O., Cole, T. M., and Chilgin, R. A.: Sexual options for paraplegics and quadraplegics, Boston, 1975, Little, Brown & Co.
69. Morrisseau, P. M., and Leadbetter, G. W.: Myelomeningocele and the urologist, J. Urol. **107:**322, 1972.
70. Paul, S. W.: Bracing in myelomeningocele. In American Academy of Orthopaedic Surgeons: Symposium on Myelomeningocele, St. Louis, 1972, The C. V. Mosby Co., p. 219.
71. Pekarovic, E., et al.: Indications for manual expression of the neurogenic bladder in children, Br. J. Urol. **42:**191, 1970.
72. Pyles, C. V., and Eliot, C. R.: Pyuria and bacteriuria in infants and children, Am. J. Dis. Child. **110:**628, 1965.
73. Raezer, D. M., et al.: The functional approach to the management of the pediatric neuropathic bladder: a clinical study, J. Urol. **117:**649, 1977.
74. Report by a working party: Ethics of selective treatment of spina bifida, Lancet **1:**85, 1975.
75. Schoenberg, H. W., et al.: Changing attitudes toward urinary dysfunction in myelodysplasia, J. Urol. **117:**501, 1977.
76. Scott, F. D., Bradley, W. E., and Timm, G. W.: Treatment of urinary incontinence by an implantable prosthetic urinary sphincter, J. Urol. **112:** 75, 1974.
77. Section on urology: Myelomeningocele: Suggested minimal urologic evaluation and surveillance, Pediatrics **56:**477, 1975.
78. Shapiro, S. R., Lebowitz, R. L., and Colodny, A. H. Fate of ninety children with ileal conduit urinary diversion a decade later: analysis of complications, pyelography, renal function and bacteriology, J. Urol. **114:**289, 1975.
79. Sharrard, W. J.: Posterior iliopsoas transplantation in the treatment of paralytic dislocation of the hip, J. Bone Joint Surg. **46B:**427, 1964.
80. Sharrard, W. J., and Grosfield, I.: The management of deformity and paralysis of the foot in myelomeningocele, J. Bone Joint Surg. **50B:**456, 1968.
81. Sherk, H. H., and Ames, M.: Functional results of iliopsoas transfer in myelomeningocele hip dislocations, Clin. Orthop. **137:**181, 1978.
82. Shillito, J., Jr.: Surgical approaches to spina bifida and myelomeningocele, chapter 8, Clin. Neurosurg. **20:**114, 1973.
83. Smith, E. D.: Follow-up studies on 150 ileal conduits in children, J. Pediatr. Surg. **7:**1, 1972.
84. Smith, E. D.: Urinary prognosis in spina bifida, J. Urol. **108:**815, 1972.
85. Spence, B., Stuart, W., and Cass, A. S.: Use of a double lumen catheter to determine bacteriuria in intestinal loop diversions in children, J. Urol. **108:** 800, 1972.
86. Stark, G. D.: Spina bifida. Problems and management, London, 1977, Blackwell Scientific Publ.
87. Stein, S., Schut, L., and Borns, P.: Lacunar skull deformity (Luckenschadel) and intelligence in myelomeningocele, J. Neurosurg. **41:**10, 1974.
88. Stewart, B.: Sex and spina bifida—an outline of sex and sexual relationships for young people and their parents, London, 1978, the Association for Spina Bifida and Hydrocephalus.
89. Tanagho, E. A.: Myelomeningocele: urologic considerations, West. J. Med. **121:**293, 1974.
90. Thompson, M. W., and Rudd, N. L.: The genetics and treatment of spinal dysraphism. In Morley, T. P., editor: Current controversies in neurosurgery, Philadelphia, 1976, W. B. Saunders Co.
91. Wilcock, A. R., and Emery, J. L.: Deformities of the renal tract in children with meningomyelocele and hydrocephalus compared with those of children showing no such central nervous system deformities, Br. J. Urol. **42:**152, 1970.
92. Williams, B. I.: Urology in childhood, New York, 1974, Springer-Verlag New York, Inc.

6

The child with significant developmental motor disability (cerebral palsy)

Israel F. Abroms
Panos G. Panagakos

Medical and neurological aspects

Israel F. Abroms

Significant developmental motor disability is a group of chronic nonprogressive disorders of the brain occurring in infants and young children, producing abnormalities of posture and motor function. The term "significant developmental motor disability" (SDMD) is used in preference to "cerebral palsy."

THE PRIMARY CARE PHYSICIAN'S ROLE

The primary care physician who is knowledgeable and interested in children with developmental disabilities can and should be responsible for major aspects of assessments and the ongoing multifaceted treatment of the child in his care. The primary care physician is the best person to be the overall coordinator of the child's care. Having special knowledge of the child and the family, the physician can help judge the impact of exhaustive tests or potentially painful therapies. The greater the involvement of the primary care physician with the multiply handicapped child, the less the parents and the patient need to move about among different clinics and subspecialists. This physician remains the ombudsman and advocate for the patient; the opinion of the physician regarding the patient's best interests should be heard by all professionals and allied health workers.

CLINICAL CLASSIFICATION

There is some variation in terms and definitions among American,[18,69,75] British,[5,59] and Swedish[48,49] authors in describing SDMD syndromes.

Following is a working classification using terms currently acceptable in the United States. It is traditional to use the suffix -plegia, which is derived from the Greek "plege," meaning a "strike" to the brain, or *paralysis*. In this chapter we will often interchangeably use the suffix-paresis from the Greek "parienai," to let fall, or *weakness*, which is more appropriate in most cases.

A. Spastic syndromes
  1. Hemiplegia: Unilateral paresis—arm affected more than leg (Hagberg classification[48]—spastic hemiplegia).
  2. Bilateral spastic hemiplegia or double hemiplegia[59]: Paresis—usually asymmetrical, involving all four limbs with arms affected more than the legs (Hagberg classification[48]—spastic tetraplegia). This clinical syndrome is rare.
  3. Diplegia: Paresis of both lower limbs with little or no involvement of the arms (Hagberg classification[48]—spastic/ataxic diplegia). Tone may be reduced initially or indefinitely; this would be hypotonic diplegia.
  4. Quadriplegia: Paresis of all four limbs with legs affected more than the arms. (Ingram[59] and Hagberg classifications[48]—spastic/ataxic diplegia). In severe cases hypotonicity predominates initially and sometimes indefinitely.
B. Dyskinetic syndromes: (Crothers and Paine classification[18]—extrapyramidal syndromes). Involuntary movements interfering with activity and function of all four limbs, usually with more disability in the lower limbs than the upper. Involuntary movements can include one or more of the following:
  1. Chorea: Rapid, irregular, unpredictable, spasmodical contractions of individual muscles or small muscle groups of the face, bulbar muscles, and mainly distal parts of the extremities.
  2. Athetosis: Slow, smooth, writhing movements, mostly involving distal musculature with dysnergia of opposing muscle groups, such as flexion and extension or pronation and supination.
  3. Dystonia: Rhythmical, usually sustained changes of tone with twisting distortions of trunk and largely proximal limb musculature.
  4. Ballismus: Wide flinging or jerking movements of the extremity.
C. Ataxic syndromes: Imbalance and incoordination of voluntary movements of the trunk and limb musculature. Lower limbs are usually more involved than upper.
D. Mixed syndromes: These have features of spasticity and dyskinesia, for example, mixed spastic/dyskinetic quadriparesis, mixed spastic/dystonic hemiplegia, and mixed spastic/dystonic diplegia.

INCIDENCE OF SIGNIFICANT DEVELOPMENTAL MOTOR DISABILITY

Prior to 1962, it was estimated that there were between 4.7 and 7.5 cases of SDMD per 1000 live births in the United States.[75] Inherent difficulties remain in conducting large-scale surveys of this group of diseases in this country, since many children are not reported to state or local authorities because of minor signs or for fear of stigmatization. Furthermore, many families cease to seek outside help after some years because of the chronic nature of the disease and the realization that no cure can be anticipated for their child with SDMD. An estimate of the incidence of chronic motor handicapping conditions in children in Great Britain between 1953 and 1967 was 2.41 per 1000 live births and in Sweden between 1954 and 1974, 1.63 per 1000 liveborn infants.[46] Table 6-1 shows the changing prevalence of SDMD in a referral clinic in Boston.

Many recent long-term follow-up studies have involved infants of low birth weight, cared for in neonatal intensive care units.* There is no doubt that the prognosis for normal neurological

*See references 2, 21, 24, 26, 32 to 36, 47, 50, 52, 67, 73, 78, 82, 86, 89 and 90.

Table 6-1. Changing prevalence of types of significant developmental motor disability in a referral clinic

Type of disability	Crothers and Paine (1959)[18]		Abroms (1969 to 1972)	
	Number	Percentage	Number	Percentage
Spasticity				
Monoplegia	2	0.4	2	1.2
Hemiplegia	189	40.3	30	17.6
Quadriplegia	89	19.0	59	34.7
Paraplegia (diplegia)	13	2.8	49	28.8
Triplegia	9	1.9	3	1.8
Dyskinesia	103	22.0	0	0
Mixed types	61	13.0	4	2.4
SDMD plus cord injury	3	0.6	0	0
Others	0	0	23*	13.5
TOTAL	469	100	170	100

*Twenty-three additional cases were evaluated during this time. Eight had mild coordination difficulties suggesting "minimal brain dysfunction"; 1 had learning difficulties alone; 6 had hydrocephalus; 3 had mental retardation without motor disabilities; 1 had a brain tumor; 1 had muscular dystrophy; 1 had dystonia musculorum deformans; and 2 children were normal.

Table 6-2. Disposition at early school age of infants of 1.35 kg and under at birth*

Disposition	Cohort born between 1950-1954	Cohort born between 1955-1959	Cohort born between 1966-1970
Normal school			
Class for age	14%	25%	70%
Educationally slow	39%	41%	17%
Special school			
Physically and/or mentally handicapped	33%	31%	9%
Ineducable	14%	3%	4%
Number of cases	43	32	57

*From Drillien, C.: A longitudinal study of low birth-weight infants. Presented at the Symposium on Perinatal Factors and Developmental Disabilities, May 17, 1978, The University of Massachusetts Medical Center, Worcester, Mass.

development for low birth weight infants weighing over 1200 to 1500 has improved dramatically in the last two decades.

Drillien[26] has shown that the percentage of children in normal schools at age 7 who as infants weighed 1367 g or less at birth in the same Edinburgh maternity unit rose from 14% from 1950 to 1954 to 70% in those born between 1966 and 1970 (Table 6-2).

In Sweden, Hagberg and co-workers[49] (Table 6-3) have been able to document a statistically significant reduction in the incidence of cerebral palsy between 1954 and 1970, but not between 1971 and 1974. Between 1954 and 1958 the incidence was 2.2%, whereas from 1966 to 1970 this dropped to 1.3%. This improved picture is mainly due to the decrease in the number of cases of spastic diplegia (called spastic/ataxic diplegia by these researchers) associated with low birth weight.[32,46-52,90] Other workers have also reported significant decreases in the incidence of major motor neurological handicaps in their follow-up studies of premature infants.*

Choreoathetosis and dystonic forms of SDMD are still seen. In the Swedish survey (called dyskinetic syndromes) they constituted

*See references 21, 33, 35, 67, 73 and 78.

Table 6-3. Relative frequency of types of significant developmental motor disability in southwest Sweden by date of birth*

Type of disability	1959 to 1962	1963 to 1966	1967 to 1970
Spastic hemiplegia	28%	38%	41%
Spastic bilateral hemiplegia	4%	1%	5%
Spastic diplegia and quadriplegia	46%	35%	31%
Ataxic syndromes	6%	8%	12%
Dyskinetic syndromes	16%	18%	11%
Number of cases	172	182	141
Incidence per 1000 live births	1.89	1.67	1.34

*Modified from Hagberg, B., Hagberg, G., and Olow, I.: Acta Paediatr. Scand. **64:**193, 1975.

between 10% and 15% of the series. Perinatal asphyxia accounted for the majority of these cases. Since 1962, kernicterus due to hyperbilirubinemia as a cause of SDMD has been virtually eliminated.[46,49]

ETIOLOGY OF SIGNIFICANT DEVELOPMENTAL MOTOR DISABILITY

Hemiplegia. The majority of hemiplegia cases are ''congenital'' and are due to prenatal or perinatal causes,[27] such as maternal threatened abortion, toxemia of pregnancy, multiple pregnancy, maternal infection, abruptio placentae, abnormal presentation of the fetus, intrapartum hypoxia, intracranial hemorrhage, and exchange transfusion. Perhaps 10% of cases are ''acquired'' hemiplegia and are due to viral or bacterial meningoencephalitis, head trauma (automobile accidents, battered child syndrome), or cerebrovascular occlusions or are associated with fever and seizures. In many patients no causative factors can be ascertained. Hagberg[49] estimated that in 30% of the cases the cause is unknown (Table 6-4).

Bilateral hemiplegia. Many patients with bilateral hemiplegia have had severe perinatal hypoxia, maternal infections, intrauterine growth retardation, and cerebral malformations as congenital causes. Etiological factors in the acquired double hemiplegia patients are similar to those listed earlier for the acquired hemiplegia cases.

Spastic diplegia. Prematurity has been implicated in as high as 70% of the cases,[6] but overall, this form of SDMD seems less common in recent follow-up surveys of both true pre-mature infants and small for gestational age infants.[16,32,90] Intrauterine fetal infections, hypoxia,[27] hypothermia,[21] and perhaps nutritional factors can produce a spastic diplegia syndrome with damage to the most medial motor fibers in the white matter lateral to both lateral ventricles.[3,14] Furthermore, the use of computerized tomography (CT) scans in the newborn infant has revealed moderate ventricular dilation as a frequent sequela in those premature infants surviving intraventricular hemorrhage.[64,95] This may occur without an initial increase in head circumference.[63] Prolonged ventilation may be a causative factor.[85]

Spastic quadriparesis. Prenatal and perinatal factors predominate, particularly hypoxic-ischemic encephalopathy,[11,27,85] congenital fetal infections,[43,53] and cerebral dysgenesis,[60,66,77,96] and in premature infants, intraventricular hemorrhage.[64,95] Hydrocephalus, viral and bacterial meningoencephalitis, and hypoxic-ischemic encephalopathy account for most cases of postnatally acquired spastic quadriplegia.

Dyskinetic quadriparesis. Hypoxic-ischemic encephalopathy occurring during the intrapartum period is now the most common cause of this syndrome. Hyperbilirubinemia is treatable using phototherapy and exchange transfusions.[76] Rhesus factor incompatibility is now preventable using postnatal injections of anti-Rh gamma globulin given to the unsensitized Rh-negative mother after delivery of an Rh-positive infant.

Ataxic quadriparesis. Malformations of the cerebellum and the cerebellar connections are often the cause of this syndrome.[60,66,77,96] Hy-

Table 6-4. Etiology of cerebral palsy in 560 Swedish cases*

Type of disability	Number	Presumed cause			
		Prenatal origin (%)	Perinatal origin (%)	Postnatal origin (%)	Unknown origin (%)
Spastic hemiplegia	200	23	41	6	30
Bilateral hemiplegia	19	42	37	11	10
Spastic diplegia and quadriplegia	217	70	96	6	28
Ataxic forms	44	25	18	16	41
Dyskinetic forms	80	31	130	7	12
TOTAL	560	27	49	7	17

*Modified from Hagberg, B., Hagberg, G., and Olow, I.: Acta Paediatr. Scand. **64:**193, 1975.

poxic-ischemic encephalopathy and postnatal meningoencephalitis will also on occasion produce this nonprogressive syndrome.[84] Autosomal recessive inheritance has been reported.[45,83]

PREVENTION OF SIGNIFICANT DEVELOPMENTAL MOTOR DISABILITY

As suggested earlier, improved antenatal, intrapartum, and postnatal care of the mother and her infant have reduced the incidence of SDMD. Of particular importance have been the following:

1. The establishment of high-risk antenatal clinics where attention is given to teenage pregnancies, maternal nutrition, alcohol consumption, smoking, maternal Rh sensitization, diabetes and kidney disease, etc. In these referral centers the intrauterine growth and well-being of the infant can be closely followed by assessing placental function and ultrasound measurements of biparietal diameter of the fetus, lecithin/sphingomyelin ratio in amniotic fluid, and (under certain circumstances) by fetoscopy

2. Regionalization of maternal delivery services[1,62] with the capability of transporting women in labor to obstetrical units with more sophisticated services

3. The use of intrapartum electronic monitoring devices and the appropriate interpretation of their findings

4. More cautious use of intrapartum analgesics and anaesthetics

5. The judicious use of cesarean sections for fetal distress and abnormal presentations (especially breech)

6. The regionalization of neonatal intensive care units with expeditious transport systems for the desperately ill newborn infant

7. The improved expertise of staff in neonatal intensive care units and improved ventilation techniques with dramatic reduction in perinatal mortality related to pulmonary disease

8. The prevention and appropriate treatment of neonatal hemolytic disease

9. The improved management of neonatal and childhood sepsis and meningitis, immunization programs in infancy, and the lead poisoning prevention and treatment programs, which collectively reduce the incidence of acquired brain damage and the resulting significant motor disability

EARLY DIAGNOSIS OF SIGNIFICANT DEVELOPMENTAL MOTOR DISABILITY

The diagnosis of SDMD can be made in an infant under 3 to 6 months of age in the presence of a significant motor delay.[9,25,57,93] This requires a good working knowledge of the motor milestones of infancy and the range of variation, together with an understanding of the appearance and disappearance of primitive reflexes.[68,72,92] In early hypotonic quadriparesis, the infant's head control will be poor for his chronological age. This information can be initially gathered by obtaining a careful history from the parents as to when the infant developed the ability to hold the head in the upright position when sitting on the parent's lap. How and when the infant held his head up in the prone position is noted. These attainments of motor development are checked by the examiner by bringing the infant into the sitting position and then placing him in the prone position. The suspended prone position will show the early acquisition of the Landau reflex. In addition to these maneuvers, the neck tilting response can be checked with the infant in the suspended upright position. This is well developed by 3 to 4 months of age. Details of the neuromaturational examination are found in Chapter 3. The most common manifestation of quadriparesis in the first few months is hypotonia of the neck flexors, trunk, and limbs. However, in severe cases spasticity may begin to appear by 2 or 3 months of age. This will be particularly evident with opisthotonic posturing of the neck with the infant lying on his side, exaggeration of the asymmetrical tonic neck reflex to either side, increased tone in the upper and lower limbs, fisting of the hands, and persistence of ankle clonus bilaterally.

With congenital hemiparesis, asymmetrical reaching will be seen at 4 or 5 months of age; the normal hand will move way over to the opposite side to pick up an interesting toy. In the creeping position the weak arm will not be extended as well as the healthy one, and there will be a tendency to drag the leg on the same side as the weak arm.

In the case of hypotonic diparesis there is a discrepancy between function in the upper and lower limbs; for instance, at 4 or 5 months of age reaching and transferring of objects may be appropriate, although at the same time supporting of the body by the lower limbs has not developed as it should have. The lower limbs simply fold up under the infant if one tries to stand him with support. Later, the infant may learn to sit, but with creeping the arms will pull the trunk and lower limbs along, and weight support on the lower limbs may not occur until the second year.

It is therefore important to be quite critical of a significant overall motor lag, comparing one side with the other as well as upper limb function with lower limb function. Simultaneously, it is necessary to assess the level of cognitive development, early speech sounds, visual interaction, and auditory responses. Poor feeding early in infancy can be an early indicator of bilateral pyramidal or extrapyramidal involvement, which affects chewing, sucking, and swallowing.

A history of very poor adaptation to sleeping through the night, excessive quietness of the baby during waking periods or, alternatively, excessive irritability and inconsolability may point to the diagnosis of cerebral dysfunction or early SDMD.

EVOLUTION OF SIGNS IN SIGNIFICANT DEVELOPMENTAL MOTOR DISABILITY

Table 6-5 describes the changes that evolve in children with different forms of SDMD followed over many years. For instance, when kernicterus due to hyperbilirubinemia was prevalent, the changes could have evolved in the following manner:

1. On the first day of life the results of the neurological examination would be normal, but the infant would become increasingly lethargic and unable to suck and would show depressed reflexes, such as the Moro reflex.
2. If untreated within a few days, the infant would develop hyperirritability, opisthotonos, a high-pitched cry and occasionally seizures. Death may occur during this phase.
3. If the infant survives, the hypertonus gradually disappears, and by 2 to 4 months there is profound hypotonia with retention of the primitive reflexes, especially the asymmetrical tonic neck reflex.
4. Choreoathetosis with dystonia in the limbs may be delayed until the second or third year. The full-blown postkernicterus syndrome could include severe dysarthria, choreoathetosis and dystonia of the trunk and limbs, high-tone hearing loss, limitation of upward gaze, microcephaly, and yellow staining of deciduous teeth.
5. Dystonia and rigidity of the limbs increase during the first decade.
6. There is occasional progression of dyskinetic signs at or after puberty.

Table 6-5. Evolution of signs in SDMD

Clinical description	Evolutionary aspects and clinical variations at an earlier age	Etiological considerations
Spastic hemiplegia Unilateral spastic paresis affecting the arm more than the leg.	Often it is a hypotonic hemiparesis affecting the arm more than the leg in the first 2 to 4 months. After 3 to 6 years more marked dystonic posturing of the arm and hand may become more prominent. If only the arm is involved, this would be called *spastic monoplegia*	Etiology unknown in a third of patients[49] Congenital hemiplegia Prenatal causes Threatened abortion Multiple pregnancy Intrauterine fetal infection Perinatal causes Abruptio placentae Abnormal fetal presentation Intracranial hemorrhage Intrapartum fetal hypoxia Complication of exchange transfusion[49] Acquired postnatal hemiplegia (10%) Meningitis Encephalitis Head trauma—battered child Hypoxic-ischemic encephalopathy Cerebrovascular occlusions
Bilateral spastic hemiplegia Spastic paresis (usually asymmetrical) involving all four limbs with the arms affected more than the legs.	Often there is an early hypotonic phase.	Hypoxic-ischemic encephalopathy Small for date—intrauterine growth retardation Cerebral malformations Cerebral arteritis and recurrent cerebrovascular accidents
Spastic diplegia Spastic paresis of both lower limbs with little or no involvement of the arms.	May be hypotonic throughout *(hypotonic diplegia)* or gradually develop spasticity over 1 to 4 years. May be spastic early and remain so or develop dystonic features after 5 to 10 years with turning in of the feet.	Low birth weight Intrauterine fetal infections Hypoxia Hypothermia Nutritional factors (?) Hydrocephalus Intraventricular hemorrhage (?)
Spastic quadriplegia Spastic paresis involving all four limbs with the lower limbs more involved than the upper. Often associated with inability to maintain upright neck and trunk posture (dysequilibrium syndrome) and bulbar involvement. (Hagberg classification, spastic ataxia). If one upper limb is spared, this is spastic triplegia.	Often hypotonic early on with more involvement of the lower limbs than the arms. This early phase is *hypotonic quadriplegia.*	Congenital Cerebral dysgenesis Congenital infections, that is, rubella, cytomegalovirus, toxoplasmosis, herpes simplex Hypoxic-ischemic encephalopathy Intraventricular hemorrhage Acquired Hypoxic-ischemic encephalopathy Meningitis, encephalitis Hydrocephalus, lead encephalopathy
Dyskinetic quadriplegia Characterized by involuntary choreoathetoid or dystonic movements of the face, bulbar musculature, trunk, and all four limbs (with more involvement of the lower limbs, usually).	Hypotonia of neck, trunk, and limbs associated with persistence of primitive reflexes (such as the asymmetrical tonic neck reflex) is often characteristic of the first 6 to 18 months. After 4 to 12 years increasing dystonia and limb rigidity may supervene. Dyskinesia may worsen at or after puberty.	Hypoxic-ischemic encephalopathy Kernicterus (rare nowadays)

Continued.

Table 6-5. Evolution of signs in SDMD—cont'd

Clinical description	Evolutionary aspects and clinical variations at an earlier age	Etiological considerations
Ataxic quadriplegia		
Characterized by marked limb and trunk imbalance and incoordination of voluntary movements associated with trunk and limb hypotonia. Usually the lower limbs are functionally poorer than the arms.	There is often a tendency for gradual improvement in coordination and balance over 5 to 10 years.	Cerebellar dysgenesis Hypoxic-ischemic encephalopathy Meningitis Encephalitis
Mixed quadriplegia		
Characterized by features of spasticity and dyskinesia, with lower limbs more involved than upper.	Hypotonia and diminished deep tendon reflexes may be evident in first year. Dyskinesia may worsen in the second decade of life.	Hypoxic-ischemic encephalopathy Low birth weight

CLINICAL-PATHOLOGICAL CORRELATES

Spastic hemiplegia. Spastic hemiplegia can either be congenital or acquired, and the right side is involved twice as often as the left. In the *congenital form* poor function of one upper limb is noted within the first weeks of life if severe but only at 6 to 9 months in the mild form. As described by Byers in 1941,[12] the infant has a hypotonic upper limb and to a lesser extent a hypotonic lower limb on the same side. After a few weeks or months spasticity supervenes; thus the full-blown picture is that of adduction (or abduction) at the shoulder, flexion at the elbow with pronation of the forearm, flexion at the wrist, and adduction of the thumb and fingers. Sometimes the thumb is caught between the flexed fingers. In the lower limb there is adduction and flexion at the hip associated with internal rotation as well as flexion at the knee and shortening of the heel cord. The gait is toe to toe on the affected side with circumduction of the leg. An ipsilateral lower facial weakness may be present, but in 90% of the cases no hemianopia is noted. Higher cortical sensory disturbances can be profound, with complete inability to recognize objects in the hand without visual clues (astereognosis) and great difficulty recognizing numbers or letters written on the palm or fingertips (graphesthesia).[91] Marked difficulty with position sense and 2-point discrimination may be present, but the senses of touch, temperature, pain, and vibration are retained. If the syndrome is mild, early establishment of handedness will be noted, and in the contralateral limb brisker reflexes and an extensor plantar response will be seen. Handedness should not become definitely established before 12 to 18 months of age. Cutaneous reflexes, such as the abdominal and cremasteric, are retained in even severely hemiparetic patients. The hemiparetic limbs grow less well over some months or years; in mild cases the width of the thumb or large toenail on the affected side will be reduced. The neuropathology of congenital hemiparesis can range from a large hemispheral porencephalic cyst associated with marked signs to mild unilateral atrophy and gliosis of the cortex and white matter. In milder cases the lateral ventricle on the affected side will be larger than the opposite side, and an overgrowth of the skull vault and frontal and paranasal sinuses on the affected side will be noted.[30]

Acquired hemiparesis is often due to cerebral trauma or vascular occlusion. The battered child syndrome should be considered if intracerebral or subdural bleeding in a young infant or child is diagnosed. This is especially important if a discrepancy is noted between the degree of trauma and the history of how it was sustained. Acute cerebral thrombosis affecting the middle cerebral artery or branches thereof can occur in infancy and childhood and produce an acquired hemiparesis with more involvement of the upper limb than the lower. Sometimes there is an alternating hemiplegia in the moyamoya syndrome.[13] Cerebral thrombosis can occur in sickle cell disease, cerebral arteritis, homocystinuria, subacute and chronic meningitides, polycythemia, and acute dehydration in infancy.[40] Cerebral embolization can occur with congenital heart disease; acute, subacute, and marasmic endocarditis; and during cardiac catheterization and open heart surgery. Acute infantile hemiplegia has been described with venous thrombosis of the sagittal sinus and its tributaries. This syndrome is associated with raised intracranial pressure, coma, and severe, intractable seizures. Late deficits are mental retardation, severe hemiparesis, and seizures.[39]

The acute infantile hemiplegia syndrome is, unfortunately, fairly common and often has no definite cause. Infants below 2 or 3 years of age will develop a fever and intractable, unilateral, or generalized seizures. Total recovery may not occur, and the signs of hemiplegia associated with contralateral cerebral atrophy will remain.[88]

Spastic monoplegia. In spastic monoplegia one upper limb is involved; again, hypotonia may precede spasticity. The clinical findings are similar to the spastic hemiplegia syndrome, but no involvement of the lower limb on the same side is noted. Often this is a congenital syndrome and no cause can be found.

Bilateral spastic hemiplegia. Bilateral spastic hemiplegia is a rare syndrome consisting of weakness in all four limbs but more involvement of the upper limbs than the lower, often asymmetrically. This can be due to cerebral infarctions in each hemisphere, which can occur prenatally or perinatally as well as in infancy or childhood. Some causes include cerebral arteritis, sickle cell disease, homocystinuria, and sulfite oxidase deficiency. The neuropathology can show bilateral porencephaly or varying degrees of hemispheral atrophy of the cortex, deep gray matter, and white matter. With involvement of frontal lobes, retardation and speech deficits are common.

Spastic diplegia. In spastic diplegia, infants may often have hypotonia of the lower limbs with delayed lower limb functional maturation for several months. Within 4 to 8 months spasticity involving the heel cords and adductors of the thigh is noted. In severe cases spasticity of the hip flexors and the hamstring muscles at the knee can result in flexion contractures. The adductors of the thigh can produce severe adduction forces, and with time subluxation or complete dislocation of the hips can occur. Very little or no involvement of the upper limbs can be seen. Deep tendon reflexes are extremely active with extensor plantar responses. Neuropathological features include gliotic scarring and cyst formation in hemispheral white matter, known as periventricular leukomalacia[4,14] or telencephalic leukoencephalopathy.[37] Factors thought to be important in this process include hypoxia,[28] septicemia,[38] and hypothermia[21] in the infant. About 70% of patients with spastic diplegia were born prematurely.[6]

Hypotonic diplegia. In hypotonic diplegia there is delayed function and poor tone in the lower limbs with normal tone and function in the upper limbs. At 3 or 4 months, when an infant is normally beginning to support his own weight, these infants' lower limbs fold beneath them. These signs continue for about 6 to 9 months, and then upright support is learned. However, because of hip girdle weakness, the trunk remains flexed on the thighs for several months. The child learns how to stand by about 18 to 20 months and stands alone a few months later. Walking is achieved between 2 and 3 years of age. If examined then, persisting hypotonia of the feet will produce notable overpronation. Deep tendon reflexes in the lower limbs are brisk in this syndrome, with persisting bilateral extensor plantar responses. By 3 or 4 years the plantar responses may become flexor. Some patients develop mild spasticity with tight heel cords, which require a heel cord stretching exercise program. If flat-footedness and overpronation persist, orthopedic shoes with longitudinal arch inserts will be needed. In mild cases no abnormal neurological signs will be seen by 4 or 5 years. The underlying cause of this hypotonic diplegia syndrome remains unclear, and neuropathological studies are not available.

Spastic quadriplegia. Spastic quadriplegia is associated with moderate or severe delay in motor development. There may be little or no head control, even at 3 to 5 years of age in severe cases. Other motor milestones, such as turning over, grasping, and sitting, are seldom achieved. Spasticity can begin as early as 2 or 3 months of life and will involve the lower limbs more than the upper. The upper limbs may be adducted, and spasticity involves the "antigravity" muscles, particularly the biceps, pronators of the forearm, wrist flexors, adductors of the thumb, and finger flexors. The thumb may be caught in the hand by flexed fingers. In the lower limbs hypotonia may produce a froglegged appearance with abducted thighs, but spasticity may supervene and the "antigravity" muscles in the lower limbs cause flexion at the hip, adduction of the thighs, flexion at the knees, and equinus of both feet with adduction of the forefeet. Marked adduction of both thighs produces the typical "scissoring" posture of the lower limbs. The signs may be more pronounced on one side.

The neuropathology of the syndrome is varied, depending on the underlying cause. The most common causes of the syndrome are (1) hypoxic-ischemic encephalopathy;[85] (2) symmetrical cerebral malformation syndromes[60,66, 77,95] such as absent corpus callosum, lissencephaly (absence of gyral formation), and schizencephaly (deep clefts in the hemispheres); (3) congenital infections and those of early infancy,[43,53] that is, rubella, toxoplasmosis, cytomegalovirus disease, herpes encephalitis, neonatal and infantile meningitis, and encephalitis; (4) prematurity alone or associated with anoxia, sepsis, or intraventricular hemorrhage; (5) metabolic disorders such as neonatal hypoglycemia; (6) hydrocephalus due to congenital causes, such as aqueductal stenosis, neonatal intraventriculor subarachnoid hemorrhage, or meningitis.

The pathology of spastic quadriparesis associated with the hypoxic-ischemic syndrome occurring in the newborn infant will vary somewhat, depending on the degree of hypoxia versus ischemia[11] and whether the infant is premature or full term.[94] In the full-term infant in whom hypoxia predominates, there will be loss of large neurons in the cortex (particularly the hippocampus) as well as in the thalamus, basal ganglia, and brain stem. When myelin stains are used, loss of basal ganglia neurons and dysmyelinogenesis can be demonstrated with resultant status marmoratus. This is the common pathological correlate of the clinical choreoathetosis syndrome. The Purkinje cells of the cerebellar cortex are also extremely vulnerable to hypoxia. Damage to immature glial cells in the white matter of the hemispheres, brain stem, and cerebellum can be produced by hypoxia.

If ischemia predominates, the "border zones" in the brain between the major arterial beds of the anterior, middle, and posterior cerebral arteries will be most affected. Most vulnerable, then, will be the parasagittal regions of the hemispheres, the "border zone" between the anterior and middle cerebral arteries. The clinical correlate of this pathology will be weakness of the muscles of the shoulder and hip girdles.[94] Other "border zone" infarcts may be seen in the inferior temporal lobe and transverse midplane of the cerebellum.

In the premature infant the white matter of the hemispheres is particularly vulnerable to hypoxia and ischemia. The changes here may be prominent in paraventricular areas. These lesions were originally described by Banker and Larroche[4] and called periventricular leukomalacia. Necrosis of glial cells and white matter fibers is followed by gliosis. If these areas of necrosis are extensive, cysts may be evident in the white matter on both sides. These changes may be seen in brains of premature infants with spastic diplegia or quadriplegia.

The pathology of cerebral malformations is complicated.[23] There are well-described syndromes associated with the major chromosomal defects, such as holoprosencephaly in trisomy 13 syndrome. Lissencephaly is a severe malformation of the cerebral cortex in which no gyration occurs; thus the surface of the brain is quite smooth.[79] Schizencephaly is a malformation described by Yakovlev and Wadsworth,[97] in which there are deep clefts in the frontal or frontotemporal regions on both sides and in which the outer pial membrane is in apposition to the ependymal lining of the ventricles. Our understanding of the migration of neurons and of the cytoarchitecture of the brain allows us to form hypotheses as to how these major cerebral malformations take place.

The pathology of rubella encephalopathy involves focal areas of ischemic necrosis in white matter, germinal matrix, and a perivascular inflammatory response.[43] With the cytomegalovirus, subependymal necrosis is often followed by periventricular calcification. Multiple granulomatous lesions with central areas of necrosis are seen with congenital toxoplasmosis; calcifications are more scattered with this infection. In herpes encephalitis there is a widespread necrotizing hemorrhagic meningoencephalitis. Neonatal meningitis, particularly with *Escherichia coli (E. coli)*, produces a ventriculitis with inflammation of the ependymal cells and choroid plexus. With healing, atrophy of the cortex and white matter and enlargement of the lateral and third ventricles are noted.

In hypoglycemia the histological changes are similar to that of anoxia—namely, decreased numbers of large neurons in the cortex, basal ganglia, and brain stem and involvement of the Purkinje cells of the cerebellar cortex. In hydrocephalus there is predominant loss of medial fibers in the white matter of both hemispheres due to pressure exerted on the walls of the lateral ventricles.

Spastic triplegia. In spastic triplegia there is usually involvement of both lower limbs and one upper limb. Generally this is an incomplete form of spastic quadriparesis with asymmetrical white matter necrosis and gliosis in the hemispheres.

Dyskinetic quadriplegia. Dyskinetic quadriplegia was formerly seen in the child with hyperbilirubinemia and kernicterus, usually associated with Rh incompatibility. The sequence of neurological patterns has been outlined previously. A similar syndrome, often with added signs of spasticity, can be associated with the perinatal hypoxic-ischemic syndrome.

If the infant dies in the acute phase of kernicterus, unconjugated bilirubin will stain groups of cerebral neurons yellow. In the overt case this will involve all layers of the cerebral cortex, the thalamus, basal ganglia, brain stem, and cerebellum.

The classic late neuropathological changes will include status marmoratus with dysmyelinogenesis in the basal ganglia. The neurons are destroyed and resorbed. Myelinization of the axons in the adjacent internal capsule is disturbed and axons with thick myelin sheaths take an abnormal course through the basal ganglia. When the Bodian method for staining is used, the axons and myelin are blackened. Paler pockets of neurons may remain between the myelinated fibers, giving the appearance of black and white marble.

In the milder forms of choreoathetosis patients often have excellent intellectual capacity; speech is possible but may be poorly understood and dysarthric. Purposeful movements of the upper limbs are extremely difficult, and if walking is possible, it will be accompanied by much extraneous movement of the neck, trunk, and upper limbs. In severe cases speech and voluntary movements of all the limbs are impaired; thus the patient is "locked in" and has little ability to communicate.

Ataxic quadriparesis. In ataxic quadriparesis the infant remains hypotonic for months or years, has incoordinated movements of the limbs when trying to perform a meaningful act, and may never walk due to lack of balance. No involuntary movements at rest will be noted. If less severe, these children may later have marked speech difficulties, ataxia of limbs and gait, limb hypotonia, reduced deep tendon reflexes, and flexor plantar responses. A few of these children develop telangiectasia of the conjunctivas at age 4 or 5, and a revised diagnosis of ataxia telangiectasia will have to be made. Hagberg and co-workers[51] have stressed the significance of a subgroup of infants having a dysequilibrium syndrome with little or no limb dysmetria but much difficulty maintaining an upright position of the body in space.

Studies may show cerebellar hypoplasia on cerebral CT scan or pneumoencephalography.[51,83] Christensen and Melchior[15] found cerebellar abnormalities in 24 of 69 children examined neuropathologically. Interestingly, clinical spasticity and dyskinesia were more often found than ataxia. An autosomal recessive "dysequilibrium syndrome" of nonprogressive ataxia and mental retardation has been described by Ingram[59] and also by Gustavson and co-workers[45] in 10 Swedish families. Recently these patients have been found to have reduced serum dopamine-β-hydroxylase and diminished sympathetic nervous system activity.[45] Two families with associated defective thymus-dependent immunity having this neurological picture have been described.[41]

Mixed spastic and choreoathetoid form of SDMD. Mixed spastic and choreoathetoid form combines the features of spastic quadriparesis and bilateral choreoathetosis. The pathology is often that of cortical atrophy and status marmoratus, as described earlier. The most common cause of this syndrome at this time is the perinatal hypoxic-ischemic syndrome.

Transient dystonia syndrome. Ingram, in 1964,[59] described a syndrome seen between 2 and 9 months of age in premature infants with abnormal neurological signs that gradually disappeared by 1 year. This was called transient dystonia syndrome.

In the first few months the infant is irritable, jittery, and stiff to handle and has diminished spontaneous movements of the limbs. The infant's head control is poor with truncal and limb hypotonia, or, in contrast, there may be increased tone in the neck extensors and limbs. The asymmetrical tonic neck reflex may persist beyond 3 to 4 months. Abnormal postures of the upper limbs may include persistent flexion across the chest or, alternatively, the arms can be held extended. The hands may be fisted with the thumbs caught in the palms. With the child held upright, scissoring of the legs may be seen with equinus postures of the feet. The crossed adductor jerk and bilateral ankle clonus may persist for 6 to 8 months.

Drillien[25] has found an inverse relationship between birth weight and the transient dystonia syndrome. This syndrome is common in small for dates infants and has a greater incidence in males. On follow-up there may be a greater incidence of mental retardation, hyperactive behavior, and school learning difficulties.[26]

MULTIPLE DISABILITIES

Mental retardation. About 50% of children with SDMD have mild to severe retardation, and the greater the extent of the cerebral lesion, the higher this incidence.[29,61] In Crothers and Paine's series,[18] 70% of children with spastic quadriplegia had IQs below 70 (Table 6-6). More recent estimates suggest that 25% to 33% of patients can become entirely self-supporting in adult life, especially with appropriate counselling and training.[61]

Feeding difficulties.[59] Many children with hypotonic or spastic quadriparesis will need an hour or more on each feeding in the first few weeks of life. Choking spells are not uncommon due to poor integration of the sucking-swallowing mechanism. With less severely involved patients this difficulty begins to improve in a few weeks and the parents cope adequately with feeding the child. In others aspiration pneumonia occurs and a temporary or permanent gastrostomy becomes imperative. Often children with poor nutritional status will improve remarkably following a gastrostomy. This in turn may allow closure of the gastrostomy as swallowing abilities are regained.

Seizures. About a third of the children with SDMD will develop seizures, and they persist into adulthood in 10%.[61] The hemiplegic group of patients is the most vulnerable. Among the 466 patients reviewed by Crothers and Paine,[18] only 7% of the dyskinetic cerebral palsy patients had had seizures, whereas 39% of the quadriparetic group and 69% of the hemiparetic group experienced seizures. In the acquired hemiparetic group this reached 72%, with an incidence of 55% in the congenital hemiparetic patients.

Deafness. Unilateral or bilateral deafness is seen in association with SDMD.[20,61] If microcephaly and grand mal seizures accompany the motor deficit, deafness is more likely.[80] Congenital rubella encephalopathy and cytomegalovirus infection of the brain can often cause SDMD and sensorineural deafness.

Psychiatric disturbances. The problems of behavioral disturbances are often major ones in children with SDMD, particularly in adolescents.[87]

Learning disabilities. The incidence of learning disabilities is considerable in children with SDMD. These include attentional problems and visual and auditory perception defects, which contribute to delays in the acquisition of reading, mathematics, and writing skills.[19,71]

Strabismus. This is common in the quadriparetic group and the spastic diparetic group. About 43% of Ingram's[59] patients had convergent strabismus. It is less common in the dyskinetic and hemiplegic forms of SDMD. It may take the form of bilateral esotropia or exotropia with alternating fixation in either eye and re-

Table 6-6. Intelligence of patients with cerebral palsy*

IQ	Random population (%)	Hemiplegic group (%)	Quadriplegic patients (%)	Extrapyramidal patients (%)
Over 110	23	7	0	9
90 to 110	52	26	13	35
70 to 90	22	31	17	25
Below 70	3	36	70	31

*Modified from Crothers, B., and Paine, R. S.: The natural history of cerebral palsy. Cambridge, Mass., 1959, Harvard University Press.

sults in failure of binocular vision. In the presence of a unilateral lesion, amblyopia may occur if the condition is not treated by patching the fixating eye.

MANAGEMENT OF SIGNIFICANT DEVELOPMENTAL MOTOR DISABILITY

A multidisciplinary group of professionals is needed in the care of children and adolescents with SDMD. Ideally, the pediatrician or family practitioner should coordinate the care of a child with SDMD. There may be need to consult other specialist physicians in orthopedics, neurology, genetics, psychiatry, otolaryngology, dentistry, and ophthalmology. Other team members who will be needed include psychologists, physical therapists, occupational therapists, speech pathologists, nutritionists, audiologists, and special educators at school. In a clinic setting a nurse or social worker learns the family dynamics. Inner-city clinics require multilingual professionals to interact with and counsel the family whose native language is not English.

Education of the patient and the family about the disability is crucial on the first visit. This is the physician's responsibility but should be reinforced by the nurse, social worker, or psychologist. A total program must be fashioned for each child. This will include a developmental stimulation program, in which the physical therapist and occupational therapist play major roles and interact with the pediatrician, orthopedist, neurologist, speech therapist, and other members of the group when necessary. The child's needs at school should be addressed with an appropriate individualized educational plan. Whenever possible, social integration of the child with his peers should be encouraged.

For the young, inexperienced parents of a child with SDMD, a home visiting program by nurses or developmental therapists should be made available. Homemakers will be able to help a family having difficulties adjusting to the child's disabilities.

A physical therapy program is important if spasticity in the limbs is marked. Many systems have been used over the years; that propounded by the Bobath and Bobath[8,9] is acceptable to many physical therapists in this field. This program suggests that abnormal postures have to be overcome by repeated exercises before progress can be made toward the next stage of motor development. It is important for the parents to learn the exercise program so that it can be carried out in the home.[31] The physical therapist should monitor the program and, depending on the progress of the child, revise the program periodically. A vigorous physical therapy program should be tried before surgery for contractures is decided on. The parents should also understand that after the surgical procedure, physical therapy *must* be resumed.

In 1976, Cooper and co-workers[17] reported the use of chronic cerebellar cortex stimulation to alleviate spasticity. Since then, there have been several other reports with encouraging results.[22,74] However, in a recent double-blind study on a small number of children with SDMD, no lasting benefit from this procedure was found.[81]

Current studies in bioengineering research laboratories are aimed at improving motor performance in a handicapped limb with the use of computers that facilitate limb movement.

Drugs, such as diazepam (Valium) and dantrolene (Dantrium), have been used to reduce spasticity with varying degrees of success. Baclofen has been used for this reason in adults but has not been released for use in children in the United States. Augmented feedback training has also been used to improve motor performance in SDMD.[55]

LOCOMOTOR PROGNOSIS

There are a few studies that help to prognosticate whether a child will walk independently. The study by Crothers and Paine[18,70] showed that all children with hemiplegia walked. This ability may be delayed until 18 months or as late as 7 years. About 70% of the children with spastic quadriplegia learned to walk by 7 years. Thus the chances of a child walking independently after that time are small. If a child is not sitting independently at the age of 4, there is little likelihood that he will walk independently. In a study by Bleck,[7] a simple scoring system was devised for predicting independent ambulation. It used the symmetrical and asymmetrical tonic neck reflexes, the Moro reflex, the neck righting reflex, foot placement reaction, extensor thrust, and parachute reaction. This method was successful in 94.5% of the 73 preschool children studied.

It is more accurate to prognosticate future developmental milestones in an individual child when repeated assessments have been made several months apart. A graph of motor progression can be constructed and probable future progression plotted, assuming optimal orthopedic and physical therapy management. Poor nutrition, social deprivation, and the onset of seizures are factors that can influence the rate of progression in these children. The level of cognitive ability in these children will affect their motor development. A child's physical therapy program will depend on his ability to understand instruction. An integrated developmental stimulation program, including cognitive, language, social, and motor aspects, is likely to improve the child's overall motor and intellectual rate of growth.

PROGRESSIVE SIGNIFICANT DEVELOPMENTAL MOTOR DISABILITY

It is now well recognized that a small percentage of patients worsen despite optimal management.[54] This seems to occur in early adolescence and to be particularly prevalent in children with dystonic or choreoathetoid forms of SDMD. Whenever regression of motor or intellectual development occurs, it is important to review the diagnosis of the child and consider other remediable conditions, such as spinal cord tumors.[56] Other disease processes involving the cerebral hemispheres and spinal cord must be ruled out, such as cerebral tumors and degenerative diseases of white matter (e.g., metachromatic leukodystrophy). The hallmarks of spinal cord tumor include back pain, radiating limb pains, progressive weakness of the lower limbs, and bladder or bowel disturbances. Several cases of mental retardation and progressive dyskinetic SDMD associated with glutaric aciduria, an inborn error of lysine, hydroxylysine, and tryptophan metabolism, have been reported.[10,42,65]

SOCIAL AND ADAPTIVE ASPECTS AND EMPLOYABILITY

The management of children and particularly adolescents with SDMD does require a sensitivity on the part of all involved in management. Disturbed emotional development can interfere with the child's progress. The infant with delayed motor development may not be able to creep over to play with the pots and pans as a normal child of the same chronological age. Braces and crutches will profoundly affect a school-aged child's social adaptation in the classroom. Often it is during adolescence, as the child attempts to establish some kind of emotional independence from his family, that the most troublesome maladaptation is seen. There is the realization that the physical disability is not going to disappear with therapy, medication, or orthopedic surgery. In this age group more severe emotional disturbances may occur and are difficult to remediate. As schooling nears an end, the issues of employability and the overall competitive job status become very important.

Crothers and Paine[18] studied this in relation to the type of SDMD that the patient had (Table 6-7). In that study there were very few cases of spastic diplegia. The majority of this group of patients with SDMD have normal intelligence. In a study by Berenberg and Ong[6] 70%

Table 6-7. Competitive status of patients with cerebral palsy over the age of 21*

Type of disability	Competitive (%)	Competitive with concessions (%)	Noncompetetive (%)
Prenatal or natal hemiplegia	33	7	60
Postnatal hemiplegia	43	6	51
Spastic quadriplegia or triplegia	0	0	100
Extrapyramidal cerebral palsy	26	5	69
Mixed cerebral palsy	7	7	86

*From Crothers, B., and Paine, R. S.: The natural history of cerebral palsy, Cambridge, Mass., 1959, Harvard University Press.

of the children had normal intelligence but had difficulties with perception and visuomotor coordination.[6] Patients with physical handicaps now have a better chance of securing jobs (with or without concessions) due to recent state and federal nondiscriminatory statutes. Many public buildings have had physical barriers for handicapped persons removed, which allows easier access and increases the number of jobs available for this population.

Orthopedic aspects

Panos G. Panagakos

Abnormalities of motor function are present in all children with SDMD. They represent a major portion of the child's symptoms and their management consumes a large segment of the treatment effort. A basic understanding of the character and natural history of motor dysfunction is essential for making decisions on diagnosis, prognosis, and management.

NATURE OF MOTOR DEFICIT

SDMD is different from other musculoskeletal disorders, such as poliomyelitis or arthrogryposis, in which problems are usually mechanical and regional. In SDMD the primary problem is a defect in the initiation and execution of movement. Failure of normal maturation of or injury to the central nervous system may produce disorganization of movement and abnormal postures. These postures represent early developmental reflexes that are present in all normal infants up to a certain age, at which time they are replaced by voluntary motion. In SDMD, however, voluntary motion is delayed, absent, or erratic, while abnormal postures persist indefinitely, dominating the child's motor behavior. They also form the patterns on which future deformities may develop. For these reasons they must be recognized and their interference with the child's function evaluated and dealt with.

Many of the reflexes producing these postures have been identified and described. They can be elicited by appropriate stimulation. They may be present at rest or only during active function. In some instances they are weak, and the child with effort may voluntarily overcome them, or they may be obligatory and overwhelming. They may change or alternate depending on the child's position or state of mind or whether the head is flexed or extended.

It is apparent, then, that the findings from the musculoskeletal system will be, in the early stages, variable and of a dynamic nature. For example, a muscle that has normal tone in the supine position may become hypertonic when the child stands or is held upright. Similarly, a child who walks on his toes should not always be thought to have tight heel cords. Careful examination may reveal a child with a strongly positive supportive reaction or extensor hypertonus. If this child is followed long enough, hypertonus and deformity of other antigravity muscles will become apparent with the associated problems and dysfunction.

Thus it is important for the examiner not to limit observations to only one static situation, such as the child lying on an examining table. Full understanding of the child's motor behavior requires that the child be examined in several positions under stimulation and during functional activities.

DEFORMITIES

Persistent abnormal postures of the neck, trunk, or limbs are known as deformities. Although SDMD is not a progressive neurological disease, deformities can progress rapidly and severely. The reason lies in the way that muscles, joints, and bones respond to immobility. When a muscle remains immobile in a stretched position, it loses its ability to contract and becomes weak. When immobility affects a muscle in a state of contraction, which is the usual and more serious situation, a permanent shortening or contracture will develop. This type of contracture is a myostatic contracture, It is not the result of actual muscle disease and can occur in normal individuals, for example, those immobilized in a cast during fracture treatment.

Whether normal or spastic, contractured muscles can be stretched with adequate physical therapy and splinting, as long as they are not allowed to remain shortened too long and to become fibrotic. In the early stages of SDMD deformities are usually functional in that they can be corrected manually by an examiner. As time passes, however, especially with poor or no treatment, muscles will become contractured and a fixed deformity will develop. Manual correction is no longer possible. Without treatment muscle shortening will continue and deformities will progress until the muscles reach their minimum length. Since reflex postures affect many joint levels, deformities will also be multiple. Biomechanical forces also cause deformities to spread from one joint to the next in a progressive fashion. The effect on the patient is a gradual loss of function and mobility.

Muscle contracture is followed by contracture of ligaments and joint capsules, further limiting motion. Lack of function and abnormal forces on joints produce in the growing child a misdirection of normal remodelling processes, with joint deformity and frequently dislocations. Bones appear underdeveloped, and disuse osteoporosis may be severe.

A number of other factors can affect deformities. A very significant one is growth. Deformities develop rapidly when growth is fast. The first 4 or 5 years of life and the period of adolescent growth spurt therefore require special attention. Progression of deformity after maturity is usually minimal.

ORTHOPEDIC EVALUATION

The orthopedic examination, to be of value, must be systematic and include many considerations that are not strictly orthopedic factors. Considering the child as an aggregate of tight muscles is unacceptable. The type of neurological involvement is important, since hypotonia, spasticity, dystonia, etc., often tend to produce specific problems.

A good developmental history and the child's present level of functioning should be determined. A sufficient period of time for observation of the child's spontaneous activity must be allowed to establish his abilities, abnormalities of posture and deformities, and the way they affect each other. To be organized and reproducible, observations should follow the sequence of normal developmental maturation. The head, trunk, and proximal and distal joints of the extremities should be examined successively, noting function and control. The child's motor age will thereby be established. Subsequent examination will help determine the rate of progress of the child. The motor and chronological ages will tend to approach each other when the child is improving, but they will tend to diverge when development is failing.

Certain aspects of the motor developmental evaluation are particularly important. Head control is crucial, since it is the first essential developmental step. A child without the ability to control his head will have a motor age of 1 month. Sitting is another crucial step. Many children unable to sit independently will be able to do so in a modified way, for example, with the legs folded under, with the back severely curled, leaning against a firm surface, or with some support around the hips.

The ability of the child to use his hands to prevent falling is always a very positive achievement; it indicates the presence of effective righting responses, which are essential for function in the upright posture, and is of great significance regarding prognosis. The basic components of hand function include the ability to reach, grasp, retrieve, release, and exchange objects from hand to hand. Any postural or other abnormalities interfering with these functions should be evaluated.

In the lower extremities, one should look for the ability to move the legs individually and reciprocally. This is best seen during creeping, which is a revealing activity in many ways. A child able to creep on his hands and knees demonstrates the ability to overcome the usual extensor hypertonus, since in creeping, he actively flexes the hips and knees. When unable to do so, he will drag his legs behind him, stiff and probably scissored. Effective creeping also demonstrates the ability to bear weight on the outstretched hands, an ability necessary if crutches are to be used later on. The ability to use crutches for support and reciprocal movement of the legs can be further tested in the upright position.

The next step in the orthopedic evaluation takes place on the examining table. Muscle tone should be evaluated and will be found to be diminished, exaggerated, or variable to different degrees. Deformities present must now be determined and analyzed. The range of motion of all joints should be tested to determine the presence of any fixed contractures of various muscle groups. During this examination the limbs should be moved briskly to reveal the point at which the stretch reflexes become stimulated; a sudden catch will be felt at this point. This determination is important because it represents the limit to which the child will be able to use his joint spontaneously. Steady slow pressure should then be applied until the stretch reflex is overcome and maximum range of motion is determined. This will reveal any permanent contracture in the muscles and ligamentous structures and structural deformation of joints.

In examining the head and trunk, one should look for any deformities caused by prolonged immobility and poor muscle tone. For example, in some children the thorax will be flattened in the anterior-posterior diameter and the predominantly abdominal respiration will have caused the lower ribs to be flared. These children may have multiple respiratory infections and may later develop severe spasticity and multiple deformities.

Deformities in the upper extremities vary greatly, but spasticity tends to give a typical pattern. The shoulder is usually adducted and internally rotated, but stimulation during gait often produces an abducted posture. The elbow remains flexed and the forearm pronated; the wrist and fingers are flexed and the thumb adducted across the palm. Function will depend on the patient's ability to actively overcome this posture and the degree of any fixed deformities present.

In the lower extremities the predominant posture is that of extension. Hips and knees tend to remain extended and the feet are in equinus. The hips are adducted and internally rotated, often to the point of scissoring. Stiffness and inability to flex the joints is obvious, especially during walking and sitting. Despite the extensor posture, flexion deformities may develop at the knees and hips. A generalized flexion posture, with flexion at the hips and knees and dorsiflexion of the feet, is much less common. Adductor spasticity is one of the earliest signs of spasticity, together with spasticity of the heel cords. In addition, adductor spasticity and contracture is a common reason for dislocation of the hips, a very frequent occurrence in cerebral palsy, which should be watched for carefully. Even in a nonambulatory child it is important to have a good triangular base (i.e., abducted thighs) and a nonpainful hip so that sitting remains possible. To reach the point of dislocation, however, adductor spasticity will be combined with underdeveloped or deformed hip joints; increased anteversion and valgus neck shaft angle is very common.

The knees may develop a flexion contracture, but, from a functional point of view, the inability to flex is equally disturbing. A contractured quadriceps muscle pulls the patella much higher than normal, with resultant degeneration of the patella and marked knee pain.

Contracture of the heel cords is very common, associated with equinus deformities and tiptoe walking. Additional foot deformities may also develop, such as valgus, varus, rockerbottom, or cavus deformities, as well as deformities of the toes.

Asymmetry of involvement of the limbs may arise in patients with bilateral disease. It is particularly dangerous around the hips, producing adduction-internal rotation and shortening in one hip, and abduction-external rotation in the other. There is marked pelvic tilt, higher on the adducted side. This results in scoliosis (convex toward the abducted side), and without treatment, dislocation of the adducted hip is practically certain. Because of the multiple problems hip dislocation produces, it must be detected and treated early. In addition to observation and examination of range of motion, checking for the Galeazzi sign, commonly used for detection of subluxating or dislocating hips, can be useful. This is done with patient lying supine on the examining table, the hips flexed to 90 degrees, with the knees also flexed. When the hips are normal, both knees should be at the same level; with the hip subluxing, however, the knee on that side will be lower.

Examination of the back may reveal dorsal kyphosis, especially in poor sitters. The lumbar spine may be lordotic, often severely so in ambulatory patients. This is partially related to hip flexion deformity and is a common reason for low back pain in the older child and adult. Scoliosis is less likely to affect children with SDMD if they remain ambulatory, but many severely affected children develop marked progressive scoliosis.

Children with hemiplegia may develop a mild thoracolumbar curve, which relates to the asymmetry of the trunk, modest shortening of the affected leg, and adductor tightness. It is seldom progressive or worrisome.

TREATMENT

Treatment in SDMD, although not curative, can be of substantial value in decreasing deformity and in increasing function and comfort. The child with SDMD can be looked on as having both normal movement and abnormal and oftentimes disturbing reflex activity. The goal of treatment is to maximize the former and minimize the latter. Physical therapy, bracing, and orthopedic surgery are the main modalities used. Treatment is complex and based on certain well-established principles. Reflex activity, for example, can be modified or partially inhibited by various techniques, increasing the chances for better voluntary control. Such techniques are used by physical therapists and may include special positioning, handling, and manipulation of the child or the use of stimulation, such as icing, brushing, etc. Muscle tone, whether increased or decreased, may be altered by using similar techniques of relaxation or reinforcement. It is im-

portant that treatment begin early, before abnormal patterns have been firmly established and deformities interfere with function. A functional deformity may be prevented from becoming fixed by a regular exercise program of stretching and night splinting. Daily range of motion exercises may help prevent joint deterioration. Although most patients are capable of some degree of voluntary control, much of this ability is often suppressed and overshadowed by abnormal reflex movement. The trained therapist will be able to distinguish such interference, help the child improve his voluntary function, and teach him ways to compensate for abnormal postural tendencies. Therapy can also be useful in other activities that require improvement, such as strengthening hypotonic muscles and working on head control, sitting, creeping, balancing, ambulating, or performing activities of daily living (dressing, eating, going to the toilet, transferring from chair to bed, etc.).

Bracing, if properly used, can be a useful adjunct to treatment. Braces are very rarely used to correct deformity. Their use is intended to prevent a deformity from becoming fixed, to prevent a corrected deformity from recurring, or to limit undesirable motion, such as in extrapyramidal SDMD. They can also be used to assist weak muscles through the use of specially applied springs or by stabilizing selected joints. One of the most important functions of braces, however, is assisting in the prevention of deformities when used for night splinting.

As many as 30% of patients with SDMD will require one or more surgical procedures at some point in their lives. The objectives of surgery are not unlike those of conservative treatment, namely (1) prevention of deformities from becoming fixed, (2) restoration of muscle balance by weakening hypertonic muscles, (3) relief of deforming forces, (4) assistance of weak muscles by appropriate muscle transfer, and (5) prevention or treatment of joint dislocations. The specific techniques used are beyond the scope of this chapter, and they vary greatly among surgeons. Surgery should not be considered the end point in treatment. No matter how well corrected, deformities have a surprising tendency to recur unless protected by a carefully designed postoperative program of physical therapy and night splinting. Therapy, to be effective, must be integrated into the patient's daily routine and not be limited to once or twice a week in the treatment center. Parents should understand the child's disabilities and learn ways of improving function. They must be familiar with the child's therapy program and practice it at home faithfully. They are an integral part of the treatment team. Finally, treatment must be adapted to each patient's needs and potential. Obviously, the requirements and objectives for a patient living a bed and chair existence will be different from those for a patient who could become an independent and competitive member of society. Careful attention must be paid to necessary adaptive equipment, which will make the youngster more functional in the home and community. Appropriate feeding chairs, car seats, and wheelchairs will help make this possible. Equipment for aiding in bathing, as well as canes and crutches for ambulation, are important.

PROGNOSIS

Prognosis for motor function is of great concern to parents who are naturally worried about their child's future. It often affects decisions, such as potential residential placement, having additional children, educational plans for the patient, and other facets of family life.

The physician is interested in prognosis because it will allow realistic goals to be set for each patient and treatment regulated accordingly. For example, surgical correction of an equinus deformity will not be necessary if the patient is not expected to become ambulatory, unless to allow for wearing of shoes in winter.

Prognosis under the age of 4 years is highly speculative. After this age, however, experience has produced certain guidelines that can be helpful. Control of the trunk seems to be a key issue regarding both ambulation and upper extremity function. A child who has not developed the ability to sit independently by the age of 4 will probably never walk independently. Even with severe involvement of the lower extremities, ambulation with crutches will be possible as long as the child is able to bear weight on his hands. This ability can be tested long before the child is actually ready to ambulate by observing his ability to creep on the floor. The lower extremities must be free of major motor deformities. Many diplegic and quadriplegic youngsters should be able to ambulate with adequate treatment. All hemiplegics will eventually be able to walk independently. Children who, after the age of 4, continue to have obligatory tonic neck and labyrinthine reflexes and strong startle reactions will be unable to walk.

Some children seem to have an excessive amount of reflex activity following cutaneous stimulation of the forefeet with plantar grasp and extensor withdrawal responses. These children are unable to stand or walk on their feet but often walk quite well on their knees. Bracing will help them become ambulatory. When hypotonia and weakness of the lower extremities is the problem and hand function is reasonable, bracing will allow for a useful type of ambulation. The development of a significant degree of scoliosis in a preadolescent child appears to be a poor prognostic sign. Deformities increase rapidly during active growth, but remain fairly stable after maturity. Patients in whom prolonged hypotonia has produced the flat chest deformity described earlier will usually develop severe spasticity, and their prognosis is poor. Other poor prognostic signs for ambulation include unilateral dislocation of a hip, severe untreatable deformities, severe mental defect, and significant extrapyramidal disease. Ataxia, especially if mild, tends to improve spontaneously. Bracing can be helpful, but crutches usually cannot be handled by the patient. As a rule, children have acquired all of their developmental skills by the time they enter adolescence. From then on, very little spontaneous improvement can be expected.

Surgical treatment should be approached cautiously and with careful planning. As previously stressed, a vigorous physical therapy program may help avoid some surgical procedures. The success of surgical treatment will depend on the type and timing of the procedure and the cooperation of the patient, but more important is the type of therapy and support that the patient will receive postoperatively and until growth is complete.

REFERENCES

1. Alberman, E.: Facts and figures in benefits and hazard of the new obstetrics (Chard, T., and Richards, M., editors), Clin. Dev. Med. **64:**1, 1977.
2. Amiel-Tison, C.: A method for neurologic evaluation within the first year of life, Curr. Probl. Pediatr. **7:**1, 1976.
3. Armstrong, D., and Norman, M. G.: Periventricular leucomalacia in neonates, Arch. Dis. Child. **49:**367, 1974.
4. Banker, B. Q., and Larroche, J. C.: Periventricular leukomalacia of infancy, Arch. Neurol. **7:**386, 1962.
5. Bax, M. C. O.: Terminolgy and classification of cerebral palsy, Dev. Med. Child Neurol. **6:**295, 1964.
6. Berenberg, W., and Ong. B. H.: Cerebral spastic paraplegia and prematurity, Pediatrics **33:**496, 1964.
7. Bleck, E. E.: Locomotor prognosis in cerebral palsy, Dev. Med. Child Neurol. **17:**18, 1975.
8. Bobath, K.: The normal postural reflex mechanism and its deviation in children with cerebral palsy, Physiotherapy **57:**515, 1971.
9. Bobath, K., and Bobath, B.: The diagnosis of cerebral palsy in infancy, Arch. Dis. Child. **31:**408, 1956.
10. Brandt, N. J., et al.: Glutaric aciduria in progressive choreo-athetosis, Clin. Genet. **13:**77, 1978.
11. Brann, A. W., Jr., and Dykes, F. D.: The effects of intrauterine asphyxia on the full-term infant, Clin. Perinatol. **4:**149, 1977.
12. Byers, R. K.: Evolution of hemiplegias in infancy, Am. J. Dis. Child. **61:**915, 1941.
13. Carlson, C. B., Harvey, F. H., and Loop, J.: Progressive alternating hemiplegia in early childhood with basal arterial stenosis and telangiectasia (Moyamoya syndrome), Neurology **23:**734, 1973.
14. Chattha, A. S., and Richardson, E. P.: Cerebral white-matter hypoplasia, Arch. Neurol. **34:**137, 1977.
15. Christensen, E., and Melchior, J.: Cerebral palsy—a clinical and neuropathological study, Clin. Dev. Med. **25:** 1967.
16. Churchill, J. A., et al.: The etiology of cerebral palsy in preterm infants, Dev. Med. Child Neurol. **16:**143, 1974.
17. Cooper, I. S., et al.: Chronic cerebellar stimulation in cerebral palsy, Neurology **26:**744, 1976.
18. Crothers, B., and Paine, R. S.: The natural history of cerebral palsy, Cambridge, Mass., 1959, Harvard University Press.
19. Cruikshank, W. M.: Cerebral palsy. A developmental disability, Syracuse, N.Y., 1976, Syracuse University Press.
20. Cunningham, C., and Holt, K. S.: Problems in diagnosis and management of children with cerebral palsy and deafness, Dev. Med. Child Neurol. **19:**479, 1977.
21. Davies, P. A., and Tizard, J. P. M.: Very low birth-weight and subsequent neurological defect, Dev. Med. Child Neurol. **17:**3, 1975.
22. Davis, R., et al.: Cerebellar stimulation for cerebral palsy, J. Flor. Med. Assoc. **63:**910, 1976.
23. DeMyer, W.: Classification of cerebral malformations, Birth Defects **7:**78, 1971.
24. Drillien, C. M.: Aetiology and outcome in low-birth-weight infants, Dev. Med. Child Neurol. **14:**563, 1972.
25. Drillien, C. M.: Abnormal neurologic signs in the first year of life in low-birthweight infants: possible prognostic significance, Dev. Med. Child Neurol. **14:**575, 1972.
26. Drillien, C. M., Thomson, A. J. M., and Burgoyne, K.: Low birthweight children at early school age: a longitudinal study, Dev. Med. Child Neurol. **22:**26, 1980.
27. Drillien, C. M., and Drummond, M. B.: Neurodevelopmental problems in early childhood. Assessment and management, Oxford, 1977, Blackwell Scientific Publications Ltd.
28. Drillien, C. M., Ingram, T. T. S., and Russel E. M.: Comparative aetiological studies of congenital diplegia in Scotland, Arch. Dis. Child. **37:**282, 1962.
29. Durkin, M. V., et al.: Analysis of etiologic factors in cerebral palsy with severe mental retardation. Part I, Analysis of gestational parturitional and neonatal data. Eur. J. Pediatr. **123:**67, 1976.
30. Dyke, C. G., Davidoff, L. M., and Masson, C. B.: Cerebral hemiatrophy with homolateral hypertropy of the skull and sinuses, Surg. Gynecol. Obstet. **57:** 588, 1933.
31. Finnie, N. R.: Handling the young cerebral palsied child at home, ed. 2, New York, 1974, E. P. Dutton and Elsevier Book Operations.
32. Fitzhardinge, P. M.: Early growth and development in low-birthweight infants following treatment in an intensive care nursery, Pediatrics **56:**162, 1975.
33. Fitzhardinge, P. M., and Ramsay, M.: The improving outlook for the small prematurely born infant, Dev. Med. Child. Neurol. **15:**447, 1973.
34. Francis-Williams, J., and Davies, P. A.: Very low birthweight and later intelligence, Dev. Med. Child Neurol. **16:**709, 1974.
35. Franco, S., and Andrews, B. F.: Reduction of cerebral palsy by neonatal intensive care, Pediatr. Clin. North Am. **24:**639, 1977.
36. Giles, H. R., et al.: The Arizona high-risk maternal transport system: an initial view, Am. J. Obstet. Gynecol. **128:**400, 1977.
37. Gilles, F. H., and Murphy, S. F.: Perinatal telencephalic leucoencephalapathy, J. Neurol. Neurosurg. Psychiatry **32:**404, 1969.
38. Gilles, F. H., Averill, D. R., Jr., and Kerr, C. S.: Neonatal endotoxin encephalopathy, Ann. Neurol. **2:** 49, 1977.
39. Gold, A. P., Hammill, J. F., and Carter, S.: Cerebrovascular diseases. In Carter, S., and Gold, A. P., editors: Neurology of infancy and childhood, New York, 1974, Appleton-Century-Crofts, pp. 113-114.

40. Golden, G. S., and Fenichel, G. M.: Vascular diseases of the brain and spinal cord. In Swainman, K. F., and Wright, F. S., editors: The practice of pediatric neurology, St. Louis, 1975, The C. V. Mosby Co., pp. 639-646.

41. Graham-Pole, J., et al.: Familial dysequilibrium-diplegia with T-lymphocyte deficiency, Arch. Dis. Child. **50:**927, 1975.

42. Gregersen, N., et al.: Glutaric aciduria: clinical and laboratory findings in two brothers, J. Pediatr. **90:**740, 1977.

43. Griffith, J. F.: Nonbacterial infections of the fetus and newborn, Clin. Perinatol. **4:**117, 1977.

44. Gustavson, K. H., Hagberg, B., and Sanner, G.: Identical syndromes of cerebral palsy in the same family, Acta Paediatr. Scand. **58:**330, 1969.

45. Gustavson, K. H., Ross, S. B., and Sanner, G.: Low serum dopamine-β-hydroxylase activity in the dysequilibrium syndrome, Clin. Genet. **11:**270, 1977.

46. Hagberg, B.: Care of the handicapped child, Clin. Dev. Med. **67:**111, 1978.

47. Hagberg, B.: Epidemiological and preventive aspects of cerebral palsy and severe mental retardation in Sweden, Eur. J. Pediatr. **130:**71, 1979.

48. Hagberg, B., Hagberg, G., and Olow, I.: The changing panorama of cerebral palsy in Sweden, 1954-1970. Part I, Analysis of the general changes, Acta Paediatr. Scand. **64:**187, 1975.

49. Hagberg, B., Hagberg, G., and Olow, I.: The changing panorama of cerebral palsy in Sweden, 1954-1970. Part II, Analysis of the various syndromes, Acta Paediatr. Scand. **64:**193, 1975.

50. Hagberg, B., Olow, I., and Hagberg, G.: Decreasing incidence of low birth weight diplegia—an achievement of modern neonatal care? Acta Paediatr. Scand. **62:**199, 1973.

51. Hagberg, B., Sanner, G., and Steen, M.: The dysequilibrium syndrome in cerebral palsy—clinical aspects and treatment, Acta Paediatr. Scand. **226**(Suppl.): 3, 1972.

52. Hagberg, G., Hagberg, B., and Olow, I.: The changing panorama of cerebral palsy in Sweden, 1954-1970. Part III, The importance of foetal deprivation of supply, Acta Paediatr. Scand. **65:**403, 1976.

53. Hanshaw, J. B., and Dudgeon, J. A.: Viral diseases of the fetus and newborn, Philadelphia, 1978, W. B. Saunders Co.

54. Hanson, R. A., Berenberg, W., and Byers, R. K.: Changing motor patterns in cerebral palsy, Dev. Med. Child Neurol. **12:**309, 1970.

55. Harrison, A.: Augmented feedback training of motor control in cerebral palsy, Dev. Med. Child Neurol. **19:**75, 1977.

56. Haslam, R. H. A.: "Progressive cerebral palsy" or spinal cord tumor? Two cases of mistaken identity, Dev. Med. Child Neurol. **17:**232, 1975.

57. Illingworth, R. S.: The diagnosis of cerebral palsy in the first year of life, Dev. Med. Child Neurol. **8:**178, 1966.

58. Ingram, T. T. S.: Clinical significance of the infantile feeding reflexes, Dev. Med. Child Neurol. **4:**159, 1962.

59. Ingram, T. T. S.: Paediatric aspects of cerebral palsy, Edinburgh, 1964, Churchill Livingstone.

60. Jacobson, M.: Developmental neurobiology, New York, 1970, Holt, Rinehart & Winston, Inc.

61. Jones, M. H.: Differential diagnosis and natural history of the cerebral palsied child. In Samilson, R. L., editor: Orthopaedic aspects of cerebral palsy, Philadelphia, 1975, J. B. Lippincott Co.

62. Knuppel, R. A., et al.: Experience of a Massachusetts perinatal center, N. Engl. J. Med. **300:**560, 1979.

63. Korobkin, R.: The relationship between head circumference and the development of communicating hydrocephalus following intraventricular hemorrhage, Pediatrics **56:**74, 1975.

64. Korobkin, R.: The prognosis for survivors of perinatal intraventricular hemorrhage. In Korobkin, R., and Guilleminault, C., editors: Advances in perinatal neurology, vol. I, Jamaica, N.Y., 1979, SP Medical Scientific Books.

65. Kyllerman, M., and Steen, G.: Intermittently progressive dyskinetic syndrome in glutaric aciduria, Neuropaediatric **8:**397, 1977.

66. Lemire, R. J., et al.: Normal and abnormal development of the human nervous system, Hagerstown, Md. 1975, Harper & Row, Publishers.

67. Lubchenco, L. O., Delivoria-Papadopoulos, M., and Searls, D.: Long-term follow-up studies of prematurely born infants. Part II. Influence of birth weight and gestational age on sequelae, J. Pediatr. **10:**509, 1972.

68. Milani-Comparetti, A., and Gidoni, E. A.: Pattern analysis of motor development and its disorders, Dev. Med. Child Neurol. **9:**625, 1967.

69. Minear, W. L.: A classification of cerebral palsy, Pediatrics **18:**841, 1956.

70. Molnar, G. E., and Gordon, S. U.: Cerebral palsy: predictive value of selected clinical signs for early prognostication of motor function, Arch. Phys. Med. Rehabil. **57:**153, 1976.

71. O'Malley, P. J., and Griffith, J. F.: Perceptuo-motor dysfunction in the child with hemiplegia, Dev. Med. Child Neurol. **19:**172, 1977.

72. Paine, R. S., and Oppe, T. E.: Neurological examination of children, Clin. Dev. Med. **20/21:** 1966.

73. Pape, K. E., et al.: The status at two years of low-birth-weight infants born in 1974 with birth weights of less than 1,001 gm, J. Pediatr. **93:**253, 1978.

74. Penn, R. D., and Etzel, M. L.: Chronic cerebellar stimulation and developmental reflexes, J. Neurosurg. **46:**506, 1977.

75. Perlstein, M. A.: Cerebral palsy—incidence, etiology, pathogenesis, Arch. Pediatr. **72:**288, 1962.

76. Plum, P.: Aetiology of athetosis with special reference to neonatal asphyxia, idiopathic icterus, and ABO-incompatibility, Arch Dis. Child. **40:**376, 1965.

77. Purpura, D. P.: Dendritic spine "dysgenesis" and mental retardation, Science **186:**1126, 1974.

78. Rawlings, G., et al.: Changing prognosis for infants of very low birth weight, Lancet **1:**516, 1971.
79. Richman, D. P., Stewart, R. M., and Caviness, V. S., Jr.: Microgyria, lissencephaly and neuron migration to the cerebral cortex: an architectonic approach, Neurology **23:**413, 1973.
80. Robinson, R. O.: The frequency of other handicaps in children with cerebral palsy, Dev. Med. Child Neurol. **15:**305, 1973.
81. Russman, B. S., et al.: Chronic cerebellar stimulator in children with cerebral palsy—a controlled study, Neurology **29:**543, 1979.
82. Saint-Anne Dargassies, S.: Long-term neurological follow-up study of 286 truly premature infants. Part I, Neurological sequelae, Dev. Med. Child Neurol. **19:**462, 1977.
83. Sanner, G.: The dysequilibrium syndrome, Neuropaediatrie **4:**402, 1973.
84. Sanner, G., and Hagberg, B.: 188 cases of non-progressive ataxic syndromes in childhood, neuropaediatrie **5:**224, 1974.
85. Sarnat, H. B., and Sarnat, M. S.: Neonatal encephalopathy following fetal distress, Arch. Neurol. **33:**696, 1976.
86. Scherzer, A. L., and Mike, V.: Cerebral palsy and the low-birth-weight child, Am. J. Dis. Child. **128:**199, 1974.
87. Seidel, U. P., Chadwick, O. F. D., and Rutter, M.: Psychological disorders in crippled children. A comparative study of children with and without brain damage, Dev. Med. Child Neurol. **17:**563, 1975.
88. Solomon, G. E., et al.: Natural history of acute hemiplegia of childhood, Brain **93:**107, 1970.
89. Stewart, A.: The risk of handicap due to birth defect in infants of very low birthweight, Dev. Med. Child Neurol. **14:**585, 1972.
90. Teberg, H. J., Wu, P. Y. K., and Hodgman, J. E.: Developmental and neurological outcome of infants with birth-weight under 1500 grams, Clin. Res. **21:**322, 1973.
91. Tizard, J. P. M., Paine, R. S., and Crothers, B.: Disturbances of sensation in children with hemiplegia, J.A.M.A. **155:**628, 1954.
92. Touwen, B.: Neurological development in infancy, Clin. Dev. Med. **58:**1, 1976.
93. Vining, E. P. G., et al.: Cerebral palsy—a pediatric developmentalist's overview, Am. J. Dis. Child. **130:**643, 1976.
94. Volpe, J. J.: Perinatal hypoxic-ischemic brain injury, Pediatr. Clin. North Am. **23:**383, 1976.
95. Volpe, J. J.: Neonatal intracranial hemorrhage: pathophysiology, neuropathology and clinical features, Clin. Perinatol. **4:**77, 1977.
96. Volpe, J. J.: Normal and abnormal human brain development, Clin. Perinatol. **4:**3, 1977.
97. Yakovlev, P. I., and Wadsworth, R. C.: Schizencephalies: a study of the congenital clefts in the cerebral mantle, J. Neuropathol. Exp. Neurol. **5:**116, 1946.

SUGGESTED READINGS FOR ORTHOPEDIC ASPECTS

Banks, H. H., and Green, W. T.: The correction of equinus deformity in cerebral palsy, J. Bone Joint Surg. **40-A:**1359, 1958.
Banks, H. H., and Green, W. T.: Adductor myotomy and obturator neurectomy for the correction of adduction contracture of the hip in cerebral palsy, J. Bone Joint Surg. **42-A:**111, 1960.
Banks, H. H., and Panagakos, P.: The role of the orthopedic surgeon in cerebral palsy, Pediatr. Clin. North Am. **14:**495, 1967.
Bobath, K., and Bobath, B.: Control of motor function in the treatment of cerebral palsy, Physiotherapy **43:**295, 1957.
Bobath, K., and Bobath, B.: The facilitation of normal postural reactions and movements in the treatment of cerebral palsy, Physiotherapy **50:**246, 1964.
Crothers, B., and Paine, R. S.: The natural history of cerebral palsy, Cambridge, Mass., 1959, Harvard University Press.
Goldner, J. L., and Nashold, B. S.: In Keats, S., editor: Operative orthopedics in cerebral palsy, Springfield, Ill., 1970, Charles C Thomas, Publisher.
Green, W. T., and Banks, H. H.: Flexor carpi ulnaris transplant and its use in cerebral palsy, J. Bone Joint Surg. **44-A:**1343, 1962.
Inglis, A. E., and Cooper, W.: Release of the flexor-pronator origin for flexion deformities of the hand and wrist in spastic paralysis. A study of eighteen cases, J. Bone Joint Surg. **48-A:**847, 1966.
Samilson, R. L., editor: Orthopedic aspects of cerebral palsy, Clin. Dev. Med. vol. 52/53, 1975.
Zausmer, E.: Locomotion in cerebral palsy. The approach of the physical therapist, Clin. Orthop. **47:**49, 1966.

7

The child with a seizure disorder

Israel F. Abroms

THE ROLE OF THE PEDIATRICIAN

A seizure is a symptom of abnormal paroxysmal electrical discharges from the brain. There are genetic factors as well as numerous acquired disease states that must be considered in determining the cause of a seizure disorder.

Accurate statistics about the prevalence of seizures in the United States are difficult to obtain. Approximately 1% of all individuals have a seizure disorder.[2] In pediatric practice the prevalence is thought to be 0.5%. From 3% to 5% of young children will have a *febrile* seizure within the first 6 years of life.[62]

The pediatrician or primary care physician (PCP) should play a major role in the work-up and management of the child with febrile and nonfebrile seizures. Often the child who has experienced his first seizure is brought to the physician's office in great haste by distraught parents. Occasionally the pediatrician is called while the child is having a major seizure but more often the child is recovering or has recovered completely. At this point the unraveling of the cause must begin with a careful history of the ictal events and a detailed family history followed by a comprehensive general and neurological examination. Most often the parents are anxious and confused, and the PCP must be supportive of both the patient and the parents. Education about the seizure, its cause, the work-up, treatment, and prognosis must be addressed as soon as possible.

The PCP will then begin the work-up of this initial seizure. The child should be admitted to the hospital and a comprehensive study begun. If long-term anticonvulsants are indicated, the PCP is in the best position to monitor their use; previous knowledge of the patient can help to discern medicational side effects. Nonfebrile seizures in the majority of children can be totally controlled on such relatively safe anticonvulsants as barbiturates and phenytoin. Thus the need for neurological referral could be confined to the child with intractable seizures or when the variety of seizure demands more unusual anticonvulsants. The pediatrician is also in the best position to determine whether the child or parents need more expert psychological support during this early adjustment phase of what may become a lengthy pediatric management problem.

ETIOLOGY
Genetic or spike-wave pattern epilepsy

Extensive studies of families with epilepsy have established that a cerebral dysrhythmia, which shows a 2½ to 3½ Hz spike-wave pattern on an electroencephalogram (EEG), is inherited as a mendelian dominant character.[19,59,75] Lennox and Lennox,[47] in studies of monozygotic twins, found both members affected with seizures in 85% of the cases; if the twins were dizygotic, both were affected in 15.9% of the cases. Studies by Metrakos and Metrakos[59] in patients with ''spike-wave epilepsy'' have shown this disorder in 8% of siblings; in 37% of family members the EEG will show spike-wave pattern abnormalities but no seizures occur. No gross or microscopical structural abnormalities of the brain have been described in patients with spike-wave pattern epilepsy.

Acquired factors

The causes of acquired or symptomatic seizures are protean. In essence, metabolic or structural abnormalities temporarily or permanently change the electrical stability of a group of neurons in the brain. This focus, then, initiates the seizure when surrounding inhibitory neurons are not able to contain the spread of electrical excitation. Following is a summary of the prenatal, perinatal, and postnatal etiological factors associated with seizures. It is a modified version of a table by Chao.[9]

I. Prenatal factors
  A. Genetic epilepsy
  B. Cerebral and intracranial vascular malformations
    1. Porencephaly
    2. Absent corpus callosum
    3. Lissencephaly
    4. Schizencephaly
    5. Holoprosencephaly
    6. Hemispheral arteriovenous malformations

  C. Neurocutaneous syndromes
    1. Tuberous sclerosis
    2. Sturge-Weber syndrome
    3. Neurofibromatosis
    4. Linear sebaceum nevus
    5. Incontinentia pigmenti
    6. Klippel-Trenaunay syndrome
  D. Recognizable syndromes of cognitive and somatic growth retardation associated with seizures
    1. Down syndrome
    2. Trisomy 18 syndrome
    3. Trisomy 13 syndrome
    4. Angelman ''happy puppet'' syndrome
    5. Rubinstein-Taybi syndrome—25% have seizures
    6. Zellweger syndrome, cerebrohepatorenal syndrome
    7. De Lange syndrome—10% have seizures
  E. Metabolic disorders
    1. Phenylketonuria
    2. Maple syrup urine disease
    3. Glycogen storage disease
    4. Tay-Sachs disease and other lipoidoses
    5. Menke syndrome (steely-hair or kinky-hair disease)
  F. Intrauterine fetal infections
    1. Rubella
    2. Cytomegalovirus
    3. Toxoplasmosis
    4. Congenital syphilis
  G. Physical and maternal factors
    1. Radiation during pregnancy
    2. Intrauterine hypoxia, for example, toxemia of pregnancy, trauma, chronic renal disease
    3. Toxins, for example, alcohol, narcotics
II. Paranatal factors
  A. Hypoxic-ischemic encephalopathy
    1. Obstetrical complications, for example, dysfunctional labor, abruptio placentae, malpresentation, cord prolapse, difficult forceps delivery
    2. Neonatal complications, for example, prematurity, apnea, respiratory distress syndrome, drug overdosage
  B. Trauma, intracranial hemorrhage
  C. Metabolic disorders
    1. Hypocalcemia
    2. Hypoglycemia
    3. Hypomagnesemia
    4. Hypernatremia and hyponatremia
    5. Pryidoxine deficiency and dependency
    6. Hyperbilirubinemia
    7. Drug withdrawal

D. Intracranial infections
1. Meningitis, especially *E. coli* (serotype K1) and group B *Streptococcus*
2. Encephalitis, for example, herpes simplex

III. Postnatal factors
A. Head injuries
1. Cerebral contusion or laceration
2. Intracerebral hematoma
3. Subarachnoid hemorrhage
4. Acute or chronic subdural hematoma

B. Infections and parainfectious processes of the brain
1. Acute bacterial meningitis
2. Chronic bacterial meningitis, for example, tuberculosis
3. Chronic fungal and protozoal meningitis, for example, cryptococcosis
4. Acute encephalitis, for example, mumps, measles, herpes simplex, equine encephalitis
5. Chronic encephalitis, for example, subacute sclerosing panencephalitis
6. Brain abscess
7. Reye syndrome
8. Acute hemorrhagic leukoencephalopathy
9. Shigellosis

C. Vascular diseases
1. Cerebral arterial thrombosis, embolism, and hemorrhage
2. Cerebral venous thrombosis
3. Collagen diseases
4. Hypertensive encephalopathy

D. Brain tumors

E. Toxins
1. Lead and other heavy metal encephalopathy
2. Immunization reactions
3. Drug reactions
   a. Cerebral stimulants, for example, ephedrine, theophylline
   b. Antihistaminics, for example, diphenhydramine (Benadryl)
   c. Steroids
   d. Isoniazid
   e. Local anesthetics
   f. Ketamine anesthetic

F. Degenerative diseases of brain
1. Gray matter disease, for example, cerebral lipoidoses, mucopolysaccharidoses, Alpers syndrome
2. White matter diseases, for example, metachromatic leukodystrophy, Krabbe disease, multiple sclerosis

G. Metabolic disorders
1. Hypoxic encephalopathy
2. Electrolyte disorders, for example, hypernatremia and hyponatremia
3. Hypoglycemia
4. Hypocalcemia
5. Hypomagnesemia
6. Hyperthermia and febrile convulsions
7. Wilson disease
8. Juvenile Huntington chorea
9. Acute porphyria

CLINICAL CLASSIFICATION OF SEIZURES[28]
Generalized epilepsy

Grand mal seizures. Grand mal seizures are characterized by a sudden cry, upward deviation of both eyes, loss of consciousness, and a fall to the ground. The limbs are tonically extended, and at this point arching of the back is often seen. Occasionally the arms are held flexed. There is associated cyanosis because of cessation of intercostal and diaphragmatic movements. The tongue may be bitten during this phase (usually on one side) due to tonic contraction of the masseter muscles. Contraction of the bladder or bowel musculature may produce incontinence. After this tonic phase rhythmic clonic movements (rapid extension followed by slower flexion) of all extremities may follow. Copious salivation will become "frothy" with return of respiratory movements. The interval between clonic movements gradually increases, and postictal limpness, drowsiness, and prolonged sleep may follow (postictal phase). Actual temporary paralysis of one side of the body (Todd paralysis) may be seen. This usually lasts less than 6 hours, however.

It is well established that specific sensory stimuli can induce seizures. This is known as reflex or evoked epilepsy and is usually atonic, myoclonic, or generalized tonic-clonic in nature. The most common form is photosensitive epilepsy, in which stroboscopic light, a flickering television set, or even an automobile drive down a tree-lined, sunlit street can induce a seizure.[41] Seizures can be brought on by a sudden startle (either auditory or tactile), taste, smell, pain, movements of the limbs (particularly the lower limbs), reading, music, writing, or vestibular stimuli.

Petit mal form of absence seizure[5]. During petit mal seizures there is a sudden cessation of movement and speech; the patient stares straight ahead and loses consciousness.[8] This is often accompanied by rhythmical fluttering movements of both eyelids and occasionally some repetitive bilateral hand or finger movements.[66] The spell usually lasts 10 seconds or less.

The "true" petit mal syndrome usually starts after the age of 3 and is most commonly seen in girls in the 5 to 9 year old age range but may occasionally start in adolescence.[15] The pathognomonic EEG finding is 3 per second synchronous spike and wave bursts, which can be activated by hyperventilation. Absence seizures cease by the time the patient is 18 years of age in over 70% of cases. If generalized tonic-clonic seizures occur as well, only about 30% of patients stop having seizures.[10,72] Good prognostic factors include a negative family history for seizures, normal intellect, and normal background activity in the EEG.[72]

Atypical absence seizures (petit mal variant). Atypical absence seizures consist of staring straight ahead with associated fluttering eye movements and last more than 10 seconds. Occasionally this will be associated with clonic movements of the limbs or autonomic nervous system phenomena such as urinary incontinence. This variety of absence seizures is usually part of a syndrome in which myoclonic and atonic seizures also occur.[29] The EEG shows atypical slow (2 to 2½ Hz) spike and wave abnormalities, sometimes activated by both stroboscopic light and hyperventilation. Over many months or years, cognitive deterioration may be noted.[4] This syndrome is known as the Lennox-Gastaut syndrome. Myoclonic, atonic, and generalized tonic-clonic seizures may be noted as well.[55]

Myoclonic seizures. In generalized myoclonic seizures there is a sudden contraction of all muscle groups, lasting just 1 or 2 seconds. If the patient is standing, he will fall "like a log," either forward or, more often, backward. Often this type of seizure is associated with atypical absences and atonic seizures. The EEG shows 2 to 2½ Hz spike or polyspike slow wave complexes, which may occur interictally.[4,55]

Atonic seizures. Atonic seizures are associated with inhibition of tone in the trunk and limbs, and the patient crumples to the ground where he is standing. They are usually brief, lasting only 1 or 2 seconds. The EEG will often show atypical spike and wave abnormalities or polyspike and wave bursts.[4,55] Control of seizures in this group of patients is often difficult.

Infantile spasms. Infantile spasms are infantile myoclonic epilepsy, in which there is a sudden flexion of the neck, trunk, and thighs with forward extension of the upper limbs.[38] This disorder is also known as West syndrome. The seizures usually start between 6 and 12 months of age but have begun as early as 2 to 3 months. In 70% of patients this syndrome is symptomatic of some other diffuse cerebral disease, such as perinatal hypoxic encephalopathy, hypoglycemia, intrauterine infection (e.g., cytomegalovirus, toxoplasmosis, or rubella), postnatal meningitis or encephalitis, or a neurocutaneous disorder such as tuberous sclerosis. About 30% of cases are cryptogenic. This group has a better prognosis, but follow-up studies have shown that only 37% of these infants will attend normal school despite treatment.[40] In the group of West syndrome patients with known cause, no child was in a normal school and 20% were in a training center or "educationally subnormal school." Of the 150 cases in this study, 22% of the patients died, usually before the age of 4 years.[40] The EEG abnormalities are diffuse with multifocal seizure discharges. With time, there is marked delta slowing of background rhythms and asynchronous, irregular, high-voltage spikes and slow waves. In sleep, a burst-suppression pattern will be seen. All these features in the EEG are known as *hypsarrhythmia*. The treatment of choice is adrenocorticotropic hormone (ACTH), but EEG and clinical improvement is seen using valproic acid or clonazepam.[46,59]

Focal epilepsy

Jacksonian seizures. Jacksonian seizures are characterized by repetitive movements starting in one part of a limb, followed by a "march" up the limb to involve the face or the other limb on the same side of the body before, perhaps, becoming secondarily generalized and involving the other side of the body. A seizure focus may be present in the contralateral hemisphere in the frontal lobe. Another type of focal motor seizure is an *adversive seizure,* in which an excitatory stimulus, often from the prefrontal cortex on one side of the brain will produce a movement of the head and eyes toward the opposite side. In epilepsia partialis continua the seizure is confined to a distal limb or the facial muscles. Neuropathological lesions are found in or near the motor cortex in many, but not all, patients.[78]

Focal sensory seizures. The initial depolarization potentials in focal sensory seizures may originate in the sensory areas of the brain. If the somatosensory cortex is involved, the aura of a seizure may consist of paresthesia in the contralateral limb. A buzzing noise or a feeling of vertigo may precede a seizure. This aura may arise from the auditory or vestibular cortex, which is an inner gyrus of the temporal lobe, known as Heschl's gyrus. Patients with seizures originating from the parieto-occipital lobe may have an aura of bright flashing lights or patterns preceding a seizure; less often, the patient experiences an elaborate panoramic visual sequence.

There is an unusual syndrome in childhood described as sylvian seizures[50] or "benign childhood epilepsy with rolandic discharges,"[49] in which a focus appears to arise from the somatosensory (or motor) cortex, just above the sylvian fissure. This condition usually begins between 6 and 12 years of age; patients will usually wake in the early hours of the morning with peculiar sensations on one side of the face, tongue, or jaw.[48] Consciousness is often preserved, salivation increased, and there may be speech arrest due to temporary weakness of the oral and pharyngeal muscles. Tonic or clonic movements of the face and, less often, the limbs may occur. The EEG shows a central or midtemporal spike-wave focus. These patients respond well to phenytoin, and on follow-up 75% were seizure free after 5 years.[50]

Psychomotor and autonomic seizures (complex partial seizures). Many psychomotor and autonomic seizures are associated with psychic, emotional, or sensory manifestations. Auras of fear or anger can precede the seizure; unusual sensations in the epigastric region

(abdominal epilepsy)[20] which may move up to the neck, are described by patients. Consciousness can be retained throughout.

More complicated auras may include feelings of depersonalization or déjà vu—that one is doing something one has done before. The psychomotor seizure may take the form of a prolonged absence or fugue state, in which the patient remains in a confused state for minutes or hours. The motor manifestations characteristic of the psychomotor seizure may include speech arrest, adversive head movements, laughing (gelastic epilepsy), lip smacking, chewing, swallowing, fumbling with the hands, running in a circle (cursive epilepsy), and other involved motor sequences.[11] Autonomic disturbances may include excessive salivation, vomiting, flushing, pallor, or urinary and fecal incontinence.

After the seizure the patient may be lethargic and sleep for hours. There may be further vomiting and headache. The speech difficulties may persist for minutes or hours. Often an anterior temporal spike focus, activated by sleep, is noted in the EEG. Nasopharyngeal electrodes may be helpful in detecting medial temporal lobe foci.

PARTICULAR FORMS OF SEIZURES
Neonatal seizures

It is appropriate to consider this group of seizures as a separate entity because there are many unique characteristics of the seizures and etiology.[6,35,51,82] The neonatal mortality is 15% to 20%, and 17.5% to 48% of surviving infants have severe neurological sequelae, such as recurrent seizures, mental retardation, and cerebral palsy.[43,45,70,82]

The incidence of neonatal seizures is 2 to 14 per thousand live births. Tonic seizures are more common in premature infants, whereas "minor or subtle seizures" and multifocal clonic seizures are more common in full-term infants.[82] Minor or subtle seizures may be manifested as rhythmical movements of the eyes to one side, blinking of the eyelids, sucking, chewing, or lip smacking movements, apnea, posturing of one limb, swimming movements of the upper limbs, or peddling movements of the lower limbs.[70,82] There may be vasomotor phenomena with pallor, flushing, bradycardia, and lowered blood pressure. With multifocal clonic movements, the seizures may migrate randomly from limb to limb. Focal clonic hemiconvulsions may be seen; these may change from one side to the other and do not necessarily imply a focal lesion. Occasionally myoclonic seizures involving one or more limbs are noted in the newborn infant.

In the elucidation of the cause and the evaluation of the neonate with seizures, a careful history of the prenatal, natal, and postnatal events must be taken and a full examination made.

Perinatal asphyxia[81] and intracranial hemorrhage account for the majority of neonatal seizures: 75% in a recent study.[56] Perinatal asphyxia may produce the ''hyperirritable syndrome'' in an infant. Threre may be a bulging fontanelle if cerebral edema is prominent, a high-pitched cry, opisthotonic posturing, marked jitteriness, hyperreflexia of the limbs, and bilateral ankle clonus. More frequently, however, the neurological examination reveals a quiet, depressed hypotonic infant with poor head control in the traction response and hypotonia of the trunk and limbs associated with brisk deep tendon reflexes. Sarnat and Sarnat[71] believe that if this hypotonic phase lasts less than 5 days, the prognosis for normal neurological development is favorable.

The neurological picture of intracranial hemorrhage in the newborn can vary. In the case of subarachnoid hemorrhage, the hyperirritable syndrome is common, often associated with hemiconvulsive seizures. Acute subdural hematoma in the newborn infant is rare. It may occur in very large, full-term infants born by breech or midforceps deliveries.[1] There is often a period of 12 hours during which time the infant does fairly well, then hemiconvulsions begin, associated with bulging of the fontanelle and, later, dilation of the pupil on the side of the subdural hematoma. In the presence of these localizing signs, an immediate tap of the subdural space on the affected side should be done.[1]

Intraventricular hemorrhage in the premature infant is most reliably diagnosed by computerized axial tomography (CT) scan. The clinical features include sudden hypotension and neurological deterioration in a premature infant,

usually on the second to sixth day. The infant is obtunded, has a tense fontanelle, and may have pupils that are unreactive to light, as well as loss of conjugate eye movements with the ''doll's head'' maneuver. Finally, a cardiorespiratory arrest may occur, associated with flaccid quadriparesis.

Bleeding in the posterior fossa is less common, but if diagnosed early, can be surgically remediable. Subdural blood in this location usually occurs in the large full-term infant born by breech or forceps delivery. At the end of the first week the infant develops the clinical picture of a bulging fontanelle, poor feeding, a weak suck and cry, neck hypotonia, and breathing irregularities.[30] A CT scan with a low cut through the posterior fossa will show a high density shadow of blood in this location. A similar clinical and radiographic picture may be seen with intracerebellar hemorrhages close to the midline. An intracerebellar hemorrhage in the premature infant [69] is difficult to diagnose and treat; the diagnosis is often made only at autopsy. This type of intracranial hemorrhage may be associated with the respiratory distress syndrome, sepsis, and intravascular coagulation defects.

Metabolic derangements, especially hypocalcemia[12] and hypoglycemia,[45,60] are common and in recent years are invariably seen associated with perinatal asphyxia and/or in infants with low birth weight for gestational age.[56] Withdrawal seizures are frequently encountered in newborn infants of drug-addicted mothers.[34,86] Other metabolic causes for neonatal seizures are rare; they do include hypernatremia, hyponatremia, hypomagnesemia, pyridoxine dependency, and aminoacidurias such as maple syrup urine disease, and the organic acidurias. The presence of clinical and laboratory evidence of metabolic acidosis should suggest defects in protein metabolism, such as hyperammonemia, hyperglycinemia, methylmalonic aciduria, etc. At the end of the first week, maple syrup urine disease may present with seizures.

Intracranial infections still accounted for about 12% of neonatal seizures in one study.[56] Group B beta-hemolytic *Streptococcus* and *E. coli* are the most common bacterial organisms.

Nonbacterial causes include cytomegalovirus, rubella virus, *Toxoplasma,* herpes simplex, and coxsackievirus B (the latter may be associated with myocarditis). Sepsis or meningitis can present with fever, hypothermia, tachycardia, hypotension, sclerema of the trunk and limbs, hepatomegaly associated with jaundice and a raised direct bilirubin level. The fontanelle may be full with depressed neurological signs, such as sucking responses, Moro reflex, diminished spontaneous limb movements, and hypotonia of the trunk and limbs. The presence of hepatosplenomegaly and a purpuric rash associated with chorioretinitis suggests congenital cytomegalovirus infection or toxoplasmosis.

A developmental anomaly of the brain, with or without a chromosomal disorder, must be considered, particularly if other somatic congenital abnormalities are noted.

In 9% to 34.8% of cases no cause for the seizure is discovered.[43,56] Overall, about 60% of this group are normal on follow-up.[56]

After examining the infant, blood should be drawn for blood sugar, calcium, phosphate, magnesium, and electrolyte analysis. Intravenous fluids containing 10% glucose should be commenced. If sepsis is considered, cultures of the blood, nose, throat, umbilical stump, and urine should be obtained. A cerebrospinal fluid (CSF) examination is crucial; excessive red cells in both the first and fourth collecting tubes may establish the diagnosis of subarachnoid hemorrhage. High white cell counts and positive bacterial and viral cultures may suggest that the infant's seizures have an infective cause. The level of CSF protein will give a rough indication of the integrity of the blood-brain barrier, reabsorptive capabilities for protein through the arachnoid granulations, and, perhaps, the amount of breakdown of cerebral tissue. The normal upper limit of the CSF protein in the full-term infant is about 120 mg/100 ml, whereas in the premature infant it is approximately 180 mg/100 ml.

The results of these tests will indicate specific therapy, such as intravenous glucose, intravenous and oral calcium, intramuscular magnesium, etc., if these metabolic parameters are found to be abnormal. After cultures have been taken, antibiotics should be commenced without delay, if the clinical and CSF profiles suggest sepsis or meningitis. These drugs can be stopped within a few days if cultures prove negative.

The EEG at this stage is useful diagnostically and prognostically; during the tracing pyridoxine (50 mg intravenously) can be administered. Abnormalities in the EEG will revert to normal if the seizures are due to pyridoxine dependency.

Anticonvulsants such as phenobarbital (10 mg/kg) intravenously should be commenced and repeated in 30 minutes if seizures continue.[56,82] The maintenance dosage of this medication is 5 to 8 mg/kg/24 hours in two divided doses. The half-life in the first 2 weeks is approximately 115 hours. After 4 weeks this may drop to 67 hours and thus may necessitate increasing the maintenance dosage of phenobarbital.[65,67]

If seizures continue, intravenous phenytoin (10 mg/kg) should be slowly administered.[56,82] A similar dosage can be given in 30 minutes if necessary. The maintenance dosage of this drug is 5 mg/kg/24 hours in two divided doses. In *full-term* infants the mean half-life in one study was 20.7 hours.[54] It was 7.6 hours in the second week of life, and the maintenance dosage of this drug may need to be increased at that time. Repeated blood level checks of both phenobarbital and phenytoin would help to make adjustments in dosages toward the aim of maintaining therapeutic levels. In the *premature* infant there are few reliable studies. It does appear that the half-life of phenytoin is much greater in the first two weeks; therefore after the loading dose, maintenance doses may need to be only 3 to 4 mg/kg/24 hours in two divided doses.[54]

It is clear that neonatal seizures are a major cause of death and illness and should be diagnosed and treated with vigor in a specialized intensive care unit in which all modern facilities are available. Studies by Wasterlain and Plum[84] on newborn rats given daily electroconvulsive shock therapy showed significant reduction of brain weight, brain cell number, and total brain DNA, RNA, protein, and cholesterol compared with control animals. This reduction was age dependent, thus all these changes were seen in rats aged 2 to 11 days, but lesser effects were noted in groups treated similarly at age 9 to 18 days and 19 to 28 days. An important aspect of these studies is that no focal histological changes were noted when the brains were examined, suggesting that damage is at the subcellular level.

The perinatal mortality among full-term infants experiencing neonatal seizures has decreased to 15% to 25%. It remains high in premature infants with intraventricular hemorrhage, neonatal meningitis, and meningoencephalitis and perinatal hypoxia.[73] In a recent study by Marshall and co-workers[56] neurological *sequelae* of neonatal seizures, including mental retardation, motor deficits, and seizures, were noted in 35% of patients. In a study by Keen and Lee,[43] the incidence of sequelae was 17.5%.

The neonatal EEG has helpful prognostic value in full-term newborn infants with seizures.[51,70] If the initial EEG tracing is normal, the infant has a 75% chance of being normal at 5 years. This figure is below 10% if the first EEG reveals "multifocal" or "episodic" abnormalities or if the tracing is "flat." If "unifocal" abnormal patterns are present initially and persist in serial EEGs, 40% of such patients will have neurodevelopmental sequelae at 5 years.[70]

Status epilepticus

Status epilepticus is characterized by repeated or persistent tonic, clonic, or hemiclonic seizures, usually lasting over 1 hour, during which time the patient never regains consciousness.[18] "Serial seizures" are defined as frequent, generalized, focal or multifocal convulsions occurring during the course of an acute insult to the brain, in which the patient may revert to his preexisting level of consciousness between each seizure. Absence status seizures refer to sustained clouding of consciousness with no abnormal motor activity or minimal stereotypical movements. This can be due to petit mal status or, if associated with prolonged automatisms, could be called psychomotor status. The EEG will help differentiate these two conditions. Epilepsia partialis continua describes continuous clonic movements that can last days or weeks but are limited to a discrete part of the body and are not usually associated with a change in the level of consciousness.[18]

Febrile seizures

Approximately 3% to 5% of all children under 6 years will have a seizure associated with a temperature that is usually greater than 38° C.[62,63] In 85% of patients they are "simple" febrile seizures, which are generalized tonic-clonic in nature and last less than 15 minutes. There may be a family history of febrile seizures, but nonfebrile seizures are infrequent in this population.[26,62] Other than discovering the cause of the fever, diagnostic studies, such as EEG and examination of the cerebrospinal fluid, are normal. A recent long-term follow-up of infants with febrile seizures suggested an incidence of nonfebrile epilepsy of 2% in this population. Long-term therapy with phenobarbital appears justified if the infant is under 18 months, there is a preexisting neurological problem or a strong family history of nonfebrile seizures, or the seizure is atypical.[24,62] These complicated febrile seizures[83] would last longer than 30 minutes, recur on the same day, have postictal paresis, or demonstrate focality during the seizure or persistently in the EEG.

Posttraumatic epilepsy

Following head trauma, generalized, focal motor, or sensory seizures can occur.[13] The incidence of seizures within 1 week of a head injury requiring hospitalization (early seizure) is 5% in all ages and 10% in children under 5 years.[42] If an "early" seizure is noted, recurrence may be seen in 17% to 20% of patients. However, "late traumatic epilepsy" occurs in only 2% to 4% if no seizure took place within 1 week of the head injury.[42] Status epilepticus can occur in children following relatively trivial head injuries, but no neurological sequelae may follow.[33]

DIFFERENTIAL DIAGNOSIS OF SEIZURES

Fainting or syncope. Fainting or syncope is often confused with seizures. The aura before a faint is a feeling of light-headedness associated with nausea and breaking out in a cold sweat; then vision darkens and there is loss of consciousness. The patient then falls down and is quite pale before and immediately after this fall. The heart rate slows, or complete asystole may occur for a few seconds. If blood supply to the lower brain stem is not restored, a tonic seizure with extension of the arms and arching of the back may occur following this syncopal attack. Afterward the patient becomes alert rapidly; no postictal drowsiness or headache is noted.

Breath-holding spells. In infancy cyanotic breath-holding spells may lead to tonic seizures.[53] The child is thwarted, cries, becomes cyanosed, holds his breath, and then falls down. Tonic movements of the trunk and limbs may occur, followed by limpness. He then recovers rapidly, without postictal features.

Basilar migraine. Basilar migraine can produce bilateral visual aurae, vertigo, altered hearing, and brief loss of consciousness with falling to the ground. On recovery, very little postictal drowsiness is noted, and a pounding headache, located occipitally, is characteristic.[31] A prior history from the patient of unilateral throbbing headaches without loss of consciousness and a positive family history of migraine may be forthcoming.

Night terrors. Night terrors (pavor nocturnus) involve the child awakening about 1½ hours after going to sleep with visual or auditory hallucinations without becoming totally awake.[77] After 10 or 15 minutes the child goes back to sleep and has no memory of this event. This is thought to be a disturbance of sleep when the child is changing from slow-wave sleep to rapid eye movement (REM) sleep. The child with this condition often responds to a small dose of diazepam before bedtime, which prevents deep slow-wave sleep from occurring.

Benign paroxysmal vertigo of childhood. Benign paroxysmal vertigo of childhood is thought to be due to unilateral inflammation of a vestibular nerve.[44] Vertigo causes the child to fall down, but no loss of consciousness occurs with this condition, and the EEG is invariably normal. Careful caloric testing may show an asymmetry of responses, indicating unilateral

vestibular nerve dysfunction. Many of these children have a family history of migraine and may develop more characteristic patterns of recurrent abdominal pain and vascular-type headaches at a later age. This latter diagnosis should be considered in this syndrome, especially if the episodes are longer lasting and the caloric tests are normal.

DIAGNOSTIC STUDIES

When an infant or a child has his first nonfebrile seizure, it is advisable to admit him to the hospital for diagnostic studies. After a detailed history and physical and neurological examinations, the following should be obtained: a full blood count; the fasting blood sugar level (6-hour glucose tolerance test if hypoglycemia is strongly considered); the levels of calcium, phosphate, magnesium, and lead; a CSF examination; and amino acid screening of the urine. If the seizure was focal, a skull x-ray series should be made. In an infant under 6 to 9 months studies to exclude cytomegalovirus, rubella, and toxoplasmosis can be useful. It is useful to have an EEG done within a few days of the seizure. This may show some focal deficits that do not appear in an interictal EEG made several weeks or months later. It is imperative to try to obtain a sleep tracing. The best way to do this is by sleep deprivation on the night before the tracing.

If focal deficits remain after a seizure and do not begin to improve within 6 to 12 hours, it is important to consider further diagnostic studies, particularly if there are focal changes on the postictal EEG. These include a radionucleotide brain scan and a CT scan. If focal lesions are noted on either of these studies, it may be necessary to proceed to a cerebral arteriogram or a pneumoencephalogram.

PATHOLOGICAL CORRELATIONS OF SEIZURES

Generalized seizures without a preceeding aura and true petit mal seizures appear to have no histological changes in the brain. The value of establishing a focal seizure disorder by history, examination, or special studies implies a focal pathology. This lesion can be benign, such as an area of gliosis or a hematoma, or it can be more troublesome, such as a brain tumor, abscess, or an arteriovenous malformation. There may be a long delay between the onset of focal seizures and the time when a brain tumor becomes detectable.[64]

MANAGEMENT

Education of the patient, family, and school system. Any physician caring for children and adolescents with seizures must have time to spend with the patient and family, answering their questions and allaying their fears. Time devoted to these concerns on the first visit promotes trust between the physician and patient. This allows the physician to emphasize the need for good compliance relative to medication, blood level checks, EEGs, and return visits.

The issue of recurrent seizures must be raised, particularly in the case of status epilepticus with the attending risks of hypoxemia and added cerebral dysfunction. An important restriction is not to allow the patient to go swimming alone, since drowning will occur with unconsciousness during a generalized seizure. If the patient works near dangerous machinery or an open furnace, he may need to alter his occupation, either temporarily or permanently, depending on the severity of his seizure disorder. The problem of a patient driving an automobile is addressed by each state; if a patient has had a seizure involving loss of consciousness, most states in the United States will not allow that patient to drive a motor vehicle for 12 to 18 months. He will then require a physician's letter advising the registrar of motor vehicles as to whether a driver's license should be issued or renewed. A major problem arises if the patient's livelihood depends on him driving a motor vehicle or train or piloting an airplane. The patient's welfare and the public's safety must be the paramount consideration in advising the patient and his family. Temporary alteration of duties may be useful for a patient until the severity of the seizure disorder and the ease with which control is achieved can be assessed.

The most frequent reason for recurrence of seizures is noncompliance, in that medications are not being taken as prescribed. Repeated checks of blood levels of anticonvulsants can document noncompliance in the presence of

adequate dosage. However, the pharmacokinetics of one or more drugs vary in individuals and may be the explanation for spurious anticonvulsant blood levels. On occasion, high temperature and infections of any kind (even without fever) can induce seizures. Major emotional factors can trigger seizures in the susceptible patient. Other medications can aggravate seizures; this has been established with diphenhydramine hydrochloride (Benadryl) in relation to febrile seizures. Central nervous system stimulants, such as amphetamine, methylphenidate hydrochloride (Ritalin), and theophylline and some of the major tranquilizers, such as chlorpromazine (Thorazine), thioridazine (Mellaril), etc., as well as ketamine (used as an anesthetic agent), have been known to induce seizures.

It is important to discuss the first aid of a generalized seizure with the family. The most important aspect is for the parent to remain with the child and turn him over onto his side or stomach so that his tongue and secretions will fall forward and will not occlude the oropharynx. It is difficult to insert an object into the mouth to prevent the tongue from being bitten. Often the teeth are clenched during the tonic phase of a seizure and one can break teeth in an effort to insert a tongue blade or spoon into the mouth. Obviously, if the child has a seizure near a dangerous machine or fire, the child needs to be removed without delay. If the seizure is generalized and lasts more than 5 to 8 minutes, an ambulance should be called and the child taken to the nearest emergency room.

Medications. If a decision is made to treat the seizures, the rapidity with which one wants to obtain therapeutic levels of medication must be assessed. For instance, with status epilepticus intravenous medication is called for, whereas with petit mal seizures oral medication taken for a week or two to get to the full therapeutic level would be in order.

The treatment of status epilepticus. Following is a treatment plan for status epilepticus modified from Dodson and co-workers[18]:

1. Record vital signs continuously and maintain an airway and good blood pressure levels.
2. Draw blood for metabolic studies, such as

glucose, electrolyte, blood urea nitrogen (BUN), calcium, magnesium, and anticonvulsant levels (if the patient is already on anticonvulsant medications).

3. Intravenous 10% glucose in Isolyte M should be started, and fluids should be limited to 1000 to 1200 ml/m²/24 hours. An intake-output measurement system should be instituted using an indwelling catheter if necessary.

4. Hyperthermia must be treated vigorously with tepid sponging, ice packs, etc. The underlying disease producing the status epilepticus must be established and appropriate studies, such as CSF examination, blood cultures, etc., must be done and specific therapy instituted whenever feasible.

5. If raised intracranial pressure is present, intravenous dexamethasone or mannitol should be considered.

6. Specific anticonvulsants must be administered. Intravenous phenytoin (5 to 10 mg/kg) in saline solution can be given slowly over 10 to 15 minutes. This dosage could be repeated in 1 hour if necessary. It is important to rapidly determine the pretreatment level of phenytoin, if the patient was receiving this drug, to gauge further dosages. If seizures are not controlled with therapeutic levels of phenytoin alone, phenobarbital can be administered intravenously; 5 to 10 mg/kg can be given, depending on the severity of the seizures and previous dosages of this medication. A repeat dose of phenobarbital can be given in 1 hour if necessary. One must decide on that dosage after receiving the results of the pretreatment phenobarbital level check, if the patient was on that drug. Within 6 hours, maintenance doses of phenytoin and phenobarbital should commence at approximately 5 mg/kg/24 hours in two divided doses.

Intravenous diazepam can be used as the first drug for status epilepticus.[23,52] In my experience, it is more effective if the seizures are due to a structural cerebral lesion rather than a metabolic derangement. The recommended dosage is 0.25 mg/kg with a maximum of 10 mg intravenously over a 5-minute period. If seizures continue, a second dose of 0.4 mg/kg (maximum of 15 mg) could be given over a 10-minute period. This dosage could be repeated in 30 minutes if necessary. Respiratory depression may occur with this drug, particularly if phenobarbital has previously been used, because the two drugs are synergistic. Intravenous diazepam is helpful but its effect is shortlived, and phenytoin or phenobarbital should be given within 30 minutes of the intravenous diazepam to maintain seizure control. Paraldehyde can be administered rectally (0.3 ml/kg in mineral oil). This dosage can be repeated within 2 hours and then can be given every 4 to 8 hours if necessary.

Petit mal status and epilepsia partialis continua can be treated with intravenous diazepam as described earlier. Ethosuxidime and valproic acid can be used as maintenance medications for petit mal seizures, while barbiturate or phenytoin can be tried for epilepsia partialis continua. With temporal lobe status, intravenous phenytoin, as described earlier for status epilepticus, could be used. A EEG obtained at the time of this form of seizure status would be useful so that the change in electrical activity can be monitored.

Treatment of generalized seizures.[3,18,57,85] A sound approach to management of generalized seizures is to consider using one medication and obtaining therapeutic levels of this drug without producing side effects. If seizures are not controlled, a second medication should be introduced in an amount that will produce therapeutic levels within a reasonably short period of time. For generalized seizures, barbiturates and phenytoin are the most helpful drugs. Occasionally there is need for carbamazepine (Tegretol) and an additional medication, such as acetazolamide (Diamox). Valproic acid has been effective for generalized seizures on its own or together with phenobarbital or phenytoin.[41]

Treatment of petit mal seizures. The drug of choice for treatment of petit mal seizures remains ethosuximide[74] (Zarontin). Valproic acid (Depakene) and clonazepam are also effective.

Treatment of atypical absence, myoclonic, and atonic seizures. Atypical absence, myoclonic, and atonic seizures are difficult to control. There is usually a need for a major anticonvulsant, such as a barbiturate and/or phenytoin, combined with valproic acid[80] or clonazepam,[7,21,61] or acetazolamide, or methsuximide (Celontin). A ketogenic diet may be useful.[37]

The treatment of infantile spasms. Injections of ACTH for infantile spasms can be very helpful. Numerous protocols have been used. One currently being used at the University of Massachusetts Medical Center, Worcester, Massachusetts, is 60 to 80 units ACTH gel intramuscularly daily for 2 weeks, then 60 to 80 units on alternate days for 3 months, then 40 units on alternate days for 1 month followed by 20 units on alternate days for 1 month. The infant may remain on a maintenance dosage of barbiturates during this time. If seizures recur when the ACTH is withdrawn, valproic acid (Depakene)[80] or clonazepam (Clonopin)[7,21] can be introduced to take its place. If seizures are uncontrolled, other medications could be tried, as outlined earlier for the atypical absence, myoclonic, and atonic seizures.

The treatment of reflex or evoked epilepsy. It appears that valproic acid (Depakene) is very useful in photosensitive epilepsy and is the drug of choice.[59] Conditioning treatment can be helpful in the reflex epilepsies.[25]

The treatment of focal epilepsy. Focal seizures respond well to primidone (Mysoline) and phenytoin or combinations of the two. In addition, carbamazepine (Tegretol) is effective on its own or in combination with these two drugs. In the situation of intractable focal seizures that appear to arise from an accessible part of one hemisphere, neurosurgical treatment can be considered.[22,68] This requires a careful team approach on the part of the neurosurgeon, neurologist, neuropsychologist, and neuroradiologist. At operation direct electrocorticography can be helpful in further localizing an atrophic area of cortex for the neurosurgeon. Ablation of this tissue can result in complete control of seizures or significant improvement in overall seizure control in about half the patients in which this form of therapy is carried out.[22,68] A more recent development has been the use of chronic intermittent stimulation of the superior surface of the cerebellum.[32,79] Long-term follow-up results in these patients must be awaited before this form of therapy can be recommended for intractable seizures.

PROGNOSIS OF SEIZURE DISORDERS

Genetic epilepsies. The overall prognosis is good for the group of patients with genetic epilepsies. With true petit mal seizures, clinical attacks disappear by adolescence in 50% to 70% of patients.[10,15,66] With grand mal seizures, seizures often become only nocturnal and disappear totally by 18 to 20 years of age.

Atypical absence, myoclonic, and atonic seizures are often refractory to treatment. Sometimes there is a gradual tendency for clinical seizures to diminish, even though the EEG abnormalities persist. Regression in cognitive functioning as the years go by with actual decrease in IQ scores remain a most troublesome aspect in the Lennox-Gastaut syndrome.[4,29]

Infantile spasms are associated with normal development in 37% of cases, if neurological development was normal before the onset of seizures.[40] These include the cryptogenic group of patients with infantile spasms and those following immunization. In the symptomatic patients, none in this study[40] were attending normal school. Infantile spasms tend to lessen over several years, but 55% of patients in one study had other types of seizures on follow-up.[40] Focal abnormalities in the EEG may precede the hypsarrhythmic pattern and reappear several months or years later.

Focal seizures. The prognosis in focal seizures depends on the underlying disease process. Thus with an infiltrating brain tumor the prognosis would be unfavorable, but if the focal seizure relates to an area of gliosis, generally there is an improvement with time in the frequency and severity of seizures.[14] This occurs with posttraumatic epilepsy. In a third of patients with seizures, control may be incomplete. There is often a direct relationship between the difficulty with which seizures are controlled in patients and the duration of the seizure disorder. It is increasingly evident that a temporal lobe focus can, with the passage of months or years, initiate or "kindle" a "mirror" focus in the corresponding area of the opposite temporal lobe. Thus a focal EEG can change to show bilateral independent abnormalities. Therefore it is important to initiate anticonvulsant treatment as soon as possible to gain control of psychomotor seizures.

DISCONTINUATION OF ANTICONVULSANTS

If total control of seizures has been achieved for 2 to 4 years, consideration can be given to gradually withdrawing and discontinuing anticonvulsants. In one study[36] seizures recurred in 24% of patients.

Factors that would be important to take into account in this decision include the following:

1. The underlying nature of the disease process. For instance, if these seizures are due to a focal process such as a cerebral gunshot wound the likelihood of being able to withdraw anticonvulsants without recurrence of seizures would be small.
2. The severity and duration of individual seizures. If the original seizures continued for several hours, it would be wiser to continue with anticonvulsants for a longer period of time.
3. The severity of EEG abnormalities in serial tracings. If EEG seizure discharges disappear on serial EEGs done every year or 2, it would be justifiable to attempt to gradually discontinue anticonvulsant medications, one drug at a time.
4. Age factors. It is common for seizures to recur in early adolescence. This may be an inopportune time to discontinue anticonvulsants.
5. The patients with focal motor and multiple seizure types have a greater risk of recurrence than those patients having grand mal, petit mal, and psychomotor attacks.[36]

ASSOCIATED CONDITIONS, DRUG REACTIONS, AND COMPLICATIONS OF SEIZURES

Depending on the underlying disorder that is causing the seizure diathesis, there may be associated mental retardation, speech delay, significant developmental motor delay (cerebral palsy), minor motor incoordination difficulties,

behavior problems, hyperkinesis, and learning disabilities. It should be stressed that none of these conditions need to be present, particularly if the underlying cerebral lesion is confined to a localized area. Status epilepticus can produce a diffuse hypoxic encephalopathy, and it may produce regression in intellectual, speech, or motor function.

Behavior disturbances associated with seizures can be due to an underlying disturbance of the frontal or temporal lobes or their connections with the limbic system. Equally important, anticonvulsants can produce disturbed behavior. This is commonly seen with phenobarbital and primidone, particularly in infants. Hyperactivity or irritability may necessitate substituting another medication. Aberrant behavior can occur with carbamazepine and ethosuximide but is infrequently seen.

An acquired aphasia syndrome is seen occasionally in infants and children with seizures. It is postulated that bilateral temporal lobe dysfunction occurs due to seizure discharges resulting in aphasia, which may be permanent.[17,27]

The complications produced by anticonvulsants must be stressed.[3] Most anticonvulsants are central nervous system depressants. Therefore cumulative doses of anticonvulsants will produce drowsiness, lethargy, and difficulties with concentration, especially in the school setting. Following are common anticonvulsants and their complications:

1. Barbiturates: The barbiturates can produce an idiosyncratic reaction with a fever and maculopapular eruption of the skin and mucous membranes. If the drug is not stopped, Stevens-Johnson syndrome may result. The more common side effects in infants and young children are drowsiness or hyperactive behavior and poor sleeping habits.
2. Phenytoin: Within 10 to 14 days an idiosyncratic fever and a macular skin rash may occur.[16] This can develop into the Stevens-Johnson syndrome. Bone marrow suppression can occur within weeks or months, and result in aplastic anemia. Overdoses produce drowsiness, vomiting, diplopia, nystagmus, ataxia, and occa-

sionally choreoathetosis. Long-term side effects and complications with phenytoin may include hypertrophy of the gingivae, hirsutism, megaloblastic anemia, systemic lupus erythematosis, peripheral neuropathy, rickets[5] and pathological bone fractures, lymphoid hyperplasia, and lymphomas.

3. Carbamazepine (Tegretol): Despite warnings about this drug, it tends to be a relatively safe anticonvulsant. Overdoses will produce drowsiness, vomiting, agitation, ataxia, and even stupor. There are rare reports of aplastic anemia, renal and hepatic dysfunction, skin rashes, and psychotic reactions.

4. Ethosuximide (Zarontin): This drug can cause drowsiness, diplopia, skin rashes, behavior disorders, and, rarely, aplastic anemia.

5. Acetazolamide (Diamox): Drowsiness, anorexia, headaches and paresthesias can be seen with this medication.

6. Clonazepam: This drug has been associated with drowsiness, ataxia, behavioral difficulties, confusion, depression, liver dysfunction, and bone marrow suppression.

7. Valproic acid: This drug has been associated with vomiting, drowsiness and, rarely, platelet and bone marrow dysfunction. More importantly, there are several reports of fatal acute hepatic failure.[76] Thus monitoring of liver function is imperative with use of this anticonvulsant.

SOCIAL AND EMOTIONAL ASPECTS OF SEIZURES

The fact that a child has had seizures is sometimes too difficult for certain families to deal with, and denial becomes a defense mechanism. This is to the detriment of the child's emotional development. The physician must encourage a more open discussion with the family about the seizure disorder. This can be compared to many other chronic diseases, such as diabetes or cystic fibrosis. If the true facts of the child's seizure disorder are suppressed, his own fantasies about his disease may be enhanced. To foster appropriate peer relationships, simple factual explanations should be available to the patient and his friends. Similarly, in the schoolroom a level-headed approach to the child with seizures must be fostered by an understanding teacher. PCPs, especially if they are also school physicians, can be most helpful in this area by encouraging sensible and realistic attitudes in the patient, his parents, and school personnel.

Despite careful attention to these details by the primary care physician, an understanding parental attitude and an adequate education milieu, maladjustment of the patient to his seizure disorder is common. The preteen and early young adult years are particularly difficult for the patient with seizures. It is at this time that he is trying to become more independent of his family; his reliance on medication thwarts this independence. The patient with a seizure disorder should begin to take more responsibility for his medication regimen in his adolescent years. The fact that a patient with seizures continues to have spells will interfere with the consolidation of closer interpersonal relationships with his peer group. This type of maladjustment in the second decade of life may lead to rebellious behavior, manifested as rejection of medication or unrealistic choices of sport or vocational pursuits. An alternative reaction may be withdrawal from his peer group. This can be severe and will require psychological counselling. In the 11 to 15 year age group, short-term group therapy sessions can often be helpful, with the inclusion of patients with other chronic diseases, such as diabetes, chronic renal failure, congenital heart disease, and cystic fibrosis. The need for a psychiatric social worker, psychologist, or psychiatrist to help the primary care physician or consultant neurologist often becomes urgent with this age group.

PREVENTION OF SEIZURE DISORDERS

In the genetic epilepsies, very little can be done to prevent the occurrence of the first seizure, but control of subsequent seizures is important. Improved obstetrical and neonatal management of high-risk infants can prevent intrauterine and perinatal hypoxic-ischemic cerebral lesions that may subsequently herald a seizure disorder. Congenital and acquired viral infections of the brain and meninges such as rubella may be prevented by immunization programs. Early diagnosis and treatment of central nervous system bacterial infections may reduce the number of children with postmeningitic seizure states. Accident prevention in the home and in the automobile can reduce the number of posttraumatic cerebral lesions leading to recurrent seizures. The seizures in many children and adults are still difficult to control, and physicians need to continue their search for safer and more efficacious anticonvulsant compounds.

REFERENCES

1. Abroms I. F., McLennan, J. E., and Mandell, F.: Acute subdural hematoma following breech delivery, Am. J. Dis. Child. **131**:192, 1977.
2. Alter, M., and Hauser, W. A., editors: The epidemiology of epilepsy: a workshop, NINDS monograph no. 14, publ. no. (NIH) 73-390, Washington, D.C., 1972, Department of Health, Education and Welfare.
3. Berman, P. H.: Management of seizure disorders with anticonvulsant drugs: current concepts, Pediatr. Clin. North Am. **23**:443, 1976.
4. Blume, W. T., David, R. B., and Gomex, M. R.: Generalized sharp and slow wave complexes: associated clinical features and long-term follow-up, Brain **96**:289, 1973.
5. Borgstedt, A. D., et al.: Long-term administration of antiepileptic drugs and the development of rickets, J. Pediatr. **18**:9, 1972.
6. Brown, J. K.: Convulsions in the newborn period, Dev. Med. Child Neurol. **15**:823, 1973.
7. Browne, T. R., and Penry, J. K.: Benzodiazepines in the treatment of epilepsy: a review, Epilepsia **14**:277, 1973.
8. Browne, T. R., et al.: Responsiveness before, during, and after spike-wave paroxysms, Neurology **24**:659, 1974.
9. Chao, D.: Paroxysmal Disorders. In Carter, S., and Gold, A. P., editors: Neurology of infancy and childhood, New York, 1974, Appleton-Century-Crofts, pp. 132-158.
10. Charlton, M. H., and Yahr, M. D.: Long-term follow-up of patients with petit mal, Arch. Neurol. **16**:595, 1967.
11. Chen, R. C., and Forster, F. M.: Cursive epilepsy and gelastic epilepsy, Neurology **23**:1019, 1973.
12. Cockburn, F., et al.: Neonatal convulsions associated with primary disturbance of calcium, phosphorus, and magnesium metabolism, Arch. Dis. Child. **48**:99, 1973.
13. Craft, A. W.: Head injury in children (Vinken, P. J.,

and Bruyn, G. W., editors), Handbook Clin. Neurol. **23**:445, 1975.
14. Currie, S., et al.: Clinical course and prognosis of temporal lobe epilepsy. A survey of 666 patients, Brain **94**:173, 1970.
15. Dalby, M. A.: Epilepsy and 3 per second spike and wave rhythms, Acta Neurol. Scand. **45** (suppl. 40): 3, 1969.
16. Dawson, K. R.: Severe cutaneous reactions to phenytoin, Arch. Dis. Child. **48**:239, 1973.
17. Deuel, R. K., and Lenn, N. J.: Treatment of acquired epileptic aphasia, J. Pediatr. **90**:959, 1977.
18. Dodson, W. E., et al.: Management of seizure disorders: selected aspects, J. Pediatr. **89**:527 and 695, 1976.
19. Doose, H., et al.: Genetic factors in spike-wave absences, Epilepsia **14**:57, 1973.
20. Douglas, E. F., and White, P. T.: Abdominal epilepsy, J. Pediatr. **78**:59, 1971.
21. Dreifuss, F. E., et al.: Serum clonazepam concentrations in children with absence seizures, Neurology **25**:255, 1975.
22. Engel, J., Jr., Driver, M. V., and Falconer, M. A.: Electrophysiological correlates of pathology and surgical results in temporal lobe epilepsy, Brain **98**:129, 1975.
23. Ferngren, H. C.: Diazepam treatment for acute convulsions in children, Epilepsia **15**:27, 1974.
24. Fishman, M. A.: Febrile seizures: the treatment of controversy, J. Pediatr. **94**:177, 1979.
25. Forster, F. M.: The classification and conditioning treatment of the reflex epilepsies, Int. J. Neurol. **9**:73, 1972.
26. Frantzen, E., et al.: A genetic study of febrile convulsions, Neurology **20**:909, 1970.
27. Gascon, G. C., Victor, D., and Lombrosco, C. T.: Language disorder, convulsive disorder and electroencephalographic abnormalities, Arch. Neurol. **28**:156, 1973.
28. Gastaut, H.: Clinical and electroencephalographical classification of epileptic seizures, Epilepsia **11**:102, 1970.
29. Gastaut, H., et al.: Childhood epileptic encephalopathy with diffuse slow spike-waves (otherwise known as "petit mal variant") or Lennox syndrome, Epilepsia **7**:139, 1966.
30. Gilles, F. H., and Shillito, J.: Infantile hydrocephalus: retrocerebellar subdural hematoma, J. Pediatr. **76**:529, 1970.
31. Golden, G. S., and French, J. H.: Basilar artery migraine in young children. Pediatrics **56**:722, 1975.
32. Grabow, J. D., et al.: Cerebellar stimulation for control of seizures, Mayo Clin. Proc. **49**:759, 1974.
33. Grand, W.: The significance of post-traumatic status epilepticus in childhood, J. Neurol. Neurosurg. Psychiatry **37**:178, 1974.
34. Herzlinger, R. A., Kandall, S. R., and Vaughan, H. G.: Neonatal seizures associated with narcotic withdrawal, J. Pediatr. **91**:638, 1977.
35. Holden, K. R., and Freeman, J. M.: Neonatal sei-

zures and their treatment, Clin. Perinatol. **2:**3, 1975.

36. Holowach, J., Thurston, D. L., and O'Leary, J.: Prognosis in childhood epilepsy: a follow-up study of 148 cases in which therapy had been suspended after prolonged anticonvulsant control, N. Engl. J. Med. **286:**169, 1972.

37. Huttenlocher, P. R., Wilbourn, A. J., and Signore, J. M.: Medium-chain triglycerides as a therapy for intractable childhood epilepsy, Neurology **21:**1097, 1971.

38. Jeavons, P. M., and Bowers, B. D.: Infantile spasms, a Review, London, 1964, William Heinemann Ltd., for the Spastic Society.

39. Jeavons, P. M., and Harding, G. F. A.: Photosensitive epilepsy, Clin. Dev. Med. **56:**1975.

40. Jeavons, P. M., Bower, B. D., and Dimitrakoudi, M.: Long-term prognosis of 150 cases of "West syndrome," Epilepsia **14:**153, 1973.

41. Jeavons, P. M., Clark, J. E., and Maheshwari, M. C.: Treatment of generalized epilepsy of childhood and adolescence with sodium valproate (Epilim), Dev. Med. Chil Neurol. **19:**9, 1977.

42. Jennett, B.: Trauma as a cause of epilepsy in childhood, Dev. Med. Child Neurol. **15:**56, 1973.

43. Keen, J. H., and Lee, D.: Sequelae of neonatal convulsions—study of 112 infants, Arch. Dis. Child. **48:**542, 1973.

44. Koenigsberger, M. R., et al.: Benign paroxysmal vertigo of childhood, Neurology **20:**1108, 1970.

45. Koivisto, M., Blanco-Sequeiros, M., and Krause, U.: Neonatal symptomatic hypoglycemia: a follow-up study of 151 children, Dev. Med. Child. Neurol. **14:**603, 1972.

46. Lacy, J. R., and Penry, J. K.: Infantile spasms, New York, 1976, Raven Press.

47. Lennox, W. G., and Lennox, M. A.: Epilepsy and related disorders, vol. I, Boston, 1960, Little Brown and Co.

48. Lerman, P., and Kivity, S.: Benign focal epilepsy of childhood, Arch. Neurol. **32:**261, 1975.

49. Loiseau, P., and Beaussart, M.: The seizures of benign childhood epilepsy with rolandic paroxysmal discharges, Epilepsia **14:**381, 1973.

50. Lombroso, C. T.: Sylvian seizures and midtemporal spike foci in children, Arch Neurol. **17:**52, 1967.

51. Lombroso, C. T.: Seizures in the newborn period (Vinken, P. J., and Bruyn, G. W., editors). Handbook Clin. Neurol. **15:**189, 1972.

52. Lombroso, C. T.: The treatment of status epilepticus, Pediatrics **53:**536, 1974.

53. Lombroso, C. T., and Lerman, P.: Breathholding spells (cyanotic and pallid infantile syncope), Pediatrics **39:**563, 1967.

54. Loughnan, P. M., et al.: Pharmacokinetic observations of phenytoin disposition in the newborn and young infant, Arch. Dis. Child. **52:**302, 1977.

55. Markand, O. N.: Slow spike-wave activity in EEG and associated clinical features: often called "Lennox" or "Lennox-syndrome," Neurology **27:**746, 1977.

56. Marshall, R., et al.: Seizures in a neonatal intensive care unit: a prospective study, Pediatr. Res. **10:**450, 1976.

57. Menkes, J. H.: The treatment of paroxysmal disorders, Pediatrics **53:**529, 1974.

58. Menkes, J. H.: Diagnosis and treatment of minor motor seizures, Pediatr. Clin. North Am. **23:**435, 1976.

59. Metrakos, K., and Metrakos, J. D.: Genetics of convulsive disorders. II, Genetic and electroencephalographic studies in centrencephalic epilepsy, Neurology **11:**474, 1961.

60. Milner, R. D.: Neonatal hypoglycaemia—a critical reappraisal, Arch. Dis. Child. **47:**679, 1972.

61. Nanda, R. N., et al.: Treatment of epilepsy with clonazepam and its effect on other anticonvulsants, J. Neurol. Neurosurg. Psychiatry **40:**538, 1977.

62. Nelson, K. B., and Ellenberg, J. H.: Predictors of epilepsy in children who have experienced febrile seizures, N. Engl. J. Med. **295:**1029, 1976.

63. Oeulette, E. M.: The child who convulses with fever, Pediatr. Clin. North Am. **21:**467, 1974.

64. Page, L. K., Lombroso, C. T., and Matson, D. D.: Childhood epilepsy with late detection of cerebral glioma, J. Neurosurg. **31:**253, 1969.

65. Painter, M. J., et al.: Phenobarbital and diphenylhydantoin levels in neonates with seizures, J. Pediatr. **92:**315, 1978.

66. Penry, J. K., and Dreifuss, F. E.: Automatisms associated with the absence of petit mal epilepsy, Arch. Neurol. **21:**142, 1969.

67. Pitlick, W., Painter, M., and Pippenger, C.: Phenobarbital pharmacokinetics in neonates, Clin. Pharmacol. Ther. **23:**346, 1978.

68. Rasmussen, T.: Surgical aspects of focal epilepsy, Electroencephalogr. Clin. Neurophysiol. **15:**1050, 1963.

69. Rom, S., Serfontein, G. L., and Humphreys, R. P.: Intracerebellar hematoma in the neonate, J. Pediatr. **93:**486, 1978.

70. Rose, A. L., and Lombroso, C. T.: Neonatal seizure states. A study of clinical, pathological and electroencephalographic features in 137 full-term babies with a long-term follow-up, Pediatrics **45:**404, 1970.

71. Sarnat, H. B., and Sarnat, M. S.: Neonatal encephalopathy following fetal distress, Arch. Neurol. **33:**696, 1976.

72. Sato, S., Dreifuss, F. E., and Penry, J. K.: Prognostic factors in absence seizures, Neurology **26:**788, 1976.

73. Seay, A. R., and Bray, P. F.: Significance of seizures in infants weighing less than 2500 grams, Arch. Neurol. **34:**381, 1977.

74. Sherwin, A., Robb, J., and Lechter, M.: Improved control of epilepsy by monitoring plasma ethosuximide, Arch. Neurol. **28:**178, 1973.

75. Sorel, L.: The descendants of epileptic patients, Epilepsia **10:**91, 1969.

76. Suchy, F. J., et al.: Acute hepatic failure associated with the use of sodium valproate: a report of two fatal cases, N. Engl. J. Med. **300:**962, 1979.

77. Tassinari, C. A., et al.: Pavor nacturnus of non-epi-

leptic nature in epileptic children, Electroencephalogr. Clin. Neurophysiol. **33:**603, 1972.

78. Thomas, J. E., Reagan, T. J., and Klass, D. W.: Epilepsia partialis continua, Arch. Neurol. **34:**266, 1977.

79. Van Buren, J. M., et al.: Preliminary evaluation of cerebellar stimulation and biological criteria in the treatment of epilepsy, J. Neurosurg. **48:**407, 1978.

80. Viking, E. P. G., Potsford, E., and Freeman, J. M.: Valproate sodium in refractory seizures, Am. J. Dis. Child. **133:**274, 1979.

81. Volpe, J. J.: Perinatal hypoxic-ischemic brain injury, Pediatr. Clin. North Am. **23:**383, 1976.

82. Volpe, J. J.: Neonatal seizures, Clin. Perinatol. **4:**43, 1977.

83. Wallace, S.: Factors predisposing to a complicated initial febrile convulsion, Arch. Dis. Child. **50:**943, 1975.

84. Wasterlain, C. G., and Plum, F.: Vulnerability of developing rat brain to electroconvulsive seizures, Arch. Neurol. **29:**38, 1973.

85. Woodbury, D. M., Penry, J. K., and Schmidt, R. P., editors: Antiepileptic drugs, New York, 1972, Raven Press.

86. Zelson, C., Rubio, E., and Wasserman, E.: Neonatal narcotic addiction. Pediatrics **48:**178, 1971.

I search within
And more I know
That strange I am
The more I grow.

Ann Sexton, 1945

8

The child with mental retardation

Albert P. Scheiner
Neal A. McNabb

The medical care of the child who is retarded is a longitudinal responsibility that is best assumed by the primary care physician. The level of intensity of involvement will change with the age of the child and the needs of the youngster and his family. The opportunity for the physician is unique. Primary care physicians are present at the time of diagnosis, perform the preschool physical examination, share the parents' anxiety about the sexuality of adolescence, and struggle with the question of out-of-home placement. No other professional is in a better position to actively participate in the growth and development of the child who is developmentally disabled.

Physicians and allied professionals who accept the responsibility for this care must be aware of their own personal feelings and phi-losophies as they relate to persons who are intellectually or functionally deficient. There is little question that their own perceptions and feelings about handicapped persons affect their therapeutic decision-making process. We have had the repeated unpleasant experience of suggesting alternate consultation when a specialist refused to provide basic treatment for a youngster with moderate to severe retardation because the specialist did not believe that the improvement of the child's overall quality of life was of any consequence. Physicians and allied professionals should also be cognizant of the fact that, if they are going to serve children who are retarded, they must be knowledgeable in child development, empathetic to the needs of the family, and ready to give the necessary time to resolve issues during periods of need and family stress. We are somewhat chagrined that we feel compelled to present this as a prerequisite for the care of the retarded child, since it would appear that the raison d'être of a primary care physician is just these qualities.

In almost all instances, as the youngster grows older, the intensity of the medical services that are traditionally provided by the primary care physician decreases (Fig. 8-1) and the need for educational and vocational services increases. Comprehensive medical evaluation is generally completed soon after the diagnosis of mental retardation is made, and education,

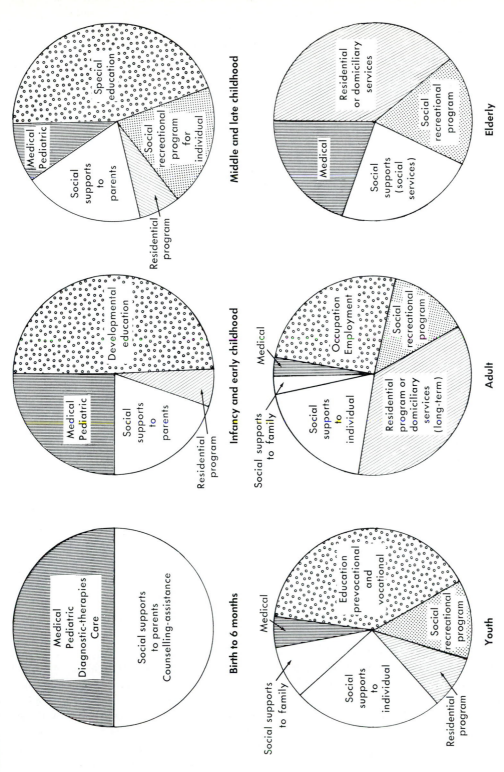

Fig. 8-1. Sequential program needs of an individual with mental retardation and other developmental disabilities. Medical needs decrease as educational and vocational needs increase. Social support needs remain reasonably constant over time while residential needs increase. Social recreational needs continue to play a permanent role throughout the life of the individual. (Developed by Cullinane, M., and presented by Crocker, A., at the Training in Developmental Pediatrics—A Transdisciplinary National Symposium, Gloucester, Mass., 1978.)

habilitation, and counselling assume primary importance. The need for primary care, however, always exists. Despite this need, a study by Kanthor[38] indicated that 27% of the children with spina bifida had no source of primary care, and a specialty clinic was the primary source of such services in the majority of cases. Specialty clinics rarely have first-hand information about a youngster's family and community milieu. They are frequently located at great distances from the habilitation services that the child and family utilize on a daily basis. It is therefore inappropriate for these specialty clinics to assume the day-to-day care of a child who is retarded or who has special needs.

The purpose of this chapter is not to provide an exhaustive review of the causes of mental retardation, but rather to define the problem and present an approach to its management. It will also address some of the current ethical and legislative issues that impact on the services provided to these children. More comprehensive reviews of the etiology of retardation can be found in such texts as *Paediatric Neurology for the Clinician* by Neil Gordon,[25] *Recognizable Patterns of Human Malformations*[55] by David Smith, and Stanbury's text, *The Metabolic Basis of Inherited Disease*.[58]

An accurate diagnosis indicates prognosis, provides for educational planning, and forms the basis for genetic counselling. However, before we discuss the approach to diagnosis, we would like to emphasize some guidelines that relate to the care of the child and his family. The presentation of these basic definitions and concepts at the onset is thought to be helpful because they could otherwise be easily lost in the traditional search for the cause of the child's retardation. These definitions and concepts include (1) the definition of mental retardation, (2) the concept of normalization, (3) the adaptation of the family to the mentally retarded child, (4) the family as a habilitator and participant in the decision-making process, and (5) the physician's awareness that habilitation is primary and requires long-term continuity and coordination.

DEFINITION AND PREVALENCE

The estimated prevalence (numbers existing in the population at a given time) of people with mental retardation in the general population is approximately 3%. Studies by Tarjan and co-workers[59] suggest that this may be an overestimation and the figure may be closer to 1.5%. The incidence (frequency with which a disorder arises anew) of moderate, severe, and profound retardation (IQ and DQ below 50) has been well established at approximately 3.6 per 1000 live births.[42] The advent of the neonatal intensive care unit has already been shown to have a substantial effect in decreasing the overall incidence of infants who were previously considered at very high risk for retardation.[19] However, with the enhanced survival of severely impaired infants, the overall prevalence of mental retardation is unlikely to be changed.

Mental retardation refers to significantly subaverage general intellectual functioning that exists concurrently with deficits in adaptive behavior and is manifested during the *developmental period*.[26] Fig. 8-2 demonstrates the distribution of intelligence as it relates to one or more standardized tests that were developed for measuring intellectual functioning. Significant subaverage function falls 2 standard deviations below the mean, or at an IQ of approximately 70. Table 8-1 relates the function and adaptation of children with mental retardation to specific IQ levels.

Adaptive behavior provides a more functional definition in that it is a measure of the degree an individual meets his social responsibility at a given age within a specific culture. For example, the ability to live independently and with a degree of self-sufficiency characterizes the adults of our society. Mentally retarded adults, except for those with mild retardation, depend on others for housing and vocational success.

This failure of adaptive skills becomes apparent in the infant or preschooler when he manifests limited capability in communication and certain self-help skills. The school-aged child who is not impaired enters school after having attained a modicum of self-sufficiency, and he is required to attain success in the educational system; the retarded youngster, in general, needs a special educational setting or additional specialized assistance in the regular classroom.

Mental retardation is therefore a symptom with degrees of adaptive failure that appears

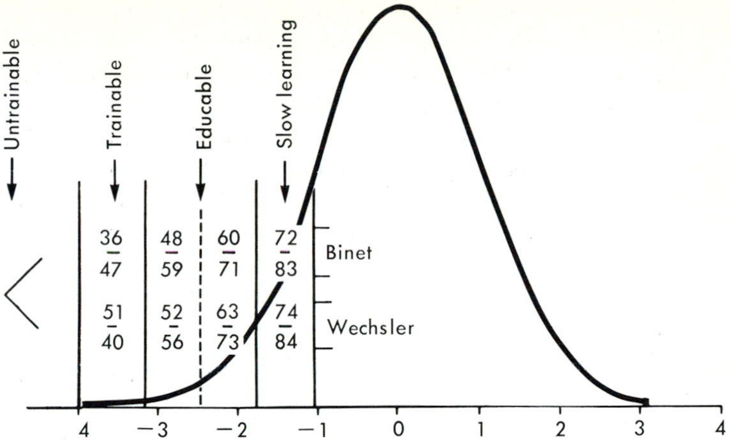

Fig. 8-2. Distribution for intelligence using the Stanford-Binet LM and the Wechsler Scale of Intelligence. The categories of untrainable, trainable, educable, and slow learner should not be interpreted as precise functional entities.

Table 8-1. Degrees of mental retardation, levels of function, and adaptation*

Maturation and development (Preschool—birth to 5 years)	Education and training (School age—5 to 21 years)	Social and vocational adequacy (adulthood)
Borderline intelligence (IQ 74 to 85) and mild retardation (IQ 66 to 73) educable		
Can develop social and communication skills	Can learn academic skills up until sixth grade level by late teens	Capable of social adequacy
Has minimal retardation in sensory motor areas	Does not do well in high school without special programs	Can live independently with proper education and training but needs assistance during crisis
May not be diagnosed until child enters school; cause usually psychosocial	Needs special education	
Mild retardation (IQ 50 to 65)/Educable		
Develops skills at approximately half the usual rate	Cannot learn beyond fourth grade level by late teens	Functions within a sheltered workshop
May have visibly impaired coordination		Can live in community with supervisor; apartment clusters, hostels, halfway houses
Moderate retardation (IQ 35 to 49)/Trainable†		
Delay apparent in infancy—associated with neurological disorders such as CP, seizures	Attends trainable class	Requires constant supervision
Cause more likely identified	Can learn necessary academic skills to function in community with supervision	Performs simple tasks when presented clearly and concretely
	Can dress and undress	May have difficulty separating from parent
		Is easily frightened, has limited judgement
Severe retardation (IQ 20 to 34) /Trainable		
Has severe delay noted in infancy	Attends trainable class	Can also be maintained in hostels, halfway houses, requirements for nursing skills greater
Has minimal speech and communication	Can only be partially trained in toileting, dressing, feeding	
Cause is frequently known		
Profound retardation (IQ 0 to 20)/Untrainable (all children are trainable)		
May not develop speech	Eligible for education that is primarily habilitation	May require out-of-home placement with skilled nursery supervision and care
May be nonambulative or noncommunicative	Attempts at developing sensory motor skills	
Has infantlike behavior		

*These descriptions have general application. Each youngster's performance varies within levels of intelligence.

†Following is true for all groups with IQ or DQ 49 or less.

between birth and 18 years of life—the time considered the developmental period (Table 8-1 and Fig. 8-2). This symptom does not relate to a specific cause but rather indicates a deficiency in cognitive, language, personal/social, fine motor, gross motor, and adaptive behavior. As noted in the outline below, the presence of impaired function in only one or two areas should always leave the diagnosis open to question. A child may have a neuromuscular disease with severe impairment in the gross and fine motor areas (as is in children with cerebral palsy) but may also be of normal intelligence.

Similarly, delays in speech can be attributable to a variety of causes in the absence of mental retardation. Following are causes of speech and motor delays:

I. Speech delay
  A. Mental retardation: Cognitive and language delay
  B. Central processing disorders
    1. Receptive-expressive
    2. Ideational
  C. Sensorineural and conductive hearing loss
  D. Environmental deprivation
  E. Emotional disorder: Selective mutism
  F. Childhood psychosis: Autism
II. Fine and gross motor delays
  A. Mental retardation
  B. Primary muscle disorders
  C. Neuromuscular disorder: Cerebral palsy
  D. Neuronal-anterior horn cell disease, polyneuritis
  E. Severe visual impairment
  F. Congenital mesenchymal disease: Ehlers-Danlos syndrome
  G. Chronic illness

In general, there is a direct relationship between the manifested severity of retardation and adaptive behavior. The severity of functional disability can be lessened, however, by the availability of training and educational resources within the community, the motivation and emotional stability of the individual, and the physical and emotional strength of the family.

NORMALIZATION: A CONCEPT OF HUMAN SERVICES

A major recent contribution to the habilitation of retarded people has been the concept that the adaptive behavior of a person can be positively altered by culturally normative expectations. Although these concepts were first attributed to Nirje,[47] Bank-Mikkelsen,[3] and Grunewald[27] in Scandinavia in the late 1960s, the appropriateness of this concept was expounded in the United States as early as 1886, when Howe,[35] in his dedication speech of a school for the blind in Batavia, New York, stated:

Such persons spring up sporadically in the community and they should be kept diffused among sound and normal persons. Separation and not congregation should be the law of their treatment; for out of their infirmity or abnormality, there necessarily grows some abnormal and undesirable effects, and unless these be counteracted by education, they disturb the harmonious development of character. These effects are best counteracted by bringing up the child among ordinary children and of subjecting him to ordinary social and family influences; but on the contrary, they are intensified by constant and close association with children who are marked by the same infirmity of peculiarity.

This philosophy of service was reintroduced in America with an almost religious fervor by Wolfensberger in 1969.[64] He coined the phrase "normalization" to describe the human service principle that advocates that services should be provided to mentally retarded persons in the same manner as their nonhandicapped peers. He redefined the normalization principle as "utilization of means which are as culturally normative as possible in order to establish or maintain personal behaviors and characteristics which are as culturally normative as possible." This concept has major implications for the location, design, staffing, and operation of habilitative service programs. It also dictates a need for major cultural changes in how people perceive of and relate to retarded persons.

The large impersonal institution, which was characterized by social distance between the staff and clients, block and assembly line treatment methods, and common dress and appearance of the retarded persons who live there is fortunately becoming the residence of the past. The concept of normalization, however, goes far beyond the character of residential treatment. As Table 8-2 indicates, the principle

Table 8-2. A schema of the expression of the normalization principle on three levels of two dimensions of action*

Levels of action	Dimensions of action	
	Interaction	**Interpretation**
Person	Eliciting, shaping, and maintaining socially valued skills and habits in persons by means of direct physical and social interaction with them	Presenting, managing, addressing, labelling, and interpreting individual persons in a manner emphasizing their similarities to rather than differences from others
Primary and intermediate social systems	Eliciting, shaping, and maintaining socially valued skills and habits in persons by working indirectly through their primary and intermediate social systems, such as family, classroom, school, work setting, service agency, and neighborhood	Shaping, presenting, and interpreting intermediate social systems surrounding a person or consisting of target persons so that these systems as well as the persons in them are perceived as culturally normative as possible
Societal systems	Eliciting, shaping, and maintaining socially valued behavior in persons by appropriate shaping of large societal social systems, and structures such as entire school systems, laws, and government	Shaping cultural values, attitudes, and stereotypes so as to elicit maximal feasible cultural acceptance of differences

*From Wolfensberger, W.: The normalization principle, and some major implications to architectural-environmental design. In Bednar, M. J., editor: Barrier-free environments, Stroudsburg, Pa., 1977, Dowden, Hutchinson & Ross.

addresses action at the person and social system level as well as at society in general.

The person level requires behavior, dress, and activities that are culturally normative for the individual, regardless of the fact that he is retarded. Long hair, moustaches, and jeans are no longer privileges that come with a normal IQ level. The manner in which a person is introduced is also important. Certain labels suggest childlike expectations and behaviors. Labelling has been identified as a major factor in how we perceive retarded children and adults. Awareness of normalization principles deemphasizes the label of retardation and facilitates interaction with a person at an appropriate level of expectation. For example, a 40-year-old man should be known as Mr. Joseph Smith. Similarly, the diagnosis of Down syndrome obviously should not bestow on a person an everlasting social level of childhood. It is apparent that an ambience of normality assists with the attainment of an environment that encourages culturally normative behavior from people. As the "person" level in Table 8-2 suggests, the skills of retarded persons are enhanced by providing mainstreaming opportunities that stress their similarities with the rest of the population, rather than their differences.

Physicians and allied professionals should be constantly aware of how they interact with their retarded clients. In the presence of adequate communication skills, the youngster or adult should be addressed directly rather than utilizing their parent or aide as an intermediary. Communication through intermediaries is a pattern of interaction that unfortunately is frequently used in addressing any member of a perceived lesser class. Physicians occasionally function this way with their clinic population when a client is accompanied by a social worker or welfare aide. It is important that physicians recognize and project the fact that they are dealing with individuals who are people first and retarded second. The sense of worth that we impart to the child in our office or in the hospital is meaningful and important and a supportive factor for the parents.

At the family and social level (primary and intermediate levels in Table 2), the concept of normalization requires the integration of the retarded child into the family, school, and community. This intermingling diminishes our perception of a person's deviance and provides him with an opportunity to be exposed to appropriate role models. The bringing together of large numbers of retarded people reinforces our perception of their behavior as different. A large number of adult retarded persons going to the museum does not appear much different from a school outing. In keeping with the concept that integration decreases deviance, the retarded individual should live in the community rather than in a large impersonal institution with other retarded people. Although community residence in itself is a goal, it should reflect a variety of levels of independence. The location of residences is also important, and every effort should be made to locate these homes in active residential communities rather than in areas that have been abandoned as a result of urban blight or in areas that are primarily industrial in nature. The variety of levels of independence of retarded people requires the availability of halfway houses as well as apartment clusters with varying degrees of supervision. Appropriate levels of independence help to decrease the perception of the individuals' inadequacies and to emphasize their strengths and capabilites.

The growth in the use of normalization principles and the concept of the least-restrictive environment for programs of daily living has been a major factor in the humanization of services. Although the goal is individual dignity and freedom, like the open classroom, it must be implemented with forethought and planning to successfully serve the needs of the retarded child. The concept of mainstreaming has proved to be controversial, and the potential for a backlash of placing retarded individuals in a more restrictive environment is possible. Parents of nonhandicapped children resent the amount of teacher time the child with a handicapping condition requires. Mainstreaming may be doomed to failure and will prove to be an injustice to teachers as well as children in the absence of adequate staff and interdisciplinary team support. We must not react impulsively in an effort to compensate for staff deficiencies and turn to the use of personnel who themselves are perceived as deviant. The use of the hard-core unemployed, conscientious objectors, elderly persons, retarded people, or other handicapped persons reinforces the concept that the care of or service to the retarded is a form of sentence or penalty delegated to persons who themselves are not competent and cannot find employment elsewhere.

Changes at the cultural level (societal systems in Table 8-2) present a mountainous obstacle. Our ability to tolerate differences in people is unfortunately limited. Society's emphasis on the best, the brightest, and the most beautiful creates anxieties within us all. How we overcome the deluge of information and advertising that stresses the need for perfect appearance and performance in ourselves and others is difficult to imagine. The cultural emphasis on upward mobility rather than the enhancement and elaboration of our current level of function also makes our acceptance of retardation difficult. Parents of retarded children more than any other group are required to overcome the frustrations created by the inflated expectations of family members and society for a child with limited capabilites.

The struggle of the parents

Ronald Mac Keith,[45] commenting on the feelings and behaviors of parents of handicapped children, noted that their response is derived from "cultural and social attitudes to children in general, to handicapped persons, and to teachers, social workers, doctors, and medical care in general." He accurately observes that reactions are influenced by "whether the handicap is evident at birth or becomes evident later," "whether there is a prospect of severe handicap or not," and "whether the handicap is obvious to others and by the attitude of other people." MacKeith describes various types of parental behaviors as follows:

1. a. The biological reaction of protectiveness toward the helpless infant would tend to produce "maternal" behavior in both the mother and father. Frequently, there is warm, normal care or there may be highly protective care. Labeling highly protective care as overprotectiveness is not an observation but a judgement, and it should involve the mother's need to behave in this way and the child's need to be highly protected.
   b. The biologic reaction of revulsion at the abnormal is a normal reaction, even if in our culture it is frowned upon. It would produce rejection of the child. Rejection may show itself as:

(1) Cold rejection;
(2) Rationalized rejection, the parents suggesting the child should be in a home with specially trained persons to care for him;
(3) Dutiful caring without warmth; or
(4) Lavish care from an overcompensation of feelings of rejection.

2. a. Feelings of inadequacies at reproduction can strike deep at a person's self-respect and may produce depression.
   b. Feelings of inadequacies of rearing can produce lack of confidence and inconsistency of rearing.
3. a. The anger of bereavement can cause aggressive behavior towards those who are trying to help the parents.
   b. The grief may cause depression, and the adjustment may come fairly quickly; although often stable, it is not always so in the face of problems that arise later.
4. The sense of shock may cause disbelief and a succession of consultation at other clinics in search for better news.
5. Guilt is frequently written about but is not felt by all parents. It is a complex feeling with undertones, for example, of punishment. It can reduce depression.
6. Embarrassment can lead to withdrawal from social contacts and consequently produce social isolation.

This excellent description of behaviors of parents can be used in a variety of ways. Not only does it give the professional insight into reactions to the birth of a retarded child, but it also can be presented to parents to initiate discussion and help them identify some of the bewildering feelings that they are experiencing. There is a need to stress that, although adjustment may come fairly quickly, instability may occur as other problems arise and new decisions are necessary. All of these behaviors may be short lived or last for many years. They may occur singularly or in a variety of combinations. It is not unusual for grief and depression to be associated with feelings of inadequacies in child rearing and reproduction. All of these behaviors and feelings, in almost all instances, are not pathological reactions but rather situationally induced; with time and appropriate support, many diminish in intensity. Chapter 17 discusses in detail the many frustrations and problems parents experience.

The overall reaction of the family is very much related to the physician's response to the birth of a defective child and the manner of support provided by the physician in the day-to-day management of that youngster. Empathy and understanding do not require that the professional decompensate with the family. If the physician is too busy managing personal emotions and is unable to provide guidance and appropriate support, efforts to help the family will be ineffective more often than not. The physician is most effective by being empathetic, sensitive, and aware of the available facts. Being an advocate for the family does not necessarily require agreement with all of the family behaviors. Inappropriate searching for cures, misplaced hostility, and misconceptions in regard to the cause of the retardation should all be addressed clearly and rationally. Once the information is provided in an understandable manner, the ultimate decision for action lies with the family. A judgment regarding the adequacy of the family's decision should not be made until the physician is reasonably certain the information presented has been truly understood.

Well-meaning advice is only helpful when based on proved philosophies that have been substantiated and are known to be effective. Such advice as encouraging a family not to see the baby because they will "get attached" only encourages the parents' fantasy, and they frequently imagine the baby as being more grotesque than the actual reality. We have yet to meet parents who are unable to deal with the appearance of their infant, except in the most unusual circumstances. Our role as physicians is not to be paternalistic but rather to facilitate self-support and decision-making capability through education and guidance.

There is no single ideal way of telling parents that they have given birth to a retarded or malformed infant. The strongest families appear frail and disrupted, and the time of telling is painful for all but the most guarded and impregnable professional. Studies[22] indicate that, whenever possible, parents want to be told together, and they want to know the full truth as soon as the physician is reasonably certain of the diagnosis and its implications. The overall initial response of the family is generally that of shock. Specific facts regarding ultimate function, diagnostic studies, and habilation are frequently forgotten during the early days of disbelief, sorrow, and anger. Repeated visits and discussions are required before parents become knowledgeable in regard to their child's disability. The importance of recognizing the infant as an individual rather than thinking of him as a disease is once again very important. Down syndrome infants are as cute and as cuddly as any other infant. This type of information should be presented along with the many problems that will follow. The introduction of families who have had similar experiences may also be helpful at this time. The attitudes of the helping parents should be well known to the professional prior to their initial contact.

The adaptation of the family to the birth of a retarded infant is a developmental process that is everchanging. Thus it requires varying types and degrees of input by the professional (Table 8-3). More than anything else, patience and understanding are required to enable the family to evolve to the point of relative adaptation and comfort—a process that may take years or may never occur at all. The stages described by Mac Keith[45] are by no means ordinal. There may be regression or, in rare instances, immediate adaptation. Parents may never be able to say the word "retardation" but may join groups for parents of retarded children and seek and provide optimal services for their youngster.

A family's adjustment to a retarded child is difficult to evaluate. What is an appropriate adjustment is not clear. Few studies are well controlled. There are no studies that describe the adjustment of families in the presence of adequate support services or that compare a family's adjustment in the presence of problems of a similar magnitude but of a different nature, for example, a child with cerebral palsy with normal intelligence. The belief that caring for severely retarded youngsters is always disasterous and disruptive to the family has not been proved. There is, however, little question that children with mental retardation are a major source of emotional, physical, and financial strain to a family. At a minimum, such supportive services as respite care, special education, habilitation, sheltered workshops, and a variety of choices for residential care must be available. Few families are interested in spending 100% of their time with their children, even in the absence of a disability. When a child requires constant ongoing care, this is especially true, and if the concepts of community living are to be implemented, there must be a whole array of services that provide not only active habilitation but also periods of relief from the physical and emotional task of caring for such youngsters.

The family as habilitators and team members

The habilitation of a child with mental retardation or any other developmental disability is a consuming task. This does not mean to imply that there is a need to constantly work with the child or that the home should be used as a structured training site. It does, however, require an understanding of what parents bring to the habilitative process. The erosion of gains a child has made in school, which is often seen after a holiday vacation when the parents are

Table 8-3. Parental reaction and the role of the primary care physician

Parental reaction and behavior	Role of the physician*
1. Shock	Provide comprehensive diagnostic assessment, support
2. Disbelief, denial, rejection 3. Grief and sorrow	Provide support, parent groups, religious groups, group and individual counselling
4. Medicalization of process	Provide comprehensive medical evaluation as needed; encourage appropiate consultation and provide necessary coordination
5. Recognition of need for habilitation and family support	Coordinate psychological, educational, occupational or physical, and speech therapy, advocacy, continuity of care, parent education, respite services

*All stages: Provide empathy, support, facts, time, and primary care.

unable to participate or are inadequately involved in a youngster's treatment program, is familiar to all of us. The role of the parent in intervention was described by Donovan in Chapter 4, and the importance of this role has been stressed by others.[24] The parents are unquestionably the most important members of the habilitation team. Not only do they provide the necessary manpower to make a program successful, but they also provide ongoing observations to develop and change the strategies of effective programming. They observe the child in a variety of free-field situations that are not cluttered with strangers or with the restrictive effects of a new and threatening environment. This day-to-day role places the parent in the unique position of having the best understanding of the needs of the child and the family.

Federal and state laws have recognized the importance of parent participation. Federal Public Law 94-142, the Education for All Handicapped Children's Act, was enacted in 1975.[36,49] This law mandates the education of all handicapped children and gives the parents a major role in its implementation. The law carefully describes the parents' participation in the evaluation conferences as well as their rights to appeal what they perceive as an inappropriate decision regarding their youngster's individual educational plan.

This law gives the parents the right to question the educational diagnostic process, including the adequacy of the medical examination. The parents are able to request alternate evaluations outside of the educational system. Parents must be notified of any evaluations, and they may be present at the meeting that determines the educational placement of their child. These rights, along with the knowledge and manpower a family brings to the diagnostic and evaluation process, makes them bona fide team members. There is little question that the stresses of time, the demands of poverty, or the presence of emotional disturbance may limit the parents' active participation in their youngster's program development. However, the number of parents who cannot contribute to some part of the decision-making process is relatively small. When encouraging parent participation, it is important to remember that one of the most important

goals of good health care supervision is to educate parents so that they will be as self-sufficient and independent of the helping professional as possible. The encouragement of dependency, although satisfying to some professionals, can be as destructive to the parents and youngster as the very disability itself.

DIAGNOSIS, EVALUATION, AND HABILITATION

The number of instances in which the establishment of a specific cause for retardation provides a cure or an amelioration of symptoms is unfortunately small. Despite these limitations, the diagnostic process is absolutely necessary for accurate genetic counselling and habilitative planning. Most families are not ready to assume the complex, ongoing process of habilitation until all possible chances of a "medical cure" have been explored and eliminated.

The evaluation of the results of the diagnostic study may indicate the need for further physical or occupational therapy, speech therapy, education, and possible corrective surgery. The goal-oriented record, which is described on p. 216, is generated directly from the diagnostic findings and their evaluation. The interdisciplinary staffing conference that follows provides the individual child with a comprehensive habilitation plan. The responsibility of the physician in this process is to provide for comprehensive assessment while simultaneously being aware of its long-term limitations in the absence of adequate program planning.

While performing these complex studies, it is important to think of mental retardation as a symptom and not as a disease. Effective habilitation and appropriate interpersonal relationships with persons who are retarded depend on this concept. A primary disease orientation may imply a short-term cure for an ongoing chronic illness and does not address the issues that are necessary for the functional success of an individual on a long-term basis. Dealing with the retarded person as a patient has led to the unfortunate development of residential facilities that are staffed and constructed as hospitals rather than homes.

In 70% to 80% of the cases the cause of

mental retardation is unknown or is attributable to multifactorial genetic and environmental factors. Environmental factors are especially important in children who's capabilities fall into the mildly retarded range. As the functional ability and IQ of individuals decrease, the number of known causes of retardation increases. The causes of mental retardation fall into three broad categories as follows:

1. Prenatally determined causes
2. Perinatally determined causes
3. Postnatally determined causes

Prenatal causes include autosomal chromosomal abnormalities, the most common of which is Down syndrome due to trisomy 21 syndrome, or translocation. Also included, but less common, are trisomy 13 syndrome, Patau syndrome, trisomy 18 syndrome, Edward syndrome, and a host of chromosomal deletions and additions that have been discovered through the technique of banding and are discussed in Chapter 9. Abnormal numbers of sex chromosomes are also associated with mental retardation. The most common sex chromosomal abnormality is gonadal dysgenesis (45,XO). Initially this abnormality was thought to be always associated with mild retardation, but studies now suggest that this abnormality is more frequently associated with learning disabilities. Klinefelter syndrome, which is characterized by an XXY genotype, may or may not be associated with mild retardation or learning disabilities.

Also included in this category is a long list of prenatally determined metabolic disorders. The prevalence of this group is exceedingly small. It includes aberrations in amino acid, lipid, carbohydrate, and mineral metabolism. Hurler syndrome is the most common member of the increasingly complex mucopolysaccharide group. An excellent review of mucopolysaccharidosis is presented by Lorincz.[44] Stanbury and co-workers[58] present an up-to-date reference for the vast majority of the other metabolic disorders.

Congenital viral infections with central nervous system involvement are relatively frequent causes of mental retardation.[29] This is especially true of congenital cytomegalic inclusion disease, which has a frequency of inapparent infection of between 0.6% and 1% and is associated with subsequent school failure in almost 30% of lower socioeconomic children.[30] The high frequency of hearing loss in this infected population is also important to note. The diagnosis of congenital cytomegalovirus infection is best made during the immediate neonatal period when specific cytomegalovirus IgM antibodies may be associated with viuria. After that time, only a presumptive diagnosis can be made. Even in the presence of positive urine culture, the diagnosis cannot be made with certainty unless there are signs of actual disease, which include microcephaly, chorioretinitis, and intracerebral calcification. These signs may also be present in congenital *Toxoplasma* infections. The diagnosis and effect of nonbacterial congenital infections have recently been extensively reviewed by Hanshaw and Dudgeon.[29]

Drillien[17] noted that many premature and small for gestational age infants have associated minor congenital malformations. These are in all probability a reflection of first trimester difficulty with subsequent premature labor. Prematurity is not in itself a cause of mental retardation unless it is a reflection of difficulties in morphogenesis or untoward perinatal events. An estimated 40% of children with severe retardation have a series of either major or minor malformations such as low-set ears, abnormal dermatoglyphics, and clinodactyly.[39] Cerebral dysgenesis associated with minor congenital malformations is a frequently overlooked cause of mental retardation. The many factors that affect the developing fetus are still unknown. Although we focus on the teratogenic effects of x rays and drugs, such factors as late or poor implantation of the fertilized egg as a cause of teratogenesis may also be important.

The causal relationship of such drugs as alcohol or hydantoin and mental retardation deserves emphasis. Although the presence of specific syndromes related to these substances have been questioned, there is little doubt about the frequent association of mental retardation with the ingestion of these substances.[31,48]

Perinatal factors and their relationship to mental retardation have been extensively discussed in Chapter 2. Asphyxia is the most common perinatal event that causes mental retardation. As noted earlier, a distinction should be made between the sequelae of prematurity and the prematurity itself as they relate to the cause of mental retardation. Birth trauma, which at one time was a frequent cause of mental retardation, is fortunately becoming less common. Kernicterus due to hyperbilirubinemia and hemolytic disease have also become rare occurrences. The role of polycythemia to subsequent developmental sequelae is unknown at this time but is thought to be a potential source of difficulty.

The most common cause of mild mental retardation during the postnatal period is psychosocial deprivation. This is primarily the burden of the poor and has been extensively reviewed by Birch[6] and others.[15,60] The inverse relationship between social class and psychological development, health, and nutrition is well documented in these texts. The transaction between the compounding effects of poor parenting and inadequate environment in infants who are placed at risk due to untoward perinatal events are reviewed in Chapters 2 and 4.

Postnatal causes of severe mental retardation are becoming less common. Accidents secondary to head truma and meningitis are the most common causes of organic postnatal mental retardation. The association of head trauma with child abuse should be noted, and a true area of prevention is the early identification of the parent who is potentially abusive. Kempe[40] indicates that potentially abusive parents can be identified during the prenatal period. Characteristics include a history of being abused themselves as children, adolescent pregnancy, financial problems, social isolation, drug addiction, alcoholism, or inadequate child care arrangements. About 15% of the child abuse cases occur with foster or adoptive parents.[46]

Inadequate intellectual performance due to chronic and acute exposure to lead has been reasonably well established.[33] All youngsters with developmental or behavioral difficulties, regardless of socioeconomic status, should be screened for lead toxicity. Children with blood lead levels of 50 to 70 μg/dl and free erythrocyte porphyrin (EP) values of 110 to 189 μg/dl should be considered lead intoxicated until proved otherwise. Those youngsters with lead levels between 30 and 50 μg/dl should be observed closely for subsequent increase in lead levels. In both instances the environment should be carefully explored for potential lead sources. Children with lead levels greater than 80 μg/dl and EP values greater than 190 μg/dl should be treated.[8,9] Chisolm[8] has described an appropriate protocol for inpatient chelation therapy for children with lead poisoning.

Meningitis, encephalitis, cerebrovascular accidents, and metabolic derangements such as hypoglycemia, hypernatremia and hyponatremia, are all known causes of mental retardation. Other postnatal causes of mental retardation are the uncommon encephalopathies related to immunization against pertussis, smallpox, and rabies.

Developmental history

The initial step of diagnosis and evaluation will vary, depending on whether or not the infant or child has been referred for consultation or has been followed in the physician's own practice. In the latter instance ongoing developmental assessment as described in Chapter 3 will assist in identifying the child who is suspected to be or actually is developmentally delayed. Figs. 8-3 through 8-8 present a pediatric developmental record-keeping system that can be easily incorporated into a routine office chart. This record-keeping system has been developed by Ashford Developmental Pediatric Research in England.[18]

The uniqueness of this system is that it enables one to easily identify developmentally delayed children while providing the necessary comprehensive information to initiate the diagnostic process. In the absence of an ongoing comprehensive record-keeping system or when a youngster has been referred for consultation, a meticulous history should be taken. The history should include the following:

A. Reason for parental concern, for example, absence of speech, delayed motor development, or bizarre behavior
B. Prenatal history
   1. Planned or unplanned pregnancy
   2. Maternal health, presence of chronic illness, such as diabetes, rheumatoid arthritis, sei-

Text continued on p. 202.

PAEDIATRIC DEVELOPMENT RECORD

DR...

Surname _____ First Name _____

Date of Birth [14] [ ][ ][ ][ ] Birth Rank [20] [ ]

Father's Age [21][22] [ ][ ] Mother's Age [23][24] [ ][ ]

Father's Occupation _____ [25] [ ]

OFFICE USE

Dr's Code (1–2) [ ][ ]

On Cols 3–13
Punch: First 8 letters of surname
First 3 letters of first name

[26] [ ][ ][ ][ ][ ] [31]

Exam. within 21 days of Birth	Date....................	[ ][ ][ ][ ]

Date of Birth [ ][ ][ ][ ][ ][ ] E.D.D. [ ][ ][ ][ ][ ][ ]

History

	Normal	Abnormal	
Ante Natal			32 [ ]
Natal			33 [ ]
Post Natal			34 [ ]

Breast Fed [No][Yes]   35 [ ]   36

Birth WT. [ ][ ][ ][ ] Grms.   [ ][ ][ ]

Maturity <36 [ ] <42 [ ] 42+ [ ]

Asymm. Symm. [ ][ ]   40 [ ] 41 [ ]

Moro Response Low Medium High [ ]   42 [ ]

Grasp	No	Yes	43 [ ]
Walking	No	Yes	44 [ ]
Placing	No	Yes	45 [ ]
Sound Resp.	No	Yes	46 [ ]
Light Resp.	No	Yes	47 [ ]

Ventral Susp. [diagrams]   48 [ ]

PHYSICAL EXAMINATION

Weight (49–52) [ ][ ][ ][ ] Grms. (53–5) [ ][ ]|[ ] Cms. (56–8) [ ][ ]|[ ] Cms. Height H.C.

	Norm.	State Abnormalities	
Skull			59 [ ]
Ears			60 [ ]
Eyes			61 [ ]
Palate			62 [ ]
C.V.S.			63 [ ]
R.S.			64 [ ]
Abdo.			65 [ ]
Spine			66 [ ]
Hernia			67 [ ]
Fem. Pulses			68 [ ]
Genitalia			69 [ ]
Hips			70 [ ]
Limbs			71 [ ]
Tone			72 [ ]
Reflexes			73 [ ]
Skin			74 [ ]
Biochem			75 [ ]

Appearance

Comments

Action

Card Code
79 [1]

If tests incomplete because of child's unco-operation put tick in box	[ ]	80 [ ]

Fig. 8-3. Profile examination form, age 3 weeks. (From Drillien, C. M., and Drummond, M. B.: Neurodevelopmental problems in early childhood: assessment and management, Oxford, 1977, Blackwell Scientific Publications Ltd. Copyright Curtis Jenkins, G. H., Developmental Paediatric Group, London.)

PAEDIATRIC DEVELOPMENT RECORD

DR. ....

	OFFICE USE
	Dr's Code (1–2) ☐☐

Surname _____ First Name _____

Date of Birth [14 ☐☐☐☐☐☐]   Birth Rank [20 ☐]

Father's Age [21 22 ☐☐]   Mother's Age [23 24 ☐☐]

Father's Occupation _____ 25 ☐

On Cols 3–13
Punch: First 8 letters of surname
First 3 letters of first name

26 [☐☐☐☐☐] 31

Exam. at **7 months**   Date. ....

Mother's Comments				
	Happy	No	Yes	32 ☐
	Sleeps	No	Yes	33 ☐
	Chews	No	Yes	34 ☐
Illness since last exam. (If yes specify nature of illness)		No	Yes	35 ☐
	Breast Fed	☐ mos.		36 ☐
	Solids started	No	Yes	37 ☐
Nursery	No	Yes		38 ☐
Minder	No	Yes		39 ☐
Hours worked per week (mother)	☐			40 41 ☐☐

Sitting	**No stability**	Sits supported	Sits un-supported	42 ☐
Standing supported	No weight Bearing	Full weight	Weight alternates foot to foot	43 ☐
Prone	No weight on hands, head up	Shoulders up weight on hands	Knee up to crawl	44 ☐
1" Brick	No grasp	Mouthing	Transfer	45 ☐
Pellet	Whole hand scrabble	Whole hand pick up	Finger-thumb pick up	46 ☐
Rolling balls	$\frac{1}{2}$"	$\frac{1}{4}$"	$\frac{1}{16}$"	47 ☐
Cover test	Squint	Doubtful	No squint	48 ☐
Hearing 3 ft.	Doubtful	Satisfactory	Good	49 ☐
Speech	Noise only	Purposeful sound	2 Syllables or more	50 ☐
Imitates shaking rattle	No interest	Interest and manipulation	Imitation	51 ☐
Reaction to Examiner	None	Resists	Co-operates	52 ☐
Attention	Poor	Variable	Sustained	53 ☐

PHYSICAL EXAM.

Weight (54–6) ☐☐/☐ K.grms. (57–9) ☐☐☐ Cms. Height (60–2) ☐☐☐/☐ Cms. H.C.

Abnormality   No/Yes (Specify below)   83 ☐

....

Appearance

Comments   Card Code

Action   79 [2]

If tests incomplete because of child's unco-operation put tick in box	☐	80 ☐

Fig. 8-4. Profile examination form, age 7 months. (From Drillien, C. M., and Drummond, M. B.: Neurodevelopmental problems in early childhood: assessment and management, Oxford, 1977, Blackwell Scientific Publications Ltd. Copyright Curtis Jenkins, G. H., Developmental Paediatric Group, London.)

Fig. 8-5. Profile examination form, age 1 year. (From Drillien, C. M., and Drummond, M. B.: Neurodevelopmental problems in early childhood: assessment and management, Oxford, 1977, Blackwell Scientific Publications Ltd. Copyright Curtis Jenkins, G. H., Developmental Paediatric Group, London.)

PAEDIATRIC DEVELOPMENT RECORD

DR.................................

	OFFICE USE
Surname _____ First Name _____	Dr's Code (1–2) ☐☐
	On Cols 3–13
14 20	Punch : First 8 letters of surname
Date of Birth ☐☐☐☐☐☐ Birth Rank ☐	First 3 letters of first name
21 22 23 24	
Father's Age ☐☐ Mother's Age ☐☐	
Father's Occupation _____ 25 ☐	26 31

Exam. at 24 months	Date...................	☐☐☐☐

Mother's Comments

	Happy	No Yes	32 ☐
	Sleeps	No Yes	33 ☐
	Eats	No Yes	34 ☐
	Imaginative play	No Yes	35 ☐
Illness since last exam. (If yes specify nature of illness)		No Yes	36 ☐

Changes in family circumstances		No Yes	37 ☐
Play group	No Yes		38 ☐
Nursery	No Yes		39 ☐
Minder	No Yes		40 ☐
Hours worked per week (Mother)	☐		41–2 ☐☐

	1	2	3	
Bowel { D				43 ☐
N				44 ☐
Bladder { D				45 ☐
N				46 ☐
Sentences	1	2	3	4	47 ☐

Kick ball	No kick	Runs into ball	Poor kick	Good directed kick	48 ☐
Throw ball	No throw	2 hands poor direct.	2 hands good direct.	1 hand	49 ☐
1" Brick column	2 or less	3 – 4	5 – 7	8+	50 ☐
Screws on table	2 or less up	3 up	4 up	5 up	51 ☐
Rolling balls	½"	⅓"	⅟₁₆"	⅛"	52 ☐
Cover test	Squint	Doubtful		No squint	53 ☐
6 Toy hearing	4 and under	5 – 6 with hesitation		6 Immediate	54 ☐
Recognition	no yes no yes	no yes	no yes no	yes no yes	55 60
Comprehension	Spoon in cup	Ball to mummy	Car on brick	Doll	Brick under cup	Cup	· · · ·
Ladybird vocab.	2 or less	3 – 8	9 – 14	15+	61 ☐
Sentences observed	None	Occasional connected words	3–4 words	5+words	62 ☐
Form board	2 or less in	3 in after mistakes	3 in immediately straight	3 in immediately reversed	63 ☐
Attention	None	Poor	Variable	Sustained	64 ☐

PHYSICAL EXAM.

Weight		Height		
(65 – 8) ☐☐☐ Cms.		(69 – 70) ☐☐ Cms.		
Abnormality	No/Yes (Specify below)			71 ☐

.... Dominant Foot	R L	72 ☐
„ Hand	R L	73 ☐
„ Eye	R L	74 ☐

Appearance	
Comment	Card Code
Action	79 ☐ 4

If tests incomplete because of child's unco-operation put tick in box	☐	80 ☐

Fig. 8-6. Profile examination form, age 2 years. (From Drillien, C. M., and Drummond, M. B.: Neuro-developmental problems in early childhood: assessment and management, Oxford, 1977, Blackwell Scientific Publications Ltd. Copyright Curtis Jenkins, G. H., Developmental Paediatric Group, London.)

PAEDIATRIC DEVELOPMENT RECORD

DR. ....

Surname _____	First Name _____

14	20
Date of Birth ▢▢▢▢▢	Birth Rank ▢

21 22	23 24
Father's Age ▢▢	Mother's Age ▢▢

Father's Occupation _____ 25 ▢

OFFICE USE

Dr's Code (1–2) ▢▢

On Cols 3–13
Punch: First 8 letters of surname
First 3 letters of first name

26 ▢▢▢▢▢ 31

Exam. at **36 months**   Date ....

▢▢▢▢▢

Mother's Comments

	No	Yes	
Happy	No	Yes	32 ▢
Sleeps	No	Yes	33 ▢
Eats	No	Yes	34 ▢

Illness since last exam. (If yes specify nature of illness)   No Yes   35 ▢

	No	Yes	
Change in family circumstances	No	Yes	36 ▢
Play group	No	Yes	37 ▢
Nursery	No	Yes	38 ▢
Minder	No	Yes	39 ▢

Hours worked per week (Mother) ▢   40 41

	1	2	3	
Eating Mode — Knife				42 ▢
Fork				43 ▢
Spoon				44 ▢
Bowel — D				45 ▢
N				46 ▢
Bladder — D				47 ▢
N				48 ▢
Dressing				49 ▢

Kick ball	Runs into Ball	Poor kick	Good direct kick	50 ▢
1" Brick	Does not try	Tries but fails	Succeeds	51 ▢
Rolling balls	½"	7/16"	¼"	52 ▢
Cover Test	Squint	Doubtful	No squint	53 ▢
7 Toy hearing	4 and under	5 – 6 with hesitation	7 Immediate	54 ▢
Ladybird Book — Speech	Less than 15 pictures	16 – 20 pictures	21 or more pictures	55 ▢
Comprehension	Less than 5 actions	6 – 10 actions	11 or more actions	56 ▢
Articulation	Not Understood	Understood with difficulty words incomplete	Understood minor errors only	Clear and understood	57 ▢

Story answers	0	1	2	3	4	5	6	7	58 ▢
Questions to Child	Name	Sex	Age	Address	Number correct	1	2	3	4	59 ▢

PHYSICAL EXAM.

Weight (60–2) ▢▢.▢ K.gms.   Height (63–6) ▢▢▢.▢ Cms.

Abnormality No/Yes (Specify below)   70 ▢

		R	L	
Dominant	foot	R	L	71 ▢
„	Hand	R	L	72 ▢
„	Eye	R	L	73 ▢

Appearance
Comment
Action

Card Code
79 ▢5▢

If tests incomplete because of child's unco-operation put tick in box ▢   80 ▢

Fig. 8-7. Profile examination form, age 3 years. (From Drillien, C. M., and Drummond, M. B.: Neurodevelopmental problems in early childhood: assessment and management, Oxford, 1977, Blackwell Scientific Publications Ltd. Copyright Curtis Jenkins, G. H., Developmental Paediatric Group, London.)

PAEDIATRIC DEVELOPMENT RECORD	OFFICE USE

DR.

Dr's Code (1–2)

Surname _____ First Name _____

On Cols 3–13 Punch : First 8 letters of surname

Date of Birth [14] [ ] [ ] [ ]   Birth Rank [20]

First 3 letters of first name

Father's Age [21][22]   Mother's Age [23][24]

Father's Occupation _____ 25 [ ]   26 [ ][ ][ ][ ] 31

Exam at 54 months   Date ....   [ ][ ][ ][ ]

Mother's Comments

	No	Yes	
Happy	No	Yes	32
Sleeps	No	Yes	33
Eats	No	Yes	34

Illness since last exam. (If yes specify nature of illness) — No | Yes — 35

....

Change in family circumstances — ° No | Yes — 36

Play group	No	Yes	37
Nursery	No	Yes	38
Minder	No	Yes	39

Hours worked per week (Mother) [ ]   40 [ ] 41

	1	2	3	
Eating Mode — Knife				42
Fork				43
Spoon				44
Bowel — D				45
N				46
Bladder — D				47
N				48
Dressing				49

Heel-toe walk	Steps wider than 15 cms. or more than 1 step to side	Gap 5–10 cms. or 1 step to side	4 steps all less than 5 cms. gap	50
Matches in box	All in 3 or more corrections	All in less than 3 corrections	All in both hands	51

6 Brick pyramid	Fails	At least 3 bricks in relation	Succeeds after more than 1 attempt	Succeeds 1st attempt		52
Vision R	6/36	6/24	6/12	6/9	6/6	53
L	6/36	6/24	6/12	6/9	6/6	54

Cover test	Squint	Doubtful	No squint		55
Hearing Toy	4 and under	5 – 6 or hesitation	7 Immediate		56
Articulation	Not under-stood	Under-stood with difficulty Words in-complete	Under-stood min- or errors only	Clear and under-stood	57

Story answers	0	1	2	3	4	5	6	7	58
Questions to child	Name	Sex	Age	Address	Number correct	1	2	3	4	59
Draw a man	0 – 4	5 – 10	11 – 14	15+					60

PHYSICAL EXAM.

Weight   Height

(61–3) [ ][ ] K.gms.   (64–7) [ ][ ] Cms.

Abnormality No/Yes (Specify below)   70 [ ]

.... Dominant foot R L   71 [ ]
.... „ hand R L   72 [ ]
.... „ Eye R L   73 [ ]

Appearance
Comment
Action

Card Code
79 [6]

If tests incomplete because of child's unco-operation put tick in box	[ ]	80 [ ]

Fig. 8-8. Profile examination form, age 4½ years. (From Drillien, C. M., and Drummond, M. B.: Neurodevelopmental problems in early childhood: assessment and management, Oxford, 1977, Blackwell Scientific Publications Ltd. Copyright Curtis Jenkins, G. H., Developmental Paediatric Group, London.)

zures, alcoholism, anemia, or drug addiction, emotional status
3. Obstetrical characteristics: Weight gain, gestation, medication (amount and duration of time used)
4. Acute maternal illnesses, chronic fatigue, sore throat, rashes (rubella or cytomegalovirus infection)
5. Obstetrical complications: Polyhydramnios, hemorrhage, difficulty in conception, previous abortions

C. Perinatal history (whenever possible, obtain birth records)
1. Intrapartum history: Knowledge of fetal monitoring, abnormal presentation, delivery method, prolapse cord, meconium staining
2. Status of the infant at the time of delivery: Apgar score, tone, need for medication or resuscitation, neurological status, or other diagnoses
3. Gestational age as determined by Dubowitz[18a] criteria: Small for gestational age, large for gestational age, head circumference, weight, physical examination, method used to determine gestational age

D. Hospital course, especially behaviors such as suck, tone, apnea, bradycardia, seizures (neurological versus metabolic, that is hypoglycemia, hypocalcemia, hypomagnesemia, polycythemia), treatments used—ventilation, hyperalimentation, exchange transfusion

E. Postnatal and developmental history
1. Developmental milestones in the fine motor, gross motor, personal/social, language, and cognitive areas; evidence of regression
2. Postnatal causes of mental retardation: Lead ingestion or exposure, meningitis, cerebral vascular accidents, suspected abuse
3. Nutritional history with a specific account of the foods ingested over a period of 3 days
4. Associated disabilities, seizures (with specific description of time and localization), presence or absence of visual or auditory problems
5. Behavior and temperament: Sleep patterns, activity, attention, distractibility, adaptation to new situations
6. Self-help capability: Dressing, toileting, feeding

F. Family history
1. Genetics: Parent pedigree exploring presence of autosomal dominant and recessive qualities and sex-linked characteristics with special emphasis on infants and children who died early due to unknown cause and children with associated school failure (reasonable certainty of the paternity of the child)
2. Age of parents: Presence of illness (past or present), including emotional difficulties
3. Family resources, including emotional, physical, and financial status

A carefully taken history should alert the physician to potential medically remediable conditions that are causing mental retardation. The clinical diagnosis of inborn errors of metabolism requires a high index of suspicion and a major knowledge of clinical manifestations of inborn metabolic errors rather than a detailed knowledge of the biochemical aspects of these disorders. Signs and symptoms listed below, such as failure to thrive, hepatosplenomegaly, vomiting, lethargy, and developmental regression, should all provoke concern regarding the presence of such inborn errors.[7] Table 8-4 refers to those conditions with neurological developmental delay in the *first few months of life* and includes those with failure to thrive but with normal cognitive development. The latter would include chronic diseases of the heart, lung, kidney, liver, and gastrointestinal tract.

Once the suspicion is raised, a more detailed literature review or appropriate consultation to rule out the many metabolic disorders listed in Tables 8-4, 8-5, and 8-6 can occur. Knowing whether or not one's particular state has a screening program for congenital hypothyroidism or specific amino acid disorders such as phenylketonuria is also important. Studies of such screening programs for hyperphenylalaninemia and congenital hypothyroidism indicate that few, if any, of the youngsters with these disorders go unnoticed.[57] Many inborn errors do not become blatantly apparent until the infant is several months old. Such diseases as Tay-Sach disease and metachromatic leukodystrophy as well as other neuronal storage diseases should be looked for when a youngster manifests regression of developmental milestones.[12]

Developmental assessment

The physical examination should be deferred until a comprehensive developmental examination is performed. The specific developmental examination used for intellectual function assessment should be mutually agreed on by the psychologist and the physician. A well-trained primary care physician or (preferably because

Table 8-4. Inborn errors of metabolism in infancy*

A. Disorders of carbohydrate metabolism
  1. Galactosemia (galactose-1-phosphate uridyl transferase deficiency)
  2. Hereditary fructose intolerance (fructose-1-phosphate (aldolase deficiency)†
  3. Fructose-1,6-diphosphatase deficiency†
  4. Glycogen storage disease, type 1 (von Gierke's disease, glucose-6-phosphatase deficiency)†
  5. Glycogen storage disease, type II (Pompe's disease, α-1, 4-glucosidase deficiency)†
  6. Glycogen storage disease, type III (limit dextrinosis, debrancher deficiency)†
  7. Glycogen storage disease, type IV (amylopectinosis, brancher deficiency)†

B. Disorders of lipid metabolism
  8. GM$_1$ gangliosidosis, type I (generalized gangliosidosis, β-galactosidase deficiency)
  9. GM$_2$ gangliosidosis (Tay-Sachs disease)
  10. Wolman's disease (acid lipase deficiency)
  11. Niemann-Pick disease, types A and B (sphingomyelinase deficiency)

C. Disorders of mucopolysaccharide metabolism
  12. Hurler syndrome (mucopolysaccharidosis I, α-L-iduronidase deficiency)
  13. Hunter syndrome (mucopolysaccharidosis II, iduronosulfate sulfatase deficiency)
  14. β-Glucuronidase deficiency

D. Urea cycle defects
  15. Carbamylphosphate synthetase deficiency (hyperammonemia type I)
  16. Ornithine transcarbamylase deficiency (hyperammonemia type II)
  17. Citrullinemia
  18. Argininosuccinic aciduria
  19. Congenital lysine intolerance

E. Disorders of amino acid metabolism or transport
  20. Maple syrup urine disease
  21. Hypervalinemia
  22. Hyperlysinemia
  23. Hyper-β-alaninemia
  24. Nonketotic hyperglycinemia
  25. Phenylketonuria (several variants)†
  26. Oasthouse urine disease (methionine malabsorption)
  27. Tyrosinemia

E. Disorders of amino acid metabolism or transport—cont'd
  28. Hypermethioninemia†
  29. Homocystinuria
  30. Hartnup disease
  31. Hypersarcosinemia
  32. Pyroglutamic acidemia

F. Disorders of organic acid metabolism
  33. Methylmalonic acidemia†
  34. Propionic acidemia (ketotic hyperglycinemia)
  35. Isovaleric acidemia
  36. Butyric and hexanoic acidemia (green acyl dehydrogenase deficiency)
  37. β-Methylcrotonyl-CoA carboxylase deficiency

G. Miscellaneous disorders
  38. Adrenogenital syndrome†
  39. Lysosomal acid phosphatase deficiency
  40. Renal tubular acidosis† (without cerebral component)
  41. Nephrogenic diabetes insipidus†
  42. Menke's kinky hair syndrome
  43. Orotic aciduria
  44. Congenital lactic acidosis
  45. Cystic fibrosis†
  46. Hypophosphatasia†
  47. Fucosidosis
  48. Crigler-Najjar syndrome†
  49. Alpha$_1$-antitrypsin deficiency†
  50. I-cell disease (mucolipidosis II)
  51. Albinism†
  52. Lesch-Nyhan syndrome
  53. Oculocerebral syndrome of Lowe
  54. Congenital hypothyroidism
  55. Other disorders of lipid metabolism
     a. Alexander leukodystrophy
     b. Globoid leukodystrophy (Krabbe disease—β-galactosidase deficiency)
     c. Infantile Gaucher disease (β-glucosidase deficiency)
     d. Canavan leukodystrophy
  56. Other disorders of amino acid metabolism
     a. Hyperprolinemia, types I and II
     b. Joseph syndrome (increased excretion of proline and hydroxyproline)

*Modified from Burton, B. K., and Nadler, H. L.: Pediatrics **61**:398, 1978.
†Usually not associated with mental retardation.

of time constraints) an allied professional can assess the developmental capability of a child between the ages of birth and 3 years. The physician performing these examinations affords an opportunity to observe the interaction between the parents and the youngster; noticing the degree to which the parents provide support during the examination is important.

The Bayley Scales of Infant Development[4] was devised to test youngsters between the ages of birth and 30 months, and the Gesell Developmental Scales[23] is used for youngsters between ages 4 weeks and 6 years. These tests are described in detail in Chapter 3. They should not be confused with the Denver Developmental Screening Test of Frankenberg and Dodd[20] or

Table 8-5. Major clinical manifestations of inborn errors of metabolism in the neonatal period*

Clinical finding	Associated disorders†
Failure to thrive, poor feeding	Essentially all
Lethargy	8,9,15-24,28,32-35,43,44,54,55a,55b
Vomiting	1-4,10,15-22,25,27,31-35,38-42,52
Diarrhea	1,10,27,30,45
Jaundice	1,2,7,10,11,15,48,49,54
Hypotonicity or hypertonicity	1,3-5,8,9,15-20,24,26,31-34,37,42, 44,47,52,55a-55d
Seizures	1,2,4,6,9,15-20,22-24,26,33,34,38- 42,44,46,55a-55c,56a,56b
Hepatomegaly	1-14,16,18,27,28,31,33,38,47,49,50 55c
Dehydration	15-19,34,38,41
Coarse facial features	8,9,12-14,50,54
Abnormal urinary odor	20,25-28,35-37
Abnormal hair	18,25,29,42-51,54
Respiratory distress	5,9,16,18,44
Gingival hyperplasia	8,9,50
Macroglossia	5,8,9

*From Burton, B. K., and Nadler, H. L.: Pediatrics **61:** 398, 1978. Copyright American Academy of Pediatrics 1978.
†Numbers refer to metabolic disorders listed in Table 8-4.

Table 8-6. Laboratory findings associated with inborn errors of metabolism in the neonatal period*

Laboratory finding	Associated disorders†
Metabolic acidosis	2-4,6,15,32-36,40,44
Hypoglycemia	2-4,6,20,27,28,33,39,44,49
Reducing substances in urine	1,2,27
Ferric chloride test (Phenistix) positive on urine	20,25-27
Hyperammonemia	15-19,22
Neutopenia	15,27,33-36,43
Thrombocytopenia	27,33-37
Vacuolated lymphocytes on peripheral smear	4,8,10-13,47

*From Burton, B. K., and Nadler, H. L.: Pediatrics **61:** 398, 1978. Copyright American Academy of Pediatrics 1978.
†Numbers refer to metabolic disorders listed in Table 8-4.

the Developmental Screening Inventory devised by Knobloch and Passamanick.[23]

It is important to make a distinction between screening tests such as the Denver Developmental Screening Test and the Bayley Scales. The former is clearly a screening examination and is not meant to be used for definitive diagnosis of developmental delay or as an instrument to measure the success or failure of intervention programs.

Psychological testing of the youngster over the age of 3 years is more appropriately performed by a psychologist who is trained in child development and educational programming. Once again, whenever possible, the physician should observe the child and parents during the testing situation. Tests for preschool and early school-aged children include the Stanford-Binet Scale L/M Revision. This test is appropriate for children between the ages of 2 and 6 years.

Although there are such motor items as bead stringing and use of formboards, the test is heavily verbal and is inappropriate for the child with an isolated developmental language delay. On the other hand, the Merrill-Palmer Scale of Mental Tests is heavily weighted in the performance area and measures sensory motor coordination in areas such as ball throwing, cutting with a scissors, and buttoning. These tests are timed and are obviously difficult for the child with a motor handicap such as cerebral palsy; they tend to overestimate the abilities of the child with good motor skills and less than optimal verbal capability. The Wechsler Preschool and Primary Scale of Intelligence (WPPSI) is a good overall test for psychological assessment of children between the ages of 4 and 6½ years. It is a good supplement to the Stanford-Binet L/M Revision, which tends to overestimate the child's verbal performance at the ages of 4½ and 5 years.

The psychological evaluation of an infant or child provides a description of the child or infant at the time of the examination. The greater the deviation from the norm, the greater the ability of the examiner to predict future deviations and the need for special education. The severely impaired child can be identified within the first year of life, and the mildly retarded youngster certainly during the preschool period. However, this is not the case in the child with a borderline performance or the child showing a scatter of skills with normal performance in some areas and delays in others.

Normal function in infancy or in the preschool period cannot provide absolute assurance of successful academic performance. The measures of language and motor capability in infancy are quite different from the thought processes that are required for the abstract problem solving of adulthood. These factors coupled with ensuing life events, including physical illness and absence of environmental support for optimal cognitive and emotional growth, can all affect ultimate performance. The repair capability of the infant in an optimal setting is also an important factor. Sameroff[51] reported the developmental improvement over time of infants who were initially identified as being delayed because of neonatal asphyxia. At no time should the IQ be considered in isolation nor should it be used for the categorical labelling of the child or for a decrease in efforts to initiate individualized educational and habilitative programs.

Obviously, the testing of youngsters with auditory and visual impairment requires special skills. Not only must the psychologist be familiar with the tests available to optimize the performance of these youngsters, but skill in the administration of the test and its interpretation is also necessary. Reynel and Zinkin[50] are in the process of developing a developmental scale for children with visual handicaps. Their initial paper described the problems in adequately assessing children with severe visual handicaps. The Hiskey-Nebraska Test of Learning Aptitude[33a] and the Leiter International Performance Scale[19] can be used for deaf children and require no verbal response.

Although psychological evaluations have been standardized in terms of clinical and intertester reliability, the true skill of the psychologist is the ability to administer a variety of tests to suit a particular situation so that an optimal habilitative program for the mentally retarded child or adult may be developed. The completion of a comprehensive psychological evaluation may require multiple visits with the psychologist, depending on the fatigability, ability, and distractibility of the youngster. On completion of the psychological evaluation, the physician may then go on to the physical examination.

Physical examination

The first impression of the appearance of the youngster with mental retardation is very helpful, but the pronouncement of a child as being a "funny-looking kid" or as having an "odd manner" bears little fruit and is not helpful to the child or his parents. Careful observation of the child's behavior along with a search for dysgenetic features is productive in providing the parents with an accurate diagnosis.

The child's behavior should be carefully noted. Whenever possible, objective measures should be used so that the effect of treatment and management plans can be adequately assessed. The scale on p. 206 is based on Touwen and Prechtl's[61] method for measurement of spontaneous mobility. The upper portion describes the youngster's behavioral state at the time of the examination. The lower portion provides a description of the youngster's social responsiveness. Both are necessary descriptions to assess the quality of the examination in terms of the cooperativeness of the child and the adequacy of the observation. The physician using these scales must consider the quality and quantity of gross and fine motor movements. These observations can then be compared to observations obtained before and after a prescription of medication or the initiation of certain management techniques. This is especially helpful in the hyperactive or behaviorally difficult child.

Measurements of height and weight give information in regard to the physical growth of the child. These measurements require special attention because of their frequent association with feeding difficulties, which may require caloric supplementation in the form of carbohydrates and medium-chain triglycerides as well as alterations of the youngster's feeding patterns.

Growth failure is frequent in children with chromosomal abnormalities or who were small for gestational age infants. This growth failure

---

SCALES THAT RECORD BEHAVIORAL STATE AND SOCIAL AWARENESS*

Behavioral state

0 = Awake, not crying
1 = Awake, not fussing
2 = Awake, crying

3 = Yelling
4 = Other (describe)

Social responsiveness

0 = Interested, agrees with proposals, no stimulation needed, facial expression alert
1 = Disinterested, agrees with proposal, no particular encouragement needed but not facially alert
2 = Reluctant, needs encouragement, appears anxious, tends to show facial expressiveness
3 = Reluctant, needs encouragement, appears sullen and withdrawn
4 = Shrinks back on approach, refuses to fulfill demands, appears frightened
5 = Refuses to fulfill demands, appears impassive
6 = Resists by pushing examiner away, tries to get away, struggles
7 = Other (describe)

---

*Modified from Touwen, D. C. L., and Prechtl, H. F. R.: Clin. Dev. Med. vol. 38, 1970.

---

may be a reflection of inherent prenatal morphological difficulties that are really not amenable to subsequent increased caloric intake. Endocrinopathies and other causes of growth failure must also be considered. The inability to feed due to neurological disorders should not be confused with the anorexia seen in association with disorders such as increased pulmonary blood flow due to a ventricular septal defect. Growth failure in this group of infants may occur even in the absence of congestive failure. The latter cause of growth failure may be altered by intracardiac surgical repair.[16]

The measurement of the head circumference is by far the best and least invasive measurement of brain growth. Microcephaly is the frequent accompaniment of cerebral dysgenesis, cerebral atrophy, and congenital infectious disease, or may be the sequela of perinatal asphyxia. In general, microcephaly suggests a poor developmental outcome. The diagnosis of primary microcephaly, which can be an autosomal recessive disorder, has important implications for future pregnancies. Following are those conditions that may be associated with microcephaly[29,39]:

A. Present at birth
  1. Cytomegalovirus infection
  2. Toxoplasmosis
  3. Rubella
  4. Paine sex-linked recessive microcephaly with aminoaciduria

  5. Chromosomal aberrations
  6. Cerebral dysgenesis
  7. Primary microcephaly
  8. First trimester radiation
B. Normal at birth, apparent at 1 year
  1. Perinatal hypoxic-ischemic encephalopathy
  2. Metabolic disorder (e.g., phenylketonuria)
  3. Degenerative brain disease
  4. Congenital rubella
  5. Congenital cytomegalovirus infection
  6. Congenital toxoplasmosis
  7. Perinatal herpes simplex virus infection
  8. Congenital varicella
  9. Craniostenosis
  10. Meningitis in infant
  11. Cryptogenic infantile spasms

The first sign of hydrocephalus may be rapidly increasing head size. The occurrence of catch-up growth in premature infants, even as late as the third month of life, can at times be indistinguishable from hydrocephalus and warrants close observation prior to surgical intervention.[53,54] Hydrocephalus in premature infants may also occur initially without an increase in the head circumference, and the CAT scan may be invaluable in showing ventricular enlargement. The head of the normal newborn grows approximately 1.2 cm per month until the fifth to sixth month, and then 0.5 cm per month until 1 year. The premature infant's head, however, grows 1.3 cm per week. Fig. 8-9 presents the growth curves of head circum-

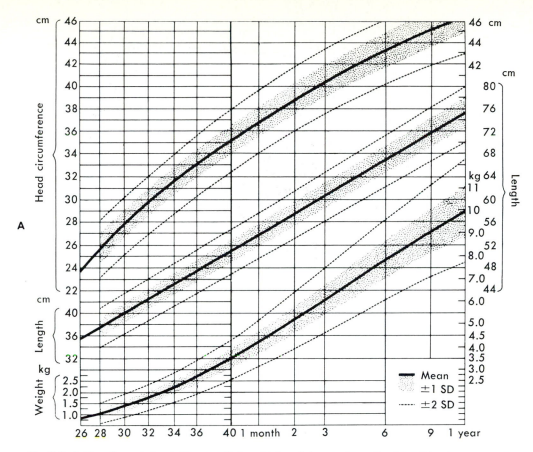

Fig. 8-9. A, Growth graph for plotting growth from birth until 1 year of age after "term" has been reached. For infants of varying gestational ages. *Continued.*

ference as well as the length and weight of premature infants.[2] The concept of adjusting for gestational age is important not only in terms of developmental assessment but also in judging the adequacy of gains in height and weight and growth of head circumference.

The physical examination of the youngster with mental retardation requires meticulous routine organ system examination as well as special attention to a child's neurological and developmental status. The presence of a cardiac lesion, organomegaly, and genital anomalies are all important diagnostic observations. Of equal importance, however, is the presence of serous otitis, which may be associated with a conductive hearing loss.

The impression that a child is odd looking must be substantiated by such measures as interpupillary distance, the length of the philtrum, and the head and chest circumferences. Chapter 9, on genetic counselling, contains percen-

tile graphs for a large number of morphological characteristics that were originally designated as "odd" on the basis of clinical impression rather than quantitative measurement. Special features bring to mind certain diagnoses and require a view more focused to particular aspects of the examination in an effort to confirm a suspected syndrome. Some of the physical characteristics associated with mental retardation are described on p. 209. These signs can be used for cross-referencing syndromes that are described in such texts as Smith[55] and Bergsma.[5] They can also be tactfully presented to parents as evidence of prenatal dysmorphogenesis. This must be done with caution and with the knowledge that the features are truly dysgenetic rather than family characteristics. The high correlation of dysgenetic features and subsequent diagnoses of mental retardation has been stressed by Drillien.[17] She noted that 45% of infants whose birth weight was 1500 g or

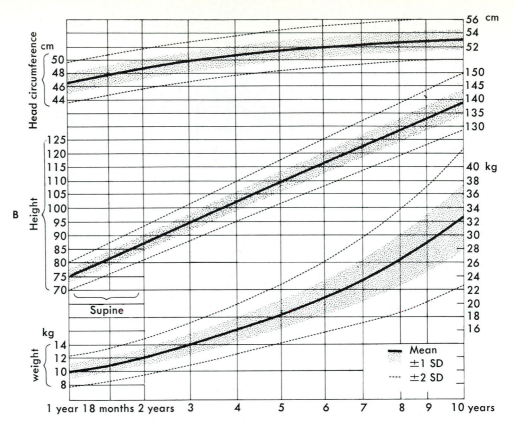

Fig. 8-9, cont'd. B, Growth graph for charting growth in three measurements until the adolescent growth spurt begins. Applicable to boys and girls from 1 to 10 years. (From Babson, G. S., and Benda, G. I.: J. Pediatr. **89:** 814, 1976.)

less and who were dysgenetic had IQs that were borderline or low as compared to 23% of infants with the same weight who did not appear dysgenetic. Smith and Simmons[56] noted that studies indicate 44% of children with severe retardation have prenatal problems in morphogenesis. The most commonly found major malformation is that of the central nervous system, including primary microcephaly, hydrocephaly, and hydranencephaly.

A special emphasis on the physical appearance and signs of the child with Down syndrome is worthwhile because of the frequent occurrence of this syndrome. Following are Hall's signs of Down syndrome noted in newborns[10]:

1. Flat face with shallow orbits
2. Upward oblique palpebral fissures
3. Dysplastic ears
4. Abundant neck skin
5. Four-finger line (single palmar crease)
6. Dysplastic middle phalanx of fifth finger (clinodactyly)
7. Dysplastic pelvis
8. Muscle hypotonia
9. Hyperreflexia
10. Lack of Moro reflex

Hall[28] noted that the presence of 6 of the 10 features listed makes the diagnosis and does not require waiting for chromosomal analysis before discussing the problem with the parents. Coleman[10] presents an updated review of Down syndrome, which addresses the physical and experimental treatment aspects of this chromosomal abnormality. Of recent interest is the implication of the father as the source of the extra chromosome in 24% of the cases, and the shift of the increased incidence of Down syndrome from the woman of over 35 to the younger mother.[34]

The physician should explain the examination process to the parents and the youngster and assure the child of the safety of the process. The retarded child is often fearful of sudden movements and heights, and the examination is best performed on a mat on the floor rather than on the prestigious, impersonal examining table. If the youngster is particularly fearful and not willing to separate from the parent, the examination should be performed with the child on the parent's lap. The examiner should then proceed carefully through each organ system, being aware of the frequent linkage of the major and minor congenital malformations that are associated with mental retardation, some of which are noted below:

- Nutrition and growth status: Height, weight, head circumference, percentiles
- General state: Somnolence, alertness, crying
- Behaviors: Hyperactivity, distractibility, emotional liability, response to environment and examiner, self-stimulation, self-abuse, cooperation
- Face: Elfin, triangular, long philtrum, coarse features
- Skin: Dermatoglyphics, depigmentation, cafe-au-lait, telangiectasia, andenoma sebaceum, cyanosis, pallor
- Hair: Texture, whorls, color
- Ears, nose, throat: Upturned nose, low-set ears, shape of mouth and nose, shape of mandible, texture of tongue, dentition, number, enamel, palate, cleft, audiological examination (all)
- Eyes: Slant and shape, cornea, Brushfield spots, funduscopic examination (all), macula, retina for chorioretinitis, papilledema, vessels, exudate, pupil shape, lashes, strabismus, vision examination (all)
- Neck: Shortness, webbing, mobility
- Chest: Shape, nipple shape and spacing, deformity, auscultation, heart murmur
- Abdomen: Visceromegaly, hernia, protuberance, masses
- Genitalia: Development, ambiguousness, testis size, urethral opening, cryptorchidism
- Back: Kyphosis, scoliosis
- Extremities: Hypermobility, limitation of movement, muscular mass, hands, polydactyly, clinodactyly, overlapping fingers, syndactyly, feet and legs, proportion distal-proximal, edema, arms carrying angle, distance between toes, arch, clubbing

Every good primary care physician knows that the traumatic and painful portions of the examination should be left to the very last. Signs of neurological disorders are difficult to elicit and observe in a crying, distressed youngster. Detecting evidence of neurological dysfunction (Chapters 3 and 6), abnormal movements, and muscular weakness is as important in the retarded child as in the normal child. A major portion of the neurodevelopmental examination should be done first, leaving the Babinski reflex and the response to pinprick to the last. The comprehensive neurological examination is described in Chapter 3.

Not infrequently, a child with neuromuscular disease and isolated psychomotor delay is referred to the clinic with an inappropriate diagnosis of mental retardation. The differential diagnosis of motor delays is presented on p. 210.

The examination of the child's eyes is a critical component of the assessment of the retarded child. This is described in detail in Chapter 11. Funduscopic examination is helpful in the identification of the cherry-red spot of Tay-Sach disease, the phakoma of tuberous sclerosis, and the chorioretinitis of toxoplasmosis, rubella, or cytomegalic inclusion disease. Retrolental fibroplasia has once again become a problem and should be carefully looked for in the premature infant who has been exposed to greater than normal oxygen tensions. All children with suspected mental retardation should have a funduscopic examination, which may require the use of such mydriatics as 10% ophthalmic phenylephrine (Neo-Synephrine). This produces mydriasis in 10 to 30 minutes and recovery in 6 hours with only slight paralysis of accommodation. The youngster should be carefully examined for strabismus, visual impairment, or cataracts. The testing of visual acuity in the retarded child is extremely difficult, and although such tests as the Sheridan[54a] Stycar Vision Test have been used by primary care physicians, the formal testing is best delegated to a pediatric ophthalmologist. The high incidence of visual disturbances in these chil-

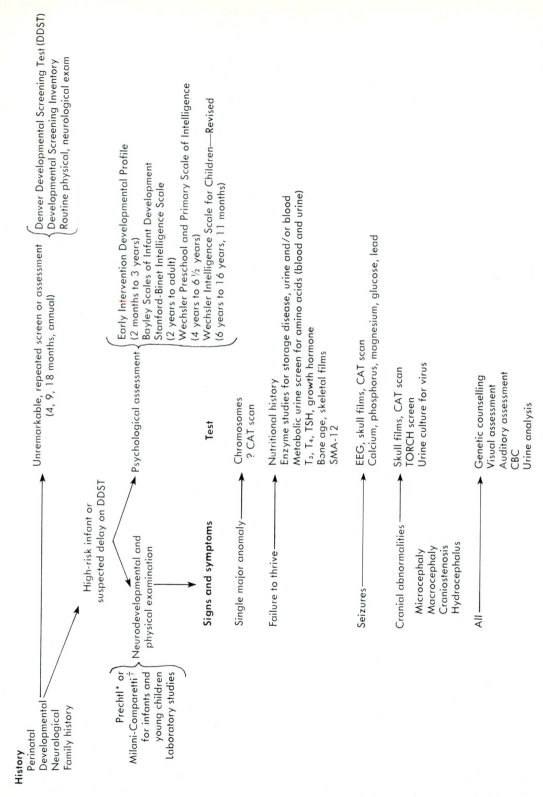

Fig. 8-10. Diagnostic process—general guide. Laboratory studies should be determined by careful history and physical examination. *Prechtl, H.F.R., and Beintema, D.: Clin. Dev. Med. no. 12, 1964. †Milani-Comparetti, G.: Dev. Med. Child Neurol. **9:**631, 1967.

dren warrant referral of all youngsters with retardation to a capable, patient, and understanding ophthalmologist.

Hearing difficulties occur in approximately 10% of moderately to severely impaired retarded children[32]; therefore they all should be referred for comprehensive auditory assessment (Chapter 10). At a minimum, such tests should include pure tone audiometry and acoustical reflex testing using an acoustical impedance bridge. Cortical audiometry correlates with graded auditory stimuli and simultaneous electroencephalographical tracings and is generally reserved for those youngsters in whom deafness is suspected and who are unable to adequately participate in traditional audiometric testing. In general, Weber, Rinne, and Schwabach testing cannot be performed with any consistent results in the moderately to severely retarded child.

After methodically proceeding through the physical examination, the decision regarding further laboratory and radiographical studies should be made. Rising medical costs in combination with the potential fears and anxieties of the child should limit laboratory studies to those that are absolutely essential and give reasonable indication that they will contribute to an ultimate diagnosis. Fig. 8-10 suggests an approach to the problem of laboratory studies. Single major or multiple minor anomalies suggest the need for chromosomal studies. Suspected sex chromosome abnormalities can be screened by using a stain of cells from the buccal mucosa. A computerized axial tomography (CAT scan) can be helpful in identifying cerebral dysgenesis or atrophy, central nervous system bleeding, or hydrocephalus. This procedure, albeit expensive, has contributed greatly in our ability to identify cerebral defects.

A review of the use of the electroencephalogram in pediatric practice by Lewis and Freeman[43] indicates that it is primarily for those youngsters in whom a seizure disorder is suspected. They stress the need for a careful history and also indicate that the management of the patient's condition depends on clinical impressions, not solely electrical criteria.

Failure to thrive associated with vomiting and hepatosplenomegaly requires, as mentioned previously, metabolic screening that includes blood tests for the detection of metabolic defects in lysosomal, lipid, carbohydrate, amino acid, and mucopolysaccharide metabolism. Growth failure may require endocrinological studies as well as urine analysis and culture, intravenous pyelography, and a host of other examinations noted in Fig. 8-10. These extensive assessments are rarely productive; however, the ongoing need to search for a correctable medical cause remains important. Although infants and children with mental retardation suffer from growth retardation possibly related to the derangement of the hypothalamic pituitary axis, it is important to remember that they also may be emotionally and physically deprived. An adequate nutritional history that consists of careful counting of calories with an assessment of the distribution of carbohydrate, fat, and protein should be obtained. This is an important initial step in all children with a history of growth failure and failure to thrive and should be done along with an assessment of the family's psychosocial qualities.

Development of a treatment plan

A treatment plan or individualized habilitative program is best developed in an interdisciplinary staffing conference with the parents present. The plan should be the result of the evaluations by social workers, occupational therapists, speech pathologists, nutritionists, audiologists, and medical subspecialists. The content of these evaluations are described in the chapters relating to specific disorders. The primary care physician should review these evaluations and plans with the parents. Treatment plans that have no basis for implementation in reality must be recognized as ego trips and academic exercises for professionals, with little functional use for the family. Although physicians should be aware of the ideal, a careful assessment of family and community resources must be made if one is to minimize the frustration of parents and professionals in response to unrealistic plans and expectations for the child.

The social service assessment performed by an allied professional such as a home visitor, social worker, or nurse practitioner should at a minimum include the following:

1. The family's emotional status and level of functioning
2. The family's conception of the handicap in terms of causal relationships
3. The family's financial situation and concerns regarding ongoing costs
4. A medical review of the family's health, that is, the presence of other acute or chronic illnesses in the family
5. The living situation (home neighborhood, extended family resources)
6. The ongoing need for counselling and advocacy to assist the family in the implementation of the program

The program implemented should at a minimum include the following:

1. Ongoing medical care or additional evaluations in regard to specific associated disabilities such as serous otitis, strabismus, scoliosis, contractures, growth failure, or seizure disorders
2. Programs to facilitate fine motor, gross motor, speech and language, self-help, adaptive, and cognitive skills as they relate to the home, school, and community
3. A psychoeducational program, including cognitive skills in terms of school and educational adaptation, skills necessary for regular school attendance or vocational placement, assessment of school learning environment, and assessment of the home and neighborhood environment as well as vocational placement

In keeping with the concepts of normalization, efforts to integrate a youngster into the regular classroom with nonhandicapped peers should be supported. The educational member of a diagnostic evaluation center, a primary care physician, or a nurse practitioner should follow the youngster into the classroom to explain the nature of the youngster's disability and how it relates to his educational needs. Those physical, emotional, and educational factors that are necessary for the child to have a positive school experience should be identified. Once identified, a judgment should be made as to how these positive qualities can be supported through proper programming and adaptation of the school environment.

Judgment of the need for respite services and recreational and social service activity should be included in the final planning program for the disabled child. Services should be made available to the family to do the following:

1. Increase their knowledge of the youngster's disability and available community rehabilitation services
2. Increase their competence and understanding in coping with adverse community attitudes
3. Provide them with the necessary skills to assist in the treatment plan and become positive members of the team
4. Attempt to develop awareness within the family of the interaction and responses that the family is having in regard to the youngster's disability
5. Decrease the burden of the day-to-day care of the youngster through respite care. Respite care should extend from such services as baby-sitting to long-term residential and home care for family vacations and special occasions

The complexity of the rehabilitation process often results in the abdication of responsibility by the primary care physician to the large, impersonal, diagnostic and evaluation center. In the absence of primary care physician participation, the identity and needs of the particular family may be lost among the hundreds of other families who are seeking similar services at the diagnostic center. The physician's ability to monitor the process depends on three major factors:

1. An appropriate allocation and organization of time
2. The use of allied professionals to assume responsibility for tasks that do not require the expertise of a physician or for which the physician is not trained
3. An adequate record-keeping system in the form of a goal-oriented record

The goal-oriented record. The goal-oriented record stems from the concept of the problem-oriented record proposed by Weed.[63] The positive implication of goals and the movement away from the traditional medical model, which considers mental retardation as a disease, has prompted this change. Like the problem-oriented record, the goal-oriented record provides a mechanism whereby the quality of the material in a record and its organization can be markedly improved. Problems are better identified and less likely to be overlooked. With explicit goals the measurement of program effectiveness becomes possible.

It is important to conceptualize the evaluative process presented in Fig. 8-11 to understand the goal-oriented record. The client must be evaluated in such a manner that all aspects of his development and environment are measurable. The individual goals are based on the evaluative observations, which will then dictate the habilitative process.

The goal of the habilitative program is the organization of a positive client and family environment for the development of the following:

1. Attitudes
2. Trust
3. Optimal physical health
4. Methods to stimulate intellectual development
5. Opportunities for the client to explore and then choose, observe, and succeed
6. Social skills to relate to and be involved with his peer group
7. Educational, vocational, and daily living skills so that he can function in such institutional settings as schools, vocational programs, and residential facilities
8. A work setting that is genuine and provides experiences with true meaning to the client, which in turn allows the client to be integrated into the mainstream of life

Physicians must remember that as they sort the data obtained during the individual evaluations they logically think from the point of view of problems. The next steps are to integrate this information into a total program and to establish positive goals. These goals must be defined in terms that are *specific, measurable,* and *observable*. It is absolutely necessary to refrain from using general terms that are not measurable, for example, "could interact better with his peers." It is obvious that interacting better has different meanings for many people and is in no way a truly measurable goal. This goal may be more specifically stated as "he eliminates rocking behavior and participates in group activities." The specific group activities should also be noted.

The development of goal-oriented records requires a standard format that includes the following:

1. The data base is gathered, consisting of historical data, examinations, and tests.

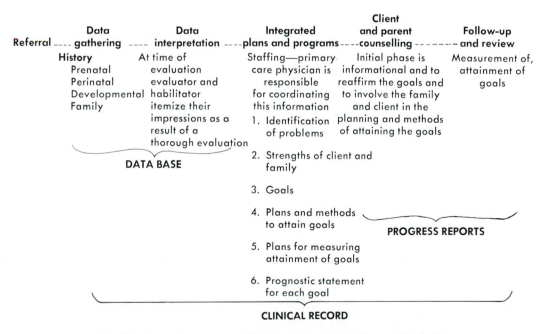

Fig. 8-11. Processing sequence of information regarding a client and his family.

This material is that obtained during the evaluation by a variety of allied professionals as well as the material obtained during the physician's physical examination. This information is then organized and itemized and the professional impressions are recorded in the first section of a clinical record.

2. A problem list is then generated as a result of the data base and may be based on the physician's own impressions or the decision of the interdisciplinary staffing conference, which includes the parents. The problem-oriented format of subjective and objective data and assessment should be used.

3. An itemized list of assets of the client and family is then determined, utilizing either the information gained from allied professionals or information that the primary care physician gathered (Fig. 8-12).

4. The goal list is then formulated and becomes a table of contents of goals that are to be achieved. It consists of an identifying number, a title, date of indexing of the goals, and where, when, and who is responsible for the attainment of the goals.

The central elements of the goals are summarized in four columns, as noted in Fig. 8-13. The identification of who is responsible and when and where the goal should be achieved are critical components of a goal-oriented record. The ''who'' relates to the name of the responsible person or agency, and the date indicates when the goal should be achieved. The

			Jones, John
			(name)
			55-55
			(consec. no.)
No.	**Problem—client and family**	**No.**	**Assets—client and family**
1.	Global retardation	1.	Appealing youngster
2.	Language development--expressive problem greater than receptive problem	2.	Ability to interact with and relate well to adults
3.	Diplegia, spasticity	3.	Has developed parallel play
4.	Grand mal seizures	4.	Appears to be motivated to try
5.	Short attention span, impulsive manipulative behavior	5.	Interested in exploring many different areas; functions best in uncontained setting
6.	Not toilet trained	6.	Indicates when wet
7.	Parental anxiety and guilt, especially mother	7.	Parental willingness to learn and be involved
8.	Lack of parental knowledge of problem and too great expectations for John	8.	With direct input, increasing mother's knowledge and providing an opportunity for parents to ventilate result in obvious reduction in anxiety level
9.	Possible marital discord	9.	Parents attempting to deal directly with pressures from in-laws

Fig. 8-12. Problem and asset list.

goals should be consecutively numbered, dated, and signed by the physician, the member of the group practice, or the allied professionals within the office. Once a goal is achieved, the number may never be used again. In general, it is well to reserve one goal for the completion of the evaluation when there is a significant lack of information. Additional procedures such as electroencephalography, vision or hearing screening, psychological tests, and others tests may be itemized under the plans and methods of attaining this goal.

A review of the final document of goals identified should satisfy the following criteria:

1. There should be enough information to proceed with a habilitative program.
2. The goal list should resolve all the existing problems listed.
3. The goals should be as specific and concise as possible.
4. The goals should be listed in order of priority, with the most important goals addressed first and the rest in the future.
5. The methods developed for attaining the goals must be clearly stated.
6. There should be evidence of active parent or client participation.
7. The availability of resources and competency of these resources should be defined.
8. Prognostic statements should be presented for each goal. They should be realistic and stated in an appropriate time frame.
9. The date for intended follow-up or reevaluation should be stated.

Following is a goal-oriented record developed after the transdisciplinary evaluation of a

---

Jones, John
(name)

55-55
(consec. no.)

Goal no.	Date received	Goal title	Disposition			
			Where	When	Who	Date achieved
1	1/7	Complete initial evaluation	Dev. ctr.	1/7 to 1/14	Smart	
2	1/7	Prevent convulsions	Dev. ctr.	1/7	William	
3	1/7	Develop parent education and couselling program to reduce parental anxiety, improve understanding of son, become primary therapists	Dev. ctr.; Arc School	1/14	Miller, Raymond	
4	1/7	Decrease manipulative behavior; increase attention span	Dev. ctr.	1/14	Kanner, Miller, Raymond	
5	1/7	Complete toilet training	Home	1/14	Raymond	
6	1/7	Improve receptive, expressive language	Dev. ctr.; Home	1/14	Miller, Raymond	

Fig. 8-13. Goal list.

2-year-old youngster with spastic diplegia secondary to perinatal asphyxia. He has been evaluated by a pediatrician, neurologist, occupational therapist, speech pathologist, and physical therapist. The primary care physician gathered data and formulated this goal-oriented record using the format on pp. 213 to 215:

A. Impression of problem
   1. Global retardation: Mild (311.90) with expressive language problems
   2. Short attention span, impulsive active behavior, brain injury secondary to perinatal asphyxia
   3. Spastic diplegia
   4. Convulsive disorder: Grand mal
   5. Manipulative behavior secondary to inconsistent management by the parents
   6. Parental anxiety
   7. Functional heart murmur of no consequence
B. Problems (Fig. 8-12)
   1. Global retardation
   2. Language development
   3. Spastic diplegia
   4. Convulsive disorder: Grand mal
   5. Short attention span, impulsive manipulative behavior
   6. Not toilet trained
   7. Parental anxieties, etc.
   8. Lack of parental knowledge, etc.
   9. Possible marital discord
C. Assets (Fig. 8-12)
   1. Appealing youngster
   2. Relates to and interacts with adults
   3. Has developed parallel play
   4. Good motivation
   5. Explores
   6. Functions best when not contained
   7. Parental willingness to learn and be involved
   8. Excellent medical care
   9. Other
D. Goals
   1. Complete evaluation
   2. Improve receptive and expressive language
   3. Improve motor function
   4. Prevent convulsions
   5. Complete toilet training
   6. Decrease manipulative behavior
   7. Develop parental education and counselling program to reduce parental anxiety and improve understanding of the youngster so that the family may become primary therapists

Fig. 8-13 demonstrates what the goal list looks like on the face sheet of the child's record. The methods of attaining the goals are not recorded but would be available in the child's records and can be used for ready reference. The goal list can be used by the physician for a regular updating of the habilitative plan of the youngster and to provide the necessary advocacy when the plan seems to lag. This not only provides the physician with an excellent record-keeping system but also provides a constant reference list of individual goals, which the physician can regularly check with the parents. Secondarily, this provides the family with a feeling of security in the physician that is knowledgeable and interested in the treatment of their child.

To follow these steps, the goal-oriented record (GOR) requires a general format divided into the standardized sections outlined below:

1. Data base: Data base consists of (1) historical data and (2) examinations and tests. This material is obtained during the assessment by individual evaluators and habilitators. This information is organized and itemized as impressions and recorded in the first section of the clinical record.
2. Problem list: The problem list is determined at the staffing conferences from the impressions (Fig. 8-12).
3. Itemized list of assets of the client and family: The itemized list of assets of the client and family is determined at the staffing conferences by the various evaluators (Fig. 8-12).
4. Goal list: The goal list is formulated at the staffing conference (Fig. 8-13). It is a table of contents of goals to be achieved. It consists of an identifying number, title, date of indexing each goal, where and when actions are to occur, and who is responsible for these actions.
5. Initial plans: Initial plans are agreed on at the time of the staffing conference. Based on the assessment of the data base, a detailed plan of action for each goal, with methods for measuring the attainment of goals and a prognostic statement, must be recorded in the second section of the clinical record. Cross-referencing of the plans will be necessary to integrate them into a gestalt. The plans should be

in such detail that they can be implemented by all program personnel.

6. Progress notes: For each goal, *as the need arises,* a record of new information, its meaning, and what should be done about it is recorded in writing by goal number.

LEGISLATIVE AND ETHICAL ISSUES

A discussion concerning the habilitation of the retarded person would not be complete without addressing the many ethical issues that this topic provokes. Ethical principles are defined as ''a generalized normative judgement about behavior based on values arising from one's experiences and beliefs and superimposed by some degree of social approval by persons who offer such principles as final justification for their choice and their decisions.''[41] Many of these judgments have been replaced by judicial and legislative actions that relate directly to the issue of the right of mentally retarded persons to medical treatment, habilitation, and education.[41]

The right to medical treatment and the sustaining of life is a major issue in the presence of the technological ability to sustain a cardiovascular system in the presence of cerebral death. There has been an ongoing controversy in an effort to satisfactorily define death. Some definitions relate to the cessation of the cardiorespiratory system (which is unrealistic with current support technology), and others focused on brain death.[1,52] The latter definition has greater applicability to retarded persons. The definition of brain death not only includes irreversible coma but also implies that the quality of life in the presence of massive brain injury is important in making the decision to sustain life. Jonsen and Garland[37] edited an excellent conference report concerning ethical issues that arise in a neonatal intensive care unit. Many of the decisions discussed at the conference relate to the subsequent quality of life of the infant in the presence of perinatal catastrophes and severe malformations.

A precedent-setting question as to who decides to terminate life support arose in the Karen Quinlan case. Here, the New Jersey court upheld that after employing the highest standard of medical knowledge that science could possibly use to determine brain death, the physician and ethics committee of the hospital involved and the parents or guardian could decide to ''pull the plug.'' In a recent decision by the Massachusetts Supreme Judicial Court, this decision was altered.[14] The court decided in the case of Saikewicz, a 67-year-old severely retarded man who had leukemia, that the physician and guardian must ask the courts to make the decision of whether or not to sustain the life of this man. The courts stated that the value and the quality of life should not be equated. In so stating, it made it very clear that the life of the mentally retarded person is worth saving, despite the severity of his retardation. Although this ruling was important in the sense that it gave dignity to the quality of life of the retarded, this court decision has proved to be very disruptive for those who work in neonatal intensive care units. This is especially true when the clinical picture, in conjunction with such laboratory studies as CAT scan, electroencephalogram, and other tests can unequivocally predict a lifetime of severe disability for a youngster and an endless burden for the family.

The issues of habilitation, education, care, and treatment prove less of a dilemma. The questioning of program costs appears to be a strawman when compared to the federal defense budget. However, the concerns of parents with normal children who see financial outlays two to three times greater for retarded children than for their own youngsters are clearly rational. Mechanisms must be identified that do not take from one youngster to give to another or the process of mainstreaming and community living may be doomed to failure.

There is little controversy regarding the right to education and habilitative treatment. In April, 1972, the Alabama case *Wyatt* v. *Stickney* set the standard for the minimal constitutionality of habilitative, educational, and medical treatment in a large state facility.[11] The case is somewhat unique in that not only does it define minimal treatment, but it also sets forth the detailed procedure for its implementation. Similar successful class action suits have been initiated by the parents of children at Willowbrook Developmental Center in New York City and at Belchertown and Monson state schools in

Massachusetts. The right to education was established in Pennsylvania in the early 1970s.[21] The states of Michigan, Massachusetts, and others have followed suit, with mandated special education beginning at birth in the state of Michigan and at 3 years in the state of Massachusetts.

Although the legal, ethical, and moral outlook for retarded people has improved markedly since the Kennedy era of the 1960s, community attitudes are still plagued with fear and ignorance about the criminality and promiscuity of the retarded person. There is little question of the disproportionately high incidence of delinquency among very mild to borderline retarded persons, in whom the cause of retardation is primarily psychosocial. This is certainly not true of the more severely impaired individual, in whom the cause is more likely to be organic. Tarjan,[59] director of the Pacific State Hospital in California, stressed the conviction that retarded people are responsive to rules of discipline and in sexual matters, without utilizing such techniques as sterilization by surgery or isolation. He stated, "the extramarital conception rate of women patients would have given pride to any college president or high school principal."[59]

This is an important statement to keep in mind when anxious parents or ill-informed professionals press for inappropriate sterilization procedures. Our experience in Monroe County, New York, with over 500 community-based retarded adults supports Tarjan's comments. The population at high risk for out of wedlock pregnancies was the borderline or mildly retarded adult whose difficulties were in most instances related to environmental factors. The moderately or severely retarded adults were at minimal risk.

In the case of *Wade* v. *Bethesda* in 1971,[62] the court stated that the denial of marriage, procreation, and the raising of children to the retarded person was a "permanent irreputable assumption" and was condemned by the United States Supreme Court. The physician who performed the sterilization procedure and the social and welfare workers who suggested the surgery were sued for a large sum of money, which resulted in a large out of court settlement on behalf of the plaintiff. This decision and our experience with retarded people living within the community suggests that the use of birth control or recommendations for sterilization should only be considered after evaluating the following:

1. The evidence of sexual activity in the individual
2. The capability of the individual to rear a child
3. The risk of potential pregnancy

CONCLUSIONS

There is little question that the welfare and treatment of people who are retarded are improving. Such concepts as normalization, deinstitutionalization, and community living have been in the forefront of that improvement. Unfortunately, primary care physicians have been conspicuous by their absence in advocating for the rights of retarded people. The reason for this lack of participation is clear. Most pediatric departments still delegate the study of developmental disabilities to the elective category, and few if any departments have effective courses in normal growth and development. The spirit of the times suggests that the lack of education is doing a disservice to both the physician and the patient. There is little question that the primary care physician will be called on time and time again to provide care to developmentally disabled and chronically ill children. As educators and interested citizens, it would seem imminently appropriate to prepare the physician for this task.

REFERENCES

1. Ad Hoc Committee of the Harvard Medical School to Examine the Definition of Brain Death: A definition of irreversible coma, J.A.M.A. **205:**337, 1968.
1a. Arthur, G.: The Arthur adaptation of the Leiter international performance scale, J. Clin. Psychol. **5:**345, 1949.
2. Babson, G. S., and Benda, G. I.: Growth graphs for the clinical assessment of infants of varying gestational age, J. Pediatr. **89:**814, 1976.
3. Bank-Mikkelsen, N. E.: A metropolitan area in Denmark changing patterns in residential services for the mentally retarded. In Kugel, R. B., and Wolfensberger, W., editors: President's committee on mental retardation, Washington, D.C. 1969, Department of Health, Education and Welfare.

4. Bayley, N.: Infant scales of development—mental, motor, and behavioral profile, New York, 1969, Psychological Corp.

5. Bergsma, D.: Birth defects, atlas and compendium, Baltimore, 1973, The Williams & Wilkins Co. for National Foundation—March of Dimes.

6. Birch, H. G., and Gussow, J. D.: Disadvantaged children—health, nutrition, and school failure. New York, 1970, Grune & Stratten, Inc.

7. Burton, B. K., and Nadler, H. L.: Clinical diagnosis of inborn errors of metabolism in the neonatal period, Pediatrics **61:**398, 1978.

8. Chisolm, J. J.: Treatment of lead poisoning, Mod. Treatment **8:**593, 1971.

9. Coffin, R., Phillips, J. L., and Staples, W. I.: Treatment of lead encephalopathy in children, J. Pediatr., **69:**198, 1966.

10. Coleman, M.: Down's syndrome, Pediatr. Ann. **7:**41, 1978.

11. Cooke, R. E.: Ethics and the law on behalf of the mentally retarded, Pediatr. Clin. North Am. **29:**259, 1973.

12. Crocker, A. C.: Inborn errors of lipid metabolism: early identification, clin. perinatol. **3:**99, 1976.

13. Crocker, A. C., Cushna, B.: Pediatric decisions in children with serious mental retardation, Pediatr. Clin. North Am. **19:**413, 1972.

14. Curran, W. J.: The Saikewicz decision: law medicine notes, N. Engl. J. Med. **298:**499, 1978.

15. Deutsch, M., Katz, K., and Jensen, A. R.: Social class, race, and psychological development, New York, 1969, Holt, Rinehart, & Winston, Inc.

16. Dobell, A. D. C., et al.: Severe feeding difficulties in infants with increased pulmonary blood flow, J. Thorac. Cardiovasc. Surg. **72:**303, 1976.

17. Drillien, C. M.: Aetiology and outcome in low birth weight infants, Dev. Med. Child Neurol. **14:**563, 1972.

18. Drillien, C. M., and Drummond, M. B., editors: Neurodevelopmental problems in early childhood, assessment and management, Blackwell Scientific Publications, Oxford, 1977.

18a. Dubowitz, L. M. S., Dubowitz, V., and Goldberg, C.: Clinical assessment of gestational age in the newborn infant, J. Pediatr. **77:**1, 1970.

19. Franco, S., and Andrews, B. F.: Reduction of cerebral palsy in neonatal intensive care, Pediatr. Clin. North Am. **24:**639, 1977.

20. Frankenberg, W. K., and Dodds, J. B.: Denver developmental screening test, J. Pediatr. **71:**181, 1967.

21. Friedman, P.: Pennsylvania civil action 71-42, mental retardation and the law, Washington, D.C., 1972, Center for Law and Social Policy.

22. Gayton, J., and Walker, L.: Down syndrome: informing the parents, Am. J. Dis. Child. **127:**510, 1974.

23. Gesell, A., and Armatruda, S.: Developmental diagnosis, ed. 3. (Knobloch, H., and Passamanick, B., editors), New York, 1974, Harper & Row, Publishers.

24. Gordon, I. J., Gumagh, B., and Jester, E. R.: Child learning through child play, New York, 1972, St. Martin's Press, Inc.

25. Gordon, N.: Paediatric neurology for the clinician, London, 1976, William Heinemann Medical Books Ltd.

26. Grossman, A. J., editor: Manual on terminology and classification of mental retardation and association of mental defects, no. 2, special publication, Baltimore, 1973, Garanmond-Predemark Press.

27. Grunewald, K.: A rural county in Sweden in changing patterns in residential services for the mentally retarded. In Kugel, R. B., and Wolfensberger, W., editors: President's committee on mental retardation, Washington, D.C., 1969, Department of Health, Education and Welfare.

28. Hall, B.: Mongolism in newborns—a clinical and aytopenic study, Acta Pediatr. Scand. vol. 1, suppl. 154, 1964.

29. Hanshaw, J. B., and Dudgeon, J. A.: Viral diseases of the fetus and newborn, Philadelphia, 1978, W. B. Saunders Co.

30. Hanshaw, J. B., et al.: School failure and deafness after silent congenital cytomegalovirus infection, N. Engl. J. Med. **295:**468, 1976.

31. Hanson, J. W., and Smith, D. W.: The fetal hydantoin syndrome, J. Pediatr. **87:**285, 1975.

32. Healy, W. C., and Karp-Nortman, D. S.: The hearing impaired mentally retarded: recommendations for action, Washington, D.C., 1975, American Speech and Hearing Association.

33. Hebel, J. R., Kinch, D., and Armstrong, E.: Mental capability of children exposed to lead pollution, Br. J. Prev. Soc. Med. **30:**170, 1976.

33a. Hiskey, M. S.: Hiskey-Nebraska test of learning aptitude, Lincoln, Neb., University of Nebraska at Lincoln.

34. Holmes, L. B.: Genetic counseling for the older pregnant woman—new data and questions. N. Engl. J. Med. **298:**1419, 1978.

35. Howe, S. G.: In Ceremonies on laying the cornerstone of the New York State Institution for the Blind at Batavia, Gennessee County, N.Y., Batavia, N.Y., 1866, Henry Todd.

36. Jacobs, F. H., and Walker, D. E.: Pediatrician and the Education for All Handicapped Children Act of 1975 (PL 94-142), Pediatrics **61:**135, 1978.

37. Jonsen, A. R., and Garland, M. J., editors: Ethics of the newborn intensive care, Berkeley, Calif., 1976, Institute of Governmental Studies, University of California at Berkeley, p. 4.

38. Kanthor, A., et al.: Areas of responsibility in the health care of multiply handicapped children, Pediatrics **54:**779, 1974.

39. Kaveggia, E. G., et al.: Diagnostic genetic studies on 1224 patients with severe mental retardation. Read before the Third Congress of the International Association for Scientific Study of Mental Deficiency, The Hague, September 4 to 12, 1973.

40. Kempe, C. H.: Approaches to preventing child abuse, Health Visit. Concept **130:**941, 1976.

41. Koppelman, L. M., and Cosman, F. G.: Rights of children and retarded persons, Rochester, N.Y., 1976, Rock Printing Co.

42. Kusblick, A., and Cox, G. R.: The epidemiology of mental handicap, Dev. Med. Child Neurol. **15:**748, 1973.

43. Lewis, D. V., and Freeman, J. M.: The electroencephalogram in pediatric practice: its use and abuse, Pediatrics **60:**324, 1977.

44. Lorincz, A. E.: The mucopolysaccharidosis: advances in understanding and treatment, Pediatr. Ann. **7:**65, 1978.

45. MacKeith, R.: The feelings and behavior of parents of handicapped children, Dev. Med. Child Neurol. **15:**524, 1973.

46. McNeese, M. C., and Hebeler, J. R.: Abused child: a clinical approach to identification and management, clinical symposia no. 29, 1977, Ciba Pharmaceutical Co. Division of Ciba Geigy Corp.

47. Nirje, B.: Normalization principle and its human management implications. In Kugel, R. B., and Wolfensberger, W., editors: Changing patterns in residential services for the mentally retarded, report of President's Committee on Mental Retardation, Washington D.C., 1969, U. S. Government Printing Office.

48. Ouelette, E. M., et al.: Adverse effects of offspring of maternal and alcohol abuse during pregnancy, N. Engl. J. Med. **297:**528, 1977.

49. Palfrey, J. S., Mervis, R. C., and Butler, J. A.: New directions in the evaluation and education of handicapped children, N. Engl. J. Med. **298:**819, 1978.

50. Reynel, J. K., and Zinkin, P.: New procedures for the developmental assessments of young children with severe visual handicaps, Child Care Health Dev. **1:**61, 1975.

51. Sameroff, A. J., and Chandler, M. J.: Reproductive risk and the continuum of caretaking casualty. In Horowitz, F. D., editor: Review of child development research, vol. 4, Chicago, 1975, University of Chicago Press.

52. Seith, F. J., Fine, J. M., and Tendler, M. D.: Brain death. II, A status of legal considerations, J.A.M.A. **238:**1744, 1977.

53. Sher, P. K., and Brown, S. B.: A longitudinal study of head growth in preterm infants and normal rates of head growth, Dev. Med. Child Neurol. **17:**705, 1975.

54. Sher, P. K., and Brown, S. B.: A longitudinal study of head growth in preterm infants—differentiation between "catch-up" head growth and early infantile hydrocephalus, Dev. Med. Child Neurol. **17:**711, 1975.

54a. Sheridan, M. D.: Vision screening procedures for very young or handicapped children. Aspects of developmental and paediatric ophthalmology, Clin. Dev. Med., no. 33, 1969.

55. Smith, D. W.: Recognizable patterns of human malformation. In Smith, D. W., editor: Major problems of clinical pediatrics, ed. 2, Philadelphia, 1976, W. B. Saunders Co.

56. Smith, D. W., and Simmons, S. E. R.: Rational diagnostic evaluation of the child with mental deficiency, Am. J. Dis. Child. **129:**1285, 1975.

57. Soriver, C. R., et al.: Screening for congenital metabolic disorders in the newborn infant: congenital deficiency of thyroid hormone and hyperphenylalaninemia, Pediatrics **60** (suppl.):389.

58. Stanbury, J. B., Wyngaarden, J. B., and Friedrickson, D. S., editors: The metabolic bases of inherited disease, ed. 3, New York, 1972, McGraw-Hill Book Co.

59. Tarjan, G.: Sex: a tripolar conflict in mental retardation. Presented at the Joseph P. Kennedy, Jr., Foundation, International Symposium on Human Rights, Retardation, and Research, Washington, D.C., October 16, 1971.

60. Tarjan, G., et al.: Natural high risk of mental retardation: some aspects of epidemiology, Am. J. Ment. Defic. **77:**369, 1973.

61. Touwen, D. C. L., and Prechtl, H. F. R.: The neurological examination of the child with minor nervous dysfunction, Clin. Dev. Med. **38:**4, 1970.

62. *Wade* v. *Bethesda,* 237 F suppl. 671 (SD Ohio 1971).

63. Weed, L. L.: Medical records, medical education and patient care, Cleveland, 1969, Press of Case Western Reserve University.

64. Wolfensberger, W.: Normalization: the principle of normalization in human services, Toronto, 1972, National Institute on Mental Retardation.

9

Genetics and the child with developmental disabilities

Louis E. Bartoshesky

Genetic factors are important in the etiology of developmental disabilities. In general, definite diagnoses are more readily determined and genetic conditions more likely to be identified in moderately and severely retarded persons. Milder forms of developmental disability are more likely to be attributed to normal variation or social and cultural factors. In these milder forms genetic factors often contribute but may not play a dominant role.

In surveys of moderately and severely retarded institutionalized persons substantial percentages with genetic diagnoses have been reported. Kaveggia and co-workers[20] studied 1224 such patients in Wisconsin and determined that "a genetic abnormality was the etiology or contributed significantly to the cause of the condition of about 600 of these patients. . ."[20] These included 145 with chromosome defects, 80 with inborn errors of metabolism, 40 with well-defined syndromes of high recurrence risk, and the remainder with conditions partially genetic in etiology.

Morton and colleagues,[28] in a reevaluation of Penrose's[33a] 1938 study of mental deficiency in England, estimated that the cause in about 30% of the moderately disabled was explainable by simple genetic mechanisms. About 10% of the people considered "dull" had genetic conditions. Larger percentages were determined to have mental retardation primarily "sociofamilial" in origin but with possible contributory genetic factors.

GENERAL GENETICS

Genetic etiologies. It can be argued that there are genetic factors involved in some known "environmental" causes of mental retardation, such as prematurity, perinatal asphyxia, placental abnormality, teratogenic effects on the fetus, and even central nervous system infections. Environmental factors, on the other hand, may alter the expression of

221

genetically determined disability, for example, the quantity of phenylalanine in the diet of children with phenylketonuria alters the degree of intellectual handicap.

Chromosomes and developmental disability. *Chromosomes* are nuclear organelles visible during certain phases of active cell division.[41] They are made up of desoxyribonucleic acid (DNA) in a protein matrix. The normal human chromosome number is 46,[44] 22 homologous pairs called *autosomes* and 2 sex chromosomes, the X and the Y. One member of each homologous pair originates from an individual's father, the other member from the mother. The reproductive cells, or *gametes,* normally have 23 chromosomes, the *haploid* number. When fertilization of an egg by a sperm occurs, the fertilized ovum or *zygote* receives 23 chromosomes from each gamete, giving the *diploid* number 46. In both sexes there are 22 homologous pairs; in addition, males have an X and a Y chromosome, whereas females have two X chromosomes.[30,40,43]

Chromosome analysis is performed on dividing cells. Blood lymphocytes are conveniently and easily obtained, but bone marrow, fibroblast, thymus, spleen, lymph node, gonad, and amniotic fluid cells are also appropriate. The cells to be analyzed are induced to divide in a nutrient medium, and after an appropriate period, cell division is arrested at the phase of the cycle in which chromosomes are visible. The cells are then ruptured and the material is spread onto a microscope slide. Sets of chromosomes are stained, identified through a microscope, and photographed, and the photographs are enlarged (Fig. 9-1). The individual chromosomes are identified and arranged according to size and shape. They are numbered according to international convention.[33]

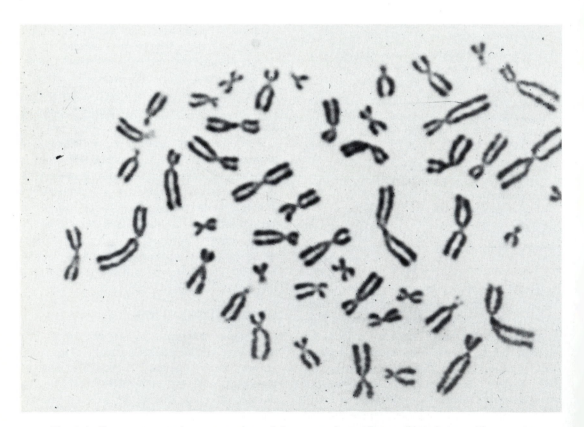

Fig. 9-1. Chromosomes as they appear prior to being arranged according to size and shape. There are 47 chromosomes in this photograph, three of which are number 21 (Down syndrome).

Precise distinction among chromosomes of similar size and shape and identification of minor abnormalities of chromosomes are possible because of specialized staining procedures called *banding* (Fig. 9-2). Banding should be routine. It should be performed on virtually all specimens collected for chromosome analysis. Many abnormalities apparent on banded material would be missed if banding were omitted.

Chromosome nomenclature. Chromosomes arranged according to size, shape, and staining characteristics constitute a *karyotype* (Fig. 9-2). Chromosomes are identified by a number assigned them according to size, staining characteristics, and location of their *centromere,* the area on the chromosome where the component strands or chromatids are joined (Fig. 9-3). In *metacentric* chromosomes (numbers 1, 2, 3, 10, 20) the centromere is in the middle; in

acrocentric chromosomes (numbers 13, 14, 15, 21, 22, Y) the centromere is near the end; in *submetacentric* chromosomes (numbers 4, 5, 6 to 12, 16, 17, 18, X) the centromere is off-center. The short arms are, by convention, on top as the chromosomes are arranged in the karyotype. The short arms are designated "p" (perhaps from French "petite"), whereas the long arms are designated "q."

Cell division. *Mitosis* is somatic cell division, the process by which cells other than germ cells duplicate. Mitosis is divided into four specific phases: (1) prophase, (2) metaphase, (3) anaphase, and (4) telophase. The period between divisions of the cells is known as interphase, a period in which genetic material is duplicated in preparation for cell division. Parent and daughter cells in the mitotic process have the diploid number (46) of chromosomes.[43]

Meiosis is the cell division process unique to

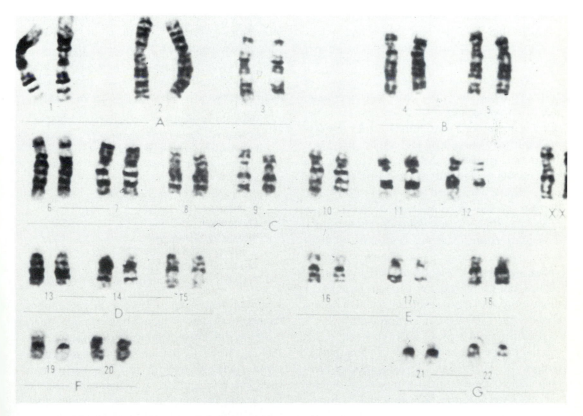

Fig. 9-2. Banded female karyotype. Note the alternating light and dark staining areas in the chromosomes.

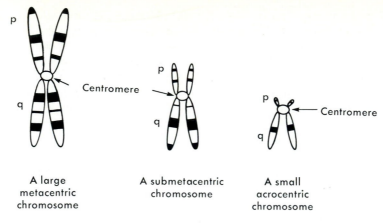

A large
metacentric
chromosome

A submetacentric
chromosome

A small
acrocentric
chromosome

Fig. 9-3

the testis and ovary. It differs from mitosis in that germ cells, sperm and ovum, with the haploid number of chromosomes (23 nonpaired chromosomes) are produced from diploid precursor cells, spermatogonia and oogonia.

Details of these processes are available in any genetics text.[30,43] It is clear that spermatogenesis, oogenesis, and fertilization are complicated and complex processes and errors in chromosome transmission can and do occur.

Chromosome abnormalities. A *zygote,* or fertilized ovum, may receive an abnormal number of chromosomes (called *aneuploidy* if the number is not an exact multiple of 23 or *polyploidy* if it is a multiple such as 69, 92, etc.). If the abnormality is the presence of an extra chromosome, it is referred to as trisomy; if a chromosome is deleted it is monosomy. The number of the extra or deleted chromosome is also mentioned in describing the abnormality. Trisomies occur relatively frequently in liveborn infants, trisomy 21 or Down syndrome occurring 1 per 800 to 1 per 1000 live births. Monosomies are rare in general except for monosomy X (Turner syndrome), which occurs about 1 per 2500 live female births.[6,39]

Duplication of parts of a chromosome occur (partial trisomy) as well as loss of parts (partial monosomy, or deletion). Translocation or rearrangement of genetic material may occur among various chromosomes or within one chromosome. A chromosome may also have its structure altered into the shape of a ring. If by error

a chromosome divides at its centromere instead of longitudinally, two abnormal daughter chromosomes result—one having two long arms, the other having two short arms. These are isochromosomes and each one has duplication and deletion of genetic material.

About one in every 200 newborns has a recognizable abnormality of chromosomes, not all clinically significant.[19] Furthermore, in a substantial percentage of pregnancies that end in first trimester spontaneous abortion the fetus had a chromosome defect. Carr and Gedeon[8] have summarized several studies as follows:

Estimated percentage of pregnancies ending as spontaneous abortion	20%
Estimated frequency of chromosome abnormality in fetal abortion material	30% to 60%
Representative cytogenetic findings in fetal material:	
Trisomies	52%
Monosomy X (45, X)	18%
Triploidy (69,XXX, 69,XXY)	17%
Tetraploidy (92,XXYY, etc.)	6%
Translocation, delections, etc.	7%

It appears that in up to 10% of all conceptions the chromosomes of the embryo are abnormal.

Causes of chromosome abnormality. It is seldom, if ever, that a specific cause of a chromosome abnormality in a fetus or liveborn child can be identified. Environmental and infectious agents have been associated with chromosome damage in laboratory animals, but extension of these observations to human aneuploidy, translocation, deletion, etc., cannot be done with precision.

SPECIFIC CHROMOSOME ANOMALIES
Down syndrome

Down syndrome occurs in 1 per 800 to 1 per 1000 live births.[10,34,39] About 95% of people with Down syndrome have trisomy 21, that is, an extra number 21 chromosome and a total of 47 chromosomes. It is believed that the trisomy results from a mistake in meiosis at either of the cell divisions that are part of meiosis or during cell division of the zygote. The term used is *"nondisjunction"* implying that the error is a failure of a chromosome pair to separate during the meiotic processes, which results in a gamete (sperm or egg) with 24 chromosomes that include two number 21s. In fact, other errors in the process may also be responsible for production of a gamete with an extra chromosome.[40]

The risk of bearing a child with Down syndrome increases with increasing maternal age. Various risks have been quoted, and recently Hook and Chambers[18] published figures for risk relative to exact maternal age at birth. The risk at age 25 is about $1/_{1200}$, at 30, $1/_{1000}$, at 35, $1/_{350}$, and at 40, $1/_{100}$. It is possible that the age-related risks are associated with aging of the ova. However, it has recently been pointed out by Holmes[16] that the extra number 21 chromosome may often be paternal in origin, perhaps in as many as 40% to 50% of children with trisomy 21 born to women under 30. Further study of paternal factors is needed.

From 3% to 4% of people with Down syndrome have chromosome mosaicism, that is, they have two or more cell lines that differ in their chromosome makeup. Most such individuals have two cell lines, some cells having 46 chromosomes, the others having 47. Mosaicism probably most often results from a trisomic zygote losing one of the number 21 chromosomes during an early cell division. Other explanations are also possible.

The clinical characteristics of mosaic Down syndrome may vary slightly from those of trisomy 21; to an extent the variation is related to the proportion of trisomic cells. Most mosaic individuals are quite similar to other Down syndrome people in physical and intellectual makeup.

A small percentage of people with Down syndrome have a translocation involving chromosome under 21. It is important to identify this group, since some of them may have received the translocated chromosome from a clinically normal parent who carries such a chromosome. In families in which there is a translocation carrier parent, recurrence risks for Down syndrome are greater than in other families with Down syndrome individuals. Precise recurrence risks are difficult to state, but may be as high as 10% to 15%. Translocation Down syndrome is not clinically distinguishable from trisomy 21.

Details of clinical features of Down syndrome are well known. Among the more common features are the following:[10,34,39]

- Midface hypoplasia
- Flat nasal bridge
- Flat profile
- Upward slant of palpebral fissures
- Hypotonia, especially in newborn period
- Short stature (approximately 100%)
- Hyperextensible joints
- Microcephaly
- Inner epicanthal folds
- Speckling of iris (Brushfield spots)
- Lens opacity
- Short neck with redundant skin
- Dental hypoplasia
- Malformed ears
- Brachydactyly
- Fifth finger midphalanx hypoplasia (clinodactyly)
- Transverse palmar crease (simian crease)
- Congenital heart disease (25% to 40%)

Less frequent but clinically significant malformations are intestinal atresias; seizures, including infantile spasms; strabismus; cryptorchidism; atlantoaxial subluxation due to hypoplasia of the odontoid process; and leukemia (about 1 per 100).

Children with Down syndrome are most frequently mildly to moderately retarded. They tend to score somewhat higher on tests of social competence (such as the Vineland[10]) than on tests such as Stanford-Binet[34] or Wechsler Intelligence Scale for Children.[39] A child with Down syndrome has the potential, because of relative social competence, to become a loving and contributing family member, sharing family joys, sorrows, successes, and failures. Social and economic independence, however, is unlikely.

It is not true that all children with Down syndrome are placid and affectionate. In fact, behavior disorders occur. Hyperactivity, affective disorders, autism, and psychoses have been observed in people with Down syndrome.[10,34]

In early childhood speech and language tend to lag behind other developmental skills, although there is a universal delay. Part of this speech and language delay may be related to the increased frequency of below-normal hearing (conductive and neural) found in people with Down syndrome. The children with normal hearing, however, also have delayed communication skills. Signing and total communication programs have been attempted with some Down syndrome children with uncertain results.

School performance is variable; a few children with Down syndrome progressing to work at seventh to eighth grade level, but the majority attaining only very simple reading and arithmetic skills.

Therapy. There have been many proposals for pharmacological therapy of Down syndrome, including thyroid hormone, procaine hydrocloride, glutamic acid, tryptophan, and serotonin. None has had any demonstrable effect on intellectual function; a few have been claimed to improve muscle tone.[10]

Home rearing is strongly recommended for children with Down syndrome, if not with biological parents, then in foster or adoptive homes. Several studies argue that Down syndrome children at home develop more advanced intellectual skills than those raised in institutions.[11,34] The presumed benefits of home rearing to the child should not blind the health professional to the emotional and psychological needs of the other family members. Parents who feel overwhelmed and unable to care for a retarded child should be given support and guidance. If they finally elect to surrender the child, the best foster placement available should be sought and efforts should be made to help the biological parents cope with their decision.

Early infant intervention and infant stimulation programs begun in the first months of life are showing great promise in management of families of children with Down syndrome. Reproducible and sustained increases in intellectual function remain to be proved, but apparent earlier attainment of developmental milestones has been observed.[14]

Early intervention programs may also provide additional compassionate emotional support to families with a Down syndrome child (Chapter 8).

Each child with Down syndrome is an individual with his own developmental potential. It is the duty of the provider of care to determine the individual strengths and weaknesses and develop a comprehensive medical, psychological, and educational program on those bases. The pediatrician should coordinate the program with assistance from medical subspecialists, educators, occupational and physical therapists, social workers, specialists in developmental medicine, etc.

Recurrence risks. Families (i.e., a mother and a father) who have one child with trisomy 21 have a 1% chance with each subsequent pregnancy of having another affected child. This risk is derived from studies of siblings of Down syndrome children. There are probably some families who are at a substantially higher risk, having undetermined genetic predisposition to nondisjunction. Unfortunately, these families cannot be reliably separated from other families with a Down syndrome member. Careful pedigree analysis with attention to spontaneous abortion, stillbirth, and infant death may provide clues and may identify some clearly high-risk families, but for the most part, 1% is the risk of recurrence quoted to families. The risk is higher than 1% for women over 40 who already have a child with Down syndrome.

Recurrence risks for families with a mosaic Down syndrome child are probably comparable to those for families with a trisomy 21 child.

In translocation Down syndrome, as noted earlier, the parents' chromosomes must be studied, since some people with translocation have a normal parent (mother or father) who carries the translocation as a so-called balanced translocation. For such a parent, risks probably range from 3% to 15% for recurrence. It is difficult to be precise, since there are a large number of possible translocations, each one probably carrying its own recurrence risk. Chromosome study of other family members is indicated when a translocation carrier is uncovered. Parents, siblings, offspring, and even more distant relatives of a translocation carrier may also be carriers and therefore be at high risk of bearing affected children.

Trisomy 18

This autosomal trisomy is seen in about 1 per 5000 live births. The affected infants have prenatal and postnatal growth deficiency and craniofacial, cardiac, musculoskeletal, urogenital, gastrointestinal, and neurological anomalies. About 90% of such babies die within 12 to 24 months after birth. Severe mental retardation is usual. Characteristic findings (Fig. 9-4) include a prominent occiput with narrow bifrontal diameter, limited motion at distal interphalangeal joints with clenched hand and overlapping of the second finger over the third and the fifth over the fourth (Fig. 9-5). A short sternum, small pelvis, and vertical talus (rocker-bottom feet) are common. Congenital heart disease is very frequent, and many other manifestations have been noted.[6,7,39]

Trisomy 13

Trisomy 13 is found in 1 per 7000 to 1 per 10,000 live births. As with trisomy 18, many anomalies have been found in affected infants, including virtually all organ systems (Fig. 9-6). Mental retardation is profound and early death the rule. Cleft lip and palate, microphthalmia,

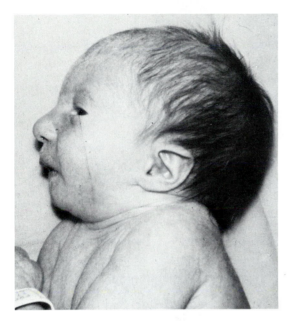

Fig. 9-4. Facial features of a child with trisomy 18.

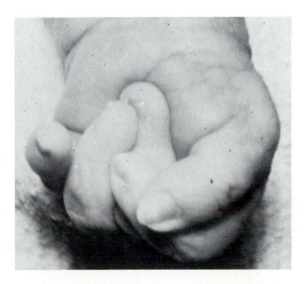

Fig. 9-5. Overlapping fingers of a child with trisomy 18.

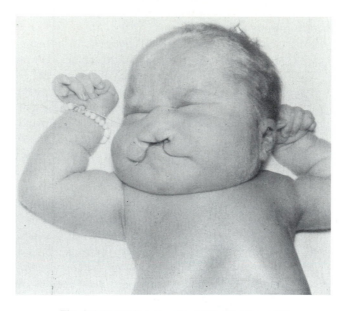

Fig. 9-6. Facial features of a child with trisomy 13.

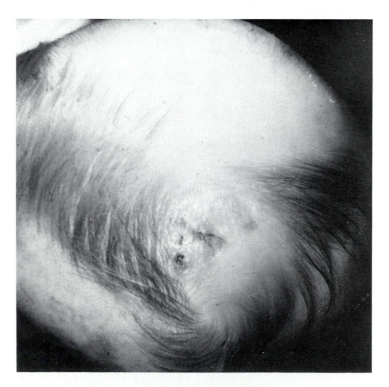

Fig. 9-7. Scalp defect in a child with trisomy 13.

iris coloboma, scalp defects (Fig. 9-7), polydactyly, and congenital heart disease are characteristic.[6,7,39] Recurrence of trisomy 18 or trisomy 13 in families is very rare. Other autosomal trisomies have been described; all are rare.

Other abnormalities

Chromosome translocation, deletions, and partial trisomies occur and are frequently associated with some degree of mental retardation. A few have occurred frequently enough with findings consistent enough to be considered syndromes:[6,39]

- 5 p−: The cri du chat syndrome is associated with a partial deletion of the short arm of chromosome number 5. Growth deficiency, microcephaly, hypotonia, ocular hypertelorism, congenital heart disease, and severe mental retardation are common. The catlike cry is not always identified and when present, may become less apparent as the child grows.
- 4 p−: The findings with partial deletion of the short arm of chromosome number 4 include growth deficiency, microcephaly, ocular hypertelorism, beaked nose, cleft lip and/or palate, micrognathia, genitourinary anomalies, and severe mental retardation.
- 13 q−: With deletion of part of the long arm of chromosome number 13 growth deficiency, microcephaly, central nervous system malformation, facial anomalies, congenital heart disease, and mental retardation are seen.
- 18 p−: There is variability in the phenotype described in association with deletion of part of the short arm of chromosome number 18. The mental retardation may be mild to severe, although most children show moderate delay.
- 18 q−: Short stature, facial anomalies, microcephaly, limb abnormalities, and mild to moderate mental retardation are characteristic of 18 q− syndrome.
- 21 q−: Low birth weight, facial and limb abnormalities and moderate to severe mental retardation are found with 21 q− syndrome.

Many other patients with somatic and/or intellectual abnormalities and associated abnormalities in various autosomes have been described in the medical literature. Developmental prognostication in children with unusual autosomal abnormalities is risky, although mental retardation of some degree is very frequent when such abnormalities are present.

Deletions and partial trisomies are important to identify because, as with translocation Down syndrome, they are sometimes passed to a child from a carrier parent with a balanced translocation, in which case recurrence risk may be high.

Balanced translocations, in which all or a portion of one chromosome is transferred to another but no significant genetic material is lost, have been identified in 1 per 500 live births.[19] Individuals with such translocations are usually normal but may be at risk for low fertility or for bearing offspring with a deletion or partial trisomy. There is much heterogeneity among the many translocations described, and generalizations are dangerous and may be misleading.

Sex chromosomes and specific abnormalities

Abnormalities in the number or structure of the sex chromosomes are seen relatively frequently (1 per 500 to 1 per 750 live births).[19] A buccal smear for Barr bodies may be a useful screening procedure in children in whom a sex chromosome abnormality is suspected. The Barr body, a densely staining mass visible at the periphery of the cell nucleus, represents an inactivated X chromosome. A normal female with a 46,XX chromosome complement will have an identifiable Barr body in 20% to 60% of her buccal mucosal cells. In normal males (46,XY) 1% to 2% of the buccal mucosal cells may appear to have a Barr body. The number of Barr bodies per cell is one less than the number of X chromosomes in a cell. Girls with Turner syndrome (45,X) have essentially no Barr bodies. Girls with trisomy X (47,XXX) have two Barr bodies. Boys with Klinefelter syndrome (47,XXY) have 1 Barr body in each cell studied. Mosaicism of sex chromosomes occurs relatively frequently. If analysis of sex chromosomes is restricted to a buccal smear study, mosaicism may be missed. Structural abnormalities of the X chromosome will not be identified by Barr body quantification. Buccal smear for Barr bodies is a screening procedure only. Definitive diagnosis of sex chromosome abnormalities is made by karyotype preparation from lymphocytes or other appropriate cells.

Turner syndrome. Frequent clinical characteristics in affected girls are short stature and gonadal dysgenesis with infertility and underdeveloped secondary sexual characteristics. Other malformations include congenital lymphedema of hands and feet (Fig. 9-8), broad chest, prominent ears, cubitus valgus, narrow palate, epicanthal folds, hyperconvex nails, renal anomalies, cardiac defect (especially coarctation of aorta), and hearing impairment.[32]

The most common karyotype found in girls with clinical findings of Turner syndrome is 45,X (monosomy X). From 50% to 70% of Turner girls are 45,X. Others have structural abnormalities of an X chromosome such as deletion of long arm or isochromosome X, while some girls show mosaicism of the sex chromosomes.[38] Some girls (and boys as well) may have many of the clinical features of Turner syndrome but normal chromosomes. This has been designated "Noonan syndrome"

or "Turner phenotype," and presumably has an etiology distinct from Turner syndrome.

Overall intellectual function is average in girls with Turner syndrome. However, specific handicaps have been reported, particularly in nonverbal areas such as figure drawing.[13]

A common developmental difficulty in Turner syndrome is in adaptation to short stature (average final height of 55 inches) and absent or underdeveloped secondary sexual characteristics. Androgenic hormone therapy to improve rate of growth and final height has been used in many centers, but efficacy remains controversial.[2,27,37] Cyclic estrogen therapy is useful at the age of usual puberty to promote breast and pubic hair development and generate menstrual periods.[2]

Trisomy X. Triple X females (47,XXX) may have minor congenital malformations and mild mental retardation, but many of the girls are normal with normal fertility.[42] The precise frequency of developmental disability in trisomy X is uncertain because many of the girls identified as 47,XXX were ascertained in a biased fashion from populations of retarded girls. A recent compilation of a number of prospective studies of trisomy X girls suggests that they have an increased risk of speech and language problems and that the average full-

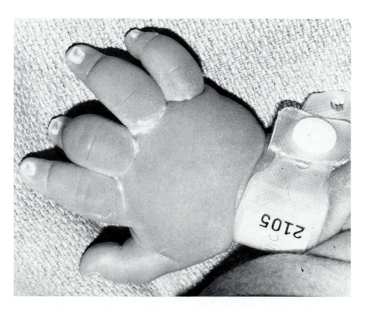

Fig. 9-8. Puffy, lymphedematous hand of a newborn with Turner syndrome.

scale IQ of these girls is lower than siblings and other controls.[36a] The frequency of 47,XXX may be 1 per 1000 female births.[19]

Klinefelter syndrome. Approximately 1 in 500 to 1 in 1000 males has a 47,XXY karyotype.[19,39] Many are tall with long limbs, "eunuchoid" habitus, gynecomastia, hypogonadism, hypogenitalism, and minor congenital anomalies such as radioulnar synostosis, hypospadias, and cryptorchidism. Others may have only minimal phenotypic abnormalities.

Normal intelligence is frequent, but 15% to 30% of the boys are low normal. The tendency toward behavior problems, immaturity, insecurity, poor judgment, and unrealistic boastful activity claimed in some studies[35] is difficult to substantiate. School problems, however, are probably often related to low intelligence and delayed emotional development.[36a]

A similar clinical picture may be seen with mosaicism or with the XXXY and XXYY karyotypes. Boys with the latter two tend to have more substantial behavioral and intellectual problems. Klinefelter syndrome may not be suspected until adolescence, when low normal performance, hypogonadism, and delayed secondary sexual characteristics suggest the diagnosis. Testosterone replacement therapy may be undertaken to bring about a more normal adolescent physical development. Adolescent adjustment problems are not uncommon.

XYY. The frequency of XYY may be 1 per 1000 live male newborns, but the abnormality is seldom detected in childhood.[19] Features are variable but may include growth acceleration, mildly abnormal facies, severe adolescent acne, radioulnar synostosis and genitourinary abnormalities. This karyotype has been argued to be associated with dull mentality and/or aggressive antisocial behavior. Studies in criminal institutions, where XYY men and boys seem to be found in high frequency, have supported the argument.[17] The existence of an association remains controversial but it is clear that most boys discovered at birth to have the extra Y chromosome are currently growing and developing normally.[7] Some 47,XYY boys were noted to have speech and language delay in a recent study.[36a] No definite evidence of school or psychiatric problems was noted among the 43 47,XYY boys followed from birth in that same study. Their risk of developing aggressive behavior is uncertain.

Recurrence risks in families with a member with any sex chromosome abnormality appear to be low.

ROLE OF CHROMOSOME STUDIES IN EVALUATION OF THE CHILD WITH DEVELOPMENTAL DISABILITY

A substantial proportion of children with delayed development and morphological abnormalities have a chromosome abnormality. Brewster and Gerald[7] reported 24 of 183 children seen in an outpatient developmental evaluation clinic had abnormal chromosomes. Twenty of the children had trisomy 21. Higher percentages have been observed in residential programs, in which the children are more likely to be moderately or severely retarded. Percentages will be lower among children with mild developmental handicaps and no or only minor morphological abnormalities. Chromosome disorders are usually associated with morphological as well as developmental abnormalities (balanced translocation and sex chromosome abnormalities are notable exceptions).

Chromosome analysis should be performed by the pediatrician as part of the initial evaluation of any child with multiple (more than 3) congenital morphological anomalies and delayed development. Children who have multiple anomalies but no substantial delay and who fit no known malformation syndrome should also have their chromosomes studied with the expectation of a lower rate of return. Children who are morphologically normal and moderately or severely retarded should have chromosome analysis when no other cause for the retardation is apparent. Chromosomes will only very rarely be abnormal in children who are morphologically normal with mild delayed development.

PRENATAL DIAGNOSIS

Amniocentesis is a relatively safe (complication rate about 1%) procedure by which Down syndrome and other chromosome abnormalities can be diagnosed prenatally.[26] Following are some conditions that have been, or theoretically could be, diagnosed in the second trimester of pregnancy:

A. Chromosome disorders: By analysis of karyotype of amniotic fluid cells obtained by amniocentesis
B. Hereditary biochemical disorders: By measurement of enzyme levels or storage products in amniotic fluid cells obtained by amniocentesis[25]
   1. Lipidoses (e.g., Tay-Sachs disease)
   2. Mucolipidoses (e.g., I-cell disease)
   3. Mucopolysaccharidoses (e.g., Hunter syndrome, Hurler syndrome)
   4. Amino acid disorders (e.g., maple syrup urine disease)
   5. Organic acid disorders (e.g., methylmalonic acidemia)
   6. Disorders of carbohydrate metabolism (e.g., galactosemia, certain glycogen storage disorders)
   7. Miscellaneous disorders with known enzyme defect (e.g., adenosine deaminase deficiency, cystinosis, hypercholesterolemia, adrenogenital syndromes)
C. Neural tube defects: By measurement of serum and amniotic fluid levels of alpha fetoprotein
D. Sex determination in fetuses at risk for X-linked conditions: By chromosome analysis
E. Certain disorders with identifiable abnormal constituents of fetal blood: By fetal blood sampling via placental puncture or sampling from a directly visualized fetal vessel[15]
   1. Hemoglobin disorders (e.g., Sickle cell anemia, thalassemias)
   2. Muscular dystrophies (elevated creatine phosphokinase)
   3. Red blood cell enzyme defects
   4. Certain coagulation abnormalities
F. Certain structural malformations: By direct visualization[5,15] of the fetus via fetoscopy, by ultrasound studies, or by fetography[31]
   1. Limb defects
   2. Craniofacial abnormalities
   3. Microcephaly
   4. Macrocephaly
   5. Malformation syndromes
   6. Skeletal dysplasias (e.g., achondroplasia)

Fluid is extracted from around the developing fetus at about the sixteenth week of gestation. Cells present in the fluid are of fetal origin and have the chromosomal, enzymatic, and biochemical characteristics of the fetus. With about 95% to 97% reliability, the chromosome complement of the fetus can be determined. Pre-

natal determination of certain metabolic and hematological disorders is also possible. Neural tube defects can be identified prenatally by measurement of amniotic fluid alpha fetoprotein.

Other prenatal diagnostic techniques such as ultrasound, fetography, fetoscopy, and fetal blood sampling may be useful in situations in which there is a high risk of various fetal malformations.

MENDELIAN TRAITS AND DEVELOPMENTAL DISABILITY

Mendelian traits or single gene defects have been estimated to be responsible for from 5% to 20% of cases of moderate and severe mental retardation.[26] It is likely that a lower percentage of children with mild developmental disability have single gene defects.

In simplified terms a *gene* is a segment of DNA specific for a given sequence of amino acids. The particular arrangement of nucleic acids making up the gene is responsible for synthesis of a specific polypeptide. The polypeptide in turn may be part of an enzyme, a structural protein, a lipoprotein, etc.

The genes are found on chromosomes. Since autosomes (nonsex chromosomes) exist as homologous pairs, autosomal genes are also found in pairs. The *locus* is the location of the gene on the chromosome. Genes at the same locus on a pair of homologous chromosomes are *alleles*. When a pair of alleles are identical in an individual, he is *homozygous;* when the alleles are different the individual is *heterozygous*. Genes on the X chromosome are X-linked. Males, since they have only one X chromosome, are *hemizygous* for X-linked genes.

An allele that is expressed clinically in either the homozygous or heterozygous state is *dominant;* an allele that is expressed only in the homozygous state is *recessive*. In fact, the observable genetic trait (the so-called phenotypic expression) is what is dominant or recessive, not the gene. Genes simply code for a specific polypeptide synthesis. In common practice, however, the terms ''dominant gene'' and ''recessive gene'' are used. This is convenient.

New alleles arise as a result of *mutation*—a change in the gene. Mutations may occur in the male or female fetal germ cells before they settle in the gonad, in the diploid germ cell precursors in the gonad, at any stage in gametogenesis, or in the mature gamete. Mutations occur on the average of $1/1,000,000$ per locus per generation. *Selection,* in simplified terms, is the process by which alleles decrease in frequency in a population. Selection occurs when a given genotype is relatively unfit compared to other genotypes, unfitness referring to the ability to reproduce.[39,42]

Autosomal dominant inheritance

Autosomal dominant traits are found in both sexes in equal proportions. Transmission is not sex related. Affected individuals, heterozygotes, either have received a mutant gene for the trait from an affected parent or a mutation has occurred in a parental gamete, the mutant being passed on. Mutation rates are slightly higher in older parents. Each germ cell of an affected individual receives one of a pair of homologous chromosomes during meiosis and therefore one of a pair of alleles, either the mutant or normal allele. Each child of an affected heterozygous parent (assuming the other parent to be homozygous normal) has a 50% chance of being affected (of receiving the mutant gene).

Autosomal dominant traits appear in every generation, with no skipping.* Unaffected individuals are those who do not receive the gene for the trait. They cannot transmit the trait. The pedigree in Fig. 9-9 demonstrates these characteristics of autosomal dominant inheritance.

Table 9-1 lists some autosomal dominant conditions in which affected individuals may have developmental disability.[6,24,39] Some conditions in Table 9-1 are also inherited as autosomal recessive and X-linked conditions. This phenomenon is known as genetic heterogeneity. A given phenotype, for example, sensorineural deafness, may be transmitted as an autosomal dominant in one family, as an autosomal recessive in another, and as an X-linked recessive in another. Sensorineural deaf-

---

*Apparent skipping of generations may occur because of low *expressivity* of a gene in some individuals. For example, some individuals with tuberous sclerosis may have no phenotypic abnormalities except for depigmented spots, which may be easily missed. Other affected individuals, also heterozygous, in the same family may have extensive dermatological abnormalities, seizures, intracranial calcifications, and mental retardation. In some autosomal dominant conditions there may be less than 100% *penetrance*. That is, some individuals with the genotype have no *detectable* expression of the trait.

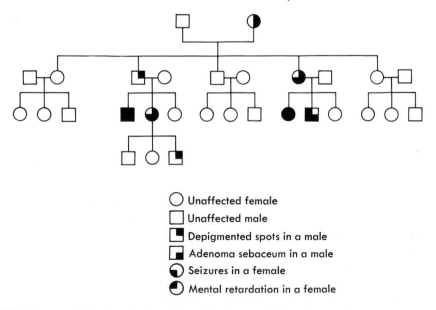

○ Unaffected female
□ Unaffected male
◼ Depigmented spots in a male
◪ Adenoma sebaceum in a male
◑ Seizures in a female
◕ Mental retardation in a female

Fig. 9-9. Pedigree of a family with the autosomal dominant condition tuberous sclerosis. Note the variable expression of the trait among affected individuals.

Table 9-1. Some autosomal dominant conditions with associated developmental disability[6,24,39]

Condition	Degree of disability	Comment
Acoustic neurinoma, bilateral	Deafness	May be form of neurofibromatosis
Acrocephalosyndactyly, type I	None to mild	Physical deformity may produce emotional problems
Acrocephalosyndactyly, type III	None	
Acrocephalosyndactyly, type V	None to mild	
Alport syndrome	Deafness	Nephritis
Arthro-ophthalmopathy (Stickler syndrome)	Progressive myopia and blindness	Joint abnormalities
Basal cell nevus	None to mild	Many organ systems may be involved
Cataracts	Blindness	Genetic heterogeneity
Charcot-Marie-Tooth disease	Normal intelligence	Progressive neuromuscular disorder
Chondrodysplasia punctata (Conradi syndrome)	None to mild	Cataracts, skeletal abnormalities
Corneal dystrophies	None to visual loss	Genetic heterogeneity
Deafness	Variable	Genetic heterogeneity
Glaucoma	Variable	Genetic heterogeneity
Huntington disease	Severe	Onset in childhood rare
Hypomelanosis of Ito	None to mild mental retardation	Dermatological problems predominate
Leopard syndrome (multiple lentigines)	Deafness, behavior problems	Cardiac abnormalities
Macular degenerations	Variable	Genetic heterogeneity
Marfan syndrome	Normal intelligence, eye disability	Cardiac and orthopedic abnormalities
Megalencephaly	Moderate	
Myopathies	Normal intelligence	Neuromuscular abnormalities, variable pathology
Myotonic dystrophy	None to moderate	Variable expression, cataracts, baldness
Neurofibromatosis	None to moderate, most are normal	Variable expression
Optic atrophy	Variable	Genetic heterogeneity
Spastic paraplegia	Variable; many are of normal intelligence	Genetic heterogeneity
Tuberous sclerosis	None to severe mental retardation	Variable expression
Waardenburg syndrome	Deafness	White forelock, iris heterochromia

ness may also be the result of an environmental insult.

Autosomal recessive inheritance

Conditions transmitted as autosomal recessive traits are expressed in persons of either sex who have received the recessive gene from both parents and are therefore homozygous. Parents are heterozygotes, or carriers. (One or both parents could be homozygous, but the conditions considered here are rare and homozygosity unlikly). Heterozygotes who mate have a 25% chance of having an affected offspring (a homozygote) with each pregnancy. Consanguinity, or marriage among relatives, may be found among parents of individuals

affected with autosomal recessive conditions.[30] Table 9-2[6,28,39] lists some autosomal recessive conditions that may be associated with developmental disability (Fig. 9-10).

Phenylketonuria (PKU) was the first autosomal recessive amino acid disorder to be identified as associated with mental retardation. Advances in early diagnosis and successful dietary therapy of PKU serve as a model of environmental treatment of genetically determined mental retardation. Other metabolic disorders are also theoretically preventable causes of mental retardation. Early diagnosis (in the newborn period of even prenatally) and treatment (in one case prenatally[1]) could be expected to prevent some 400 cases of early death or

Table 9-2. Some autosomal recessive conditions with associated developmental disability[6,24,39]

Condition	Degree of disability	Comment
Acrocephalosyndactyly, type II	None to mild	
Amaurosis congenita of Leber	Blindness	
Amaurotic "idiocy"	Visual loss and mild to severe mental retardation	Several forms exist
Amino acid disorders; organic acid disorders	Variable	Effects of some preventable by diet therapy
Ataxia-telangiectasia	Ataxia	Immune defect
"Bird-headed" dwarfism of Seckel	Mild to moderate	Characteristic facies
Carbohydrate metabolism disorders	Variable	
Cataracts	Variable vision loss	Genetic heterogeneity
Cerebrohepatorenal syndrome (Zellweger)	Severe mental retardation	Multiple anomalies
Chondrodysplasia punctata	Moderate to severe mental retardation	Dwarfism
Cockayne syndrome	Visual and auditory disability, moderate to severe mental retardation	Premature senile appearance
Corneal dystrophies	Variable	Genetic heterogeneity
Dandy-Walker syndrome (cyst)	Variable	Hydrocephalus
Deafness	Variable	Genetic heterogeneity
Dubowitz syndrome	Mild to moderate mental retardation	Eczema, short stature
Dysautonomia	None to mild mental retardation, emotional disability	
Fanconi pancytopenia	None to mild mental retardation	Heart, kidney, limbs involved
Friedreich ataxia	Normal intelligence	Progressive neuromuscular disability
Glaucoma	Variable	Genetic heterogeneity
Holoprosencephaly (familial)	Severe	Some are not genetic
Laurence-Moon-Biedl syndrome	Mild to moderate mental retardation	Obesity, retinitis, hypogenitalism
Leprechaunism	Moderate to severe mental retardation	"Gnomelike" appearance
Lipid metabolism disorders	Variable	See also genetic heterogeneity
Macula degeneration	Variable visual loss	Genetic heterogeneity
Marinesco-Sjögren syndrome	Moderate mental retardation, visual loss	Cataracts, ataxia
Microcephaly	Mild to severe mental retardation	Many causes other than autosomal recessive
Mucopolysaccharidoses	Variable	Several forms with normal intelligence
Myopathies	Variable	Genetic heterogeneity
Necrotizing encephalomyelopathy of Leigh	Progressive intellectual deterioration	Probable defect in thiamin metabolism
Retinitis pigmentosa	Variable visual loss	Genetic heterogeneity
Rothmund-Thomson syndrome	None to mild mental retardation, visual disability	Dermatological and orthopedic abnormalities
S-C phocomelia syndrome	None to moderate mental retardation	Limb deficiency, facial anomalies
Sjögren-Larssen syndrome	Moderate to severe mental retardation	Ichthyosis, retinal degeneration
Smith-Lemli-Opitz syndrome	Moderate mental retardation	Genitourinary and craniofacial anomalies, short stature
Spastic paraplegia	Variable	Genetic heterogeneity
Spinal muscular atrophy (Werdnig-Hoffmann syndrome)	Normal intelligence	Progressive neuromuscular deterioration
Spongy degeneration of central nervous system (Canavan disease)	Severe	Early death, multiple central nervous system abnormalities
Thyroid hormonogenesis defects	Severe mental retardation if untreated	Treatable
Usher syndrome	Deafness, blindness	Retinitis, sensorineural deafness
Wilson disease	Severe if untreated	Treatable defect in copper metabolism

severe mental retardation each year in the United States.[4,21,26]

Several of the mucopolysaccharidoses are autosomal recessive.[23] Not all are associated with mental retardation nor are all causes of early death. Scheie syndrome (MPS I-S) is clinically very distinct from Hurler syndrome (MPS I-H) although the same enzyme is deficient in each condition. People with Scheie syndrome are not retarded; those with Hurler have progressive central nervous system deterioration. People with Morquio syndrome (MPS IV) and Maroteaux-Lamy syndrome (MPS VI) have normal intelligence but moderate to severe orthopedic and ophthalmological disability. Diagnosis of mucopolysaccharidoses is by indentification of the enzyme deficiency in leukocytes, fibroblasts, or amniotic fluid cells.

Many conditions fall into the category of lipid metabolism disorder. Most of them share clinical characteristics, including progressive nervous system deterioration (intelligence and motor and visual systems especially). Visceromegaly is common in those that are storage diseases (Tay-Sachs syndrome, Niemann-Pick disease, etc.). A few, such as adult Gaucher disease, have later onset and no central nervous system involvement. Diagnosis is by enzyme assay in appropriate cells. None are treatable currently.

Galactosemia is a disorder of carbohydrate metabolism in which intellectual, visual, and hepathic dysfunctions occur in the untreated. Perinatal screening and treatment should prevent these disabilities.

Among the other autosomal recessive conditions noted in Table 9-1 are Wilson disease and thyroid hormonogenesis disorders in which early diagnosis is essential, since early therapy prevents central nervous system deterioration. The thyroid disorders are routinely screened for in the newborn period in several states.[22] This newborn screening is efficiently done on a small sample of blood in Massachusetts and elsewhere; amino acid and thyroid screening are done on the same sample. Diagnosis of Wilson disease in childhood may be difficult,[46] but this treatable disorder of copper metabolism should be suspected in older children with hepatitis, hemolytic anemia, or unexplained neurological or psychiatric dysfunction.

There are children with moderate to severe developmental delay and multiple congenital anomalies who do not fit any of the more common malformation syndromes and who have normal chromosomes. Kaveggia and co-workers[20] found 149 such children in the Cen-

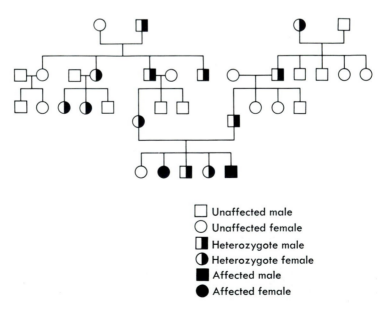

☐ Unaffected male
○ Unaffected female
◨ Heterozygote male
◑ Heterozygote female
■ Affected male
● Affected female

Fig. 9-10. Pedigree of a family with an autosomal recessive trait.

tral Wisconsin Center for Developmentally Disabled in Madison, Wisconsin. Four (from three families) were determined to have a condition with high recurrence risk, possibly autosomal recessive. A later study by Becker and colleagues[3] of 40 patients with severe mental retardation and no physical abnormalities revealed that 25% of first-degree relatives (siblings, parents, offspring) of these patients were either mentally retarded or "dull normal." The study concluded that severe mental retardation was etiologically heterogeneous, but that auto-

Table 9-3. Some X-linked conditions with associated developmental disability[6,24,39]

Condition	Degree of disability	Comment
Angiokeratoma corporis diffusum (Fabry syndrome)	Progressive	Lipidosis
Borjeson syndrome	Severe mental retardation	Obesity, hypogonadism
Cataracts, congenital	Variable vision loss	Genetic heterogeneity
Coffin-Lowry syndrome	Severe mental retardation	Characteristic facies
Deafness	Variable	Genetic heterogeneity
Hydrocephalus due to aqueductal stenosis	None to severe	Some aqueductal stenosis, not mendelian
Leber optic atrophy	Progressive visual loss	Some doubt about precise mode of inheritance
Lesch-Nyhan syndrome	Mild to severe mental retardation	Choreoathetosis; defect in uric acid metabolism
Lowe syndrome	Moderate to severe mental retardation, visual loss	Cataracts, renal defect
Menkes syndrome	Moderate to severe mental retardation	"Kinky" hair, progressive course
Mental deficiency (Renpenning type)	Moderate mental retardation	No somatic malformation
Mucopolysaccharidosis, type II	Progressive intellectual defect	Coarse facies, hepatosplenomegaly
Muscular dystrophy (Duchenne type)	Normal to mild mental retardation	Neuromuscular involvement
Norrie disease	Variable mental retardation, visual loss	Pseudoglioma
Ornithine transcarbamoylase deficiency	Severe, often lethal	Hyperammonemia
Orofaciodigital syndrome, type I	None to moderate mental retardation	X-linked dominant
Otopalatodigital syndrome	Deafness	Characteristic craniofacial findings
Pelizaeus-Merzbacher disease	Progressive defect	Diffuse cerebral sclerosis
Retinitis pigmentosa	Variable	Genetic heterogeneity
Spastic paraplegia	Variable intelligence	Genetic heterogeneity

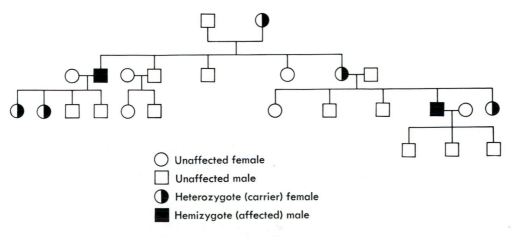

○ Unaffected female

□ Unaffected male

◐ Heterozygote (carrier) female

■ Hemizygote (affected) male

Fig. 9-11. Pedigree of a family with an X-linked recessive trait.

somal recessive inheritance very likely played a role in the condition of some of these patients. In counselling families with such children uncritical statements of low recurrence risk should be avoided and the possibility of 25% recurrence risk must be kept in mind.

X-linked inheritance

In X-linked single gene conditions the gene is located on the X chromosome. Females have two X chromosomes and therefore two alleles. Males have only one X chromosome and thus X-linked recessive conditions are much more frequent in males. Female heterozygotes are carriers who have a 50% chance of passing the gene and trait to their male offspring and the same risk of passing the gene to their female offspring, making them carriers as well. X-linked traits are never passed from father to son, since males impart a Y chromosome to their sons. All female offspring of affected males are carriers.[30] (Fig. 9-11).

X-linked dominant conditions are more frequent in females. All female offspring and no male offspring of affected males are affected. These conditions are often more mildly expressed in female heterozygotes than in male hemizygotes.

Table 9-3[6,24,39] lists some X-linked conditions in which developmental disability may occur. Of note is the syndrome of X-linked mental deficiency without somatic malformation (Renpenning's syndrome).[36] Excesses of males over females have long been noted in epidemiological studies of moderately retarded individuals without physical abnormalities. Several detailed pedigrees have been reported that are consistent with X-linked inheritance.[45]

MULTIFACTORIAL INHERITANCE AND MILD DEVELOPMENTAL DISABILITY

It has become clear in recent years that certain congenital malformations recur in families more frequently than expected by chance. Malformations such as congenital heart disease, neural tube defects, cleft lip and palate, and others are seen among siblings more frequently than chance can explain but less frequently than expected by single-gene patterns.

The precise nature of the hereditary factors in these families is not clear. If has been hypothesized that genetic and environmental factors are interacting, hence the term "multifactorial." It is hypothesized that for any given malformation each individual at conception has a genetically determined predisposition to the malformation. Predispositions are argued to be distributed in a normal fashion throughout the population. A "threshhold" predisposition is hypothesized. Those whose predisposition is high—exceeds the threshhold—will develop the malformation. Environmental factors of uncertain nature may push some individuals beyond the threshhold or may affect the severity of the lesion in others. More detailed discussions of the multifactorial concept by Carter[9] and Nora and Fraser[30] are available.

Neural tube defects, anencephaly and myelodysplasia, are found in families in a frequency consistent with multifactorial inheritance. Anencephaly is, of course, fatal, but children with myelodysplasia may survive with varying degrees of developmental disability. A family with one child with any neural tube defect has a 2% to 4% risk of recurrence with each subsequent pregnancy. This is the order of magnitude of risk in multifactorial malformations. It is likely that other central nervous system malformations responsible for developmental disability may follow a similar model.

Mild developmental disabilities, particularly mild mental retardation, may lend themselves to analysis on a multifactorial basis.[29] Severe mental retardation does not lend itself to such analysis. Severe mental retardation is more likely to have a medical or single-gene etiology. "Intelligence" in the population is more or less normally distributed as might be expected in multifactorial traits. "Intelligence" obviously is subject to influence by environmental factors such as injury, infection, toxin, poverty, nutrition, and so forth. Furthermore, the frequency of mild mental retardation among siblings of mildly retarded people is higher than the frequency in the general population.

If the multifactorial model is accepted in the absence of environmental consideration, parents of a child with *mild* mental retardation stand a risk of about 3% to 5% with each subsequent pregnancy of having a similarly affected child. If a second child is affected, the subsequent risk, according to the model, rises to 10%. These risks assume that the parents are average or above in intelligence and that no chromosomal, metabolic, single-gene, or environmental cause of the disability can be discovered, and that the child does not have a known malformation syndrome. Parents who are dull normal or mildly retarded would be expected to have higher risks consistent with the multifactorial model.

Estimates of risk have been tabulated by Reed and Reed.[35] Recurrence risks for learning disabilities, dyslexia, and related disabilities are being studied.

MALFORMATION SYNDROMES

Some children with developmental disability and morphological abnormalities may fit into a recognized malformation syndrome. A syndrome is a pattern of malformations that occur together more frequently than expected by chance. Syndromes are presumed to have a single cause but there may be separate causes associated with a similar clinical pattern (e.g., Turner and Noonan syndromes; Marfan syndrome and homocystinuria). As the cellular and biochemical bases of malformations are uncovered, specific malformation patterns will presumably be proved to be associated with specific cellular or biochemical defects, as Turner syndrome is associated with monosomy X. Marfan syndrome and homocystinuria, which can be distinguished clinically only with difficulty, can be clearly distinguished by measurement of tissue activity of cystathionine synthetase.

Environmental teratogenic agents such as viruses and drugs may produce well-defined syndromes, for example, rubella embryopathy, fetal alcohol syndrome; chromosome abnormalities are also associated with specific malformation patterns, and malformation syndromes are found in lists of autosomal dominant, autosomal recessive, and X-linked single gene defects, some with identifiable biochemical defect but many with unknown etiologies.

In many malformation syndromes associated with developmental disability, the inheritance pattern is not determined (or the syndrome is not inherited) and etiology is unclear. De Lange, Rubinstein-Taybi, Beckwith-Wiedemann, Prader-Willi, Sturge-Weber, and Williams syndromes are some well-known disorders in which recurrence risks are low.

Diagnosis of a syndrome is made by identifying malformations in an individual and matching those with a previously described pattern. Of course, x-ray and laboratory studies may be as useful as morphological findings. Prognostic and genetic counselling can then be supplied based on previous observations of people with the identified syndrome. In many syndromes there is normal intellectual function.

Familiarity with syndrome literature is often necessary to make a definitive syndrome diagnosis. The assistance of a "syndromologist" or dysmorphologist may be helpful. Recognition of morphological abnormalities, however, does not require specialized tools. Major malformations (microcephaly, congenital heart defects, abdominal wall defects, major limb defects, etc.) are readily apparent; recognition of minor abnormalities requires careful observation, measurements, and reference to standards. The pediatrician should be the person to make the observations and identify children who appear to fit a malformation syndrome. The physician must then decide if referral to a specialist is indicated. The specialist may confirm the diagnosis or offer a new one.

Feingold and Bossert[12] have published a monograph of normal measurements of various physical features. Smith[39] includes similar standard measurements in his book, as well as discussions and photographs of some minor malformations. Other similar but more specialized texts are also available.

It should be noted that a few minor malformations may be found in any normal person. When a larger number are present in an individual, a syndrome should be suspected.

Morphological abnormalities

Some of the more frequent dysmorphic features are discussed below.

Head. Abnormalities of skull shape may reflect premature closure of sutures, which may be isolated or part of a syndrome.

Large fontanelle or delayed closure may be found in skeletal dysplasias, metabolic abnormalities (hypothyroidism), and chromosome defects. Standards for fontanelle size are found in Smith.[39] Scalp defects (Fig. 9-7) occur in trisomy 13. Anterior upsweep of scalp hair is described in certain microcephaly syndromes.

Face. A flat face is seen in Down syndrome, certain skeletal dysplasias, and certain other syndromes. A round face is characteristic of Prader-Willi, cri du chat, and Laurence-Moon-Biedl syndromes.

An expressionless face suggest myotonic dystrophy, and this autosomal dominant condition should be considered.

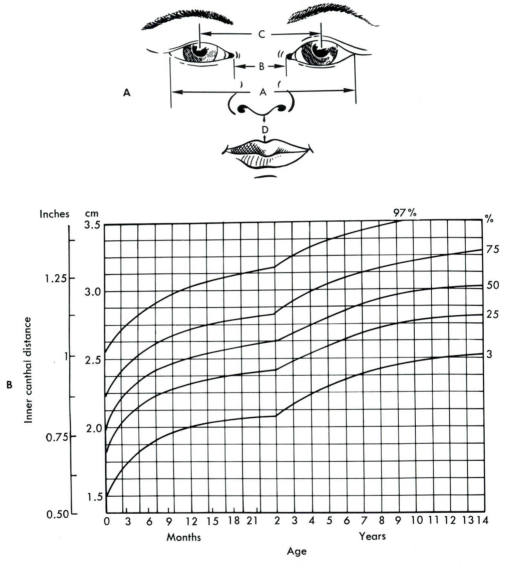

Fig. 9-12. A, Various ocular distances. Distance *A* is the outer canthal distance, distance *B* the inner canthal distance, distance *C* the interpupillary distance, and distance *D* the nasolabial (philtrum) length. Ocular hypertelorism exists when distance *C* is increased. When distance *A* is normal but distance *B* is increased, telecanthus (or laterally displaced inner canthi) is present. **B** to **D,** standard curves for various ocular distances. (From Feingold, M., and Bossert W.: "Normal Values for Selected Physical Parameters," Bergsma, D. (ed). White Plains: The National Foundation—March of Dimes, BD:OAS, X(13), 1974.)

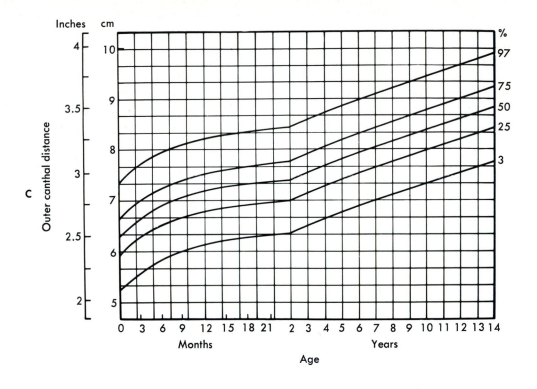

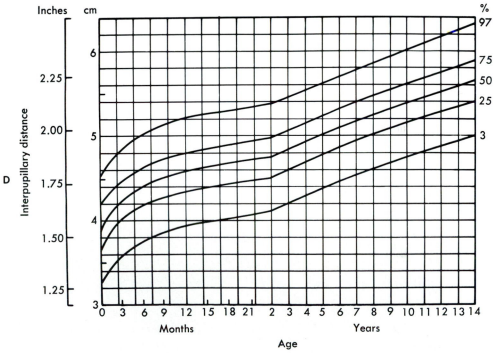

Fig. 9-12, cont'd. For legend see opposite page.

Coarse facies with prominent features are seen in mucolipidoses, mucopolysaccharidoses, and hypothyroidism syndromes, to name a few. Children with mucopolysaccharidoses do not have coarse features at birth. Those with mucolipidoses may. Children with Williams syndrome are described as having "elfin" facies.

Eyes. Ocular hypertelorism (wide-set eyes) and hypotelorism (close-set eyes) may be accurately diagnosed by measurement of distances between inner canthi and outer canthi or by direct measurement of interpupillary distance in a cooperative patient (Fig. 9-12, A-D). Standards for these distances are available (Fig. 9-12, D).[12,39] Inner epicanthal folds or telecanthus (lateral displacement of inner canthi) may give a false impression of ocular hypertelorism.

Short palpebral fissures are found in children with fetal alcohol syndrome. These are determined by measuring inner canthal to outer canthal distance and comparing to standards. With ptosis, but *not* shortened fissures, this measurement is in the normal range but the upper lid is in a lowered position. Upward slanting or downward slanting of palpebral fissures occur in some syndromes.

Synophrys, or meeting of eyebrows in the midline, is seen occasionally in normal people but with great frequency in de Lange syndrome.

Colobomata are developmental defects and occur in the iris, the retina, and elsewhere (Fig. 9-13).

Nose. Minor upturning of nares or flat nasal bridge are seen in normal newborns, but a more substantially upturned or flatten bridge is abnormal. Prominent noses of various kinds are described in Seckel, Rubinstein-Taybi, and trichorhinophalangeal syndromes and certain chromosome defects.[6,39]

Ears. Low-set ears are definitely present when the ear is positioned below a line drawn horizontally from the medial canthus of the eye to the side of the head, the person being erect when examined. Posterior positioning exists when the angle the ear makes with the horizontal line is greater than 10 to 15 degrees (Fig. 9-14, A).

Preauricular skin tags, incompletely developed helices, "squared" helices, prominent ears, and large or small ears (based on comparison to standards) (Fig. 9-14, B) may suggest a syndrome. Substantial structural ear abnormality may be associated with hearing loss.

Oral area. The philtrum or nasolabial area may be long in some syndromes (Williams) and short in others (orofacodigital syndrome) (Fig. 9-14, C). Micrognathia and glossoptosis (posteriorly placed tongue) with or without a cleft palate constitute the (Pierre) Robin anom-

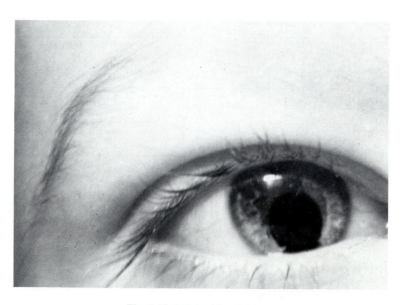

Fig. 9-13. Inferior iris coloboma.

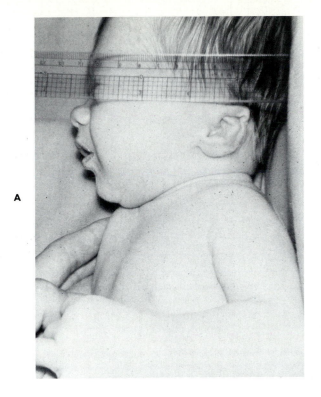

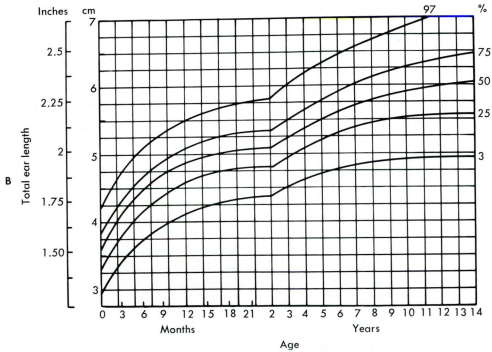

Fig. 9-14. A, Low-set posteriorly rotated ear, verified by method noted on p. 242. Note also the folded helix and prominent anthelix. **B,** Standards for ear size.

Continued.

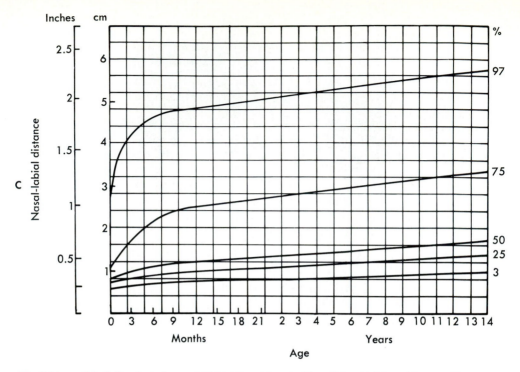

Fig. 9-14, cont'd. C, Standards for nasolabial (philtrum) length. (From Feingold, M., and Bossert, W.: Normal Values for Selected Physical Parameters, Bergsma, D. (ed). White Plains: The National Foundation—March of Dimes, BD:OAS, X(13), 1974.)

aly. The Robin anomaly may occur as an isolated malformation or as part of a malformation syndrome (trisomy 18, Zellweger syndrome, and many more). Children with isolated Robin anomaly are at risk for airway obstruction in the newborn period; they are generally normal intellectually.

Cleft lip and/or palate are apparent, but submucosal cleft of the soft palate may not be obvious and may be associated with middle ear fluid, hearing loss, or speech difficulty. A bifid uvula suggests the possibility of a submucous cleft; palate palpation is indicated.

Chest. A variety of chest shapes are seen. Children with spondylothoracic or spondyloepiphyseal dysplasias have a barrel chest. The chest is narrow in other skeletal dysplasias. Children with progeria may have a pear-shaped chest, while girls with Turner syndrome often have a broad chest ("shield-like").[6,39]

Turner girls (as well as children with certain other syndromes) have also been described as having widely spaced nipples. Standards for internipple distance are available. Some believe the internipple/chest circumference ratio to be

a more useful measurement.[12] As many as one child in a hundred may be born with one or more supernumerary nipples (polymastia).[6] These are found along the so-called milk line running from the axilla to the groin. Nipples above the normal mammary are lateral, whereas those below are medial. The lateral ones are more likely to develop functional breast tissue. Nipple hypoplasia may be seen in Poland anomaly and de Lange and other syndromes.

Pectus excavatum (posterior dislocation of the lower sternum, costal cartilages, and anterior ribs) occurs as an isolated anomaly or as part of a syndrome (Marfan, XYY, skeletal dysplasias, Noonan, and others). Generally no treatment is required. Occasionally pulmonary function may be compromised or cosmetic effect may be substantial so surgical repair is considered.

Pectus carinatum ("pigeon breast") is a prominent sternum with lateral depression of the anterior ribs. It is also seen as an isolated malformation or in association with other malformations. In syndromes such as Marfan, homocystinuria, osteogenesis imperfecta, Mor-

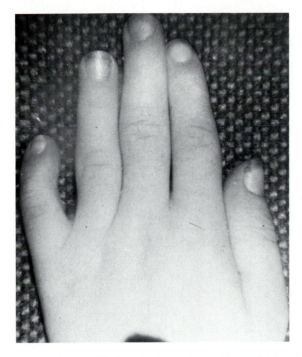

Fig. 9-15. Fifth finger clinodactyly. The fifth finger is short and curved in a radial direction because of a short, wedge-shaped middle phalanx.

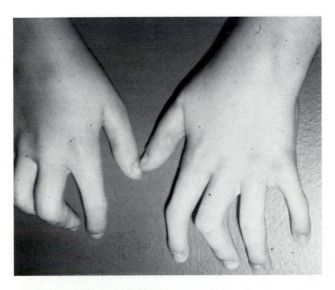

Fig. 9-16. Camptodactyly. Note fixed flexed interphalangeal joints on both hands. The thumbs are abnormally positioned as well, and there are abnormalities of creases on all fingers.

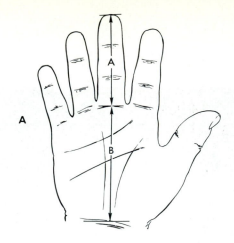

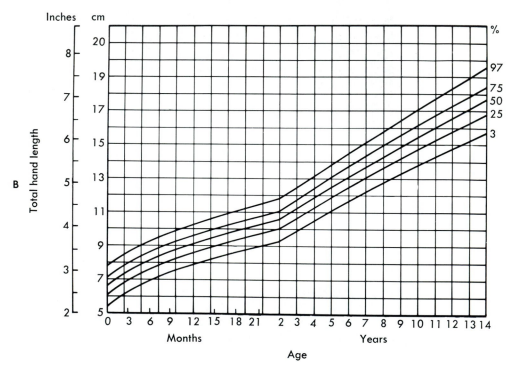

Fig. 9-17. **A,** Hand measurement hallmarks. **B** to **D,** Standards for these measurements. (From Feingold, M., and Bossert W.: "Normal Values for Selected Physical Parameters," Bergsma, D. (ed). White Plains: The National Foundation—March of Dimes, BD:OAS, X(13), 1974.)

quio and others, pectus carinatum may be found. Both pectus excavatum and pectus carinatum are inherited as autosomal dominant traits in some families.

Limbs. Dermatoglyphics, a study of dermal ridge patterns, is almost a science unto itself. Abnormalities of patterns may suggest a malformation syndrome.

Syndactyly, nonseparation of digits, is ob-

vious when complete and osseous, but may be missed when incomplete and cutaneous. Partial cutaneous syndactyly involving second and third toes is common among normal individuals.

Clinodactyly, or curved finger, most frequently involves the fifth fingers. Frequently it results from hypoplasia of the midphalanx of that finger. Clinodactyly is common in Down, de Lange,

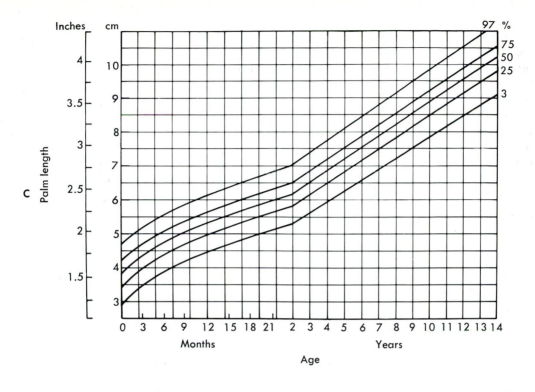

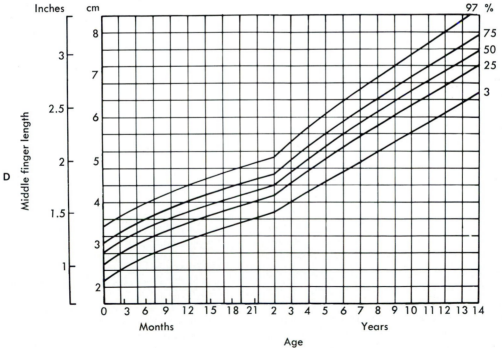

Fig. 9-17, cont'd. For legend see opposite page.

and Seckel syndromes and many others (Fig. 9-15). Camptodactyly is fixed, flexed digits (Fig. 9-16).

Standards for hand, palm, and finger length are available; thus brachydactyly (small hand), arachnodactyly (long fingers), and large hands can be detected with some precision (Fig. 9-17, *A-D*).

Genitals. Hypospadias frequently is seen as an isolated finding, but may be part of a syndrome (Smith-Lemli-Opitz, Robinow, 13 q−, etc.).

Micropenis[39] occurs in Prader-Willi, Noonan, and Robinow syndromes, while labia majora hypoplasia may be seen in trisomy 18 and other syndromes.

• • •

Despite careful examination and investigation of children with morphological abnormalities and delayed development, a specific diagnosis cannot be determined in 60% to 80% of the cases (Down syndrome excluded).[12,21]

SUMMARY

Genetic counselling of a family with a developmentally disabled child begins with determination of diagnosis. Environmental insults, chromosome defects, single-gene traits and known malformation syndromes must be eliminated as causes of the disability. Prenatal and perinatal history; developmental history; detailed pedigree analysis, including reports of infant deaths and miscarriages; physical examination; and appropriate laboratory studies are indicated. Much of this can be performed by the pediatrician alone or in consultation with a geneticist or developmental specialist. If a cause is determined, appropriate recurrence risk counselling is provided. If no diagnosis is determined, the condition is assumed to fall into the multifactorial category. Quoted recurrence risks depend on the number of affected individuals in the pedigree and the severity of those affected, in keeping with the principles of multifactorial inheritance. Because of X-linked mental retardation possibilities, recurrence risks will be slightly greater if the patient is a male. Some families probably have a 25% recurrence risk because of unidentified autosomal recessive syndromes, whereas others have a very low

risk because of an unidentified environmental agent. The 5% risk quoted to families is probably a weighted average of many risks, a concept consistent with the multifactorial model.

A pediatrician who feels comfortable doing genetic counselling can of course do so, particularly if a diagnosis is apparent. Comprehensive genetic counselling, however, is a communication process that involves more than simply stating recurrence risks; in complicated situations the pediatrician will probably wish to make a referral to a genetic counselling clinic. Access to the "syndrome" literature and to specialized diagnostic tools such as assay of fibroblast enzymes is not always available to the pediatrician. The pediatrician might not be familiar with available and appropriate specialized services for the developmentally disabled child with a rare genetic condition. Detailed genetic and prognostic information about unusual conditions may also be difficult for the busy pediatrician to locate. Finally, information about alternatives to further reproduction (adoption, contraception, artificial insemination, prenatal diagnosis, etc.), which families often require as part of the counselling process, may not be information the pediatrician is familiar with in detail. For these reasons referral to a geneticist-dysmorphologist is often indicated. However, primary care of the child remains with the pediatrician, the genetic clinic serving only consultant and continuing education roles.

REFERENCES

1. Ampola, M. G., et al.: Prenatal therapy of a patient with vitamin B-12 responsive methylmalonic acidemia, N. Engl. J. Med. **293:**314, 1975.
2. Arye, L.: Androgens, estrogens and the ultimate height in XO gonadal dysgenesis, Am. J. Dis. Child. **131:**648, 1977.
3. Becker, J. M., et al.: A biologic and genetic study of 40 cases of severe pure mental retardation, Eur. J. Pediatr. **124:**231, 1977.
4. Bennett, A.: New England regional newborn screening program, N. Engl. J. Med. **297:**21, 1977.
5. Benzie, R. J.: Fetoscopy, Birth Defects **XIII**(3D): 181, 1977.
6. Bergsma, D., editor: Birth defects compendium, ed. 2, New York, 1979, Alan R. Liss, Inc. for the National Foundation—March of Dimes.
7. Brewster, T. G., and Gerald, P. S.: Chromosome disorders associated with mental retardation, Pediatr. Ann. **7:**22, 1978.
8. Carr, D. H., and Gedeon, M.: Population cytogenetics of human abortuses. In Hook, E. B., and Porter,

I. H., editors: Population cytogenetics—studies in humans, New York, 1977, Academic Press, Inc., p. 1.

9. Carter, C. O.: Multifactorial genetic disease. In McKusick, V. A., and Claiborne, R., editors: Medical genetics, New York, 1973, HP Publishing, p. 199.

10. Coleman, M.: Down's syndrome, Pediatr. Ann. **7:**36, 1978.

11. Cornwell, A. L., and Birch, H. G.: Psychological and social development in home reared children with Down syndrome, Am. J. Ment. Defic. **74:**341, 1969.

12. Feingold, M., and Bossert, W.: Normal values for selected physical parameters, Birth Defects **X**(13):12, 1974.

13. Garron, D. C., and Vander Staef, L.: Personality and intelligence in Turner syndrome, Arch. Gen. Psychiatry **21:**339, 1969.

14. Haskins, R., Finkelstein, N., and Stedman, D.: Infant stimulation programs and their effects, Pediatr. Ann. **7:**99, 1978.

15. Hobbins, J. C., and Mahoney, M. J.: Fetoscopy and fetal blood sampling: the present state of the method, Clin. Obstet. Gynecol. **19:**341, 1976.

16. Holmes, L. B.: Genetic counseling for the older pregnant woman: new data and questions, N. Engl. J. Med. **298:**1419, 1978.

17. Hook, E. B.: Geneticophobia and the implications of screening for the XYY genotype in newborn infants. In Milunsky, A., and Annas, G., editors: Genetics and the law, 1976, New York, Plenum Publishing Corp., p. 73.

18. Hook, E. B., and Chambers, G. M.: Estimated rates of Down syndrome in live births by one year maternal age intervals for mothers aged 20-49 in a New York state study, Birth Defects **XIII**(3A):123, 1977.

19. Hook, E. B., and Hamerton, J. L.: The frequency of chromosome abnormalities detected in consecutive newborn studies. In Hook, E. B., and Porter, I. H., editors: Population cytogenetics—studies in humans, New York, 1977, Academic Press, Inc., p. 63.

20. Kaveggia, E. G., et al.: Diagnostic/genetic studies on 1,224 patients with severe mental retardation. Proceedings of the Third Congress of the International Association for the Scientific Study of Mental Deficiency 82, 1973.

21. Levy, H. L., Madigan, P. M., and Shih, V. E.: Massachusetts metabolic disorders screening program, Pediatrics **49:**825, 1972.

22. Levy, H. L., et al.: Screening for congenital hypothyroidism, J.A.M.A. **239:**2348, 1978.

23. Lorincz, A. E.: The mucopolysaccharidoses: advances in understanding and treatment, Pediatr. Ann. **7:**64, 1978.

24. McKusick, V. A.: Mendelian inheritance in man, ed. 5, Baltimore, 1978, Johns Hopkins University Press.

25. Milunsky, A.: The prenatal diagnosis of hereditary disorders, Springfield, Ill., 1975, Charles C Thomas, Publisher.

26. Milunsky, A.: The prevention of genetic disease and mental retardation, Philadelphia, 1975, W. B. Saunders Co.

27. Moore, I. C., et al.: Studies of anabolic steroids. VI, Effect of prolonged administration of oxandralone on growth in children and adolescents with gonadal dysgenesis, J. Pediatr. **90:**462, 1977.

28. Morton, N. E., et al.: Colchester revisited, a genetic study of mental defect. J. Med. Genet. **14:**1, 1977.

29. Morton, N. E., et al.: Genetic epidemiology of an institutionalized cohort of mental retardates, Clin. Genet. **13:**449, 1978.

30. Nora, J. J., and Fraser, F. C.: Medical genetics, principles and practice, Philadelphia, 1972, Lea & Febiger.

31. Omenn, G. S., et al.: The use of radiographic visualization for prenatal diagnosis, Birth Defects **XIII**(3D): 217, 1977.

32. Opitz, J. M.: Turner syndrome. In Bergsma, D., editor: Birth defects compendium, ed. 2, New York, 1974, Alan R. Liss, Inc. for the National Foundation—March of Dimes, p. 870.

33. Paris Conference (1971), Birth Defects **XI**(9): Suppl., 1975.

33a. Penrose, L. S.: A clinical and genetic study of 1280 cases of mental defect, Medical Research Council spec. rep. no. 229, London, 1938, H. M. Stationary Office.

34. Penrose, L. S., and Smith, G. F.: Down's anomaly, Boston, 1966, Little, Brown & Co.

35. Reed, R. W., and Reed, S. C.: Mental retardation: a family study, Philadelphia, 1965, W. B. Saunders Co.

36. Renpenning, H., et al.: Familial sex-linked mental retardation, Can. Med. Assoc. J. **87:**954, 1962.

36a. Robinson, A., et al.: Summary of clinical findings: profiles of children with 47,XXY; 47,XXX and 47,XYY karyotypes. In Robinson, A., et al., editors: Birth Defects **15:**261, 1979.

37. Rosenfield, R., and Weky, A.: Oxandrolone therapy for children with Turner syndrome, J. Pediatr. **91:**854, 1977.

38. Schmid, W., et al.: Cytogenetic findings in 89 cases of Turner syndrome. Humangenetik **24:**93, 1974.

39. Smith, D. W.: Recognizable patterns of human malformations, Philadelphia, 1976, W. B. Saunders Co.

40. Stevenson, A. C., and Davison, B. C. C.: Genetic counseling, ed. 2, Philadelphia, 1978, J. B. Lippincott.

41. Sutton, W. S.: The chromosomes in heredity, Biol. Bull. **4:**231, 1903.

42. Tennes, K., et al.: A developmental study of girls with trisomy X, Am. J. Hum. Genet. **27:**71, 1975.

43. Thompson, J. S., and Thompson, M. W.: Genetics in medicine, Philadelphia, 1973, W. B. Saunders Co.

44. Tijo, J. H., and Levan, A.: The chromosome number of man, Hereditas **42:**1, 1956.

45. Turner, G., Turner, B., and Collins, E.: X-linked mental retardation without physical abnormality: Renpenning's syndrome, Dev. Med. Child Neurol. **13:**71, 1971.

46. Werlin, S. L., et al.: Diagnostic dilemmas of Wilson's disease: diagnosis and treatment, Pediatrics **62:**47, 1978.

10

The child with a hearing loss

Burton F. Jaffe
David M. Luterman

A severe hearing loss occurs in 1 per 1400 newborns and is far more common than many metabolic disorders routinely screened. In addition, there is probably a tenfold greater number of children with a mild to moderate hearing problem.

Most experts agree that this severe hearing loss causes far more devastating consequences than the other major sensory deficit, blindness. A child with a hearing loss may be developmentally delayed in many ways. To prevent or ameliorate the devastating effects of a hearing loss, the primary care physician must be aware of this sensory deprivation.

Following terms appearing in the text are defined as follows:

deaf A hearing loss which exceeds 80 decibel (dB) average in the speech frequencies (500 to 2000 hertz, or Hz) in the better ear, or a child who even with amplification will not be able to understand speech without some other sensory help.

hearing impaired Generally refers to all categories of hearing loss. It is frequently modified with the adjectives mild (20 to 40 dB), moderate (40 to 60 dB), and severe (60 to 80 dB).

Medical aspects

Burton F. Jaffe

MANAGEMENT BY THE PRIMARY CARE PHYSICIAN

In most instances the pediatrician, primary care physician, or family practitioner is the first professional person that is consulted by the parents of a hearing impaired child. Deafness is seldom considered as a diagnostic category by parents, and by the time the parents have confided their fears to their primary care physician, they have been through considerable emotional turmoil. Their initial concern, whether it is ever expressed or not, is usually that the child may be mentally retarded.

By the time the infant is 3 or 4 months of age, the parents begin to suspect in a vague way that something is wrong. They recognize that the child is not as responsive as they had expected. Frequently it is the mother who begins to actively question the hearing and it is the father who denies the existence of a problem. From about 6 to 12 months of age, the parents begin to embark on a program of testing the child's hearing, usually by means of calling to him when his back is turned, banging two objects together, or stamping their feet. The problem in testing the hearing of a young child in this manner is that there are many opportunities to obtain a pseudoresponse. The hearing impaired child rapidly learns to compensate for his reduced acuity by a heavy reliance on the other sensory modalities. He is, therefore, very attuned to any visual or vibratory information and will frequently respond to a vibratory or visual aspect of the stimulus rather than to the auditory aspects. For example, the clapping of hands creates a pressure wave that the child might respond to, or he might respond to the information from his peripheral vision. Moreover, deafness in childhood is seldom total; thus if the stimulus is of a high enough intensity, the child can make a legitimate auditory response. It is during this time that the parental anxiety level is at its highest, and parents have described this time as being on an "emotional rollercoaster"; their feelings are of elation when they obtain a response or a pseudoresponse and of despair when the child does not respond. It is only with the greatest trepidation that they approach the pediatrician; it is so very difficult for parents to admit that there might be something wrong with their child.

When the diagnosis of a hearing loss is made, new problems arise for the parents. In the early stages of the child's diagnosis of hearing impairment they go through a crisis reaction; they move through stages of shock, active mourning, denial, acceptance, and, finally, constructive action. The pediatrician or family physician is very much part of the supportive and coordinating services needed by the parent. The early stages are fraught with a great deal of anger on the part of the parents, including anger at the child, which can seldom be expressed. Frequently the anger is turned inward onto the parent and becomes depression, or is deflected to the primary care provider for some imagined slight. A major complaint of some parents was that the physician did not listen to them; not just in terms of not accepting their own diagnosis of deafness, but not being accepting of and willing to listen to the parents' feelings.

In fact, information at this point tends to be confusing, since the parents have no stored data to use to evaluate new data. In the early stages of crisis parents need to be listened to rather to be given much information. They need to feel free to talk about their fears and angers and to have these accepted in a nonjudgemental fashion. Feelings are important because only after tensions are relieved can the desired goals be approached. Parents need to feel the acceptance and warmth of a caring professional. The primary care physician is in just such a position to help foster healthy positive attitudes in the parents that can be of help to future professionals, and of course, of considerable benefit to the hearing impaired child.

The primary care physician will be seeing the hearing impaired child at normal interviews for routine physicals, school and camp physicals, and with acute illnesses. At each visit the physician can be aware of the importance of the hearing aid, ask if the hearing aid is working properly, and encourage the use of the hearing aid as much as possible. An ear canal examination is important to rule out impacted wax or to detect an external otitis from the ear mold. At regular intervals the physician should take the time to assess the developmental progress, discuss the proposed educational plans, and evaluate the emotional status of the child and family.

The primary care physician can obtain a family history of hearing loss and encourage all members of the family with or without hearing loss to obtain a family audiogram to detect even an unsuspected partial loss. Genetic counselling may be indicated if positive results are encountered.

The primary care physician can act as an ombudsman for the family. The physician may contact the specialist to obtain facts for the family and may discuss how to handle the large financial burden by seeking help from various social agencies as well as the state health department or March of Dimes.

It is incumbent on the primary care physician to know the choices of education available to the hearing impaired child. Knowledge of appropriate resources such as residential schools and day schools and such philosophies as mainstreaming will help the parents sort out the necessary issues. Obviously no one professional can know all the details of the various programs, but the primary care physician should be aware of the choices. The physician should also be supportive and encourage the parents to investigate a number of programs before making any final decision.

NEWBORNS WHO ARE AT A HIGHER RISK FOR DEAFNESS

In the past decade a series of national studies has been held to identify which infants at birth have a higher risk for deafness. Most authorities believe that the following eight categories should alert the primary care physician to the fact that a newborn might have a hearing loss.

1. Familial hearing loss
2. Congenital rubella, cytomegalovirus infection, toxoplasmosis, or herpes simplex infection
3. Low birth weight (less than 1500 g)
4. Hyperbilirubinemia (20 mg/ml of blood or higher or an exchange transfusion done)
5. Congenital malformations of skull or pinna or cleft lip or palate
6. Meningitis
7. Ototoxic drugs (i.e., kanamycin, neomycin, ethacrynic acid)
8. Significant perinatal asphyxia

In all cases the at-risk newborn should be referred to an audiologist for evaluation within the first 2 months of life. These categories constitute a screening that requires sophisticated testing by a trained professional. Each of these categories is amplified in the following discussion.

Familial hearing loss. If the history indicates that one parent or a sibling is deaf or hard of hearing, arrangements should be made for a hearing test for any newborns in the family. In most cases a recessive or dominant deafness may be the only abnormality. Audiograms are recommended for the entire family of a deaf newborn to detect an unsuspected familial partial loss, since these can affect only low, mid, or high frequencies and have no obvious effect on someone's ability to hear. However, even if a slight familial loss should be detected,

genetic counselling would clearly be appropriate. Recessive sensorineural deafness occurs in 1 per 4000 births, while dominant isolated deafness occurs in 1 per 40,000 births.

Some forms of familial deafness are merely one part of a larger syndrome. Following are familial syndromes that have deafness as a component.

Mucopolysaccharidoses. Mucopolysaccharidoses occur in 1 per 10,000 births. The mucopolysaccharidoses are inherited metabolic disorders due to defective lysosomal degradation. Characteristic findings include thick facies, mental deficiency, and hepatosplenomegaly. Due to the swollen tissues of the nose, nasopharynx, and probably the eustachian tube, there is a higher risk for chronic otitis media. In addition, some of these patients have an associated sensorineural loss.

Pendred syndrome. Pendred syndrome occurs in 1 per 20,000 births. This autosomal recessive syndrome is characterized by a hearing loss present from birth and a goiter that is usually present by age 5 but may not develop until puberty. The hearing loss is a bilateral severe sensorineural loss.

Usher syndrome. Usher syndrome occurs in 1 per 20,000 births. This autosomal recessive syndrome is characterized by a mild to severe congenital sensorineural hearing loss, a progressive visual loss, and possible mental retardation. The retina examination reveals bone spicule pigmentary changes clustered around vessels.

Familial hyperlipoproteinemia type I. Type I hyperlipoproteinemia occurs in 1 per 33,000 births. Eruptive xanthomas, hepatosplenomegaly, lipemia retinalis, and abdominal pain characterize this syndrome.

Waardenburg syndrome. Waardenburg syndrome occurs in 1 per 40,000 births. The most characteristic features of patients with Waardenburg's syndrome are widely spaced medial canthi and a flat nasal root with confluent eyebrows. Frequently those affected have variably colored irises as well as a white forelock. At least a fifth have a hearing loss.

Alport syndrome. Alport syndrome occurs in 1 per 200,000 births. There is often a history of renal failure, and in some cases a renal transplant is required. The syndrome is characterized by hematuria and albuminuria, which may occur before a hearing loss is detected. The hearing loss develops after age 10 and slowly progresses.

Jervell and Lange-Nielsen syndrome. Jervell and Lange-Nielsen syndrome occurs in 1 per 200,000 births. This recessive inherited syndrome is characterized by fainting spells and sudden lapses of consciousness, usually appearing about age 5. An ECG will reveal a prolonged QT interval, and sudden death may occur. All patients have a congenital bilateral severe sensorineural hearing loss.

Rubella and other ototoxic infections during pregnancy. Epidemics of *rubella* have each been followed by a wave of congenitally deaf children. Rubella during any trimester of pregnancy can cause deafness, and the incidence ranges from 69% in the first trimester, to 23% in the second trimester, to 8% in the third trimester. Even subclinical rubella, which occurs in 50% of the mothers so infected, can give rise to rubella-infected newborns. It has been estimated that 15% of women of the childbearing age are not immune to rubella and should be vaccinated.[6] Only Colorado requires a premarital serological test for rubella, but hopefully other states will pass similar preventive measures.

Cytomegalic inclusion disease may prove to be the most significant cause of congenital deafness in newborns since rubella vaccine is now commonly used. Cytomegalovirus infection (CMV) occurs in about 0.6% to 1% of all live births. Only 5% of those infants have a clinical disease, which consists of low birth weight, hepatosplenomegaly, jaundice, microcephaly, thrombocytopenia, and hemolytic anemia; the other 95% have subclinical infections.

About 35% of infants with congenital symptomatic CMV have a congenital sensorineural hearing loss. Congenital subclinical CMV infections, detectable only by viral antibody studies, will cause sensorineural hearing loss in 15% of the newborns.[8] The hearing loss is usually bilateral and moderate to profound but may be confused with a high-frequency loss. Less often, a progressive sensorineural hearing loss occurs and may be due to viral replication within the cells of the organ of Corti and neurons of the spiral ganglia.

Because of the large number of newborns with CMV and a hearing loss, estimated at 4000 hearing impaired newborns a year, this is clearly a major health problem. Fortunately, natal acquisition of CMV, which occurs in 3% to 5% of live births, does not seem to give a hearing loss.[8]

Toxoplasma gondii is a protozoon causing multiple problems in the newborn and frequently involving the central nervous system, with seizures, microcephaly or hydrocephalus, and intracranial calcifications. Hearing loss is uncommon in infected newborns, but it may occur and a progressive loss may ensue. In a group of children with neurological disease due to toxoplasmosis, 17% had deafness.[1]

Low birth weight. A newborn with a low birth weight who is small for gestational age has a small risk for hearing loss. In 1066 infants under 1.8 kg at birth who were followed, 19 (1.8%) had a hearing loss.[5] In contrast, a newborn with a low birth weight but a normal gestational age has almost no increased risk for a hearing loss.

The problems of the low birth weight infant, often associated with such factors as jaundice and sepsis in addition to the use of ototoxic drugs, places him in a vulnerable position for a hearing loss.

At present, the exact percentages of infants with a hearing loss at 1500 g, 1800 g, and 2000 g is not known but it appears that the risk increases at lower weights.

Hyperbilirubinemia. Hyperbilirubinemia occurs in 6 per 1000 newborns, and of this group 2% to 4% will have a hearing loss due to Rh incompatibility.[4]

Currently, antibody screening in Rh-negative pregnancies and treatment during pregnancy or after birth is reducing this problem by over 97%. Other forms of neonatal jaundice are being treated with phototherapy and exchange transfusions; thus these methods should also reduce the incidence of hearing loss in jaundiced newborns.

Nevertheless, an infant with a bilirubin level of over 20 mg/100 ml or a rapidly rising bilirubin level with the last documented level at

15 mg/100 ml or a low birth weight newborn with a lower bilirubin—possibly as low as 10 mg/100 ml—are at risk and should have a follow-up hearing test. It is estimated that 2% to 4% of these newborns will have a hearing loss.

Congenital malformations. Certain malformations of the head are more commonly associated with a hearing loss.

Foremost among these is the newborn with a *cleft lip* and/or a *cleft palate,* who has a 99% chance of having bilateral serous otitis media that continues unabated for 2 to 6 years. Unfortunately, even though this hearing loss may be mild (15 to 30 dB), it occurs during the early formative years of speech and language development. When coupled with the other speech problems of cleft palate children (i.e., hypernasality, articulation problems, and possible tongue sensation abnormalities), the added loss of 15 to 30 dB handicaps the child even further. Myringotomy and repeated insertion of tubes into the eardrums to allow for middle ear drainage can overcome the hearing handicap.

Skull abnormalities should also signal the need for an early hearing test. Abnormal skull shapes, as in Crouzon and Apert syndromes, may be associated with a conductive hearing loss due to abnormal middle ear ossicles. Microcephaly and hydrocephalus are more commonly associated with a sensorineural hearing loss.

Pinna abnormalities such as a prominent ear, a cup ear, or helix-anthelix abnormalities may occasionally be associated with a hearing loss.

Meningitis. Neonatal meningitis may be caused by a wide variety of bacteria, and group B *Streptococcus* is the most common infectious agent. About 1% to 3% of all newborns and young children with meningitis will have a hearing loss. This may be due to involvement of the auditory nerve at the base of the skull or due to the infection spreading to the inner ear via the internal auditory canal, the endolymphatic sac and duct, or the cochlear duct. Clearly each newborn or child with meningitis should have a hearing test to assess any deafness after recovery. In most cases the sensorineural loss

is permanent, but we have seen a few children spontaneously improve over a period of months.

Ototoxic drugs. The aminoglycosides cause a hearing loss by damaging the hair cells of the cochlea. Kanamycin, gentamycin, neomycin, and streptomycin are currently potentially damaging drugs. It is difficult to predict what dosage is dangerous, since serum levels fluctuate and may not be related to perilymph or endolymph levels. Prospective studies relating serum levels in newborns to hearing loss are presently underway. These studies will aim at deciding if the significant factor is the peak serum level, the "trough" level, or other factors.

Since ototoxic drugs are given to newborns with multiple high-risk factors for hearing loss, each newborn given an ototoxic drug should have a hearing test by 2 months of age.

Significant perinatal asphyxia. In a number of series of congenitally deaf children, hypoxia or anoxia at birth has been recorded as a factor. In lieu of other known causes, a low Apgar score has been indicted as a high-risk factor for deafness. Research in animals has shown that hypoxia alone does not cause a sensorineural loss. Therefore one suspects that cofactors which may result in a hearing loss, such as prematurity or ototoxic drugs, may be present.

• • •

The Joint Committee* on Newborn Hearing Screening stated that an infant falling into these high-risk categories should be referred for an in-depth audiological evaluation within 2 months after discharge from the nursery. This is the most important step in management, since early diagnosis can lead to earlier and more successful intervention, which may minimize educational, speech, language, and behavioral problems.

WHEN TO SUSPECT A HEARING LOSS IN INFANTS OR CHILDREN

Parental concern. Very often a parent or a grandparent will suspect a hearing loss and report it to the primary care physician. Our policy as specialists is to accept the parental concern, and we recommend this acceptance to all physicians. In all cases the suspected child should have an audiological evaluation as soon as possible, regardless of the age. Testing can be done from the first day of life. When a physician takes the responsibility to decide that the parents are overanxious or that the infant indeed responds to some loud sounds and fails to refer the child for evaluation, the detection of the hearing loss may be delayed unnecessarily with resultant irrevocable harm to the child.[7] The burden should not be on the primary care physician to document the hearing loss. For parents even to voice this concern means that they have made multiple observations at home, have reason to suspect a loss, and have overcome a fear of voicing their concern. The physician *must* respect their observation and obtain direct referral to refute or sustain their concern.

History of otitis media under 6 months of age or recurrent otitis media under 2 years of age. Otologists and pediatricians are becoming increasingly aware that newborns can have middle ear effusions and/or otitis media. Such factors as low birth weight associated with being small for gestational age, sepsis, need for intensive care, and prolonged nasogastric intubation seem to place certain newborns at greater risk for middle ear disease. Regardless of the etiological factor or factors, the newborn is at risk for a chronic middle ear effusion, which may be sterile or associated with bacteria. Unfortunately, this fluid tends to remain for months or even 1 to 2 years, producing a mild bilateral hearing loss. At this age no speech or language problem exists, and it may not ever be noticed until age 3 or 4. (Yet, the time to detect this hearing loss is when the infant is as young as possible, since early management can avoid the sequelae of abnormal speech or delayed language.) In general, parents notice that their children seem to have a speech or language problem by the age of 3 to 4 years. Parents become aware of their child's hearing loss a short time before the awareness of speech problems. Although the hearing loss was probably present earlier, parents may have lower expectations of language development and are simply not knowledgeable about subtle symptoms. On obtaining a history, it is often discovered that a diagnosis of otitis media was made before 6 months of age and infrequently found that the infant had drainage from the ears before 6 months of age.

Why the fluid should persist has not yet been researched, but multiple factors could be implicated. First, the eustachian tube function may have been altered ever since birth, and this may be chronic in nature. Second, the eustachian tube size may be smaller than normal. There probably is a random distribution of sizes of the eustachian tube lumen, and since the normal size is 1 mm at its narrowest portion, any decrease in size might prevent the viscous middle ear fluid from flowing down the eustachian tube. Third, the fluid in the middle ear may be gluelike, that is, so viscous and tenacious that it would not even pass down a normal-sized eustachian tube. Fourth, it is possible that the neonatal infection established a chronically inflamed middle ear mucosa, which pours out a mucoid or serous fluid, constantly filling the middle ear. This fluid may remain asymptomatically in the middle ear and produces no pain, fever, or discomfort, such as pulling on the ears.

On the other hand, the fluid in the middle ear is a good culture medium. Thus whenever some children have an upper respiratory infection, they have an associated otitis media with recurrent episodes of otitis media before age 2 years.

Chronic serous otitis media. It should be axiomatic that fluid in the middle ear does cause a hearing loss. Typically the fluid accumulation occurs in both ears, with the hearing impairment ranging from mild to moderate. In some of these children language delay and speech, educational, behavioral, social, and psychological problems may occur temporarily or, uncommonly, permanently.

Failure in school hearing test. There is a wide variation of how and when hearing tests are performed in schools throughout the country. Some are well performed and can be accepted as reliable. Others are done poorly, such as those with inadequately calibrated audiometers. Nevertheless, when a child does fail a school hearing test, the child should be referred for audiological evaluation. It is not enough to examine the ears and find no wax and a normal middle ear and thus declare that the ear is normal and therefore the test must have been in error. There are sensorineural losses as well as an occasional ossicular problem that are invisible to the examining physician. Only a carefully administered audiogram will determine the extent, the nature, and the seriousness of the loss.

Speech problems and language delay. Although there are many reasons for speech and language problems in children, examination of hearing must be included as part of a basic evaluation. A bilateral hearing loss in an otherwise normal child is capable of producing problems of either phonology (such as articulation, phonation, and inflection) or syntactics (semantical content of language) for the child.

Children with mental retardation or cerebral palsy may have speech and language problems due to their basic disorders. Rather than attributing a speech and language problem solely to the neurological disorder, a hearing test should be routinely requested. From 10% to 30% of these children will have an associated hearing loss and specific remediation is important; the child with a speech problem and a hearing loss will require a habilitative program quite distinct from the neurologically damaged child who has a speech problem and normal hearing. A hearing aid, parental counselling, teaching-listening skills, and utilization of the services of a teacher for the deaf or hard of hearing make up the early habilitative package for a hearing impaired child.

OFFICE ASSESSMENT FOR DETECTING A HEARING LOSS

History. The physician must be alert to the at-risk categories (p. 252) for hearing loss. In obtaining information specific to a potential hearing problem, it may be helpful to ask the parents the following questions:

1. Have you any worry about your child's hearing?
2. Does he turn his head toward an interesting sound or when his name is called?
3. Does he try to imitate you if you make his own sounds?
4. Is he beginning to repeat some of the sounds that you make?

In assessing the answers to the questions, the physician must bear in mind that deafness is seldom total and that a youngster with a significant hearing loss might not be detected by the answers to these questions. Therefore it is also necessary to observe the infant's responses to sound.

Behavioral observation. Table 10-1 gives the normative localization responses in infants. The sound source is usually something of interest such as a bell or rattle.

In testing the child the physician must use extreme care to avoid a pseudoresponse. The hearing impaired child is invariably visually alert and will respond to almost any movement in his peripheral vision. He is also very alert to vibratory and tactile information, and it is not uncommon for the child to make nonauditory responses and thus avoid detection. Therefore the physician must be sure that the sound source is out of the child's visual field. The sound must be moved from one side of the head to the other to determine the relative acuity of each ear. The tester must use a variety of sound sources such as bells of varying intensity and frequency or rattles to help keep the child interested in the localizing task.

Older hearing impaired children will respond to tuning fork testing, although these give only estimates of the degree and type of hearing loss. The comprehensive audiometric evaluation is by far the best method for assessing degree of loss. A 512 Hz tuning fork should be used, not a 128 Hz as used for neurological testing of vibration sense. The Rinne test is performed as follows: after striking the tuning fork, the tine is placed 2.5 cm from the pinna (air conduction) and then firmly pressed on the mastoid process (bone conduction). Normally air conduction is louder than bone conduction (a positive Rinne

Table 10-1. Development of the localization response in infants*

Age (months)	Response	Final	Initial
3	Infant turns head to side at which sound is presented		
3 to 4	Infant turns head toward sound and eyes go in the same direction		
5 to 6	Infant turns head to one side and downward, if the sound is made below the ear		
6	Infant turns head to one side and then upward, if the sound is made above the level of the ear		
6 to 8	Infant turns head in a curving arc toward the sound source		
8 to 10	Infant turns head diagonally toward the sound source		
13 to 15	Infant turns eyes and head upward to sound source		

*From Murphy, K.: Hear. News **29**:9, 1961.

test). In an ear with a hearing loss, a positive Rinne test would indicate a sensorineural loss (i.e., due to a problem of the cochlea or auditory nerve). If bone conduction is louder than air conduction (a negative Rinne test), the hearing loss is conductive (i.e., due to a problem in the ear canal, tympanic membrane, or middle ear).

The Schwabach test is performed by holding the tuning fork near the child's ear until he reports no sound, and then placing the tuning fork near the physician's own ear. If the physician hears a loud tone, there may be a severe loss at the frequency of the tuning fork; if the physician hears a soft tone, there may be a mild loss.

There are children who may have near normal hearing at 512 Hz and whose hearing drops precipitously above that frequency. This kind of loss can only be detected by using a higher frequency tuning fork or formal audiometry.

Physical exam of the ear

Pinna. The pinna is remarkably similar from person to person. Any malformation of the pinna may be associated with a middle ear or inner ear anomaly, since both regions develop from the first and second branchial arches. Fig. 10-1 demonstrates that the pinna can be simplified by recalling two lines: an outer curved helix and an inner anthelix, which divides into a superior and inferior crus.

Any missing cartilage fold or any extra fold may be a harbinger of a malformation affecting hearing, at least in that particular ear. Examples are shown in Fig. 10-2.

Ear canal examination. The size of the ear canal may be another subtle clue to a middle ear malformation. At the following various ages, specific otoscope speculum tip sizes can be used.

Age of child	Size of speculum (mm)
Birth to 6 months	2
6 months to 2 years	3
2 years to 5 years	4
5 years and older	5

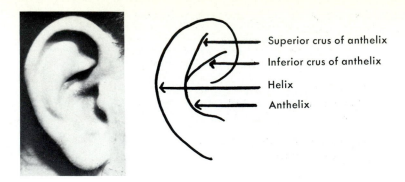

Superior crus of anthelix

Inferior crus of anthelix

Helix

Anthelix

Fig. 10-1. Comparison of the normal pinna, left, with a sketch, right, showing how to draw a pinna utilizing only two lines.

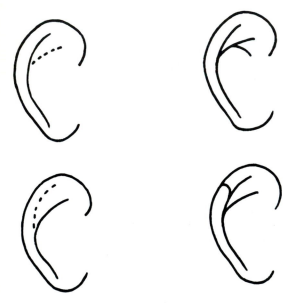

Fig. 10-2. A "missing line" on a pinna, both on left; an "extra line" on a pinna, both on right. A congenital malformation of the middle or inner ear may coexist with these minor anomalies.

When a speculum used is two sizes smaller than anticipated, a diagnosis of "canal stenosis" seems reasonable. That is, a 4-year-old child with an ear canal that admits only a 2 mm speculum tip has a canal stenosis. An associated middle ear ossicular problem causing a hearing loss should be suspected.

Tympanic membrane. The entire eardrum should be examined. Often this requires considerable moving of the otoscope or patient's head to readjust the directional view. Positive identification of the short process of the malleus should be the first goal, since it is a constant

and important eardrum landmark (Fig. 10-3). Noting that the short process is normal is more important than looking for the light reflex, which is so often unrelated to disease of the middle ear. Changes in the appearance of the short process are well correlated with middle ear disease.

The eardrum should be translucent gray. The light reflex only means that the light is striking the drum and reflecting back into the examiner's eye. Much pathology can exist even with a normal light reflex. On the other hand, an absent light reflex may not relate to significant ear disease.

The malleus is examined for anomalies. The malleus handle may be broadened and shortened, thin and discontinuous, grossly malformed, etc. If the eardrum moves inward on pneumatic otoscopy, the short process and handle should move. If they fail to move but the drum moves, a malleus fixation may be present.

The incus is then sought, and it can be detected in approximately 50% of children. Just because it is not seen does not mean that an anomaly is present. However, if it is seen and is discontinuous or grossly malformed, a resultant hearing loss of up to 60 dB will occur.

The stapes is never normally seen. If the round stapes head is seen (Fig. 10-4), it means that part of the incus long process is absent due to infection, a congenital anomaly, or trauma.

Pneumatic otoscopy. It is most important in children that the eardrum movement be assessed with pneumatic otoscopy. Normally the middle

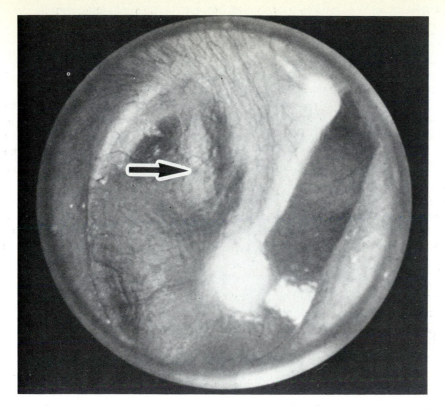

Fig. 10-3. Normal right tympanic membrane. Long process of the incus (arrow) is visible behind the normal tympanic membrane.

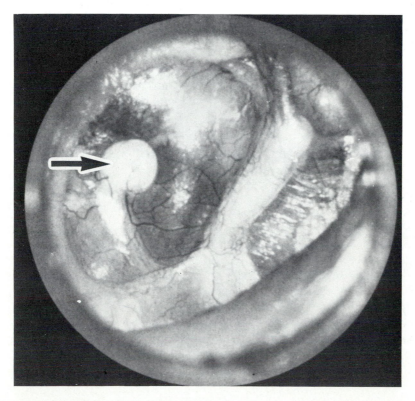

Fig. 10-4. Round head of the stapes (arrow), indicating destruction of a portion of the incus long process.

ear is filled with compressible air, so the tympanic membrane can be moved inward with positive pressure and then outward with negative pressure. The most common cause of hearing loss in children is fluid in the middle ear, which is noncompressible and will impair the brisker inward movement of the tympanic membrane.

The pneumatic test is reliable if a tight seal exists at all joints in the otoscope head and between the ear canal and ear canal speculum tip. If the tympanic membrane fails to move, it is important to test the system for leaks. First, place a finger over the speculum tip, squeeze the bulb, and make certain a resistance is felt while squeezing the bulb. If there is a leak, the bulb resistance to squeezing is poor and an air leak will be heard as air emerges from the open site (i.e., where the rubber bulb attaches to the nipple of the otoscope head, where the magnifying lens fits into the otoscope head, or where the speculum base pushes onto the otoscope head).

Choosing the largest possible speculum tip will provide a better seal with the ear canal. Even this area may leak, however, so one must listen for air leaks while examining the tympanic membrane.

THE OTOLARYNGOLOGICAL CONSULTATION

When to refer. As discussed more fully earlier, a referral should be considered in any of the following cases:

1. Newborn with a high risk for deafness (p. 252)
2. Infant or child in whom a parent even *suspects* a hearing loss (p. 251)
3. Infant with otitis media onset under 6 months of age
4. Infant or child with four or more bouts of otitis media per year
5. Infant or child with chronic serous otitis media (i.e., over 6 weeks)
6. Child who fails a school hearing test
7. Child with speech abnormalities or language delay
8. Child with failure of office screening

The otolaryngologist's evaluation. The oto-laryngologist will review the history in more detail and will reexamine the child. This physician can more easily clean out wax to better assess the tympanic membrane.

The next task is to determine if a *conductive loss* is present. Common middle ear problems exist, such as fluid or infection in the middle ear. The otolaryngologist will be able to recognize uncommon problems, such as a fixed malleus head, by observing the absence of the malleus motion during pneumatic otoscopy or a malformed incus that might be fixed to surrounding bone by observing a bulky mass in the posterior superior quadrant of the middle ear. The otolaryngologist may detect an attic retraction that has otherwise gone undetected, sometimes giving rise to a cholesteatoma, which destroys the incus long process. This physician may detect a perforation that is hidden by a bulging canal wall but which can be detected by hearing air rush out of the ear canal when performing a Valsalva maneuver (i.e., ask child to squeeze nose shut, close mouth, and blow nose hard). The otolaryngologist may remove a crust from the tympanic membrane that obscures a chronic perforation.

The pneumatic otoscope is the basis for any ear examination, although increasingly more otolaryngologists have operating microscopes available in the office, too. A frightened child must be handled carefully, both emotionally and physically. Delicate instruments used under the microscope can clean out wax or crusts that obscure the true pathology.

If no middle ear pathology is found, a *sensorineural loss* is considered. The otolaryngologist will look for congenital syndromes associated with sensorineural loss, which are listed on p. 254.

THE AUDIOLOGICAL EVALUATION

After the otolaryngologist completes the physical examination, the patient will be referred for an in-depth audiological evaluation. An audiologist holds a masters or a doctorate degree and may possess a certificate of clinical competence (CCC) in audiology issued by the American Speech and Hearing Association. The audiologist may work in a speech and hearing clinic in a hospital, in a community, in a private clinic, or in an otolaryngologist's office. Close cooperation between the audiologist, otolaryngologist, and primary care physician is essential for the best patient management.

Audiological tests are administered at comprehensive audiological facilities; they may not be within the scope of a practicing physician's office area because of the sound proof chamber and sophisticated equipment needed to administer a definitive test to a child. These tests are included here to acquaint the physician with the kinds of tests that are available for the very young child and to make audiological reports more understandable.

Current technology is such that reasonably definitive statements about a child's hearing can be made from birth onward in most cases. The method of choice for most audiologists is behavioral and observational techniques. By the use of graded noisemakers (squeaky toys for high frequency, cellophane for mid frequency, drum for low frequency) and carefully calibrated speech stimuli, startle responses in the newborn infant are readily observable. This can be used as a screening device in the primary care setting, employing the precautions previously noted. The somewhat older infant can be conditioned to respond to a light source by use of the Conditioned Orientation Reflex (COR) audiometry.[6] This procedure employs lighted transparent toys that are flashed on simultaneously with the presentation of an audi-

tory signal. Responses are noted when the sound is presented without the lights as the child searches for the lighted toys. In play audiometry, the clinician conditions the child to respond in some overt manner to an auditory stimulus, for example, placing a block on a ring stand. Conditioning can be entirely programmed using an operant procedure, a technique known as Tangible Reinforcement Operant Conditioning Audiometry (TROCA).[6] It was developed for use with retarded children and has also been very successful with normal young children.

There are several so-called objective tests that do not require the active participation of the child. Probably the most revolutionary and exciting development has been impedance audiometry, sometimes referred to as tympanometry. This technique involves the measurement of the reflected energy from the tympanic membrane. Examination of the tympanogram enables one to distinguish among the various middle ear pathologies and can also determine if there is a normal middle ear function. This is important in determining that a sensorineural loss is present in that it can eliminate the possibility of a conductive loss. Impedance audiometry is usually quite easy to administer and does not require the active cooperation of the child, although it takes a skilled clinician to obtain a good seal and to interpret results.

Considerable research attention has been paid the last few years to Evoked Response Audiom-

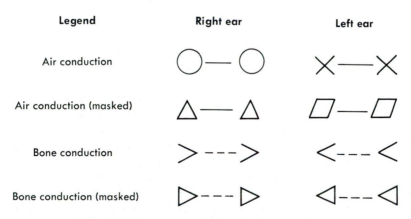

Fig. 10-5. Standard legends for audiogram recording.

etry (ERA).[6] In this technique the cortical and brain stem response to auditory signals are read through a computer to separate auditory responses from the random "noise" of cortical activity. The application of these results to clinical testing is being intensively investigated; these tests are generally used when all others have failed to yield reliable results, such as in the cases of mentally retarded and autistic children. It is important to remember the children with autistic behavior may also be hearing impaired or deaf.

The interested physician might wish to consult *Hearing in Children* by Northern and Downs[6] for detailed information on these tests.

By far the most common audiological test is the pure tone audiogram. This test is administered by using a calibrated audiometer that emits pure tones in octave bands from 125 to 8000 Hz. The results are recorded on an audiogram in which the frequency (pitch of the sound) is recorded on the horizontal axis and intensity in decibels (dB) is recorded on the vertical axis. Generally the right ear is recorded in red and the left ear in blue.

Air conduction hearing levels are tested with earphones, generally using specific frequencies of 250, 500, 1000, 2000, 4000, and 8000 Hz pure tones. This tests the entire system from ear canal to the auditory cortex via the middle ear, cochlea, eighth nerve, and brain stem.

Bone conduction hearing levels are tested by a mastoid vibrator using specific frequencies from 500 to 4000 Hz pure tones. This tests the hearing from the cochlea to the auditory cortex.

Fig. 10-5 shows standard legends used for audiometric recording. Normal levels of air and bone conduction hearing should be between −10 dB to 15 dB. The larger the dB number required for hearing, the greater the loss. A mild loss is 20 to 40 dB, a moderate loss 40 to 60 dB, a severe loss from 60 to 80 dB, and a profound loss over 80 dB.

Masking is given to the better hearing ear to prevent it from hearing a louder sound presented to the poorer ear. If not done, it would appear that the hearing level of the poor ear was better than it really is because the sound was actually heard in the unmasked better ear. Masking is therefore essential if the difference in hearing acuity between the two ears is approximately 40 dB for air conduction and approximately 10 dB for bone conduction.

Conductive hearing losses. A conductive loss refers to results of an audiogram with a normal bone conduction level but a depressed air conduction level. The difference between the bone and air levels is referred to as the "air-bone" gap. The maximum air-bone gap is 60 dB. That is, if the entire middle ear is destroyed, there will still be hearing in the ear with a threshold at 60 dB. A conductive loss refers to a problem involving the ear canal, tympanic membrane, and/or middle ear.

Fig. 10-6 demonstrates a small conductive loss with an air-bone gap of 20 dB. Fig. 10-7 demonstrates a large conductive loss with an air-bone gap of 50 dB.

Sensorineural hearing losses. A sensorineural loss refers to results of an audiogram with equal air and bone conduction levels. No air-bone gap exists. The maximum sensorineural hearing loss is 110 dB. A sensorineural loss refers to problems involving the cochlea ("sensory" hair cells) or auditory nerve ("neural").

Often the ability to discriminate words is impaired even if presented loudly enough and above the threshold at which the words should be discernible and clear.

Fig. 10-8 demonstrates a sensorineural loss involving high frequencies, and Fig. 10-9 demonstrates a sensorineural loss involving low frequencies. Speech discrimination is worse in the case presented in Fig. 10-8 because of the severity of the high-frequency involvement. Fig. 10-10 demonstrates a total bilateral sensorineural loss. Fig. 10-11 demonstrates a sensorineural dip at 400 Hz that does not interfere with communication.

Mixed hearing loss. In some children there is a combined conductive and sensorineural hearing loss. The bone conduction will be abnormal but the air conduction will be even more depressed. Fig. 10-12 demonstrates a mixed loss with a depressed bone conduction and air-bone gap.

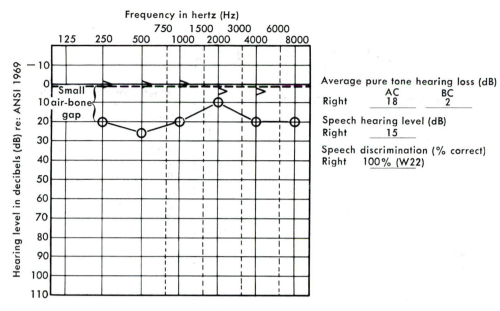

Fig. 10-6. Conductive hearing loss with a small (20 dB) air-bone gap, often seen with (1) acute otitis media, (2) serous otitis media, and (3) moderate-sized tympanic membrane perforation. (From Jaffe, B.: Hearing loss in children—a comprehensive text, Baltimore, 1977, University Park Press.)

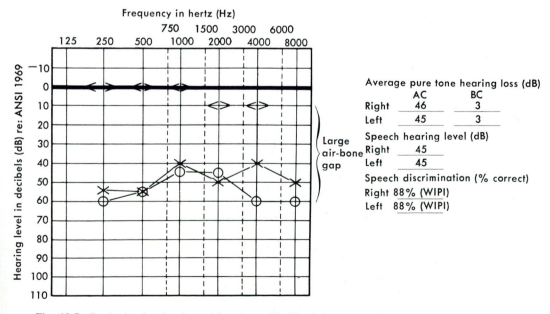

Fig. 10-7. Conductive hearing loss with a large (50 dB) air-bone gap, often seen with (1) middle ear congenital anomaly and (2) ossicular chain disruption. (From Jaffe, B.: Hearing loss in children—a comprehensive text, Baltimore, 1977, University Park Press.)

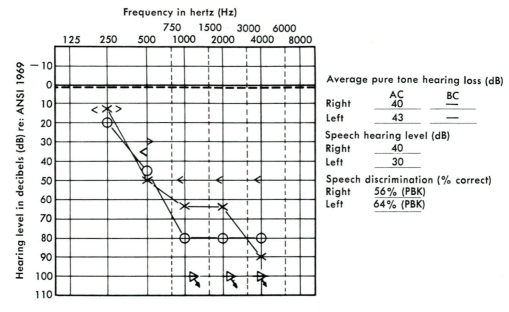

Fig. 10-8. Sensorineural hearing loss involving high frequencies with no air-bone gap, often seen with (1) prematurity and (2) dominant progressive sensorineural hearing loss. (From Jaffe, B.: Hearing loss in children—a comprehensive text, Baltimore, 1977, University Park Press.)

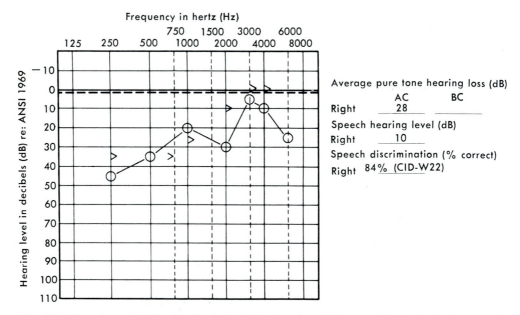

Fig. 10-9. Sensorineural hearing loss involving low frequencies, often seen with (1) Meniere disease and (2) others as dominant low-frequency sensorineural hearing loss. (From Jaffe, B.: Hearing loss in children—a comprehensive text, Baltimore, 1977, University Park Press.)

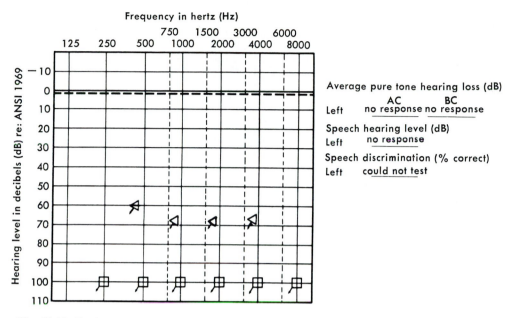

Fig. 10-10. Total sensorineural hearing loss, often seen with (1) meningitis and (2) congenital deafness. (From Jaffe, B.: Hearing loss in children—a comprehensive text, Baltimore, 1977, University Park Press.)

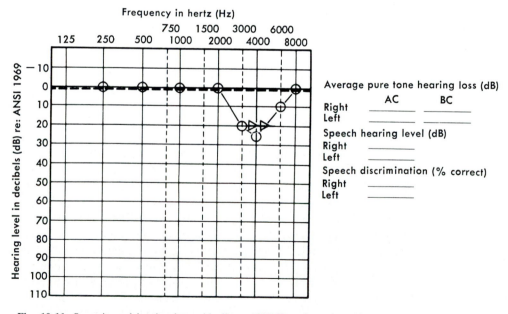

Fig. 10-11. Sensorineural hearing loss with dip at 4000 Hz, often seen with (1) "noise-induced" hearing loss and (2) viral cochleitis. (From Jaffe, B.: Hearing loss in children—a comprehensive text, Baltimore, 1977, University Park Press.)

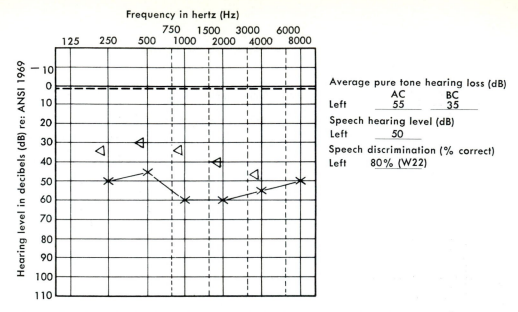

Fig. 10-12. Mixed hearing loss, often seen with (1) chronic otitis media and (2) some congenital or hereditary disorders. (From Jaffe, B.: Hearing loss in children—a comprehensive text, Baltimore, 1977, University Park Press.)

Educational implications

David M. Luterman

The extent of the handicap of deafness is seldom appreciated. The children look normal and the effects of the hearing defect are not immediately apparent. The congenitally deaf child is, in the main, a severely language impaired child. Language is the medium by which our culture and the bulk of information is transmitted to the child; consequently, the deaf child has a formidable handicap in all areas of education. The results of educational programming for the deaf have been very discouraging. "More than one half of the deaf population does not complete high school and 28% have only an eighth grade education or less. The average achievement of the deaf on the Stanford achievement test is equivalent to grade 4.3."[6a] Helen Keller herself, when asked which sensory defect she most minded, replied the deafness, ". . . . it keeps me from the sound of the human voice that brings language, sets thoughts astir and keeps us in the intellectual company of man."

All educators of the hearing impaired agree on the need for early identification and for early amplification. Beyond that there is little agreement in the field. The major controversy lies in whether or not some forms of manual communication should be introduced into the educational program. The dispute between those using some form of manualism (now called Total Communication) and those not permitting any (oralists) has been present in one form or another for over 200 years, and it does not look amenable to solution. What is beginning to clearly emerge is that each method is right and appropriate for certain children. The orally successful children seem to have somewhat better hearing, be otherwise intact, and have very supportive families. Any community should be able to provide both Total Communication and oral forms of education, and the responsible physician must see that the community provides such alternatives. The pediatrician must also keep informed as to referral sources in the community. In particular, the physician should be aware of the nearest facility containing a comprehensive audiological-otological program.

Educational programs for the deaf child have been expanding rapidly. Formerly there were very limited educational alternatives, and almost all severely hearing impaired children were educated within a school for the deaf. This was generally a highly restricted environment and most programs were residential in nature. Recent educational thinking has tended to promote the inclusion of handicapped children within the general educational milieu. Recent federal legislation, PL 94-142, has mandated that handicapped children be educated in the least restricted environment, which means that many more hearing impaired children will be integrating with normally hearing children; the integration of the handicapped with the non-handicapped is referred to as mainstreaming. The federal legislation calls for the formulation of an education plan known as the "individualized educational plan" (IEP) for each child. The plan will be written by the school personnel in conjunction with the child's parents. When possible, information and suggestions from other professionals, including physicians, are actively solicted, and it is expected that primary care physicians will have an increasingly more active role in determining the child's educational future.

HEARING AIDS

The hearing aid is often thought of as having corrective powers. The parents frequently use eyeglasses as an analogy, "If you have an eye problem, you put on glasses and you can see; therefore, the hearing aid will enable my child to hear." Unfortunately this reasoning is not appropriate to the congenitally deaf child. In the first place, the hearing is actually a central phenomenon in which the cortex interprets the neural impulses generated by hair cell activity in the inner ear. If there is no stored information in the cortex to process the incoming impulses, the child will remain functionally deaf, and this is the case with the congenitally impaired child. Second, the hearing aids themselves are merely amplifying systems, they take sound and make it louder. They cannot do anything to correct the distortion produced by a malfunctioning inner ear; consequently the child perceives a distorted signal with the aid. It is only after extensive training and use that the hearing impaired child begins to respond to sounds, and seemingly very deaf children can be taught to utilize their remaining residual hearing.

All hearing aids have three component parts. There is a microphone that converts sound energy to electrical energy, an amplifier that increases the flow of electrons, and a receiver that converts the electrical energy back into acoustic energy. There must also be a power source, which is usually a nickel alloy battery, although there are several hearing aids on the market that have rechargeable batteries. The hearing aid is fitted to an ear mold, which is individually constructed to conform to the child's external auditory meatus. The ear mold must be kept clean; the lumen can be cleared regularly with a pipe cleaner. Constant use of the hearing aid will tend to cause an accumulation of wax in the external meatus. The primary care physician must be alert to this possibility and must examine and clean the aided ear, if needed.

As a general rule, the larger the hearing aid, the more powerful the unit, although the limiting factor is not so much the size of the unit as the distance between the microphone and the receiver. When these two parts of the hearing aid are not shielded from one another, a feedback squeal is heard, rendering the aid inoperative. It is imperative that the child have a tight fitting ear mold. One way of determining if the aid is operative is for the physician to take the ear mold out and place it near the microphone to see if there is a feedback squeal.

There are generally three kinds of hearing aids: an on the body aid, a behind the ear instrument, and an all in the ear unit. Selection of the proper hearing aid is a matter of careful audiological testing; when possible, speech materials are used to select the aid. For the very young child, speech materials may not be possible and the audiologist must rely on controlled observation and input from the parents and teachers to select the aid. Initial aids are usually chosen for their versatility as far as power and frequency response are concerned to allow the audiologist to adjust the aid in accordance with the increased data obtained from repeated tests.

EFFECTS ON THE COMMUNITY

There is a cost to society for hearing handicapped children. For those with mild to moderate hearing losses who are not diagnosed, there will be unexplained difficulties in school that may be labeled as learning disabilities. Special education teachers must be hired and supported through local or state taxes. Because speech development is usually impaired, speech therapists will be needed in larger numbers to correct articulation and phonological problems in these children.

For those with moderate to severe losses, schools will need specialized classrooms or programs for hearing impaired children. Special schools may even be needed. Forces within the community will either favor this decision or will consider the needs as being too special or too expensive to meet. Yet this is specious thinking. A productive hearing impaired citizen yields varied benefits to society and himself, whereas a poorly educated, nonproductive hearing impaired citizen wastes his own life and continuously drains services from society. It is the responsibility of all concerned professionals to identify the hearing impaired child as early as possible and to rapidly institute a habilitative program.

REFERENCES

1. Eichenwald, H. F.: Human toxoplasmosis. In proceedings of the Conference on Clinical Aspects and Diagnostic Problems of Toxoplasmosis in Pediatrics, Baltimore, 1956, The Williams & Wilkins Co.
2. Horstmann, D. M.: Letter to editor, N. Engl. J. Med. **283:**1292, Dec. 3, 1970.
3. Jaffe, B.: Hearing loss in children—a comprehensive text, Baltimore, 1977, University Park Press.
4. Keaster, J., Hyman, C. B., and Harris, I.: Hearing problems subsequent to neonatal hemolytic disease of hyperbilirubinemia, Am. J. Dis. Child. **117:**406, 1969.
5. McDonald, A.: Children of very low birth weight, Spastics Society Medical Education and Information Unit Research Monograph no. 1, London, 1977, William Heinemann Medical Books Ltd.
5a. Murphy, K.: Development of hearing in babies, Hear. News **29:**9, 1961.
6. Northern, J., and Downs, M.: Hearing in children, Baltimore, 1975, The Williams & Wilkins Co., pp. 122-123.
6a. Schein, J., and Delk, C.: The deaf population of the United States, Silver Springs, Md., 1974, National Association of the Deaf.
7. Shah, C. P., et al.: Delay in referral of children with impaired hearing, Volta Rev. **80:**206, 1978.
8. Stagno, S., et al.: Auditory and visual defects resulting from symptomatic and subclinical congenital cytomegaloviral and toxoplasma infections, Pediatrics **59:**669, 1977.

11

Ophthalmic aspects of developmental disabilities

Richard M. Robb
Carol M. Donovan

Ophthalmic considerations in the developmentally disabled child

Richard M. Robb

The pediatrician or general physician is in an ideal position to identify eye or vision problems and to make appropriate referrals to an ophthalmologist, the medical eye specialist who deals with the broad range of eye disorders that can occur in childhood. Occasionally minor problems, such as conjunctivitis, corneal abrasions, or surface foreign bodies, can be dealt with directly by the pediatrician, but most of the more serious eye diseases require the special diagnostic skills and treatment modalities of the ophthalmologist. Any physician who performs well-child examinations at regular intervals can offer the important service of checking the eyes and vision of patients in a manner appropriate to the child's age. In addition to the obvious advantages of early recognition and treatment of disease, there is the special gain of ensuring that both eyes of the child will be used to their full potential during the early years, thus avoiding any loss of vision from disuse, the so-called amblyopia ex anopsia that accompanies some pediatric eye disorders. This form of visual loss does not occur in adults; it is characteristic of the more pliable visual system of a child and can be successfully reversed only during childhood years. In developmentally disabled children the effort to recognize eye and vision problems carries the added reward of restoring one of the major avenues of sensory contact with the environment to individuals who may lack other sources of stimuli.

OPHTHALMIC EVALUATION
Assessment of vision

Any eye examination should begin with an attempt to assess visual acuity. The examination of a developmentally disabled child is no exception to this rule, although for such a child it is often difficult to obtain a quantitative estimate of vision when behavioral responses are limited. In infancy, testing of vision is usually based on visual fixation and following responses.These are tested by moving an object of visual interest in front of the child and watching to see whether the eyes turn toward the object and follow its movement back and forth in the visual field. The object of visual interest can be a face, a flashlight, or a brightly colored toy. Although adding sound to the test object might theoretically compromise its purity as a visual stimulus, in practice a light that rattles or a toy that squeaks is often more effective in gaining an infant's visual attention. The size of the object and its distance from the patient are not critical, since one is not trying to quantitate visual acuity. Full-term normal infants under ideal circumstances can fix and follow objects at birth, but such responses become much more obvious to parents at 6 weeks to 2 months of age.[9] If visual fixation and following are not present by 4 months of age, further eye examination is certainly indicated. Of course, an eye problem will not always be found, since visual inattention may be based on delayed development of the brain as well as on a specific ocular problem. Nevertheless, an eye examination should be done, and it should include examination of the ocular fundus through dilated pupils. The best view of the interior of the eye at this age can be obtained with the indirect ophthalmoscope, an instrument seldom used by nonophthalmologists. In practice, then, this examination should be done by an ophthalmologist. Anesthesia is almost never needed for this initial assessment.

In addition to the fixation and following responses, other clinical findings may be helpful in evaluating an infant's vision. Pupillary reactions to light are present at birth, and their absence or asymmetry is a definite abnormality. Inequality of the pupillary reactions to light due to an afferent defect is known as the Marcus Gunn pupillary sign. It is easily tested by swinging a flashlight from one eye to the other. Both pupils dilate when the light is directed toward the eye with the afferent defect, and they constrict when it is shifted back to the more normal eye. The test is useful in distinguishing unilateral retinal or optic nerve disease. Unsteadiness of the eyes, either rhythmical nystagmus or irregular wandering movements, is also abnormal at this age. The nystagmus may arise from a primary oculomotor neurological defect, or it may reflect poor vision of any cause. The latter sensory type of nystagmus is characteristically present when vision is lost before 2 years of age.

A number of more elaborate methods of testing infants' vision have been used in recent years, each an attempt to quantitate the vision of patients unable to give subjective responses. These methods are mentioned briefly because of their possible applicability to individuals with developmental retardation. Optokinetic nystagmus, the rhythmical oscillation of the eyes induced by passing a pattern of alternating black and white stripes in front of the eyes, can be elicited from the time of birth and is linked to visual acuity measurements by adjusting the stripe width of the testing drum.[6] Evoked occipital potentials have also been used as a parameter of visual function. These electrical potentials, representing brain activity in the visual cortex, are induced by repetitive light stimuli. The relatively small individual responses are summated by computer and can be observed to vary with the check size of the patterned stimuli.[25] Preferential looking tests, which offer another means of measuring visual function, have been modified for clinical use in early infancy.[8] They measure vision by noting an infant's preference for a patterned stimulus over a plain one when the two are presented simultaneously (Fig. 11-1). This preference disappears when the pattern is too fine to be resolved by the infant's visual system. The preferential looking test appears to be especially helpful in infants whose behavioral responses are delayed. When available, these several kinds of tests may supplement the information gained from an initial

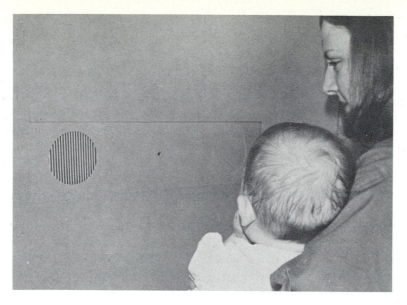

Fig. 11-1. Testing an infant's vision by preferential-looking technique. Infants tend to look toward the striped disc rather than the plain one when the stripes are wide enough to be distinguished. Observer judges infant's fixation pattern from behind screen through the small central hole.

clinical examination, but, of course, they are not a substitute for it.

Subjective testing of visual acuity

When a child is able to respond by naming pictures or by pointing in the direction of the "fingers" of an E symbol, a subjective visual acuity can be obtained.[1] Some examiners prefer to use the Screening Test for Young Children And Retardates (STYCAR), in which the letters T, H, V, and O on a distant chart are matched with similar letters on flash cards within reach.[27] For a normal child, subjective testing is usually possible by 3 years of age. For an individual with developmental retardation, these early tests may be useful at a much later age. As soon as possible a whole chart of symbols should be used, since single symbols may give a falsely optimistic estimate of vision, especially in an amblyopic eye. Ideally, testing is done at 6 m, so that nearsightedness (myopia) will be picked up. In the near range myopes may have normal acuity. With this one reservation, vision can be tested at less than 6 m if the test symbols are appropriately reduced in size. 20/40 is usually accepted as normal visual acuity at 3 years of age. 20/30 is normal at 4

years, and many children attain 20/20 vision by age 5 to 6. The numerator in the fraction represents the test distance (in feet) used; the denominator is the distance at which a normal adult should see similar symbols. The eyes are usually tested separately with the aid of an eye patch or a lorgnette occluder. With this technique one must be alert to identify the occasional patient with occlusion nystagmus (p. 278), for whom the visual acuity will be falsely low when tested with one eye covered and more nearly normal when both eyes are tested together. Since most children with farsightedness (hyperopia) can accommodate to overcome their refractive error, small to moderate degrees of hyperopia may be overlooked in these tests of visual acuity. Significantly large degrees of hyperopia usually are recognized when they cause accommodative crossing of the eyes or when the necessary accommodation cannot be sustained and the vision becomes blurred, whatever the testing distance. It must be borne in mind that visual function can be expressed only partially in numerical terms. For many patients with retarded development a descriptive statement may be as helpful as a numerical expression in conveying visual capabilities.

Recognition of strabismus

The ability to detect overt misalignment of the eyes in children is of great importance because strabismus is such a common eye problem in childhood and because early detection is at the heart of successful management of the condition. The recognition of strabismus is made much easier when a child's point of fixation is known and can be controlled. The simplest and best device to control fixation is a small hand-held flashlight. Most infants will look at such a light and follow it with interest, and when the light is directed toward their eyes, it provides a useful additional landmark—the corneal light reflex—by which to judge which eye is straight and which is deviated. The corneal reflex is usually centered in the pupil of the fixing eye and somewhat off center in the deviated eye. The examiner chooses which eye is fixing directly on the light and covers that eye with a hand or an occluder, watching for a jump of the other eye as it takes up fixation. This is the cover test, which can be done easily in the pediatrician's office. Since a very small jump of the nonfixing eye can be seen, this test is highly sensitive and can be used to recognize even small degrees of misalignment. The test can be repeated as long as the child is willing to look at the flashlight. An attempt by the child to look around the occluder held before one eye may indicate poor vision in the fellow eye, especially if the objection to occlusion is more marked on one side than the other.

It is also quite helpful to have a fixation device, usually a noise-making toy, located at some distance from the patient and examiner. With the patient fixing on this distant target, the cover test can be repeated. An outward deviation of the eye (exotropia) is more frequently seen with this distant fixation, whereas an inward deviation or crossing of an eye (esotropia) is more often brought out by testing in the near range.

If the patient has a strong preference for fixation with one eye, the preferred eye will usually jump back to the straight position when the cover is removed from it. With an alternating fixation pattern, the deviation may seem to change as the cover test is done first over one eye and then over the other. A latent ocular deviation (phoria) may become manifest if the occluder is alternated from one eye to the other, but such a phoria should never induce a jump in the simple cover test.

Tests for binocularity are occasionally used to screen vision and detect strabismus.[21] They customarily measure stereoacuity or look for simultaneous perception of objects that are seen independently by the two eyes. These tests are not specific for strabismus, since they are failed by individuals with poor vision from any cause and occasionally they do not pick up children with true strabismus. In their present form these tests are not a substitute for the direct measurement of visual acuity and the cover test for strabismus detection.

Since the medical management of strabismus is the province of an ophthalmologist, children who are found to have ocular misalignment should be referred without delay. There is no reason to wait until an arbitrary age is reached for referral. The vast majority of true squints (another name for strabismus) do not disappear with time, and there are many advantages in early assessment. The best management may be observation without intervention, or it may be occlusion therapy for amblyopia, glasses for clear vision or control of the deviation, or eye muscle surgery to realign the eyes. The ophthalmologist is in the best position to decide. In most instances the proper management of strabismus requires repeated examinations over a period of years and a degree of patience and persistence on the part of the patient, the parents, and the physician. A quick and definitive cure is rarely possible for this disorder.

Measuring refractive errors

It is possible to determine the refractive status of the eye at any age, even without subjective responses from the patient. In young children the technique most commonly used is retinoscopy, a method that depends on the way light is refracted as it enters the eye and is reflected from the eye back to the observer. Lenses can be interposed in the path of the light to neutralize the patient's refractive error, and a glass correction can be arrived at as long as the patient is able to fix on the light of the retinoscope. Occasionally with uncooperative patients

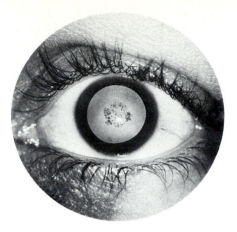

Fig. 11-2. Fundus reflex photographed as an examiner would see it through a direct ophthalmoscope. The granular central opacity, seen as a shadow against the usually clear fundus reflex, is an early cataract caused by prolonged systemic use of corticosteroids.

this procedure must be done under anesthesia, usually as a part of a more extensive eye examination. Older children, like adults, can assist in deciding what is clear and what is less clear (a manifest or subjective refraction) and thus refine their glass correction. But it is most important to recognize that accurate refractions can be performed at any age in an objective fashion, and glasses can be prescribed and worn from about the time of the first birthday. Occasionally, when indicated, as after early extraction of congenital cataracts, contact lenses can be worn well before 1 year of age.

Anatomical examination of the eye

Examination of the eye itself usually rests on visualization of its anterior segment and most of its interior parts. Optical instruments are highly useful to this end, but much can be done with simple equipment. The anterior segment of the eye can be inspected with a flashlight and magnifying glasses. The slit lamp reveals more detail because of its higher magnification and its intense, well-focused slit beam. The lens of the eye can be examined by direct illumination with a flashlight or by retroillumination with the ophthalmoscope. The ophthalmoscope is set at +5 or +6 diopters, and its light is directed into the pupil. Any imperfections in the lens appear as shadows against the usually clear fundus re-flex (Fig. 11-2). The ocular fundus itself can be seen with a direct or an indirect ophthalmoscope, and in either case more easily through dilated pupils. The direct ophthalmoscope gives about 12× magnification and a correspondingly small field of view, whereas the indirect ophthalmoscope gives a wide field of view at about 2× magnification. The indirect ophthalmoscope, which is used mainly by ophthalmologists, offers many advantages in examining children, especially young or uncooperative ones, since the whole posterior pole of the eye can be seen in one glimpse. With this instrument it is usually possible to examine the interior of the eye in an office setting without resorting to an anesthetic examination. Ophthalmologists usually employ general anesthesia for measurement of the intraocular pressure, electroretinography, and special examinations of the retina (for example, fluorescein angiography or scleral depression for the visualization of the peripheral retina) when these are necessary in early childhood.

Visual field testing

Although some form of visual field testing can be done at any age, use of the perimeter to quantitate visual fields is usually possible only after 6 to 7 years of age. Prior to that age some form of confrontation testing may be helpful in demonstrating quadrantic or hemianopic defects. Asking the child to grab the physician's wiggling fingers as they are brought into view from behind the child's head is a method that avoids many of the distracting clues of face to face testing.

Examination of the central fields and blind spots with the tangent screen is a difficult task for most children because of the temptation to shift fixation in the direction of the stimulus. Fortunately, the information that might be obtained from this kind of testing is seldom of critical importance. Central field defects are, of course, often heralded by a marked drop in visual acuity.

OCULAR PATHOLOGY IN PATIENTS WITH DEVELOPMENTAL DISABILITIES

What follows is an account of a few of the ocular defects associated with developmental disabilities. The entities are grouped anatomically according to which part of the eye is affected. The list is far from exhaustive.

Eyelids and orbit. Unusual configurations of the *eyelids and orbit* and blepharoptosis are individually or collectively associated with many syndromes of abnormal development. The epicanthus of Down syndrome, the shallow orbits of Crouzon disease, the hypertelorism of Waardenburg syndrome, and the lower lid deformities of Treacher Collins syndrome are among the best known. Among the phakomatoses, the port-wine stain of the forehead and upper eyelid in Sturge-Weber syndrome (Plate 1, *A*) and the plexiform neuroma of neurofibromatosis (Fig. 11-3) are cutaneous markers of potential underlying eye pathology. Childhood glaucoma is associated with both diseases, and optic nerve glioma is frequently a part of the wide-ranging neurological involvement of neurofibromatosis.

Microphthalmia. Mild *microphthalmia* may be an isolated abnormality, but it is also a characteristic feature of the maternal rubella syndrome and the fetal alcohol syndrome. More severe degrees of microphthalmia, especially in association with iris colobomas and retinal dysplasia, are often seen with trisomy 13.

Cornea. The *cornea,* which is ordinarily crystal clear, loses this clarity in response to a number of pathological processes. Corneal opacification, when associated with photophobia and corneal enlargement, is highly suggestive of congenital glaucoma. The glaucoma, which can only be confirmed by measuring elevated ocular pressure, is often associated in childhood with systemic diseases, such as the maternal rubella syndrome, neurofibromatosis, Lowe syndrome, or the Pierre Robin anomaly. Another important cause of diffuse corneal clouding in childhood is abnormal deposition of mucopolysaccharide, such as occurs in the Hurler syndrome and some of its variants. In the mucopolysaccharidoses ocular pressure is normal and the corneas are not enlarged. Vision may be severely impaired. Focal corneal opacification is exemplified by the white corneal

Plate 1. **A,** Port wine stain of Sturge-Weber syndrome, especially when it involves the upper eyelid, may be associated with childhood glaucoma. The syndrome includes a calcified vascular malformation of the meninges and cerebral cortex and usually a contralateral seizure disorder. **B,** Brown Kayser-Fleischer ring of hepatolenticular degeneration (Wilson disease). The ring (arrows) is due to copper deposition deep in the cornea and is best seen by slit lamp. **C,** Waxlike tan nodules (arrows) on this blue iris are nevoid hamartomas, highly characteristic of neurofibromatosis, a disease with multiple neurological manifestations. **D,** Nearly complete cataract in the eye of an infant with the congenital rubella syndrome. Live virus has been cultured in such cataractous lenses of children up to 3 years of age. **E,** Retrolental fibroplasia in a prematurely born infant exposed to supplemental oxygen in the newborn period. The gray-white membrane behind the lens encroaches on the pupillary axis from the temporal side. Further progression of the process might lead to complete retinal detachment. **F,** Cherry-red spot of Tay-Sachs disease is actually the normal fovea surrounded by opaque, white lipid deposited in the retinal ganglion cells. Optic atrophy and blindness ensue in the course of this degenerative disease of the nervous system. **G,** Rubella retinopathy, a granular pigmentary change in the congenital rubella syndrome. **H,** Lacunar lesions in the retina of a patient with Aicardi syndrome. The edges of the lesions are variably pigmented. This retinal picture is highly characteristic when found in association with infantile seizures and absence of the corpus callosum.

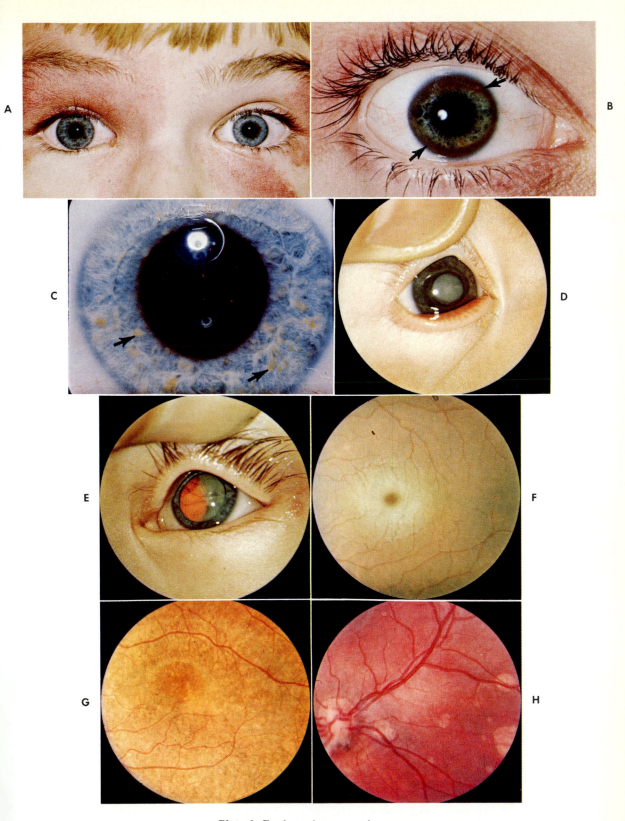

Plate 1. For legend see opposite page.

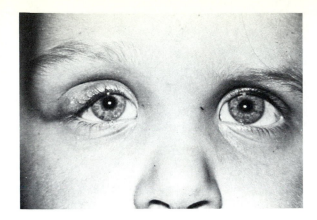

Fig. 11-3. Characteristic S-shaped upper eyelid of a patient with neurofibromatosis (von Recklinghausen disease). The lid deformity (patient's right) is caused by a plexiform neuroma. Childhood glaucoma and gliomas of the optic nerve are part of the clinical spectrum of this dominantly inherited disease.

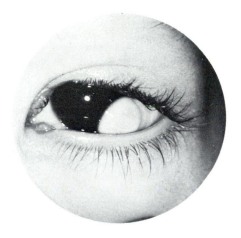

Fig. 11-4. Congenital dermoid tumor overlying the cornea of a patient with Goldenhar syndrome. Note also the colobomatous defect in the medial aspect of the upper lid, a characteristic location for such a defect in this syndrome.

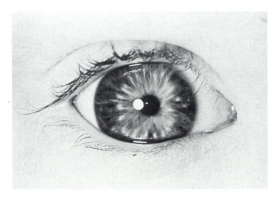

Fig. 11-5. White Brushfield spots of Down syndrome are easily seen against the blue iris background of this patient. The spots may appear tan when the iris color is brown.

dermoids of Goldenhar syndrome, which occur in association with preauricular skin tags and vertebral anomalies (Fig. 11-4). One of the most striking corneal abnormalities to be seen in association with a systemic disease is the Kayser-Fleischer ring of Wilson disease, a brown ring deep in the peripheral cornea due to deposition of copper (Plate 1, *B*). The Kayser-Fleischer ring can be identified or ruled out with assurance only by examination with the slit lamp. Its presence is virtually pathognomonic for hepatolenticular degeneration.

Iris. The *iris,* which is one of the most readily seen structures of the eye, may bear the marks of a number of generalized developmental abnormalities. These range from the Brushfield spots of Down syndrome (Fig. 11-5) to the nevoid hamartoma of neurofibromatosis (Plate 1, *C*); they include the peripheral iris stromal thinning of the maternal rubella syndrome, the iris transillumination of albinism, and the colobomas of both the trisomy 13 and the Schmid-Fraccaro ("cat's eye") syndrome.[17]

Lens. The *lens,* although not rich in its expression of pathological processes, can be an important marker of systemic disease as well as a critical determinant of visual disability. Cataracts are the most obvious problem. They occur in children as an isolated, dominantly inherited disorder; sporadically without recognized cause; in more or less characteristic form with the maternal rubella syndrome (Plate 1, *D*), galactosemia (Fig. 11-6), hypoparathyroidism, and Down syndrome; they are also associated with prolonged use of sys-

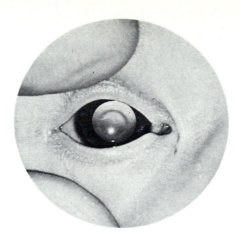

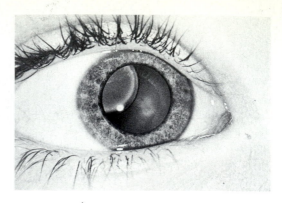

Fig. 11-7. Dislocated lens in a patient with Marfan syndrome. The lens has been displaced up and temporally so its edge can be seen in the pupil.

Fig. 11-6. Oil droplet cataract of galactosemia in an 11-day-old infant. Such a lens opacity might become densely white if the disease was not recognized and dietary therapy started.

temic steroids (Fig. 11-2). Surgery for childhood cataracts has improved remarkably in recent years. It can be performed at any age. The lens material can be aspirated from the eye through a small incision under microscopic control. Repeated operations and severe postoperative inflammation can be avoided. Contact lenses or spectacles are readily available for the necessary refractive correction. These technical advances, taken together, mean that children with bilateral congenital cataracts have a favorable visual prognosis. Unfortunately, eyes with unilateral congenital cataracts still have a much poorer prospect for useful vision, even with technically satisfactory surgery. This is because it is rarely possible to get a child to use the operated eye in preference to the normal fellow eye, and the eye that has had the cataract extraction usually remains functionally amblyopic.

In addition to cataract formation, lens dislocation is an important pathological process in patients with developmental disabilities (Fig. 11-7). The dislocation occurs because of a defect in the formation of lens zonules, the thin fibers that suspend the lens within the eye. When these zonules become lax, the lens may move to an eccentric position with respect to the pupil, or it may actually prolapse through the pupil into the anterior chamber of the eye. The latter event is an ophthalmological emer-

gency because of the rapid rise of intraocular pressure that accompanies the dislocation. If the lens cannot be returned to its usual position behind the plane of the pupil, it must be extracted without delay. The causes of lens dislocation that are pertinent to developmental disability are Marfan syndrome, homocystinuria, and sulfite oxidase deficiency.[23] The former is usually recognized by its characteristic changes in body habitus, and the latter two by the presence of abnormal amino acids in the urine.

Fundus of the eye. Examination of the *fundus of the eye* can be of paramount importance in evaluating developmental disabilities. A few examples will illustrate the point. Prematurely born infants who require supplementary oxygen during the neonatal period have an increased risk of developing retrolental fibroplasia (Plate 1, *E*). If oxygen is sharply curtailed to avoid retrolental fibroplasia, these children have a higher risk of developing signs of anoxic brain damage. It is difficult with present oxygen monitoring techniques to pick a safe middle ground between these two hazards.[15] The fundi of prematurely born babies must be examined, therefore, to determine whether any retinopathy has developed. This examination can be done when the infant is sufficiently stable to be taken out of the incubator. It is not intended as a way of monitoring the use of supplemental oxygen, but as a way of knowing which babies have developed vascular retinopathy.[3] Since most of the vascular changes occur in the temporal periphery of the retina, the examination is best done with dilated pupils and the indirect ophthalmoscope. Unfortunately, there is no satisfactory treatment for retrolental fibroplasia once it has developed. It does appear that many patients with early active retinopathy undergo spontaneous regression without treatment and are left with only an inactive scar in the peripheral retina. A few of these patients may later develop a retinal detachment due to traction from the scar, so follow-up examination is important.

A number of the cerebral lipidoses are associated with distinctive changes in the ocular fundus.[26] One can see actual lipid accumulation in the perifoveal retina of patients with Tay-Sachs disease (Plate 1, *F*) and Niemann-Pick disease, the lipid setting off the fovea as a "cherry-red spot." In Krabbe leukodystrophy early loss of retinal ganglion cells results in optic atrophy and blindness within the first year of life. In Fabry disease dramatic tortuosity of retinal vessels is present along with characteristic lipid deposition in the cornea and lens. These latter changes are subtle enough to require slit lamp examination.

Prenatal and postnatal infections with important developmental consequences can manifest themselves in the retina. The maternal rubella syndrome frequently is accompanied by a granular pigmentary retinopathy, which fortunately causes very little visual disability (Plate 1, *G*). Congenital toxoplasmosis and cytomegalic inclusion disease can cause focal and often multiple chorioretinal inflammatory scars. Neonatal herpes simplex encephalitis may result in widespread retinitis.[5] Subacute sclerosing panencephalitis related to earlier measles infection may become manifest as a focal retinitis associated with personality changes and a seizure disorder.[22]

Two seizure disorders of infancy may be associated with distinctive retinal changes. One is tuberous sclerosis (Bourneville disease), in which retinal gliomata are found in approximately 50% of patients (Fig. 11-8). The other is Aicardi syndrome, in which chorioretinal lacunar lesions (Plate 1, *H*) are nearly always present in association with absence of the cor-

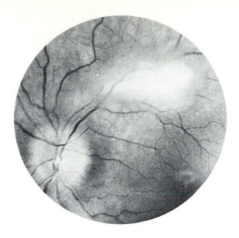

Fig. 11-8. Retinal glioma along superior temporal vessel of a patient with tuberous sclerosis (Bourneville disease). Intracranial calcification and seizures are other hallmarks of this disease.

pus callosum and infantile flexion spasms.[12] In both these disorders subsequent neurological development is severely retarded.

Optic nerve hypoplasia is a developmental abnormality that can be recognized ophthalmoscopically in infants with poor vision and nystagmus.[28] The optic discs appear small, pale, and abnormally pigmented. The condition is congenital and stationary. It can occur as an isolated entity without other neurological involvement, with limited midline cerebral defects, or with extensive cerebral anomalies such as anencephaly. Optic nerve hypoplasia is one of the commonest developmental causes of poor vision in pediatric patients. Although the pathogenesis is uncertain, a known predisposing factor is maternal diabetes mellitus.[18] No treatment is available, but recognition is important in clarifying what may otherwise be a puzzling neurological entity.

Optic atrophy, which must be distinguished from optic nerve hypoplasia (in optic atrophy the disc is not small), may be found in children with hydrocephalus, cranial synostosis, subacute necrotizing encephalitis of infancy (Leigh syndrome),[19] metachromatic leukodystrophy, Krabbe disease, and adrenoleukodystrophy[20]— all pediatric neurological disorders with serious developmental implications. Papilledema due to elevated intracranial pressure is distinguished by elevation and blurring of the optic disc margins. When it develops acutely there may be hemorrhages and cotton-wool spots on or near the disc and the retinal vessels may be engorged. Usually the vision is not affected by papilledema. Optic neuritis may cause the same clinical picture (or may occur retrobulbarly without fundus changes), but in that case the vision is profoundly reduced and intracranial pressure is normal.

Retina. Finally, there is a group of pigmentary degenerations of the retina that can be recognized ophthalmoscopically. These can occur as isolated, inheritable disorders of the eye or as components of more generalized systemic diseases, but in either case they have profound visual significance because of their characteristic progressive course toward blindness. Leber congenital amaurosis is the earliest and most common of the primary pigmentary degenerations of childhood.[16] The visual deficit is usually profound at birth, and the electroretinogram is universally diminished or absent. Later acquired pigmentary degenerations are associated with abetalipoproteinemia, the Laurence-Moon-Biedl syndrome, Refsum syndrome, and spinocerebellar degenerations. In Batten disease the pigmentary degeneration is more restricted to the macular area and may be due to accumulation of ceroid and lipofuscin in the retinal pigmented epithelium.[2]

Disorders of ocular motility

Disorders of ocular motility occur frequently in patients with developmental disabilities. This is undoubtedly because eye movement and alignment are controlled by the nervous system, and they therefore reflect more general disorders of neurological function. Nystagmus and strabismus are the two most important disorders of ocular motility to consider.

Nystagmus. *Nystagmus* may be primarily a motor defect, as in congenital motor nystagmus, or it may be secondary to various types of ocular sensory defects. Children with congenital motor nystagmus often develop a head turn to use their eyes in a position of gaze in which the nystagmus is least marked, the so-called null point. Since this is the position in which their vision is best, they should not be dissuaded from using it. In children with congenital motor

nystagmus the vision is characteristically good, whereas it is usually reduced in children with sensory nystagmus. The most familiar ocular causes of sensory nystagmus are ocular albinism, congenital color blindness (achromatopsia), aniridia, optic nerve hypoplasia, and Leber congenital amaurosis. Any cause of early reduction of vision, such as optic atrophy from hydrocephalus or neonatal anoxia or congenital cataracts of any cause, may lead to sensory nystagmus. In disorders that also affect the brain, such as the maternal rubella syndrome, it is sometimes difficult to determine whether nystagmus is due to a reduction in vision or whether it is directly related to pathological involvement of the brain stem. In either case the unsteadiness of the eyes is detrimental to vision.

Two kinds of nystagmus have relatively little effect on vision. One is spasmus nutans, in which the nystagmus is typically unilateral, fine and rapid, and associated with head nodding and a head tilt. The nystagmus is intermittent and usually (but not always) disappears by 3 years of age. Since this condition is sometimes associated with acquired strabismus, ophthalmological examination and follow-up are advisable. The second benign form of nystagmus is occlusional nystagmus, which may be present alone or in association with other disorders of ocular motility. The occlusional element is not present when both eyes are open, but when one eye is occluded, jerk nystagmus develops in both eyes, thus reducing the vision. Occlusional nystagmus therefore makes monocular testing of vision unreliable. In these patients it is best to test the visual acuity binocularly as well as in each eye, since the binocular vision may be significantly better than the vision of either eye alone.

Strabismus. *Strabismus* is many times more common among patients with developmental disabilities than in the general population. It may reach a prevalence of 40% to 50% among children with cerebral palsy.[24] Although some strabismus seems clearly related to abnormal orbital development (as in the craniofacial dysostoses) and some is traceable to paretic extraocular muscles (as with congenital fourth cranial nerve palsies or acquired abducens nerve palsies with increased intracranial pressure) in the vast majority of patients ocular misalignment is not attributable to either of these factors and is best thought of as a kind of neuromuscular incoordination. If one considers how many separate factors contribute to the maintenance of single binocular vision—six cranial nerves, twelve extraocular muscles, two complex optical systems, a neural mechanism linking accommodation and convergence, and the cerebral cortex, which must be able to put together disparate images from the two eyes—it is not surprising that occasionally the eyes are out of alignment and cannot be used together.

Although in some ways every child with strabismus is unique and must be dealt with individually, there are several common types of strabismus that can be distinguished. The first is *congenital esotropia,* which is usually defined as crossing of the eyes that becomes manifest in the first few months of life. In infants with congenital esotropia there is often an alternating fixation pattern and a reluctance or inability to abduct the eyes. Whirling the child around in one's arms may bring out fuller abduction by stimulating the labyrinth. As long as the eyes are used alternately, the vision of each eye develops normally, and in time the abduction deficit may disappear. Surgery is usually required to straighten the eyes. Since it takes some time to evaluate this kind of strabismus, to decide whether glasses will be helpful in reducing the turn, or to know whether patching will be necessary, it is well to refer children with congenital esotropia to the ophthalmologist early. Usually a full assessment of the strabismus can be made by 18 months of age and surgery can be planned thereafter. One difficulty with relatively early surgery for this type of strabismus is that the eyes may spontaneously diverge in later years. If this spontaneous divergence is added to an early operative correction, a consecutive exotropia develops. Certain factors, such as high hyperopia, a small and variable turn, amblyopia in one eye, or the presence of other neurological disease, are known to be associated with spontaneous divergence. The presence of these factors may dictate a delay in surgery.

A second common type of strabismus is *intermittent exotropia.* This is characterized by an outward drift of one eye, usually when the patient is looking off at a distance. The drift is usually reported to be more frequent with fatigue or illness, and the exotropic eye is often squinted closed in bright sunlight. Since the eyes can be kept straight with near fixation and at times of increased alertness, this type of strabismus may be missed at the time of initial examination. The vision is usually good in both eyes, and the eyes are used together when they are straight. This type of exotropia may first become apparent in the early years, but it does not change rapidly with time. Since the turn is only intermittent and the vision is good, there is less pressure to intervene surgically than with congenital esotropia. Glasses may be useful to provide clear vision in each eye, but patching is seldom required. Exercises are of no help. The decision whether to perform surgery is usually based on the amount and frequency of the turn; the operation can be done at any age.

A third type of strabismus is *accommodative esotropia.* This type of esotropia is nearly always associated with hyperopia (farsightedness), and the crossing occurs because of the extra convergence induced by accommodating to overcome the farsightedness. The turn occurs more often with fixation in the near range. It often begins shortly after the first birthday and is intermittent at the start. Fully accommodative esotropia is by definition completely correctable with glasses for the farsightedness. Bifocal additions may be necessary to control the deviation in the near range. Partly accommodative esotropia is a form of acquired esotropia for which glass correction for the farsightedness provides only a partial straightening effect. Surgery may be required for the residual deviation. It is important to recognize that surgery cannot be substituted for glasses to correct the accommodative part of the turn, and if glasses are required before surgery they will usually be necessary after surgery.

A few general remarks about the treatment of strabismus may be useful for the nonophthalmologist. An ideal result of the treatment of strabismus would be perfect realignment of the eyes and a return to normal binocular vision.

In practice this ideal is achieved in only a small percentage of patients, especially if one sets aside those with accommodative esotropia for whom glasses provide full correction. It is almost always possible to correct the angle of misalignment so that it is not apparent on casual inspection, but the development of binocular vision depends more on whether binocular vision existed before the strabismus developed and how quickly the eyes were realigned. It follows that the prospects for binocular vision are poorest in children with congenital esotropia, who have never used their eyes together. Some may learn a kind of partial binocularity, but many continue to use their eyes independently despite adequate anatomical realignment. It should, however, be stressed that alternating fixation with good vision in each eye and a small angle of deviation is a perfectly acceptable therapeutic result for a child with strabismus. There is no handicap for day-to-day activities or for school work.

One of the most important goals in strabismus management is to obtain good vision in each eye. Occlusion of one eye for a period of time is often necessary to achieve this goal. It is the most direct and useful way to treat strabismic amblyopia, and few shortcuts are available. Eye exercises are generally ineffective. Surgical realignment does not in itself improve the vision. Drugs are of no help. The timing of amblyopia therapy is important: the earlier occlusion is begun, the more rapid its effect. If, after surgery, a small angle of strabismus remains, the patient must be followed carefully to avoid a return of amblyopia in the crossing eye. Rarely, when the visual potential of an eye is limited or when strabismic amblyopia has been overlooked until well after school age, occlusion of the good eye becomes a practical impossibility. Under these circumstances the patient can be advised of the special importance of the better eye and precautions can be taken to avoid injury to it. The functional handicap associated with strabismic amblyopia in one eye is relatively minor. The good eye can be used alone without harm or strain, and a limited kind of depth perception is available. The peripheral vision of the amblyopic eye is usually intact. There is no reason to think that strabismic amblyopia in itself is the cause of poor developmental progress, reading problems, or learning disabilities.

Program planning for the visually impaired child

Carol M. Donovan

The primary care physician, therapist, or teacher involved in caring for or treating any high-risk infant or developmentally disabled child is in a perfect position to observe how the visual status of the child affects his overall development. This should be part of a routine developmental screening or assessment. As with other areas of development, visual function develops in an orderly sequence as follows:

Neonate	Alerts with widening of palpebral fissures to visual stimulation by an object or face presented 20 to 30 cm from the eyes
	Makes momentary eye contact with adult
	Follows a visual stimulus in a horizontal arc 30 degrees on either side of the midline
	Turns head toward a diffuse source of light
	Blinks at a flashlight shone in the eyes
1 month	Follows a visual stimulus in a horizontal arc 60 degrees on either side of the midline
	Follows a visual stimulus vertically 30 degrees above and below the horizontal meridian
	Shows looming response—blinks at approaching object
2 months	Tracks horizontally across midline
	Follows a moving person 1.8 m away
	Makes prolonged eye contact with adult
	Smiles in response to a smiling face
3 months	Eyes and head follow smoothly through 180 degree arc
	Regards own hands
	Looks at objects placed in hand; initiation of visuomotor coordination

4 to 5 months	Shows spontaneous social smile in response to familiar adult
	Reaches on sight to a 2.5 cm cube presented 30.5 cm from the infant
	Notices a raisin presented 30.5 cm from the infant
5 to 6 months	Smiles at mirror image
7 to 8 months	Picks up a raisin by raking
8 to 9 months	Pays visual attention to details of objects, such as facial features of dolls, or poking at holes in pegboard
9 months	Shows neat pincer grasp
12-14 months	Gains skill in perceptual motor items, that is, stacks blocks, uses formboards, places peg in round hole

Techniques in the assessment of vision in the infant and young child are addressed in the earlier part of this chapter. Once visual impairment in this group is suspected and confirmed by an ophthalmologist, the primary care physician should assist in the formulation of the management plan. A developmental program should be initiated by a developmental specialist experienced in working with the visually impaired infant and child. Visual impairment may occur in isolation but is more frequently associated with cerebral palsy, hydrocephalus, or other handicapping conditions. The frequent association of visual disorders with other handicapping conditions is emphasized in the earlier portion of this chapter. The associated visual difficulty of these children makes their basic disabilities more difficult to manage. There has been a continued resistance to serving the needs of the severely retarded or multiply handicapped child; however, appropriate ophthalmological treatment often results in significant improvement in performance and overall functioning of these youngsters.

Of equal concern is the child who presents with visual impairments and has been allowed to develop maladaptive behaviors, thus appearing retarded and or emotionally disturbed.

"Blindisms"[13] are examples of self-stimulating behaviors that are frequently observed in visually impaired children. These behaviors are undesirable because they serve to further isolate the child in his own world and inhibit normal

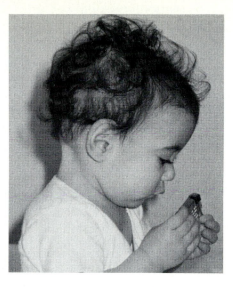

Fig. 11-9. Gina (15-month-old with RLF) inspects objects by holding them close and turning her head to the left.

interactions with his environment. Following are alerting signs and blindisms:

A. Alerting signs suggesting referral to an ophthalmologist
　1. Failure to pass screening items, such as on p. 280 and above; other items at a similar level are passed
　2. Appearance of any strabismus (squint) after 2 months of age
　3. Wandering uncoordinated eye movements
　4. Nystagmus
　5. Holding items close (within 15 cm) for visual inspection (Fig. 11-9)
　6. Cocking head habitually to look at items
　7. Turning head then eyes to look at people or object (ocular motor apraxia)
　8. Disregard of objects presented in peripheral field
B. Blindisms
　1. Prolonged handwatching past developmental age 5 months (shadowing)
　2. Staring at lights in preference to people or objects
　3. Poking at eyes
　4. Rubbing eyes
　5. Flicking finger (stimulus presented peripherally)
　6. Rocking
　7. Spinning
　8. Banging head
　9. Smelling, sniffing, "rooting"
　10. Prolonged mouthing of objects

DEVELOPMENT OF VISUALLY IMPAIRED INFANTS

Primary care physicians, ophthalmologists, and early intervention professionals should work together with the families of children who have visual difficulties. Infants with moderate to severe visual impairment will show an altered developmental pattern that can make it difficult for parents to incorporate the child into the family routine. Parents need guidance to understand why the child is responding differently and having difficulties performing certain activities. The relationship among developmental delays due to lack of vision is not always readily apparent. Fraiberg[7] has contributed much to our understanding of the development of blind infants. She meticulously followed 10 infants that were considered totally blind from birth. They did not have major physical or mental handicaps. She also acted as a consultant to many other families with young children who had a variety of visual difficulties that ranged from legal blindness to multiple handicaps with associated cortical blindness. Although 10 children is a small number on which to make reliable judgments of the norms of development in blind infants, the description of their development in her book *Insights From the Blind* as well as many other articles will help parents and professionals to understand the developmental patterns of these infants. Her data provide "insights" and methods of intervention that can be used to facilitate the normal development of these youngsters.

Social and emotional aspects

The attachment process described in Chapter 4 is complex and can be easily disturbed if the primary caregiver and the infant are not able to accurately interpret each other's signals. Much of this progress is mediated by visual cues, that is, mutual gazing and prolonged eye contact, preferential smiling in response to the mother's face, and the infant's ability to keep in contact with the mother via visual regard. Early smiling may be elicited in all infants by a familiar voice. The true social smile, which develops into the preferential smiling of a 5-month-old normal child, is often seriously delayed in the visually impaired infant. When the infant hears the familiar voice during the early

months it is not associated with the person he has come to know as "mother" until the voice and person come together in some form of physical contact as well as auditory signal. The physical contact is necessary to provide the voice with a physical presence that the infant can be sure of. When he hears only the auditory signal it is interpreted as an isolated event that does not represent a permanent object or person in his environment. Until the visually impaired infant develops the concept of object permanence he is unaware that sounds represent the things that he "knows" when he is in contact with them in a tactile kinesthetic sense. Sounds by their very nature are discontinuous events that are most often heard when they are acted on by a human force. The infant's rattle and musical teddy bear require that someone activate them to give the blind child the information that they still exist. The visually impaired infant must learn to develop an attachment to his caregivers by gaining an awareness of the individual differences in people who hold him. He develops this through his sense of smell and tactile and propriokinesthetic awareness, which differentiate how individuals hold him. The infant needs to be taught how to reach out to feel the face of the caregiver and build the schema that associates the voice with the tactile and olfactory cues. This internal image connects the voice with the person who has recently held him. Besides the difficult task of developing the initial attachment, the visually impaired child also faces a slightly different course in the separation and individualization process. Separation has always been part of this young infant's experience because he experiences contact and lack of contact in a way different than the normally sighted infant. Theoretically it follows that the visually impaired child will show some distress when not in contact with the mother. The infant then develops alternate ways of keeping in contact with the mother by connecting the voice at a distance with the person who has held him. Once the infant is able to localize a sound source and reach out toward it he should develop the mobility that will give him the freedom to initiate separation while simultaneously maintaining contact with the mother through auditory cues. It is this personal growth that should allow separation anxiety to wane while communication via symbolic language improves. Communication through vocal and auditory channels would help, therefore, to improve contact with the mother.

Prehension

In the sighted child the development of reach, grasp, and the use of the thumb and forefinger in opposition takes place during the first 9 to 10 months of life. These milestones are achieved by developing motor skills that are facilitated by the infant's awareness of his environment. The 2-month-old child who lies in an asymmetrical tonic neck reflex becomes aware of his hands as part of himself and then sees his hands in relation to objects, which are then reached for. Between 4 to 5 months of age the infant will immediately reach for an object on sight, whether his hand is in view or not. He knows his hands are extensions of himself that can be used as tools for bringing the object in close proximity so that he may examine it further. During this period he also becomes visually aware of the differences in the size of objects before he reaches for them. At the end of the first year he adjusts his hand position prior to reaching for the object and consequently uses a pincer grasp to pick up small objects. The visually impaired child is obviously without these important cues and must learn to substitute auditory cues for the visual cues as an incentive for reaching. The substitution of the auditory stimuli for the visual cues delays directed reaching. As discussed previously it is not until the infant develops an appreciation for the fact that sounds represent real objects or people that he will reach on sound cue alone. Fraiberg's[7] 10 children developed this reach at a median age of 8.8 months, with a range from 6 to 11 months. Even at this age, when sighted children are developing isolation of the index finger and a pincer grasp, the blind child relies on raking an object up to more efficiently locate it. This raking remains an adaptive mechanism for locating the object, but the visually impaired child still also needs the opportunity to develop the pincer grasp.

Gross motor

Fraiberg[7] compared the attainment of major motor milestones between visually impaired and sighted children (Fig. 11-10 and Table 11-1). Visually impaired and sighted children attained major milestones that involved stable positions

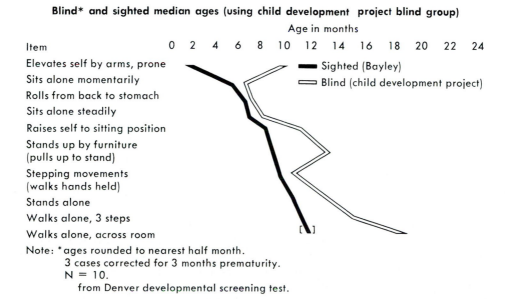

Blind* and sighted median ages (using child development project blind group)

Age in months

| Item | 0 2 4 6 8 10 12 14 16 18 20 22 24 |

Elevates self by arms, prone
Sits alone momentarily
Rolls from back to stomach
Sits alone steadily
Raises self to sitting position
Stands up by furniture (pulls up to stand)
Stepping movements (walks hands held)
Stands alone
Walks alone, 3 steps
Walks alone, across room

Sighted (Bayley)
Blind (child development project)

Note: *ages rounded to nearest half month.
3 cases corrected for 3 months prematurity.
N = 10.
from Denver developmental screening test.

Fig. 11-10. Median age of attainment of major motor milestones for Fraiberg's blind infants and the norms for sighted children based on the Bayley Motor Scales. (From Fraiberg, S.: Insights from the blind, New York, 1977, Basic Books, Inc., Publishers, © 1977 by Selma Fraiberg.)

Table 11-1. Gross motor items and age achieved by blind (Child Development Project) and sighted (Bayley)*

Item	Age range†		Median age		Difference in median ages
	Sighted	Blind*	Sighted	Blind	
Elevates self by arms, prone‖	0.7 to 5.0	4.5 to 9.5	2.1	8.75	6.65
Sits alone momentarily	4.0 to 8.0	5.0 to 8.5	5.3	6.75	1.45
Rolls from back to stomach‖	4.0 to 10.0	4.5 to 9.5	6.4	7.25	0.85
Sits alone steadily	5.0 to 9.0	6.5 to 9.5	6.6	8.00	1.40
Raises self to sitting position‖	6.0 to 11.0	9.5 to 15.5	8.3	11.00	2.70
Stands up by furniture‖ (pulls up to stand)	6.0 to 12.0	9.5 to 15.0	8.6	13.00	4.40
Stepping movements¶ (walks hands held)	6.0 to 12.0	8.0 to 11.5	8.8	10.75	1.95
Stands alone‖	9.0 to 16.0	9.0 to 15.5	11.0	13.00	2.00
Walks alone,§ steps‖	9.0 to 17.0	11.5 to 19.0	11.7	15.25	3.55
Walks alone, across room#	11.3 to 14.3#	12.0 to 20.5	12.1#	19.25	7.15

Note: All ages given in months.
*From Fraiberg, S.: Insights from the blind. New York, 1977, Basic Books, Inc., Publishers, © 1977 by Selma Fraiberg.
†Age range includes: 5% to 95% of Bayley sample, 25% to 90% of Denver sample, and 10% to 90% of Child Development Project sample.
‡Ages rounded to nearest half month.
§Cases corrected for 3 months prematurity.
‖One child had not achieved by 2 years.
¶Not observed for one child prior to walk alone.
#Item from Denver Developmental Screening Test.

at the same times. However, in any of the achievements that required an infant to assume a specific position or to move the milestones were generally delayed. Mobility positions, which required the infant to raise the head from the prone position, creep, and walk unassisted, were the most severely hampered. It is known that two factors cause the very young infant to raise his head in the prone position. One is the stimulus from the labyrinths in the middle ear, which causes the activation of the prone righting response. This automatically brings the head up to a horizontal position (Chapter 3). Also, very quickly after birth the neonate lifts his head in an effort to visually scan his environment. In the absence of visual reinforcement the visually impaired child has little reason to lift his head and maintain it in the upright position; to do so the infant must be encouraged by auditory and tactile stimuli. Creeping and walking usually develop when the infant has the neuromuscular maturation to attain the quadruped and bipedal positions. However, there must be an incentive to go forward to attain a desired object or person. The visually impaired infant must have the incentive of

knowing that something or someone is in the void to give them the courage to venture forward. Mobility is not achieved until the infant learns to reach on sound cue.

Cognition

Piaget describes the first 2 years of life as being the sensory motor phase of intellectual development. During these early years vision is the single most important factor that allows the infant to learn about his world. As has been described previously, the lack of vision will alter the way the infant develops in the social-emotional, gross motor, and fine motor areas. These all are linked with the way the infant must learn about his world by substituting his other senses and making whatever vision he has become a meaningful experience. Fraiberg[7] mainly discusses the development of object permanence and symbolic play. However, the development of appropriate concepts involving causality, imitation, and spatiality also are altered by the visual impairment. Entrance to Piaget's stage III is hallmarked by the infant's ability to combine schema. The visually impaired infant should learn to deliberately bring items placed in his hand to his mouth at around the same time that normal children do, 3 to 4 months. Mouthing will be an important avenue for the visually impaired infant to learn about his world and if not accomplished should be encouraged. This mouthing behavior will also continue in visually impaired infants long beyond the point that it drops out of the repertoire of normally developing children. This behavior is often considered more permissible in young visually impaired infants. The other two major skills that involve combination of schema, the hearing of sound and turning to locate it and the seeing of an object and reaching for it, are obviously delayed. The infant, however, can be guided into a developmental path by teaching him to substitute his other senses, mainly tactile and auditory, for the visual channel.

Causality. The visually impaired infant will experience the phenomenon of simultaneously making a movement and hearing a sound and will attempt to reproduce the effect with repeating the motion; thus if given the opportunity to hold objects, he should develop shaking ability, an early cause and effect behavior. Banging, however, usually develops when the young infant sees a relationship between the supporting surface of a tray in front of him and the item that he holds in his hand. The visually impaired infant will have to be helped to feel the relationship so that he develops banging as an activity. Other causality tasks that emerge in Piaget's stages IV through VI often depend on insightful understanding of the objects and how they relate to each other, for example, seeing a string attached to a ring, he learns to pull it to retrieve the ring; seeing the mark that is produced by a crayon, he learns to duplicate the mark; or knowing that by moving a chair and standing on it he can obtain a desired object that is placed beyond his reach. The visually impaired child is severely hampered because he is not able to take in all of his environment but rather must experience bits of it over time. The infant will learn by adults working with him to help him to feel and understand relationships. At the same time the adult will interpret for him what he is feeling. For example, the adult can help him feel the relationship between the string and the ring or use a stick and modelling clay to illustrate the idea of a

writing utensil. The constant verbalization of the adult eventually helps the blind child understand these relationships.

Imitation. Visually impaired children should develop vocal and verbal imitation within the same time frame as normally developing children. They have the disadvantage of not being able to see models, which would give additional cues to forming the sounds, but they can be encouraged to feel the adult's mouth and throat as well as their own, in addition to using their auditory channel. They should be encouraged to experiment with various sounds. Imitations of simple motor acts will obviously not occur, but a different approach can be used by having the child move through the actions while the adult uses the hand over hand approach. With enough repetition the infant or young child should eventually pick up from the model what has been demonstrated on him. The disadvantage is that there will be a difference in the time frame. The seeing child has the advantage of being able to watch the model and adjust his actions to more nearly conform to the model. The visually impaired child will have to experience the model first and then try to repeat the action after a time delay. This makes the imitation task more complicated; thus good imitations of motor acts probably will not be accomplished until the child is functioning within Piaget's stage VI of cognitive development (18 to 24 months), when it is expected that young children can perform delayed imitations.

Object permanence. Nothing is permanent in the very young visually impaired child's world, but he must come to know that objects exist by picking up on cues that indicate where the objects are in the environment. An example of this is what Fraiberg[7] considers to be a stage III task. The child is repeatedly presented with appropriate toys when he is seated in his high chair, and he comes to know that by touching a tray an object will be there. The notion that the object is there is reinforced by the parent giving a sound cue when the toy is placed in front of the child. Piaget's stage IV object permanence is said to have been accomplished when the infant can reach on hearing the sound cue when it is presented from any point in space. The final stage of object permanence is when the blind child can retrieve an object by remembering where he has put it. This would be similar to the advanced object permanence in a seeing child.

Play. The symbolic play that one expects to see in the 1- to 2-year-old child is, according to Fraiberg,[7] the most serious delay in the visually impaired infant. Conclusions again are based on a small number of children, so it is impossible to say whether this finding would hold true for a more generalized population of blind infants. However, knowing that this stage may be delayed would guide the professionals and parents into encouraging this type of activity. This encouragement could be in the form of introducing an infant who seems to be functioning at about a 12 to 15 month developmental level with appropriate toys, such as dolls and dishes,

and encouraging him to use those objects in relationship to each other rather than just in relationship to themselves. Similar activities would include other types of pretend play, such as allowing the infant to experience what a vacuum cleaner is by feeling and hearing and then giving him a toy similar to a vacuum cleaner and encouraging him to pretend or mimic this domestic activity of the parents.

Spatiality. The visually impaired child must be encouraged to feel the differences between objects and to experience their relationships to each other through the tactile kinesthetic sense. He must be able to manipulate the objects with his hands and also use his body to experience items that are near as opposed to things that are far from him. As with all these tasks, it

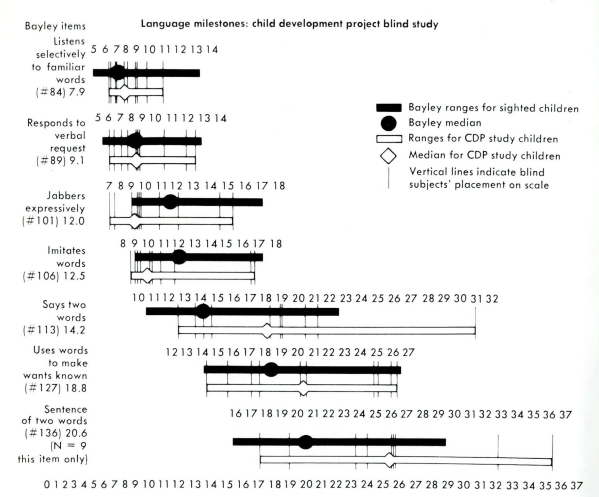

Fig. 11-11. Language milestones for Fraiberg's blind infants and the norms for sighted children based on the Bayley Scale of Infant Development (From Fraiberg, S.: Insights from the blind, New York, 1977, Basic Books, Inc., Publishers, © 1977 by Selma Fraiberg.)

will be extremely important that the adult continue to give him verbal labels for the things he is experiencing, such as round or square, full or empty. As the child hears the verbal description and feels the objects he will begin to get some sense of what the words mean. This will continue to play an increasingly important part in helping the growing child learn about his world.

Language

In Fraiberg's[7] sample many of her infants developed those speech and language skills that did not involve recognition of items and pictures, which obviously require vision, at about the same time as normal children. This included using single words, following simple commands, and combining two words (Fig. 11-11). The visually impaired child must learn to recognize objects by determining the way that they taste, feel, and sound. This recognition could be tested at a receptive level by asking the child to select a named item or on an expressive level by having him name the item. If the child is totally visually impaired, he will never experience representational pictures and drawings but will eventually need to learn Braille, which involves attainment of a conceptual level advanced enough to understand that symbols substitute for objects, people, and ideas.

PROGRAMMING

Programming for visually impaired infants must include the building of compensatory skills. Many blind infants are not *totally* lacking in vision, and the smallest amount of light perception can be helpful in aiding their independent functioning. Many educators of the visually impaired advocate formal visual training. They start with using very bright lights directed at the infant and looking for any type of behavioral response as an indication of the infant's awareness. If a response is present, this awareness is then shaped into the child orienting to, focusing on, and then following the light. If this works well, the process is continued, initially using shiny and then colorful objects.

Simultaneously, the infant is encouraged to use his other senses. This enables him to get some meaning from the blur of sounds, odors, and propriokinesthetic stimuli and helps him to be in touch with his environment. The overall goal of programming is to help the infant develop communication patterns that will facilitate positive interactions. This should inhibit development of maladaptive behaviors and promote more normal growth patterns. This will allow the infant to achieve full human potential.

Following is an actual program designed for the parents of a 4-month-old girl with profound visual impairment due to optic hypoplasia. Many of the program's suggestions are applicable to other visually impaired infants.

Home program

Here are a few suggestions that you might find useful when you care for and play with Katie. Infants who have visual difficulties need to use all of their senses to learn about you and to develop attachment and trust, since they are unable to use their vision to keep in contact with you.

1. If Katie enjoys cuddling and a high degree of closeness to you, you may find it enjoyable to get an infant carrier, which is a sling or harness arrangement that allows you to carry an infant in front of you and frees your hands to do housework. As Katie gets bigger, other types of carriers will allow you to carry her on your hip or back.

2. When you are caring for Katie (holding and cuddling her), help to bring her hands up to your face to explore it. Help her to feel your facial features (eyes, nose, mouth, ears, and hair) as well as to feel them on her own body, naming the body parts as you go along. Always bring Katie's hands in contact with your face until she starts to initiate this action on her own.

3. Select one or two scents, such as perfume, cologne, or after-shave, that you enjoy wearing and wear them on a consistent basis if you do not already do so. Katie will come to know you by a number of things, scents being one of them. When you use a perfume that lasts a long period of time and can be smelled from a short distance away, it will help Katie to keep in contact with you when you are not holding her.

4. Infants with visual difficulties learn to smile, as Katie has, in response to familiar voices, but the most reliable smiling and laughing responses often come from enjoyable physical play. Select any or all of the following activities that Katie enjoys.

a. Give her a bath followed by drying her with a soft towel, naming her body parts as you dry them, and then massaging with baby lotion or powder.

b. Play any form of rocking, stroking, tickling, whispering, blowing, cuddling, or "I'm going to get you" games; move her about in the air, such as holding her up and slowly spinning her about while securely holding her, bouncing her, etc.

Motor suggestions

1. Visually impaired infants usually learn to sit and stand at the same time as other children, but they do not necessarily learn how to change positions as sighted children do. Work on Katie's head control by placing her over a small bolster or rolled-up towel about 3 to 4 inches in diameter and encouraging her to hold her head and upper chest up while you are sitting next to her. Eventually eliminate the bolster and encourage her to lift her head with a minimum of manual guidance on your part, until she does so on her own.

2. To attain sitting balance, when you hold Katie on your lap, hold her slightly away from your body with your hands around her chest, tipping her body from side to side, making her right herself to a normal position. As she increases her head and trunk control, move your hands down around her hip and continue this same tilting game. You can also try keeping Katie sitting on the floor between your legs, helping her to prop her hands in front of her while you offer as much support as she needs around her lower chest or hips.

3. Work on her independent sitting balance by moving her into a sitting position. Have her push up from a side lying position and then encourage her to sit, propping her hands in front of her or to the sides.

4. Reaching is another activity that is associated with a visual stimulus. To encourage Katie to reach, rig up dangling, noisy objects in her crib that are easily touched when she moves her hands or feet.

5. Improve Katie's reach and grasp by directing her face toward a noisy object and allow her to have contact with it. Then remove it from her hands for a very short distance and help her hand to come in contact with the object again. Gradually she should be able to build the skill of reaching on a sound cue alone, before she has had any tactile contact with the object.

6. Use a high chair or feeding table with a wide surface and a built-up rim and support for her feet. This type of chair would give her boundaries and help her to feel more secure. Furthermore, the wide surface expanse provides a play area for toys.

7. Katie should be moved around a great deal. Carry her in close contact with you. Later try movements without contact with you like dancing or gentle swinging motions as she is held in space.

General stimulation activities

1. Turning on a sound cue to locate the source of sound on either side is normally a 4-month-old task. This may be delayed in visually impaired infants. Katie is already starting to turn toward your voice. Continue to reinforce this movement by rewarding her with pats, kisses, and hugs when she turns toward you. Help her to complete the turn if she does not turn all the way. Gradually increase the distance between you and Katie so that she will turn toward you as you enter the room and call her name.

2. Whenever you are talking to Katie, try to bring her into a face to face position so that she is making some eye contact with your face. Talk with Katie on an ongoing basis and use words consistently for the same object.

CONCLUSION

In the first 2 years of life vision plays a critical part in the social and emotional development of the child and facilitates a healthy attachment to the primary caregiver, which allows for the child to develop appropriate autonomy. It plays an equally important role in the sensory motor phase of cognitive development and the early development of gross motor skills, which allow the child to explore his world. When there is some impairment to vision, either as a single impairment or in conjunction with others, it makes the task of raising such a child very difficult. It behooves all the professionals that will come into contact with this infant and his family to understand how this type of impairment alters the normal developmental course and to prepare themselves to offer ongoing guidance to the family on this developmental process as well as ways of intervening to ameliorate the effects of this type of impairment. Once again, the primary care physician who will have an ongoing relationship with this family and child must be aware of all the medical and educational factors to provide the ongoing support that this family will need.

REFERENCES

1. Allen, H. F.: A new picture series for preschool vision testing, Am. J. Ophthalmol. **44:**38, 1957.
2. Armstrong, D., Dimmitt, S., and Van Wormer, D. E.: Studies in Batten disease. I. Peroxidase deficiency in granulocytes, Arch. Neurol. **30:**144, 1974.
3. Cantolino, S. J., et al.: Ophthalmoscopic monitoring of oxygen therapy in premature infants, Am. J. Ophthalmol. **72:**322, 1971.
4. Catford, G. V., Oliver, A.: Development of visual acuity. Arch. Dis. Child. **48:**47, 1973.
5. Cogan, D. G., et al.: Herpes simplex retinopathy in an infant, Arch. Ophthalmol. **72:**641, 1964.
6. Dayton, G. O., Jr., et al.: Developmental study of coordinated eye movements in the human infant. I. Visual acuity in the newborn human: a study based on induced optokinetic nystagmus and electro-oculography, Arch. Ophthalmol. **71:**865, 1964.
7. Fraiberg, S.: Insights from the blind, New York, 1977, Basic Books, Inc.
8. Fulton, A. B., Manning, K., and Dobson, V.: A behavioral method for efficient screening of visual acuity in young infants. II. Clinical application, Invest. Ophthalmol. Vis. Sci. **17:**1151, 1978.
9. Gesell, A., Ilg, F. L., and Bullis, G. E.: *Vision. Its Development in infant and child,* New York, 1967, Hafner Publishing Co., p. 84.
10. Goldberg, H. K., and Drewry, R.: Ophthalmologic examination of the handicapped child, Pediatr. Clin. North Am. **20:**45, 1973.
11. Harley, R. D., editor: Pediatric ophthalmology, Philadelphia, 1975, W. B. Saunders Co.
12. Hunt, C. S., et al.: Ocular features of Aicardi's syndrome, Arch. Ophthalmol. **96:**291, 1978.
13. Jan, E. J., Freeman, R., and Scott, E.: Visual impairment in children and adolescents, New York, 1977, Grune & Stratton, Inc.
14. Jan, J., et al.: Blindness due to optic nerve atrophy and hypoplasia in children: an epidemiological study, Dev. Med. Child Neurol. **19:**353, 1977.
15. Kinsey, V. E., et al.: Pa_{O_2} levels and retrolental fibroplasia: a report of the cooperative study, Pediatrics **60:**655, 1977.
15a. Lippman, O.: Vision of young children, Arch. Ophthalmol. **81:**763, 1969.
16. Noble, K. G., and Carr, R. E.: Leber's congenital amaurosis. A retrospective study of 33 cases and a histopathological study of one case, Arch. Ophthalmol. **96:**818, 1978.
17. Petersen, R. A.: Schmid-Fraccaro syndrome (''cat's eye'' syndrome). Partial trisomy of G chromosome, Arch. Ophthalmol. **90:**287, 1973.
18. Petersen, R. A., and Walton, D. S.: Optic nerve hypoplasia with good visual acuity and visual field defects. A study of children of diabetic mothers, Arch. Ophthalmol. **95:**254, 1977.
19. Pincus, J. H.: Subacute necrotizing encephalopathy (Leigh's disease): a consideration of clinical features and etiology, Dev. Med. Child Neurol. **14:**87, 1972.
20. Powell, H., et al.: Adrenoleukodystrophy. Electron microscopic findings, Arch. Neurol. **32:**250, 1975.
21. Reinecke, R. D., and Simons, K.: A new stereoscopic test for amblyopia screening, Am. J. Ophthalmol. **78:**714, 1974.
22. Robb, R. M., and Walters, G. M.: Ophthalmic manifestations of subacute sclerosing panencephalitis, Arch. Ophthalmol. **83:**426, 1970.
23. Shih, V. E., et al.: Sulfite oxidase deficiency. Biochemical and clinical investigations of a hereditary metabolic disorder in sulfur metabolism, N. Engl. J. Med. **297:**1022, 1977.
24. Smith, V. H.: Strabismus in cerebral palsy, Br. Orthop. J. **22:**84, 1965.
25. Sokol, S.: Measurement of infant visual acuity from pattern reversal evoked potentials, Vision Res. **18:**33, 1978.
26. Spaeth, G. L.: Ocular manifestations of the lipidoses. In Tasman, W., editor: Retinal diseases in children. Harper & Row, Publishers, New York, 1971, pp. 127-206.
27. Ulrich, S.: Elizabeth, a mother's account of raising a blind child, Ann Arbor, Mich., 1972, University of Michigan Press.
28. Walton, D. S., and Robb, R. M.: Optic nerve hypoplasia, Arch. Ophthalmol. **84:**572, 1970.

SUGGESTED READINGS

1. Brown, S., and Donovan, C. M.: Stimulation activities, Ann Arbor, Mich., 1977, University of Michigan Press. Activities presented in cognitive, social, self-help, language, perceptual, fine motor, and gross motor areas. Shows how to adapt them for blind children.
1a. Davidson, I.: Handbook for parents of preschool blind children, Toronto, 1976, Ontario Institute for Studies in Education. Publication sales, 252 Bloor Street West, Toronto, Ontario, Canada M5S 1V6.
2. Fraiberg, S.: Insights from the blind, New York, 1977, Basic Books, Inc. Detailed observations of the development of blind infants. Theoretical implications of how their developmental course is altered.
3. Raynor, S., and Drovillard, R.: Get a wiggle on—a guide for helping visually impaired children grow, Michigan, 1975, Ingham Intermediate School District. Available free to parents. 2630 West Howell Road, Mason, Mich. 48854. Simple games and activities to use with blind infants.
4. Scott, E., Jan, J. E., and Freeman, R.: Can't your child see? Baltimore, 1977, University Park Press. Written for parents as an introduction to problems that blind children face at different ages. Suggestions for activities and assistance.

12

The child with speech and language deficits

Anthony Bashir
Howard C. Shane

The prevalence of communication disorders in children is difficult to determine with accuracy in view of the variability of definitions, samples, and methods employed in a wide variety of studies. Recent figures[42] indicate that approximately 7% to 10% of the general population have deviations in one or more aspects of communicative functions. The impairments result from a wide variety of causes and are associated with an even greater diversifica-

☐ This paper was supported in part by Grant 928, Maternal and Child Health Services, United States Department of Health, Education and Welfare.

tion of acute and chronic medical and developmental conditions. Males are more frequently affected than females. As of yet no systematic data are available on variation of prevalence within different social classes.

An impairment of communication is present when a person's speech pattern deviates from what is accepted by the social group. Communication is considered impaired when the manner of communication interferes with the speaker's ability to be understood or when attention is detracted from the communicator's intent or the message, and focused on the way in which the message is spoken. Disorders of communication should be viewed in terms of the effects they have on the speaker-listener relationship. The individual handicapped by a disorder of speech and/or language may well experience significant obstacles to the development of an adaptive life-style and a place within a social milieu.

Following classification of communicative disorders will be followed in this discussion:

resonance disorders Deficits arising from a disruption in normal oronasal sound balance and most commonly heard as hypernasality or hyponasality.

voice disorders Deviations in the quality, pitch, or loudness of the voice. The basis of these deficits may be psychological and/or physiological in nature.

fluency disorders Disruption in the natural flow of connected speech. The most common form of the disorder is stuttering.

articulation disorders Problems in speech sound production.

language disorders Disruption in the individual's ability to comprehend and/or use the symbol system of language.

In general, communicative disorders do not have a common cause. A multitude of factors give rise to the presence of communication deficits in children. It is for this reason that early identification and assessment of deficits should occur. Only in this way can appropriate therapeutic strategies be formulated and amelioration of the developmental consequences be brought about for the child.

The evaluation of communicative skills in children will involve a thoughtful and thorough assessment of speech, hearing, and language skills by a qualified speech and language pathologist and an audiologist. In addition, consultation will be requested frequently from and with other professionals to establish the medical-neurological status of the child, the child's social setting, and the cognitive and emotional development of the child. A knowledge of normal speech and language development will provide the background against which judgments will be made concerning the adequacy of any given child's communicative skills.

THE DEVELOPMENT OF A COMMUNICATION SYSTEM

For the vast majority of children diagnosed as developmentally disabled, the acquisition of speech and language represents a major achievement. Indeed, disorders of communication are associated with a wide variety of developmental disabilities of childhood, including hearing impairment,[26] mental retardation,[47] affective disorders,[3] and specific language learning disorders. A careful understanding of the ways in which the communicative system is disrupted in each of these groups of children is essential to appropriate planning of both remediation and education.

For the child, the development of a communicative system represents the chief means by which the individual will understand and express ideas, wants, and emotions as well as develop social controls and appropriate social interactions. For this discussion, language is viewed as an organized system of rules that govern the use of symbols. This system becomes the chief mode through which the individual child will represent thought. This system, whether spoken, written, or signed, becomes, as Cazden[9] has pointed out, "both curriculum content and learning environment, both the object of knowledge and a medium through which other knowledge is acquired."[9]

In becoming communicatively competent, the child must learn to perceive his world in an organized and systematic manner. It is only then that he can learn the grammar of the language and its use to convey intent within the social milieu. In acquiring and developing language, the child masters at least four somewhat different yet interrelated systems that form the basis for oral communication, that is, skills in sematics, syntactics, phonology, and pragmatism.

The child will acquire a vocabulary (lexicon) that will mark objects, events, and actions. This vocabulary becomes the primary means of marking meaning through the development of semantical systems.[6,8] For the child, the first 3 years of life is a critical period for the development of cognitive requisites to language learning. The child learns to realize self as separate from the environment and capable of controlling it. The child comes to appreciate the independence of objects, the functions of these objects, and the ways in which objects act on each other and in concert with environmental events. This early learning forms the basis for language development, the system that the child will rely on for representing what he knows about the world.

The child will acquire a syntactical system, or the rules needed to organize words hierarchially into different sentence types, for example, declarative sentences, questions. These rules will be learned over time and will be reflected in the child's utterances through time.[35,36] These systems are not learned on an imitative basis, although imitation plays a role in learning. Children make comments about their world and their concerns. Families respond to these comments and observations and their responses potentially enhance the child's utterances and provide exemplar targets of utterances. For example, the child might say "big truck" and the family respond "Yes, it's a big truck. Let's push the truck." (demonstrating the act). Dialogues like this confirm the child's observations and expand information about grammatical structure. Models are provided to the child that allow the enhancement of their own sentence productions.

The early statements of children do not have the characteristics of well-formed adult sentences. This type of speech is characterized as "infantile" or "baby talk." The early sentences of children are characterized by word deletions. Phrases such as "big truck," "no a shoe," "where boat?" reflect the child's sentence-building skills at that time. As the child matures in abilities and masters rules for sentence building these early patterns will change gradually. For example, "big truck" becomes "that big truck," and then "I want that big truck." Similarly, the statement "no a shoe" will emerge as "that's not a shoe." It is important not to view these examples as absolute. Variation does occur as does the time it takes any given child to achieve knowledge of the various rules necessary to build sentences of the different types. The examples are provided to demonstrate that the acquisition of language is not a random, chance occurrence, but rather proceeds systematically with later achievements capitalizing on earlier accomplishments.

The child will acquire a phonological or sound system for purposes of coding semantical and syntactical information. The acquisition of this system may be viewed as the learning of an auditory-motor act.[45] This information that the child has acquired about language is then ultimately mapped into coordinated muscular actions, which result in speech behavior. Over time the child learns to adapt the structures and functions of the oral, nasal, pharyngeal, laryngeal, and respiratory systems for purposes of speech sound production. It is the auditory mechanism that is the primary system by which information about speech sounds is gathered and determined. Based on auditory targets[37] or features, the child learns progressive motor

Table 12-1. Age of phonological accomplishment in children*

Age (years)	Sounds
3†	/m/,/n/,/ng/,/p/,/f/,/h/,/w/
3.6	/j/
4	/k/,/b/,/d/,/g/,/r/
4.6	/s/,/sh/,/ch/
6	/t/,/th/ (voiced), /v/,/l/
7	/th/ (voiceless), /z/,/zh/,/dz/

*Modified from Templin, M.: Certain language skills in children, Minneapolis, 1957, University of Minnesota Press.
†All vowels are 75% correct by 3 years.

selection and balistic maintenance strategies for producing the acoustic spectrum called speech. Table 12-1 is a developmental chart for speech sounds after Templin[56] and can be used as a general guide to speech accomplishment. Speech reaches its complete development by the eighth year of life.

Finally the child learns a system for using language to convey intent within the social context. Indeed, an awareness develops from early in the child's life of how to use language to mean different things and how to change the language system depending on needs and goals of a particular situation.

RESONANCE DISORDERS

The coupling and effective separation of the oral and nasal cavities is essential for normal speech sound production. Maintenance of the relationship between the cavities occurs as an operative result of the velopharyngeal mechanism. When disturbances in the balance of sound energy in the oral and nasal cavities occur, disorders of resonance are heard. The resulting acoustic features are hypernasality or hyponasality. The principal reasons for a disturbance in acoustic energy balance are (1) incompetence of the velopharyngeal mechanism giving rise to hypernasality or (2) obstructions of the nasal passageways or nasopharyngeal space, giving rise to hyponasality.

Normal operation of the velopharynx results in a sphincterlike movement.[53,54] The anterior portion of the sphincter is formed by the velum, or soft palate, when, on activation, it is elevated with posterior elongation. The pharyngeal component is in the simultaneous reduction of the nasopharyngeal space as a result of symmetrical and bilateral movement of the lateral and posterior walls to center, leading to a reduction of the superior and medial pharyngeal space.

The coupling or separation of the oral and nasal cavities depends on the activation or deactivation of the velopharyngeal system. Varying degrees of velopharyngeal seal are essential for the production of all English consonants and vowels, except /m/, /n/, /ng/. For production of these three speech sounds, the oral and nasal cavities are coupled through a lowering of the velum and change in the pharyngeal space.

Hyponasality

Hyponasality results from (1) nasal and nasopharyngeal obstructions, (2) enlargement of the adenoids, and (3) chronic allergic conditions with subsequent edema of the mucosal linings. These conditions lead to an alteration in the normal oronasal balance by disrupting the coupling relationship and alteration of the acoustic spectrum. For children presenting with hyponasality, treatment should be medical and/or surgical. The child should be referred to an otolaryngologist for assessment and subsequent care.

A word of caution should be given. In the surgical management of obstructions or in consideration of adenoidectomy, presurgical examination of the velum should be done to rule out conditions of congenital foreshortening of the velum or submucosal cleft. If these are not considered appropriately, postoperative recovery of normal air balance may not be possible due to a surgical unmasking of velopharyngeal incompetence. The child will now sound hypernasal and have the characteristics to be described below.

Hypernasality

Three primary explanations can account for velopharyngeal insufficiency, which gives rise to hypernasality. The first condition is abnormal formation of the palate seen in complete and partial clefts of the palate, submucous clefts, or congenital foreshortening of the palate. A child with no overt cleft but with hyper-

nasality may suffer from these latter conditions, and careful evaluation by a plastic surgeon or otolaryngologist is essential to rule them out. A second group of causes are adventitious and relate to acquired oral injuries from impalement of the structures with sticks or lollipops or through surgical creation secondary to treatment for oral pathologies. The third group results from weakness or paralysis of the velum and pharyngeal complex secondary to neurological damage, for example, pseudobulbar palsy, peripheral neuropathies, or acute myopathies such as dermatomyositis.

As a result of velopharyngeal incompetence speech sound production may be adversely affected, since adequate intraoral breath pressure and oral airstream direction cannot occur or be maintained. There is also an increase in nasal tone and/or nasal emission of air. Vowels can be nasalized and consonants distorted or misarticulated, frequently with errors of sound substitution or sound omission occurring. The most commonly affected consonants are those belonging to the plosive class, for example, /p/, /b/, /t/, /d/, /k/, /g/ and the sibilant, affricate, and fricative classes, for example, /f/, /s/, /ch/, /sh/, /zh/. Problems in the production of other consonants tend to be minimal, if affected at all. Finally, studies attempting to correlate the severity of the degree of hypernasality and speech disability with the degree of velopharyngeal incompetence have not succeeded in indicating a one-to-one relationship between these parameters. This resulting dilemma requires individualization of case assessment and management. Indeed, it raises the complex problem of structural and functional processes as they underlie adequate speech production and resonance maintenance.[6,25]

Not all communicative disabilities seen in patients with velopharyngeal incompetence and associated craniofacial abnormalities can be attributed to the velopharyngeal dysfunction per se.[43] Intellectual status, the individual's understanding and use of language, additional dental and oral anomalies, and physiological changes due to alteration of neuromuscular status and hearing status may all impact on the speaker's ability to achieve adequate communication. Consequently, assessment of these parameters will assist the delineation and selection of management methods for each aspect of the presenting communication problem.

Special management strategies are essential for the child with orofacial and craniofacial anomalies. Adequate intervention should be coordinated through a team approach that will plan a comprehensive and integrated habilitative program. The members of the team include a plastic surgeon, pediatrician, dentist, orthodontist, prosthodontist, otolaryngologist, speech and language pathologist, audiologist, social worker, and psychologist. Although an extensive literature exists on children with oral and cranial structural problems,[21] several observations are warranted.

Children with oral and craniofacial abnormalities have a higher incidence of middle ear disease with consequent conductive hearing loss, which may fluctuate significantly over time.[44] Recent evidence[40] suggests that persistent middle ear disease related to chronic serous otitis media can affect the course of language and speech development. Consequently, rigorous otological management and audiological following of these children is necessary to assess the child's hearing status and to maintain a facilitating auditory basis for development of communication skills.

Children with velopharyngeal incompetence may evidence a higher than expected incidence of vocal pathology. This may well be due to the increased vocal effort seen in these children. The child increases vocal effort to compensate for loss of airstream pressure due to the disruption in the normal functioning of the velopharyngeal system. Consequently, hyperfunction of the larynx may set in and give rise to pathological change in the vocal folds leading to changes in pitch, quality, and/or loudness of the voice.

In general, the conservative management of speech for the child with velopharyngeal incompetence with or without other craniofacial abnormalities consists of facilitating the development of normal oromotor patterns for speech sound production; correction of maladaptive learned oral and/or pharyngeal and laryngeal patterns, for example, pharyngeal fricatives and glottal stops; and assistance in achieving appropriate airstream direction and intraoral breath pressure. When a lack of speech and/or resonance change occurs in the child following conservative treatment, other management issues should be considered.

Surgical intervention or prosthetic management[21] are the two options available to conservative management. Even when these are employed, renewed use of speech therapy may be necessary to ensure the desired outcome of adequate speech and resonance balance. Surgical intervention is directed toward reconstruction of the bony environment and/or reconstruction of the velopharyngeal system through, for example, superior-based velopharyngeal flaps. The best candidates for such intervention are those children with structural basis for continued velopharyngeal incompetence.

Children whose problems result from neuromuscular deficits, for example, dysarthria, or velar and pharyngeal incoordination or from oral dyspraxia are best treated through the use of prosthetic devices. Whether surgical or prosthetic management is eventually employed to facilitate speech, the decision should be based on careful evaluation of structure and function, which relies on the use of speech fluoroscopy and endoscopy. Through these measurement techniques information critical to an understanding of the physiology of motion in the velopharynx can be achieved and become the basis for rational decision making.

VOICE DISORDERS

Clinical management of voice disorders requires an appreciation of normal vocal functions. According to Wilson[65] the parameters of a ''normal'' voice include

. . . (1) pleasing voice quality, (2) proper balance of oral and nasal resonance, (3) appropriate loudness, (4) an habitual pitch level suitable for age, size and sex, and (5) appropriate voice inflections involving pitch and loudness. The rate of speaking should be such that it does not interfere with the five essential characteristics of a normal voice. This basic definition of a normal voice must be broad enough to allow a wide range of variation in any one or more of the essential positive characteristics.[65,p.1]

It is thus deviation from the norm that signals the presence of a voice disorder.

Voice disorders refer to a complex of deviations in voice quality, vocal pitch, and vocal loudness. Pitch relates to the vibratory cycle or frequency of vibration of the vocal folds. Typically male voices have a fundamental frequency of approximately 130 hertz (Hz). A normal female voice vibrates one octave higher or at approximately 260 Hz. In classifying disorders of pitch consideration is given to whether the habitual pitch level of the voice is too high or too low for the individual's age and sex.

The parameter of vocal loudness is related to an interaction between air pressure below the level of the vocal folds, that is, subglottic air pressure, and the length, mass, and tension of the folds themselves. Disorders of loudness are based on subjective judgment of whether the vocal intensity is too loud or too soft.

Quality disturbances arise when the normal vibratory pattern of the vocal folds is disturbed. Most often vocal fold growths, for example, vocal nodules, contact ulcers, or vocal polyps, or changes in the condition of the folds such as edematous vocal folds influence the normal vibratory pattern and result in such vocal disorders as hoarseness, harshness, huskiness, and/or breathiness. To the trained ear the underlying pathology can be diagnosed because of its unique acoustic symptomatology.[2]

Voice disorders in children occur most frequently because of (1) vocal abuse, for example, excessive talking, yelling, or singing, most often leading to vocal nodules, (2) vocal misuse, for example, speaking at an inappropriate pitch level or vocal loudness level, most often leading to vocal nodules, (3) allergic conditions, most often leading to edema of the laryngeal membranes, and (4) nonmalignant growths, for example, juvenile papillomata.

Not all voice disorders arise secondary to structure changes. Children may consistently use an inappropriate pitch or voice quality because of faulty learning, that is, a functional voice disorder. A psychogenic explanation can also underlie a perceived voice disorder. For example, an aphonic or dysphonic condition can arise in which the individual is seemingly unable to produce voice and thus speaks in a whisper, known as psychogenic aphonia. Furthermore, emotional issues are thought to lead to disturbances of laryngeal structures in the following way. Anxiety can produce increased tension of the extrinsic and intrinsic laryngeal musculature, which in turn leads to structural change following faulty usage over time. Similarly, a child's management of aggression or anger may result in his use of unusually high or low vocal intensity or may result in vocal abuse through excessive screaming. This in turn leads to structural change, that is, vocal nodules. Finally, disturbances in normal hearing can result in changes in vocal loudness.[7]

There is a lack of unanimity with regard to the underlying cause of some voice disorders. Such is the case with the condition known as mutational falsetto, in which the expected lowering of pitch associated with puberty does not occur. The resulting acoustic phenomenon is a high-pitched voice spoken in the falsetto register. Although a functional reason is often given to account for this condition, other clinical descriptions suggest a psychogenic explanation.[31]

Management of voice disorders will vary as a function of the underlying cause. Initially referral should be to an otolaryngologist for examination of the laryngeal structures and functions. With knowledge from this examination, treatment decisions can be generated based on an integration of these physical findings and historical data. Medically based voice disorders such as those associated with allergies or juvenile papillomata will require medical or surgical consideration and management. For those conditions requiring vocal education or reeducation, for example, vocal nodules, treatment by a speech and language pathologist will be required. This includes those vocal pathologies related to vocal abuse, with or without structural change. Nonsurgical management is preferred. It is our opinion that surgical removal of vocal nodules is contraindicated in children, since noninvasive therapy can ameliorate the condition. Furthermore, surgical removal without attention to underlying cause will merely result in regrowth of the nodular tissue.

Generally a threefold treatment approach is elected. That treatment deals with (1) monitoring and manipulating vocal use in the environment, (2) providing normal vocal habits, and (3) preventing reoccurrence of the disorder.

FLUENCY DISORDERS

Stuttering, the most common form of fluency disorder, has been an enigma to man since ancient times. Since Satyrus treated the stuttering Demosthenes, considerable speculation, writing, and research have been accomplished to explain the basis of stuttering and effective remediation strategies.[57]

Hypotheses of the cause of stuttering can be grouped into three major areas. These include (1) psychoanalytical theories,[19] (2) physiological or organically predisposing theories,[57] and (3) learning theories.[57] No attempt will be made to review these concepts in this chapter. The reader is referred to the specific studies for detailed information.

The manner in which stuttering is defined both suggests the principal cause and describes the therapeutic management of the child. A three-factor definition[23] of stuttering can be stated. (1) Stuttering is a disruption in the natural flow of speech, that is, nonfluencies or dysfluencies, which are often heard as repetitions of sounds or whole words, prolongation of sounds, excessive pausing or the addition of words in connected speech. (2) Stuttering is an evaluative judgment on the part of the listener who perceives certain speech nonfluencies just noted as abnormal or unacceptable. (3) Stuttering represents the speaker's assessment of self, based on how others have reacted to his communicative style and how he perceives those reactions. Such a definition of stuttering defines the behavior as learned over time and extended by factors such as anticipation and judgment as well as negative social and communicative experiences.

The vast majority of children who are called stutterers are identified between the third and fourth years of life. Stuttering may also appear, however, during a child's first school experiences or as the child approaches adolescence. While this is not as common as preschool dysfluent behavior, the appearance of stuttering at these times may represent problems of a deeper emotional nature, in which the dysfluency is a symptom among many others and signals the need for careful appraisal of the child's emotional concerns and well-being.

In the course of normal language development all children evidence periods of normal, nonfluent speech or disruptions in the natural flow of language.[66] This occurs during the second to fifth years of life. These nonfluencies should be considered as normal occurrences consisting of pauses, repetitions of sounds, sound prolongation, revision of sentences, and pauses in responding to a speaker. While the explanation for normal nonfluent behavior is not firmly established, it is hypothesized that while children may understand language and possess the rules needed for sentence building, they lack the practiced automaticiy of speech that adult speakers possess. Consequently breaks occur in the natural flow of their oral language formulation.

One possible explanation for stuttering is that it represents a judgment of abnormality on the part of the listener to these normal, nonfluent patterns present in the child's speech. Consequently, a change in the interaction between the speaker (child) and listener (family members) results. Through explicit or implicit behaviors on the part of the listener, such as telling a child to slow down, think before speaking, take a deep breath and then talk, the child begins to feel his inadequacy as an effective communicator. While the child may not recognize what is aberrant about his speech behavior, he senses that speech is inadequate. Following sufficient negative experiences, the child may begin to anticipate problems with speech and perceive himself as a poor, ineffective communicator. The child begins to attempt avoidance of the behavior that inevitably leads to dysfluent speech.

Clinically, one also encounters those children who use their speech dysfluencies as a means of gaining attention and controlling their families. Issues surrounding secondary gains from stuttering need thoughtful management. Careful psychological assessment and speech and language evaluation should be conducted involving both the child and his family.

For the reasons noted, a careful management of parents' complaints concerning nonfluent behavior must occur. Also, a careful analysis of these behaviors and the parent's attitudes must be made. Counselling with regard to the nature of the child's behavior and the methods for dealing with it should be provided. The assistance of experienced professionals is frequently necessary. Early intervention may prevent a true disability from occurring by reversing negative attitudes and correcting management of children.

This concept suggests that stuttering is not predominantly a physiological problem. Although there are instances of stuttering associated with wider neurological dysfunction, this is not the general rule. While stuttering may appear in families, it should not be regarded as genetically transferred to children. Rather, the attitude of the family to normal nonfluency and familial expectations about communication and the subsequent changes in family-child interaction may explain its occurrence in different generations. Current knowledge suggests that stuttering is not learned through imitation. While children may occasionally mimic dysfluent speech in other children, they do not adopt the dysfluent pattern as their own. However, the reactions of people toward the child's imitation may establish the stuttering behavior as his typical speaking pattern.

ARTICULATION DISORDERS

Disorders of speech sound production or articulation are the most frequently encountered speech problems in children, estimated to account for 75% of recognized communication disorders.[42] Articulation disorders are characterized by four types of errors:

1. *Substitutions* occur when the child replaces one sound with another, such as in the production of /w/ight for /l/ight.
2. An error of *omission* occurs when the production of the child lacks the inclusion of a particular speech sound as in boo/ / for boo/k/.
3. The third type of articulation error is referred to as *distortion,* for example, lisping.
4. Addition of sounds is a seldom occurrence.

Speech sound production errors may vary from one speech sample to the next. One might note, for example, that a youngster is capable of producing a certain sound in a specific word or position and not in other words. Also, production errors might vary from single words to connected speech. For example, he might be able to accurately produce a sound in one word, but be unable to articulate the same word when it appears in a phrase or sentence. In addition, the child may commit errors of all three types within any single speech sample, that is, combinations of substitutions, omissions, and distortions.

Variability is observed in the number of consonants and vowels that are misarticulated. The child's errors may range from only a few sounds being misarticulated to a child who is capable of only producing a limited number of consonants and vowels. In this latter instance, the child may well be unintelligible to the listener. Regardless of the number of speech sounds involved, children exist who are unable to produce sounds with facility and consistency. To this extent they differ from normal speaking children.

Etiology of articulation disorders

Failure to develop normal speech production skills may not be readily explained by any single factor. In fact, a complex of interacting variables may be present and responsible for the child's inability to produce intelligible speech. The purpose of the following discussion is to briefly discuss some commonly considered causes of articulation disorders.

The normal production of speech occurs because of the integrated action of several different systems and structures. The respiratory system; the laryngeal mechanism; the pharynx; the nasal cavity; the oral cavity with such structures as the palate, tongue, and teeth; and the lips are all component parts of the speech mechanism. It is the integrated function of this system that gives rise to such processes as articulation, voice, and resonance. Changes within the structure and/or function of this system may have an effect on speech sound production ability. A problem arises, however, in establishing a clear causal relationship between changes in the oral structure and articulation skills. This often results from the difficulty in weighing the importance of any one deviation in structure over another to the resulting speech problem.

Dental irregularity is seen as one cause of speech disorder. The production of certain consonants does require at least reasonable dental alignment. This is particularly true of such labiodental sounds as /f/ and /v/, or linguodental sounds like /th/ (thing) and /th/ (this). Sounds such as /s/, /z/, /sh/, and /zh/ (vision) require the approximation of the teeth and tongue for direction of the airstream across the cutting edge of the teeth. It is generally agreed, however, that persons are usually capable of achieving compensation in production of sounds when the normal dental alignment is altered.

In conditions in which the normal relationship between the upper and lower teeth is disturbed or excessive spacing and turning of the teeth are present, problems in speech sound production may occur. It is an error to assume, however, that all changes in dentition lead directly to speech impairment. Similarly, it would be inaccurate to assume that normal speech is not possible without perfect dental spacing and alignment. Careful consideration by qualified professionals is necessary to determine the factors affecting speech production and a judgment of the relationship between structural change and the speech sound errors that the individual is producing should be made.

Lingual functions in conjunction with other parts of the oral cavity create constrictions, channel the airstream, and shape the general contour of the oral resonator. Lingual activity influences the oral environment and changes oral resonant cavities, giving rise to different speech sounds. For example, when the tip of the tongue is placed behind the teeth and then released, the sound /t/ is produced. In this instance the voice tone is not produced. With few exceptions, research on the role of minor incoordination of the tongue as a basis for articulation deficits is inconclusive. Several instances of lingual involvement that cause speech problems should be mentioned, however.

The shape of the hard palate may restrict the mobility of the tongue when the hard palate is highly arched and narrow. This condition may restrict the contact between the tongue and the hard palate in the formation of certain speech sounds and result in distorted speech sound production.

Tongue-tie (foreshortened lingual frenulum) is often viewed as responsible for speech articulation problems. Judgments concerning the relationship of tongue-tie to articulation problems should be made conservatively. Unless the tongue is severely reduced in its range of movement, that is, protrusion, elevation, etc., it is in all likelihood unrelated to the speech problem. Careful examination is warranted before a causal relationship is assumed.

Recent evidence suggests that some individuals who demonstrate articulation disabilities have difficulty in using sensory information from the mouth (somesthetic and kinesthetic feedback). It is hypothesized that such a deficit in the use of sensory data can interfere with speech sound production. Although the exact method by which such a deficit may interfere with speech is not clearly explained, it seems reasonable to say that in some selected cases, reduced use of oral sensation may result in reduced articulation skills. The diagnosis of such cases must remain in the hands of professionals well versed in using the available assessment tools. Similarly, it should not be concluded that all children with speech disorders experience problems in the use of oral sensory information.

Conditions that cause paralysis of the tongue musculature will have an obvious effect on speech production. Those speech disorders which result from a disturbance of motor movement for speech because of weakness, paralysis, or severe incoordination of the speech musculature are referred to as the dysarthrias.[11,12] Dysarthrias are most frequently encountered in children with cerebral palsy, although not limited to this condition. The speech and behavioral symptoms associated with dysarthria are many and are related to the location of central and/or peripheral nervous system lesions. Not only will these children have varying degrees of speech involvement, but also they will often demonstrate problems in feeding. The speech involvement may be seen in reduced ability to produce articulated speech. Resonance and voice disorders may also be noted. Careful description of the problem is essential for therapeutic planning. Such children should be seen for a speech and language evaluation before plans are made for their therapy. This group of children is at great risk for not developing intelligible speech. Consequently, assessing these children as potential users of nonvocal communication systems is essential (p. 307).

Another group of children have a developmental apraxia of speech. These children are unable to select voluntarily, direct, and organize sequences of movement for purposes of speech sound production even when the musculature is strong. They are often of normal intelligence and hearing sensitivity. They make attempts at speech, but often fail, frequently groping when attempts are made to imitate a sound. The degree of speech present is variable and may be a severe limitation in sound production skills or may represent problems in the sequencing of movements for the production of multisyllabic words. Because these symptoms are common to a number of other disabilities, careful differential diagnosis of speech and language function along with neurological and psychological studies is warranted.[68] Care must be taken before a decision regarding the cause of the speech problem is made.

The ability to hear plays a crucial role in the development of speech and language. It is obvious that hearing loss, regardless of the degree, may have far-reaching impact on the child's ability to not only acquire language, but also to act as an efficient user of language. The symptoms and problems arising in language development because of hearing loss have been discussed in Chapter 10. The role of hearing in the acquisition and maintenance of speech is not limited, however, to questions of normal sensitivity.

Individuals are not only capable of detecting the presence of a sound, but are also able to tell the differences between sounds (auditory discrimination), remember sound sequences (auditory sequential memory), and select a message from a generally noisy environment (attention

and figure ground). These capacities of the organism are not necessarily totally developed at birth and are generally regarded as improving with age. Learning and maturation play mutual roles in the emergence of these skills.

For some children, difficulties in speech sound production are said to be caused by their inability to tell the differences between sounds. Research to date indicates that such relationships may not be real. However, documentation of the general effects of an inability to remember sounds or of problems in the child's ability to attend to speech as causal bases for articulation disorders has yet to be firmly established. It is obvious that a thoughtful evaluation of the child is needed before decisions are made.

While it is reasonable to have noted these causes of articulation disorders, it must be pointed out that in the vast majority of cases no significant cause for the problem can be isolated. Inaccurate learning of sounds is often used to explain speech problems. Those factors which cause learning to be a problem are, however, not obvious, and increased research into this question is needed before thoughtful statements can be made.

Factors such as deficient speech models in the environment, a lack of good speech stimulation, reduced motivation on the part of the child to improve speech, disruption in the relationship between the family and the child, and poor self-image are additional reasons for articulation problems. The evidence to suggest these factors is largely clinical and represents the accumulated experiences of many professionals in the diagnosis and management of children with communication disorders. Research is required before the nature of the interaction between these conditions and articulation disorders is clarified.

LANGUAGE DISORDERS

The search for primary causes of language disabilities has been abandoned in favor of those approaches that describe the child's knowledge of the grammar system and the use of that knowledge in communicative contexts. While this more generic approach to a description of the communicative process is in use clinically, extensive literature concerning the language status and special problems of the hearing impaired child,[26] the mentally retarded individual,[47] and the child with atypical development[3] is available. Since this exists, avoidance of redundancy and belaboring of the point has special appeal to us. It is the intent of this section to describe a set of clinical observations most frequently seen in that group of children considered to manifest specific developmental language disorders. These are children who have often been referred to as "aphasic" children. For various reasons that term is not considered appropriate when referring to children with nonacquired disorders of language.[24]

Recent studies[13,14,32] have identified disorders of language and the processing of auditory-verbal information as major components of later reading disabilities in children. These language deficits are present generally from the preschool years and for many children persist into the school years.[55,63] The early forms of language disorders are seen as varying problems in the comprehension and/or use of language symbols as well as disturbances in the social use of language. In addition, many of these children present deficits in their ability to use and organize incoming auditory-verbal information.

It should be noted that public education assumes that a child has knowledge of the language system before entering school and that language is a given in the formulation of the early school curriculum and an important vehicle for learning thereafter. Because of this presuppositional stand, children with developmental language disorders are at high risk for academic failure of varying degrees and types during the school years.

It is also becoming increasingly apparent that language disorders do not represent a homogeneous type of deficit. Recent evidence of children with reading disabilities, for example, indicates clusters of deficits that differentiate groups of children within the general category of those with reading problems. This is also becoming apparent in cases of language impairment. Knowledge of the clusters of different behaviors associated under the general topic of language disorders is emerging.[1,4]

A recognition of the multifaceted nature of language disorders encountered in childhood reduces the likelihood of professionals adopting a single-process etiological model in both assessment and treatment. The language impaired child is thus viewed in a holistic perspective as a child who demonstrates problems in both language knowledge and use (the social manifestations of language deficits) and in the affective domain and regulation and also as an individual with the potential for disruption in the learning of language forms in the school curriculum.

The clinical findings usually encountered in language disordered children are presented as follows. Understand that although categorical presentation is used here for purposes of symptom display, this distinction does not occur with such clear lines in actual clinical encounters.

Disorders of understanding or comprehension

Understanding refers to the individual's ability to derive meaning from the spoken message by way of reference to words, relationships, and sentence structures. In addition, the individual understands against a background of shared experiences, presuppositions about the speaker's message and knowledge, and an ability to integrate the context in which the message is heard. In understanding a message the listener will apply reasoning abilities.

The listener makes a judgment concerning the speaker's intent. The utterance, "Your face is dirty," by a mother to a child who is about to leave for school is often interpreted as a request or command to do something about one's condition. This is an interpretation of the message and is not derived from the literal meanings of the words but from the listener's understanding of the speaker's intent.

Children with specific disorders of understanding demonstrate a number of cardinal clinical signs. In general, these children are characterized by predominant problems in understanding symbol-object associations or relationships, difficulties in interpreting and distinguishing different sentence types, and problems in the interpretation of social conversations. For some of these children the inability to know and interpret sound of any type, for example, running water, honking horn, may also be present. These are more severe cases, and their problems extend beyond the management of meaning and grammar and include difficulties in the consistent management of sound meanings in general.[39]

On initial encounter, the children may present clinically with a question of hearing loss. Similar factors, such as Rh and ABO incompatibility, prematurity, anoxia and congenital rubella and cytomegalovirus infections, that give rise to hearing loss may also be associated with specific problems in understanding. These factors may also be used to determine a child at risk for hearing impairment, specific language disorder, or other developmental problems. Clinically, determining the hearing status in the child with specific understanding problems may be difficult, since the child may not understand how to perform the auditory task involved in the testing situation, whether the testing is done using pure tone or free field audiometric techniques. While some of these children may have hearing impairments of the sensorineural type with bilateral involvement, the presence of the hearing impairment per se often does not explain completely the difficulty the child has in understanding. In other cases, the hearing will be shown to be within normal limits, and an audiological explanation of the child's comprehension problems is not possible.

Affectively, these children will relate to others and enter into reciprocal relationships. However, some may appear shy and overdependent on their families. For language impaired children, in general, disturbances in the principal means by which they relate to caretakers and peers may give rise to the development of overdependence, the lack of age-appropriate means for dealing with self-control issues and interfere with the effective development of peer and other social relationships. Also, children with problems in understanding may appear to demonstrate appropriate social skills when, in fact, they lack these skills. Smiling and nodding during a conversation and following requests that are made with contextual support may allow the child to give the erroneous impression of understanding what is said.

The psychological assessment of the language impaired child poses several critical problems. The first comes about because of the reliance on verbal skills in the assessment of intelligence. Clearly some nonverbal assessment of cognitive skills should be made. Scales like the Leiter International Scale, the Hiskey Nebraska, and the performance subtests of the revised Wechsler Intelligence Scale for Children are useful for this purpose. Children with problems in language, specifically children with problems in understanding, usually demonstrate age appropriate functioning on performance measures. This does not, however, exclude the possible presence of visuomotor, spatial, or integration deficits.

The second problem encountered in the psychological assessment of the language impaired child is in the area of emotional status. Interpretation of the child's use of play material and observations of how the child manipulates others and controls himself are important aspects of the assessment.

Problems of impulse control, delayed personal skill mastery, expression of anger, separation and independence from the family, and social misperception pose special problems. A thoughtful assessment will be necessary both for the planning of the child's therapeutic and educational programs and the family's ability to adjust and deal effectively and reasonably with the child.

Expressive language disorders

Expressive language disorders are a group of deficits in the use of language for purposes of representing thought and self within the social context. Deficits are evidenced in the ways the child expresses ideas and concepts in spoken verbal symbols. In describing the oral language abilities of a child, reference is made to the following:

1. The context of communication
2. The intent of the speaker
3. The main means of communication, whether expressed through pointing, signs, gestures, jargon, words, phrases, or sentences
4. The words known and used by the child for specifying objects and events

5. The underlying relationships expressed through words
6. The child's overall sentence-building skills
7. The child's word-finding skills
8. Appropriateness of narrative to context
9. The child's ability to elaborate narrative and maintain organization
10. The child's ability to communicate in unsolicited versus solicited and confrontationally constrained situations
11. The child's conversational skills.

Specific clinical problems can be detected through measurement of each of these behaviors. Although advances have been made in this area,[5,14,28] subjective clinical decisions continue to be the bases for formulating a description of the child's expressive language skills. Following is a transcribed dialogue with a 9-year-old boy after his return from spring vacation to Florida and Connecticut. The child was first seen for assessment of language at the age of 4 years. The sample provides a number of examples of deficits in conversation and makes explicit material pertinent to an understanding of the areas just described. R. J. is a child with normal hearing. On nonverbal assessment his intelligence is within normal limits. He has problems in visuomotor coordination. His speech evidenced a mild to moderate articulation deficit believed to have its basis in oral dyspraxia. He is an appealing child, eager to please, but one who profited from tasks being broken down into their component parts and material provided to him slowly, with repetition and clear separation of tasks.

Therapist: Well the lightning can happen in the country too, can't it?

R. J.: Right . . . ah . . . some . . . that happened too.

Therapist: Is the lightning as scary in the country?

R. J.: Yes and you know what . . . ah . . . ah . . . sometimes . . . well we went to Florida anicut . . . and um . . . Susan and that was scary too . . . we went on a airplane . . . and um . . . and it was . . . it was almost scary, I mean, it was scary on the airplane.

Therapist: You had some difficulty on the airplane.

R. J.: Yep, because you know what . . . uh . . . then it got dark and we couldn't see and . . . and . . . no . . . no . . . and all the airplanes had the light burned out.

Therapist: Well, that sounds very scary. How did it feel?

R. J.: Yep, the motor . . . um . . . got some lightning and then you know what we got some food on the airplane and then when there's no . . . no . . . no lightning and storm and thunder and lightning and rain the lights came back on. I mean, no, it was on.

Therapist: When you were in the plane?

R. J.: Yes, and it was very scary.

Therapist: Can children play in an airplane?

R. J.: No toys.

Therapist: What do you do?

R. J.: Just sit and get the seatbelts on and then . . . it went down the um . . . wheels to the runway and then you know what . . . we . . . we went to the runways down and then we came back up to the sky and then you know what the lights came back off.

Therapist: What's the first thing the airplane does?

R. J.: Get on and get the suitcases back one and then . . . it has these pressers.

The example points out the child's problems with sentence building, which continue to persist at age 9. His difficulty in finding the appropriate word when he needs it, the problems he has in cohesive narrative building, deficits in answering the questions requested of him are all seen in many children with language impairment. As in the case of other language impaired children, R. J. has problems in reading, both in acquiring analytic decoding skills and in understanding printed material.

What follows is a description of clinical findings that are important during the assessment of the child with an expressive language disorder. The aspects of oral language usage listed in the initial part of this section have generic applicability to the assessment of all children with developmental disabilities. For these purposes we will describe the findings generally associated with children having specific language learning problems.

The parents of children with disorders of expressive language complain that their children have difficulty conveying their ideas through words. In addition, parents will note that they have difficulty following their children's conversations and understanding the child's communicative intent. Frequently the children become frustrated when not understood and will in many instances refuse to repeat themselves when they are not understood. This is especially true of those children with expressive language problems and articulation deficits. The children may resort to the use of gestures, taking the parents to what is desired, or showing what it is they mean to say. Parents react to these frustrations on behalf of their children and themselves and experience difficulty in managing their feelings about the role they have played in their child's problems. They have significant concerns, and realistically so. They are concerned about the impact of the child's communication problems on his social growth and on the child's educational progress.

In many instances parents begin to overcompensate and place subtle demands on their children for growth in areas other than communication. Denial plays a role in the extent to which realistic adjustment may be brought about for the family and the child. Care should be taken to assist the family in understanding the child and the ways in which language deficits interfere with normal growth and development. Indeed, for many families assistance through psychological intervention is necessary.

Language impaired children present with a broad array of behavioral styles. They generally relate to others and can be engaged in reciprocal relationships. Play is often present, but there are those children for whom restricted development of play may be noted. This is seen as part of the continuum of disruption in the development of the representational continuum.[30] For some children, the restricted play and use of toys seems to reflect the lack of socioenvironmental experience with toys. In others, the child's emotional styles, for example, rigidity or lack of personal options, interferes with the degree of elaborate play and representation in play.

Characteristics such as overdependence and lack of age appropriate independence may be seen in the children as a group during the preschool years. In addition, the children will evidence awareness of their problem and in new and different situations become reticent to communicate or to interact. This reluctance seems secondary to the child's awareness and fear concerning the consequence of communicative ineffectiveness. In addition, the management

of agression may be difficult for the children as they evidence problems in age-appropriate means of expressing control over those with whom they interact, for example, striking out, refusal to respond and other withholding behaviors, or overemphasis of monster fears and "superheroes." Again, we emphasize the need for a child psychologist familiar with the problems of the language impaired to assist in defining the needs of the child and assisting the parents with their reactions to behavior and management issues.

Traditionally children with predominant oral language formulation and use problems were presumed to have appropriate comprehension abilities. Recent studies and clinical experience indicate that this may not be the case for all children. Indeed, there is good evidence to suggest that as the complexity of a verbal understanding task increases, the child will evidence increasing problems in comprehension. As research methodology and study and the ability to measure comprehension of increasingly complex language improve this point will be further clarified. Just because the parent reports that the child understands everything, the child follows simple commands during an office visit, or he turns his head during conversation as the parent does, there is no assurance that comprehension is intact. If the parent or pediatrician has some basis for concern, careful study is needed and referral to a speech and language pathologist is urged.

A review of the communication literature reveals a debate concerning the question, "Is the language production skill of those children with language problems different from those of normal children or are they simply delayed?" The debate on this topic is long and arduous.[5,27,29,36] Because of language sampling differences across these studies, a quick and reasonable answer to the problem is not readily apparent. Nevertheless, we support the position that the language formulation skills of language impaired children are different from those of normal children, and although acquisition of structures does occur, there is evidence that even in later childhood unresolved aspects of language acquisition and development are noted.[61,63]

''What we gonna do?''
''Michael have a big monster, can knock me down.''
''Why you have a mail box in here?''
''In the morning Laurie run right out the door.''
''Then the boy getting a cookie, then he gonna fall down, hurt hisself.''

All of these utterances are produced by 5-year-old M. J., who has normal intelligence and hearing sensitivity. Her understanding skills, as well as measurement allows, appears to be normal. These utterances, however, characterize her expressive language problem. M. J.'s case is also important for the following reason. On certain standard assessment tools of expression, this child appeared to be functioning at expected levels for her chronological age. However, she did not incorporate her knowledge of language into general conversational skills and descriptions. Because a child appears to be functioning normally along certain assessment parameters, it is not sufficient to preclude breakdown in production processes during free-speaking situations or in situations of solicitation and confrontational speech requests, for example, description or specific dialogue about certain topics.

The appearance of apparent superficial ''immaturity'' in sentence-building skills, the presence of telegraphic structures, and the use of less mature rule ordering and inclusion devices are the hallmarks of children with problems in sentence formulation. Indeed, the work of Wiig and Semel[63] and Vogel[61] and the case report of Weiner[61a] suggest that even by late childhood, these problems persist and sentence-building skills continue to be deficient.

Approaches to the description of the child's use of semantic relationships[5] or to an analysis of the syntax of children's utterances[27,28] are available. These methods will allow a clinician to generate the basis of the child's rule systems. On this analysis clinical intervention can be planned. Reference to the methods of analysis then becomes the main way for the clinician to establish an accountability base and to measure growth and development of expressive skills.

Not only do children have problems in sentence building and the specification of meaning but also in word retrieval. This problem, re-ferred to variably as word-finding deficits, dysnomia, or semantic aphasia, is a condition seen as a momentary inability on the part of the child to recall the name of an object or event of which the child has previous knowledge. It is most commonly observed under confrontational naming situations, such as answering questions and in extended descriptions and explanations. Parents will report, ''He can't say what he wants,'' ''I can't follow him when he talks,'' or ''It's like it's on the tip of his tongue and he can't get it out.''

The isolation of the behavior takes place under conditions of confrontational naming. A series of pictures are presented to the child, and the nature of his behaviors during picture naming is noted. Certain behaviors during word finding are associated with children who have language disabilities[46] as well as with children who have language learning disabilities.[14,67] It is important to point out that while the child has difficulty accessing to the vocabulary that he has available to him, recent evidence suggests that these children may have reduced rates of growth in vocabulary per se.[67] Therefore, not only is the child not able to retrieve from what he has, but there may also be a reduction in the total lexical options available to the child.

Among the behaviors noted in these children the following are most often encountered. The child may attempt to represent through gestures or the shape of the object. For some children descriptions or illusions will be used, for example, ''fish scooper'' for pelican, ''hump horse'' for camel, ''something the doctor uses to listen to your heart'' for stethoscope. Sometimes a word that sounds like the one sought after will be used, for example, slow for low, tornado for volcano. The similarity of the number of syllables in the word error and the distribution of accent within the word gives evidence that not all of the word is lost to retrieval. Additional behaviors are seen in the creation of phonemic errors or sequence of phonemic errors, such as ''hart'' for harp, ''donimos'' for dominos, ''racacus,'' then ''rhinocerole'' for rhinoceros. In their narratives these children may evidence the use of indefinite words, and although speaking in sentences, on closer listening one finds they are not using substantative words; for example, ''Oh and then he did that to him before it was done,'' is a description of the rescue of an individual who was saved from the sea.

In the course of language development, these children with language and word finding problems may develop nonfluent speech. This usually occurs between the ages of 3 and 7 years. A speaker's ability to maintain fluency during communication is based on a number of factors, one of which is the person's ability to preserve meaning through the quick and accurate retrieval of the desired words. For the language impaired child this may not be the case, as can be seen in the previous example of a conversation with R. J. The manner in which parents and teachers react to these dysfluencies and the methods used to provide the child with compensatory strategies will affect the eventual outcome of the dysfluent behavior. Stress for confrontational dialogue and adverse reactions to the child's attempts to communicate can precipitate true stuttering behavior. One is faced then with a language impaired child who now stutters. There is an obvious need for careful management of the child by the speech and language pathologist.

Children with word-finding problems, as well as those with sentence formulation deficits, frequently have difficulty with narrative and maintenance of narrative. While they may be topically correct in their narratives, several problems are noted. For some children there is a reduction in their ability to comment on the content of situations or events. In addition, they evidence reduced story-telling skills. Some have difficulty elaborating on a story or speak only in the most immediate and basic way about events. Others have difficulty in maintaining organizational features and seem to ramble and build incoherent narratives.

Therapy for the language impaired child will vary, depending on the degree and types of deficits present. Approaches emphasizing the cognitive basis of language are used frequently to assist the child in acquiring the abilities to represent in general and from there to use language to mark thought. For some children placement in a classroom for language impaired children emphasizing adaptive teaching and stylistic management will be necessary.[38] Still others will require behavioral management before they profit from individual intervention. Therapy will provide a basis for accommodating to the necessary styles of the child, for example, the need to have external structure, in which tasks are broken down into their component parts for teaching, the need for repetition and slower modes of providing information; the need for care in facilitating attending behaviors; the need for assistance in moving from one task to another. In addition, therapy should focus on the functional teaching of language, beginning where the child is and progressively assisting the child to develop strategies that will facilitate the understanding and use of more complex language.

The consequences of language impairments are grave. They disrupt social growth and development. They can limit the child's adaptive skills. They can interfere with the expression of feelings and the development of self-concept. Many of these children who demonstrate preschool problems in the comprehension and use of language will also experience problems in reading and writing language during the school years. There is an urgency in saying that just because professionals are itinerant in the language impaired child's life, the language problems are not. The educational problems that these children encounter will manifest themselves throughout the school years as a function of the learning tasks involved and the stresses placed on the child for higher order thinking and production.

AUGMENTATIVE COMMUNICATION SYSTEMS

Professionals dealing with communicatively handicapped persons have come to the unsettling realization that they cannot induce oral communication in all persons. This point has long been claimed by educators of deaf children emphasizing hand signals but only recently applied to individuals whose communication deficits were not caused by hearing loss. Paralleling this realization has been a movement of more handicapped citizens into the public sector. Consequently clinicians are faced with developing communication strategies for persons whose speech is ineffective in all or most situations.

To meet the communication needs of the estimated 1 million Americans who will not develop sufficient speech, augmentative communication systems are gaining greater acceptance. Two generic terms can represent the available augmentative communication system options: *manual communication systems* and *communication prostheses*. The manual systems include formal sign language and gestures. Sign language, which is usually associated with communication by the hearing impaired, has been reported of late to benefit persons who are considered mentally retarded[18,20] or autistic.[41] Gesture systems can be either idiocratic (reflect creation by an individual) or more developed and culturally recognized as in the case with the American Indian sign language. American Indian sign language, or Amerind, has been introduced to nonspeaking persons who are mentally retarded,[16] glossectomized,[52] or have an acquired apraxia of speech.[51] Although no published reports have documented the success of manual communication procedures with children having developmental apraxia of speech, it has been our clinical experience that such procedures are often useful.

Communications prostheses include both the electronic and nonelectronic communication devices and systems. Such devices allow communication to take place through the nonspeaking person's indication of symbolic information (representing his communicative intent) contained on a communication display (e.g., lap tray, Etran chart). Desired information can be indicated through either direct selection or scanning or encoding procedures,[58] and the mode of indication will be based on the nonspeaking person's cognitive and motor status at the time of the evaluation.

In recent years engineering advances have led to the development of electronic communication prostheses having a variety of sophisticated outputs. These include typewritten, liquid crystal, cathode ray tube (i.e., television screen), and speech (synthetic or prerecorded) output or some combination of these. The availability of such output options can allow for greater interaction between the nonspeaking and speaking persons as well as among nonspeaking individuals. Furthermore, these output modes can also allow the nonspeaking person to create his autobiography, correspond in writing, or communicate at a later time.

A number of symbol options can be placed on the display, including traditional orthography, Blissymbols, photographs, pictures, line drawings, or a combination of these stimuli. The selection of the symbol material will depend on a consideration of motor, cognitive, linguistic, and environmental factors.

Communication prostheses have been used most often with persons having cerebral palsy.[33,60] Recently, however, these methods have also been tried with persons who are ambulatory and have a variety of diagnostic labels, such as mental retardation, autism, or apraxia of speech.[48,49]

The long-term effects of introducing an augmentative communication system, whether it be of a manual or communication prosthesis type, are unknown. Some clinical reports have suggested that such procedures, when implemented appropriately, have led to increased speech. Greater knowledge concerning which children, when fitted with a particular system, will develop greater oral speech awaits further study.

Determining candidacy for an augmentative communication system (termed here election) has been considered by several clinical investigators.[10,22,33,50] Selection, on the other hand, refers to the choice of the appropriate system and instructional methodology for the individual deemed a candidate.

Election is based on a review of multiple factors, including cognitive, linguistic, and motor status; previous intervention; and a number of environmental considerations. The interaction of these factors in the overall consideration of candidacy determination was considered by Shane and Bashir.[50] The branching type decision matrix generated by Shane and Bashir[50] is on p. 307. The intent of using the decision matrix is to help define the parameters of decision making. It should be noted that the matrix is an attempt to provide guidance or a structure in which to approach election. It is our opinion that effective decision making requires the in-

ELECTION DECISION MATRIX*

Level I   Cognitive status

Greater than stage V sensorimotor intelligence; greater than 18 months mental age; or ability to recognize at least at photograph level?
> YES → Go to II
> NO → *Delay*

Level II   Oral systems—reflex behavior factors

Persistent (1) rooting, (2) gag, (3) bite, (4) suckle/ swallow, or (5) jaw extension reflex?
> YES → *Elect* → Go to X
> NO → Continue to III

Level III   Language and motor speech production factors

A. Is there a discrepancy between receptive and expressive skills?
> YES → Go to III B
> NO → Go to V

B. Is the discrepancy explained predominantly on the basis of a motor speech disorder?
> YES → Go to V
> NO → Go to III C
> UNCERTAIN → Go to IV

C. Is the discrepancy explained predominantly on the basis of an expressive language disorder?
> YES → Go to VII
> NO → Go to VI
> UNCERTAIN → Go to V

Level IV   Motor speech—some contributing factors

Presence of neuromuscular involvement affecting postural tone and/or postural stability?
Presence of praxic disturbance?
Vocal production consists primarily of vowel production?
Vocal production consists primarily of undifferentiated sounds?
History of eating problems?
> YES → Evidence to support motor speech involvement
> If less than 3 years evidence to support *elect* → Go to V
> NO → Evidence against motor speech involvement

Level V   Production—some contributing factors

Speech unintelligible except for family and immediate friends?
Predominant mode of communication is thru pointing, gesture, facial-body affect?

Level V   Production—some contributing factors—cont'd

Predominance of single word utterances?
Frustration associated with inability to speak?
> YES → Evidence to *elect* → Go to VII
> NO → Evidence to *delay* or *reject*

Level VI   Emotional factors

A. History of precipitous loss of expressive speech?
> YES → Go to VIII
> NO → Go to VI B

B. Speaks to selected persons or refuses to speak?
> YES → Go to VIII
> NO → Go to V

Level VII   Chronological age factors

A. Chronological age less than 3 years?
> YES → Go to VIII A

B. Chronological age between 3 and 5 years?
> YES → Go to VIII A

C. Chronological age greater than 5 years?
> YES → Go to VIII A

Level VIII   Previous therapy factors

A. Has had previous therapy?
> YES → Go to VIII B
> NO → Go to IX, weigh evidence—*delay* with trial therapy or *elect* → Go to X

B. Previous therapy appropriate?
> YES → Go to VIII C
> NO → *Delay* with trial therapy

C. Therapy progress too slow to enable effective communication?
> YES → *Elect* → Go to X
> NO → *Delay* → continue therapy

D. Therapy appropriately withheld?
> YES → *Elect* → Go to X
> NO → *Delay* with trial therapy

Level IX   Previous therapy—contributing factors

Able to imitate (with accuracy) speech sounds or words, gross motor or oral motor movements?
> YES → Evidence to *delay* → Go to VII
> NO → Evidence to *elect*

Level X   Implementation factors— environment

Family willing to implement (use, allow to be introduced to) nonspeech system recommendation?
> YES → *Implement*
> NO → *Counsel*

*Shane, H. C., and Bashir, A. S.: Election criteria for determining candidacy for an augmentative communication system: preliminary considerations. Presented to the American Speech and Hearing Association, San Francisco, Nov. 1978.

SCREENING QUESTIONNAIRE

From 2 weeks to 4 to 5 months

Do loud noises awaken the child?
Does the child startle or cry to loud noises?
Does the child look to where noises are coming from?
Does the child appear to "listen" to speech?
Does the child coo and produce other gurgling sounds?

From 6 to 9 months

Does the child respond to his name?
Does the child react to different uses of the voice, for example, "no"?
Does the child "notice" new sounds and voices and look for their source?
Does the child "attend" to speech by quieting, observing the speaker?
Does the child babble, that is, make consonant-vowel strings, for example, buh-buh-buh?
Does the child attempt to imitate sounds made by the caretaker?
Does the child's babble include different consonant-vowel groups, for example, buh, buh, guh?
Does the child, at times, communicate with voice to the caretakers and use differential cry and vocalizations?

From 9 to 12 months

Does the child show increased interest in looking at and listening to people talking to him?
Does the child respond differentially or prefer to listen to different kinds of sounds, for example, the caretaker's voice, music of different types, strangers?
Does the child look up when called?
Does the child respond to requests?
Does the child use vocalizations and pointing to communicate?
Does the child imitate the caretaker's babble?
Does the child engage in games, for example, pat-a-cake, peekaboo?
Does the child use words intended to specify object names, wants, or surprise? (The child's pronunciation may not be accurate.)

From 18 to 24 months

Does the child follow simple requests or two consecutive requests?
Does the child show evidence of differentiating meaning in the caretaker's speech?
Does the child speak in two-word phrases?
Does the child ask questions, for example, "Where truck?"
Does the child produce speech that is intelligible to the caretaker?
Does the child show evidence of an "easy" learning of new words and their consistent use?
Does the child make requests for repetition of what is said?
Does the child repeat in part or whole what the caretaker says?

From 30 to 36 months

Does the child participate in conversations?
Does the child ask questions about objects and events in his environment?
Does the child ask what something means?
Does the child use language to make his needs known?
Does the child relate prior experiences?
Does the child use simple sentences?
Does the child request?

put of an interdisciplinary team experienced in the clinical management of the nonspeaking individual.

In summary, determination of the candidates for an augmentative communication system and the most appropriate system itself requires the review of multiple factors by a variety of medical and paramedical specialists. Careful documentation of the effectiveness of these communication systems on both the nonspeaking person as well as the individuals with whom he interacts will lead to improved management procedures in a clinical area with a limited experiential or research basis.

SCREENING AND THE PEDIATRICIAN

The pediatrician is frequently the first professional consulted by the family when a question in the child's development occurs. In screening for children with communication disorders the use of a careful developmental history as well as direct observations of the child's speech, language, and hearing status during the office visit are the beginning of the screening process. Opposite are a series of questions, divided into groups by age from birth to 3 years, that we hope will guide the pediatrician in determining children at risk for communicative disorders. It is better to overrefer early than to let time pass and problems become complicated.

In addition to the areas covered in the questionnaire scales such as the Vineland Social Maturity Scale,[15] The REEL Scale, and the Meecham Scale[34] may structure an interview about communicative status. Screening assessment tools such as the Preschool Language Scale[69] and the Fluharty Speech and Language Preschool Screening Test[17] can also be used when directly engaging the child in the office.

REFERENCES

1. Aram, P. A., and Nation, J. E.: Patterns of language behavior in children with developmental language disorders, J. Speech Hear. Res. **18**:229, 1975.
2. Aronson, A. E.: Psychogenic voice disorders, Philadelphia, 1973, W. B. Saunders Co.
3. Baltaxe, C. A., and Simmons, J. Q.: Language in childhood psychosis: a review, J. Speech Hear. Disord. **40**:439, 1975.
4. Bashir, A. S.: Language disorders in children with

learning disorders. Presented at the Sixth Annual Conference of The New York Branch of the Orton Society, New York, March 1979.
5. Bloom, L., and Lahey, M.: Language development and language disorders, New York, 1978, John Wiley and Sons, Inc.
6. Bloomer, H. H.: Speech defects associated with dental malocclusions and related abnormalities. In Travis, L. E. editor: Handbook of speech pathology and audiology, Englewood Cliffs, N.J., 1971, Prentice-Hall, Inc., pp. 715-766.
7. Boone, D.: The voice and voice therapy, ed. 2, Englewood Cliffs, N.J., 1977, Prentice-Hall, Inc.
8. Brown, R.: A first language, the early stages, Cambridge, Mass., 1973, Harvard University Press.
9. Cazden, C. B.: Problems for education: Language as curriculum content and learning environment, J. Am. Acad. Arts Science pp. 135-148, Summer 1973.
10. Chapman, R., and Miller, J.: Analyzing language and communication in the child. In Schiefelbusch, R., editor: Nonspeech language intervention, Baltimore, 1980, University Park Press.
11. Darley, F. L., Aronson, A. E., and Brown, J. R.: Clusters of deviant speech dimensions in the dysarthrias, J. Speech Hear. Res. **12**:462, 1969.
12. Darley, F. L., Aronson, A. E., and Brown, J. R.: Differential diagnostic patterns of dysarthria, J. Speech Hear. Res. **12**:246, 1969.
13. Denckla, M. B.: Minimal brain dysfunction and dyslexia: beyond diagnosis by exclusion. In Blaw, M. R., Rapin, I., and Kinsbourne, M., editors: Topics in child neurology, New York, 1977, Spectrum Publications.
14. Denckla, M. B., and Rudel, R.: Naming of object drawings by dyslexia and other learning disabled children, Brain Lang. **3**:1, 1976.
15. Doll, E. A.: Vineland social maturity scale, 1965 ed., Circle Pines, Minn., 1965, American Guidance Service, Inc.
16. Duncan, J. L., and Silverman, H.: Impacts of learning American Indian sign language on mentally retarded children: a preliminary report, Percept. Motor Skills **44**:1138, 1977.
17. Fluharty speech and language pre-school screening test, Boston, 1978, Teaching Resources.
18. Fristoe, M., and Lloyd, L.: A survey of the use of non-speech systems with the severely communication impaired, Mental Retardation **16**:99, 1978.
19. Glauber, I. P.: The psychoanalysis of stuttering. In Eisenson, J., editor: Stuttering: a symposium, New York, 1958, Harper & Row, Publishers, pp. 71-120.
20. Goodman, L., Wilson, P. S., and Bornstein, H.: Results of a national survey of sign language programs in special education, Mental Retardation **16**:104, 1978.
21. Grabb, W. C., Rosenstein, S. W., and Bzoch, K. R., editors: Cleft lip and palate: surgical, dental and speech aspects, Boston, 1971, Little, Brown & Co.
22. Harris-Vanderheiden, D. W., et al.: Symbol communication for the mentally handicapped: an application of Bliss symbols as an alternate communication mode for

nonvocal mentally retarded children with motoric involvement, Mental Retardation **13**:34, 1975.

23. Johnson, W.: The onset of stuttering, Minneapolis, 1959, University of Minneapolis Press.
24. Kleffner, F.: Language disorders in children, New York, 1973, The Bobbs-Merrill Co., Inc.
25. Koepp-Baker, H.: The treatment of orofacial clefts: surgical, orthopedic and prosthetic. In Travis, L. E., editor: Handbook of speech pathology and audiology, Englewood Cliffs, N.J., 1971, Prentice-Hall, Inc., pp. 783-800.
26. Kretschmer, R. R., and Kretschmer, L. W.: Language development and intervention with the hearing impaired, Baltimore, 1978, University Park Press.
27. Lee, L. L.: Developmental sentence types: a method for comparing normal and deviant syntactic development, J. Speech Hear. Disord. **31**:311, 1966.
28. Lee, L. L.: Developmental sentence analysis, Evanston, Ill., 1974, Northwestern University Press.
29. Leonard, L.: What is deviant language? J. Speech Hear. Disord. **37**:427, 1972.
30. Liebergott, J. W., and Swope, S.: An application of Piaget to language therapy: a child's play is serious work, Audio J. Communication Disord. vol. 1, no. 7, 1976.
31. Luchsinger, R., and Arnold, G. E.: Voice—speech—language: clinical communicology: its physiology and pathology, Belmont, Calif., 1965, Wadsworth Publishing Co. Inc.
32. Mattis, S., French, J. H., and Rapin, I.: Dyslexia in children: young adults: three independent neuropsychological syndromes, Dev. Med. Child Neurol. **17**:150, 1975.
33. McDonald, E., and Schultz, A.: Communication boards for cerebral palsied children, J. Speech Hear. Disord. **38**:73, 1973.
34. Mecham, M.: Verbal language development scale, Circle Pines, Minn., 1971, American Guidance Service, Inc.
35. Menyuk, P.: Sentences children use, Cambridge, Mass., 1970, The M.I.T. Press.
36. Menyuk, P.: The acquisition and development of language, Englewood Cliffs, N.J., 1971, Prentice-Hall, Inc.
37. Menyuk, P.: The development of speech, New York, 1972, The Bobbs-Merrill Co. Inc.
38. Monaco, J. L., and Zaslow, E. L.: Hey, I got sump'n to tell you an' it cool, Rockville, Md., 1972, Board of Education of Montgomery County.
39. Myklebust, H. R.: Auditory disorders in children, New York, 1954, Grune & Stratton, Inc.
40. Needleman, H.: Effects of hearing loss from early recurrent otitis media on speech and language development. In Jaffe, B. F., editor: Hearing loss in children, Baltimore, 1977, University Park Press, pp. 640-649.
41. Oxman, J., Webster, C. D., and Konstantareas, M. M.: The perception and processing of information by severely dysfunctional nonverbal children: a rationale for the use of manual communication, Sign Lang. Stud. **21**:289, 1978.

42. Perkins, W. H.: Speech pathology: An applied behavioral science, ed. 2, St. Louis, 1977, The C. V. Mosby Co.
43. Peterson, S. J.: Speech pathology in craniofacial malformations other than cleft lip and palate. In orofacial anomalies: clinical and research implications, ASHA report no. 8, Rockville, Md., 1972, American Speech and Hearing Association.
44. Pollock, K. C.: The influence of hearing impairment, In Grabb, W. C., Rosenstein, S. W., and Bzoch, K. R., editors: Cleft lip and palate: surgical, dental and speech aspects, Boston, 1971, Little, Brown & Co., pp. 681-690.
45. Rutherford, D.: Auditory-motor learning and the acquisitions of speech, Am. J. Phys. Med. **46**:245, 1967.
46. Rutherford, D.: Speech and language disorders and MBD in Millichap, J. G., editor: Learning disabilities and related disorders: facts and current issues, 1977, Year Book Medical Publishers, Inc., pp. 45-50.
47. Schiefelbusch, R. L., and Lloyd, L. L., editors: Language perspectives—acquisition retardation, and intervention, Baltimore, 1974, University Park Press.
48. Shane, H. C.: Approaches to assessing people who are nonspeaking. In Schiefelbusch, R., editor: Nonspeech language intervention, Baltimore, University Park press (in press).
49. Shane, H. C.: Decision making in early augmentative communication system use. In Schiefelbusch, R., editor: Early language intervention, Baltimore, University Park Press (in press).
50. Shane, H. C., and Bashir, A. S.: Election criteria for determining candidacy for an augmentative communication system: preliminary considerations. Presented to the American Speech and Hearing Association, San Francisco, Nov. 1978.
51. Skelly, M., et al.: American Indian sign (Amerind) as a facilitator of verbalization for the oral verbal apraxic, J. Speech Hear. Disord. **39**:445, 1974.
52. Skelly, M., et al.: Amican Indian sign: a gestural communication system for the speechless, Arch. Phys. Med. **56**:156, 1975.
53. Skolnick, M. L.: Video velopharyngography in patients with nasal speech, with emphasis on lateral pharyngeal motion in velopharyngeal closure, Radiology **93**:747, 1969.
54. Skolnick, M. L., and McCall, G. N.: Competence and incompetence following pharyngeal flap surgery: video-fluoroscopic study in multiple projections, Cleft Palate J. pp. 1-12, 1972.
55. Strominger, A. Z., and Bashir, A. S.: A nine year follow-up of language delayed children. Presented at the American Speech and Hearing Association, Chicago, Nov. 1977.
56. Templin, M.: Certain language skills in children, Minneapolis, 1957, University of Minnesota Press.
57. Van Riper, C.: The nature of suttering, Englewood Cliffs, N.J., 1971, Prentice-Hall Inc.
58. Vanderheiden, G., and Harris-Vanderheiden, D.: Communication techniques and aids for the nonvocal

severely handicapped. In Lloyd, L., editor: Communication assessment and intervention strategies, Baltimore, 1976, University Park Press.

59. Vellutino, F. R., Steoer, J. A., and Kandel, G.: Reading disability: an investigation of the perceptual deficit hypothesis, Cortex **8:**106, 1972.

60. Vicker, B.: Nonoral communication system project: 1964/1973, Iowa City, Iowa, 1974, Campus Stores Publishers.

61. Vogel, S. A.: Syntactic abilities in normal and dyslexic children, J. Learning Disabilities **7:**47, 1974.

61a. Weiner, P.: A language delayed child at adolescence, J. Speech Hear. Disord. **39:**202, 1974.

62. Wiig, E. H., and Semel, E. M.: Logico-grammatical sentence comprehension by learning disabled adolescents, Percept. Mot. Skills **38:**1331, 1974.

63. Wiig, E. H., and Semel, E. M.: Language disabilities in children: adolescents, Columbus, Ohio, 1976, Charles E. Merrill Publishing Co.

64. Wiig, E. H., Semel, E. S., and Crouse, M. B.: The use of English morphology by high-risk learning disabled children, J. Learning Disabilities **6:**457, 1973.

65. Wilson, D. K.: Voice problems in children, Baltimore, 1972, The Williams & Wilkins Co.

66. Winitz, H.: Repetitions in vocalizations and speech of children in the first two years of life, J. Speech Hear. Disord. Monogr. Suppl. **7:**55, 1961.

67. Wolf, M. A.: The relationship of disorders of word finding in reading in children, unpublished doctoral dissertation, Harvard University, 1979.

68. Yoss, K. A., and Darley, F. L.: Developmental apraxia of speech in children with defective articulation, J. Speech Hear. Res. **17:**399, 1974.

69. Zimmerman, I. L., Steiner, V. G., and Evatt, R. L.: Preschool language test, Columbus, Ohio, 1969, Charles E. Merrill Publishing Co.

There is a soul in me
It is asking
To be given its body

Gemini, 1971
Louise Glück

13

The child with learning disabilities

Melvin D. Levine

The concept of learning disability has evolved to account for a group of children whose academic struggle and/or failure is associated with well-circumscribed areas of constitutional deficit or handicap.[22] These children are said to have "low severity–high incidence handicaps," in contrast to the more severely affected, but less prevalent retarded or multiply handicapped youngsters. Actual prevalence figures have been extremely variable, ranging from 4% to 20% of school-aged children.[18] Imprecise definitions and a lack of criteria for inclusion have hampered studies of the epidemiology of learning disabilities.

A developmental pediatric model of a learning disabled child is based on a series of empirically derived concepts.

1. A learning disabled child may reveal impairment in one or more aspects of a broad range of functional areas comprising such processes as attention, memory, visual perception, receptive language, expressive language, motor output, and higher order conceptualization.

2. A child may be learning disabled without failing in school. It is possible that compensatory strategies or alternative learning pathways facilitate success despite handicaps.

3. At times it may be difficult to differentiate a learning disability from a "cognitive style." A handicap of one function may be associated with excellence in another area and preferential use of the strength.

4. Learning disabilities often have a broad impact affecting not only learning, but also social interaction, self-esteem, affect, and personality development.

5. Children with learning disabilities are a heterogenous group etiologically and with respect to the pathogenetic pathways culminating in their failures. Genetic transmission, perinatal stress events, early illnesses, nutritional deficiencies, specific deprivations, critical life events, and the nurturing environmental support system blend in infinite patterns to shape a child's learning abilities, strategies, attitudes, motivation, and ultimate performance.

6. Learning disabilities must be regarded as

developmentally dynamic. Specific handicaps will manifest themselves to varying degrees at specific ages, as discussed below. This relates to the maturation of the central nervous system, to experience, and to cultural and educational expectations as they emerge. The symptoms of developmental dysfunction undergo a steady metamorphosis with age. A complex "nature-nurture" interaction allows constitutional predispositions to be potentiated, altered, or thwarted by time and circumstance.

Following are common signs suggestive of developmental dysfunction* grouped by age:

A. Preschool years (ages 3 to 5)
   1. Delayed acquisition of intelligible speech
   2. Delayed acquisition of motor skills
   3. Poor peer interactions
   4. Overactivity, insatiability, poor selective attention, difficulty sitting in a chair
   5. Failure to acquire preacademic skills (e.g., letters, colors, name writing) despite adequate exposure
   6. Behavior problems in preschool setting
   7. Difficulty following directions
   8. Extreme confusion about time relationships
B. Early school years (ages 5 to 9)
   1. Delayed acquisition of reading skills despite average or near average IQ
   2. Overactivity, task impersistence, impulsivity, poor selective attention, distractibility
   3. Difficulty following directions
   4. Problems with peer interaction
   5. Chronic anxiety, depression, diminished self-esteem
   6. Motor incoordination
   7. Difficulty retaining and applying new skills
   8. Confusion over sequences and poor retention of multiple-step instructions
   9. Delays in left-right discrimination, telling time, tying shoelaces
C. Middle school years (ages 10 to 14)
   1. Any of the signs described under B
   2. Difficulty mastering multiplication tables
   3. Severe spelling problems
   4. Awkward word finding and oral narration

5. Problems with pencil control and sustained writing
   6. Apparent poor motivation, "laziness," deteriorating attitude toward school
   7. Emergence of antisocial behaviors
   8. Reluctance, failure, or inability to complete assignments
D. Late school years (ages after 14)
   1. Any of the signs described under C
   2. Increasing depression and/or antisocial behaviors
   3. Inability to keep pace with increasing volume demands for academic output
   4. Progressive alienation from adults

Primary care physicians are in an excellent position to observe these interactions, and there are a variety of service models through which pediatrically oriented evaluation and advice in the field of learning disabilities may be provided. In some cases pediatricians do much of their own assessment. In other instances allied personnel, such as special educators, nurse practitioners, and clinical psychologists, perform much of the evaluation and offer ongoing monitoring and advice-giving services. Some neighborhood health centers and private practice groups now employ a part-time or full-time educator or psychologist. In such cases pediatricians can offer traditional medical and developmental insights and/or serve as case coordinators and ombudsmen. Regardless of the role played by physicians, their identity as team members is critically important. However, the diagnosis and management of a learning disability can never fall exclusively in their domain.

DESCRIPTIVE EVALUATION

In describing learning disabilities as a clinical problem, I will consider the diagnostic process to be descriptive and developmentally based. The major areas of school-aged development and the specific functional deficits that may be encountered within each area will be reviewed. The hazards of labelling will be circumvented, since such terms as "dyslexia" and "minimal brain damage (MBD)" are poorly defined and not helpful to those children so branded. It will be assumed that the pediatrician is an active participant in formulating the comprehensive

---

*It must be emphasized that any one of these signs may result from causes other than specific disabilities. On the other hand, they represent many of the common clinical manifestations of underlying developmental dysfunctions.

description of a child's strengths, strategies, and weaknesses. Together with providers from other disciplines the pediatrician or health care professional helps to formulate a functional profile that is based on developmental principles and that has prescriptive implications for the child.

The pediatric evaluation of a child with learning disabilities should include a historical compilation as outlined below:

A. Account of perinatal stresses
    1. Illness, trauma, bleeding, etc., during gestation
    2. Details of delivery
    3. Birth weight and gestational age
    4. Delivery room complications
    5. Congenital abnormalities
    6. Health stresses during first month
B. Early health
    1. Significant illnesses, trauma, hospitalizations, and chronic or recurrent disorders during the years leading up to school
C. Early temperament
    1. Feeding, crying, and sleeping problems in infancy
    2. Colic, constipation, other recurrent somatic dysfunctions
    3. Behavioral organization: Attention, activity, adaptability, predictability, rhythmicity
    4. Emotional lability, irritability, consolability
D. Early development
    1. Motor, language, social "milestones"
    2. Preschool experiences
E. Social and family history
    1. Demographic data
    2. Family history of learning and/or behavioral problems
    3. Current family structure
    4. Critical life events
F. Current skills and performance
    1. Parent and teacher account of abilities in cognitive and academic areas
G. Current effectiveness of activity and attention
    1. Parent and teacher ratings of selective attention and control of activity
H. Current behavioral profile
    1. Parent and teacher accounts of social interaction, affect, self-esteem, personality, etc.

This history includes a description of any perinatal stress events, of health status in the early years of life, of early temperament, of critical life events, and of motor, language, and social development. Early psychosocial stresses are documented. The history then should turn toward a comprehensive description of the child's present functional status. There should be a review of current physical health. Competence in specific skill areas should be elicited. An account of the child's patterns of activity and selective attention should also be sought. In addition, it is important to obtain data on function and behavior at school. In general, one wishes to know how a child functions at home, in the neighborhood, and in school. Standardized questionnaires can be used for this assessment. One should also identify and assess the effects of any current family or environmental stresses.

The pediatric examination of a child with learning disabilities should include a standard physical assessment to uncover medical conditions that may be aggravating or predisposing to learning problems. This should include assessment of vision and hearing. A standard neurological examination should be undertaken in an effort to demonstrate any localizing findings or "hard" neurological signs. Skull x-ray examinations, blood tests, and electroencephalograms are only indicated if there exist compelling medical symptoms suggesting a metabolic defect, a specific central nervous system disease, anemia, seizure disorder, or other specific conditions.

A controversial area of evaluation is the search for minor neurological signs.[23-31] These indicators of possible delay in the maturation of the central nervous system are common and normal in younger age groups, but become increasingly rare as children mature or age. Their delayed disappearance is often associated with learning and behavior disorders. Table 13-1 summarizes the content of a suggested neuromaturational examination. The interpretation of results from such an assessment can be difficult. The signs have no direct therapeutic implications, but they may be helpful in defining the extent to which constitutional inefficiencies or immaturity may be contributing to a child's functional failure.

A pediatrician active in the diagnosis and

Table 13-1. Neuromaturational assessment

Sign	Description	Comments
Synkinesis	Child is asked to appose fingers of one hand (singly or in sequence). Mirror movement in opposite hand is sought. Can also be elicited with rapid pronation-supination of hand.	Common finding before age 7. Associated with dysfunction increasingly beyond 7. Examiner should also seek other associated movements (e.g., "mouthing") during these tasks.
Dysdiadochokinesis	Child shows flailing of arms, deviation of elbow from trunk during rapid pronation-supination of hand.	Increasing efficiency after age 6. One can look for synkinesis. Simultaneously, one can try to have child suppress dysdiadochokinesis voluntarily.
Choreiform sign and motor impersistence	Child stands straight with arms out directly in front, fingers spread, mouth open, tongue protruding, eyes closed. Rotary (choreiform) movements of fingers and/or tongue are noted, as is inability to sustain stance for 30 seconds (impersistence).	Choreiform sign has high association with learning and behavior problems in older school-aged children. Impersistence common in children with neuromaturational delay and attentional deficits.
Finger agnosia	Child sits facing examiner with palms on knees, fingers spread, eyes closed. Must say whether two or one of his fingers is touched by examiner. Older children can state how many fingers, or child can imitate examiner's finger movements with arms extended.	Inability has been associated with variety of developmental dysfunctions. May be seen often with fine motor problems and with sequencing deficits.
Stimulus extinction	Child sits facing examiner with palms up, eyes closed. Examiner touches child on each hand, then each cheek, then cheek and hand simultaneously. Child tells where he is being touched.	Immature child may not perceive distal stimulus (on hand) when simultaneously touched proximally (on cheek). Common finding in normal preschool children.
Delayed or poorly established dominance	Hand: Child observed pretending to comb hair. Eye: Child given a telescope to peer through. Foot: Child asked to kick a ball.	Consistent hand dominance usually established by 4, eye dominance by 6, foot variable; poorly established or late dominance are signs of delay. Mixed dominance is controversial.
Delayed left-right discrimination	Child asked to identify left and right on own body parts, then to cross midline ("touch your right shoulder with your left hand"); then to transfer to examiner ("touch my right knee with your left hand").	Simple laterality usually achieved by 6; midline crossing by 8; transfer to other body by 10. Task depends somewhat on language processing *and* experience.
Propriokinesthetic signs: agraphesthesia, astereognosis	Child asked to identify numbers written on palm or back without seeing them (graphesthesia) or to identify or match objects placed in hand behind back (sterognosis).	Of limited value. Norms not well established. Difficult to interpret findings.
Immature separation of movements	Child asked to follow examiner's finger with eyes, but to keep head still (may need a second reminder *not* to move head). Can also be assessed by having a child "wink" just one eye at a time.	5- and 6-year-olds usually cannot separate eye and head movements. This should diminish between 7 and 8 and represent maturation lag after 8. The "wink" is not as well standardized but usually can be accomplished in both eyes by 9, in one by 7 or 8.
Visual tracking	Child asked to follow examiner's finger back and forth in "horizontal" plane and is observed for nystagmus, ease of crossing midline, and general smoothness of visual pursuit.	5- and 6-year-olds often show uneven tracking. Older children with such findings may also have problems with visual attention and with keeping their place in reading.

management of a learning disabled child must observe the child's function directly. It is helpful to parents and teachers if the physician contributes direct observational data to the diagnostic and therapeutic team. Each physician will need to adopt tools for the direct sampling of performance. Later sections of this chapter will suggest some tools that can be incorporated into the pediatric neurodevelopmental assessment.

A schema of the learning process can aid in differential diagnosis and also help organize one's thinking about learning disability as a subject. Fig. 13-1 depicts a simplified conceptual model. It illustrates some cognitive phenomena that are accessible diagnostically. On the first level of this diagram there is basic arousal and selective attention. From there one proceeds to the processes entailed in decoding:

INFORMATION PROCESSING MODEL

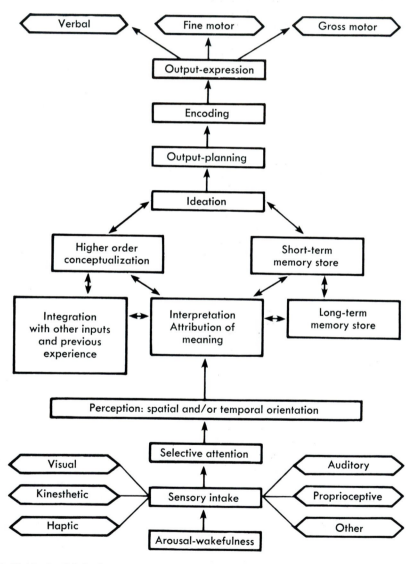

Fig. 13-1. Highly simplified schema illustrates one model of the intake and processing of stimuli, their storage, and the generation of relevant responses. These components can be considered during the evaluation of a child with school failure.

various forms of perception, organization of time and space, and the attribution of meaning to incoming written or spoken symbolic information. On the next level there is storage: immediate recall, short-term memory, and long-term memory. On another level are the various encoding processes generating and executing an appropriate response, or output. Encoding can occur through one or more modalities of expression, including gross motor output, fine motor function, and expressive language (both written and spoken). Higher order conceptualization entails the organization of experience into rules and generalizations about the universe, associations, and relationships (perhaps creativity and imagination) from which one can develop systems of logic and reasoning. The integration of various sensory and memory pathways relates intimately to this process. The child with learning problems (like all children) encompasses a range of strengths and/or weaknesses within the schema. Developmental evaluation should result in a broad profile of strengths, weaknesses, and preferred pathways of function.

Following is a continued elaboration of Fig. 13-1, elucidating those areas of development which should be scrutinized in the child with learning or behavioral disorders. It deals with specific functional areas, their normal properties, their clinical assessment, and deficits commonly encountered in school-aged children. We will begin with a discussion of attention and the closely related issue of activity control.

Selective attention

Chronic inattention in children is one of the most common complaints related to behavior and learning. Overactivity is often (but not always) an accompanying symptom. Deficient attention is a symptom rather than a diagnosis. The differential diagnosis is broad.

It is helpful to define the qualities of "normal" attention. At each instant we engage in a perpetual selection process: an extraordinary array of stimuli are scanned and one or two selected for conscious focus or "concentration." The foci of our consciousness are chosen from within various sensory channels (especially auditory and visual), from memory, from so-

matic sensation (e.g., pain, comfort), from fantasies, and from the free flow of ideas. Although in daily life we make attentional choices that are frivolous or purposeless, it is expected that a reasonable proportion of the objects of our attention will be selected because they lead to some planned and worthy objective, such as knowledge acquisition or work accomplishment. At each instant we "decide" whether to continue focusing on the same stimulus or stimuli or whether to attend to a new focus. When selective attention yields good, useful, or pleasurable information, it is likely that one will continue to pursue the same selection for an appropriate period. When selective attention is not reinforced with good data, one is likely to keep changing foci, not unlike the process of turning a channel selector in search of a good television program.

The child with an attentional deficit presents a history of erratic, purposeless, or randomlike selection of stimuli or focus. Such a child may often select background instead of foreground stimuli. He may "tune in" to what the rest of us would consider distraction. There may be an effort to focus on too many stimuli simultaneously. A child may demonstrate impersistence, or a tendency to shift attentional focus too frequently.[25,30] Children with attentional deficits tend to show a cluster of behaviors or characteristics. These are listed below and may be manifested to varying degrees in different children:

1. Tendency to "tune in and out" of focus unpredictably
2. Distractibility: Difficulty sorting out foreground-background phenomena; poor differentiation between noise and central stimuli
3. Impulsivity: Apparent inability to act reflectively, to plan and monitor output, to engage in deep thought or careful problem solving, to inhibit inappropriate behavior
4. Poor modulation of activity: Overactivity (in some cases), fidgetiness, purposeless motor output, inappropriate hypoactivity (in some cases)
5. Insatiability: Difficulty reaching a state of satisfaction or contentment, constant

wanting, restlessness, whining (in young children), irritability

6. Poor reinforceability: Lack of appropriate response to reward and/or punishment

7. Easy fatigability: Struggle to remain fully aroused and alert during day, frequent yawning, tendency to become excessively tired during activities

8. Sleep problems: Difficulty falling asleep at night

9. Task impersistence: Trouble finishing what is started

10. Social imperception: Problems understanding and nurturing social relationships

11. Superficiality: Reluctance to develop strong areas of intellectual interest, hobbies, preferred games, skills. Often a finding in adolescents with life-long attention problems

12. Developmental dysfunction: Neuromaturational delay and/or any conceivable combination of "specific learning disabilities." (NOTE: Some children with attentional deficits have *no* learning disabilities.)

There are varying degrees of these manifestations or associated findings in children with attentional deficits. For example, the symptom of overactivity or purposeless motor output may not be discernible; some children are "hypoactive-hyperactive," being highly distractible and inattentive but lethargic rather than overactive. Activity is the product of a selection process, just as is attention; from instant to instant one selects a specific activity. It is hoped that this process is purposeful, since it is the quality of the selection that matters more than the quantity of activity selected. A child may be overactive and yet exploratory and efficient. Such a youngster may be a management problem, but he should not be viewed as having a deficit of any kind! The emphasis should be on the efficiency of attention and activity rather than on ergs of activity or spans of attention. For this reason the term "hyperactivity" may be misleading or an oversimplification.

A frequent concomitant of attentional weakness is impulsivity. Some children demonstrate this as their major symptom and experience difficulty engaging in what has been called "reflective behavior."[17] They do not seem to plan their activities. They almost never engage in thoughtful problem solving. They seldom monitor their work. They rarely "look before they leap." They may be proficient only in performing tasks or mastering skills that require minimal sustained pursuit of information or "deep thought." Children who are chronically impulsive engender difficulties that compromise both academic and behavioral performance. Their impulsivity often impairs social interaction at the same time it interferes with classroom learning.

In evaluating a child with a history of ineffective attention, it is important to describe the clinical manifestations in each of the areas listed on p. 314. Each symptom component may have implications for educational planning and the counselling of parents, teachers, and children. In a diagnostic descriptive account of a child's attentional deficit, it is essential that the clinician account for variable manifestations in different settings or circumstances: Is the attentional weakness present in almost all situations? Is it evident both at home and in school? Is attention weaker when materials are presented visually or when they are presented through auditory channels? Are there particular kinds of academic challenges or cognitive experiences that are more likely to result in inattention, distractibility, and impulsive behavior? These questions can be helpful in determining whether a child's weak attention is a primary handicap or whether it is secondary to another learning problem or to emotional preoccupation.

A youngster may have a secondary attentional deficit when chronic inattention is caused by inefficiencies of processing in a particular cognitive area. For example, if a child has a receptive language disability, it may be difficult for him to decode complex verbally presented information. In the classroom, when there is a great deal of discussion or when complicated instructions are being transmitted, such a youngster may become very distractible, impulsive, inattentive, and hopelessly disorganized. On the other hand, when copying from the blackboard or following written instructions, the same child may be more attentive. The reverse phenomenon may also occur.

Another form of secondary attentional deficit can be seen in children who harbor significant emotional turmoil. A chronically anxious or depressed child may be drained of attention. In the classroom such a youngster may stare out the window and have great difficulty focusing on academic materials. When there are many problems at home, a youngster attending school may have difficulty sustaining concentration.

A child may demonstrate "situational inattention." The difficulty rests in the discrepancy between the youngster and the setting in which he finds himself. Disparities in expectations, in cultural backgrounds, or in learning styles may result in a child's tendency not to focus or sustain attention in the classroom. Thus a child from a home where little value is placed on the learning of mathematics and where no other family member is adept with numbers may feel little incentive for concentration and may have difficulty focusing when he is in a mathematics class.

Thus in the evaluation of children with chronic inattention of great relevance is the determination of whether a youngster has a primary attentional deficit, whether he is inattentive secondary to other learning disabilities, whether there are strong emotional preoccupations that are competing for attention, or whether the learning situation is inappropriate in one way or another. Mixed manifestations commonly occur; a youngster may have a primary attentional weakness and have endured years of chronic failure and approbation from the adult world. Such a child may have become quite anxious and depressed about performance. The secondary emotional issues further drain an already diminished attentional capacity. Alternatively, a student may have a primary attentional deficit and also have associated specific learning disabilities. The latter may render learning tedious, leading to a further reduction in selective attention.

A child who can focus well on a ghost story or television cartoon may nonetheless have a serious attentional deficit. It is necessary to assess attentional strength at normal daily levels of motivation rather than at the extremes of high motivation. A child's demonstrated capacity to watch television should not be used as evidence against him when seeking specialized services for an attentional deficit. Direct measures of selective attention are not yet available for general clinical use. The most reliable indicators of an attentional deficit are derived from historical and questionnaire materials. Standardized attention questionnaires have been developed and are widely used in clinical practices.[4,19] Parent and teacher ratings become an important part of our understanding of inattention. Such ratings or questionnaires do not differentiate well between primary attentional deficits and those which are secondary to other causes. Diverse youngsters may appear very similar in their outward manifestations of inattention. Diagnostic testing, further historical data, and direct observation may be necessary to differentiate among the groups.

An inattentive or overactive child often performs much better on a one-to-one basis than in a classroom or large group. This can impair the pediatrician's appreciation of a child's problem. Typically, a youngster with an attentional deficit may appear very well organized, normally active, and quite attentive during a routine pediatric examination. This may engender disbelief in the pediatrician who has heard horrendous tales of this child's frenetic social and academic life. Pediatricians need to be aware that they are not observing a reliable sample of a child's function. A clinician can observe a child's selective attention more directly through neurodevelopmental testing. Having a child perform at an age appropriate level in a number of cognitive areas may elicit distractibility, impulsivity, impersistence, easy fatigability, as well as other symptoms of attentional inefficiency. Neurodevelopmental assessment also affords the opportunity to discern differences in attentional focus in varying conditions. For example, it may be observed that a child is more reflective and focused when copying forms than when following verbal instructions or repeating a span of numbers.

Since a large number of children with attentional deficits have associated or causative underlying handicaps, no evaluation of an inattentive child is complete without a careful search for specific learning disabilities. Subtle processing handicaps can be seen in youngsters who are not failing in school. Despite their apparent academic success, such children may be struggling and may be at risk for later academic failure. The fact that a second grade child is reading adequately does not preclude the possibility that a specific learning disability exists that, at least in part, accounts for attentional difficulties. In some cases there is a tendency to assume that if a child is inattentive and/or overactive and he appears to be learning fairly well in school, the problem must be purely emotional. Such an assumption may be quite unjustified. A child's disorganization and inattention may be the only manifestations of a barely compensated processing problem. For this reason, the diagnostic evaluation of an inattentive child should always include a broad developmental assessment.

Basic decoding of data and experience

In this section we will look at three interacting areas of development: *visual processing, temporal-sequential organization,* and *receptive language*. Children with learning problems may demonstrate underlying deficits in one or more of these areas. Such handicaps may lead to deficits of attention and to diminished or significantly delayed learning. They may interfere with personality development, social interactions, self-esteem, and affect.

Visual processing. During the earliest days of life newborns begin to learn about visuospatial relationships. As they move their bodies through space, the constancy of spatial relationships becomes "programmed" and forms a critical element of their understanding of the universe. The acquisition of such knowledge has been described by Piaget as occurring in a period of "sensorimotor intelligence."[24] Babies also learn about space by studying their body parts; rules and relationships emerge governing the difference between the tops and bottoms of things, the fronts and backs, etc. It has been speculated, however, that because of the symmetry of our bodies on either side of the mid-sagittal plane, concepts of left and right are more difficult for children to master.[7]

Children with difficulties in interpreting visually presented stimuli may appear to develop normally through infancy and the toddler and preschool years. It may only be when subtle discriminations between similar visual symbols are called for that a child's visuoperceptual weakness may become apparent. It may be observed that a child has difficulty catching a big ball or participating in other activities that require precision in visuospatial judgment. Some children may manifest their visual processing difficulties when drawing, tracing, using scissors, recognizing colors, identifying numbers, or orienting letters. Of course, any one of these symptoms should suggest a differential diagnosis and may derive from a variety of developmental and environmental sources instead of, or in addition to, visual processing deficits. A child who has difficulty tracing may indeed have visuospatial confusion, but alternatively he could be manifesting fine motor deficits, attentional weakness, or inexperience. It is only by assessing a variety of task performances that one can rule out other possibilities and pinpoint specific visual processing handicaps. Some children with visuospatial disorientation may be late in acquiring left-right discrimination. However, it is important to recognize there is a strong language component in the identification of left and right; thus a youngster may have difficulties in this area because of underlying language rather than visual processing problems.

It is likely that children with visuospatial difficulties meet their greatest challenge in the earliest grades of school. This is a time when the educational system places heavy emphasis on the recognition and identification of symbols, on subtle visual discriminations (such as *b* versus *d*), and on a variety of fine motor tasks that involve visual input. A child with moderate visual processing problems who is strong in all other areas of development has an excellent prognosis if he can progress through the first few grades of school without developing significant emotional problems and learning inhibitions! Given appropriate educational support, such a youngster ultimately may perform adequately as school becomes increasingly oriented toward "auditory learners" in the higher grades.

The assessment of visual processing deficits can be difficult. Historical cues can be elicited. The usual screening procedure involves having a child copy forms that have been standardized for his age. Following is an assessment process:

I. Historical hints
   A. Delay in learning directionality concepts, telling left from right, mastering visuospatial tasks (e.g., tying shoelaces, catching a ball)
   B. General clumsiness
   C. Extreme visual distractibility, problems with figure-ground relationships
   D. Difficulty learning to recognize and discriminate between visual symbols (e.g., letters, numbers)
   E. Problems drawing, tracing, using scissors
   F. NOTE: Many of these harbor a second variable—motor function
II. Screening observations
   A. Form copying
      1. Norms: See Fig. 13-3 for specific forms
      2. Comments: Form coyping also measures fine motor and/or pencil control, experience or practice, visual attention, and eye-hand integration
   B. Dressing-undressing, writing, catching a ball
      1. These are difficult to standardize, but can provide some cues to visuospatial confusion
      2. Visuomotor *integrative* function plays a key role in these acts

Such assessments are "contaminated" through the involvement of other functions, including visual attention to detail, fine motor skill, intersensory integration, and pencil control. Often, however, it is possible for the clinician to differentiate between poorly reproduced forms resulting from a lack of pencil or fine motor control and those which represent visuospatial confusion. One can also make the clinical judgment as to how impulsively a form is copied and how organized and/or attentive the child appeared. Standardized tests such as the Beery Visual Motor Integration Test can be utilized.[9] In a screening assessment it is possible to have a child copy those forms that are developmentally appropriate for his age. Fig. 13-2 illustrates some of these forms. Signs of visuo-

FORMS TO COPY FOR THE SCREENING OF VISUAL PERCEPTUAL-MOTOR FUNCTION

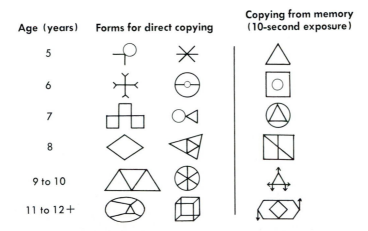

Age (years)	Forms for direct copying		Copying from memory (10-second exposure)

Fig. 13-2. Forms that may be used by the clinician in the process of screening. The child should be asked to copy them using a sharp pencil and unlined paper. Immature performance may reflect any of a variety of problems, including visuospatial disorientation, inexperience, fine motor weakness, impulsivity, and difficulty with visual–fine motor integration. This screen should never be used as a definitive diagnostic test. Suspicious findings should be validated through the history and more comprehensive standardized examinations.

spatial disorientation might include difficulty with whole-part relationships, confusion over the relative sizes of the components of a form, distortions in the relative position of components of a form, changes in overall spatial orientation of parts of a form or of the whole form itself, and poor appreciation of a detail or pattern. It is helpful to watch a child while he draws. In addition to judgments about fine motor and pencil control, one can also observe revealing compensatory strategies. A child who has confusion about overall Gestalt or pattern may perceive a diamond shape as four separate lines. Such a youngster may look back at the original stimulus and draw one line at a time without ever recognizing or perceiving the entire form as a single entity (a diamond).

As children grow older and more experienced in school, one can learn a great deal about developmental function through analyses of their tasks and the errors that they typically commit. A child with visuospatial difficulties may have an impaired sight vocabulary (memory for the appearance of words); because of inefficiencies in visual processing, it may take too long to decode words. Such a youngster may also have problems orienting letters properly. This is particularly true with *p* and *q* or *b* and *d*. He may demonstrate awkward and labored letter formation techniques. Ultimately, spelling errors may reflect a poor sense of the visual configuration or detail of words. Errors may reflect a good sense of language (i.e., words spelled phonetically correct), but suggest problems with visual memory and more specifically the visual appreciation and retention of patterns.

Letter reversals do not necessarily indicate a problem with visual processing. Impulsivity can result in letter reversals. If a child is heavily preoccupied with the mechanics of writing, spelling, and verbal expression he may not be able to concentrate on directionality and may thereby lapse into symbol reversals.[11]

Standardized tests may help to confirm the presence of a visual processing deficit. Subtests of the Wechsler Intelligence Scale for Children (WISC) may be particularly useful.[26] In particular, the block design, object assembly, and picture completion subtest scores may be used as part of the evaluation of visual processing.

Each of these does have a motor component. Other assessments include the Developmental Test of Visual-Motor Integration[9] and the Frostig Developmental Test of Visual Perception.[11] Tests involving matching figures, picking out two identical forms from an array of similar ones, or finding embedded shapes in pictures are ways of eliciting visual processing data that are relatively free from the "contamination" of motor output.

Temporal-sequential organization. Just as a child with spatial disorientation may encounter academic difficulties, a child who experiences confusion over time and sequence may be handicapped in learning. Deficits in sequential organization can result in problems with reading, spelling, mathematics, verbal expression, and complex motor activities. Sequencing problems are commonly associated with weaknesses of short-term memory. Typically an affected child has difficulty following directions in a classroom; if a teacher gives a four- or five-step instruction, the child may only be able to decode and carry-out one of the steps. Similar phenomena may be noted at home; the child may be labelled or condemned for frequent failure to listen or follow directions.

Sequential organization may be learned very early in life. An infant sucking on a nipple may come to recognize that particular sequential patterns have the highest yield of nutriment. Daily routines and various body rhythms may further reinforce temporal order. Young children who have sequencing problems may reveal their difficulties during the preschool years as they struggle inordinately to master the vocabulary of time. Prepositions such as "before" and "after" and words such as "earlier" and "later" and "now" and "then" may baffle such a child. As he progresses there may be problems learning the days of the week, the months of the year, and other concepts involving serial order. There may be delays in learning how to tell time. There may also be problems with motor tasks that require a complicated sequence of operations, such as those involved in tying shoelaces. An affected child may also manifest impaired organization of spoken language or narrative. Parents might report their exasperation listening to the child "muddle through" a story or joke! Often the child is frustrated in narrating events in a logical order, and sometimes in coping with rules of syntax. Occasionally such a child will blatantly reveal his time-related disorientation, as one youngster did when he said, "Daddy, I sure hope you come home late tonight so we can play before it gets dark!"

Historical evidence of difficulty following directions, problems utilizing time-related vocabulary, delay in learning how to read clocks, and deficiencies with short-term memory may lead one to suspect a sequencing deficit in a young child. As children grow older analyses of errors may yield valuable information suggesting sequencing problems. Sequential errors in spelling or reading (e.g., *was* for *saw*) may be present. Many children with sequencing difficulties encounter major obstacles in mathematics, particularly in learning the multiplication tables. In some cases a sequencing problem is noted almost exclusively in auditory-verbal tasks. Other children may have problems with serial order or memory when a sequence is presented visually. In many cases, however, difficulties in three areas (visual, language, and motor) are noted when a child has significant temporal-sequential disorganization.

The screening of a child's sequencing can be achieved in a physician's office. Interpretation can be hazardous. Primary attentional deficits, slowness of processing, anxiety, or just a bad day can mimic a sequencing handicap. It is important that direct observations be supplemented by historical evidence of sequential disorganization at home and in school. Following are some of the tasks that can be used to screen a child's sequencing abilities*:

I. Hints from the history
   A. Child shows delay in learning temporal prepositions (e.g., before, after), days of the week, order of months.
   B. Child shows delay in learning to tell time.
   C. Child has problems with number concepts.

---

*Historical hints and screening observations should lead to hypotheses to be confirmed by additional evidence. Children with sequencing deficits may *not* show problems in *all* areas listed. Some of these historical hints and task weaknesses may indicate delays in areas other than sequencing.

   D. Sequencing errors in narrative organization, syntax, spelling, reading are evident.
   E. Child shows weakness of short-term memory: Difficulty following multistep directions, taking telephone messages, complying with instructions at home.
   F. Child has tendency to perform tasks (e.g., dressing) in the wrong order.
II. Screening observations
   A. Digit spans: Examiner recites list of numbers at 1 per second. Child repeats in same order.
      1. Norms: Ages 4 to 6—four numbers; ages 6 to 8—five numbers; ages 9 to 12—six numbers forward, four to five numbers repeated by child in reverse order.
      2. Comments: Task also tests attention, meaningfulness of numbers, and rate of processing. Performance adversely affected by anxiety.
   B. Object spans and block tapping: Examiner taps in various sequences a series of objects or blank squares on a table. Child then does this in the same order.
      1. Norms: Ages 4 to 6—four objects (or squares); ages 7 to 9—five objects; ages 9 to 12—six objects.
      2. Comments: Success also depends on good visual attention. Object span affected by meaningfulness of objects to the child.
   C. Serial commands: Examiner gives a sequence of simple commands. Child then carries out the commands in the appropriate order, e.g., "Put the pencil on the chair. Open the door. Put the pencil in the drawer and sit down."
      1. Norms: Ages 4 to 6—three commands; ages 6 to 8—four commands; ages 8 to 10—five commands; ages 10 to 12—six commands.
      2. Comments: Several sets of commands should be given. Look for omissions and sequencing errors. Children with receptive language problems may also perform poorly in serial commands.

In the auditory modality digit spans and serial commands have been used. Imitative block tapping and object spans can assess visual sequencing. Motor sequential organization can be screened in a series of visuomotor sequencing tasks.

Substantiation of a sequencing problem can be sought with standardized tests; digit span and picture arrangement subtests of the WISC might be part of confirmatory evidence.[26] The auditory and visual sequential memory components of the Illinois Test of Psycholinguistic Abilities (ITPA) might also be utilized.[15] The Detroit Tests of Learning Aptitude (DTLA) has subtests dealing with visual, motor, and auditory sequencing.[8]

Receptive language. Developmental language disabilities are covered in Chapter 12. Within the context of a discussion of learning disabilities, such handicaps are of critical importance. A child who is slow or inefficient at understanding language may manifest serious academic and behavioral problems. Secondarily, such a youngster may be inattentive, impulsive, and anxious about school-related activities. There may be great difficulty following classroom instructions, learning to read, and ultimately mastering the highest form of language: written expression.

In other sections there is a discussion of auditory attention and memory. These critical components of language processing will be omitted from this section. Fig. 13-3 shows a simplified hierarchy of language processing. At the lowest level are arousal, acuity, and auditory attention, or the effort to "tune in." Above these is the process of auditory discrimination, or the differentiation between similar units of sound (e.g., bald and bold, tag and tug). Then come the processes of segmentation and blending; one breaks down words to their individual sound or syllabic components and reassembles them in such a way that specific clusterings of sound units constitute "morphemes" or words. Then there is the attribution of meaning or idea to the received word units. Finally there is the appreciation of syntax and the morphology of sentences in such a way that comprehension can occur.

Children with developmental language disabilities may display deficits anywhere along this chain of processing. A child may demonstrate developmental delay in the capacity to proceed through the "strata" of receptive language. Alternatively, a child may be able to accomplish linguistic operations, but the process may be too slow, inefficient, and tiring to allow for keeping pace with peers in the classroom. A youngster who takes an inordinately long time to decode the first halves of the teacher's sentences may be missing most of the second halves!

Children with developmental language disabilities may show certain "risk factors" in their early histories. Perinatal stresses, such as prematurity or toxemia, are common. One may encounter a history of recurrent ear infections and chronic serous otitis during the first 3 years of life. Preschoolers with receptive language difficulties may show behavior problems, including maladaptive social interaction. They may appear to be chronically inattentive, and they may be delayed in speaking full sentences. They may be more apt to use motor than verbal forms of expression and interaction, so aggressive behavior is observed by the preschool teacher and parents. A child with developmental language disabilities may point at what he wants rather than ask for it. The child may overuse short sentences, evading the rules of syntax. He may frequently request repetition of instructions or directions from parents and teachers. The child may be suspected of being partially deaf and in extreme cases even autistic. Sometimes a language-impaired youngster is mislabelled as "spoiled," while therapy is delayed unnecessarily. When the child with a receptive language disability reaches school, there may be difficulties following instructions and learning to read, write, and spell. Some children with strong visual processing may be able to bypass their auditory-language problems because of superior visual recognition abilities. Such youngsters may encounter obstacles in their later years as verbal and written communication become increasingly complex and essential to academic proficiency.

The office screening of receptive language disorders is difficult. Physicians should rely heavily on careful history taking. The suspicion of a language disability should be pursued with a complete language evaluation by a qualified specialist. Traditional psychological testing may not cover many of the important areas of receptive language. It may not be sufficient to refer a child to a clinical psychologist for evaluation of a learning problem. Language assess-

HIERARCHY OF AUDITORY-LANGUAGE FUNCTION

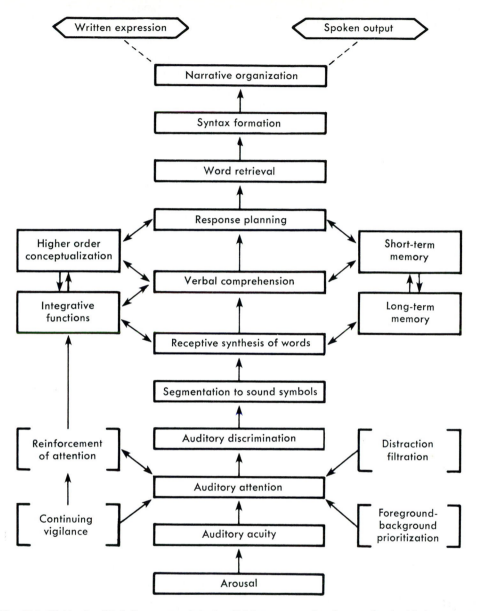

Fig. 13-3. Highly simplified diagram may help the clinician conceptualize the steps involved in language reception and expression. Children with developmental language disabilities characteristically may reveal deficits at one or more points in this schema.

ment may be of the greatest importance. Following is a list of historical hints that may be used by the pediatrician in determining whether a school-aged child could benefit from a comprehensive language evaluation in school or at a specialized center:

1. Developmental delay in the utilization of phrases or full sentences
2. History of recurrent otitis media during the first 4 years of life
3. Immaturity of articulation
4. Family history of language disability

5. Frequent need to have instructions repeated
6. Problems finding the right words, describing experiences, applying syntax, and organizing narrative
7. Extreme social passivity or quietness in school
8. Excessive use of circumlocutions, definitions rather than precise words
9. Confusion over similar-sounding words (e.g., fluent and fluid)
10. Immature vocabulary
11. History of hearing loss (transient or permanent)
12. Verbal hesitancy
13. Difficulty associating sounds and symbols for reading and spelling
14. Spelling errors that are phonetically bizarre (in older children)
15. Attentional weakness in "verbal settings" in a child who focuses appropriately on visuomotor tasks

Memory

Many learning disabled children demonstrate real or apparent deficits of either short-term or long-term memory. In an earlier section I described a characteristic memory deficit associated with the inability to preserve the serial order of incoming data. Other patterns of impaired memory can be seen in failing youngsters. In evaluating memory there are some principles that must be applied. First, it may be difficult to distinguish between chronic inattention and deficiencies of memory. One must remember in order to forget! If a child fails to attend, there is no way he can retain information. Second, one must be highly specific about the kinds of content a child has difficulty retaining. A youngster may have a poor memory for numbers, but excellent retention of words or sentences. Some children can store quantities of meaningful information but not abstractions or symbolic material. Finally, one must distinguish between recognition memory and retrieval. A child may recognize familiar patterns, symbols, faces, or words, while the same youngster may be handicapped in word finding or in reproducing a word or picture from memory. The active retrieval of information from the memory store is often more of a problem than the passive recognition of previously met words, images, or symbols.

Deficiencies of memory may exist selectively in one sensory modality. A child with a problem in visual memory for pattern or Gestalt may have a normal auditory memory for words or sequences. A child with a visual memory problem may be slow to acquire a sight vocabulary for reading. Such a child may reveal labored, hesitant, word-by-word reading. He may be proficient at word analysis (phonetic decoding and reblending of words), but limited in the visual recognition of symbols.

The act of spelling in particular requires retrieval rather than recognition. Analysis of errors may reveal that words are spelled phonetically, but are inaccurate in their visual configuration. An affected youngster may have difficulty with the revisualization of words he could recognize easily. It may be that words within a sight vocabulary for reading cannot be "mobilized" for spelling. This phenomenon can be demonstrated in a standardized test used to evaluate children with spelling and reading difficulties.[2]

There is a close relationship between the meaningfulness of data and their retention and accessibility. A child with perceptual problems in one sensory modality may have difficulty retaining information conveyed through that vulnerable channel.

Some children appear unable to store information from one week to the next, suggesting deficiencies in long-term memory. Effective long-term retention depends in part on the perceived relevance of material. Frequently children with long-term memory deficits have problems dealing with higher order conceptualization. They have difficulty classifying or categorizing data. They may have problems comprehending the common properties of such classes as animals, plants, etc. They have problems associating new information with their current knowledge of the universe. An inability to relate new data to previous experience and existent concepts may result in poor storage of such input.

Children with deficiences of memory often

show both academic and behavioral disorganization. Impulsivity may be seen in a youngster with limited short-term memory who acts quickly to avoid forgetting his intentions. Chronic inattention can be seen in children with retention problems. If attention leads only to transitory information, sustained focus does not get reinforced and distractibility often supervenes.

The clinician can screen for deficits of short-term memory. Sequential memory can be examined using the items described on p. 323. Visual memory for pattern can be evaluated by having a child copy forms from memory (Fig. 13-2). One can ask a child to pick out shapes or forms that previously have been presented to him from among a collection including those he has not seen before. Long-term memory capacity is more difficult to evaluate. It usually is inferred from a child's general level of information.

Standardized tests of memory are scanty. Digit spans are common in many examinations, but are subject to the contaminations noted earlier. The Detroit Tests of Learning Aptitude contains subtests dealing with memory.[8] In addition, The Benton Visual Retention Test has been used to identify children with such deficiencies.[1] It suffers from requiring a fine motor response. Traditionally long-term memory has been assessed by looking at the information vocabulary subtests of the WISC. Historical evidence of a long-term memory deficit as related by parents and teachers may be more reliable.

Output and encoding

I have been examining areas of development that facilitate the reception, storage, and interpretation of incoming data. An essential ingredient of academic success is what might be termed "output," or productivity. Gross and fine motor function along with expressive language constitute the three most widely studied human output processes. These are the media through which "performance" is judged. Although output functions are significant in themselves, they also are the channels through which children can let us know whether reception, comprehension, and memory are intact. There

are children whose receptive, decoding, and retentive capabilities are age appropriate but who falter in the struggle to communicate or perform. Such children may succeed in the earliest grades of elementary school when only small volumes of output are required. As they approach the late elementary and junior high school years their academic performance may deteriorate significantly because they are required to increase their productivity and the efficiency of their output to meet demands, such as four- or five-page book reports, oral presentations to the class, and increased participation in competitive sports. Some youngsters who present initially with perceptual problems in the early grades may improve greatly in the areas of attention, comprehension, and memory but then perform less well when output demands increase. Conversely, certain children learn better by performing than through the passive infusion of data. Such youngsters may accelerate when there is more emphasis on expression.

As the output demands increase in the late elementary school years, vulnerable children may experience "developmental high output failure" (to borrow a term from the cardiologists). They may demonstrate that their learning capacity outstretches their working capacity. They may fatigue easily and falter in written and oral expression. They may be reluctant to focus on tasks involving prolonged, continuous performance. Such youngsters frequently are accused and "convicted" of poor motivation, "primary emotional disturbance," attitudinal problems, and laziness. Although low motivation and the fear of failure can play a role in output disorders, such "diagnoses" may be made too casually, while overlooking underlying developmental problems. At this point, it will be useful to look at some of the components of output and the kind of deficits one may encounter clinically.

Expressive language. Verbal expressive skill can facilitate learning, personality development, and social interaction. Children with handicaps of expressive language may experience failure and anguish in a verbal and language oriented educational system. The effective and rapid encoding of ideas into words, phrases, sentences, and narratives represents a pivotal academic challenge for school-aged children. Cultural influences and early experience can contribute to a child's verbal proficiency. Intrinsic language-processing abilities are critical.

A child with expressive language problems may demonstrate one or more of a number of deficiencies; there may be problems with word finding or the ability to associate ideas with precise word symbols. A youngster may be hesitant at finding the right word to encode a thought or to identify a familiar object. In some instances a child can find the precise words, but the process is too time consuming and fatiguing. Other youngsters have difficulty organizing words into sentences or applying syntactical rules effectively. In other cases there are problems with narrative organization, or the sequencing of events. Frequently the physician can detect such impairments in normal conversation with the child. One can often discern expressive handicaps when the child is trying to describe recent events or narrate an experience.

Although many children with expressive language problems tend to be "nonverbal," a child may be delayed in expressive language and yet highly loquacious. It may be that such a youngster's verbal outflow is accomplished with a vocabulary that is immature or limited to relatively few words and with relatively primitive syntax. The child may often use circumlocutions, overindulging in words such as "thing" and "whatchamacallit." Such a child may be noted to be extremely talkative or verbal at home, but comparatively taciturn in the classroom, where more stringent demands are placed on expressive vocabulary.

A child with expressive language handicaps may present with the same historical findings noted in children with receptive language difficulties (pp. 324 to 326). Expressive language problems may be accompanied by a history of articulation difficulties (Chapter 12). Some children with expressive language problems are reluctant or slow to participate in class discussions. As one 14-year-old boy commented, "I can understand what the class is talking about when we discuss current events. I have some good ideas, but by the time I figure out how to say my ideas, the class is always talking about something else."

Expressive language problems can lead to a failure to communicate easily in social settings and consequently to difficulties controlling relationships with peers. Some children with emotional problems find it difficult to talk about their feelings. In a child with expressive language impairment, this may be aggravated by his difficulty finding the words to describe emotions. Such a handicap should be understood by the psychotherapist treating the youngster.

Writing constitutes the highest hurdle for the child with expressive language problems. A youngster with expressive deficits may be inhibited about committing to paper such imperfect prose. Writing is likely to be perplexing, inordinately time consuming, and extremely fatiguing to such a child. When one blends expressive language problems with deficiencies in fine motor or graphomotor function, one has some ingredients for academic failure. Such an outcome is frequently encountered in junior high school children, in whom increased demands for expression plunge a child into panic and failure. Typically the youngster continually denies the existence of any homework, fails to finish assignments, or tends to submit illegible, poorly organized written work (often several days late). He becomes inhibited and defensive about school and is likely to develop an exaggerated posture of indifference, "coolness," defiance, or, at worst, antisocial or even sociopathic behavior. It is not uncommon to hear adolescent delinquents lament on how much they hate to write.

Poor writing may be more than a manifestation of fine motor and/or expressive language problems. Written encoding is the culmination of multiple underlying developmental functions. Attention, memory, and sequencing abilities are among the many prerequisite functions that contribute to effective writing.

Standardized tests of output capacity are difficult to administer and score. Word finding can be measured through picture-naming tests and other assessments of verbal fluency. Tests of written expression have been developed, but these have been inadequately standardized and difficult to score. In general, the clinician should evaluate output by sampling it. It is helpful to watch a child write and listen to him speak. It is essential to get good data from the parents and school about output efficiency. It is often helpful to talk to the child to acquire further information about the stress and strain associated with writing and verbal expression. At the same time one can attend to cues about the child's word finding, fluency, and narrative organization.

Fine motor function. Deficits in fine motor function may impair a child's writing ability. ''Dysgraphia'' can be a manifestation of any of a number of underlying developmental dysfunctions and not necessarily be symptomatic of a fine motor delay. On the other hand, children with fine motor deficits encounter great difficulties when the demands for written output increase (fourth grade and beyond in particular). Fine motor activity can involve distal function in many regions of the body (for example, tongue, toes). Generally speaking, however, fine motor performance most frequently refers to activities of the hands and fingers.

School-aged children with fine motor deficits may have an early history of problems establishing a pencil grip or mastering manipulative tasks during the toddler years. It is common to find such youngsters delayed in learning to use feeding utensils and in tying their shoelaces. In the school-aged child the most common presenting complaint is illegible or labored handwriting. Here again, there exists a differential diagnosis; some children may have apparent fine motor problems, but in reality their difficulty is chronic impulsivity! No one could write as rapidly as they are attempting to do. Often the physician can learn about a child's fine motor function through simple observations. Undressing and dressing for the physical examination can provide data about fine motor ability as well as other areas of development. Careful observation of buttoning, shoelace tying, and the adjustment of socks can yield information about dexterity and eye-hand coordination. Observing a child copying forms as part of the visuospatial assessment can help to gauge pencil control (graphomotor function). The clinician should note the pencil grip, since many youngsters with fine motor problems re-

veal bizarre and inefficient hand postures during writing. The coding subtest of the WISC and the motor speed parts of the Detroit test may also suggest fine motor deficiencies.

It is important to assess not just the quality of fine motor output but also its rate and efficiency. Many children with output difficulties appear to have adequate fine motor function, but the rate of performance is so slow that sustained output is likely to be tedious. In observing a child completing a fine motor task, the clinician should consider the following components of productivity:

1. The reception and decoding of the instructions
2. Previous experience with the requested fine motor task
3. The capacity to integrate previous experience with current demands
4. Reflectivity, or the planning of the fine motor response
5. Eye-hand coordination and the execution of the plan.
6. Persistence and continuity of the performance
7. Feedback and monitoring of the quality so that performance can be refined or improved with time

It can be seen from this that youngsters with primary attentional deficits, visuospatial problems, and difficulties decoding verbal instructions may all ''masquerade'' as children with fine motor problems.

Gross motor function. Coordination, balance, body position sense, and motorsequential organization are not in themselves prerequisites to academic success. Many individuals who could never catch a ball or win a sprint have become great scholars, artists, and national leaders. It might be argued that such individuals were not ''distracted'' by competitive sports and were therefore able to devote their full energies toward academic pursuits. On the other hand, the effectiveness of gross motor output plays a role in personality development. Youngsters who are not able to compete in team sports will generally lack a sense of ''motor mastery'' and may suffer from diminished self-esteem, social rejection, and general feelings of inadequacy.

The assessment of gross motor function has counselling implications for the clinician. The child with excellent gross motor abilities may utilize these to sustain his self-image when other developmental areas are deficient. Through gross motor activity, a major channel of output or expression may be opened. For these reasons, the assessment of gross motor function can be an important part of developmental description. In addition, gross motor handicaps may be the outward indicators of central nervous system dysfunction.

Children with gross motor delays often present a history of reluctance to participate in games or sports. Sometimes children will partake selectively of those events that require little visuomotor integration, or they may participate in physical activities that offer privacy from peers and are less directly competitive. A history of difficulty catching a ball, general awkwardness, poor balance, and trouble learning to ride a bicycle, to hop, and to skip may lead one to suspect a gross motor lag. Following is a list of some screening items to sample gross motor performance in a school-aged child; such observations can be helpful in one's overall neurodevelopmental examination:

I. Historical hints
   A. Child shows reluctance to participate in competitive physical activities and fear of gym classes.
   B. Child has difficulty catching or throwing a ball, skipping, jumping, and balancing.
   C. Mastery of bicycle riding and other learned motor tasks is delayed.
   D. Child shows clumsiness, motor disorganization at home.
   E. NOTE: Some children with visuomotor integration problems may have particular difficulty with motor activities requiring considerable visual input and feedback (for example, baseball, volleyball), but perform much better when the inputs are largely proprioceptive or kinesthetic (for example swimming, skiing, gymnastics).
II. Screening observations (examples)
   A. Stressed gaits: Stressed gait tests provide an opportunity to observe incoordination of gait, particularly in younger children. One should look at overall performance and upper limb posturing.

1. Ages 4 to 5: Skipping, hopping, walking on heels
2. Ages 5 to 8: Tandem gaits (forward and backward)
3. Ages 9 to 10: Sidewise tandem gait
   B. Eye–upper limb coordination: This area of coordination can be observed by having a child throw a ball or beanbag at a target and catch a ball thrown by the examiner. In children under 9 a beach ball or volley ball should be caught with both hands. In older children a tennis ball should be caught with one hand.
   C. Body position sense and regulation: This parameter is observed by having a child sustain balance or stance.
      1. Ages 5 to 6: Standing on one foot, eyes open (10 seconds)
      2. Ages 7 to 9: Standing heel to toe, eyes closed (15 seconds)
      3. Ages 9 to 12: Standing on tiptoes, eyes closed (15 seconds)
   D. Complex motor organization: Planning, sequencing, and coordinating complex output should be observed.
      1. Ages 5 to 7: Imitating examiner's gestures—clap hands twice over head, twice behind back; clap hands three times in front of chest, twice behind back, once in front of chest; clap hands twice in front of chest, once behind back, once in front of chest, once behind back
      2. Ages 7 to 9: Hopping twice on each foot in succession in place (repeat four times without stopping)
      3. Ages 10 to 12: Jumping jacks; simultaneous jumping and clapping

Higher order conceptualization and integration

I have described the phenomena associated with the receipt, understanding, storage, and transmission of data. In a learning child these processes work synergistically. They connect and interrelate in a fully integrated central nervous system. Higher order cognitive function governs and renders meaningful much of the raw data entering the system. Some children with perceptual, attentional, and/or memory problems are likely to find redemption in their capacity to conceptualize, to generate rules about the universe, to deal with abstractions, and to perceive consistent relationships or common denominators in their learning experience. A child with a poor visual memory may learn to spell because he is adept at applying rules, such as "i before e except after c." On the other hand, children who have difficulty conceptualizing have great problems in learning.

The measurement of higher order conceptualization is indirect, relating closely to overall intelligence. The WISC similarities subtest is one index of higher order conceptualization.[26] Other tests specifically evaluate a variety of higher order cognitive functions.[3,13]

The most complete and influential theoretical framework for understanding the development of higher order conceptualization has been formulated by Piaget and his colleagues.[24] The diagnostic applications of their work have not yet materialized to aid in the assessment of learning disorders.

Integrative processes are essential to learning. Children with learning problems may reveal poor intersensory integration or defective blending of information entering through more than one sensory pathway. There may be problems integrating activities on both sides of the body simultaneously or carrying out two separate functions at the same time. For example, when asked to read aloud, a child might say, "Do you want me to read it or understand it?" He is saying that he can translate visual symbols into meanings or into oral sound symbols, but that he cannot integrate the two processes. It is sometimes said that a person (often an American president!) can either chew gum or walk, but cannot do both at the same time!

The capacity to integrate functions and to carry out simultaneous receptive or output processes in critical to academic performance. The clinician may encounter children whose integrative disorders are limited to specific pairs of receptive and/or output channels. A child may be adept at encoding a verbal response to an auditory input, but, characteristically, may have great difficulty traversing modalities, transforming an auditory input into a fine motor or graphomotor response. Such a youngster may not have a primary motor problem but rather difficulty integrating or "anastomosing" auditory and graphomotor "circuits." Prob-

lems with intersensory integration may be one cause of the failure of a young child to master the visual sound symbol associations crucial for reading and written encoding. Thus it is not isolated functional areas that generate performance, but rather a network of individual elements or processes in development that must act in concert and often simultaneously for optimum learning and output.

Assessing a child's integrative function involves direct observation of how the child performs tasks that entail cross-modal or simultaneous process. Many of the items suggested in this chapter require the integration of one input modality (e.g., verbal instruction) with a different output (e.g., gross motor). A child may repeatedly have difficulty with a specific "linkage." By analyzing the integrative component of tasks, the clinician can make useful observations in this important area of function.

OLDER CHILDREN AND ADOLESCENTS

The older child or adolescent with learning problems offers a unique set of challenges. Following factors complicate evaluation:

1. Most standardized tests for learning disabilities "ceiling out" at younger ages, thus normative data on adolescent development are scanty.
2. Specific tests for learning disability in adolescents generally are not available.
3. Most neuromaturational assessments have little or no yield in this age group, since fewer maturational signs are elicitable.
4. Children have only minimal tolerance for chronic failure. An older child who has waged a losing battle against learning is likely to superimpose over his constitutional deficiencies a dense matrix of learning inhibitions, defenses, and maladaptive strategies. These secondary symptoms may appear to be "the whole problem," thus the youngster is diagnosed as having a purely emotional, attitudinal, or motivational cause for failure.
5. In the early adolescent years a child often exercises heavy denial with respect to underlying handicaps, wanting to appear as "normal" and "regular" as possible.

6. Teachers and other school personnel are less apt to be sensitive to learning disorders in older children and adolescents.

7. It can be very difficult for the physician to establish close rapport with older children (especially during early adolescence). Children at this age feel self-conscious about seeing a physician. They are reluctant to discuss any "rough edges" or shortcomings. They have an enormous desire to be "normal," "cool," and inconspicuous. There is a commensurate fear of such labels as "retard," "mental," or "fag." This hypertrophied sensitivity can impair diagnostic evaluation.

8. Because children do not like to pursue activities in which they are chronically deficient, adolescents have their learning disorders aggravated by a relative lack of practice or experience. If a child writes poorly, he is likely to write infrequently. By the age of 16 an adolescent with dysgraphia has written a great deal less than his smooth-writing contemporary. It is ironical that the less competent a child is, the less opportunity he will give himself to improve. This effect is especially potent in adolescence.

9. Some adolescents make remarkable progress in dealing with learning disorders because of an increasing capacity to order the universe through higher order logic and abstract reasoning. This capability may help compensate for persistent handicaps of perception, attention, and memory. Piaget has called these late-acquired processes "formal operations."[24]

The diagnosis and management of adolescents with learning problems have been further hampered in the past by misconceptions about the natural history of developmental dysfunctions; many clinicians believe that "hyperactivity" ends at puberty. In fact, children with learning disorders and attentional problems are likely to have increasing trouble during adolescent years if they are not managed properly. The association of underlying handicaps with the later development of antisocial behaviors has been well established. Chronic depression, affective disorders, and sociopathy may

be late complications. Although some children show remarkable developmental resiliency, others continue their spiral of failure throughout junior and senior high school. The clinical manifestations may change. An earlier problem with reading may transform into an adolescent's struggle with writing and organizing reports.

The clinician can be aware of these limitations while offering useful insights and solid support to an adolescent. The diagnostic evaluation of an older child requires a meticulous, methodical review of the history. The kinds of developmental and academic problems encountered during elementary school years should be reconsidered along with any early test data. The clinician should develop hypotheses about the presence of learning disabilities during the early school years. It is then possible to trace these up to the present. The process of task analysis, which is critical to any developmental assessment, is particularly germain in the evaluation of adolescent function. The clinician should analyze the tasks in which a particular child is succeeding and those in which he is failing to develop a sense of where specific developmental strengths and weaknesses may rest. Much of the diagnosis in older children should be conducted through direct observation of performance. One should review samples of the child's writing and arithmetic. One should listen to the child read. Spelling errors should be analyzed. From this type of data, along with past history, one can create a natural history of the learning disability. Older adolescents are adept at talking about themselves. With appropriate encouragement it is possible for such a youngster to describe in vivid detail the kinds of learning situations that are most difficult for him. As one chronically inattentive 16-year-old boy said, "Doc, let me tell you what my head is like. It's just like a television set. Only, it's got no channel selector. All the programs come on my screen at the same time. It's real noisy up there!"

During the adolescent years attentional deficits and/or specific learning disabilities may be complicated by the development of antisocial or sociopathic behaviors. In this age group it is common for youngsters who have never been able to succeed to form strong alliances with peers who have shared the same plight. There is increasing evidence of an association between developmental dysfunction of various types and the problem of delinquency during adolescence. Social and cultural factors are woven into the fabric of sociopathy, together with feelings of inadequacy secondary to academic failure. The avoidance of antisocial behavior patterns is certainly one of the major goals of preventive developmental pediatrics!

MANAGEMENT OF LEARNING DISORDERS

The "treatment" of learning disorders, while widely undertaken, has been subjected to only the crudest scientific scrutiny. There are few well-controlled studies of specific curriculum materials, individualized educational programs, medications, counselling, or special diets. Randomized clinical trials of specific therapies would be difficult to design and to carry forth ethically. It is hoped that increasing investigative efforts will take place in the coming years. In the meantime children with learning disorders need to be treated responsibly within the limits of the state of the art.

Special education

Individualized education does not have the most immediate or dramatic "payoff," but it is a critical ingredient of a management program. Special educational legislation in the United States now mandates individualized educational plans drawn up by multidisciplinary teams to meet the special needs of children with learning problems.[10] The design of a child's educational program can be derived from team efforts. From diagnostic findings one can determine how much special help a child needs. For example, children with attentional deficits certainly benefit from very small group or one-to-one teaching situations for part of each day. The extent to which this can be helpful depends in part on the severity of a child's attentional deficit but also on the degree of academic delay. Children may leave the regular classroom for part of each day to receive specific assistance in weak academic areas, as well as individualized exercises to strengthen delayed developmental functions. Programs designed to enhance lan-

guage development, sequencing ability, or visual-perceptual-motor function might be utilized in appropriate cases.

As youngsters enter the junior and senior high school years, less emphasis is placed on intervention to bolster weak developmental areas, with greater stress on specific support in academic subjects. This propensity requires further investigation. The assumption is often made that helping a child in high school to improve visual perception, memory, or receptive language is futile, thus any additional assistance is focused on helping the youngster with mathematics, social studies, science, etc., or on bypassing deficient areas altogether.

Many standardized curriculum packages have been developed to help children with weaknesses in specific learning areas. The best way for a clinician to learn about these is to become involved actively in the educational planning process and to review the materials available in the local school systems. In addition, several books review current forms of educational intervention for learning disabilities.[12,16,18,28]

A recurring dilemma in the management of learning disorders is whether to strengthen a child's weaknesses or to enhance and utilize only his strengths. "Bypass strategies" can be formulated to enable a youngster to apply strengths almost exclusively, thereby avoiding undue frustration and failure. Children with certain kinds of writing disorders might be taught to type. Youngsters who have difficulty with prolonged written assignments might be allowed to present oral book reports or at least to shorten written presentations. Children described as "visual learners" might be given most of their instructions in writing or with visual "demonstration models" rather than through complex verbal communication. Such custom-made, "delivered to your door" teaching can be expensive and sometimes can represent a gross capitulation to a child's handicaps. An ideal educational program should combine appropriate bypass strategies or developmental concessions with concerted efforts to strengthen weak areas. A youngster with a receptive language disability can benefit from appropriately designed language therapy, while at the same

time the classroom teacher can simplify or reduce the length of verbal instructions and offer
more visually presented materials.

Part of educational management involves
helping regular classroom teachers to understand and to cope with a child who is not learning. Many issues require consideration: the
child's seating in the classroom, the appropriate
expectations for volume of output or information intake, the choice of curriculum materials,
the methods of positively or negatively reinforcing the child, the choice of subject matter (such
as the introduction of foreign languages for an
older youngster), and the appropriate classroom
routine (degree of structure, amount of free
choice, etc.). These issues are best decided by
the interdisciplinary team who employ a wide
range of perspectives and varying kinds of
knowledge about the child and the school.

Counselling

Counselling is an essential part of any management program. The professional responsible
for a child with a learning disorder must be able
to deal with the parents and the child on several
levels. First, it is essential that the parents have
a good understanding of the child's learning
disorder. They must be helped to understand his
strengths, weaknesses, and styles. They need to
appreciate the degree to which maladaptive behaviors result directly from or secondary to the
child's developmental handicaps. They need to
be helped to decide when to hold the child ac-
countable for his actions, and when to attribute
them to constitutional weaknesses. They need
support in dealing with many of the difficult
temperamental qualities of children with learning disorders. Parents of learning disabled children need considerable assurance that they have
not caused their child's problem. The allevia-
tion of guilt is an important counselling objective. The clinician working with parents must
be nonaccusatory, while helping them achieve a
balanced view of their child. They need to be
primed as strong advocates for their youngster's
service needs; on the other hand, it is important
that they not become so intensely impassioned
over their child's handicaps that the learning
problems become an obsessive interest. In
counselling parents it is essential that the clini-

cian remain available to help them manage
specific situations or predicaments as they arise
at home, in school, and in the neighborhood.
This becomes an important part of follow-up
management.

The direct counselling of children with learning difficulties is crucial. Too often the youngster is left out of direct discussions of the learning disorder. Such a child may fantasize, inflat-
ing the problem and rendering it far more devastating. An effort should be made to be as open
as possible with the child. Whenever it is feasible, he should be allowed to read reports and
attend conferences. The direct one-to-one counselling should focus on his concerns about
being "dumb." The child should be helped to
see strengths as well as weaknesses. An effort
should be made to simplify or "demystify"
learning problems. Children should be supported in the effort to control their feelings of
inadequacy and to see the possibilities for success. It is important to help them overcome
their feelings of guilt about academic failure. In
follow-up visits a child should be encouraged to
describe specific experiences relating to his own
learning styles or handicaps. The clinician
should be able to ask questions such as, "How
is your attention problem coming along?"
"Have you been able to stay 'tuned-in' a little
better lately?" "Has your doing things without
thinking caused trouble lately?" "Tell me
about some good control you have had." The
child should describe recent experiences he has
had in grappling with school and other areas of
performance.

A learning disorder is a family problem. The
clinican should involve the siblings of an affected child. Brothers and sisters constitute a
major part of the environment. Their peculiar
styles, strengths, weaknesses, and attitudes toward the handicapped youngster are of great
importance and must be understood by the
clinician. Jealousy or resentment should be
managed. The siblings of a learning disabled
child become partners in his care. They need to
understand the nature and extent of the child's
struggles so as not to feel rejected themselves. It
is important to observe the ways in which a
handicapped child measures himself against
siblings. A highly competent, achieving sibling

may hamper the academic effort of a learning disabled child. Developing the mechanisms through which all family members can interact meaningfully and cooperate with the affected youngster can be a powerful strategy.

The counselling of teachers is another critical component; by ascertaining that the teacher is sensitive to a child's learning style and acknowledges the neurological or constitutional predispositions to failure, one can reduce the level of moral condemnation doled out in the classroom. The clinician must interpret neurodevelopmental and biomedical findings for the teacher while collaborating to gauge their impact on learning and behavior. The overall objective should be to create a school environment in which the system is likely to take a nonaccusatory, highly supportive attitude toward a failing child.

Medical therapies

A variety of pharmacological agents have been used to help children with learning problems. These range from minor to major tranquilizers, to antidepressant drugs, to anticonvulsant agents, and to stimulant medications. In rare cases tranquilizers, antidepressants, or anticonvulsants may be indicated. This chapter will be limited to a discussion of the stimulant medications. These agents have been utilized widely to treat children with attentional deficits.[5,21,29] At best they can enhance selective attention, promote the filtration of distractions, foster reflectivity, and potentiate task persistence. They help to decelerate some youngsters who are overactive, while they may benefit some underactive children with attentional deficits.

The indications for stimulant therapy have not been well established; however, general guidelines can be suggested. First, medication is never the ultimate panacea for a child. Youngsters with attentional deficits are likely to have special educational and counselling needs that must supplement the use of medications. Second, it is important that parents and the child feel comfortable with the use of stimulant medication. It is inappropriate to coerce or "sell" parents on the use of such drugs when they are very apprehensive about them. Third, a full neurodevelopmental and medical assessment should be performed on a child prior to the introduction of stimulant medications. Fourth, it is often advisable to implement an individualized educational plan for a child prior to the prescription of stimulant medication; it may be that counselling and educational programming will obviate the need for pharmacotherapy. Finally, when the child is put on such medication, ongoing monitoring and careful management is important.

Table 13-2 lists three commonly used stimulant medications and their dosage ranges. It is best to start with the smallest possible dosage and increase this gradually if necessary. There is a difference of opinion as to whether children should take stimulant medications on weekends and during school vacations. Many clinicians prefer to utilize them only on school days. Children who are put on medications deserve close and consistent follow-up. The clinician should be easily accessible by telephone to alter dosage schedules. It is important to see the child regularly to discuss his feeling about the medication and to measure the effectiveness of such drugs. Questionnaires are available to monitor progress.[4]

There has been widespread interest in special diets to help children with learning problems and "hyperactivity."[6,20,27] Diets free of chemical additives and various forms of low-carbohydrate regimens have been tried. There is some evidence that additive-free diets may be of some benefit to some children; exaggerated claims have been rampant. If parents feel strongly about the pursuit of an additive-free diet, the clinician should ensure that the child receives appropriate nutrition and that the psychological effects of the diet do not become inordinately oppressive. Anecdotal evidence on the efficacy of low-carbohydrate diets and other special nutritional measures has not been substantiated by scientific data. In fact, such intervention can be dangerous. Parents should be discouraged from engaging in such programs until responsible studies can be undertaken and interpreted.

An important part of management involves helping parents (and often teachers) to reject medically related therapies that have no scien-

Table 13-2. Stimulant medications in the management of attentional deficits

Medication	Dosage range	Possible side effects	Additional comments
Dextroamphetamine (Dexedrine) 5 mg tablets; 5, 10, and 15 mg Spansules	2.5 to 30 mg (up to 40, rarely)	Anorexia, weight loss, sleep problems, emotional lability, oversensitivity, facial tics (?), growth retardation, "bleary-eyed" appearance	Begin at 5 mg/day, increase by 5 mg/wk until optimum dosage is attained In children 4 to 6, begin at 2.5 mg
Methylphenidate (Ritalin) 5, 10, 20 mg tablets	5 to 40 mg, usually in 2 divided doses (up to 30 mg bid in very unusual circumstances)	Similar to dextroamphetamine	Approximately half the potency of dextroamphetamine Duration of action about 4 hours, peak effects in 2 hours
Pemoline (Cylert) 18.75, 37.5, 75 mg tablets	18.75 mg to 112.5 mg (mean dose is 56.25 to 75 mg)	Insomnia, anorexia, abdominal pain, nausea, headache, dizziness, fatigue, depression	Long-acting (up to 12 hours) Begin at 18.75 to 37.5 mg, increase by 18.75 mg/week until optimum effects are noted; may take 2 weeks to show benefit

tific basis. Such treatment programs are highly appealing, since they promise over-simplified glib answers to a child's dysfunction.[27] Included are optometric exercises, megavitamin therapy, allergy desensitization, a variety of bizarre metabolic interventions, motor patterning, and transcendental meditation. Since there is a nonspecific beneficial effect of almost any kind of increased supportive attention, programs of this type can offer potential consumers abundant testimonial evidence of success. However, they represent an expensive effort that can divert attention from the child's true educational and emotional needs.

Medical management includes the evaluation and treatment of associated symptoms such as seizures, recurrent abdominal pains, headaches, encopresis, enuresis, and other disorders that commonly cluster in children with learning disorders.

Other referral services

A clinician must consider the need for other kinds of intervention; referral for psychotherapy, language therapy, and physical or occupational therapy may be indicated. The clinician should be a highly informed consumer advocate in helping parents to find the appropriate and most effective professionals in these areas.

A variety of special activity groups are emerging in various parts of the country to help children who have low self-esteem and feelings of inadequacy. They may include special summer camps, music groups, clubs, and other programs designed to bring together children who have special needs. The health provider can provide a kind of clearinghouse for such resources.

Finally, a critical part of management involves ongoing monitoring and follow-up. Children and their families need continuity of support from the clinician. The learning problem must be managed and "titrated" as a chronic illness; ongoing availability is critical.

THE ROLE OF THE PEDIATRICIAN

The pediatric role in the evaluation and management of learning disorders is a matter of some controversy. Some physicians wish to take a leadership position, while others do not believe it is legitimately a part of pediatrics. Recent studies have indicated that parents are turning to pediatricians increasingly for help with children who are failing in school.[14] Special educational legislation is mandating an increasingly prominent role for the physician as part of the diagnostic and management team.[10] As expectations rise, pediatricians need to respond in a manner that is likely to be helpful to parents, children, and educators. The degree of involvement will vary. However, the following common components of the medical role can be described.

Early detection and screening. As physicians and other professionals continue to learn about the early cues to developmental dysfunction, it will be important for the pediatrician to become an informed observer and an early diagnostician of learning disorders. P. 313 provides a brief summary of some of the outward clinical signs of underlying learning disorder. An attentive physician should have a high degree of suspicion for learning disorders when confronted with the various symptom complexes that include these signs.

Traditional medical evaluation. The physician plays an important role in ruling out traditional medical predispositions to learning failure. The educational impact of medical conditions and treatments should be assessed. For example, if a child is taking antihistaminic or anticonvulsant drugs, he may be more fatigable in the classroom. For the child who has chronic allergic rhinitis, the condition may become a powerful distractor. It is also important for the physician to diagnose and interpret for the educational team any neurological conditions such as seizure disorders. On rare occasions an undiagnosed seizure disorder may in itself interfere with learning.

Historical formulation. The physician can assemble a child's medical and developmental history as it bears on current functional problems. The content is summarized on p. 314.

Neurodevelopmental examination. The importance of direct observation of developmental performance has been stressed. Standardized neurodevelopemental examination packages are available.[19] These may be valuable office tools for the physician. The screening items tabulated earlier in this chapter can be included as part of a neurodevelopmental assessment. Many clinicians are compiling their own evaluation or screening packages. In doing so one must be careful to administer well-standardized items and to be cautious about their interpretation. Such an evaluation should not be considered the exclusive or final diagnostic procedure. Neurodevelopmental findings or hypotheses should be confirmed by historical data and in many cases by other standardized tests as well as teacher observations. The diagnostic descriptive "hunt" should seek out developmental strengths as well as deficits.

Psychosocial evaluation. By maintaining the greatest continuity with the family, the primary care physician can play a valuable role in elucidating stylistic, social, psychological, and family dynamics issues that may have a bearing on a child's function in school. While it is important to protect the family's privacy, certain kinds of psychosocial information can be very helpful in educational planning and in sensitizing oneself and others to the child's total predicament.

Participation in a transdisciplinary diagnostic and management team. Team evaluation and the treatment of children with learning disorders is becoming a well-established process. Members should overlap in the kinds of skills they possess and the observations and recommendations that they make (hence the term "transdisciplinary"). In some cases the pediatrician may serve as a team member and in others as the coordinator or team leader.

Informed advocacy. The pediatrician can represent a potent social force on behalf of a child or for all children in the community, advocating the enhancement of services. When an individual school or an entire educational system seems unresponsive to the needs of handicapped children, a pediatrician can be an influential catalyst. It is essential, however, that advocacy be based on real knowledge of the kinds of problems that constitute the special needs of specific children. The physician's role should extend to the area of consumer advocacy, as mentioned earlier; it is important to protect families from irresponsible intervention programs, while seeing that they obtain appropriate services.

Medical therapeutics. The use of various medications and other forms of medical management may be a key role of the pediatrician. This will vary from case to case.

Counselling of parents, children, siblings, and teachers. The ongoing counselling described earlier is a job that can often be assumed by the developmentally oriented pediatrician.

The role in resource utilization. The pediatrician can serve as an agent of referral to help parents seek out appropriate higher order diagnostic and treatment services.

Monitoring and follow-up. The ongoing longitudinal surveillance of a developmental dysfunction is crucial. Follow-up is combined with anticipatory guidance. The support of families in coping with the threat of failure and the constantly evolving manifestations of handicaps is critical.

Independent evaluation. In most cases a failing child can be assessed and served optimally under the auspices of the public school in cooperation with the primary care physician. In some instances the school or parent may request ''a second opinion.'' A parent may not feel satisfied with the educational diagnosis and/or plan. There may be a suspicion of conflict of interest in the school when the budget, specific personality issues, or the nonavailability of certain services may unduly influence the evaluation. Independent evaluation may be coordinated by the primary care physician or it may be performed in a medical center outpatient department or a child development unit. A truly independent evaluation must always be free of disciplinary biases and political or economic ties to the schools. The physician may shift between service as an informed child advocate and a mediator between the school and the parents.

SUMMARY

In summary, learning disability in a child is a potentially severely handicapping condition, which has major educational, vocational, financial, and emotional implications for the child and his family. Early identification and specific educational programming and counselling are very helpful in dampening many of the undesirable long-term effects. The role of the primary care physician will vary, depending on the age and needs of the child, but there is little question that it should include active participation in the diagnostic, evaluative, and educational programming process.[19]

REFERENCES

1. Benton visual retention test, New York, The Psychological Corporation.
2. Boder, E.: Developmental dyslexia: a diagnostic approach based on three atypical reading-spelling patterns, Devl. Med. Child Neurol. **15**:661, 1973.
3. Boehm test of basic concepts, New York, The Psychological Corp.
4. Conners, C. K.: A teacher rating scale for use in drug studies with children, Am. J. Psychiatry **126**:884, 1969.
5. Conners, C. K., and Eisenberg, L.: The effects of methylphenidate on symptomatology and learning in disturbed children, Am. J. Psychiatry **120**:458, 1963.
6. Conners, C. K., et al.: Food additives and hyperkinesis: a controlled double blind experiment, Pediatrics **58**:154, 1976.
7. Corballis, M. C., and Beale, I. L.: The psychology of left and right, New York, 1976, John Wiley & Sons, Inc.
8. Detroit tests of learning aptitude, Indianapolis, The Bobbs-Merrill Co., Inc.
9. Developmental test of visual-motor integration, Chicago, Follett Corp.
10. The Education for All Handicapped Children Act of 1975, PL 94-142, Washington, D.C., 1975, U.S. Government Printing Office.
11. Frostig developmental test of visual perception, Palo Alto, Calif., Consulting Psychologists Press.
12. Gearheart, B. R.: Learning disabilities: educational strategies, ed. 2, St. Louis, 1977, The C. V. Mosby Co.
13. Goldstein-Scherer object sort test, New York, The Psychological Corp.
14. Haggerty, R. J., Pless, I. B., and Roughman, K. J.: Child health and the community, New York, 1975, John Wiley & Sons, Inc., p. 95.
15. Illinois test of psycholinguistic abilities, Urbana, Ill., University of Illinois Press.
16. Johnson, D., and Mykelbust, H.: Learning disabilities: educational principles and practices, New York, 1967, Grune & Stratton, Inc.
17. Kagan, J.: Reflection-impulsivity and reading ability in primary grade children, Child Dev. **36**:609, 1965.
18. Lerner, J. W.: Children with learning disabilities, Boston, 1976, Houghton Mifflin Co., p. 11.
19. Levine, M. D., Brooke, R., and Shonkoff, J. S.: A pediatric approach to learning disorders, New York, 1980, John Wiley & Sons, Inc.
20. Levine, M. D., and Liden, C.: Food for inefficient thought, Pediatrics **58**:145, 1976.
21. Millichap, J. G.: Drugs in the management of minimal brain dysfunction, Int. J. Child Psychother. **1**:65, 1972.
22. National Advisory Committee on Handicapped Children, Special Education for Handicapped Children: First annual report, Washington, D. C., 1968, Department of Health, Education and Welfare.
23. Peters, J. E., Romine, J. S., and Dykeman, R. A.: A special neurologic examination of children with learning disabilities, Dev. Med. Child. Neurol. **17**:63, 1975.
24. Piaget, J.: The origins of intelligence in children, New York, 1952, International Universities Press.
25. Ross, A. O.: Psychological aspects of learning dis-

abilities and reading disorders, New York, 1976, McGraw-Hill Book Co., pp. 38-61.

26. Sattler, J. M.: Description and evaluation of WISC subtests, in assessment of children's intelligence, Philadelphia, 1974, p. 174.

27. Silver, L. B.: Acceptable and controversial approaches to treating the child with learning disabilities, Pediatrics **55:**58, 1975.

28. Spache, G. D.: Diagnosing and correcting reading disabilities, Boston, 1976, Allyn & Bacon, Inc.

29. Sroufe, L. A.: Drug treatment of children with behavior problems. In Horwitz, F. D., editor: Review of child development research, Chicago, 1975, University of Chicago Press, p. 347.

30. Tarver, S. C., and Hallahan, D. P.: Attention deficits in children with learning disabilities: a review, J. Learning Disabilities **7:**36, 1974.

31. Touwen, B. C. L., and Prechtl, H. F. R.: The neurological examination of the child with minor nervous dysfunction, Clin. Dev. Med. vol. 38, 1970.

14

The preschool child: prediction and prescription

Paul H. Dworkin
Melvin D. Levine

WHY THE PRESCHOOL CHILD?

Educators have in recent years increasingly stressed the importance of the early identification of preschool children who may subsequently encounter problems in academic learning. Much evidence has been provided to support the critical influence of the early childhood years on later competence. In addition, for the child who has already sustained failure due to developmental dysfunction in the early childhood years, emotional problems, such as loss of self-esteem and a lowering of self-confidence, make school-aged intervention far more difficult.

Increasing emphasis on the early identifica-

tion of children with potential learning disorders is also reflected in state and federal legislation. Many states require screening for readiness skills prior to school entry, as well as the provision of appropriate services for those children found to have developmental and educational handicaps. Federal legislation such as The Education for All Handicapped Children Act (Public Law 94-142) requires that to receive federal funds states must provide a "free appropriate public education" for all handicapped children residing in that state. State and local agencies are obligated to develop programs allowing identification, evaluation, and appropriate educational intervention, with all children receiving a "full educational opportunity."[10]

THE VALUE OF EARLY IDENTIFICATION

For children with physical, sensory, and gross developmental problems, the reasons for early identification and diagnosis are obvious. These handicaps differ significantly from potential learning failure:

1. The conditions identified are already manifest in the child.
2. Once the condition is recognized, a specific treatment is usually initiated.
3. For many conditions the sooner the treat-

ment is begun, the greater is the likelihood of enhanced outcome.

4. For some disorders, such as phenylketonuria, treatment will prevent the development of further damage to the child.[23]

Screening for potential learning disorders is quite different. The condition (i.e., school failure) has not yet developed. Even after the identification of factors predisposing to school failure, it is not always possible to determine the optimal intervention. Critics of early identification and intervention cite a "similarity of remedial recommendations" for these children, for example, nursery school is commonly the recommendation for the preschooler with delayed readiness skills regardless of the child's specific developmental profile. Furthermore, the beneficial effects of treatment are far more difficult to document. If a child "fails to fail," despite being identified via screening as predisposed to school failure, the reasons for this outcome are complex. Was the child inappropriately identified? Which aspects of intervention, if any, prevented school failure? With developmental screening, the danger of creating a "self-fulfilling prophecy" also exists. Will the child identified as manifesting delayed readiness skills be viewed differently by his teachers? Will problems with performance be more glibly accepted as documenting school failure? Thus those professionals assessing the preschool child must be secure in their belief that the beneficial effects of identification outweigh possible negative effects.

Notwithstanding the differences between screening for more conventional handicapping conditions and potential learning failure, attempts at the latter should not be abandoned as futile. Early identification of potential school failure should provide guidelines for appropriate early intervention and careful ongoing monitoring of developmental attainment, as well as crucial support to avoid secondary emotional problems, such as loss of self-esteem, noted earlier. However, because of difficulties with early identification, problems with the similarity of recommendations, and the danger of self-fulfilling prophecy, screening and assessment of the preschool child should be undertaken with great care.

THE ROLE OF THE PEDIATRICIAN

Pediatricians have been increasingly advised to assume a primary role in the early identification of learning disorders. The pediatrician is frequently called on by parents and educators to offer opinions with regard to a child's readiness for school. In addition, pediatricians strongly support the idea that screening for potential learning disabilities in the preschool child should be a routine part of primary pediatric care. In a survey of New England pediatricians, 60% strongly agreed and 25% agreed with this concept.[9]

The opportunity for involvement by the pediatrician is present at various levels: as medical consultant to preschool programs such as Head Start, as an active participant in preschool screening programs, and as a referral source for a child with evidence of developmental dysfunction. Whatever the role, a general appreciation of the components of assessment is critical, while a general overview of the normal development of the preschooler is an essential ingredient of pediatric evaluation

GUIDELINES FOR EVALUATION OF THE PRESCHOOL CHILD

Certain guidelines should be kept in mind when evaluating the preschool child.[23] To start with, one must be certain that the proper questions are being asked. To attempt to predict a child's college potential on the basis of early screening would be foolish! Rather, for the preschooler the appropriate question to pose is whether or not the child has the skills to succeed in kindergarten. Similarly, the kindergarten child should be assessed for potential for successful first grade performance. Asking the proper question is crucial—abilities assessed should, as far as possible, resemble those required in the next immediate educational setting.

The child must also be considered within the context of the situation in which he must function. The expectancies, for example, placed on a child entering an "open classroom" are quite different from those of a child in a more conventional setting. Those programs which stress early academic achievement require a different composite of strengths than the classroom stressing social interaction. Thus some awareness of the specific classroom situation into which a child is entering is relevant.

Any screening or identification techniques must also be designed to produce information that can translate into intervention programs. Services may include specific instructional procedures, some form of treatment, observation, or reassurance. Educators speak of the need to "operationalize" such approaches, that is, results from screening must readily lead to specific action.[4]

Finally, the purpose of screening and assessment should not be viewed as merely confirming deficits. Equally valuable for a child is a description of competence and relative strengths. Awareness of a child's learning characteristics and style is also helpful. Teachers can readily utilize such information in planning a child's educational curriculum, bypassing areas of weakness, and increasing self-esteem and self-confidence.

DIFFICULTIES WITH PRESCHOOL ASSESSMENT

There are certain difficulties inherent in the assessment of the preschool child. First, a number of functions are emerging at age 5 or 6 that cannot be studied adequately in earlier years. The real skills in question—reading, writing, spelling, and arithmetic—have not yet been developed. Thus "readiness skills" for reading, etc., are examined. The relationship between such readiness skills and actual academic performance is often speculative.

The relationships between single specific preschool test findings and later school achievement are too variable to allow definitive prediction in an individual case. No single assessment tool exists that is comprehensive in scope.

Preschool screening and assessment based on standardized test instruments are faced with another problem. Often such assessment screens out important evaluative information. Observations relating to a child's behavior in a classroom and problem-solving strategies are not usually provided during formal screening. Such limitations in information provided by screening and assessment utilizing standard instruments probably account for the greater ac-

curacy of preschool teachers as compared to pediatricians or psychologists in predicting school achievement.[11]

A further difficulty inherent in evaluation of the preschool child is that assumptions with regard to developmental, behavioral, temperamental, and environmental factors may be erroneous and misleading. Experience in a consultation clinic evaluating preschool children referred with disorders of function and behavior demonstrated that assessment of only one discrete area of performance as suggested by the presenting complaint would result in a failure to identify important factors relating to the child's dysfunction. Thus the need for a comprehensive evaluation of the child presenting with evidence of behavioral and/or developmental dysfunction is stressed.

The pediatrician, with a continuing relationship with families and young children, is in a unique position to assimilate various components of assessment and provide an important overview and perspective. The next section of this chapter will deal with methods of pediatric preschool assessment. Areas to be evaluated will be identified, methods of observation discussed, and clues regarding later academic performance suggested. Some of the examples of assessment items are very similar to those included in the Pediatric Examination of Educational Readiness[25] (p. 354).

COMPONENTS OF ASSESSMENT OF THE PRESCHOOL CHILD

Assessment of the preschool child must take into account multiple factors. Fig. 14-1 suggests many of these factors. Although certain aspects of assessment have traditionally been assigned to a specific discipline, that is, education or medicine, few components are limited to the confines of only one discipline. Assessment must not be considered the responsibility of only one group of professionals. An interchange of ideas and communication between professionals—an interdisciplinary approach—is indicated. Redundancy of observation of specific skills is not to be discouraged; multiple observations within different settings offer an important opportunity to increase the reliability of assessments. The pediatrician can

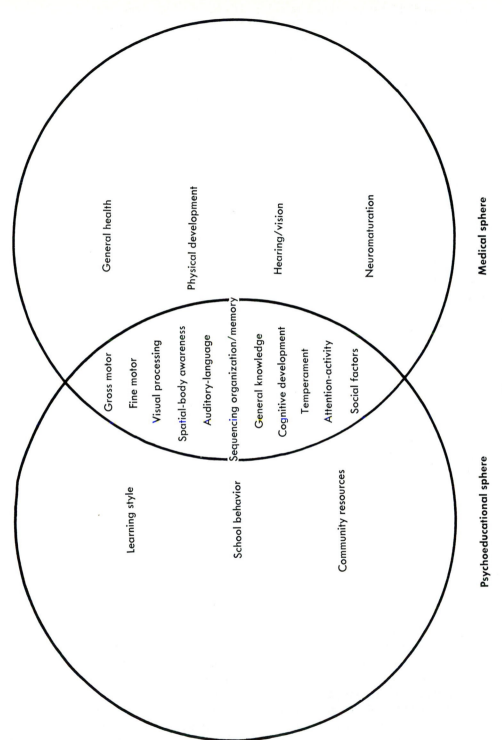

Fig. 14-1. Assessment of the preschool child: multidisciplinary task.

compare and contrast years of office observation of a particular child with the perceptions of the preschool teacher and results of any formal preschool readiness testing. Similar observations can be interpreted as highly reliable, while discrepant observations should be questioned. For example, a child may perform poorly on that portion of a readiness evaluation administered by the school system dealing with fine motor function. However, the pediatrician who has been monitoring the growth and development of that child over the years may not be concerned with fine motor function. If the nursery school teacher is similarly not worried, then the results of readiness screening must be viewed with caution. Repeat testing at a later time rather than intervention is indicated. As noted earlier, the pediatrician is in a unique position by virtue of years of contact with a child to provide such an overview.

SPECIFIC AREAS OF ASSESSMENT

General health. Little is known of the association between learning problems and chronic medical diseases. Although the effects of certain conditions, that is, seizures, chronic serous otitis media, etc., are evident, the role of others in affecting academic performance is unclear. The relevance of such chronic medical problems as lead poisoning, mild iron deficiency anemia, cystic fibrosis, congenital heart disease, and chronic renal disease is not obvious. Results of past studies attempting to answer these questions have been inconclusive. Even for those conditions in which the child will miss many school days due to illness, the impact on academic performance must be viewed cautiously.

Information relating to general health is obtained via the medical history. The perinatal history should be reviewed in depth. In weighting the perinatal history, it appears that clusters of complications rather than single perinatal events may be more important in predicting later performance. Questions relating to the prenatal period should include the areas of maternal nutrition, prior reproductive and gestational adequacy, infectious disease during gestation, other maternal illnesses, weight gain, toxemia, hemorrhage and anemia, medication,

smoking, and alcohol intake. Events during labor and delivery must also be reviewed: duration of labor, type of delivery, presence of fetal distress, cyanosis, trauma during delivery, gestational age, birth weight, congenital anomalies, etc. The postnatal period should also be reviewed for clues related to hyperbilirubinemia, respiratory distress, sepsis, seizures, hypoglycemia, dehydration, etc. The length of the neonate's hospital stay may provide a helpful clue as to the presence of perinatal problems.

Health problems during infancy and throughout the preschool years should also be evaluated in attempting to define "at riskness" for learning problems. Parents should be asked about recurrent ear infections, meningitis, seizures, asthma, slow weight gain, problems with vision or hearing, hospitalizations, allergies, anemia, lead poisoning, and other health problems. Although, as noted earlier, the relationship of such illnesses to subsequent academic performance is inconclusive, the information is valuable as one factor in the comprehensive assessment.

Physical development. The effects of gross developmental defects on a child's subsequent school performance are obvious. The general physical examination may provide some clues helpful in identifying the preschooler at risk for subsequent educational dysfunction. For example, a small head circumference correlates with suboptimal brain growth and indicates a child's at-risk status.[1] More controversial is the possible association between minor anomalies of physical development and subsequent academic performance. Several studies have noted an increased incidence of minor congenital anomalies in preschoolers at risk for educational dysfunction.[42] Anomalies observed include electrical hair (very fine hair that will not comb down), epicanthal folds, low-set ears, high-arched palate, curvature or deformity of the fifth finger, and a gap between the first and second toes.

Problems exist with such studies, however. The children evaluated for the presence of minor anomalies were selected, in the main, because of problems with hyperactivity and behavior. Such children thus represent a diverse group of patients, rather than a homogeneous one. Also, the results of studies are contradictory. Better designed prospective studies are necessary to definitively settle this issue. For the present, anomalies detected on physical examination should be noted, with an awareness concerning a possible correlation with subsequent learning problems.

General examination at time of school entry should also include a screening of hearing and vision.

Neuromaturation. The significance of neurological signs indicative of maturational lag is controversial in the literature. The findings in a neuromaturational examination that are indicative of inefficient or immature function of the central nervous system are most commonly referred to as "soft neurological signs." There is much misunderstanding about these signs, with some professionals believing that the term "soft" means equivocal. However, such findings can be very well-documented.[41]

Most of these signs are normal at very young ages, and become increasingly unusual and more likely to be associated with learning problems as children mature. Thus for the preschooler certain neurological findings are normally present and will disappear as the child reaches the early school years. The neuromaturational examination of the preschooler involves looking for the presence of findings expected to have already disappeared. Although norms for such findings are not solidly established and implications with regard to later school problems are unclear, neuromaturational assessment can be viewed as a kind of "window" on the development of the nervous system.

In Table 14-1 a series of observations are presented that suggest neuromaturational delay in a child at the time of school entry.

Gross and fine motor skills. During the preschool years the child demonstrates significant maturation of both gross and fine motor skills (Table 14-2). The 2-year-old has just mastered running and is able to kick a ball on command. Fine motor abilities include turning the pages of a book, holding a glass securely, and building a

Table 14-1. Findings suggestive of neuromaturational delay in a child observed at time of school entry

Task	Description	Observations
Heel walking	The child is asked to walk across the room on his heels.	Is there extreme dystonic positioning of the hands and arms?
Pronation— supination	The child is asked to imitate the examiner; arm is bent at a 90-degree angle at the elbow, the elbow touches the ribs and the child rapidly pronates and supinates his hand.	Does the child show deviation of the elbow from the chest wall of more than 45 degrees?
Motor stance	The child is asked to put his feet together, put his hands straight out in front, close his eyes, stick his tongue out, and maintain this posture for 15 seconds.	Is there marked choreoathetoid movements of the fingers?
Finger opposition	The child is asked to imitate the examiner; the thumb and forefinger are rapidly opposed at a rate of 3/second.	Does the child show marked "mirroring" movements, virtually undistinguishable between the two hands?
Pencil grasp and utilization	The child is asked to write his name.	Does the child show marked tongue movements or extreme stretching of the lips or mouth?
Drawing of figures	The child is asked to copy a series of figures.	Is there constant variation in hand utilization for drawing?
Horizontal visual tracking	The child is asked to follow a pencil with his eyes, and not with his whole head; the pencil is held 15 cm in front of the child and moved from left to right very slowly.	Does the child give up in the midline?
Speech	The child's speech is observed during conversation.	Are there major articulation errors?

Table 14-2. Some examples of a child's increasing abilities during the preschool years

Area of function	2 years	3 years	4 years	5 years
Gross motor	Running Kicking a ball	Walking up stairs by alternating feet Pedalling a tricycle	Performing a standing broad jump	Skipping smoothly Balancing on one foot for 20 seconds
Fine motor	Turning pages of a book Holding a glass securely Building a tower of six blocks	Pouring from a pitcher Scribbling with a crayon Building a tower of 9 to 10 blocks	Buttoning clothes Lacing shoes	Brushing teeth Combing hair Washing face
Visual processing	Imitating a circular stroke while drawing	Copying a circle	Copying a cross Drawing a man with two parts	Copying a triangle Drawing a recognizable man
Auditory-language	Using I, me, and you, although not necessarily correctly Verbalizing immediate experiences	Using an active vocabulary of 1000 words Speaking so strangers can understand	Engaging in long narratives	Speaking using adult sentence structure

tower of blocks. By the age of 3, we find the child walking upstairs unaided while alternating his feet, and he is even able to pedal a tricycle. A block tower of 9 to 10 cubes can be constructed, and scribbling with crayons is seen. With age 4 far more complex gross motor activities, such as a standing and even a fair running broad jump, are possible. The 4-year-old can button his clothes and sometimes lace his shoes. By 5 the child demonstrates a well-developed sense of equilibrium and is able to skip quite smoothly. Sophisticated fine motor tasks such as brushing teeth, combing hair, and washing the face are accomplished.

Delayed motor development may indeed be a significant clue in the identification of the preschool child with a potential learning disability. Most experts agree, however, that the cause of the delay (anoxia, myopathy, etc.) is a more important clue than its presence per se.[27] The academic success of children with significant motor impairment, (e.g., severe cerebral palsy) is frequently observed. Although the presence of delay must be considered a predisposing factor or possible predictor of school problems, delayed motor milestones or delayed motor development certainly to not preclude successful learning.

Assessment of the preschooler's motor skills takes several forms. Review of developmental milestones, although fraught with hazard when

done retrospectively, may be useful. The parents may be asked the age of accomplishment of such gross motor activities as sitting without help, crawling, walking alone, walking up stairs, and catching a big ball. Fine motor milestones include the age at which the child employed fingers to feed himself, used a spoon successfully, was able to dress himself, and was able to tie shoelaces. As noted earlier, when such information is gathered in a retrospective manner the exact ages suggested must be viewed with caution.

Far more useful may be inquiry related to the child's present level of motor functioning. The parents may be asked to describe how well their preschooler can perform various skills. Often it is useful to suggest that the parents compare the child to other children of the same age. Gross motor skills such as balancing, throwing a ball, carrying objects, running, hopping, jumping, and skipping can be considered. Using a pencil for drawing, cutting with scissors, pouring water into a cup, and using a knife and fork while eating are examples of fine motor skills.

Motor skills can also be directly observed. Examples of some gross and fine motor skills that may be assessed at the time of school entry examination are presented in Table 14-3.

Visual processing. Numerous studies have examined the visual perceptual functioning of

Table 14-3. Examples of some gross and fine motor skills that may be observed at the time of school entry

Task	Description	Observations
Heel walking	The child is asked to walk across the room on his heels.	Does the child walk well on the heels for 2 m without faltering?
Standing on one foot	The child is asked to imitate the examiner; the child stands up, one foot is placed in the popliteal fossa of the other leg while the eyes are kept open for 15 seconds.	Is the child able to maintain the position without faltering more than once?
Tandem gait	The child is asked to walk in a straight line as if walking on a tightrope and to put his heel right in front of his toe each time.	Is the child able to walk well without faltering for 2 m?
Sequential finger opposition	The child tries to imitate the examiner; first the thumb and forefinger are opposed and then, one by one, the remaining fingers on the hand.	Does the child perform the task without more than one or two errors, or only minor difficulty getting started?
Pencil grasp and utilization	The child is asked to write his name on a blank piece of lined paper.	Does the child properly grip the pencil with the first three fingers of the hand? Is the grip fairly distal? Does he demonstrate a fistlike grasp?
Rhythm tapping	The examiner asks the child to imitate from memory a series of rhythm taps, such as two taps with the left and one with the right hand.	Is the child able to successfully imitate two of three sequences?

preschool children in an attempt to predict subsequent academic achievement. During the preschool years the child demonstrates increasing competence in copying geometrical forms (Table 14-2). The 3-year-old imitates a circular stroke. At age 4 copying a circle is perfected, and copying a cross, but not a triangle, is possible. The 5-year-old is able to draw a recognizable man, and copy a square and even a triangle, thus demonstrating some mastery of the diagonal plane. A diamond is still a formidable task.

Considerable controversy exists among both professionals and nonprofessionals regarding the predictive value of perceptual tasks.[43] Visual processing delays present in the preschool years often persist in the early school years.[31] One must be cautious, however, in predicting reading failure on the basis of such delays. Although there is evidence to suggest that visual processing delays (such as difficulties with spatial relations and visual discrimination) are probably in some way related to difficulty with reading in the early school years, there are no data demonstrating how a delay in visual processing alone can account for reading retardation. This is particularly true for the later school years. Although it appears that adequate perceptual development is important in beginning reading, the minimal perceptual skills required are not well appreciated. Many children with delays in this area are excellent readers. This finding probably reflects the abilities of children to compensate for areas of weakness and the abilities of teachers to employ different strategies.

The assessment of visual processing skills may contribute importantly to the child's overall assessment. The predictive value of perceptual tasks increases as testing items approximate actual academic tasks. For example, those studies measuring visual discrimination employing letter shapes appear to have greater predictability than those employing "nonliteral" shapes. Examples of some visual processing tasks that may be presented to the child entering school are presented in Table 14-4.

Spatial orientation—body awareness. This component of function refers to a child's orientation in space and understanding of such fac-

Table 14-4. Examples of some visual processing tasks that may be presented to the child entering school

Task	Description	Observations
Copying figures	The child is asked to copy a series of figures. Examples are:	How accurate are the drawings from the standpoint of orientation, relative size of various parts, relative position of various parts, quality?
Block construction	The child is asked to construct, by direct imitation, some stairs made with six blocks, like so:	Does the child copy the staircase accurately?
	The child is asked to construct from memory a three-block bridge, like so:	Is the child able to reproduce the bridge in 10 seconds?
Object span	Four items (key, pencil, penny, block) are placed before the child. The examiner points to each one in a certain order, and the child is asked to point to each in the same order after the examiner finishes.	This is a test of visual sequential memory. Is the child able to correctly repeat two of three sequences?
Matching figures	The child is asked to match identical figures on a card, like so:	Is the child able to correctly match letters within 10 seconds?

tors as body position, left-right discrimination, and farness versus nearness. It is closely related to other components including gross motor, propriokinesthetic (the ability to interpret information coming from the sensory end organs in muscles), and visual-perceptual function. Spatial orientation difficulties are often demonstrated in children with learning problems.

Although consistent identification of left and right is usually not found until age 6, the preschooler is aware that there are two sides to things. The child at time of school entry should be able to cross the midline when given directions. For example, although he may not be correct, he should show a contralateral response when asked to first raise his right hand, then his left foot.

Some appreciation for a child's spatial and body awareness can be obtained by parent interview. Is the child always tripping and falling? Does the child appear clumsy and awkward? How is the child's balance? Does the child often get lost or have difficulty orienting himself relative to his surroundings? Examples of tasks assessing spatial orientation and body awareness are presented in Table 14-5.

Auditory-language skills. The preschool years are characterized by a dramatic growth in language skills (Table 14-2). Language skills of the child at age 3 include an active vocabulary of about 1000 words, the ability to speak in a

Table 14-5. Examples of some tasks evaluating spatial orientation and body awareness skills that may be presented to the child entering school

Task	Description	Observations
Body parts	The child is asked to point to his nose, then knee, then heel, then waist.	Is the child able to correctly identify three of four body parts?
Simple laterality	The child is asked to show his right hand, then his left foot, then his left hand, then his right foot.	This is not usually attained by preschool children. Does the child cross the midline with his responses?
Graphesthesia	The child is shown a card with each of the following: — ○ □ ✗ The child is asked to name each shape. While he views the cards, the examiner takes the child's hand behind his back and traces one of the shapes on the child's palm. The child is asked to point to the one the examiner has drawn.	Is the child able to correctly identify three shapes?
Stereognosis	Four shapes are put in front of the child while identical shapes are held by the examiner. ○ ■ ● ▲ One of each shape is placed in the child's hand, out of view, and he is asked to point to the identical shape in front of him.	Is the child able to correctly identify three shapes?

manner comprehensible to strangers, and the capacity to name a familiar object when presented with its picture. These accomplishments seem meager compared to the sophisticated language of the child at school entry. During the fourth year the child's use of language truly blossoms. He will talk about everything, frequently questioning, and engaging in long narratives. By age 5 the child remarkably resembles a "little adult" in his use of language; all of the basic sentence structures utilized by adults can be found in the language of children at school entry!

Given the remarkable development of language skills during the preschool years, it is little wonder that language-related variables frequently are identified in children with learning problems. An important point must be considered, however; language skills will often change as a function of interaction with the environment and thus are not a stable trait allowing long-term prediction.[12] For example, the language ability of a 4-year-old may be significantly different following a year in a nursery school that encourages verbal output. Language skills are highly dynamic during the preschool years; therefore an evaluation at any one point in time should be cautiously interpreted with regard to long-term prediction.

Because language undergoes such dramatic change during the immediate preschool years and it is prerequisite to the task of reading, its evaluation is essential. Misgivings over language skills are a frequent developmental concern of parents of preschool children. Language delays often can be incorrectly perceived. Children with such delays are often incorrectly viewed as being hyperactive, emotionally disturbed, or even retarded.

Information concerning the preschooler's language function can be obtained via the interview; milestones should be sought but cautiously interpreted. How old was the child when he spoke his first words? First put words together? Spoke two or three word sentences? Spoke clearly, so strangers understood? Questions relating to the child's present level of functioning will probably be more helpful. How well does the child understand spoken instructions? Recite a nursery rhyme? Sing a song? Tell a story? Pronounce words? Find the right words for things? How does the child's

Table 14-6. Examples of some tasks evaluating language function utilized in the assessment of the child at school entry

Task	Description	Observations
Sound memory	The examiner presents to the child a series of phonemes, repeating each set twice. The child is asked to then repeat the set. Examples are "laudy-tu-dum," "above and below," "behind and ahead," "quack duck quack."	Is the child able to repeat the sounds accurately with only one or two errors, requiring assistance only once or twice?
Sentence memory	Similar to sound memory, a series of sentences or phrases are read to the child, and the child is asked to repeat each one immediately, "my big black dog," "please pass the meat and peas," "we had lots of fun playing at the park."	Similar to sound memory.
Serial command	The child is asked by the examiner to do some things, but to wait until he has finished with all the instructions. He is asked to do exactly what he is told in the right order, "I want you to put the pencil on the chair, and then open the door, and then come back here and give me a block, and sit down."	Auditory sequential memory and patterned motor output are involved. Is the child able to perform the command without more than one mistake?
Object naming	The child is told, "Bread and meat are good to eat. Tell me other things you can eat. Name as many as you can, as fast as you can."	Is the child able to name six foods in 30 seconds?
Definitions	The child is asked to define words, such as, "What is a ball? . . . river? . . . street?"	Is the child able to define word in terms of use, shape, composition, or general category?

overall use of language compare to his peers?

Direct observation is an important method of gathering clues relating to language function. Examples of some tasks appropriate for use in assessing the preschool child are presented in Table 14-6.

Sequential organization—memory. The ability of a child to orient himself and the outside world in dimensions of time has important implications for the child's level of functioning. Children with sequencing problems may have problems perceiving auditory or visual stimuli in a particular order. Such children also frequently have difficulty with short-term memory. Deficits of sequential organization and memory are frequently identified in children having problems in school. When a preschooler who has difficulty following a series of instructions in the home enters school, problems are likely.

A number of clues suggesting deficits in sequential organization and memory can be elicited via the interview. How well does the child remember spoken instructions or telephone messages? Does the child have difficulty remembering things in the proper order? Does the child understand time relationships, such as before, after, etc.?

The child's sequential organization and memory can be observed directly. Examples of tasks relating to auditory memory include those of sound and sentence memory, digit span, and serial commands presented earlier. Some tasks also relating to visual memory include object span and copying a figure from memory.

Cognitive development. One would assume that intelligence or cognitive abilities would strongly affect a child's academic performance, so intelligence testing in the preschool years would enable accurate prediction regarding later school achievement. However, although there is a statistical relationship with school achievement across the wide range of intellectual ability, when IQs that are borderline or above are considered, the correlation is significantly weakened.[23] It is obvious that children with IQs below borderline have difficulty in school, yet why is there not a stronger correlation between the preschooler's cognitive abilities and educational performance?

There are several reasons for this phenomenon. By definition, "learning disabilities" involve a discrepancy between predicted achievement based on IQ and achievement measured by achievement tests. Furthermore, intelligence and cognitive abilities are developing functions, not stable traits. Intelligence testing thus becomes more reliable as a child grows older for a variety of reasons, and assessments of intelligence made during the early preschool years may be inaccurate.

Thus, although the relationship between cognitive development and school performance is not as specific as one might imagine, cognitive factors are certainly important contributors to accurate predictions regarding later school performance. Estimates of intelligence based on experience alone are fraught with hazard. If intelligence is to be assessed, a standardized test is necessary. There are tools that can be readily utilized in the clinic setting, which provide a crude screening of cognitive ability. Some of these, such as the Ammons and Ammons Quick Test and Goodenough Draw-A-Man Test, will be mentioned on pp. 353 to 355.

Temperament. Temperament or behavioral style refers to those intrinsic characteristics of an individual that interact with the environment in the development of personality. Temperamental factors contribute to the child's adjustment to and success in the new school setting. A relationship has been demonstrated between certain temperamental characteristics and low academic achievement. The preschooler who characteristically withdraws from new stimuli and does not easily adapt to new situations may be expected to have some difficulties in school. These are the typically "slow to warm up" children, as described with results of the New York Longitudinal Study (NYLS) by Thomas and Chess.[38] Other traits considered related to educational dysfunction to some degree include activity level, intensity of reaction, attention span, persistence, and the intensity level of stimulation necessary to evoke a response, referred to as sensory threshold. The preschooler who is highly persistent and attentive is better suited to academic tasks than the child who has difficulty completing a task and demonstrates high distractability.

Information on temperament can be acquired via the history. Questions relating to both early function during the infancy and toddler years and to present behavioral style are helpful. Such retrospective information must be interpreted cautiously. Carey[6] has demonstrated the useful-ness of contemporaneous temperament determinations in assessing school adjustment and academic achievement. The relationship between infant temperament and school adjustment is viewed as being of "uncertain significance." The Behavioral Style Questionnaire, developed by McDevitt and Carey,[28] offers a practical tool for determination of temperament in the 3- to 7-year-old child. These researchers[28] propose that the questionnaire may well be appropriate for use in the clinic. This is in contrast to the questionnaire developed in the New York Longitudinal Study,[38] which is only appropriate for use in the research setting.

Following are some examples of descriptions of children relating to behavioral style. Parents are asked to say whether each characterization definitely applies, applies somewhat, or does not apply.[26]

1. His body is in constant motion.
2. His body is underactive.
3. His mind seems overactive.
4. He has trouble sitting through a meal.
5. He does things without thinking.
6. He starts things, but does not finish them.
7. At times he does not seem to hear what I say.
8. He does things in the wrong order.
9. He does not realize when he has made a mistake.
10. He has trouble *falling* asleep at night.
11. He has trouble *staying* asleep at night.
12. He yawns often during the day.
13. He breaks things around the home.
14. He seems to do things the hard way.
15. He stares at things for long periods.
16. He listens to outside noises for long periods.
17. He gets distracted easily.
18. He likes to keep changing games.
19. He is hard to control on a long car trip.
20. He can not keep his hands to himself.
21. He seems to want things all the time (is seldom satisfied).

In addition to information obtained during the interview, direct observation of the child provides important insight with regard to temperament and behavioral style. Is the child impulsive? Does the child display frequent fidgetting? How distractible is the child? How well does the child monitor his own performance? How difficult is attracting the child's attention? Does the child appear overactive? Underactive? How cooperative is the child? One must be aware, however, that behavior in a physician's office may not be typical of the child's behavior in other settings. These factors, including the issue of attentional deficit, are discussed in greater detail in Chapter 13.

School behavior. For the child in a nursery school or another preschool setting, teacher observations regarding school behavior, learning style, and social competence provide invaluable information. There is much evidence available

to suggest that teachers can, when provided with a framework for observation, recognize developmental and behavioral characteristics important in school performance.[19] When used in combination with the results of developmental assessment, teachers' ratings are useful in selecting children at risk for educational dysfunction.[36]

Caution should be taken, however, when considering preschool behavior problems as predictive of later disturbances. The situational peculiarity of many preschool behavior problems stresses the need for better differentiation between those which are likely to persist and those which are more transient.[7] The key here is the theme expressed repeatedly throughout this

Table 14-7. Examples of some questions that may be asked of the preschool teacher to survey various areas of function

Area of function	Sample questions
Gross motor skills	Is the child always tripping and falling? Is the child clumsy and awkward? Does the child appear to have poor balance? Is the child able to pour liquids into containers without spillage?
Fine motor skills	Does the child have difficult using scissors? Is the child's pencil or crayon grasp awkward? Is the child able to tie shoelaces? Is the child able to manipulate zippers and buttons?
Visual processing ability	Is the child able to match shapes or forms? Is the child able to differentiate larger from smaller? Is the child able to copy simple figures or letters? Is the child able to draw a circle? A cross? A square?
Language	Does the child often ask to have words repeated? Does the child have difficulty understanding what is being said? Is the child able to follow directions? Is the child able to answer questions about stories read to him? Is the child's speech often difficult to understand? Is the child's expressive vocabulary limited?
Spatial orientation — body awareness	Does the child often get lost in the school or playground? Does the child have difficulty orienting himself relative to surroundings?
Sequencing organization — memory	Does the child have difficulty remembering words to nursery rhymes or songs? Does the child seem to have poorly developed time concepts? Does the child have difficulty remembering the order of things?
Attention — activity	Is the child in constant motion? Is the child easily distracted? Does the child seem to "tune out"? Is the child very impulsive?
Social — emotional status	Is the child usually quiet and withdrawn? Sad? Does the child get upset easily? Does the child appear to have little self-confidence? Is the child disliked or rejected by peers?

chapter; developmental, maturational, and behavioral components must be integrated to form a complete and reasonable formulation. The pediatrician occupies a unique position in being able to aid with this integration.

Communication with the preschool teacher is a vital component in assessment. Unfortunately, such communication is often limited. A telephone call to the preschool teacher, a written report, or a completed teacher questionnaire are some of the mechanisms by which information can be acquired. The teacher should be asked to describe the child's difficulties and strengths and specific questions relating to the child. Details concerning the child's educational setting, community resources for children with special needs, and the results of any testing performed are helpful. A profile of the child's strengths and weaknesses can be compiled by surveying the child's performance in various areas of development. For example, with regard to gross motor function, is the child always tripping and falling? Is the child clumsy and awkward? Appear to have poor balance? Unable to pour liquids into containers without spillage? In a similar manner, questions can be posed relating to such functioning as fine motor, visual perception, language, spatial awareness, sequencing and memory, and social-emotional status. In addition, questions relating to behavioral organization and attention-activity can be presented. Examples of some of these questions are presented in Table 14-7.[30]

EXAMPLES OF PRESCHOOL ASSESSMENT TOOLS

A variety of tools are presently used in health programs to assess the preschool child.[16] Following is a sample of preschool assessment tools presently used in health programs. The list is by no means complete, nor does inclusion necessarily represent endorsement.

- Preschool Readiness Experimental Screening Scale (PRESS)[32,33]
- Sprigle School Readiness Screening Test (SSRST)[35,37]
- Goodenough-Harris Draw-a-Man Test[17]
- Pediatric Examination of Educational Readiness (PEER)[25]
- Preschool Screening System[18]

- Denver Developmental Screening Test (DDST)[13,14,15]
- Head Start Developmental Screening Test and Behavior Rating Scale (HSDS)[8]
- Cooperative Preschool Inventory (CPI)[5]
- School Readiness Survey (SRS)[21]
- Thorpe Developmental Inventory (TDI)[39]
- Physician's Developmental Quick Screen for Speech Disorders (PDQ)[24]

Several factors account for the large number of such tests. All suffer to varying degrees from problems of reliability and validity, as well as the need for well-established norms. The tools are designed to serve various purposes. Some are designed as screening instruments and are utilized to identify those children who may be at risk for educational dysfunction. Others serve as diagnostic measures, yielding definitive information concerning various developmental areas and strengths and weaknesses.

The multidisciplinary nature of preschool assessment also accounts for the wealth of assessment tools. The expertise of the examiner as well as practical considerations dictate the choice of a given test. For example, the requirements for the mass community preschool screening performed by teachers on a given summer date will be quite different than those for consultation by a psychologist, evaluating a given child in an office. For the busy pediatrician or nurse specialist who wishes to screen a child's readiness skills at school entry, other factors become important; the test must be short and easily administered. Interpretation must be straight forward, yielding information that is readily communicable to parents in a concise, objective manner.

A knowledge of school readiness screening can serve a number of functions for the physician and/or nurse; for the physician serving as a consulting member of a multidisciplinary team performing community preschool screening, familiarity with assessment techniques will allow more meaningful participation. For the pediatrician referring a child to a psychologist for evaluation, some knowledge will afford a more critical appraisal of the consultant's recommendations and facilitate counselling. For the physician desiring to perform some office screening at the time of school entry, some expertise in administering a screening test is necessary. Finally, for the pediatrician desiring to monitor a patient's developmental status, a collection of tasks informally assembled from various tools may be helpful.

The ideal tool to serve all purposes does not exist. A few tests are discussed below to provide a sampling of the variety and limitations of preschool assessment techniques.

Preschool Readiness Experimental Screening Scale (PRESS). This test represents an interesting attempt to integrate readiness screening into the preschool office visit.[32] Based on several motor and social skill tests adapted from Gesell, the PRESS was devised to be administered during the physical examination. According to the authors, it is really more a set of questions that a formally administered standardized test. Some limited validity information is available.[33] The PRESS does not offer a picture of a child's strengths and weaknesses in various developmental areas, and questions with regard to reliability and validity exist. Many factors crucial in predicting school success are not included.

Sprigle School Readiness Screening Test (SSRST). This test is also proposed for use in the pediatrician's office and is an example of a somewhat more detailed instrument.[35] Administration is estimated to take 8 to 12 minutes. Nine areas—verbal comprehension; size relations; verbal discrimination; reasoning; and understanding of numbers, information, analogies, vocabulary, and spatial relations are included. Although scores do appear to correlate well with IQ scores, correlation with school achievement is less secure.[37] Furthermore, certain developmental areas, such as visuomotor, are not included.

Goodenough-Harris Draw-a-Man Test. Although not an assessment of school readiness, this nonverbal test of mental ability is included because of its popularity in health programs. The child is asked to draw a man, a woman, and himself, and performance is scored according to norms.[17] Further information regarding reliability and validity is desirable.

Pediatric Examination of Educational Readiness (PEER) and Preschool Screening System. These screening tests are presented to-

gether because of their similarities, with the former incorporating some items from the latter.[18,25] The PEER places more emphasis on observations of a child's efficiency and observed attention patterns. Both survey gross and fine motor, speech, language, and visuomotor development, as well as behavior and social skills. Both are proposed as screening instruments to assess school readiness. A parent questionnaire accompanies both. Some normative data are available for these instruments.

Denver Developmental Screening Test (DDST). This popular screening test covers four areas of function—gross motor, language, fine motor–adaptive, and personal-social behavior.[13] Although reliability and validity issues have been addressed, the applicability of norms in different population groups, such as among minority children, is questionable.[14] The test does afford the opportunity to evaluate a broad range of behavior, and results are easily interpreted. A Prescreening Developmental Questionnaire (PDQ) has been devised to identify those children requiring screening with the DDST.[15]

Head Start Developmental Screening Test and Behavior Rating Scale (HSDS), Cooperative Preschool Inventory (CPI), School Readiness Survey (SRS), and Thorpe Developmental Inventory (TDI). These tests all represent screening inventories currently utilized in health programs.[5,8,21,39,40] All assess gross and fine motor abilities, communication skills, and personal-social behavior. Although predictive validity for all inventories is lacking and norms often have limited applicability to the children screened, each can provide a description of a child's strengths and weaknesses. These instruments may be best utilized in a setting in which continuity of care is provided.

Physician's Developmental Quick Screen for Speech Disorders (PDQ). Although assessing only one area of development, language, the PDQ is presented as an example of a screening instrument that is self-instructional and economical with respect to time and necessary materials and readily yields information regarding parental counselling and referral.[24] The instrument uses a combination of interview and direct observation. More information regarding validity and reliability is necessary.

PRESCRIBING FOR THE PRESCHOOL CHILD

The clinical assessment of the preschool child is only worthwhile if evaluation readily leads to helpful suggestions that can be implemented readily. For many assessments—particularly those serving a screening function—more questions will be raised than answered, and further investigations and referrals will be indicated. At times, a specific medical intervention will be suggested. Counselling should always accompany assessment, in some instances serving to clarify the nature of problems, while at other times serving a more specific therapeutic function. Assessments may lead to specific educational strategies or to utilization of available community resources. Fig. 14-2 depicts various modes of action that may follow clinical assessment.

The role adopted by the pediatrician will determine the extent of involvement with various recommendations. Certainly the pediatrician is called on to assume a major role when specific medical intervention is indicated. The pediatrician will also suggest and coordinate further investigations and referrals. This is appropriate for both the physician serving a screening function and the subspecialist with fellowship training in child development. Counselling has long been viewed as a traditional pediatric role. The pediatrician can also ensure appropriate utilization of community resources, assuming the role of ombudsman in the delivery of services to the

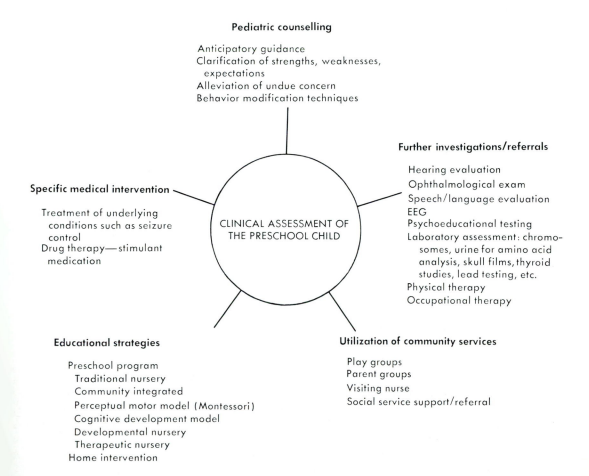

Fig. 14-2. Various modes of action may follow clinical assessment. Prescribing for the preschool child.

handicapped child.[2] The pediatrician allied with a multidisciplinary team can even be involved in the development of a child's educational program, as well as the monitoring of progress.[20]

Specific medical intervention. The treatment of underlying medical conditions such as a seizure disorder is the most traditional of pediatric roles. Medical therapy for the hyperactive child—including stimulant medication and more controversial treatments—are discussed in Chapter 13.

Counselling. Pediatric counselling is an important method of intervention, serving many different functions; it is hoped that the clarification of a child's strengths and weaknesses will lead to more appropriate expectations. In some instances undue concerns can be alleviated. Counselling can also provide important information regarding normal but ''problematic'' behaviors frequently encountered in the pre-school years.[3] Anticipatory guidance can be provided relating to commonly occurring difficulties at time of school entry. The maturational aspects of such problems as enuresis can be explained.

Counselling can also serve a more direct ''therapeutic'' function. Stressing the constitutional nature of developmental dysfunction and a child's temperamental traits can alleviate inappropriate parental guilt and anxiety. For parent-child interactional problems, the identification of specific areas of undersirable interaction and pointing out the temperamental traits of the child and parental behaviors contributing to the stress can be very helpful. The goal of such counselling is an appropriate match between a child's temperamental traits and parental attitudes and practices.[38]

Specific behavioral management advice can also be provided during counselling. Depending on the experience and expertise of the pediatrician, approaches such as behavioral modification can be recommended.

Further investigation and referrals. As mentioned earlier, assessment may raise more questions than it answers. For some children specific medical concerns will suggest laboratory assessment, such as lead screening, thyroid studies, etc. By the preschool years, major developmental concerns attributed to chromosomal abnormalities or inborn errors of metabo-lism should have already been raised. An electroencephalogram (EEG) is rarely indicated, unless a seizure disorder is suspected.

Assessments frequently lead to referrals for further investigation. With a child who has a history of frequent episodes of otitis, for whom the parents or teacher is concerned regarding hearing acuity, who evidently has language delay or chronic serous otitis on examination, or who performs unsatisfactorily on routine hearing screening at time of school entry, a full audiological evaluation is indicated. For the child not passing a screening of visual acuity or with evident strabismus, an ophthalmological evaluation is indicated. Poor performance in specific areas during developmental assessment will also indicate the need for further assessment. For the child not performing satisfactorily in the auditory-language area, a speech and language evaluation by a speech therapist is indicated. When the level of a child's cognitive functioning is a concern, for example, when the child demonstrates general developmental delay, formal psychological assessment should be sought. For the child whose behavior appears truly pathological or when interactional problems are more formidable, psychiatric referral may be indicated.

Educational strategies. For the preschool child with evidence of developmental dysfunction, recommendations frequently include participation in a preschool program. For many children the structure imposed by such a program as well as opportunities for peer interaction probably account for the apparent beneficial effects observed. Far more difficult to ascertain is whether different types of preschool programs are more beneficial for different children.

There is probably as much variation in the quality and content of preschool programs as there are programs.[34] Traditional nursery school programs emphasize social and emotional development rather than specific areas of function. Models exist, however, for nursery programs with curricula oriented toward intervention in specific areas of development. Cognitive development programs attempt to improve such functions as memory, concept formation, general information, and comprehension. The Montessori program is an example of a perceptual motor development model, stressing visual discrimination and visuomotor integration. Programs attempting to provide some direct instruction in language, reading, and arithmetic prior to first grade fit the acacemic skills development model. Because the curricula were only recently developed, limited information is available concerning effects of the various models. Studies conducted have evaluated effects on disadvantaged children. Interestingly, in one study a highly structured well-supervised traditional program proved as effective as the other approaches.[44]

Preschool programs may be organized according to the problems demonstrated by their students. For the child with developmental delay, for whom a specific program of intervention aimed at areas of weakness—whether cognitive, motor, language, etc.—is desired, a developmental nursery is indicated. For the child with a severe behavior problem or who manifests psychopathology, a therapeutic nursery may be well suited. For the disadvantaged child, a community-integrated nursery affords an opportunity to experience a traditional preschool program with middle-class children.

As is evident, the nature of preschool programs vary greatly. It is unlikely that the pediatrician will be independently selecting a specific program for a child. However, the physician can participate in the decision with other professionals, and a familiarity with the different types of programs is therefore important.

Educational intervention is not limited to the preschool setting. Particularly in situations in which no preschool program is available to the child, home intervention may be utilized. Programs have been established that instruct parents in techniques aimed at promoting cognitive development. Parents are requested to work with their children at home using age-graded play material. Some modest benefits from such programs have been demonstrated. The pediatric clinic has even been utilized as the basis for one parent-education program.[29]

Utilization of community services. The pediatrician can serve an important role as coordinator in introducing parents to appropriate community resources. By gaining familiarity with play groups, parent groups, and other agencies, families can be directed toward valuable sources of support. Similarly, by making known their interest in such problems, community resources will also contact pediatricians.

SUMMARY

The importance of early identification of preschool children who may encounter difficulty in school is receiving increasing emphasis. The pediatrician, as the professional concerned with monitoring the growth and development of children, is suited uniquely to contribute to such assessments. Certain specific areas of assessment, such as general health, physical development, and neuromaturation, clearly fall within the confines of pediatrics. The pediatrician can also provide important observations regarding the preschool child's level of function in other areas of development. Even if the observations of educational and medical personnel overlap, multiple perspectives from different settings increase the reliability of assessments. The pediatrician can also assimilate the results of various assessments, providing an important overview and sense of perspective.

To participate meaningfully in the management of the preschooler, the pediatrician must appreciate the guidelines for and difficulties with preschool assessment. The components of assessment must be recognized, as well as the manner in which they fit together into a whole greater than the sum of its parts. It is important to appreciate that the relationship between single specific preschool test findings and later school achievement is too low to allow definitive prediction, although a comprehensive assessment can be predictive and educationally relevant. Some familiarity with assessment tools is necessary, as is an awareness of different modes of intervention. It is hoped that by directing attention to the preschooler prior to school entry, the pediatrician can collaborate in the effort to prevent later school difficulties, avoiding the inevitable consequences for a child who eluded early detection.

REFERENCES

1. Barber, C. R., and Hewitt, D.: Changes in head shape, J. Neurol. Neurosurg. Psychiatry **19**:54, 1956.
2. Battle, C.: The role of the pediatrician as ombudsman in the health care of the young handicapped child, Pediatrics **50**:916, 1972.
3. Brazelton, T. B., Snyder, D. M., and Yogman, M.

W.: A developmental approach to behavior problems. In Hoekelman, R., et al., editors: Principles of pediatrics: health care of the young, New York, 1978, McGraw-Hill Book Co.

4. Buktenica, N.: Identification of potential learning disorders, J. Learning Disabilities **4:**35, 1971.

5. Caldwell, B. M.: Cooperative preschool inventory, rev. ed., Berkeley, Calif., 1970, Educational Testing Services.

6. Carey, W. B., Fox, M., and McDevitt, S. C.: Temperament as a factor in early school adjustment, Pediatrics **60:**621, 1977.

7. Chamberlin, R. W.: The use of teacher checklists to identify children at risk for later behavioral and emotional problems. Am. J. Dis. Child. **130:**141, 1976.

8. Dodds, J.: The Head Start developmental screening test and behavior rating scale, CAP-HS form 56, G.S.A. D.C. 68, Washington, D.C., July 1967, Government Printing Office.

9. Dworkin, P. H., et al.: Acquisition of knowledge and training needs in developmental pediatrics. Presented before the Society for Pediatric Research, New York, April 1978.

10. The Education for All Handicapped Children Act of 1975, PL 94-142, Washington, D.C., 1975, U.S. Government Printing Office.

11. Fargo, G., Roth, C., and Code, T.: Evaluation of an interdisciplinary approach to prevention of early school failure, technical report, Honolulu, 1968, University of Hawaii.

12. Faust, M.: Cognitive and language factors. In Keough, B. K., editor: Early identification of children with potential learning problems, J. Spec. Educ. **4:**307, 1970.

13. Frankenburg, W. K., and Dodds, J. B.: The Denver developmental screening test, J. Pediatr. **71:**181, 1967.

14. Frankenburg, W. K., et al.: Reliability and stability of the Denver developmental screening test, Child Dev. **42:**1315, 1971.

15. Frankenburg, W. K., et al.: The Denver prescreening developmental questionnaire (PDQ), Pediatrics **57:**744, 1976.

16. Frost, J., and Minisi, R.: Early childhood assessment list, Hightstown, N.J., 1976, The Northeast Regional Resource Center.

17. Goodenough-Harris draw-a-man test, New York, 1963, Harcourt, Brace, Jovanovich, Inc.

18. Hainsworth, P. K., and Hainsworth, M. L.: Preschool screening system, start of a longitudinal-preventive approach, Pawtucket, R.I., 1974, Preschool Screening System.

19. Haring, N. G., and Ridgway, R. W.: Early identification of children with learning disabilities, Except. Child. **33:**387, 1967.

20. Jacobs, F. H., and Walker, D. K.: Pediatricians and The Education of All Handicapped Children Act of 1975 (public law 94-142), Pediatrics **61:**135, 1978.

21. Jordan, F. L., and Massey, J.: School readiness survey: ages 4-6, Palo Alto, Calif. 1967, Consulting Psychologist Press.

22. Keough, B. K.: Psychological evaluation of exceptional children: old hangups and new directions, J. School Psychol. **10:**141, 1972.

23. Keough, B. K., and Becker, L. D.: Early detection of learning problems: questions, cautions and guidelines, Except. Child. **40:**5, 1973.

24. Kulig, S. G., and Baker, K. A.: Physician's developmental quick screen for speech disorders (PDQ), Galveston, Texas, 1975, The University of Texas Medical Branch, Department of Pediatrics.

25. Levine, M. D.: Pediatric examination of educational readiness, Brookline, Mass., Brookline Early Education Project.

26. Levine, M. D., Dworkin, P., and Yurchak, M. J.: Parent questionnaire for functional and developmental assessments of the preschool child, Boston, 1977, The Children's Hospital Medical Center.

27. Leydorf, S. M.: Physical-motor factors. In Keough, B. K., editor: Early identification of children with potential learning problems, J. Spec. Educ. **4:**307, 1970.

28. McDevitt, S. C., and Carey, W. B.: The measurement of temperament in 3 to 7 year old children, J. Child Psychol. Psychiatry **19**(3):245, 1978.

29. Morris, M. G., London, R., and Glick, J.: Educational intervention for preschool children in a pediatric clinic. Pediatrics **57:**765, 1976.

30. Oberklaid, F.: Preschool and kindergarten teacher questionnaire, Boston, 1977, The Children's Hospital Medical Center.

31. Robinson, M. E., and Schwartz, L. B.: Visuo-motor skills and reading ability: a longitudinal study, Dev. Med. Child Neurol. **15:**281, 1973.

32. Rogers, W. B., Jr., and Rogers, R. A.: A new simplified preschool readiness experimental screening scale (The Press), Clin. Pediatr. **11:**558, 1972.

33. Rogers, W. B., Jr., and Rogers, R. A.: A follow-up study of the preschool readiness experimental screening scale (The Press), Clin. Pediatr. **14:**253, 1975.

34. Spicker, H. H.: Intellectual development through early childhood education, Except. Child. **38:**629, 1971.

35. Sprigle, H. A., and Lanier, J.: Validation and standardization of a school readiness screening test, J. Pediatr. **70:**602, 1967.

36. Stevenson, H. W., et al.: Longitudinal study of individual differences in cognitive development and scholastic achievement, J. Educ. Psychol. **68:**377, 1976.

37. Switzer, F., et al.: The efficiency of the Springle school readiness screening test (SSRST) at various intelligence and socioeconomic levels. Presented at annual meeting of Canadian Psychological Association, Winnipeg, Manitoba, Canada, May 1970.

38. Thomas, A., and Chess, S.: Temperament and development, New York, 1977, Brunner/Mazel, Inc.

39. Thorpe, H. S.: The Thorpe developmental inventory: ages three to six years, instruction manual, Davis, Calif., 1972, Office of Medical Education, University

of California at Davis, School of Medicine (ed. 2 published 1973).

40. Thorpe, H. S., and Werner, E. E.: Developmental screening of preschool children: a critical review of inventories used in health and educational programs, Pediatrics **53:**362, 1974.

41. Touwen, B. C. L., and Prechtl, H. F. R.: The neurological examination of the child with minor nervous dysfunction, London, 1970, Spastics International Medical Publications.

42. Waldrop, M. D., Pedersen, F. A., and Bell, R. Q.: Minor physical anomalies and behavior in preschool children, Child Dev. **39:**391, 1968.

43. Wedell, K.: Perceptuo-motor factors. In Keough, B. K., editor: Early identification of children with potential learning problems, J. Spec. Educ. **4:**307, 1970.

44. Weikart, D. P.: Comparative study of three preschool curricula. Presented at the biennial meeting of the Society for Research in Child Development, Santa Monica, Calif., March 1969.

Not even stooping from its sphere,
It asks a little of us here.
It asks of us a certain height. . . .

Choose Something Like a Star
R. Frost

15

Behavioral aspects of pediatrics and chronic illness

Edwin A. Sumpter

The behavioral and emotional impact of chronic illnesses on a child and his family so strains the ingenuity and commitment of the primary care physician that it is tempting to avoid this dimension of care altogether. However, if the physician is to be the ombudsman and coordinator discussed in Chapters 1 and 17, the child and family must be helped to realize and mobilize all of their resources in coping with their problem. This chapter will suggest some ways of enhancing the responsiveness of the primary care resource to these areas of concern, some diagnostic and management principles and limitations, the role of the primary care physician in the management of some chronic

psychiatric illnesses, and, last, the emotional implications of chronic diseases.

THE RESPONSIVE PRIMARY CARE RESOURCE

The usual image of the ''typical'' office providing primary care for children is one of ceaseless activity, cacophony, harried personnel, and a panting physician charging from room to room. Although it is not always true, those who have been in practice would find this picture at least partially familiar. Most primary care offices or clinics are geared to the care of children with short duration acute illnesses and those needing routine well-child care. The large number of patients requires tight schedules, long days, and a high overhead, resulting in a serious compromise in flexibility. Any problem other than the ''usual'' throws the day out of rhythm. Such a situation hardly lends itself to the thoughtful and time-consuming consideration required for the management of the child with complex behavior problems and/or chronic illnesses. Without accommodative planning, these patients may present to the physician at such inopportune times that the visit produces hurried and superficial assessment and recommendations, a tendency to make hasty referrals, and ultimately a sense of dissatisfaction on the part of both patient and physician. Mechanisms for dealing with complex problems in the "busy office" are suggested in Chapter 17.

It is not enough to respond to the problems as they present themselves. Chamberlin[16] and others have noted that major parental concerns are often not expressed to the physician. The reasons for this are many, but significant among them is the feeling that only somatic issues are appropriate for discussion in a visit to the physician. (This may well be true in the case of some physicians, to whom this chapter will be quite irrelevant!) Clearly this impression undermines comprehensive care and raises important questions regarding the effectiveness of health maintenance visits, history taking, and the responsiveness of the facility.

Following are only examples of some measures that may improve the development of a more effective therapeutic alliance between the physician and the patient and/or parents.

Institution of the prenatal conference,[52] particularly for the primiparous couple, provides the parents with an opportunity to discuss their expectations and anxieties, and to assess their resources for handling the stresses of caring for a new baby. When the possibility of a high-risk pregnancy exists, such conferences are of even greater value. If the new baby has a medical problem or birth defect, even this brief previous encounter with the pediatrician assists the physician in assuming a supportive role.

During well-child visits initial and interval histories should contain questions designed to elicit information about behavior and development with full cognizance of the limitations of parental recall.[25] Anticipatory guidance and health education on these visits should include information about behavior and development as well as nutrition and physical growth. Although the short duration of a well-child visit cannot accomplish everything, the physician should nonetheless be alert to indications of family instability. Clues may be present in the manner in which the baby is handled and how the mother acts in the examination situation.[28] How much is the father involved in the care of the baby? What effect does the introduction of this new person have on the marriage? Do the baby's health and temperamental characteristics represent more of a challenge than the family's

resources are currently able to handle? It is not the purpose of this chapter to reiterate the often discussed content of health maintenance visits,[1,42,53] but rather to cite their pivotal importance in setting a tone that transmits to the patients a sense of the responsiveness of the practice. History taking will be discussed in more detail below.

An office in a community that provides sophisticated and easily accessible services obviously has requirements quite different from those of the relatively isolated practice on which a wide range of demands are made. Nurse practitioners and other allied health workers may be of great importance in some settings, while underemployed or redundant in others. Some practices have a part-time psychologist, social case worker, or home visitor working directly out of the office.

The telephone conversation is often the first as well as the most frequent interface between the patient and the office and is a common source of patient dissatisfaction and physician irritation. The most experienced and wisest of office personnel should be assigned to this area, and careful attention given to telephone protocols, style, and record keeping. The telephone contact is the "ticket of admission" and can provide important information regarding the request for service.

Medical records for chronically ill children require a design that continually jogs the memory of the physician or assistant about special problems and strengths. Outpatient adaptations of problem-oriented records and chronic disease flow sheets are useful in achieving this aim. Examples of these are indicated in the references[33,46] and discussed in Chapter 8.

The physician obviously must be familiar with the resources and agencies of the community and their strengths and limitations. It is also important to be informed about public laws that affect the patients such as the "Education for All Handicapped Children Act of 1975."[38]

HISTORY

Assuming an already recorded and adequate pediatric history, a further expansion of the data base is needed for the assessment of behavioral and emotional problems, whether in the physically healthy or in the handicapped child. This kind of history requires time and attention to detail. It is best that it be taken from both parents without the child being present. The younger child is a continual distraction and the older is to be given a separate opportunity to present his own version of the history at another time.

A second-year medical student taking his first medical history from a patient is painfully aware of how difficult it is to gather data without some concepts of health and disease as a guide. A conceptual framework is no less necessary when taking a behavioral and developmental history. An example of such a framework is summarized below:

A. Cognitive and developmental history (Chapter 3)
   1. Motor developmental milestones
   2. Developmental tasks—age specific
   3. School performance
B. Temperamental profile (Table 15-1)
   1. Activity level
   2. Rhythmicity
   3. Approach-withdrawal
   4. Adaptability
   5. Threshold of responsiveness
   6. Intensity of reaction
   7. Quality of mood
   8. Distractibility
   9. Attention span and persistence
C. Family and environmental profile
   1. Family stability
   2. Family life-style
   3. Parental adequacy
   4. Neighborhood
   5. School
D. Presenting problem
   1. Physical symptoms and signs suggestive of psychosocial problems
   2. Specific behaviors of concern to parents
   3. Parental responses to the behavior in question
   4. "Typical day"
   5. History from child
E. Contact other sources of history
   1. School or nursery school teachers
   2. Other physicians or professionals involved with child

Cognitive and developmental history. In the consideration of the cognitive and developmental history (Chapter 3), at least a skeletal appreciation of Piaget's[39] massive work is nec-

essary. Of especially practical value is his concept of continual self-regulation. Whether physiological, affective, or intellecutal, "need" is a state of disequilibrium that generates anxiety. This anxiety requires some remedial response, the nature of which depends on the child's cognitive development and temperamental endowment. A child's interactions with his world will change as he develops, both because there are real environmental changes occurring and because of his awakening intellect, which alters his perceptions of that environment. Therefore anxiety is expected in the self-regulating developmental process and, in fact, is necessary as is the "energetic" and the sense of discontent, which stimulates the child to seek resolutions to those needs.

Temperamental attributes. Fundamental to the child's style of response to developmental anxieties are his temperamental attributes. Few works in child psychiatric literature are as practical in the primary care setting as that of Thomas, Chess, and Birch,[54,55] whose longitudinal studies focus on the individuality of the child. They have analyzed temperament according to nine categories (p. 363). Three clinically significant combinations of characteristics have been observed. One group, the "easy child," which comprised about 40% of the original New York Longitudinal Study sample, exhibits regularity in biological functions, positivity of mood, adaptability to new situations, and a mild to moderate mood intensity. A second group, about 10% of the sample, is characterized by irregularity of biological functions, poor adaptability, negativity of mood, and negative withdrawal responses when confronted by new stimuli—a "difficult child" by anyone's criteria. A third group has been labelled "slow to warm up," about 15% of the sample. The negative attributes of the "difficult child" are coupled with reactions that are of mild intensity and low activity level. This might be illustrated by the child who quietly and solemnly withdraws and huddles in a corner when faced with a new environmental situation. There is evidence that the latter two categories are at higher risk for later behavior disorders.

This work is not to be interpreted as meaning that a child's responses are predestined or im-

TEMPERAMENTAL PROFILE*

Category, definition, and scoring	History question†
GENERAL APPRAISAL	**OPEN QUESTION**
Activity level: Motor component of functioning; active and inactive periods (Score: High, medium, or low)	"What was he like in the first few months of life?"‡ How much did he move around? Did he wiggle so much he was hard to dress? Did he sleep quietly or did you have to arrange his covers after he had been asleep?
Rhythmicity: Predictability of sleep-wake cycle, hunger, elimination (Score: Regular, variable, or irregular)	Could you tell by 2 or 3 months of age about when he would be hungry? sleepy? How much variation?
Approach or withdrawal: Nature of initial response to a new stimulus (Score: Approachable, variable, or withdrawal)	How did he respond to new events such as first bath, a new food, a new person?
Adaptability: Modified toward adaptation, regardless of initial responses (Score: Adaptable, variable, or nonadaptable)	Did he get used to the tub, the new food, the new person, after a short time or a long time?
Threshold of responsiveness: Intensity of stimulation needed to elicit a response, regardless of the nature of that response (Score: High, medium, low)	How sensitive to noises, temperature changes, and changes in appearance of a parent and how easily aroused from sleep?
Intensity of reaction: Energy level of responses, regardless of whether positive or negative (Score: Positive, variable, or negative)	How did he express hunger—with loud protest or whimper? Was pleasure or displeasure made known loudly or softly?
Quality of mood: How much joyful and friendly as contrasted with crying and unfriendly (Score: Positive, variable, or negative)	Was he more often contented or fussy and complaining and why do you think so?
Distractibility: Effect of extraneous stimuli in altering current activity (Score: Yes, variable, or no)	While sucking bottle or breast, would a sound stop his sucking? If crying with hunger, how quickly and easily could you divert his attention and stop his crying, if at all?
Attention span and persistence: How long and how determined the continuation of an activity (Score: Yes, variable, or no)	How long could he remain attentive to a solo activity? If he tried to get something out of reach, how long and hard would he try before giving up?

*Modified from Thomas, A., and Chess, S., editors: Temperament and development, New York, 1977, Brunner/Mazel, Inc.
†Illustrative only.
‡Similar questions to be asked regarding the patient's current response patterns.

mutably set by his genes, but rather that from infancy he does make a unique contribution to his own development in the complex interactions between himself and his child-rearing milieu. This individuality of temperament is often ignored in the history-taking process and in the formulation of the genesis of a behavior problem.

Much of these data may emerge from clues in the medical and developmental history. The reader is referred to Thomas and Chess[54] for a suggested list of questions appropriate to the nine categories, samples of which are above.

These are easily included in the history-taking process. Carey[13] has developed a questionnaire to be administered to parents of infants, and Thomas, Chess, and Korn[56] have published some for parents and teachers of 3- to 7-year-olds.

More detailed discussion of developmental assessment appears in Chapter 3. This history should include questions relative to developmental landmarks, a subject best introduced by asking "What is the child doing now?" followed by more directed questioning if this is not sufficiently productive. ("Is he reaching yet?'' is not a particularly good question if he isn't!) Age-appropriate developmental tasks are explored. Behavioral and developmental questionnaires,[45,58] which can be completed while the parent waits, are sometimes useful as catalysts in initiating discussion about sensitive or embarrassing issues. They cannot serve as substitutes for the interview, however.

Family and environmental profile. Of particular concern are indicators of family instability, such as marital stress, inadequate economic resources, serious physical or emotional illness in the family, frequent moves, job dissatisfaction or unemployment, and the disruptive or helpful role of the in-laws or other extended family. Some aspects of family life-style may be pertinent, such as how they spend their time and money and what kinds of attitudes and habits they exhibit. A couple's adequacy as parents is affected by their own upbringing, education, intellectual capacity, previous experience with children, and expectations of their own children. A ''family functioning index'' has been developed by Pless and Satterwhite[40] (Chapter 17, Appendix), which characterizes these issues by use of a questionnaire that is designed to be administered in a primary care setting. Other important circumstances include the kind of neighborhood and school in which the child must live, the opportunities for contact with peers, and the availability of special resources for those children with special needs.

In gathering this information the physician has to be particularly sensitive to any major differences between his own values and standards and those of the patient and family. To be judgmental and irritated by how a family ''chooses'' to live is to undermine the effectiveness of one's efforts; it is difficult to mask such feelings. If there were no other reason for exploring the parents' own background, the better understanding it generates and the greater likelihood of acceptance of their ''style'' would be sufficient justification.

Presenting problem. Having collected the foregoing background data, the history is now focused more specifically on the presenting problem. As already suggested, parents do not always express their concerns to the physician and may not interpret a symptom as having an emotional basis. One must therefore be alert to those unspoken signs of stress, or ''lack of fit,''[15] which may first manifest themselves as physical signs or developmental delays. In the infant these may be eating or sleeping problems, motor delay, ''failure to thrive,'' apathy, physical signs of neglect suggesting passive child abuse, or signs of unexplained trauma. In the toddler the complaints are usually identified as behavioral by the parents. Most frequently cited are annoying habits such as whining and thumb sucking, tantrums, and hard to control behavior. In the preschool child sleeping and eating problems may still be present. The child may complain of vague aches and pains, be enuretic or encopretic, show poor growth, slow development of skills, or be unusually accident prone. Parents most often express concerns about fear of new situations or reticence around new people, sibling relationships, immature behavior such as failure to toilet train, and reluctance to separate from the parents.[16] The older school-aged and adolescent youngster may have recurring abdominal pain or headaches, become hypochondriacal, hyperventilate, exhibit conversion symptoms, tics, be ''tired all the time,'' have menstrual problems, anorexia, or obesity.

Details of the behavior or symptom must be pursued with the thoroughness used in tracking down any pain symptom. Since the physician often does not witness the behavior itself or the parents' response to it, the behavior must be pictured as accurately as possible. The ''typical day'' interview is of value in this regard.[14,41] To be fully informative, the incident in question must be explored to its final resolution, with detailed reconstruction of what each involved party said and did in response to the other. This technique may have a therapeutic effect in itself as parents see how they may be reinforcing the very behavior they are trying to change.

In school-aged and adolescent youngsters, indications of progress toward achieving developmental social tasks are sought. ''How are things going in school, with peers, and at home?'' In the adolescent these same areas are important along with indications of progress toward some responsible independence of thought and action, heterosexual relationships, and the development of a value system. This is further discussed later in the chapter.

Interview and examination of the child. The physician working with children has developed a personal style for drawing them out and easing their apprehension. The pediatrician has seen enough children of all ages to make a reasonable assessment of office behavior and of the interactions among the child, his parents, and the physician. "Monsters" becoming "angels" from one visit to the next is commonly seen; thus the physician is properly cautious in making judgments and prognostications. The developmental evaluation may include a simple battery of screening tests (Chapter 3) to help determine whether more comprehensive evaluation is necessary, but again, caution is used in their interpretation.

The interview with the child can establish the physician as an advocate for the child. His own history may reveal a perspective on the issues quite different from that of his parents. In the case of pubescent and adolescent youngsters, the physician must be comfortable with the developmental turmoil likely in this age and be willing to relate directly and confidentially to the patient rather than only through his parents.

Decision to refer. The decision to refer to a psychiatrist, psychologist, or specialized facility must depend on the physician's training, experience, and interest. With complete historical information and examination, the physician may decide to (1) manage the problem in the pediatric practice, (2) refer to a specialist for diagnosis and treatment, or (3) refer to a specialist for diagnostic clarification, the further definition of the physician's own function deferred pending the consultation. (Fig. 15-1). If there is good family functioning and the child is achieving major developmental tasks, the physician may initiate counselling with the likelihood that the child's symptoms are developmentally or situationally related, involving child-rearing strategies and techniques. If, after several sessions and a passage of a few

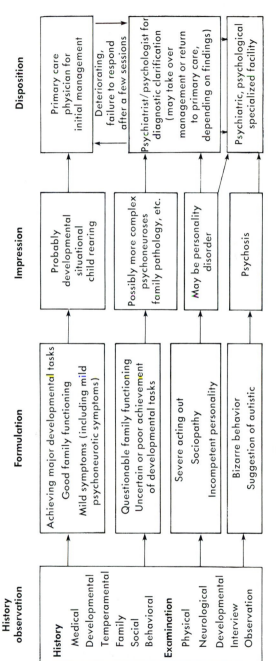

Fig. 15-1. Initial assessment of behavior problems.

months, there is no progress or if there is deterioration of behavior and of family functioning, referral to a psychiatrist or psychologist for diagnostic clarification is advisable. Depending on the findings, the consultant may either continue management or send the patient back to the referring physician for care, perhaps in concert with the consultant.

If the initial assessment indicates failure to achieve developmental tasks and questionable family functioning, the referral for diagnostic clarification is indicated without further delay. Children with severe symptoms of acting out, sociopathic behavior, or incompetent personalities or those with symptoms indicative of psychosis should be referred for diagnostic and probably for continued management.

Principles of management. As indicated earlier, if a family is fundamentally healthy, the child-rearing issues that arise in infants and preschool children usually require no more than a few counselling sessions and are appropriate for most primary care physicians to undertake. During the initial interviews, including perhaps a "typical day" history, the physician assesses the family's style and coping ability. Information about developmental variations and individuality is provided and related to the presenting complaint. Specific tactical recommendations for more effective responses to the child's emotional needs and to objectionable behavior are made to avoid the self-perpetuating "vicious circle"[14] that may develop. Parents are encouraged to look for alternative limit-setting techniques and to think of "discipline" in an educational rather than a punitive sense. They are advised to concentrate on a single issue at a time and to prepare responses carefully in anticipation of problems instead of reacting impulsively at times of irritation and anger. A few visits with parents and a follow-up period of a few months should determine whether the physician's intervention is sufficient for the needs of this family. Evidence of continued or worsening behavior and/or indications of increasing family stress and discouragement require reevaluation and possible consultation or referral for management.

"Listening" to more than a child's words is necessary at every age, but it becomes particularly important by school years as a child begins venturing out of the home and learning the art of getting along with the outside world. As already discussed, such stress has to produce anxiety, and how this anxiety is expressed is individual to the child. Parents should be helped to understand this developmental principle and given some specific examples of how to respond. For example, the 10-year-old who mysteriously becomes moody and irritable may not really know why he feels as he does and an impatient, "What in the world is the matter with you today?" may lead to a slammed door and a "wise guy" response. On the other hand, a perceptive parent who simply says, "Some days are hard to take, aren't they?" is requiring no response from the child but is eloquently expressing understanding and accessibility, and this parent is far more likely to initiate a fruitful interchange.

Not until later childhood are most children able to work verbally with the physician, since younger children may require play therapy for which most primary care physicians are not equipped or trained. Most of such visits will be an exploration of the child's feelings about his world, an opportunity for him to ventilate about the younger brother who is "getting in his hair," and a time for the physician to inform and support the child in a manner appropriate to his level of cognitive development. Some knowledge of cognitive levels of understanding is important so as not to discuss issues that go "over the head" of the child. The older child or adolescent who continues to achieve most important developmental tasks despite his presenting problem is likely to be amenable to this kind of supportive, reality-oriented counselling, which the family practitioner or pediatrician should be able to offer.

CLINICAL EMOTIONAL DISORDERS

For detailed information concerning the following specific clinical disorders, the reader should consult the many references available.[3,49] Developmental crises, situational crises, some neurotic and psychosomatic symptoms, and adolescent problems can often be managed by the physician. Personality disturbances usually require consultation for diagnosis and probably for management as well. The psychoses require psychiatric management.

Developmental crises

By definition self-limited, these account for the largest number of behavioral concerns expressed by parents. They do not represent emotional illness unless they become unusually severe or are reinforced or perpetuated by a suboptimal child-rearing environment. As indicated previously, the quality and severity of the behavioral manifestation is partially determined by the child's temperamental attributes. There are no hard criteria for making the differentiation between the developmental crisis and a significant emotional disturbance. It must be a clinical judgment based on the physician's experience, knowledge of the individual situation, and a period of careful observation. Most primary care physicians have had the statement "he'll grow out of it" come back to haunt them, yet predictability of behavior and thus the value of intervention is uncertain at best.[17]

A few examples of developmental crises causing parental concern are as follows:

Early infancy	Organization of sleep-wake cycles, feeding problems
9 to 12 months of age	Fear of strangers, awakening at night, head banging
12 to 24 months of age	Discipline, anorexia, "bad" habits such as thumb sucking, testing, independent behavior, temper tantrums
2 to 4 years of age	Stuttering, separation anxiety, phobias, increased motor activity, sibling conflicts
School age	School phobia, mood swings, unsuccessful experiments in relating to peers, recurrence of phobias, sexual experimentation, masturbation, "bad words"
Puberty and adolescence	Moods, emotional distance and ambivalence in parental relationships, testing, challenging standards and values of the family, identity struggle

Situational crises

Real stresses and fears may be the causes of transient emotional disturbance. The death of a parent, a sibling, or of a pet; a move to a new community; a hospitalization or other frightening experience; a divorce; or the birth of a severely handicapped sibling all may result in a wide range of expressions such as fits of crying and depression, regression, aggressive outbursts, school failure, and psychosomatic symptoms. The following case illustrates a situational reaction in a basically healthy girl in a stable family.

A 9-year-old girl presented with a sudden inability to read or to see the blackboard at school although she was able to get around quite normally. A screening vision test indicated extremely poor visual acuity and she was referred to an ophthalmologist who found a central scotoma physiologically unexplainable in the absence of other findings. It was eventually learned that while walking home from school the patient had seen her father stop his car and pick up her dead cat from the side of the road. On arriving home she was told by her father that someone had hit her cat and killed it, but he made no further explanation. It was the patient's impression that her father had actually hit the cat, when in fact he had merely seen it by the side of the road on the way home from work and had recognized it. When she learned that her father was not really responsible for her pet's death, her loss of vision was replaced by a more normal grief reaction. There were no recurrences of such reactions and no subsequent evidence of the emotional disorder. She graduated from high school after an outstanding career both scholastically and socially.

The basic health of the family and the child and the degree to which the family is also reacting to the same stress influence the duration and severity of the symptoms. As in a developmental crisis, prior knowledge of the family and child help in deciding when a symptom has "gone far enough" and specific interventions become necessary.

Neurotic and psychosomatic symptoms

The anxieties necessary to the developmental process may become internalized to the point of becoming crippling in some older children, with the appearance of the same kinds of neurotic patterns seen in adults. Free-floating anxiety attacks; obsessive-compulsive, phobic, hypochondriacal, dissociative, or psychosomatic symptoms; and conversion reactions all may be seen. Following is a classification of psychoneuroses[42]:

anxiety type Diffuse, "free-floating" feelings of apprehension, less common in children than the "symptom" neuroses. To be differentiated from an acute situational panic reaction.

phobic type Unconscious, irrational displacement of a conflict into an environmental object or situation to which the child consciously reacts, such as fear of an animal, a high place, school, dirt, etc. To be distinguished from the frequently seen transient and developmentally related phobias of the healthy preschool or late childhood age youngster (spooks, monsters, a dark basement, a new situation).

conversion type Displacement of a conflict into a somatic dysfunction involving a disturbance in function of bodily structure or organs supplied by the voluntary portion of the central nervous system, that is, striated muscles and somatosensory apparatus. The symptom has symbolic meaning, results in primary and secondary gain, usually in an hysterical personality (next column)

dissociative type Conflicts lead to temporary personality disorganization with fugue states, amnesia, catatonia, pseudodelirium, consciousness disturbances. To be distinguished from toxic, psychotic, or seizure disorders.

obsessive-compulsive type Conflict is counteracted by recurring thoughts, impulses, or both to act in a manner apparently unrelated or opposite to the original conflict, such as ritualistic counting, touching, or washing, in an apparent subconscious effort to "manage" the threatening impulses.

depressive type May result in eating and sleeping disturbances, hyperactivity, acting out, suicide threats, inconsistent behavior in response to feelings of guilt, poor self-image, ambivalence toward a parent. To be distinguished from developmental and situational crises, which may cause transient depression in healthy children.

Despite the symptoms, or with the aid of them, a child may continue to manage his developmental tasks. Judgment and full information are needed to determine "how much is too much." To be unusually neat or to have a low threshold of tolerance for physical discomfort does not necessarily require the labelling of the child as "obsessive-compulsive" or "hypochondriacal." Some neurotic symptoms may be seen in mild form as manifestations of developmental crises. In such cases the physician is in a favorable position to manage the problem, although psychiatric consultation may be sought for reassurance of the accuracy of the diagnosis. Recurring physical symptoms such as abdominal pain or headache are among the commonest complaints brought to the physician. One should be able to manage most of these cases without referral.[2,23]

It is of particular importance that psychosomatic or conversion symptoms not be so labeled by a process of exclusion. These diagnoses require positive evidence, not merely proof of the absence of physical disease. If the recurring abdominal pain in a 9-year-old youngster is based on developmental or environmental stresses, the physician must include these possibilities among his initial diagnostic considerations, both in personal thinking and in discussion with the family and the child. Otherwise the investigation lacks completeness and integrity. "Since we found nothing physical, it must be emotional," is a statement that will be received by the family with skepticism, prove to be of very little therapeutic value, and is likely to send them seeking another diagnostic opinion.

Friedman[20] has summarized the features necessary to the diagnosis of a conversion reaction. A symptom usually has symbolic meaning to the child, is more commonly seen in a hysterical personality, and is reported by the patient in a characteristically dramatic style with an inappropriate lack of concern about its seriousness. There is usually found to be a "primary gain" of reducing anxiety and a "secondary gain" of helping the patient cope with a stressful situation. The child is often living in a home with overly protective parents where health issues frequently arise in family communication and where there is often a model for the particular symptom. A history of unexplained symptoms is typical with a physical examination that is inconsistent with the anatomy and physiology expected for the complaint. Unless most of these features are present, the diagnosis of "conversion" is made at both the physician's and patient's peril.

Adolescent problems

An appreciation of adolescent developmental processes is necessary even for a limited role in counselling. The ambivalence of the dependent-independent struggle of early adolescence may lead to partial withdrawal and rebellion, which is often reflected in moods of sadness, feelings of fatigue, irritability, loss of motivation in school work, and a loss of interest in normal activities. The patient may begin to look to other "objects" in which to invest his affection and for support of his crumbling ego— for example, the heros of his culture, certain of his peers, or important adults. Fantasies about great achievements, feats of daring, or sexual experiences may occupy significant amounts of his time. His evolving sexuality may produce transient homosexual feelings and activities that may frighten a youngster who is concerned about what is "normal" and what is "mental." The identity search continues throughout the teens, requiring examining and sometimes experimenting with values and standards quite unlike those of his home. The late adolescent resolution of the identity search requires a commitment to standards and values that are clearly identifiable as having come from within and are therefore "owned by" the youngster. Plans for a life work and a return to a parent-child relationship but at an "adult-adult" level completes the maturational process.

Behavior problems arising in adolescents present a special challenge to the primary care physician. If as a child the patient has always identified the physician as primarily serving his parents' needs, he may as an adolescent wish to distance himself from the physician as he does from his parents. This may undermine any direct counselling efforts the physician may attempt.

The differentiation is not always clear between the self-defeating and hostile acting-out of a disturbed adolescent and the merely rebellious, negative behavior of one in the throes of what will be an ultimately successful identity struggle. Delinquent, self-destructive behavior, anorexia nervosa, panic, and schizophrenic symptoms all deserve consultation. Although even these symptoms may undergo spontaneous resolution, most pediatricians are likely to feel uneasy attempting to manage them without assistance.

Even a referral may require a significant investment of the physician's efforts. Few adolescents will admit to the need for or willingly consent to intervention by a "shrink," but they may agree to talk with their own physician, however unenthusiastically, who may then be able to persuade them of the need for further counselling.

Personality disorders

Personality disorders are not often identified prior to later childhood. These youngsters are usually characterized as disorganized, socially incompatible, poorly adaptive, and seemingly incapable of making the multitude of day-to-day judgments required to maintain "synchrony" with their environment. During puberty and adolescence, these disorders may become more "public," taking the form of antisocial behavior, but the major manifestation may simply be social ineptness. The guarded outcome and the difficulties encountered in the therapy of these children require referral to a specialist.

Psychoses

It would be a foolhardy pediatrician indeed who would wander into the continuing controversy among authorities regarding the classification and etiology of childhood psychoses. Bender[6] formulates a developmentally associated continuum with autism at one end and schizophrenia at the other. Rutter[44] and others see schizophrenia and autism as separate entities. Shirley[48] describes childhood schizophrenia as a generic term only, similar to "juvenile delinquency," under which are classified patients with certain ego-development problems in common. That it is "an early decompensation in genetically vulnerable individual"[7] seems generally acceptable.

To the pediatrician with a disturbed child and his family in the office, the major issues are similar to those considered in dealing with handicapped children (pp. 375 to 387, as follows:

1. Alertness to the diagnostic possibility of a severe disturbance
2. Gathering the history necessary to make an appropriate referral

3. Support and interpretation for the family through an often prolonged and arduous work-up
4. Attentiveness to their needs in formulating immediate and long-term treatment plans
5. Ongoing involvement as the primary care physician
6. Monitoring the quality of resources in the community for these special needs

However ultimately related to each other, the following clinical disorders should at least be familiar to the physician.

Anaclitic depression. Anaclitic depression was first described by Spitz[51] and is most familiar to the pediatrician as the infant with "failure to thrive," apathy, and developmental retardation on the basis of maternal deprivation. Characteristically, these children have reached 6 to 9 months of age and are then separated from their mothers without an adequate surrogate being supplied. Although some of these children may prove to be autistic, unlike autistic children, their symptoms seem clearly related to an environmental cause.

Autism. "Autism" must take its place with the multitude of medical conditions that continues to defy precise definition as to etiology or pathology. Controversy continues regarding which clinical presentations qualify for the label. Following are symptoms of autism:

A. Disturbances in social development
  1. Failure to assume "pick me up" posture as infant
  2. Flaccidity or stiffness when picked up
  3. Relating to persons as objects; aloof, no eye contact
  4. Temper outbursts, inappropriate giggling
  5. Inability to play appropriately with children
B. Disturbances in speech and communication
  1. Inability to use speech for communication
  2. Pronominal reversal
  3. Atonal, monotonous speech
  4. Delayed echolalia
  5. Speech development may begin but becomes arrested or regresses
C. Disturbance in perception and intellectual development
  1. Resistance to learning skills or new behavior
  2. Inability to play with toys or persons imaginatively

  3. Failure to respond appropriately to auditory stimuli
  4. Lack of fear of realistic dangers
  5. Resistance to change in routine and environment
  6. Good rote memory
  7. Special mechanical or musical aptitude
  8. High incidence of mental retardation
D. Disturbances in motor and neurological functions
  1. Rhythmic, ritualistic, repetitive activity
  2. Seizures in about a sixth of such children
  3. Disturbances in sleeping, eating, elimination
  4. Alteration in galvanic skin resistance activity

The literature is massive and confounding to the physicians who may be involved with such patients only a few times in their professional career. Although they cannot be the primary diagnostician and therapist, they nonetheless can be useful to the child and family if they are sufficiently informed to avoid the attitude of hopelessness often associated with this diagnosis. Because a pediatrician may well be part of the management team, this entity is discussed in more detail than the others in this section. For comprehensive works on autism, see the references.[43,59]

Clinical description. Kanner[26] originally described a syndrome characterized by failure during infancy to assume anticipatory posture before being picked up, failure to use speech for communication, good rote memory, delayed echolalia, inability to use abstract concepts, pronominal reversal, an anxious desire to maintain sameness, monotony of activity, panic or increased excitement in unusual situations, unawareness of other people, an inability to play imaginatively with toys or with other children, normal physical development, and a course that tends toward improvement after 5 or 6 years of age.

This describes the "nuclear" syndrome, but there is great variability in the severity and range of the manifestations. Although the diagnosis may not be made until the child has reached 2½ to 3 years of age, in many cases the mother recalls wondering about her infant's unusual behavior even during the first year. She may have sensed a lack of "synchrony." There may be an aversion to human contact with either stiffness or flaccidity when picked up.

The child may alternate between intense, inconsolable irritability and placidity. There may be absence of playful social responses; a lack of the curious exploratory activity expected of the age; feeding, sucking, and sleeping problems; and prolonged head banging or rocking. Although this pattern may be apparent during the first year, there are a number of infants who appear to develop normally until 18 to 24 months of age. This group may have a somewhat more favorable prognosis.

Problems may become more apparent in the 2- to 5-year age range when rapid developmental strides are normally being made. Disturbances of speech development and language reflect the inability of the child to make appropriate use of incoming stimuli. There may be normal early development of speech, that then becomes arrested or there may be life-long mutism. What speech there is may be atonal, lacking in inflection, inappropriate, and echolalic. Unlike deaf children, children with autism may be unable to substitute gestures for speech, a further indication of profound intellectual disorganization.

Deviations from the normal sequence and rate of development are apparent in motor and social milestones as well as in language. These children may unexpectedly develop special musical or mechanical skills that do not depend on language for their expression. There may be surprisingly durable rote memory, the content of which may be totally lacking in logical priority and application.

Other impairments suggest extensive neurological involvement. Responses to visual and auditory stimuli are unpredictable and inappropriate to the degree that the child is sometimes thought to be blind or deaf. There is often a tendency to use peripheral instead of central vision. The sometimes total indifference to sensory stimuli may be abruptly replaced by great excitement or agitation at the sight of a spinning top or at the sound of a barking dog.

Motor control and activity may be bizarre with flapping, rocking, or swaying involving the hands, the head, or the whole body and alternating with periods of posturing and an almost trancelike immobility. Disturbances of sleep, elimination, eating, and resistance to vertigo suggest vestibular and autonomic effects.

Problems in social development and behavior may be secondary to the perceptual impairments. As noted in the discussion of deaf children on p. 381, inability to hear language is itself sufficient to interfere with the development of social interactions. Language that may be heard but not decoded and associated with the complex cognitive problems of autism must have an even more profound effect on social development. These children are described as aloof and indifferent, responding to other persons as though they were objects. They may relate only to a part of a person, such as to the hand that is holding an interesting object or favorite food. Instead of indicating a request for a cookie by a word or gesture, the child may take the concrete action of pulling a parent's hand toward the cookie jar. Reactions to people may be completely lacking in sensitivity and appropriateness. There may be inappropriate public behavior such as undressing; prolonged temper outbursts; or sudden screaming, crying, or laughing. Exaggerated fear of new situations and resistance to slight changes in the environment or in daily routines may be seen in the same child who recklessly and fearlessly charges into a dangerous situation. Games and toys are used only as objects, not as stimulants to the imagination. Play is likely to be stereotyped and inflexible. There may be compulsive collecting of particular objects, such as gum wrappers, bottle caps, or specially colored bits of plastic.

After 5 or 6 years of age there tends to be some improvement in these behavioral problems, but the wide variations in expression and severity of the syndrome become more apparent and suggest the natural course and prognosis.

Rutter[44] studied 64 psychotic children when they reached 15 to 29 years of age. In all but four the onset of their psychoses was prior to 30 months of age. One was considered "normal," 19% had made a "fair" adjustment, 5% of those over 16 were employed, 50% were in full-time residential care, 64% were considered too severely handicapped to lead any kind of independent life, 33% has seizures, 50% were unable to use language, and all had profound problems with social relationships. A definite correlation was noted between IQ and prognosis. Lack of speech and failure to respond to sound were unfavorable prognostic signs. Not surprisingly, the less severe the manifestations, the better the eventual outcome. Although these observations appear gloomy, it is important to note that a significant minority of these children did improve with appropriate schooling.

Epidemiology. Because the definition of the syndrome is not universally accepted, epidemiological data vary. Most of these indicate a male to female ratio of 2 or 3 to 1 and an age-specific prevalence of 4 to 5 per 10,000.[61] The geographical distribution is universal, and there is no correlation with birth rank, maternal age, or prematurity. There is no increase in prevalence of schizophrenia or psychosis among parents, but there is a significantly increased representation of parents from the higher socioeducational level.

Diagnosis and differential diagnosis. In considering a diagnosis, the physician must address the following points, as listed by Wing[60]:

1. The pattern of behavior
2. The child's level of ability including language development and abnormalities, performance on cognitive tests, perceptual functions, special skills, self-care, and practical competence
3. Any associated neurological handicaps
4. Any other physical handicaps
5. The underlying etiology and pathology, if known
6. The child's social and emotional environment

Some of the protean expressions of autism may be shared by other diagnoses. Such differentiations will require the efforts of the experts, but the primary care physician should be aware of the following possibilities. Childhood schizophrenia is characterized by some adult schizophrenic features such as hallucinations and delusions. Other features are discussed on p. 374. Autistic features may be seen in deprivation syndromes as already discussed, sensory deficits, developmental aphasia, and brain damage syndromes associated with rubella, phenylketonuria (PKU) metabolism disorder, degenerative brain diseases, and some seizure disorders.

Management. The management of the child with autism should be planned and implemented by those with the special experience and resources necessary to deal with complex educational and developmental issues. The physician still has an important role, however, as with every chronic disability. The physician may be confronted with questions from the parents, who are concerned about the first subtle signs of unusual behavior in their child. Their poorly defined complaints may be explained away merely as transient, developmental, parent-child conflicts and the parents labelled as "overanxious." They already may be doubting their "parenting" instincts, and it takes very little reinforcement from an authority to convince them of their own ineptness. When the diagnosis eventually is made, the physician may become the target of hostile criticism for failure to respond helpfully to their initial concerns. If the family should continue under the physician's care despite this stress, the relationship may be further imperiled if psychotherapy for the parents and/or institutionalization for the child is inappropriately suggested under the assumption that these are universally necessary recommendations.

Schopler[46] has eloquently discussed the treatment program developed at the University of North Carolina. Citing the inadequacy of either psychiatric or pure operant-conditioning modalities, a problem-oriented approach is used, which is individualized and responsive to specific situations. This rejects therapeutic adherence to a preconceived framework. Problems are addressed in a logical sequence of priorities: (1) risks to life, (2) risks to living in the family, (3) risks to access to special education, (4) risks to access to normal education.

Parents become cotherapists in this approach, which also involves them in ongoing counselling. Again, the burden of the counselling probably lies beyond the purview of most physicians, but the physician will be seeing the child regularly for health maintenance and acute illnesses and will become at least peripherally involved in the family's reactions and concerns.

If community resources are relatively limited, the physician may at least be a coordinator of management and support.

Schopler discusses parental counselling problems in terms of (1) *general* and (2) *specific* reactions. *General reactions* are exemplified by the frustrations, discouragement, and disappointment associated with the handicap. There is confusion about the disability and its causes. Many expectations prove to be unrealistic. A continuing tension may develop between the parents and the many professionals involved in their child's care. As stated previously, these may be well-educated and critical persons who are likely to challenge the professionals with whom they have contact. In their desperation to find answers, they may bombard the physician with articles about new approaches in management. The physician may feel less informed than the questioners and unless secure in the knowledge of the handicap and of the dynamics of these parental reactions, the physician may respond with defensiveness and irritation and, without realizing it, maneuver to avoid the parents.

Specific problems in counselling are those involving the day-to-day tactics of behavioral management.

1. Can the child be taught responses to solve the particular management issue?
2. Can environmental changes be made to solve the problem?
3. Can parents be helped to accept the unmodified behavior?

Because a high percentage of children with autism are retarded, it is a particularly sensitive task to establish treatment goals that fit the severity of the handicap, still further indication of the need for individualized and expert planning.

Sexual behavior may become a particularly difficult management problem. An adolescent child with autism may develop an undiscriminating desire for physical contact, which is embarrassing for parents and puzzling, if not alarming, to others. Teaching the child that masturbation should be private and how to care for the hygiene problems of menstruation require patience and tactical guidance.

The role of drugs in management of autism is very limited. Despite the number of physiological, attentional, and affective disturbances that would seem logical targets for drug therapy, their usefulness has been disappointing. Stimulants have generally worsened the symptoms, as have antidepressants in most cases. Barbiturates have done little and tended to increase agitation in many. The major tranquilizers along with behavioral modification have been selectively useful. Haloperidol has also been helpful in some cases but its therapeutic margin of safety is narrow.

In summary, the primary care physician's role in the care of a child with autism will of necessity vary with the quality of the community resources available. Even in the unlikely event that the physician's training and experience have been extensive in this area, a team of diagnostic and management specialists is needed, although such expertise may require considerable travel for the family. The physician's major functions are those to be described in the discussion of other chronic handicaps: early suspicion and appropriate diagnostic referral, coordination and interpretation of diagnostic and therapeutic measures, the formulation of a life plan, and the continual comprehensive medical care of the child, including the emotional support of the family, which such care implies. The various professionals involved should have defined, mutually agreed on responsibilities and a clear "team" leader, with whom the physician and family maintain good two-way communication.

Symbiotic psychosis. The intimate young infant—mother attachment, so necessary to both, must gradually give way to the mutual recognition that the child is, in fact, separate from his mother and from the world and must exercise his independence. He is neither part of his mother nor the center of the universe, but rather a being among beings. To remain psychologically merged with his mother, unable to identify himself as a separate and distinct organism, is the serious psychotic disorder symbiotic psychosis, described by Mahler.[30] The child may present a disturbing exaggeration of the commonly seen 2- to 4-year-old

THE PRACTICAL MANAGEMENT OF THE DEVELOPMENTALLY DISABLED CHILD

separation anxiety. Many children of this age may become transiently panic stricken if the mother is hospitalized or if a new sibling appears on the scene. The child with a symbiotic psychosis, however, may even be unable to tolerate being in a separate room from his mother. The total immersion in the mother may reach the point of paralysis of function for both, and the child may eventually regress to an autistic-like state. The mother's investment in the relationship may be such that treatment is very difficult.

Schizophrenia. The term schizophrenia seems most useful as a description rather than a diagnosis. As with most of the body's systems, the mental apparatus has a limited repertory of responses, so a number of causes may give rise to similar manifestations. Those features usually associated with schizophrenia are an onset late in childhood, usually puberty or later; initial presentation with symptoms of extreme anxiety and bizarre behaviors; flat, withdrawn affect with loss of interest in parents, friends, and normal activities; purposeless, perserverative activity; impulsive, destructive, or self-destructive behavior; and delusions and hallucinations of the kind seen in adult schizophrenia.

O'Neal and Robins[37] discussed childhood patterns possibly predictive of adult schizophrenia in a 30-year follow-up study. In this study 284 children seen in a child guidance clinic 30 years previously and 68 controls from the public school records were interviewed. Of the former patients, 28 with the diagnosis of schizophrenia were compared with 57 described as having "no disease." The schizophrenic group was found to be predominently male and between 7 and 17 years of age at the time of the original referral. More of the preschizophrenic children had severe infections in the first 2 years of life, histories of physical handicaps, particularly hearing problems and disfigurement, and difficulties in locomotion. Among males, particularly, there was significantly more physical acting-out and pathological lying in the preschizophrenic group. More than half of the preschizophrenics were considered incorrigible, over half had juvenile arrest records, and more than a third had a history of running away.

Among girls, there seemed to be a higher incidence of passivity, dependency, hypersensitivity, and characteristics of poor social adjustment. In summary, the authors found that the preschizophrenic children had more total symptoms, more areas of function involved, a higher rate of mental hospitalization, and a higher arrest rate than the "no-disease" group. Schizophrenics were "often treated as criminals rather than mentally ill persons."[37]

Bender[6] reviewed the life course of 100 children with schizophrenia, in which she includes 32 children with autism, 27 with symbiotic psychosis, 28 with onset of psychosis in mid-childhood, and 13 with onset at puberty. Of these children, 68 were chronically institutionalized and 37 were living in a community in some sort of adjustment. Every kind of socioeconomic and family setting was represented and there was no evidence of environmental factors in the eitology. There were frequently strong family histories of psychosis. Remissions were seen to occur in some girls in late childhood and in some boys at puberty. The prognosis was good for a marginal community adjustment in about a third.

Despite these apparent patterns of behavior, there are still significant areas of overlap between the behavior of those later diagnosed as schizophrenic and those considered healthy. A primary care physician would be on uncertain ground at best to interpret a set of symptoms as preschizophrenic or schizophrenic without psychiatric support. Even if the diagnosis is relatively certain, terms themselves are so imprecise and so electrifying to most people, that they probably serve no useful purpose in discussions with the family.

Most of these children can reside at home, depending on the health of the family, the severity of the problem, and the supportive community resources available. Child psychiatric management is necessary and usually of an intensity that leaves little role for the primary care physician, who may have considerable difficulty maintaining an even superficial touch with the complex and subtle therapeutic proceedings. A family often assumes that there is good interprofessional communication, and it is disconcerting to hear, "Didn't Dr. X tell you that Boris is on a tranquilizer now?'' when the physician and Dr. X have not communicated in 6 months! Just as a patient-physician contract is appropriate, so should there be a specialist–referring physician contract with mutually understood definitions of respective roles. The referring physician may only be a peripheral support for the family, but even this requires knowledge of what is happening in therapy.

Summary of management

The primary physician's role in management of emotional problems requires the following:

1. A knowledge and understanding of cognitive, emotional, and physical development and their variations
2. An appreciation of the individuality of responses to environmental and developmental stresses
3. Sensitivity to the multifarious forces that bear on the child's development
4. Willingness to commit time and effort to mobilizing this information and special understanding on behalf of the child and family
5. Sufficient appreciation of clinical disorders to sort out the problems that can be managed independently from those requiring more sophisticated resources
6. Commitment to continue support of the family and child, although ''standing in the wings'' of the direct management of the more serious disorders

EMOTIONAL IMPACT OF CHRONIC AND DISABLING ILLNESS

This section will address the inevitable emotional impact of a chronic physical disability on the child and family (Chapters 8 and 17). The primary care physician's role, so pivotal in the coordinated care of the disabled child, is especially critical here. A broad summary of these tasks is as follows:

1. Ongoing interpretation of problems for the family and coordination of general care
2. Support of the family during the critical initial diagnostic period
3. Assisting in the formulation of a life plan

4. Anticipation of developmental crises and of the emotional difficulties, which may be unique characteristics of the child's particular disability
5. Sensitivity and response to marital and/or sibling stresses
6. Knowledge of community and specialized professional resources needed in habilitation and treatment

The impact of chronic disability on the child and the family will be affected by the nature and extent of the problem, its age of onset and duration, the degree to which physical pain is part of the child's experience, and the stability and resources of the family. These many variables obviously preclude the prediction of individual patient or parent reactions. However, there are broad response patterns seen with sufficient frequency to enable the physician to better understand some of the developmental agonies of the patients and their parents and thus to be more helpful to them in the development of a life plan. Following is a discussion of these general responses; some conditions will be examined that present specific problems of management.

Family reactions to chronic disability

The major problems facing the family involve exaggerations and variations of the complex developmental struggles of all children and families, whether or not there are disabilities. It is perhaps important at this point to focus on these family reactions, which are the major emotional issues in the child's first years.

The child is a complex developing organism, consistently effecting change on his environment and in turn being changed by his perceptions of it. So also is the family into which he is born. Miller[34] discusses the stages of family development and how a child's disability may be disruptive to the evolution of these stages. A couple progresses from being childless, to having an infant, to having children of preschool, elementary school, junior and high school age, and finally to being childless again. It is a progression that is a deeply ingrained expectation in our society. Each stage produces its special problems and concerns, but part of the immense satisfaction of parenthood is the successive mastering of these stresses as child and family develop. There is consolation in the fact that these difficulties are, after all, a part of "growing up" experienced by all families. There is a plethora of friends, relatives, books, and talk shows, which, whether helpful or not, are at least addressing familiar and universal child-rearing issues.

By contrast, the parents of the handicapped child are isolated. Progression of development may be distorted or arrested. Traditional sources of support are uninformed or irrelevant. Even their medical professionals may be inexperienced with their particular problem, further adding to their sense of helplessness. Numerous authors discuss the dynamics of parent reactions to the birth of a handicapped child.[21,22,29,36] The initial impact of the diagnosis will be quite different, depending on whether it is apparent at birth or at a later time after "parent-child bonding" has occurred. In either case the reaction is quite predictably one of shock and disorganization. Relative to the immediately evident disabilities such as spina bifida, Mac Keith[29] accurately presents the reactions of parents. This is described in detail in Chapter 8.

It is during this emotionally tumultuous period that parents are often faced with difficult and complex decisions regarding treatments and procedures, at a time when there is inevitably a degree of personality disorganization.

Sensitive, experienced professionals who are fully cognizant of their own reactions to the handicap in question are urgently necessary. Forthright, gentle, and full disclosure of the diagnosis must be made as soon as possible to both parents.[22] If the physician's information is incomplete, so must be the discussion with the parents, a situation as demanding of artful communication and support skills and ingenuity as a physician is likely to face in any practice. If the physician is unable or uncomfortable providing this type of support, it is incumbent on the physician to arrange for it from another source.

Out of this immediate period of shock and disorganization denial defenses form, which in the extreme may be paralyzing to planning and acceptance, but without which families would

not be able to function at the outset. Olshansky[36] describes the sometimes life-long tension between partial denial and partial acceptance of their child's problem as "chronic sorrow." A degree of denial protects them as they gradually struggle to mobilize their resources, make plans appropriate to their now drastically altered expectations, and move toward acceptance. They will learn to derive satisfaction from very limited developmental and motor achievements, but a degree of bereavement persists as awareness of their child's disadvantage is exaggerated by the approach of landmarks of normal childhood development such as entering kindergarten, promotion to high school, and graduation. The continuing dependency and "chronic sorrow" does not keep most families from becoming reintegrated, however, and doing their best with their resources.

The introduction of any child into a family effects some change in already existing relationships, thereby causing stress. This may be creative and ultimately enriching, but if the family's stability is already marginal, this new stress can be threatening and divisive.

Gath[21] studied the impact on 30 families of the birth of a child with Down syndrome. These and 30 control families with normal newborn infants were interviewed six times over 18 to 24 months. The nature and severity of the emotional reactions of mothers with children with Down syndrome were similar to those experienced by mothers with normal children faced with rearing them under difficult circumstances. The incidence of depression was about the same as that found in mothers of normal twins, or about one third. Most marked were the effects on the quality of the marital relationship. In 9 of 30 of the study parents there were evidences of serious discord, with two divorces already having occurred. No significant hostility was noted in the control group. However, there was also evidence of more positive changes in the marital relationship among the study parents than among the controls. Similar observations were made by Burton,[11] who found that 64% of mothers and 53% of fathers of children with cystic fibrosis considered their marriage strengthened by the presence of the handicapped child. Whether or not the new child is handicapped, it therefore seems apparent that the marital relationship is likely either to move toward greater strength or toward divisiveness, but clearly it does not remain unaffected.

Siblings already in the family and those to follow are profound participants in the developmental struggles with their handicapped brother or sister. A younger sibling passes by the developmentally delayed child, further intensifying the pain of the child's disrupted staging. Whether older or younger, a sibling may be overtly or subtly resentful of the concentration of effort, time, and family resources on the patient. The adolescent siblings express concerns about who will care for the child when the parents are no longer able to and about the likelihood of their own children being similarly affected. Some are reticent to bring friends home because of their "strange" brother or sister. A child harboring these resentments is very likely to pay some emotional price for them. The attitude of siblings toward the handicapped child often reflects parental responses and attitudes. Parental response to the child may be influenced in turn by the manner in which they see the child affecting the siblings, thus completing a complex transactional cycle.

This discussion only touches on these complex issues. Chapters 8 and 17 provide additional perspectives on these important issues.

Emotional reactions in the child

It is not clear whether or not actual psychiatric disorders are more common in children with nonneurological disabilities than in healthy youngsters. In a survey of all crippled children between 5 and 15 years of age in three London boroughs, Seidel and co-workers[48] found neurologically impaired children of normal intelligence to have an incidence of psychological problems twice that of children with similar physical disabilities but without neurological impairment. There was a scattering of psychiatric diagnoses without relationship to the particular type of neurological disorder. The authors suggest that the brain lesion per se represents a "biological vulnerability" to psychosocial stresses, the nature of the behavioral response

to those stresses being individual. But of particular importance is the observation that three fourths of the brain-damaged children had no evidence of psychiatric problems.

The developmental stage of the child is obviously a major determinant in his reaction to a handicap. The very basic age-related developmental tasks of the normal child discussed in Chapter 3 clearly require alteration appropriate to the handicap. The child's struggle to achieve these and other subtler tasks of his development require the continual reassessment of himself in relationship to his world. It is not possible to divorce cognitive, physical, and emotional maturation from each other. His efforts to maintain an equilibrium between his understandings and his observations of his environment must be reflected in his emotional development.

The handicapped infant's needs are those of every infant. Early parent-infant attachment may have been severely compromised during the difficult adjustments and procedures necessary in the neonatal period. If grief, resentment, and rejection are the prominent reactions of a family, optimal emotional nuturing of the infant is at risk.

As the healthy child progresses physically and cognitively into preschool years, he becomes increasingly mobile, independent, and excitedly interactional with his family and environment. The pain, hospitalizations, and separations from parents, siblings, and home environment that occur so frequently in the handicapped child are wrenching experiences, often interpreted by the child as punishment. Until 3 or 4 years of age this separation and punishment constitutes his major concept of illness. By 4 or 5 years of age, when still "preoperational" in cognitive development, he associates illness with sensory experiences, sights, sounds, and colors. *Red is the Color of Hurting* is the apt title of a symposium on the hospitalized child.[50]

In the school-aged child, the social deprivation limits the breadth of his experiences and relationships, further delaying his progress and undermining his self-image. Continued dependency may lead to depression as he becomes more aware of the independence and mobility of other children. Hospitalization now becomes increasingly stressful as it may mean even more immobilization, pain, and a fear of further mutilation. There may be a resentment and blame directed at parents who are the "cause" of the disability. They may think in terms of "catching" an illness, obviously not because of an understanding of microbial contagion, but by a kind of direct transmission of the manifestations of the disease itself, as, for example, the spots of measles or the runny nose of a cold. There may be a magical self-blame that they have somehow brought on their problems by their own action, negligence, or "bad thoughts."

At the level on "concrete operations," usually during the early years, the child may make clear distinctions between what is "inside" and "outside" his body. Here the concept of contagion takes on more of the aspect of contamination. The effects of an illness are caused or alleviated by "surface" contact. Bibace and Walsh,[8] in a very useful study correlating the cognitive development of children with their concepts of illness, cite examples from interviews of children. Headaches are caused by "being noisy when your brother wants you to be quiet" and is treated by rubbing something on it; cancer is caused by "smoking without permission."

By late childhood, at a more sophisticated level of logical thinking, the child tends to internalize illness, but still in a concrete fashion, for example, "stomach aches are caused by swallowing germs," but people may have some control, in that by taking proper care of themselves, they can avoid sickness. On the other hand, the converse is also true, and they may develop illness if they do something they "shouldn't"; for example, arthritis may result from running around too much or diabetes from eating too many sweets.

During the early "formal-operational" stages, puberty and early adolescence, a more physiological concept of illness develops. An external agent may be the cause, but the illness itself is an internal derangement of the body. Even psychosomatic concepts develop, such as "headaches are caused by worrying" and "heart attacks are due to stress."

Bibace and Walsh[8] emphasize two dimensions in the development of concepts of illness in children; (1) the sequence of their cognitive developmental processes and (2) the parental and environmental understandings of illness as they are perceived by the child. It is obvious, then, that the management of ill children requires the physician to be sensitive to their cognitive development level. It is less obvious, but no less important, that the physician must also know something of the concepts of illness expressed in the environment with which the child is continually interacting.

Many of these reactions represent exaggerations of the developmental coping efforts of nonhandicapped children. This is particularly apparent in the adolescent. Puberty is the beginning of the drive for emotional distance from the family, independence of function, and increased association with peers as issues around sexuality become emergent. When physical limitations are inhibiting in these areas, there may be an explosion of resentment and anger, depression, and self-deprecation. In a discussion of sexuality and the handicapped adolescent, Blos and Finch[9] discuss the difficulties confronting the youngster attempting to adapt to the biological changes occurring in a body that may be limited and distorted. The severity and the character of the reactions differ according to the nature of the handicap. Blos and Finch[9] classify these categories as follows:

1. Physical handicaps that are obvious and visible, such as cerebral palsy, amputation, and congenital defects such as myelodysplasia
2. Visible but concealable handicaps, such as a colostomy, hypospadias, and cryptorchidism
3. Invisible handicaps, which have perceivable effects and limitations, such as diabetes, seizure disorders, heart disease
4. A miscellaneous group including mental retardation and schizophrenia

It is not difficult to visualize the impediments to normal socialization, learning, and thus to the development of an operational self-image and sexuality that each of these categories of handicap presents to the youngster. Continued dependence must undermine confidence, which in turn increases the tendency to withdraw.

Motivation, so much associated with confidence and self-image, may be tentative and lacking in determination and direction. With perhaps a limited forum in which to test values, ideas, and styles of human interaction, emotional responses may become fixed and stereotyped. Among the developmental tasks of the adolescent is the formulation of a value system identifiable as his own, a formidable task indeed given the physical dependence, lack of privacy, and truncated pleasures and social contacts of the handicapped child. Three major groups of maladaptive states have been observed by Mattson[31] in adolescents with handicaps:

1. A passive personality with great dependence on the mother, a lack of interests and initiative, and a timidity and fearfulness about any but the most protected and controlled situations.
2. An overcompensating daring and independence with defiance of reasonable caution and a denial of the existence of realistic hazards to safety.
3. A withdrawn, lonely, sullenness and hostility toward others in contrast to the timidity of the first group. These youngsters have usually had families that isolated them and otherwise gave poor support

Superimposed on these basic personality patterns may be the same spectrum of psychiatric illness seen in other young people; anxiety, depression, psychosomatic symptoms, conversion reactions, and acting-out antisocial behavior.

These observed behavioral patterns further reinforce the need for parental acceptance of the child's handicap to help him incorporate it into his own self-concept. Parents may need special counselling to help them order the conflicting and confusing feelings they have about their child, and physician sensitivity may be required to point out when they are being oversolicitous or rejecting.

Every child needs a secure resource for education about his body as it develops and particularly about his sexuality. This is more crucial, not less, in the handicapped child. It is often assumed that the child with cerebral palsy, myelodysplasia, or mental retardation has no

sexual drive or interests. Sexual activity among such "unattractive" persons is so unthinkable to some that they deny the existence of the painful longings some of these children may face. Sex education must be individualized in terms of the handicapping condition and the cognitive level of the child and is usually best carried out by parents with the help of professionals. Parent groups, teenage groups, and individual counselling all may have their place. However it is done, the physician must be alert to the need, take the initiative, and be satisfied that it is being addressed in a manner appropriate to the needs of that patient.

The disrupted emotional adaptations of most disabled children cited in the foregoing discussion are summarized in Table 15-1 and exemplified in the following conditions, which, by the nature of the associated handicap, may also present special problems in emotional adjustments. These are juvenile rheumatoid arthritis, deafness, blindness, seizure disorders, and myelodysplasia.

Juvenile rheumatoid arthritis. Juvenile rheumatoid arthritis is one of the most common chronic illnesses in childhood. The two peak ages of onset are under 5 years and between 10 and 15 years of age. Clinical manifestations range from the pauciarticular, to the acute febrile, to the persistent polyarticular forms. Prognosis depends on the clinical form, the polyarticular being the most likely to cause permanent joint disability, the pauciarticular being most often associated with uveitis. The onset may be subtle and insidious, giving rise to the consideration of many diagnostic possibilities. A child may be hospitalized repeatedly for inconclusive fever of undetermined origin (FUO) work-ups, or have many months of recurring "leg aches" before unequivocally objective findings become manifest. The emotional stress of the disease may therefore begin even before the diagnosis is made.

McAnarney and co-workers[32] studied 42 children with chronic arthritis and an equal number of matched controls with respect to (1) the extent of psychosocial problems as compared to healthy children and (2) the relationship between the severity of the disease and the extent of psychosocial problems. As ex-

Table 15-1. Problems of adaptation of disabled children

Problems	Management
Physical deprivation	
Compromised mobility	Development of means of independent mobility, ongoing orthopedic care, environmental alterations
Sensory deprivation may partially arise from mobility limitation even without sensory handicap per se, due to prolonged hospitalizations, limited access to environment	Special attention to enrichment of environment, sight, sound, tactile experiences, human sensory contact
Emotional deprivation	
Parental interactional problems, grief, ambivalence, etc.	Ongoing family counselling
Peer interactional problems; contacts few and distorted; isolation common	Enrichment of opportunities for contact, social groups, counselling groups, association with others with handicaps, individual counselling
Cognitive deprivation	
Physical and emotional deprivation limit new and varied stimuli needed for normal developmental process	Special educational needs addressed from infancy
Distortion of cause of disability	
Arising from cognitive-developmental understandings, magical thinking, punishment, fixation of self-concept at developmentally appropriate level	Need for continual opportunity to discuss self-concepts, unspoken distortions, reality reinforcement
Distortion of body image	
From own perceptions and from the reactions of others to his handicap	Need for counselling with parents and directly with child to develop areas of special strength and to accept handicap as part of self; reality reinforcement
Distortion of sexuality	
Which must grow out of distortion of body image	Direct and thorough education about body, its limitations and capabilities; confrontation of ''morality'' issues, masturbation, fantasies, with special emphasis on parent education and support, ''rap groups''
Depletion of ego	
Inevitably resulting from unresolved maladjustments above	All of above; psychiatric consultation

pected, children with arthritis were more likely to be maladjusted in the view of the school, parents, and in measures of the child's own self-esteem. The children with arthritis were then divided into those with moderate to severe disability, those with mild disability, and those without disability, and their psychological test scores compared. An almost linear negative relationship was found between severity and maladjustment. Approximately twice as many nondisabled children had poor adjustment ratings when compared to those with disability. The authors interpret their findings cautiously, but the suggestion is clear that in the child with minimal or invisible disability, environmental

conflicts may be heightened. Teachers, peers, and parents may unconsciously expect ''normal'' activity from a ''normal'' appearing child, yet he often may not feel well. He is continually reminded that he is ''sick'' by constant medical attention and enforced limitations on his activity.

R. S. is a girl who presented at 7 years of age with recurring pain and swelling in her knees and wrists, low-grade fever, and an evanescent, macular skin eruption, clearly supporting the diagnosis of juvenile rheumatoid arthritis. For at least 2 years prior to this time, however, she had had intermittent knee pain of variable frequency and severity, but sufficiently distressing to require several medical consultations. The pain was either explained as "growing pains" or as psychosomatic, repeated observations and work-ups having failed to clarify the symptoms. Following the acute episode during which the diagnosis was made, the patient was treated with salicylates, which eliminated fever, swelling, and rash, but she continued to have considerable discomfort. Her return to school was marked by a long period of depression, poor performance, deterioration of peer relationships, and increased anxiety on the part of her parents. Because she "looked fine," expectations of teachers and friends did not make allowances for her limitations. Unable to run well, or even walk fast, she was chided for not keeping up. Though an average student previously, she fell behind in the classroom work because of her long absence and her deteriorating self-esteem. A succession of somatic symptoms appeared, such as recurring abdominal and midback pain, and she was seen periodically by a rheumatology consultant, but in addition to the medical management of her arthritis, it was necessary for the pediatrician to communicate with teachers and to arrange for regular visits for purposes of parental support and for talks with the child. These talks were brief, exploring "how things are going" with friends, teachers, school work, and with her feelings about her illness, but with minimal discussions about her various symptoms. At one point, psychological counselling was also necessary to help the family, the child, and the pediatrician to cope with the many complex and subtle issues. These efforts have been rewarding as she has become much happier and more successful, both in the classroom and socially. (However, two younger siblings are now complaining of a variety of unidentifiable aches and pains.)

This vignette illustrates the problem of "marginality" discussed by McAnarney.[32] The primary care physician was involved in several levels of care, including initial diagnostic evaluation, coordination, interpretation, and working in partnership with a rheumatologist, psychologist, and physical therapist. The physician was a patient advocate at school, an important resource for parental support, and an understanding ear for the child, as well as being the "sore throat and earache doctor."

Sensory deprivation. Mention already has been made of the potential developmental effects of the isolation experienced by physically handicapped children due to limited mobility and social opportunity. When isolation is the result, not of limited physical access to the environment, but of the means of receiving signals from it, learning and personality problems assume some unique qualities. Hearing and vision are the "lead senses" in humans. Myklebust[35] discusses their fundamental characteristics in the process of the "mediation between inner needs and external circumstances."

Vision is undirectional, a foreground sense. If an individual has only this lead sense, he must look toward the object or person to receive the message. Vision is a "receiver," which is turned off completely by closing the eyes or turning out the lights.

Hearing is mandatory, a background sense, an unceasing scanning operation. The listener is able to sort out, classify, organize sounds and their interpretations, and be alerted to changes or hazards in his environment. Three physical attributes of sound—frequency, intensity, and complexity—have their psychological counterparts in the listener's organization of interpretations of these sounds as to pitch, loudness, and timbre. These are exquisite and subtle differentiations. Visual experience, by contrast, is stereotyped and stable, with limited subtlety and a narrower range for interpretation.

One need only consider the uniqueness of each human voice and the inflections of speech that infuse words with affective value to appreciate the enormous disadvantage of hearing loss in the development of human interactions. Chapter 10 discusses the etiology and classification of deafness. The emotional impact in a given case does relate in some measure to its degree of severity and age of onset. Obviously the child who has begun some speech development prior to loss of hearing may have less difficulty with language skills and less severe psychological effects. Even if the child has reached 2 years of age before loss of hearing, there may be some verbal benefit, and if he has reached school age, there is sufficient language function to enable fairly normal cognitive development, although peer relations are still likely to be problematic.

Early diagnosis of deafness is of paramount importance. Although actual use and comprehension of words do not occur for many months, language development begins immediately after birth. Appropriate referral should be made as soon as hearing loss is suspected to institute whatever remedial and educational efforts are possible.

Most infants will respond to loud noises in the newborn period, but a child with normal hearing and a generally high threshold of response to environmental stimuli will sometimes appear unresponsive to sound, and raise parental concerns about hearing. Infants may respond to their mothers' voices at birth and by 3 to 4 months of age even these infants should be responding to and turning toward a parent's voice. Questions relative to these responses must be part of health maintenance visits.

The deaf infant does not hear the baby talk and cooing sounds of his mother, and therefore by the second half of the first year his own random noises cease. Parental sounds transmit much feeling and must be replaced by enriched visual and tactile experience. This important parental intervention may not "come naturally" and specific guidance is usually necessary. Skilled medical, language, and educational efforts should be under way as soon as the hearing impairment is identified.

This is a vulnerable time for family and child as the implications of the handicap become apparent. Not only do they see a child with whom communication is difficult, but they may begin to see physical mannerisms that appear unusual when compared to other children. The deaf child, having been surprised countless times by a sudden environmental change, will frequently look up from play and visually explore his surroundings, since he lacks the continual scanning of ambient sounds that his hearing would provide. Being unable to use language to compare feelings and experiences with his peers, his identification with them is difficult and he becomes isolated, manifesting withdrawn or physically aggressive behavior. As he gets older, he is likely to find more comfort associating with other deaf children.

Of no small significance to child and parent is the reaction of other adults. The deaf child may look perfectly normal, but his performance, mannerisms, and unusual speech classify him as "strange," in contrast to the blind child who immediately elicits the utmost compassion from the observer. As illustrated in the case of R. S.,

the youngster with arthritis, normal behavior is expected from a child who looks normal.

Delayed and aberrant language development may affect thought processes and intellectual growth as well as communication. Differences have been noted in memory and in the ability to deal with abstractions, particularly when verbal symbolism is involved. Rigid, aggressive, and competitive personality characteristics have been noted, with a tendency to develop emotional and social problems. Their choices are often unrealistic and immature, tending to favor the situation offering the more immediate gratification.

Even though these difficulties relate to the communication deficit and its effect on cognitive and emotional growth, they are not inevitable. Remarkable progress is being made in the understanding and education of the deaf, but the physician may have to help guide the family to the best resources available. A hearing aid salesman does not so qualify. Although the issues may be largely educational and beyond the expertise of the primary care physician, the role of assuring that there is parental understanding of the cognitive and emotional implications of the handicap and that appropriate plans are being formulated is important.

Although the blind child (Chapter 11) may have more difficulty with his physical environment, he does have an advantage over the deaf child in his ability to form relationships. However, until he is able to understand speech, he must be stimulated by other means. He cannot imitate by watching, and he is limited in his capacity for physical exploration. There must therefore be a rich array of tactile and auditory stimuli. A parent should talk a great deal from all sides of the child and help him to experience a variety of sounds. Toys of a wide variety of sizes, textures, shapes, and weights should be provided in addition, obviously, to a great deal of human contact. It is the blind child without such compensating stimulation who develops the mannerisms and affect suggestive of autism. Blind children rarely crawl, and motor function may be delayed in other ways as well. An environment that is orderly, safe, and predictable must be provided to enable them to explore without fear of injury.

The development of unpleasant mannerisms is a major problem, which may begin at a very young age. Habitual movements, such as rolling and rocking, rubbing and poking at eyes and ears, flapping of arms and waving hands when upset or excited, and self-protective gestures such as constantly reaching out to avoid bumping into objects, all require a gentle "unlearning" process. Although speech and language may be excellent, there is no way to imitate gestures and expressions. We continually monitor reactions to our speech by the facial responses and gestures of the listener. To the child who is old enough to be aware of being seen but is not able to see the person to whom he is talking, there may be a very painful self-consciousness. Coaching in these areas is necessary, but doing so without creating a nagging kind of interaction may require considerable tactical ingenuity.

As in the case of hearing loss, age of onset and severity make a difference in the educational and emotional impact of vision loss. Even some visual experience in early life or a less than total loss of vision may make some visual perspective possible and learning easier.

Although recordings are being used increasingly, education still depends a great deal on Braille. Parents should begin to learn it when the child is young so that they are ready to help him when he reaches reading age.

Although he may be able to communicate verbally and emotionally, the child's sensory limitation makes social isolation a major problem, particularly during that time in childhood when intellectual interests are at a minimum among his peers. What can he do physically in play with one or a group of children? How can he understand untouchable experiences in his environment such as clouds, an airplane in flight, a rainbow? Bakwin and Bakwin[4] cite personality characteristics often developing in the blind. They may be suggestible, hypersensitive, and lacking in social competence with many fear reactions, lack of initiative, and a sense of inferiority.

These observations are not intended to stereotype the personality of the deaf or blind child, but to sharpen the sensitivity of the physician to the problems that may arise as a direct result of these sensory deprivations and require appropriate developmental interventions.

Seizure disorders (Chapter 7). Epilepsy is singled out for discussion because its emotional impact may be qualitatively different in some ways from that associated with other chronic illnesses. To witness a sudden and unexpected seizure is a frightening experience for a layperson whose knowledge and understanding are derived from superstition, folklore, and misinformation. Ward and Bower[56] have published a comprehensive study of psychological considerations of epilepsy. In this study 81 children who had seizures unassociated with other major disabilities were drawn from pediatric neurology practice in Oxford. Their parents were interviewed over a period of 20 months to elicit their reactions, feeling, and understanding about their child's condition and its impact on their family.

As might be expected, the first impact was related to witnessing of the seizure itself. There was fear of impending death, of choking, of the "spooky" loss of contact, and of the motor manifestations of the seizure. Even after the diagnosis was established and treatment instituted, a fear of coping with the next episode remained, particularly when the seizures were of a major motor type. This is a critical time for the physician's concentrated efforts to educate and anticipate, but this process must include exploration of the family's fears and understanding of processes and language. Seizures, convulsions, fits, epilepsy, spells, all terms medical professionals may use interchangeably, may have very different connotations to a layperson. When told her child had had a febrile seizure, a mother said to me with great relief, "I'm glad it was a seizure. I was afraid it was a convulsion!" This frequent confusion of terms is further documented in Ward and Bower's study[57].

As the initial investigation and treatment get under way, questions begin to surface about the development of mental retardation, a common lay concept being that each seizure leaves the child with a little more brain damage. Combined with the real and/or imagined effect of drugs, parents may believe they see a "slow down'' in their child's performance. They and the teachers are uncertain about what demands are appropriate, what behavior is due to ''his condition,'' how protective they must be, and what situations are realistic hazards to the child. The kind of grief reaction arising from altered expectations may become apparent as it so often does with other chronic illnesses.

Even if the physician has successfully allayed these fears in the immediate family, visions of witches and supernatural possession may still lie beneath the reactions of others. The child becomes ''peculiar,'' ''strange,'' ''different,'' and the cooling of responses from others is sensed as rejection, even when it is not overt. A grandparent or parent of a friend may be too frightened of a seizure to have the child visit overnight. Particularly when seizures have been public or when their control requires heavy medication affecting reaction time and coordination, teasing and name-calling may result, but Ward and Bowen's[57] study indicates that this occurs much less often than feared by parents. If the family learns to be confident and accepting of the condition, the child will be less embarrassed and isolated and be able to develop a forthright, matter-of-fact attitude in his peer relationships.

Although they indicated concern about reactions of school personnel, once their children were acutally in school 63% of parents expressed satisfaction with the accepting and helpful attitude of the schools, and another 26% indicated satisfaction with some qualifications.

The setting of limits and the development of behavior problems produces a number of parental dilemmas. With all children it is sometimes difficult to define the line between reasonable parental caution and overprotectiveness. This is even more difficult when there is concern that a seizure may occur when a child is in a vulnerable situation or when there is uncertainty about the degree to which medication may compromise reaction time or coordination. It takes very little time for some children to learn the manipulative possibilities in such a situation and little longer for his siblings to feel that they are not getting equal treatment.

In summary, the primary care physician's role, in addition to maintaining seizure control, is as follows:

1. Education of parents and child about epilepsy, which must include exploration into misunderstandings, myths, and confusion about terms
2. Anticipatory guidance, as specifically articulated as possible, in the areas of behavioral and performance expectations, hazards, and limitations
3. Personal contact with teachers to discuss these same issues
4. Follow-up visits that include, in addition to discussion of seizures and medications, alertness to evidences of stress in the family and sibling
5. Periodical personal discussions with the school-aged child and adolescent to assure his understanding of the disease, his feelings about himself, his peers, his school, and his compliance with treatment
6. Formation of counselling groups, particularly among adolescents and young adults with seizures, which may have special value in dealing with problems of sexuality, career planning, and social interactions

Myelodysplasia. Following vignette illustrates a very typical history for a child with myelodysplasia.

M. D. is a Caucasian girl who was born with a thoracolumbar meningomyelocele. By the time she was 3 years of age she had been hospitalized 12 times. Surgical procedures included excision of the meningomyelocele, a ventriculoatrial shunt, two shunt revisions and finally shunt removal, and three hip operations. When she was 5 years old, she was admitted three times for procedures on her dislocated hip and three times more at 8, 9, and 10 years of age. Between 12 and 13 there were four admissions for spinal fusion because of her rapidly progressing scoliosis, and at 15 she was admitted twice for treatment of a fracture of her femur.

In addition, there were frequent visits to the clinics for urinary tract infections, problems with obesity and constipation, and in recent years acne and the development of alopecia have been problems. Although she is confined to a wheelchair, she might be ambulatory with braces and crutches if her weight could be reduced. She is of average intelligence and does reasonably well in school. Her peer contacts are minimal and superficial, and if she has had sexual drives and motivations in the past, she has never discussed them. The parent-patient interaction is one of almost total dependence and resistance to efforts to make her more independent. Seemingly accepting and resigned to her handicap, she is content to do handwork with older women in her church, which is her major social outlet. Always pleasant and uncomplaining, she is quite comfortable with adults.

Myelodysplasia is the prototype of the multiple-system disability, calling on the skills of a variety of medical professions, community agencies, and special educators. Unless there is a carefully planned convergence of these resources, care may be fragmented and these various elements may at times find themselves working at cross-purposes.

As discussed in Chapter 5, a team consisting of a neurosurgeon, orthopedist, urologist, psychiatrist, and pediatrician is best equipped to manage the overlapping and complex medical problems. There must be an effective, two-way communication between the primary care physician and this team if the family and child are to receive optimal benefit from the alliance. Particularly during the initial period of shock, rapidly moving events, and agonizing decisions, a family needs a single, reliable, coordinating authority to inform, educate, interpret, and support them. It is my bias that this person should be the primary care physician, with the myelodysplasia team functioning as a consultant and resource. The physician must understand the surgical procedures and the problems likely to arise therefrom and the likely course and complications of the particular combination of disabilities the patient suffers, as far as these can be foreseen.

Neonatal period. During the immediate period after birth, at least the following tasks are necessary:

1. Informing the family as fully as available knowledge permits. Decisions regarding immediate treatment are discussed in Chapter 5.
2. Providing frequent opportunity for discussion and questioning. During the initial period of multiple consultation and decision-making regarding diagnostic and therapeutic procedures, the dynamics of grief reactions are such that repetitive explanations and clarifications are necessary.
3. Assessment of family support. It is necessary that important supporting members of the extended family, friends, and clergy be reinforcing of the therapeutic efforts decided on by family and physicians. Well-meaning and concerned persons can be a source of great strength, but they can also be undermining if ill-informed. Because a physician may not share a patient's religious faith, it may be ignored as an important resource for a troubled family and thus no effort to communicate with clergy is made.

Infancy. During the first several months, most parents become involved in the routines of daily care and physical therapy and begin to accommodate themselves to the immediate care problems and to the child's physical limitations. As questions begin to surface about the child's future and the family begins to search for more concrete signs of intellectual progress, it is important for both medical personnel and family to formulate a "life plan" as early as the parents are able. Goals beyond immediate care must be established, recognizing that the unpredictability of a child's development will necessitate many revisions. Battle[5] and Bunch and co-workers[10] have suggested outlines for such a plan, which should be continually referred to and reevaluated as the child grows and develops.

Included should be consideration of the following:

1. Physical status problems: Eventual goals are for independent means of locomotion, control of urine and feces, and maintenance of good kidney function. What medical and surgical management will be necessary to achieve these ends? What complications can be foreseen?
2. Overall health maintenance: As should be provided for every child, but is sometimes lost in the midst of the continual attention

to the medical demands of the organ-specific disabilities.

3. Developmental, social, and emotional issues: The effects on parents, siblings, marriage stability, impact of social life, in addition to those issues relative to the child's own adjustment to his handicap.

4. Maximum development of intellectual potential: Developmental and psychological assessment and educational planning from early intervention in infant through adolescence.

5. Anticipated life needs: Shelter, nurture, protection for child and parents. What is the status of family's financial security? Is there serious illness in a parent? Are parents intellectually or emotionally limited?

6. Recreational and social opportunities: For example, minimizing the effects of isolation imposed by the disability.

7. Vocational training and opportunities.

8. Eventual financial independence.

9. Attention to special concerns and needs of the parents.

The task of working out this "life plan" is formidable and time consuming, requiring a realistic grappling with many difficult and emotion-laden issues. As this plan becomes part of the child's record, the physician and family periodically reassess the child's progress toward the goals that have been defined.

Preschool. Even though the child may have minimal or no intellectual impairment, repeated hospitalizations and physical limitations may keep him out of the normal flow of explorations and experimentation with contemporaries, which is so fundamental to the development of the personality. Early educational intervention and enrichment of social experience is important. The frequent surgical interventions that may be necessary during the first few years are usually completed by about 3 years of age and attention turns to school placement.

School age. The degree of physical and intellectual handicap, widely varying in children with this diagnosis, obviously affects the nature of the school placement. Unfortunately, many communities do not have access to the resources required to make optimal educational plans for a child who has possible intellectual and emotional limitations, is in a wheelchair or uses braces or crutches, and who must use some special technique, which does not always work, to keep from soaking himself with urine.

The ever widening gap between the child's own capacities and those of his peers becomes increasingly apparent to both child and family. The reactions of others to an obvious handicap become a heavily influential factor in the complex process of shaping his self-image. It may be a delicate balance indeed for family and teachers to recognize and respect realistic limitations, yet to maintain expectations that challenge and develop the child's potential.

Fox[19] cites a combination of disabilities of particular concern to the psychologists and teachers in their formulation of educational plans for these children. (1) It was found that 25% have visual defects which may compound the already existing visuospatial difficulties of some hydrocephalic youngsters. (2) There may be a sensory deficit of the upper extremities that compromises fine motor coordination. (3) Some children with hydrocephalus have aberrant language development, characterized by "cocktail party chatter," a deceptively appropriate-sounding loquacity with little content and coupled with poor comprehension of speech.

In later elementary grades the child's peers are rapidly accelerating in intellectual and physical skills, a new body consciousness, achievement in athletics, and pride in their accomplishments. The clubs, cliques, comraderie, and cooperative adventures, which are so much a part of this age, may drive the child with myelodysplasia even further into isolation and depression unless alternative gratifications and contacts are generated.

Adolescents. Dorner[18] reports an interview study of 46 adolescents, 21 boys and 25 girls, with spina bifida. Girls were generally more unhappy than boys, but were also the more severely handicapped. About half the girls had expressed feelings of hopelessness and not wanting to live within the previous year. In both sexes there was depression related to future career plans and to problems around marriage and having a family. However, 11 of the group were leading reasonably satisfying lives with good peer and family relationships and had positive feeling about school. Only a few patients had been able to establish heterosexual relationships. Even those with reasonable mobility may have urinary appliances or diversions, the embarrassment of which inhibits them from sexual activity. Even among the minority of boys who can achieve erection, the ability to ejaculate is doubtful. Girls may or may not have some degree of genital sensation depending on the level of the lesion, but intercourse is generally possible in most cases, as is pregnancy and the vaginal delivery of an infant.

Of primary importance, however, is the clear evidence that the majority of these youngsters have the drives and concerns about sex and marriage of all adolescents and therefore the profound need for sensitive and competent counselling. An all too common assumption is that because the patient may not bring up the issue, it must not be important to him. It is a confident youngster who will initiate such discussions. If we are reticent to discuss sexual matters with our healthy adolescent patients, we are struck dumb when confronted with a handicapped one!

Although some of the success among the 11 patients in Dorner's[18] study was related to the lesser degree of severity of their handicap, a more social life seemed to be an issue of greater importance in their adjustment. This study points up the need for energetic efforts to provide easily accessible, informed, and competent counselling as sexual problems and career planning become urgent realities. Although many are able to maintain at least superficial friendships among school mates, their major need is for regular peer contact outside of school. This will not usually just "happen" as with healthy youngsters, but rather must be planned actively.

The successful passage through each developmental period prepares the youngster for the next, whether healthy or disabled. The child with myelodysplasia will be less isolated as an adolescent if, from infancy, his family and physicians have helped him maintain as lively a contact with his peers as his mobility and limitations will allow. As Dorner[18] and others have stated, serious problems are not inevitable.

SUMMARY

In summary, the chronically ill or disabled child and his family require comprehensive, coordinated health care and support. Families work through problems in their own way and in their own time, but may need help doing so. The child needs sensory stimulation and social contact to lessen the boredom, apathy, shame, and humiliation accompanying his disability and continual challenge to avoid resignation, defeat, and regression; there must be a monitoring for emotional developments that may require psychiatric referral.

Although no primary care physician can be expected to have the knowledge, competence, and time to "do it all," who else has the global perspective to coordinate and direct the resources that can fulfill those needs? Many of these children do succeed, and they deserve the most energetic of professional advocates.

REFERENCES

1. Alpert, J. J.: Infancy and early childhood. In Green, M., and Haggerty, R. J., editors: Ambulatory pediatrics II, Philadelphia, 1977, W. B. Saunders Co., pp. 384-401.
2. Apley, J.: The child with abdominal pains. ed. 2, Oxford, 1975, Blackwell Scientific Publications, Ltd.
3. Bakwin, H., and Bakwin, R. M., editors: Behavior disorders in children, ed. 4, Philadelphia, 1972, W. B. Saunders Co.
4. Bakwin, H., and Bakwin, R. M.: Part 3—Care of the physically ill or handicapped child. In Bakwin H., and Bakwin, R. M., editors: Behavior disorders in children, ed. 4, Philadelphia, 1972, W. B. Saunders Co., pp. 121-193.
5. Battle, C. V.: Chronic physical disease, behavioral aspects, Pediatr. Clin. North Am. **22:**525, 1975.
6. Bender, L.: The life course of children with schizophrenia, Am. J. Psychiatry **130:**783, 1973.
7. Bender, L.: A career of clinical research in child psychiatry. In Anthony, S. J., editor: Explorations in child psychiatry, New York, 1975, Plenum Publishing Corp., p. 457.
8. Bibace, R., and Walsh, M.: Development of childrens' concept of health and illness, Pediatrics (in press).
9. Blos, P., Jr., and Finch, S. M.: Sexuality and the handicapped adolescent. In Downey, J. A., and Low, N. L., editors: The child with disabling illness, principles of rehabilitation, Philadelphia, 1974, W. B. Saunders Co., pp. 521-540.
10. Bunch, W. H., et al.: Modern management of myelomeningocele, St. Louis, 1972, Warren H. Green, Inc., chapter 6, pp. 181-209.
11. Burton, L.: The family life of sick children, London, 1975, Routledge and Kegan Paul, Ltd., p. 231.

12. Carey, W. B.: Clinical applications of infant temperament measurements, J. Pediatr. **81**:823, 1972.

13. Carey, W. B., and McDevitt, S. C.: Revision of infant temperament questionnaire, Pediatrics **61**:735, 1978.

14. Chamberlin, R. W.: Early recognition and modification of vicious circle parent-child relationships, Clin. Pediatr. **6**:469, 1967.

15. Chamberlin, R. W.: Syllabus for developmental pediatrics, University of Rochester School of Medicine and Dentistry, unpublished data.

16. Chamberlin, R. W.: Syllabus for developmental pediatrics, Pediatr. Clin. North Am. **21**:1, 1974.

17. Chamberlin, R. W.: Can we identify a group of children at age 2 who are at high risk for the development of behavior or emotional problems in kindergarten and first grade? Pediatrics **59** (part 2, suppl.):971, June 1977.

18. Dorner, S.: Adolescents with spina bifida. How they see their situation, Arch. Dis. Child. **51**:439, 1976.

19. Fox, A. M.: Review: the special educational needs of physically handicapped children, Child Care Health Dev. **2**:45, 1976.

20. Friedman, S. B.: Conversion symptoms in adolescents, Pediatr. Clin. North Am. **20**:873, 1973.

21. Gath, A.: The impact of an abnormal child upon the parents, Br. J. Psychiatry **130**:405, 1977.

22. Gayton, W. R.: Down syndrome: informing the parents, Am. J. Dis. Child. **127**:510, 1974.

23. Green, M.: The management of long-term non life-threatening illness. In Green, M., and Haggerty, R. J., editors: Ambulatory pediatrics I, Philadelphia, 1968, W. B. Saunders Co., pp. 443-450.

24. Haggerty, R. J.: Adolescence. In Green, M., and Haggerty, R. J., editors: Ambulatory Pediatrics II, Philadelphia, 1977, W. B. Saunders Co., pp. 425-425.

25. Hoekelman, R. A., Kelly, J., and Zimmer, A. W.: The reliability of maternal recall: mothers' remembrance of their infants' health and illness, Clin. Pediatr. **15**:261, 1976.

26. Kanner, L.: Autistic disturbances of affective contact, Nerv. Child **2**:217, 1943.

27. Kanthor, H., et al.: Areas of responsibility in the health care of the multiply handicapped child, Pediatrics **54**:779, 1974.

28. Klaus, M. H., et al.: Maternal attachment. Importance of the first postpartum days, N. Engl. J. Med. **286**:460, 1972.

29. Mac Keith, R.: The feelings and behavior of parents of handicapped children, Dev. Med. Child Neurol. **15**:524, 1973.

30. Mahler, M. S., and Gosliner, E. J.: On symbiotic child psychosis, Psychoanal. Study Child **10**:142, 1955.

31. Mattson, A.: Long-term physical illness is childhood: a challenge to psychosocial adaptation, Pediatrics **50**:801, 1972.

32. McAnarney, E. R., et al.: Psychological problems of children with chronic juvenile arthritis, Pediatrics **53**:523, 1974.

33. McConnochie, K.: Structure of the pediatric record. In Hoekelman, R. A., et al., editors: Principles of pediatrics: health care of the young, New York, 1978, McGraw-Hill Book Co.

34. Miller, L.: Toward a greater understanding of parents of mentally retarded children, J. Pediatr. **73**:699, 1968.

35. Myklebust, H. R.: The psychology of deafness, New York, 1964, Grune & Stratton, Inc.

36. Olshansky, S.: Chronic sorrow: a response to having a mentally defective child, Soc. Casework **43**:190, 1962.

37. O'Neal, P., and Robins, L.: Childhood patterns predictive of adult schizophrenia: a 30-year follow-up study, Am. J. Psychiatry **115**:385, 1958.

38. Palfrey, J. S., Mervis, R. C., and Butler, J. A.: New directions in the evaluation and education of handicapped children, N. Engl. J. Med. **298**:819, 1978.

39. Piaget, J., and Inhelder, B.: The psychology of the child, New York, 1969, Basic Books, Inc.

40. Pless, I. B., and Satterwhite, B.: A measure of family functioning and its application, Soc. Sci. Med. **7**:613, 1973.

41. Provence, S.: Developmental assessment. in: Green, M., and Haggerty, R. J., editors: Ambulatory pediatrics II, Philadelphia, 1977, W. B. Saunders Co., pp. 374-383.

42. Psychopathological disorders in childhood: theoretical considerations and a proposed classification, New York, 1966, Group for the Advancement of Psychiatry.

43. Ritvo, E. R., editor: Autism, New York, 1976, Spectrum Publishing.

44. Rutter, M.: Autistic children: infancy to adulthood, Semin. Psychiatry **2**:435, 1970.

45. Schmitt, B. D., Duncan, B. R., and Riley, C. M.: Ambulatory pediatrics. In Kempe, C. H., Silver, H. K., and O'Brien, D., editors: Current pediatric diagnosis and treatment, Los Altos, 1974, Lange Medical Publications, pp. 152-170.

46. Schopler, E.: Towards reducing behavior problems in autistic children. In Wing, L., editor: Early childhood autism, Oxford, 1976, Pergamon Press, Ltd., pp. 221-245.

47. Schutt, W. H.: Critical issues in the management of adolescents with handicaps, Proc. R. Soc. Med. **68**:309, 1975.

48. Seidel, V. P., Chadwick, O. F. D., and Rutter, M.: Psychological disorders in crippled children. A comparative study of children with and without brain damage, Dev. Med. Child Neurol. **17**:563, 1975.

49. Shirley, H. F.: Pediatric psychiatry, Cambridge, Mass., 1963, Harvard University Press.

50. Shore, M. F., editor: Red is the color of hurting, Bethesda, Md., 1967, USPHS pub. no. 1583, U. S. Public Health Service.

51. Spitz, R. A.: Anaclitic depression, Psychoanal. Study Child **2**:313, 1946.

52. Sumpter, E. A.: Behavior problems in early childhood, Pediatr. Clin. North Am. **22**:663, 1975.

53. Sumpter, E. A., and Charney, E.: Health promotion in the four to ten year old child. In Green, M., and Haggerty, R. J., editors: Ambulatory pediatrics II,

Philadelphia, 1977, W. B. Saunders Co., pp. 401-414.

54. Thomas, A., and Chess, S., editors: Temperament and development, New York, 1977, Brunner/Mazel, Inc.

55. Thomas, A., Chess, S., and Birch, N. G.: Temperament and behavior disorders in children, New York, 1968, New York University Press.

56. Thomas, A., Chess, S., and Korn, S.: Parent and teacher temperament questionnaire for children 3-7 years of age. In Thomas, A., and Chess, S., editors: Temperament and development, New York, 1977, Brunner/Mazel, Inc., Appendix 8, pp. 222-247.

57. Ward, F., and Bower, B. D.: A study of certain social

aspects of epilepsy in childhood, Dev. Med. Child Neurol. **20**(suppl. 39): entire issue, 1978.

58. Willoughby, J. A., and Haggerty, R. J.: A simple behavior questionnaire for preschool children, Pediatrics **34**:798, 1964.

59. Wing, L., editor: Early childhood autism, Oxford, 1976, Pergamon Press, Ltd.

60. Wing, L.: Diagnosis, clinical description and prognosis. In Wing, L., editor: Early childhood autism, Oxford, 1976, Peragmon Press, Ltd., chapter 2, pp. 15-52.

61. Wing, L.: Epidemiology and theories of etiology. In Wing, L., editor: Early childhood autism, Oxford, 1976, Pergamon Press, Ltd., chapter 3, pp. 65-72.

16

The dental care of the developmentally disabled child

F. Edward Gallagher

The recognition and management of oral problems in the child with a developmental disability is an area that until recently has been both misunderstood and poorly documented. This situation has existed despite the importance of and concentration on the development of feeding and language in these children. Dental consultation has frequently been overlooked in the planning for their care because of overriding medical concerns in some instances and the lack of accessibility in others. The result has often been the failure to resolve difficulties to the detriment of the patient. It is now recognized that an understanding of oral growth and development can impact strongly on the diagnosis and effective management.

Dental disease is the most prevalent chronic disease faced by society at large. Approximately one third of Americans receive either no care or purely symptomatic treatment. This appalling fact is magnified in the developmentally disabled youngster. Dental caries or decay is an entity that can be prevented in most cases with early screening and education. A multitude of developmental problems can be ameliorated by early diagnosis and treatment, when assessed in an appropriate context. The guidance of oral maturation, not simply dental development, can improve an individual's health, function, and psychological image.

It has been observed that a caste system exists within the health care complex. The socially, economically, or physically disadvantaged patient may have discernible difficulty in obtaining services. Access to dental evaluation and treatment may be the most difficult. The location and utilization of these services in the community is important. With the advent of the concepts of ''deinstitutionalization'' and ''normalization'' the emerging population of ambulatory and semiambulatory patients has outstripped the normally identified available services. Families often are discouraged in their search for care by the barriers of acceptability and cost. These are surmountable problems,

☐ Supported in part by Project 928, Maternal and Child Health Service, Public Health Service, Department of Health, Education and Welfare.

particularly if appropriate referrals are made by the pediatrician at the earliest possible date. The role of the pediatrician as the primary diagnostician and most practical interface with the health care community cannot be stressed enough.

As a general rule, most children should be seen for dental consultation by their third birthday, although many practitioners ascribe a date as early as 1 year of age. This is especially true for nutritional review and counselling, assessment of potentially aberrant feeding patterns, and the deliverance of expository preventive materials. This becomes particularly important for the child with any perceived developmental delay because the remediation of their problems is difficult. Team consultation at this stage enables planning for many related areas to proceed rationally and ensures the maximum in oral health.

THE DEVELOPMENT OF THE ORAL STRUCTURES

To recognize and appreciate divergence from the norm, it is necessary to briefly outline the expected sequence of oral development. The dental lamina of the embryo begins its ectodermal invagination at the six week, or 11 mm stage. By the fourth month of the pregnancy, ameloblasts derived from the horseshoe-shaped lamina have begun the deposition of the matrix of the primary dentition, with the initiation of the crowns of the maxillary primary central incisors.[7,16] Sequentially, the 20 primary teeth

Table 16-1. Chronology of the human dentition and relative caries susceptibility*

Tooth	Amount of enamel formed at birth	Enamel completed	Eruption	Relative caries susceptibility
Primary dentition				
Maxillary				
Central incisor	5/6	1½ months	10 months	
Lateral incisor	2/3	2½ months	11 months	
Canine	1/3	9 months	19 months	
First molar	½ to ¾ crown	6 months	16 months	Very susceptible
Second molar	Cusps united	11 months	29 months	Very susceptible
Mandibular				
Central incisor	3/5	2½ months	8 months	
Lateral incisor	3/5	3 months	13 months	
Canine	1/3	9 months	20 months	
First molar	Cusps united	5½ months	16 months	Very susceptible
Second molar	Cusps united	10 months	27 months	Very susceptible
Permanent dentition				
Maxillary				
Central incisor		4 to 5 years	7 to 8 years	
Lateral incisor		4 to 5 years	8 to 9 years	
Cuspid		6 to 7 years	11 to 12 years	
First bicuspid		5 to 6 years	10 to 11 years	
Second bicuspid		7 to 7 years	10 to 12 years	Very susceptible
First molar	Sometimes a trace	2½ to 3 years	6 to 7 years	Highly susceptible
Second molar		7 to 8 years	12 to 13 years	Highly susceptible
Mandibular				
Central incisor		4 to 5 years	6 to 7 years	
Lateral incisor		4 to 5 years	7 to 8 years	
Cuspid		6 to 7 years	9 to 10 years	
First bicuspid		5 to 6 years	10 to 12 years	
Second bicuspid		6 to 7 years	11 to 12 years	Very susceptible
First molar	Sometimes a trace	2½ to 3 years	6 to 7 years	Highly susceptible
Second molar		7 to 8 years	11 to 13 years	Highly susceptible

*Courtesy Dr. Edward Sweeney, Harvard School of Dental Medicine.

begin to calcify after the matrix is deposited, with all primary enamel being deposited by the child's first birthday. The analogous process for the permanent dentition begins within the first 6 months of life and is completed for the second permanent molars by 8 years (Table 16-1).

The result of this process is a documented chronological calendar of development that becomes evident with the eruption of each tooth, both primary and permanent. This calendar can be marked by developmental interferences, which interrupt or arrest the function of the ameloblast, causing hypoplastic lines or spots to appear. Knowing that calcification begins at the biting edge or surface and proceeds to the gingival margin, temporal estimates of developmental interruptions can be made (Fig. 16-1).

Other oral structures also undergo much of their definition midway through the first trimester. Between the fifth and seventh weeks of embryonic development, the maxillary process coalesces with the median and lateral nasal processes to form the upper lip.[7,16] The median nasal processes also form the philtrum of the upper lip, the incisor section of the maxilla, and the triangular primary palate. Similarly, at 6 weeks deep outgrowths of the maxillary process appear. At 7 weeks the tongue drops down from between these structures and the palatal shelves rise, fusing anteriorly-posteriorly from the incisal foramen to the uvula. The tongue begins its development around the fourth week

of embryonic life anteriorly as a coalescence of swellings of the mandibular arch and posteriorly by mesodermal components of the second, third, and fourth arches. The body of the tongue is innervated by the mandibular branch of the trigeminal nerve, while the base of the tongue receives most of its innervation from the glossopharyngeal nerve. Interruptions in development during this period lead to the variety of clefts and a plethora of related oral developmental problems.

EARLY PROBLEMS AND EARLY DIAGNOSIS

The initial entry of a developmentally handicapped child into the health care delivery system is often prompted by a perioral finding or event. Although obvious syndromology or the determination of anomalous development is a flag, more subtle affectations may be noted due to difficulties in early feeding, the eruption of the dentition, or the delay in the development of speech. These may be among the earliest signs of a more overriding delay.

The feeding process

The feeding process is a complex physical and psychosocial blend that reflects early structural and neuromuscular development.[6] The ability to suck depends on the competency of the lip structure, the relationship of the mandible to the maxilla, and the integrity of the

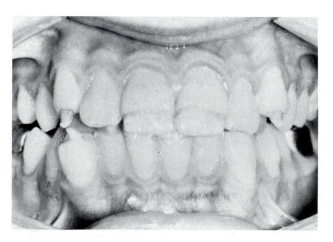

Fig. 16-1. Linear hypoplasia of the anterior teeth caused by a serious illness with high temperatures at approximately 1 year of age.

palatal components. Infants with difficulties in early feeding behavior or infants whose developmental milestones are delayed beyond normal expectations should receive a thorough oral examination to ascertain potential problems. There is a distinct need for early intervention to counteract any perceived nutritional deficits, since the young child is at substantial risk. Parents may not be aware of actual intake, ascribing feeding difficulties to normal fussiness.

There are several components that interrelate to the complex feeding process, notably reflex-ivity and tone. The formation of an effective oral seal is necessary for the management of liquids and food. To obtain this seal requires that the lips meet with sufficient muscular tone to prevent a reflux of any bolus out of the mouth and that the oral cavity has the integrity to prevent reflux into other areas. Interruptions of this seal obviously diminish the amount of food actually swallowed. Such breaks in the seal can result from a decreased tone in the orbicularis oris complex, a physical break in this complex as with cleft lip, or a relationship of the mandible and maxilla precluding normal apposition

Table 16-2. Normal oral reflexes

Reflex	Description
Moro reflex	A proprioceptive response elicited by dropping the head back suddenly; the response includes a rapid extension and abduction of the limbs, followed by flexion and adduction of the limbs Normal occurrence: Birth to 4 months Retention produces: Total body responses to stimuli Interferes with: Sitting balance; hand-to-mouth activities
Asymmetrical tonic neck reflex	A proprioceptive response elicited by turning the head from side to side; increased extension is seen on the side to which the face is turned and increased flexion in the opposite limbs Normal occurrence: Birth to 4 months Retention produces: Asymmetrical postures Interferes with: Sitting balance; hand-to-mouth activities
Hand grasp	A stimulus to the palm of the hand (from the ulnar side) elicits finger flexing and grasping of the object Normal occurrence: Birth to 3 or 4 months Retention produces: Fisted hands; difficulty in opening hands Interferes with: Holding utensils
Suckle-swallow	A stimulus introduced into the mouth elicits vigorous sucking followed by a swallow if liquid is present Normal occurrence: 1 or 2 days after birth to 3 to 5 months Retention produces: Suckling response to any oral stimuli Interferes with: Taking food from spoon with lips; cup drinking; chewing
Rooting	A stimulus to the oral area (corners of the mouth, upper and lower lip) causes lips, tongue, and finally head to turn toward the stimulus Normal occurrence: Birth to 3 to 5 months Retention produces: Asymmetrical oral response to stimuli; head turning to oral stimuli Interferes with: Maintaining head position for appropriate feeding

Gag	A stimulus to the posterior tongue or soft palate causes constriction of the posterior oral musculature to bring stimulating substance forward
	Normal occurrence: Birth to adulthood
	Retention produces: Increased oral sensitivity
	Interferes with:
	    Hyperactive gag—Food is constantly pushed forward and out of the mouth
	    Hypoactive gag—Food can passively enter the esophagus or trachea

Bite	Pressure on the gums elicits a phasic bite and release Normal occurrence: Birth to 3 to 5 months Retention produces: Biting all objects placed in the mouth Interferes with: Mouthing activities; ingesting food; more mature biting; chewing

From Nutrition in clinical care by Howard, R. B., and Herbold, N. Copyright © 1978 McGraw-Hill Book Co. Used with permission of McGraw-Hill Book Co.

of the lips. Any of these can result in an open mouth, allowing more than normal extrusion or loss during swallowing.

The swallowing process in the newborn is initially governed by a set of reflexes that persist through the early months of life. The extension of these reflexes beyond normal dates is an indication to observe the actual feeding process. The initial rooting reflex is complemented by the suckle-swallow reflex, which also requires adequate tone of the lip structures. Flaccidity in this area or lack of ability to sustain the suckle-swallow burst can reduce the efficiency of feeding. This process is mediated by the posterior section of the tongue and is primarily an anterior-posterior movement transferring the food to the posterior pharynx for swallowing. The size of the bolus is regulated by both the gag and extrusion reflexes. The gag reflex appears to be more anteriorized from birth through 6 months before becoming an essentially posterior process. Early manifestation of this reflex on stimulation is not necessarily notable. The extrusion reflex is a tongue reaction that persists through 4 months of age with excessive food being pushed out of the oral cavity. By the time the youngster is 5 months of age the lips can approximate to a cup and the sucking reflex becomes voluntary (Table 16-2).

The evaluation of the feeding process should include a look at this normal framework. It should take into account the positioning of the child. A child fed in an extended body and neck position may be more prone to gagging and have more difficulty in swallowing than the child who is fed while flexed forward with head and body support. The reflexes should also be assessed. A child with developmental problems may exhibit immaturity of these reflexes from an early age, having either intense or almost absent responses. Persistent rooting may lead to excessive head motion and interfere with feeding in the child with central nervous system dysfunction. Persistence of the suckle-swallow reflex may interfere with the acquisition of cup and utensil skills and the introduction of textured foods to the diet. The bite and gag reflexes may be increased in hypertonic children and diminished or absent in hypotonic youngsters.

In severely affected individual these findings can remain for life. The child's response to the manipulation of the oral tissues may also give an indication of his experience with oral sensation, becoming more rigid or remaining hypotonic when stimulated. This may parallel the findings in the jaw, lips, and tongue and be an indication of overall motor development. Similarly, a child with a shortened or impaired palatal velum may exhibit considerable difficulty in the swallowing process, with gagging and nasal reflux. The velum should be inspected for potential problems. Certainly these examinations cannot represent a thorough diagnostic procedure but they can be indications of delays in the oral developmental process. Much of the interaction between parent and child surrounds feeding, and the interpersonal aspects of this process cannot be overlooked (Table 16-3).

The speech process

A second area of concern to parents is the early development of speech in their children. The development of speech and language is a complex process related to the maturation of cognitive and motor skills and can be substantially delayed by neurological or anatomical deficits in the oral motor area.[11] A definitive analysis of these problems is not appropriate at this point, but a brief synopsis of several systems is pertinent (Chapters 3 and 12).

The difficulties associated with cleft lip and palate are well recognized. More subtle, however, is the problem of velopharyngeal incompetence. Submucous clefts, insufficient velar length (or increased pharyngeal depth), or neurological impairment of the soft palate can lead to the inability to effect nasopharyngeal closure. This may not only allow food reflux but also a hypernasal vocal quality. In the child who additionally has difficulties with motor control of the tongue, speech can be markedly impaired. Some of this impairment can be compensated for by the mass of palatine tonsils and adenoidal tissue. Although the hypertrophy of this tissue may also cause difficulties, the child's development and speech must be carefully assessed before surgical removal is recommended.

Table 16-3. Development of feeding skills

Age	Oral and neuromuscular development	Feeding behavior
Birth	Rooting reflex	Turns mouth toward nipple or any object brushing cheek
	Sucking reflex	
	Swallowing reflex	Initial swallowing involves the posterior of the tongue; by 9 to 12 weeks anterior portion is increasingly involved which facilitates ingestion of semisolid food
	Extrusion reflex	Pushes food out when placed on tongue; strong the first 9 weeks
		By 6 to 10 weeks recognizes the position in which he is fed and begins mouthing and sucking when placed in this position
3 to 6 months	Beginning coordination between eyes and body movements	Explores world with eyes, fingers, hands, and mouth; starts reaching for objects at 4 months but overshoots; hands get in the way during feeding
	Learning to reach mouth with hands at 4 months	Finger sucking—by 6 months all objects to into the mouth
	Extrusion reflex present until 4 months	May continue to push out food placed on tongue
	Able to grasp objects voluntarily at 5 months	Grasps objects in mitten-like fashion
	Sucking reflex becomes voluntary and lateral motions of the jaw begin	Can approximate lips to the rim of cup by 5 months; chewing action begins; by 6 months begins drinking from cup
6 to 12 months	Eyes and hands working together	Brings hand to mouth; at 7 months able to feed self biscuit
	Sits erect with support at 6 months	Bangs cup and objects on table at 7 months
	Sits erect without support at 9 months	
	Development of grasp (finger to thumb opposition)	Holds own bottle at 9 to 12 months
		Pincer approach to food
		Pokes at food with index finger at 10 months
	Relates to objects at 10 months	Reaches for food and utensils including those beyond reach; pushes plate around with spoon.
		Insists on holding spoon not to put in mouth but to return to plate or cup
1 to 3 years	Development of manual dexterity	Increased desire to feed self
		15 months—begins to use spoon but turns it before reaching mouth; may hold cup, likely to tilt the cup rather than head, causing spilling
		18 months—eats with spoon, spills frequently, turns spoon in mouth; holds glass with both hands
		2 years—inserts spoon correctly, occasionally with one hand; holds glass; plays with food; distinguishes between food and inedible materials
		2-3 years—self-feeding complete with occasional spilling; uses fork; pours from pitcher; obtains drink of water from faucet

From Nutrition in development by Getchel, E., and Howard, R. B. In Comprehensive pediatric nursing, ed. 2, by Scipien, G., et al. Copyright © 1979 McGraw-Hill Book Co. Used with permission of McGraw-Hill Book Co.

Irregularities in the dental arches can also affect these processes. Certainly a cleft of the alveolar ridge, with an associated cleft lip and the resulting malpositioning of teeth, may allow excessive air leakage from the mouth. This leakage also results from a malalignment of the jaws (a retrognathic or prognathic mandible or maxilla) or from a bite altered by either local (thumb or finger) or congenital factors. A contributing cause also might be an inappropriately sized tongue. Although true macroglossia and microglossia are rare, their effect on speech is obvious. The more common occurrence is a relative macroglossia, in which the tongue is "normal" size but the lower two thirds of the face are altered (for example, as in Down syndrome), creating an insufficiently large oral cavity to accommodate the tongue. Alterations of the alveolar ridges may also contribute to speech problems. Severe phenytoin (Dilantin) hyperplasia or increased ridge size (as in Down syndrome) may constrict the movements of the tongue and impede the normal airflow.

These conditions exist separately and in combination. Their presence in a youngster with overlying developmental problems complicates an already complex process. Remediation is sometimes available through dental treatment. The prosthetic placement of an obturator limits the escape of air from the compromised palate while creating a stabilizing surface for the pharyngeal muscles, enabling some closure to exist. This appliance, also known as a speech bulb, consists of an anterior stabilizing segment, usually acrylic, covering the hard palate and a posterior "bulb component," also of acrylic, filling the tissue void (Fig. 16-2). The orthodontic realignment of the permanent teeth also provides more competent dental stops, as can the placement of prosthetic "denturelike" appliances even in the deciduous dentition. Finally, surgical recontouring of bony defects, removal of hypertrophied tissue, and the repositioning of jaw components can be of great assistance when indicated. These procedures should be undertaken judiciously with a reasonable understanding of the overall benefit. Most often the appropriate forum for such a decision is in a team consultation. This team might include a speech pathologist, nutritionist, and psychologist in addition to the pediatrician and dentist.

ORAL EXAMINATION AND EVALUATION

Having delineated some of the developmental and functional aspects of the oral-motor complex, it is essential to understand at least one technique for the evaluation of its components. This is based on the experiential format and is not meant to preclude alternative approaches. It does try to include the philosophy of looking at the whole child and not just the mouth.

In the developmental model the examination of the oral structures should proceed in an ordered fashion, considering each component in relation to the entire milieu. The evaluation should have a progressive rationale similar to a review of systems or a physical examination. It should be designed to garner the easily accessible information first, leaving the more difficult components to the end of the session. It is essential to proceed slowly because many children are extremely reticient about oral examination. Three reasons may be considered for this. First, the developmentally disabled child may have had less oral stimulation and be increasingly sensitive. Second, many youngsters may have had multiple previous examinations, and, finally, most children are afraid of the unknown. Autistic children, particularly, are extremely anxious about this perceived invasion as are children whose sensory deprivation preclude full awareness of events. Also, the triggering of hyperactive reflexes can diminish a child's cooperation.

An effective introductory technique is to seat the child, if possible, on an examining table. Standing or kneeling at a slight distance, and preferably at eye level, the child's fingers can be counted by the examiner while presenting the analogy that the teeth will be counted in a similar fashion. This establishes initial tactile contact in a nonthreatening manner and enables the examiner to gather several pieces of in-

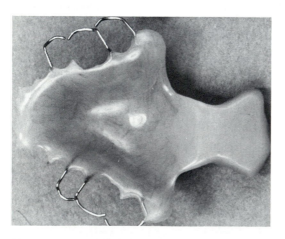

Fig. 16-2. Obturator appliance. (Courtesy Dr. Robert Mason, Orofacial and Communicative Disorders Program, University of North Carolina, Chapel Hill, N.C.)

formation. Initial observation of the child's facial structures, symmetries, and eye contact can be noted as well as evidence of oral habits such as drooling, tongue protrusion, mouth breathing, or digital habits such as thumb sucking. The latter is best noted by a whitened or callused finger or thumb. One can also assess the child's ability to relate to the process and his attention span. A patient that withdraws or squirms will have to be positioned for further examination.

Stabilization of the developmentally disabled child is a major component in the success of the examination. Patients with neuromuscular involvement or increased activity levels need head support for effective observation. This might appropriately be rendered in a supporting wheelchair if the child uses one or it can be effected by placing the child in a supine position near the end of an examining table and examining from the head of the table in an inverted manner. The head can be gently restrained from lateral motion with the forearms while the parent reassures the child and restrains the hands. For the smaller child a similar effect may be achieved by sitting ''knee to knee'' with the parent, positioning the child's head in the examiner's lap. All necessary instruments should ideally be in place before positioning the patient, especially some aid to assist the child in maintaining an open mouth. Persistent reflexes or neuromuscular involvement make this more important. In the clinical setting a rubberized bite-block with a string attached for easy retrieval or several taped tongue blades should suffice.

Perioral assessment—the lips, cheeks, and temporomandibular joint

Consistent with the philosophy of ''easiest first,'' the examination should proceed from extraoral to intraoral. Having already noted the size and shape of the head from the frontal view, a lateral observation should be made, documenting any superficial anomalies (ear tags, swellings, etc.). The relationship of the upper jaw to the lower jaw and the profile give an indication of the underlying bony, or basal arch, relationship. A flat, or orthognathic, profile is considered normal. Marked discrepan-

cies such as a retruded mandible (Pierre Robin syndrome) may have implications on the early feeding process, since food may not be maintained within the mouth. This disparity may also limit the approximation of the lips, decreasing food stasis and sucking if severe. If there is substantial soft tissue or if there is a prominent chin, the maxillomandibular relationship may be masked. A more accurate impression of this juxtaposition may be attained by placing a finger and a thumb just above and below the lips and pressing inward to establish the position of the dental arches. In the child with a prognathic mandible the gonial angle at the bend in the mandible should also be noted. An approximation of this angle can be obtained by placing a tongue blade along the back of the ramus by the ear and another along the inferior border of the jaw. The more obtuse this angle appears, the less chance the child has for outgrowing this pattern because it is an indication of a vertical growth pattern associated with this type of development.

The lips should also be observed in lateral profile before returning to a frontal examination. Large lip structures can mask some incompetence of these structures. Lip competency is defined as the ability to approximate these structures and form the anterior oral seal. The band of muscles surrounding the mouth, the orbicularis oris complex, must be able to generate sufficient tone to maintain this seal (Fig. 16-3). If the jaw alignment or a cleft does not preclude this, the tone should be assessed

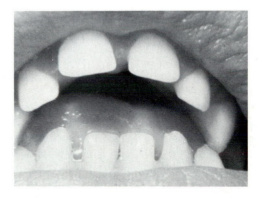

Fig. 16-3. Incompetent oral seal with an anterior open bite. (Courtesy Dr. Manouch Darvish, Worchester, Mass.)

by having the child "suck" with the lips closed. A child with good tone can make it difficult for the examiner to place a finger in the mucobuccal area with this exercise. A child with insufficient tone will have a flaccid feel to the lips, may have a problem with drooling, and can offer little resistance to examination. This youngster will also have a limited ability to kiss, which has both clinical and interpersonal implications. It may relate to a generalized hypotonicity or to a local neurological deficit. Hence drooping of one corner of the lip or an asymmetrical smile should be documented at this point. This impressionistic approach can be quantified with the use of a tonometer or can be assessed by placing a button on a string inside the lips and determining the child's ability to resist displacement. One should also determine whether an opened mouth appearance with a perceived weakness is related to these factors or to pharyngeal causes. Large tonsils and adenoids, chronic upper respiratory infections with blocked nasal passages, nasal incompetence, or a relative macroglossia can cause mouth breathing and underutilization of the lips, resulting in weakness. Exercises such as resistance to button displacement already mentioned can help to increase tone if the cause for the weakness is understood or has been eliminated.

Similarly, the tone of the cheek muscles should be examined. Although the techniques for this assessment are imperfect, this parameter should not be ignored, since a marked weakness in the buccinator muscles can result in the inadvertent "squirreling" of food in the mucobuccal pouch. It is sometimes impossible for the tongue with limited lateral movement to retrieve food from this area if the musculature cannot constrict to force the bolus back toward the center of the mouth. Some youngsters will compensate by clearing this area of food with their finger during a meal. By placing an index finger into the mucobuccal fold external to the teeth, one should gain a crude impression of the child's ability to suck inward or resist lateral displacement. Needless to say, this should be done with some caution in a child whose bite reflex is still prominent.

The temporomandibular joint represents the hinge on which the mandible swings. It should allow for both vertical and lateral motion of the lower jaw as well as a sufficient width of opening to introduce foods. The chewing cycle is not simply an up-and-down motion but is more elliptical. Up-and-down closure would limit the mobility of foods within the mouth and inhibit mastication. This elliptical motion is governed by the competency of the joint as well as the muscle mass that guides the lower jaw, the masseteric sling. The examination of these components should begin by having the child open as wide as possible while the examiner's fingers rest over the joint in front of the ears. This allows documentation of the width of opening as well as any deviation on opening. Arthrosis of one or both of the joints due to trauma is more common in a population of youngsters with balance and coordination difficulties. Palpation of the joint on opening and closing may also reveal crepitation or clicking. These findings may again relate to trauma, particularly in the symphysis or chin area or might be a result of a disharmony of the maxillomandibular relationship, a malocclusion, or bruxism. These discrepancies or habits can affect the joint itself as well as place inordinate stress on the supporting musculature with resultant spasm. Both hypertonicity and hypotonicity of the masseteric sling can affect the ease and efficiency of chewing. While local therapy such as heat or muscle relaxants may ameliorate this condition, a dental consultation might be necessary to define the cause.

Intraoral examination

Having completed the peripheral examination, the intraoral section should initiate with a notation of the breath. Although odors are hard to define, certain types, such as the ketone odor of diabetes, can be most significant. Dentally, however, most odors are caused by local factors. The stasis of food on and around the teeth is the most recognized cause. Its elimination results from the removal of this debris, which incorporates brushing and flossing as well as restorative dentistry to reduce the entrapment of food within open cavities. Its occurrence may be greater in the developmentally delayed population because the difficulty of oral hygiene increases. Also, many youngsters with chronic underlying disease can be prone to dehydration, which alters the oral environment by increasing the precipitation of calcium salts from the saliva. There may be a notable increase in plaque and calculus as well as an alternation of the oral flora. Debris can also lodge on the tongue, contributing to the odor. Brushing the tongue can remove much of this. If these odors persist the next and perhaps more prevalent cause may be the pharynx. The odors of this origin are more notable in the morning, approaching fetidness on awakening. They may result from debris accumulation in palatine tonsillar crypts or from mucostasis at night. The flow of saliva is decreased in the sleeping child, resulting in less clearance of debris and a drying effect, which may be enhanced in the mouth-breathing child. Usually these odors will diminish after rinsing of the mouth, although with chronic upper respiratory infections they may not be elininated. Often these odors will disappear after a tonsillectomy. This is generally not an indication for surgery, but the presurgical patient with hypertrophied tonsils is more prone to these odors.

The tongue. The tongue is another area where assessment is difficult because it is not static, particularly in children. Observation of the tongue with notation of its size and relative position is the best initial examination. As has been discussed, a child with a "small" oral

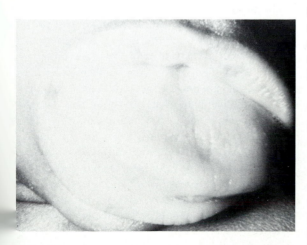

Fig. 16-4. True macroglossia interferes with feeding and speech.

environment and a "normal" sized tongue will have to keep it in a relatively protruded position to accommodate its size. These children are generally able to retrude the tongue within the mouth from its "convenience" position. It is impossible to arbitrarily define the line between a relative and a true macroglossia, but from a functional standpoint the ability to bring the teeth into occlusion may be considered one demarcation (Fig. 16-4). The youngster incapable of this is also incapable of mastication and will have marked difficulty in the manipulation and transference of liquids and pureed foods as well. Feeding problems may also exist in the patient with a relative macroglossia or protruded tongue but will decrease in intensity along the spectrum. Protrusion may be a result of hypertrophied tonsillar tissues or nasal blockage, creating the necessity for chronic mouth breathing, but the range of motion may not be impaired. The tongue should be capable of protrusion, intrusion, and lateralization. These parameters may be limited by the anatomical alterations discussed, neurological difficulties that are exemplified by deviation on extrusion, or immature development, which can limit the acquisition of lateral skills. The retention of components of the extrusion reflex can cause a "tongue thrust" or "reverse swallowing" pattern as well. Although this aberrant swallow is not treated in the general population until the early teenage years and in some delayed children can never be broken, it can cause alterations in the dental arches, speech patterns, and feeding. This pattern is noted when the anterior tongue protrudes through or pushes strongly against the anterior teeth when swallowing.

Another anatomical limitation must be ruled out on this examination—the presence of a prominent lingual frenum. Although a true ankyloglossia is rare, varying degrees of "tongue tie" may exist. Philosophies in this area vary, but most speech pathologists believe that the frenum must attach extremely closely to the tip of the tongue to constitute an impediment. It is important to consider this problem in the examination of the floor of the mouth. It can be accomplished by having the child place the tongue on the roof of the mouth. Failing this a digital examination should be done, since even though speech might not be impaired, the ability to lateralize the tongue and retrieve foods may be compromised.

Knowing that the tongue is of normal size and has a normal range of motion on random movement does not preclude the existence of motor sequencing problems. In certain types of central nervous system dysfunctions such as cerebral palsy the ability to coordinate the movements of the tongue is impaired. A coarse but effective screen is to determine the child's ability to protrude the tongue, then curl it to touch the upper lip with the tip. A child who should have speech should also be able to protrude the tongue and lateralize it from one corner of the mouth to the other in reasonably rapid succession. These are difficult to explain to a child and are best demonstrated by the examiner with the patient mimicking the actions. Since much of a child's development is perceived through his speech and language skills, a speech pathologist should be consulted when there is a question of a language delay or articulation problem.

Salivary problems. In children with difficulties in tongue control, drooling may be noted as a problem. This can result from an inability to control secretions intraorally because of a relative flaccidity of the tongue and a protruded rest position. The "drooling syndrome" can encompass the following areas, however, and these should be scrutinized. Lip competency and tone, poor buccinator tone, anterior displacement of the tongue because of hypertrophied tonsils and adenoids, chronic mouth breathing, or wide alveolar shelves (Down syndrome) may contribute to this picture. If these aspects appear normal, the possibility of increased secretions or increased viscosity should be considered. Salivation is both a conditioned and unconditioned reflex predicated on masticatory or gustatory involvement. The major glands—submaxillary (mixed), parotid (serous), and sublingual (mainly mucous)—contribute disproportionate amounts to the saliva.[9,14] All three receive both sympathetic and parasympathetic innervation, and the child with sensory problems may have increased salivation tendencies. Hypersalivation is also

reported as a feature in some syndromes (acrodynia) or may be theoretically caused by the eruption and/or exfoliation of teeth.[5] It may also be the result of concentration on a particular task with the head down, causing gravitational drooling.

Increased viscosity of the saliva can be a manifestation of chronic dehydration and present difficulties in the clearance of secretions due to the "ropiness" of the saliva. Historical context and examination of the structures, including palpation of the glands and ascertainment of duct patency, can help to centralize the cause. This increased viscosity can also cause the formation of calculus, or tartar, particularly on the lingual surfaces of the lower incisor teeth.

Alteration of the gingiva. The presence of calcified deposits on teeth can be an indication of salivary viscosity or can be a manifestation of chronic food accumulation and poor oral hygiene. This is often seen in the mouth-breathing youngster. When dryness contributes to this deposition the primary result of these deposits is the beginning of periodontal, or gum, disease as the particulate matter forms an irritant to the tissue around the teeth. Chronic irritation most commonly leads to an erythematous response with shrinkage of the tissue and loss of underlying bone support to the teeth. Although this is more prevalent in the older developmentally delayed individual, it can be seen at a very early age if hygiene is neglected. The marginal tissue around the tooth may exhibit loss of tone and normal stippling with puffiness and redness of the tissue. The gums in this instance may bleed easily on gentle probing and the papillae between the teeth may be inflamed or potentially necrotic. This finding indicates that a thorough cleaning and sound oral hygiene instruction are necessary. The gums should also be inspected for the presence of fistulae, most commonly called "gum boils," which result from the chronic abcess of a tooth. Also, recession of the gingival tissues from around the tooth, even with the absence of inflammation, should be considered as pathological, especially in the younger population. Loosely termed "juvenile periodontosis" this finding is associated with specific (Papillon-

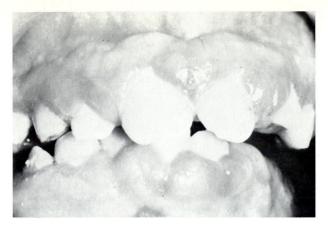

Fig. 16-5. Gingival hyperplasia caused by phenytoin use and poor oral hygiene.

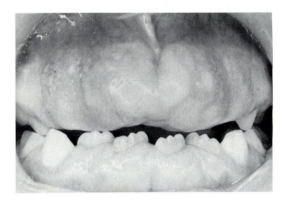

Fig. 16-6. Phenytoin gingival hyperplasia stimulated by the eruption of the permanent teeth in an 8-year-old with good oral hygiene.

Lefèvre syndrome) and nonspecific entities. It probably always relates to some chronic low-grade infection, however.

The overgrowth of gingival tissue can be associated with pregnancy, puberty, or hereditary gingival fibromatosis, but in the developmentally disabled population is almost always caused by phenytoin (Dilantin). Of the 2 million people in the United States receiving phenytoin therapy probably 25% to 50% are affected with gingival hyperplasia[1] (Figs. 16-5 and 16-6). The initiation of the process can occur at any time after the onset of medication. Although there is no sex predisposition, it is apparently related to dosage and is seemingly more common in the younger population. Although the mechanism is not clearly understood, phenytoin seems to

cause an exaggerated gingival response to local irritation with resulting fibrotic tissue changes. The irritation can be debris accumulation, orthodontic bands, poor dental restorations, or the eruption of the permanent or primary teeth. Phenytoin appears to be the only drug capable of causing this response and the process slowly reverses on cessation of the medication or replacement with an alternative anticonvulsant. If the substitution of medication cannot be considered, therapy is limited to the surgical excision of the tissue. This should be considered if:

1. The *risk* of general anesthesia with substantial blood loss is minimal
2. The *benefit* in feeding, speech, or aesthetics is substantial
3. The *reoccurrence* can be limited by the establishment of sound oral hygiene

Prevention is the most important factor. Scrupulous oral hygiene can minimize the recurrence of this process. It is essential that these procedures be initiated with the medication.

The pharyngeal area. An area that poses moderate difficulty in examination is the soft palate–posterior pharyngeal complex. Whereas the presence of a cleft palate is obvious, the existence of a submucous cleft or velopharyngeal insufficiency is more difficult to discern, particularly since a language delayed child may not develop speech at a normal rate and deviations in speech patterns may not be as easily identified as in a nondelayed child. Many youngsters are amenable to the normal examination approach, but developmentally delayed children may have receptive language and behavioral problems that make this difficult. In these children it may be necessary to employ a mouth prop to visualize the pharynx. Areas that need assessment are the competency of the soft palate, the size of the tonsils, the velar length, the velar lift, and the configuration of the uvula. Transillumination of the soft palate will reveal a bluish hue if an underlying cleft is present. This cleft should be palpable in some children, depending on access and the activity of the gag reflex. Tonsillar size contributes to the adaptive process (although edenoidal size is probably more important) and should be noted since tolerance limits are quite small. (Some practitioners believe that a 3 mm freeway space in the posterior pharynx can cause hypernasality.) The tonsils and adenoids reach their peak growth at approximately age 12 (although other ages are sometimes given) and thereafter begin to involute. This involution may be compensated for by some palatal stretch, but stretching may not occur if the soft palate's growth is restricted. Hence some assessment of velar length, especially in the raised position, should be obtained. Phonation of the vowel "oo" or the more involuntary response of the gag reflex

can locate the palatal dimple. Ideally this should occur at about 80% of the velar length, near the uvula. The dimple indicates the attachment of the levator muscle of the velum palatini. If this attachment is at the 50% level (i.e., nearer the end of the hard palate) the ability of the velum to close off the nasopharynx is questionable. In this situation the posterior tissue curtain will resemble an **A** configuration on extension (Fig. 16-7). The configuration of the uvula should also be noted. About 1 out of 76 individuals has a bifid uvula. Although there is no definite correlation between its presence and that of a submucous cleft, most individuals with these clefts have a bifid uvula. The converse is not true. However, an alteration in the configuration of the uvula, whether it is bifid, short, or rotated, should lead to further investigation. Certainly compensatory growth does correct some velopharyngeal insufficiency after tonsillectomy and adenoidectomy, but this will occur only within the first 2 to 3 postsurgical months, after which time other types of remediation will probably be necessary.

Dental examination

The examination of the teeth and their relationship to each other constitutes the final segment of a thorough oral evaluation. This can be approached segmentally, using the format popularized by Law, Lewis, and Davis,[8] beginning with an assessment of eruption. It is an area that is often misunderstood when rigid eruptive patterns and timing are applied to various individuals. In general, the primary teeth begin to erupt around 6 months of age with the appearance of the mandibular central incisors. This event can occur months earlier or later, however, with no necessary implication. Similarly, the eruption of the permanent teeth theoretically begins around age 6 to 7 years, although perfectly normal patterns can occur 2 years on either side of these dates. It is important to recognize this range before ascribing abnormality. Natal teeth, for instance, occur infrequently (1 per 2000)[9] but are normally the primary central (mandibular) incisors. If left in the mouth they will develop root structure and become a viable part of the dentition. There are indications (excessive mobility or laceration of the

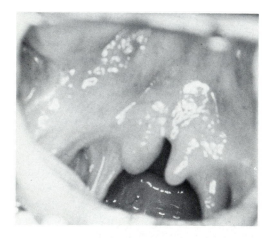

Fig. 16-7. A configuration of the soft palate in a patient with a submucous cleft. Note how anteriorly the soft palate is hinged. (Courtesy Dr. Robert Mason, Orofacial and Communicative Disorders Program, University of North Carolina, Chapel Hill, N.C.)

tongue) for their removal. This can result in space loss. There are also certain associations with difficulties in eruption and exfoliation that are not as benign. Down syndrome (delayed eruption) is the most widely recognized entity in which this is common but it can also be seen with cleidocranial dysostosis and certain endocrine dysfunctions (hypothyroidism, hypopituitarism). Early loss of teeth can result from hypophosphatasia, acrodynia, and histiocytosis X (Hand-Schüller-Christian disease).[14]

Structural anomalies. Structural aberrations of teeth can be loosely categorized as either hereditary or acquired. The latter group includes the broad area of hypoplasia, seen primarily on the permanent teeth and most commonly the result of febrile illnesses or trauma. The ameloblast appears to be sensitive to notable changes in systemic temperature, and in instances of chronic and subacute disease can undergo a temporary diminution of enamel deposition. This deposition normally resumes at the end of the insult, but the process can leave a band of hypoplastic enamel on all teeth developing at that time.

A more local hypoplastic defect can result from trauma to the primary dentition, normally in the maxillary anterior, causing damage to the developing bud. This can result from actual physical damage to the bud from intrusion or displacement of the primary tooth. Although intruded primary teeth will generally reerupt without assistance, they should be assessed (by lateral radiograph if possible) to determine the juxtaposition of the root to the permanent bud and hence the possible neces-

sity of extraction. Displaced teeth can often be repositioned to eliminate interferences with the bite. There is unfortunately a high incidence of this type of trauma in the child with seizure activity, neuromuscular disorders, or syndromes affecting motor development.

The sequela to trauma of this type can include ankylosis, or fusion of the tooth to the alvelous with subsequent eruption and exfoliation problems. More commonly the tooth will discolor due to intracoronal hemorrhage and limited blood flow within the confined pulpal area. The resultant increase in intracoronal pressure and, possibly, the phenomenon of anachoresis (the localization of bacteria at an inflammatory site) can lead to the formation of an abscess, which can impair the development and eruption of the permanent tooth (Fig. 16-8). Often this process is asymptomatic and is seen only by mobility of the primary tooth or the formation of a fistulous track or "gum boil." Drainage through the tooth and extraction where indicated are the preferred treatments.

Alternative causes for acquired dental hypoplasias are metabolic. This finding may occasionally occur with hypophosphatasia, hypothyroidism, pseudohypoparathyroidism, vitamin D resistant rickets, and vitamin deficiencies, notably of the fat-soluble type.[14] It is also commonly seen in cases of prematurely born infants (Fig. 16-9).

The hereditary forms of structural anomalies focus on aberrations in the enamel and dentin. The former category includes hereditary enamel hypoplasia, in which the enamel is present in

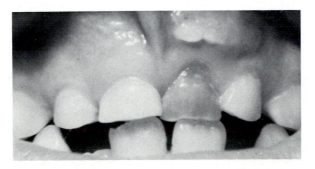

Fig. 16-8. Chronic abscess of a discolored primary tooth, resulting in bone loss and abnormal eruption of the permanent tooth. (Courtesy Dr. Manouch Darvish, Worcester, Mass.)

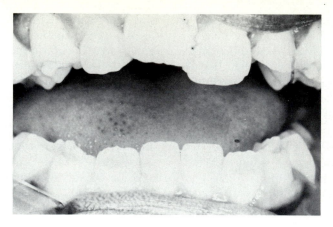

Fig. 16-9. Interruption of enamel formation (hypoplasia) of metabolic origin. (Courtesy Dr. George M. Richardson, Burlington, Vt.)

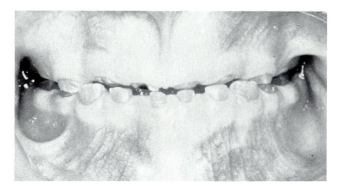

Fig. 16-10. Discoloration and attrition of the teeth in dentinogenesis imperfecta.

reduced quantity but is of normal structure, and hereditary enamel hypocalcification, in which the enamel quantity is sufficient but the quality of the calcification is impaired. These are classified together as amelogenesis imperfecta.[8] Alternately, there is hereditary dentinogenesis imperfecta, in which the internal dentin is compromised, leading to changes in the refractive index of the teeth. These teeth take on a translucent brownish grayish to bluish hue and have been characterized as opalescent (Fig. 16-10). They suffer rapid attrition, often with the fracture of the enamel, subsequent to a compromised dentinoenamel junction. Clinically they are most similar to the teeth seen with osteogenesis imperfecta. They require full prosthetic coverage if they are to be maintained.

Nursing bottle syndrome and dental caries. Although not truly a developmental

hypoplasia, the decalcification seen with nursing bottle syndrome can initially appear to be a hypoplastic event and is very common in children who have a chronic exposure to juice, flavored drinks, and milk given by bottle at bedtime. A variant of the caries process, it results from the pooling and stasis of liquid in the sleeping child's mouth, unabated by normal salivary flow and muscular actions, providing the perfect environment for bacterial proliferation and the adherence necessary for the acid destruction of teeth. Most prevalent on the maxillary anterior teeth and infrequent on their mandibular counterparts, the process also effects the primary molars, depending on age. The "syndrome" is characterized by progressive chalky decalcification of the smooth dental surfaces with eventual flaking and dissolution of the entire enamel structure (Fig. 16-11). It is

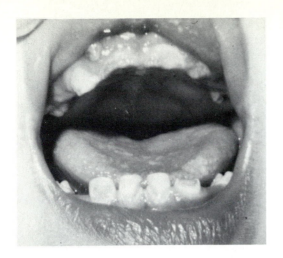

Fig. 16-11. Rampant dental decay and decalcification from the nursing bottle syndrome in an 18-month-old child. (Courtesy Dr. Manouch Darvish, Worcester, Mass.)

often seen in developmentally delayed children whose feeding maturation is retarded and who maintain bottle supplements for a longer period than nondelayed children. Admittedly, there are cases in which there is little or no effect from this exposure. This may indicate a variable buffering capacity within the saliva of some individuals, but researchers cannot yet predict which ones. Prevention by the elimination of the bottle at bedtime is the most effective approach. Restorative treatment is awkward at an age often not greater than 2 years.

Although dental caries is not an anomaly, the completion of the examination of dental structures should include notation of the prevalence of decay. This process can be enhanced substantially by structural defects but is normally the result of local factors. Advanced or rampant decay can be threatening to the child with cardiovascular or renal disorders or to the youngster with a blood dyscrasia and should be treated as early as possible.

Dental size, shape, and color. The remaining section of the dental examination should focus on alterations in the size, shape, color, and number of the teeth. It is difficult to delineate absolute parameters for tooth size and shape. Microdontia and macrodontia have been reported in a variety of syndromes but usually without much consistency. They are thought to be associated with pituitary dysfunction syn-

drome.[5] Alterations in shape include fusion (two independent tooth buds fusing to form one anomalous structure), gemination (one bud splitting to form two crowns), and problems of the root structure such as concresence and dilaceration. Although these most often occur as isolated events, certain alterations are associated with specific developmental entities. In this category are the ''mulberry molars'' and Hutchinson's (notched) incisors of congenital syphilis and taurodontism (body and root of tooth have a block rectangular shape), which has also been associated with Klinefelter's syndrome.[5,9,14]

The shape of the teeth can also be altered by local factors, of which the most common is bruxism, or grinding. These teeth will be flattened with notable wear facets posteriorly, while the anterior teeth will be shortened considerably if they are in occlusion. The causes for bruxism are unknown although tension, occlusal dysharmony, self-stimulation, aberrant bite reflex, and pinworms have all been advanced as possibilities. Although often annoying and potentially damaging to the nerves of the teeth, it does limit stasis of food on the teeth and generally decreases the rate of decay. It may diminish with the eruption of the permanent teeth or can persist for life. Treatments range from the fabrication of splints to decrease dental trauma to the use of ataractic medication such as diazepam (Valium).

The color of teeth can be affected by two types of staining: extrinsic and intrinsic. External stains are common in children, removable, and relatively benign although they can lead to gingival irritation and erythema. These are most commonly green (chromogenic microbial organisms), black or brown (often from iron supplements), or white (debris accumulation). The intrinsic or internal stains are generally more specific in their origins and cannot be removed although some can be successfully masked. The most well-known is the yellow-black spectrum associated with tetracycline ingestion. White opacities are generally idiopathic but can be associated with high-level fluoride ingestion. The reddish brown to dark brown staining of congenital porphyria is a result of changes in hemolysis and increased quantities of free porphyrins in the dental structures. A similar hemolytic process stains teeth greenish blue in erythroblastosis fetalis. Discoloration of teeth also occurs in biliary atresia, in which the circulatory levels of bilirubin and biliverdin cause the developing dentition to take on a green hue.[15]

As with the shape of teeth, it is often difficult to ascribe much meaning to an isolated alteration in the number of teeth. Many individuals are congenitally missing third molars (wisdom teeth) or other particular teeth. Yet the percentage of the population having either missing or extra teeth (1% to 3% in normal population)[16] increases to 43%[2] in Down syndrome. Another syndrome of this nature is ectodermal dysplasia, in which the spectrum runs from oligodontia to anodontia (Fig. 16-12). On the other side, individuals with cleidocranial dysostosis have problems with multiple supernumerary teeth as well as with the eruption and exfoliation of the expected dentition. This alteration of numbers must be measured and assessed individually, since it fits with a pattern of anomalous development. It should also be considered in relation to an individual's abilities to cope with a diet of textural significance. As with the premature loss of deciduous or permanent teeth through dental caries or periodontal disease, congenital absence of teeth can restrict the development of feeding by limiting the introduction of textured foods.

Occlusion. Although the teeth are normally examined with the mouth open, they must also be assessed while biting, or in occlusion. Parameters for evaluation are the ability to have all teeth meet in a balanced form and the ability to bring the front teeth "edge to edge." Without this a child cannot incise or grind food effectively. The developmentally disabled child has a higher incidence of malocclusions due to structural anomalies and the persistence of abnormal habits. Both tongue thrust and habits such as thumb sucking can cause the bite to be open anteriorly, often with only minimal posterior occlusion. An enlarged or inappropriately sized tongue can cause lateral open bites or preclude occlusion entirely. Some of these alterations will correct themselves given the elimination of the habitual cause, although others will require orthodontic correction in the amenable child. Certain alterations, however, cannot be treated due to patient intolerance, and dietary adjustments must be made. The type of malocclusion characterized by an open bite or protruding teeth also places a child at substantial risk from trauma, especially in the individual with a neuromuscular disease or a seizure disorder.

DENTAL TREATMENT FOR THE DEVELOPMENTALLY DISABLED CHILD

The dental experience for the developmentally disabled child should be tripartite, consisting of the determination of the oral status, the re-

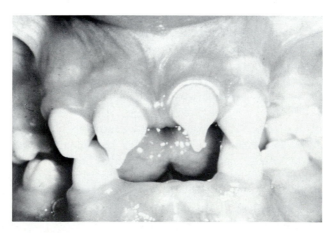

Fig. 16-12. Alteration in the shape and number of the teeth in a patient with anhidrotic ectodermal dysplasia. (Courtesy Dr. George M. Richardson, Burlington, Vt.)

mediation of dental needs, and the prevention of continued or potential difficulties. Having dealt with the initial area, some misconceptions surrounding dental treatment should be eliminated.

The approach to dental care for the handicapped has matured greatly in recent years with the addition of psychological and pharmacological adjuncts to conventional therapy. Modern dental offices are more physically accessible and more responsive to the needs of this population. Working in conjunction with other allied professionals, dentists are trained in behavior modification and adaptive techniques. With a greater understanding of the patient and the patient's needs, care can be delivered to all individuals. The spectrum of care ranges from normal ambulatory delivery to more specialized considerations, including physical adaptation of the facilities (e.g., the use of a beanbag chair to more adequately contour a dental chair for support) and the use of medication and/or analgesic agents such as nitrous oxide to effect behavioral alteration and sedation. A standard approach to this latter area includes the assessment of the child without medication on the initial visits and then the incremental use of medication (chloral hydrate, hydroxyzine [Vistaril], diazepam [Valium]). Some practitioners supplement their premedication with the in-office use of nitrous oxide with good results, although many developmentally disabled youngsters are not amenable to the nose piece. It should be noted that the term "premedication" is more standardly applied to the antibiotic prophylaxis used with cardiac patients, patients with certain renal disorders, and youngsters with ventriculoperitoneal and ventriculoauricular shunts. These modalities have helped to substantially alter dental experiences for many of the handicapped and retarded. Admittedly, general anesthesia must still be employed in selected individuals, but it is being used less frequently and usually in the appropriate hospital setting.

The results of these adaptations has been that developmentally delayed individuals have greater access and greater acclimatization to dental services. This enables not only routine dentistry to be performed but also use of some advanced prosthetics (for individuals with anterior clefts or a history of missing teeth or trauma patients) and, in instances where tolerated, orthodontic care.[17] These are the types of benefits that may be garnered from extended contact and mutual understanding. The identification of resources and the referral of the patients in these areas is an integral segment of the health plan and essential to the elimination of dental disease.

Home dental care by brushing. Dental de-

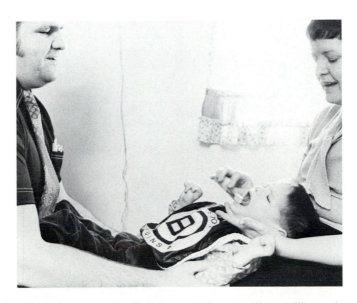

Fig. 16-13. Parents can effectively brush child's teeth while seated knee to knee.

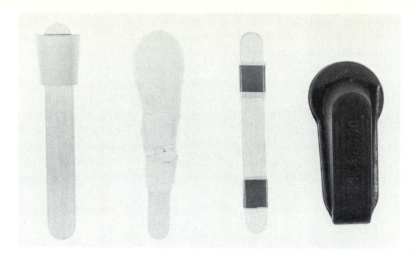

Fig. 16-14. A variety of mouth props can be adapted for home use.

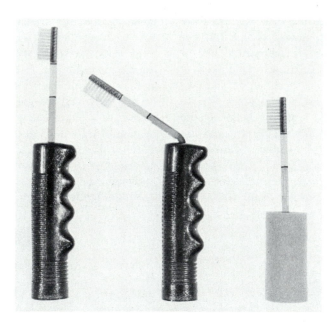

Fig. 16-15. Modifications of toothbrush handles to fit a child's particular grasp.

cay remains the most prevalent disease in this country, although it is practically preventable. It is initiated by the plethora of oral bacteria that utilize refined carbohydrates as a substrate. Colonizing in the plaque—a mucopolysaccharide film—on the teeth, the bacteria excrete acid that dissolves the tooth enamel. It is a process that once initiated usually cannot be cured without treatment.

As has been mentioned, dental caries and periodontal disease can be almost entirely pre-

vented. With the exception of some of the aforementioned developmental difficulties, the proliferation of disease can be checked by home oral hygiene measures. These fall into several areas and must be modified in the retarded or developmentally disabled population.

Toothbrushing, the standard weapon, is routinely abused in the normal population. Its effectiveness with special groups is contingent on use. To achieve success, several tenets must be considered. Primarily, a child must be placed

Table 16-4. Multiple use of fluorides, based on the severity of dental disease, the ability of the patient to cooperate, and the route of administration

Severity of dental disease	Ability of patient to cooperate			
	Independent		Dependent	
	Systemic	Topical	Systemic	Topical
Mild	Water fluoride *or* Fluoride tablets adjusted to age and concentration of fluoride in water	Home Fluoride dentifrice Office Semiannual topical gel	Water fluoride *or* Fluoride drops adjusted to age and concentration of fluoride in water	Home Fluoride dentifrice Office Semiannual topical gel
Moderate	Water fluoride *or* Fluoride tablets adjusted to age and concentration of fluoride in water	Home Fluoride dentifrice Daily fluoride rinse (after 6 years of age) Office Semiannual topical gel	Water fluoride *or* Fluoride drops adjusted to age and concentration of fluoride in water	Home Fluoride dentifrice "Therapeutic" fluoride regimen Brush on gel Office Semiannual topical gel
Severe or rampant	Water fluoride *or* Fluoride tablets adjusted to age and concentration of fluoride in water	Home Fluoride dentifrice "Therapeutic" fluoride regimen Brush on gel Gel in tray Office Semiannual topical gel	Water fluoride *or* Fluoride drops adjusted to age and concentration of fluoride in water	Home Fluoride dentrifrice "Therapeutic" fluoride regimen Brush on gel Gel in tray Office Semiannual topical gel
Root caries		Home "Therapeutic" fluoride regimen Brush on gel Gel in tray Rinse		Home "Therapeutic" fluoride regimen Brush on gel Gel in tray Rinse

From Nowak, A. J.: Prevention of dental disease. In Nowak, A. J., editor: Dentistry for the handicapped patient, St. Louis, 1976, The C. V. Mosby Co., p. 180.

in a stable position for brushing.[12] This can be accomplished with the parents seated knee to knee with the child across their laps (Fig. 16-13). It can also be effected by a child lying on a bed or a couch with his head on a pillow or lap. Alternatively, a parent working from the rear of a child seated on either the floor (with the parent in a chair using legs for stabilization) or in a wheelchair can accomplish satisfactory brushing in a stable environment. Imagination and flexibility are crucial to the program, and it should be recognized that a bathroom, with its obvious obstacles, is not necessarily the only acceptable location.

Good hygiene cannot be achieved unless access can be gained. Mouth props of either the taped tongue blade or bite-block variety are useful in a youngster with difficulty in maintaining an opening (Fig. 16-14). A standard rubber doorstop has great value in this endeavor because it can be trimmed to size, is sturdy but not hard, and can be cleaned. It can be inserted on its flat side and tipped to provide stability. The initial reaction to its use is generally disbelief, but it is among the most functional of aids.

Brushing itself may be modified to suit the needs of the child (Fig. 16-15). All surfaces should be brushed by the parent, however, at least twice a day. This should begin with the eruption of the primary teeth, when cleaning can be done with a gauze pad or a soft washcloth, and continue until the child is capable of assuming this responsibility. In the normal child this is around age 7. Fluorinated toothpaste should be used when practical, but even in the absence of its use, brushing is beneficial. The areas between the teeth should be flossed in children with the aid of a floss holder. This device frees one hand for stabilization. Obviously not all children will acclimate readily to this protocol. It may be awkward at first but it is as necessary as changing diapers. With time and positive reinforcement these procedures can be implemented on a routine basis—after meals and particularly before bed—and can become an event of satisfaction and accomplishment. It is one very visible area in which the parents can have a dramatic impact on the health of their child.

Fluorides. Supplemental processes can also ameliorate a child's dental health. Fluoridation of water supplies is the safest, most effective, and most economical method. Where this benefit is not available, fluoride supplements (with or without vitamins) provide substantial systemic effect for the developing dentition, while the newer fluoride rinses provide a daily topical benefit (Table 16-4). The use of standard mouthwashes is more cosmetic than therapeutic. These modalities must be employed individually and should suit the child's particular need.

Of course it is ideal to integrate the child into the oral hygiene procedure. The methods listed should be initiated by the parents, but the child's participation should be encouraged. This is part of an ongoing learning process. Adaptations of the brush specifically can increase a child's participation. For a child with a limited grip, the brush handle can be inserted into a bicycle grip or a sponge rubber hair curler. It can also be fastened to a contoured nailbrush handle. Electric brushes (of the cordless variety) have thicker handles and are effective in the more self-sufficient child.

These measures are effective ways of limiting the incidence of caries but are not solely effective. Cariogenic bacteria must have carbohydrate to support growth. Diminution of this parameter will obviously reduce the incidence of decay. Control of dietary intake and substitution of snack foods constitute little deprivation and improve oral health immeasurably. Reduction of the frequency of carbohydrate consumption also limits the overall elevation of sugar levels. Hence sweets given for desserts or on a controlled basis at meals, when oral hygiene measures can be instituted with some predictable immediacy constitute a rational approach to caries prevention.

SUMMARY

An understanding of the nature and extent of oral development and disease is essential to complete evaluation of the developmentally delayed child. The value of such an understanding, however, is minimized unless translated into active education. Certainly the individuals who have primary contact with these children and their families are the most important. The primary care physician and other helping professionals have the responsibility of informing the parents of existing difficulties and potential solutions. Early recognition of problems is the obvious key to early intervention and the maximization of treatment. The restorative aspects of dentistry are the benchmark of the profession. These are deserved and available services that, when coupled with a sound preventive program, can be of immense benefit. Yet the overall importance of complete oral evaluation must not be overlooked. The translation of this information to the parent and the referral for appropriate assistance will make the early and most malleable years the most productive.

REFERENCES

1. Braham, R. L., et al.: The dental implications of epilepsy, publ. no. 78-5217, Rockville, Md., U.S. Department of Health, Education and Welfare.
2. Brown, H. R., and Cunningham, U. M.: Some dental manifestations in mongolism, Oral Surg. **14:**664, 1961.
3. Finn, S. B.: Clinical pedodontics, ed. 4, Philadelphia, 1973, W. B. Saunders Co.
4. Gallagher, F. E., and Cohen, M. M.: The effect of maternal rubella on the primary dentition, J. Dent. Res. **55:**B156, 1976.
5. Gorlin, R. J., Pindborg, J. J., and Cohen, M. M., Jr.: Syndromes of the head and neck, ed. 2, New York, 1976, McGraw-Hill Book Co.
6. Howard, R. B., and Herbold, N.: Nutrition in clinical care, New York, 1978, McGraw-Hill Book Co.
7. Langman, J.: Medical embryology, ed. 2, Baltimore, 1969, The Williams & Wilkins Co.

8. Law, D. B., Lewis, T. M., and Davis, J. M.: An atlas of pedodontics, Philadelphia, 1969, W. B. Saunders Co.

9. McDonald, R. E., and Avery, D. R.: Dentistry for the child and adolescent, ed. 3, St. Louis, 1978, The C. V. Mosby Co.

10. Nowak, A. J., editor: Dentistry for the handicapped patient, St. Louis, 1976, The C. V. Mosby Co.

11. Perkins, W. H.: Speech pathology: an applied behavioral science, ed. 2, St. Louis, 1977, The C. V. Mosby Co.

12. Schey, L. S., and Gallagher, F. E.: Home dental care for the handicapped child, Waltham, Mass., 1976, The New England Developmental Disabilities Communications Center.

13. Scipien, G., et al.: Comprehensive pediatric nursing, ed. 2, New York, 1975, McGraw-Hill Book Co.

14. Shafer, W. G., Hine, M. K., and Levy, B. M.: A textbook of oral pathology, ed. 2, Philadelphia, 1967, W. B. Saunders Co.

15. Shapiro, B. M., Gallagher, F. E., and Needleman, H. L.: Dental management of the patient with biliary atresia, Oral Surg. **40:**742, 1975.

16. Shaw, J. H., et al.: Textbook of oral biology, Philadelphia, 1978, W. B. Saunders Co.

17. Wei, S. H. Y., and Casko, J., editors: Orthodontic care for handicapped persons. Proceedings of workshop, May 8 to 10, 1977, University of Iowa, Iowa City, Iowa, 1978.

18. Wolfman, M., Cohen, M. M., and Gallagher, F. E.: The effect of Down's syndrome on the primary dentition, J. Dent. Res. **55:**B108, 1976.

17

Practical problems and their management

I. B. Pless

Over the past 30 years at least 50 texts dealing with the care of "handicapped children" have been published. This term is used as the one that deals most broadly with the wide range of disorders now included within the rubric "developmental disorders." Despite this outpouring of well-intentioned advice, however, few of the preceding publications have attempted to focus specifically on the nitty-gritty aspects of day-to-day practical management. The reason for this is quite simple; there are very real obstacles to implementing most of the recommendations usually offered. This is particularly the case when those recommendations are aimed at the primary physician, the main target of this text. The reasons for this will be discussed in a subsequent section of this chapter; at this point it is important to emphasize that the principal goal of this chapter is to provide guidelines whereby many, if not most, of these obstacles can be overcome.

Our focus on the central role of the primary physician is deliberate. It is our conviction that those in primary care are in the best position to provide the wide range of services these children and their families so desperately need. Moreover, it is our belief that by doing so physicians will find a sense of reward and gratification unique in their repertoire of activities. There can be little doubt that the management of a child with a developmental disorder is a formidable challenge for most physicians. It is not an exaggeration to suggest that the successful diagnosis, assessment, treatment, *and* management of a child with a chronic disorder of any kind is the ultimate test of the physician's skill in both the art and science of medicine. No other group of conditions poses as many problems for the conscientious physician. Their mastery depends on a complex interplay of the physician's skill, knowledge, temperament, and training and a realistic recognition of the practice situation and the available resources. But it must also be emphasized that the family, too, plays a major role in determining the outcome. The nature of the specific illness combined with a full appreciation by all concerned of the child's personal assets are of particular importance. Accordingly, the interplay becomes still more complex; physician and pa-

Table 17-1. Characteristics of some typical diseases

Disease	Nature of disability	Duration	Therapy
Cerebral palsy	Complex, multiple (locomotor)	Permanent	Complex (team)
Spina bifida	Complex, multiple (locomotor)	Permanent	Complex (team)
Epilepsy	Episodic, restrictive (social)	Uncertain	Drugs
Cystic fibrosis	Restrictive	Progressive	Drugs and other
Asthma	Episodic, restrictive	Uncertain	Drugs and other
Diabetes	Episodic, restrictive	Progressive (?)	Drugs and diet
Learning disorders	Educational (social)	Uncertain	Education (? drugs)
Arthritis	Restrictive	Progressive (?)	Drugs and other
Blindness	Restrictive (social)	Permanent	Education (? surgery)
Deafness	Restrictive (social)	Permanent	Education (? aids)

tient as well as other professional helpers and the resources of the community all combine to determine whether and how well the child and family will succeed over the long term.

But what is "success" in the case of a child with a developmental disorder? Is it really measurable, or even recognizable? In our view it is both, since ultimately it is nothing less than the emergence of a young adult who has learned to cope successfully with an illness, that is, an adult who is able to function well despite his disability. Having stated this, however, it must be acknowledged that success, even when defined as "functioning well," can never be assessed by a single parameter alone. It must be measured in a myriad of ways. It is particularly important not to equate success only with "good" medical results because, although this must remain central to the physician's "game plan," this objective must be balanced against a broader range of goals that the child and family view as reasonable and desirable.

In this chapter the term "developmental disability" is used in a very broad sense, perhaps more broadly than the interpretation applied by authors of some other chapters. It is intended to indicate the entire range of mental and physical disorders of childhood that may adversely affect normal growth and development. It therefore encompasses not only the "traditional" group of handicapping conditions, such as cerebral palsy and mental retardation, which clearly and specifically affect development, but also the more recently recognized array of disorders, the impact of which is primarily or predominantly in the area of school performance (the so-called "learning disorders" or "dyslexias"). In addition, most of the remaining chronic conditions of childhood also fall within this definition. Thus we are as concerned about the management of children with diabetes, asthma, or epilepsy as we are about those with blindness, deafness, or muscular dystrophy. The fact is that any of these disorders has a clear potential for interfering with normal development—physical, intellectual, emotional, and social (Table 17-1).

Some additional terms also require clarification. The emphasis of this chapter is on the "practical" aspects of "management." Both terms, "practical" and "management," are subject to a variety of interpretations. For example, the word practical in one sense refers simply to that which relates to everyday practice. Used in this sense it is "normative"—it is based on determining what most people actually do. But in the case of most physicians caring for these children, as will be shown later, such a standard would be insufficient. In other words if we are to assume that it is only "practical" for physicians who care for children with cerebral palsy to rely exclusively on referrals to a neurologist or to a local community Cerebral Palsy Association clinic (on the grounds that any more extensive involvement is "impractical"), this definition becomes misleading. Whatever the norm may be, it is our intention to provide guidelines whereby the conscientious primary care physician who is challenged by the problems of these children will adopt a more aggressive approach to care. Thus the second meaning of the word "practical"—inclined to action as opposed to theory or speculation—is more appropriate in this context. Much of what has been written to date is either speculative or theoretical. As such it provides guidelines that are ideal and often utopian. Our goal is to bring these ideas down to earth and to recognize clearly the many realistic limitations that confront both parents and physicians when they try to follow the advice so often offered by "experts" whose situation, it might be added, often differs markedly from that of those on the front line of care.

As has been suggested, we also wish to consider what is practical from the viewpoint of the parents as compared with that of the physician. This point also applies in connection with the word "management," since it must be clear that we do not intend this to be used as synonymous with "treatment." The latter is a very narrow, isolated facet of management as a whole. It refers only to the medical aspects of the disease. Moreover, in everyday use, particularly in medical writing, management has an active connotation; for example, the physician "manages" the patient by telling the child or family what they are to do and how they are to do it. Although in a very real sense this is clearly part of the physician's task, in the case of the child with a chronic disorder it is essential to also consider fully the issue of self-management or management by parents, guided by, but nonetheless somewhat independent of, the physician's orders.

This chapter will therefore range over fairly wide territory. It will examine what is actually done as well as what needs to be done by the physician, parents, and others who are helping provide care for these children. The emphasis throughout will indeed be on that which is practical (i.e., realistic and possible), as opposed to that which is simply theoretical. In making this distinction, however, it must be emphasized that what is possible, reasonable, or practical for some may be difficult or even impossible for others. Knowing which is which and who is who (i.e., what can reasonably be expected of a particular family or physician) and what the family or child's most pressing needs and highest values are lies at the heart of successful management.

Thus the issue of practicality will be considered equally from the viewpoint of the physician and that of the family. In this chapter both will be discussed, together when possible, but also separately, since in reality many of the most urgent and difficult problems of the family are beyond the scope of the physician's ability to intervene. Certainly the reverse is also true; that is, many of the limitations that surround the physician due to the constraints of time or other resources must also be understood and accepted by the family.

Much of the chapter is built around one dominant source—the verbatim comments of parents of handicapped children—which serves to highlight the day-to-day realities of life for these families. The specific quotations are taken from a film entitled: *Stress: Parents with a Handicapped Child.*[11] This film, produced in England with the cooperation of many agencies and organizations, is a poignant, highly realistic documentary. It takes a slice out of the lives of five families: one has a preschool child with mild spastic cerebral palsy, another has a 20-year-old girl with athetoid cerebral palsy whose intelligence is thought to be within the normal range, a third has an only child who has been diagnosed as autistic, another has a child with a severe seizure disorder, and the last has a retarded, mildly spastic child who is in residential care but who visits home on weekends. In addition to this principal source, other qualitative and quantitative insights into the problems of management are drawn largely from two other groups of studies: the Isle of Wight survey conducted in England in 1965[30] and those which took place in Rochester, New York, between 1967 and 1975.[8] Together these studies provide a conceptual and empirical framework on which these basic ideas are presented.

THEORETICAL CONSIDERATIONS

Although the primary orientation of this chapter is toward practical aspects of management, as physicians, allied professionals, and scientists it is helpful to understand some of the theoretical bases for the problems described and the solutions proposed. Regrettably there is still too little empirical data available from which strong support can be provided for many of these propositions. The data we have are none-theless useful because an improved understanding of the underlying issues point the way to solutions that may in time prove more effective than those attempted to date. Although there are many orientations that could be considered, three seem immediately applicable to the main theme of this discussion.

The first approach is essentially an appreciation of the fundamental nature of developmental disabilities and some of the rationale for considering what are biologically very diverse disorders within this broad rubric. What do the wide range of disorders dealt with in this text have in common? The answer is deceptively simple: they are each of significant duration, if not permanent, and each has the potential of affecting the daily lives of the child and family in some significant manner. (By definition, a "chronic disorder" is one which persists for longer than 3 months.) Although this is an arbitrary definition, in practice it serves to distinguish between the vast majority of childhood illnesses (for example, those of infective origin such as respiratory and gastrointestinal disorders, most of which are of short duration) and those which are usually of several years duration and generally more serious. Moreover, with very few exceptions, most of the disorders that fall within the category of developmental disabilities are relatively unaffected by medical or surgical treatment. In effect, this is simply another way of saying why these conditions are usually of long duration—because they are rarely cured, do not tend to improve spontaneously, and are rarely fatal. Although there are clear exceptions to this somewhat sweeping generalization, it does hold true when the natural and clinical history of these conditions is compared with the more common, prosaic illnesses so commonly seen by physicians who treat children (for example, the frequent episodes of tonsillitis, pharyngitis, and otitis), which occupy so much time and attention.

A second theoretical consideration is derived from the existence of an illness over a substantial period of a child's formative years. It is assumed (and there is considerable evidence to support this assumption[22,39]) that when a child lives with a disorder for any significant period of time, some type of psychological adaptation is required. The presence of any condition that makes a child different from his peers in some important way poses a potential threat to psychological development (Chapter 3). It does so either by interfering with the development of a positive self-concept, a sound ego, or by exposing the child to forms of stress beyond the ability of his coping mechanisms. Although it may seem too obvious to emphasize, it is worth stressing that our society continues to place high value on appearance and conformity. Accordingly, any expression of deviance, particularly over a prolonged period, is unwelcome by one's peers and ultimately by oneself. Stated even more simply, those who are forever different from the majority must pay a price, even when the differences are not of their own choosing. The price may well begin with changes in self-concept, accelerated or modified by the way in which parents, peers, and others react to the child when he is recognized by himself and these important "others" as being different. The price is perhaps greater when the differences are obvious and visible,[27] whether they take the form of an unusual gait, the use of crutches or wheelchair, a squint, or abnormal speech.

But even for those with "hidden" disorders, such as diabetes or renal conditions, the child knows they are there, the parents know, and eventually, whether they are informed openly or not, it is usual for most others with whom the child and family have regular contact to know, too. This knowledge and the behavior it elicits from others further reflects on the child. When, as is so often the case, there is an element of negative reaction in the behavior of parents, teachers, or friends, the impact on the child's already threatened self-concept is inevitably increased. Eventually, unless adequate support is provided by the family or others, the child's adaptive abilities are exceeded and various forms of "unhealthy coping mechanisms" come into play (Chapter 15).

The third important theoretical concept that must be considered may best be described as the "sociology" of health care for the handi-

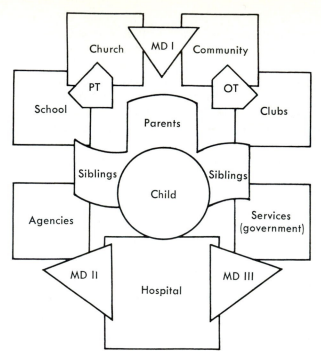

Fig. 17-1. The complex interaction of the child with the family, professionals, agencies, institutions, and the community.

capped.[21] This is a highly complex area, encompassing such facets as the role of primary and tertiary medical care, of voluntary agencies and government organizations, of services in the community, and of the economics and organization of health services. The list of social factors that impinge on the management of these children is almost endless. To suggest that there is a well-developed theoretical framework for considering all these factors is a gross exaggeration. But every physician recognizes that the care of these children does not exist in a vacuum; it must be viewed in a broad social context in which the family is but the first in a series of ever-expanding, overlapping circles of influence that each have some bearing, potential or actual, on the outcome of the illness (Fig. 17-1). It is the very complexity and wide range of these influences that makes the physician's task so challenging and demanding, yet at the same time may provide some form of relief for physicians and their colleagues. When they work well or are made to work well the resources of the community can be used to lighten the burden of the physician and also reduce the

load placed on the family. All too often, however, these social forces remain unharnessed or, worse still, work at cross purposes, so instead of helping they may actually add to the problem. The political, social, organizational, and other realities that invariably impinge on the care of these children are forces that cannot be ignored and must, therefore, to the best of our abilities, be better appreciated by the practicing physician.

PRACTICAL PROBLEMS FOR THE CHILD AND FAMILY

This section will describe some of the common practical problems that many children with developmental disorders face, as follows:

A. Day-to-day stress
  1. Constant attention
  2. Reactions of others
  3. Social relations
  4. Effect on siblings
  5. Marital relations
B. Life maintenance stress
  1. Financial stress
  2. Housing

3. Transportation
4. Clothing and appliances
5. Need for support
C. Worries about the future
1. Further children
2. Schooling and vocational training
3. Residential care

Of course, not all families have the same problems, and obviously some problems are much greater under certain circumstances than others. A child with diabetes does not have a wheelchair to contend with, whereas a child in a wheelchair does not have to face many of the conflicts that surround what to do when eating out. But the common thread should be clear; the range of everyday living problems extends well beyond the scope of medical care in its narrow sense. Treating the disease, with the best drugs, appliances, surgery, or whatever available form of therapy, is for many children at best only half the battle. In actuality it is often the smallest part of the struggle and in some respects the simplest. The conventional formula for success is relatively easy: "follow the doctor's orders." But as many families soon discover, compliance with the treatment is often more difficult than they (or the physician) anticipated, and even when it is successful, there are still more obstacles to overcome.

Hewett[9] has pointed out that many of the systematic studies of the problems of families of handicapped children reach somewhat conflicting conclusions. Casework studies alone tend to generate the impression that most such families are overwhelmed with emotional and social problems. Conversely, more scientific studies, that is, those which attempt to assess problems objectively and which may include some form of "controls" for purposes of comparison, while far from unanimous, do make it clear that the amount and nature of problems range enormously. Strikingly, they also suggest that this variation is by no means a direct reflection of the severity of the disability itself. The quality of the family is perhaps of equal if not greater importance in predicting the type of problems that will be encountered and in determining how successfully they will be managed. Nevertheless, Hewett notes that two themes appear consistently in most research findings, thus suggesting that they have general significance.

The first are the practical problems that require resources, usually money, for their solution. The second kind of problem requires "not money but thought, imagination, time and effort,"[9] and since they cost nothing (or relatively little) "they are or should be, more susceptible to solution than the others."[9] These then, are the underlying themes to which the following section will refer repeatedly.

Day-to-day stress

Constant attention

Oh he does get me down at times because I have to be with him the whole time.[11]

Perhaps more than any other, the most demanding drain on the emotional and physical resources of some parents is that which stems from the obligation to attend constantly to the needs of a disabled child. It is not the magnitude of problems, but the unrelieved demands from hour to hour and day to day that dominates their lives. Even in the best of families, unless they can find some relief from the need for constant supervision, the drain can be stultifying.

Admittedly, this problem is largely confined to those with major physical handicaps or to the severely retarded and may be greater during the preschool years than later, but it is nonetheless a major problem for many families. It is perhaps more extensive than we realize because many parents of children with less demanding disorders also believe they must provide continuous supervision. Parents of children with diseases like asthma, certain other allergic disorders, poorly controlled seizures, diabetes, or hemophilia often believe that some form of surveillance is needed at all times. The anxiety that results from the possibility that at any moment such a child may have a medical crisis (an asthmatic attack, a seizure, a bleed, a hypoglycemic episode, etc.) is a prevalent worry that cannot be dispelled easily.

It is even conceivable that it may be easier to help parents in the first group than the second. That is, those with preschool children with, say, cerebral palsy are increasingly likely to be able to find specialized day care programs—providing, of course, they live in urban areas where such programs exist. In such cases some relief may be available for a part of the day, but, nonetheless, for the remainder of the day and on weekends and holidays these children require much more attention than do their healthy siblings. They cannot be left alone in a room "to play quietly" by themselves without the nagging fear that some harm may come to them. Nor can the child be left with others outside the family, since few "sitters," neighbors, or relatives have the confidence or generosity to accept such a heavy burden of responsibility.

An extension of this problem into the night and its effect on sleep patterns of the family can be equally troublesome. In one of the large-scale studies of families with handicapped children, that of the Carnegie United Kingdom Trust,[2] one mother's comments sums it up well:

We were frantic for 8 years. That's one of the reasons why we wanted residential care for him, because we'd never had a night's sleep for 8 years. He used to go to bed and he used to cry and shout—oh, for 2 or 3 hours. . . . I was tired, my husband was tired, we were irritable and snapping at the others . . . most nights he does wake up. . . . It was a horrible thing—I loved him and yet I resented him for the ill-feeling and unhappiness he was causing the rest of us, you know.[2]

In Hewett's[10] study of children with cerebral palsy in Nottingham it was found that about 26% of the children over the age of 5 were still having trouble getting to sleep or were waking during the night. As noted, although the problem may not be great numerically, its importance to individual families cannot be minimized. One potential solution—having a child sleep in the same room as the parents—can hardly be recommended other than as a last resort.

Reaction of others

People are very nice as a rule, though sometimes if I'm going down the street they come up to me and say how sorry they are and they go on so—they're really not interested. . . . Yesterday I went in to a baker and L. had an [epileptic] attack and the woman looked at me and said "Wouldn't it be better if he was dead?"[11]

While this type of reaction is, it is hoped, the exception rather than the rule, many families, particularly those whose children have severe visible disabilities and those with stigmatizing disorders such as epilepsy, are often subject to public reactions of this nature. In place of tolerance, support, and understanding they too often find what amounts to sheer indifference at best and at worst pity or even hostility. It is difficult to explain why this should be so without delving deeply into some of the complexities of social psychology. Generally people fear what they do not understand. They resent the unfamiliar. They dislike being made to feel uncomfortable and being confronted with their own vulnerabilities and mortality. As a society we have not learned how to interact with the handicapped and rather than make the effort to learn, we have learned instead how to avoid such encounters.

The Isle of Wight survey[30] provided some perspective on the extent of the problem. From 4% to 5% of the families of children with central nervous system dysfunction or "other physical disorders" reported that the reactions and attitudes of others—friends, neighbors, relatives, and strangers—posed problems of this kind. In the Rochester study[8] "embarassment" was a problem for between 10% and 15% of families. The frequency of this problem was directly proportional to the severity of the condition. Interference by relatives, often in an attempt to be helpful, but interference nonetheless, was less common and was not related directly to the degree of disablement.

Although in general the reaction of the public toward persons with various types of handicap is negative, some disabilities are more likely to generate strong adverse reactions than others. Much of the basic work in this area has been done by Richardson and co-workers,[29] who have demonstrated a widespread and deep-seated "pecking order" among the preferences (or dislikes) of children and adults toward disabilities. As a rule those with cosmetic or obvious disorders are less preferred than those with less obvious disorders. One striking example of such differences is noted in a comparison of attitudes toward blindness and deafness. Ashley,[1] a British member of Parliament who became deaf during adulthood following surgery to correct a minor hearing loss, wrote the following in his autobiography, *Journey into Silence:*

The poverty of the organization for the deaf is a reflection of the striking difference in the public attitude to the two disabilities. The average person feels gratified helping a blind man across the road; . . . But cooperation with the deaf involves positive and continuous help rather than a gesture which is soon over and done with. . . . Equating the deaf with the daft is not confined to music halls; the public readily assume that one malady is synonymous with another. This may be due to a general inability to identify with the deaf [since] the deaf man looks normal and it requires imagination to appreciate his difficulty and it is impossible to simulate it.[1]

In a later section Ashley describes how this type of reaction affects the feelings of the deaf person. There is no reason to suspect that the problem would be much different for children than for adults.

I spoke of the inability of the deaf to accept deafness in the way that other people accept their disabilities. Self-conscious, almost ashamed, the deaf suffer a loss of self-confidence and an increasing embarassment which can destroy relationships already seriously impaired. . . .

Ashley concludes by stating that he had no doubt that deaf people are commonly regarded as second-class citizens.

Social relations

We don't usually go out because we never can get a babysitter to look after him.[11]

The effect on the family's social life, whether it be that of parents or the siblings, is frequently reported in many studies. In a review of the Rochester studies Satterwhite[31] summarizes data from several reports in which this area was explored. Of 404 interviews approximately 40% of those with severe to moderate disabilities reported some effect on the families' social life compared with less than 20% of those in which the disability was judged to be mild or not present. There is no doubt that the restriction on social activities for most families with

children who have reasonably severe disabilities is considerable. After some time many families adapt to this quite effectively, but nonetheless it seems likely that it must inevitably take its toll.

This is one good example of the need for the physician to put such parents in contact with others with similar experiences so that, to some extent at least, they can share the burden. It is also a specific area in which voluntary agencies can on occasion provide concrete assistance. Providing assurance from the physician and clear guidelines for babysitters and others who may take care of the child when the parents wish to go out is a simple but highly effective method of assisting in this area. The public needs to be better educated to understand that it is unlikely that children with these disabilities will run into severe problems and in general better education and much reassurance is in order.

Effect on siblings

Of course L. is overprotected and she [the sibling] is completely ignored. . . . She feels as if she's lost. . . .

My wife and I have largely adjusted our lives to A. coming home each weekend, but we are increasingly recognizing that for A.'s brother and sister his regular weekend arrivals represent a turbulent and unwelcome intrusion into their lives.

I'm glad I had a second child *now,* but at the time when I was pregnant and discovered that M. was handicapped—I couldn't tell you what I was thinking. But now that she's really here she's really rather a joy to look after. . . .[11]

These quotations, like the previous ones, emphasize the consequences of a developmental disorder on the psychological well-being of the disabled child's normal siblings. In general, the literature on the effects of handicap supports the belief that siblings are often adversely affected by this situation. But, as the quotations suggest, it is not invariably the case that the effects on siblings are negative. Some families are firmly convinced that the illness has helped to draw them closer together or helped the other children develop personality attributes that might not otherwise have arisen. Whether they are correct or not is relatively unimportant; the important point is that not all families perceive that the presence of a handicapped child is stressful for the other siblings.

Nonetheless, in several of the Rochester studies[37] between 15% and 30% of families reported some adverse effects on the siblings. Again, it should not be assumed that the parents are correct in attributing these problems to the presence of the illness, but, as before, it is their perception that is of salience. Very few studies have used such adequate control groups that it is possible to conclude with certainty that the problems noted are indeed causally related to the presence of the handicap. In some cases the controls chosen are inappropriate; for example, one study controlled by matching the handicapped child with a "normal" child but failed to match the siblings. In a study of nephrotic syndrome, in which close matching on several key variables was accomplished for both the nephrotic child and the siblings, there were few important differences found suggesting adverse consequences for the siblings.[37] The same general conclusion was reached in a study of children with cystic fibrosis and their siblings.[6]

Despite recent findings such as those which cast some doubt on the matter, the conventional wisdom for a long while has been that the presence of handicap poses problems not only for the family as a whole, but particularly for the siblings. It is assumed that one of the principal reasons this is so is because parents are forced to neglect the needs of the normal children in favor of those with a medical illness. This in turn is thought to lead to resentment or hostility. Parents may also feel guilty over this neglect, real or imagined, and may attempt to compensate their normal children in various ways, some of which may be unhealthy psychologically. Children too may feel guilty about the illness of a sibling, and may try to compensate for these feelings by adopting abnormal patterns of behavior. In the Carnegie Trust Study[2] a fairly typical set of findings is reported for a group of physically handicapped children. "In only two cases [out of the 12 studied] did the presence of the handicapped child have any

deleterious effect on other siblings, and family atmosphere was good."

In the more systematic Isle of Wight study[30] it was postulated that "a handicapping condition of childhood has an effect not only on the child but also on the others, and in particular on other members of his family." It was recognized, however, that the impact on the family is the result of many factors, among which the family's normal coping abilities are paramount. Several studies have also attempted to determine the relative importance of such factors as the affected child's sex, age, and the nature and severity of the disorder, as well as the demands made on the family for providing medical care. Few studies have been successful in doing so, and, in general, apart from global assessments of the family's coping strengths, there are not many reliable predictors of the effects that an illness will have on normal siblings. It is, however, of interest to note that in the Isle of Wight study the parents judged that 9% of the siblings of children with central nervous system dysfunction were unwilling to invite their friends into the home (presumably because of embarrassment), whereas the same was true for only 4% or 5% of the children with other physical disorders and for only 2% of the children with asthma. Generally, the effects were greatest among children with behavioral disorders, particularly those with antisocial-type behaviors. In the Rochester studies[31] about 12% overall reported that they thought the child's siblings were resentful of the sick child and much fewer, about 5%, received any evidence of neglect. Generally, the effects, at least in these two areas, were proportional to the severity of the disorder.

The problem for the physician, of course, is to determine the circumstances under which problems of this nature are most likely to occur and to take whatever steps possible to prevent or minimize them. At the most practical level, the simplest step is to ask parents directly how the other children appear to be affected by the child's illness. Parents must be encouraged to deal with this problem openly, and the physician must realize that this may be a sensitive and embarrassing topic for some. Thus efforts may be needed to help parents admit that this is a problem, for example, by reminding them that it is commonly seen and that it is quite natural for normal children to harbor feelings of resentment, frustration, or anger. In some extreme cases family therapy may be indicated and the help of professional counsellors may have to be sought. More often, however, visits by a public health nurse or sessions with the hospital social worker may be sufficient to help the family sort out problems of this nature.

Marital relations

All that was worrying me was coming home and telling my husband. . . .

Well the strain really falls on my wife's shoulders physically but mentally I feel it sometimes, especially when D. cries a lot during the night and stops about four in the morning and I find I've got about two hours sleep and have to be out at six to get to work. . . .

It does put a stress on the marriage—having a handicapped child. . . .

I feel with her at home we are never bored and [we] have a sense of purpose in life—which is keeping J. happy and occupied. I feel that through J. we lead a much fuller life than we would have done under more normal circumstances. . . .[11]

These quotations typify the wide range of opinions and assumptions that are held about the effect of a disabled child on the relationship between parents. For the most part the literature emphasizes the stress and strain, and, although there are few systematic data to support this assumption, it is probably more often correct than not. It stands to reason that any stressful event in the family will have shock waves that touch on the often fragile relationship between parents. There can be few more sensitive or more stressful events in the life of a family than to give birth to a child with a major disability or to have a previously healthy child become ill with a serious chronic disorder.

Marital problems have been extensively studied, usually in the context of more generalized studies of the "impact on the family" of disorders ranging from Tay-Sachs disease[13]

to cystic fibrosis,[35] cerebral palsy,[28] and spina bifida[32]—to cite but a few. For the most part the conclusions reached in these studies suggest that major marital problems do exist for a majority of families, or at least that such problems are reported consistently and attributed to the presence of the child with a disability. Unfortunately, again, most such studies fail to include a suitable comparison group of normal families ("controls"), so it cannot be concluded that marital difficulties are truly more prevalent among those families than they are in the general population. It is all too easy to attribute any such problems to the existence of disability in the family, but it is not necessarily true that this and this alone is responsible for the difficulties some parents experience.

These disclaimers aside, common sense forces us to accept the proposition that for most families marital stress is one of many manifestations—perhaps the most important, if not the most frequent—of the effects handicap can have on other family members; the reasons for this are many and for the most part, readily apparent.

Life maintenance stress

Financial stress

I suppose in a way you are only asking society to pay part of the price for advances in medical science that have benefitted millions and also resulted in the birth and survival of many handicapped children. You have to recognize that part of this price may mean a much higher cost for their education than looking after a normal child.[11]

The costs of education were but one of the many additional financial burdens families of the handicapped had to bear. In recent years special education has finally come to be regarded as one of the social obligations that can be claimed as a "right," based in large measure on the above argument. But the same does not apply to all other costs of care; only a relatively small part of the medical bills are assumed by some states, whereas in Canada, as in most of Europe, some form of national health insurance covers the entire costs of physician visits as well as hospitalization. In few places, however, are medications or appliances "free," and nowhere does the state reimburse the families for special or all too quickly worn out clothing, diapers, or shoes. Nor is there any compensation for travel when visiting the physician or the sick child in hospital, for special diets, or for architectural modifications to the home. This is only a partial list of some of the direct costs to these families. Those which are more indirect, such as the loss of income through time off from work to attend clinics or visit the hospital or the inability of one spouse to seek work (usually the mother because of added caretaking responsibilities), are rarely acknowledged.

No one has been able to put meaningful figures to this most practical problem of all, save to note that few families who have a child with any chronic disorder are unaffected to some degree. The staggering costs of wheelchairs (particularly motorized ones), their maintenance, and of architectural changes that ensure mobility within the home or simply access to it are easy to appreciate. It is perhaps less easy to realize that even purely "medical" conditions such as asthma may also be very costly. Vance and Taylor,[36] based on the records of 35 asthmatic children in California, estimated that the costs of care ranged from $61 to $3200 per year, with an average figure of $1245, or nearly 15% of gross income. This study was reported in 1968 and presumably some of the costs would now be defrayed under Title IX. However, others would be considerably greater due to inflation and generally rising costs. In a similar report Meyers and co-workers[19] found that 42% of 70 patients with hemophilia living in New Hampshire and Vermont estimated that their medical expenses alone exceed $1000 annually. It is worth noting that more than 50% of this group had been denied health insurance at least once. And even those covered by Blue Cross and Blue Shield must pay for factor VIII concentrates or any other medication given on an outpatient basis. In total, these researchers estimate an annual cost of $60,000 for medical care alone for the group as a whole. They conclude, "Until the bleeder is reduced to poverty levels by the cost of his illness, no effective financial relief is available."

The litany of dollar and cents add-ons is almost endless. The salience of this burden should not be underestimated, for its ramifications extend well beyond simple financial hardship. It must be clear that because of it some resentment toward the child is almost inevitable—resentment not only by the wage earner but often too by siblings who eventually recognize that they are also in various ways being deprived of some of life's basic needs or pleasures because of the costs incurred by their brother or sister's illness. In addition to one spouse being deprived of wage-earning opportunities, the reverse may occur—a spouse may be forced to seek employment to help "make ends meet" when by preference the parent would rather be home helping care for the children.

The obvious inequity of this situation should not need to be spelled out. It is tragic enough to have a child who is disabled or chronically ill; to add often heavy financial insult to the basic physical and emotional injury is simply wrong and unjust. Increasingly, however, even in a land of rugged individualism, popular sentiment is recognizing the basic inequity and moving through the extention of various forms of insurance and state and federal programs to recognize the rightful claim of these families for assistance. But rugged individualism is not completely dead—for example, it lives in the rights of individual states and counties to determine for themselves the extent to which they will implement crippled children's programs, the level of eligibility, the diseases to be covered, and so forth. Overall, we are left with a situation whereby, within some broad limits, the degree to which the costs of illness will be softened by some forms of social assistance remains largely a matter of chance.

To the extent that services which may help soften the financial blow are available through private agencies, this is also all too often a matter of chance of another kind: the specific disorder the child happens to have! This is so because some agencies are relatively speaking "wealthy" while others are poor. For example, most communities of reasonable size have fairly generous programs available through the Cerebral Palsy Association, The Association for the Blind, or the Cystic Fibrosis Association. Not only are these groups well financed and hence able to provide many forms of assistance short of direct subsidies, they are also more effective lobbyists than many of their "country cousins."[4] In Britain, for example, public support for the blind is 200 times greater than that for the deaf—a reflection, no doubt of both a deep-seated popular attitude toward these equally tragic disorders, but also a tribute to the greater fund raising abilities of the wealthier of the two. Unfortunately, however, for most diseases there are no voluntary agencies to which parents can turn for help.

Insurance of some kind is needed to eliminate not only the costs of hospital care but also those associated with all forms of ambulatory care. The next major line of help must be to provide full coverage for disease-related medicines and appliances without the extraordinary "red tape" that is now customary.

Housing

I wish I wasn't living in a place like this—because of the stairs. . . .

The neighbours are very understanding, especially the people beneath because they are the ones who have to suffer the most . . . And that's another reason why I think if we had a ground floor flat I wouldn't worry so much about him making a noise.[11]

Problems related to housing may be almost insurmountable for some families, particularly those with a child who has a severe locomotor disorder like cerebral palsy. Middle-class families rarely consider how much more difficult and stressful everyday life would be if three or four children were sharing one or two rooms. Reasonable living space is taken for granted. However, in the context of having to cope with a child with a major handicap affecting mobility, one who may have to be carried from place to place, housing problems take on a new perspective. The lack of play space, the need to climb stairs, and the lack of basic amenities—these and many more problems that fall under the rubric of "inadequate housing,"—may be

the straw that breaks the camel's back. It is therefore incumbent on the physician who really cares about relieving such burdens to do whatever is possible to help these families secure better housing or such modifications to existing premises as are needed. Frequently low-income families are eligible for housing assistance or may earn a higher priority for public housing if the physician is willing to bring to the attention of the local authorities the added burdens of the handicapped child's special needs.

In a study of the housing problems of a sample of handicapped young adults VanVechten and Pless[38] found that 40% had difficulties related to architectural barriers in their own homes. Adaptations are usually expensive and frequently the needed "know-how" is not easy to locate. Often basic alterations are necessary to permit a child in a wheelchair to enter and leave his home unaided, for example, using ramps or widening doorways to accommodate the passage of a wheelchair. For older children a whole range of additional adaptations are needed to permit them to make full use of the home and its facilities and thereby enable them to take part in the daily life of the family. Counters may need to be lowered, taps and outlets adapted, or telephones placed at a special height. Not only are such adaptations desirable for increasing the independence of the child, they are often essential for his safety. Basically they are all fairly simple, but finding the funds and designers willing to invest time and energy in their construction is much less simple.

Inaccessibility of public places is a major problem in most communities. What is less well appreciated is the extent to which they restrict the social experiences and hence the development of the handicapped. At a later age such barriers also interfere with the availability of employment or higher education. In fact, it is worth noting that many handicapped children receive their education in "special" schools or classes entirely because these are the only facilities that are architecturally accessible.[12] In other words, many more children could become or remain part of the mainstream of education were it not for the existence of these barriers in most regular schools.

Transportation

Alongside these considerations are those pertaining to transportation for the handicapped, both public and private. Consider for a moment the difficulties in transporting a child confined to a wheelchair in a standard automobile. The basic physical problem of lifting and carrying the child from chair to car and back again with each trip increases as the child grows older and heavier. At all times he is completely dependent on such assistance. Not only must the child be carried, but the chair must also be collapsed, stowed in the trunk (or elsewhere), and the process repeated in reverse at the end of the trip. This must be done for each and every journey. For older teenagers and young adults this degree of dependence is unacceptable, but the only alternative is a van, preferably one with a hydraulic lift. Unfortunately, these are extremely expensive and the technology is such that they are often unreliable to the point of posing real dangers to the handicapped driver.

In the area of public transportation the picture is, if anything, even more depressing. Very few communities have buses that are capable of transporting handicapped persons. Thus the only alternative is the use of very expensive wheelchair ambulances or private transportation of the type described. Some communities have adopted the idea of using a dial-a-ride bus to respond to the needs of a variety of handicapped persons. The costs involved are still greater than normal public transportation and accordingly this service requires subsidization by the community. Nonetheless it is the only way that persons in wheelchairs, for example, may be able to gain independence through employment. In our studies[8] approximately 35% of the persons indicated that there were major problems pertaining to transportation difficulties of this nature.

Considerations such as these, although they pertain primarily to adults, are also relevant to discussions of management of the handicapped child. Certainly the physician responsible for providing this care must be aware of the practical problems associated with moving the child from home to school and to places of therapy and recreation. Each of these have an important impact on the ultimate development of the child, and the physician should take whatever steps possible to facilitate these transportation arrangements.

Clothing and appliances

Mundane as it may seem, for many families, particularly those on marginal incomes, the provision of clothing can often be a major hassle. The replacement of ordinary clothes becomes a problem because wear and tear are inevitably excessive in the case of children who spend a lot of time crawling or moving about in an abnormal manner. In addition, to achieve some degree of independence many handicapped children require clothing that has been specially designed and adapted to meet their needs. Velcro fasteners in place of buttons and zippers, shirts and blouses that are not pulled over the head but wrapped around, and trousers or skirts that allow for urine or fecal collection sacs are all obtainable (with some difficulty) and invariably at a greater cost. Physicians, apart from finding additional financial resources, may be unable to help very directly with this problem but referrals to occupational therapists with experience in such matters or to voluntary private agencies may facilitate the solution of these difficulties.

A closely related practical problem for many parents of severely disabled children has to do with securing the needed devices, appliances, and gadgets that may help compensate for the underlying disability. Unfortunately, most such devices are costly, and, moreover, it is usually difficult for any physician to be fully aware of the wide range of appliances available. Several recent publications provide a fairly comprehensive listing, but a more practical approach for most primary care physicians would be to obtain the help of physical or occupational therapists. Not only are they likely to be more familiar with what is available but also of equal importance, these co-workers are usually able to judge the suitability of a particular device relative to the child's developmental level and other considerations.

Need for support

If you have a handicapped child in the family you need support—you don't want to be done good to.[11]

The English phrase "to be done good to" has no exact American equivalent. The closest may be something like "receiving handouts," but in both instances the meaning is clear—these families, like most self-respecting families, do not want to be demeaned in the process of accepting help. They do not want the assistance, financial or otherwise, to be regarded by the donor as a "charitable" gesture, reflecting the kindness or discretion of the giver rather than a rightful claim of the recipient. (Few of us regard the receipt of an income tax refund as an act of generosity on the part of the government. It is a sum to which we are entitled—a simple balancing of the books, and help for the handicapped must be seen in the same way.) Although charity is unwelcome, many families, however, openly acknowledge their great need for assistance. As well as financial support, families need advice and guidance from a sympathetic and knowledgeable source—preferably, but not necessarily, the physician. Cooke[3] notes that several levels of support can be valuable. "Repeated contact with the physician is essential for the family even though no specific therapy is given. . . . Continued interest by the physician is an enormous supporting factor."[3] As well, "Introduction of the family to others with similar problems may permit some emotional outlet but even more importantly may provide the family with details of management worked out by others with years of experience."[3]

A later section will examine more closely how much of this task can be expected of the physician in practical terms. The purpose here is simply to emphasize the pervasive need for a range of services that are neither strictly speaking medical nor financial. Support, guidance, counselling—all these terms apply. For most disabilities the demands are too great for parents (or physicians) to do the job alone and do it adequately. Help of all kinds is needed, and while most physicians can easily appreciate why this is so, what many fail to realize is how poorly our "system" of care is designed to respond adequately to those needs. And as a corollary, physicians may rightfully ask how much of the "supporting role" they should be expected to play.

Worries about the future

The worry is what will happen when you're dead and the child is still alive, with no one to take him out and no one to bother about his birthday.[11]

This poignant observation certainly dominates the minds of many parents of disabled children, whether the child is placed in residential care or kept at home. No matter what arrangements are made, the child's dependence on parental support is an ever-present fact of life for many families. Our society is not yet oriented toward providing much in the way of easily acceptable alternatives to home care for most dependent children or adults. If anything, the situation is worse for adults, and it is therefore quite reasonable that many sensitive parents should be preoccupied about the future.

This preoccupation—the worry about what will happen at some later point in time—ranges through a gamut of fears and anxieties. For the child with a progressive illness the dominant worry is that at some future time he will die. Not knowing when this will be, whether it will be a matter of months or years, and not being able to fully prepare oneself or the rest of the family is a constant burden. Some families are able to come to terms with the inevitability of an early death for children with progressive illnesses on their own. Others will require careful, sensitive guidance from experienced health care workers. Only occasionally is this help given by clergy[7] or friends.

Further children

I'm glad I had a second child now.[11]

One further, often quoted indicator of the immense impact that a severely disabled child has on the family is the way in which it influences attitudes about subsequent reproduction. This is not confined exclusively to situations in which the genetic pattern is known. It also extends to situations in which the sheer burden of day-to-day care makes problematic the question of any additional children, sick or healthy. Whether having a normal child will in various direct or indirect ways add to the difficulties of an already stressed family is difficult to assess. Yet it is precisely this question with which parents need help and advice. At the very least they need support while they go through the agonizing decision-making process. In the case of parents who decide that they cannot cope with another child even if it is normal, the physician should arrange for effective contraceptive advice. Sexual problems, on top of those which already exist, are easily prevented when the parents feel confident that the contraceptive approach chosen will prove to be successful.

The physician must ensure that careful, well-informed, and sensitive genetic counselling is provided in almost all instances. The physician must not believe, however, that after having done so, the problem has ended. At least one study[18] has shown that many parents who receive such counselling still view with perplexity the final decision about whether to have more children. Although they may fully understand the statistical risk of having another child with a defect, the ultimate decision is often seen in terms of the numerator alone rather than as a statistical probability. In other words, while understanding that the risk may be ''1 in a 100,'' the question in their mind is whether or not they will be that *one*. The decision for these parents is essentially a dichotomy—will it or won't it happen *to them,* despite the odds? For these couples many other factors are taken into account as they approach the final decision. They examine their personal resources and their values and look closely at what another disabled child would mean to them as a family. The dilemma is aggravated by the fact that most genetic counselling in North America is aimed at helping parents understand their situation rather than trying to persuade them to make what the counsellor believes to be a ''rational'' or ''correct'' decision based on the odds alone.

In the last decade there have been an increasing number of disorders for which primary prevention is available through prenatal diagnosis (Chapter 9). Through amniocentesis, subsequent enzyme assays, and chromosomal analyses, it is often possible to identify deformed fetuses in utero. When it is virtually certain that a pregnancy has resulted in a fetus with a serious disorder, parents have an opportunity to have the pregnancy terminated through legalized abortion in most parts of the country. This

choice is not as easy as it may sound and again the primary care physician has a key role to play in helping parents make the wisest possible decision, taking a variety of factors into account. Although many physicians view prenatal diagnosis as a great blessing by removing much uncertainty, it should not be assumed that parents will necessarily view it in the same manner. For despite generally liberalized religious attitudes toward abortion under these circumstances, this decision is a major obstacle for many parents. Health care workers themselves may have to struggle to avoid imposing on their patients their own religious biases. As Travis[34] notes, even parents who assert that religion is meaningless or a form of escape may not continue to hold this view when faced with intolerable grief or anxiety. Faced with situations of this nature, in which questions about subsequent pregnancies are being raised, most physicians will want the help of geneticists and often of social workers as well. Physicians in this situation cannot remove themselves completely from this difficult issue. The physician must be familiar with the services and attitudes of colleagues. The physician must know, for example, whether genetic counselling will be presented only as an objective statistical statement of risks or whether it will include a comprehensive assessment of the burden a subsequent handicapped child may impose for each family on an individual basis.

Schooling and vocational training

A second major concern about the future that practically every parent of a disabled child shares relates to questions about schooling and work opportunities in later life. ''What kind of schooling is best for my child, that is, how do I make the compromises that might be needed between the best possible educational experience and the needed allowances for his disability? At what stage and in what manner must we begin to think about job opportunities for a person with this type of disability and how do we decide if the preparation for these is adequate or even appropriate?''

Both questions are tough ones, and because of certain customs and rigidities in our educational system, they are probably tougher than they really need be. The fact is, however, that many disabilities make it difficult for a child to be educated properly in a regular classroom. The difficulties range from fundamentally strategic and pedagogical ones in the case of the blind and the deaf and those with major dyslexias, for example, to simply architectural considerations for those in wheelchairs or on crutches. For the great majority of children of roughly normal intelligence there now seems to be widespread agreement that every effort should be made by parents and physicians to ensure that most of the child's educational experience takes place within the mainstream of regular classroom settings. The reasons are both educational and sociopsychological. Whatever the arrangements, parents must struggle to avoid making undue allowances for the disability in terms of their expectations or those of the child's teachers or peers; if anything the goals for these children should be higher than their peers, since for many it is their mental skills alone that may compensate for their physical limitations. The primary care physician cannot avoid dealing with the question of special educational arrangements and must be prepared to help parents weigh the arguments. For those with lesser disabilities who are in the mainstream, the physician must maintain close contacts with the school to be sure that teachers and others do not out of misguided ignorance overprotect or otherwise hamper the child's educational and social development.

To help parents help their disabled child make the most appropriate decisions about employment, the physician must include among the list of goals during the early years of adolescence sessions devoted specifically to these considerations. Whenever possible these should include inputs from, if not the actual participation of, vocational counsellors and other school representatives as well as, of course, the parents and affected child.

Residential care

And I think for anybody I'd advise them—at least I myself—I'd always keep my baby. The only thing I'm dreading is later on when I'm gone and I don't know what's going to become of him. But still as long as I'm alive he'll always be with me.

. . . Once a child has been in residential care the main strain has been taken away from you. The worry is what will happen to him when you're dead and the child is still alive.

It's not that I wouldn't let him go away—I would—but he's likely to be put in with other kinds of handicap and he's not going to get the special attention he requires.

When A. went to residential care we didn't want him to go completely. We weren't rejecting him. It was just that the strain of having him with us seven days a week, 24 hours a day was too great and we needed help.[11]

Concerns such as these about the effects of institutional care are dominant in the mind of most parents faced with this agonizing decision. It is also a concern that has been shared by investigators who have examined the effects of residential care on handicapped children. Until quite recently the concensus was that whenever possible this should be avoided, since almost invariably it was assumed that the effects on the child's development are adverse. Tizard and Grad[33] were among the first investigators to examine the effects of institutional care objectively. From the field experiments that they described and evaluated it seemed clear that the usual form of residential program in large institutions is undesirable. However, newer, smaller units appear to be less of a problem and have fewer undesirable effects on the child's development. In fact, some studies, such as those of Kushlick[17] and his colleagues, suggest that with imagination, adequate resources, and opportunities for flexibility, small family-like units are feasible and attractive alternatives to helping the severely retarded child at home—both for the family and for the child.

Most of the studies in this field have dealt with children with mental subnormality and it is only recently that some attention has been directed toward the physically handicapped and chronically sick child. Perhaps the most extensive study of this nature is that reported by Miller and Gwynne.[20] The authors note:

Institutions vary greatly in the extent to which they go beyond simply providing physical care [by making] provisions for their inmates to occupy other roles besides that of patient—the extent, in other words, to which they provide for inmates to exercise independence.[20]

They conclude, however, that

The problems of providing residential care for the physically handicapped are in many ways intractable and will remain so until and unless there is a pronounced change in the values of society, which may make the parasitism of some of its members more acceptable to all.[20]

PRACTICAL PROBLEMS FOR THE PRIMARY CARE PHYSICIAN
Practical implementation

To implement some of the practical vitally important measures outlined so far, many fundamental changes are needed in the way health care professionals approach the care of these children (Table 17-2). The most important change is for primary care physicians to accept fully the key role they alone have to play in the management of the disabled child. Several studies[14-26] have clearly demonstrated that with few exceptions it cannot be assumed that disease specialists, for example, pediatric neurolo-

gists, orthopedists, allergists, or rheumatologists, are willing (or able) to play the roles of manager, coordinator, and ombudsman for these families, yet it is equally clear that these are essential roles. They demand the time, skills, and devotion that many primary care physicians already possess or (in the case of skills) can readily acquire. Unfortunately it is also clear that at present it is uncommon for primary care physicians, be they pediatricians or family physicians, to accept this role to the extent that it is required. A typical pattern is one in which a primary care physician who suspects a child to have a disability or who makes such a diagnosis immediately refers the child to the appropriate subspecialists. Implicit in such referrals is the assumption that specialists will provide most of the ongoing and comprehensive care required. The primary care physician may also easily assume that the specialist will take on the managerial role and provide all of the needed coordination of services. Not only is this the exception rather than the rule, but also it frequently implies a subtle or gradual transfer of responsibility, both for the

Table 17-2. Problems and some practical steps in their solution

Problems	Practical steps
How to manage a complex set of inputs	Develop a formal "plan"; specify goals and time for attainment (Chapter 8)
How to maximize compliance with goals of care	Ensure parent participation in determining goals; consider practical obstacles
How to prevent secondary psychosocial problems	Include in treatment plan; assess family and child; provide counseling; focus on self-concept (Chapter 15)
How to find the time needed to counsel and educate	Schedule regular blocks *or* use nonprofessional family counselors, social workers, or public health nurses
How to provide day-to-day help and services to lighten the load	Contact community agencies; lay counselors, etc.
How to decide about residential care	Explore all alternatives; weigh pros and cons; consider "temporary" placement initially
How to provide relief from need for constant attention and limited social life	Consider day care programs, respite and residential care, voluntary agencies and parent groups
How to deal with embarrassment due to reaction of others	Participate in public education efforts; help parents to "role-play"
How to deal with effects on siblings and parents	Discuss problem with parents directly; use other therapists and helpers, genetic and other counseling
How to solve financial, housing, and transportation problems	Ensure family receives all help it is entitled to, especially use of voluntary agencies; lobby for "barrier free" legislation
How to use adaptive devices	Consult occupational or physical therapist, voluntary agencies

illness and for the child's acute and preventive health care. It is unusual to find a specialist able and willing to assume complete responsibility for all the child's needs. Similarly, parents wanting to ensure that the child receives the best possible care would also welcome the advice of specialists. Without a doubt high-quality care must be equated in part with the awesome technology that most specialists in tertiary hospitals have at their fingertips—but only in part.

Because most families have an equally urgent desire to find someone willing to serve as "captain of the ship," to help them steer through the rough seas, to help them chart a course for the future, both in theory and in practice the primary care physician is best suited to play this decisive role. It is, after all, the physician who knows the child and family best. Moreover, the physician knows the community best and should be familiar with the schools, agencies, and other resources. Ultimately, therefore, to obtain the best possible balance between excellent medical "treatment" and good "management" it is usually necessary for the primary care physician to share the responsibility for the child's care with one or more specialists. Under this shared responsibility model the referral should explicitly state, in writing, who will do what and a copy should be provided to the parents.

Unfortunately, circumstances such as the volume of patients, the availability of time, financial considerations, and the complex nature of the child's disorder make it impossible for the primary care physician to assume the complete responsibility for the patient. However, if the physician is to be the "captain of the ship" certain basic changes in the office routine must be made, the knowledge base expanded, and certain philosophies of service developed. It requires that the physician be committed to the concept that services to the developmentally disabled, chronically ill child and his family are a significant part of the primary care mandate. The fact that some pediatricians have succeeded in fulfilling this mandate speaks for itself. McInerny,[18a] in a symposium concerning chronic illness indicated that his large, busy group practice has successfully

integrated the coordination of comprehensive care of the chronically ill child into the practice without financial sacrifice and with a high level of patient satisfaction. The mechanism of implementation would require major changes for some pediatric practices and relatively minor alterations for others. Needless to say, starting out with the "proper" initial organizational format would be exceedingly helpful.

Having a basic knowledge in child development and developmental disabilities is obviously essential. In a study of 100 New England pediatricians Levine noted a basic lack in knowledge of child development. The acquisition of knowledge and skills in this area can be obtained by attending minifellowships (several of which offer stipends to compensate for the time away from the office), by participating in university-affiliated developmental clinics, and by attending symposia, all combined with a great deal of self-teaching. Once a basic core of knowledge is established, the following organizational changes can be initiated:

1. Children who are identified as high risk or who are developmentally disabled should be "red tagged" and receive a more comprehensive evaluation. They would, in general, require a longer visit. One afternoon per week should be allocated for these more complex, difficult to manage youngsters. Health maintenance and acute illness for these children also require some additional time. This seems to balance out; the brief "otitis visit" pays for the somewhat longer visit for the chronically ill child.

2. Approximately 50% of primary practice is well baby and child care. 50% of this could be successfully handled by a pediatric nurse practitioner. This would liberate a pediatrician for 25% of the working time.

3. The use of allied professionals such as nurse practitioners for developmental and behavioral screening and case management. McInerny and associates,[18a] in addition to using nurse practitioners, rented space to a clinical psychologist and a social worker who provided services to many of their patients.

4. These patients should be charged an appropriate hourly fee. Most parents would gladly pay for these services rather than having to go unnecessarily to impersonal tertiary care settings.

5. Finally, a problem- or goal-oriented record-keeping system with a developmental perspective should be established (Chapter 8).

Working with allied health personnel

Most chronic illness requires a wide range of help from health care workers besides the physician. Broadly speaking, both ''technical'' and ''supportive'' services are needed. Included in the first category are the contributions of nurses, physical therapists, occupational therapists, speech therapists, prosthetists, laboratory services, and geneticists. In the second category are included social workers, psychologists, guidance counselors, family service workers, home aides, vocational counselors, and school personnel. These distinctions are somewhat arbitrary, and there are obviously several overlapping areas. Regardless of the category to which they belong, the more such services are mobilized the greater the opportunities for fractionization and hence the greater the need for skillful coordination and integration. Without active leadership a wide variety of well-intended services may easily end up adding to the family's burdens and confusion.

Much has been written about the advantages of the team approach, but it must be recognized that these potential advantages are not without hazards. The difficult challenge of providing services to the developmentally disabled child cannot be met simply by bringing all the needed personnel together in one place at one time. Procedures must be developed to ensure that each member of the team understands and shares a common set of objectives. Whenever possible these objectives must be reached with the participation of the parents.

Although every effort should be made to share the burden of care between both parents, realistically it must be recognized that it is the mother who usually needs the most support and guidance and perhaps above all the ear of the sympathetic listener. Up to a point the physician can and should play this role, but for some parents more time and help is needed than the physician can practically provide. It was for this reason that the idea of using nonprofessional ''family counselors'' was introduced on an experimental basis in Rochester.[23] Six carefully selected nonprofessional women were recruited from among a pool of applicants for this task. After a short period of training in which the basics of counselling techniques were introduced and some familiarity with the more common chronic disorders of children was provided, each was assigned to eight families in which there was a child with a chronic medical condition. After a year of counselling, therapeutic listening, advising, helping, and providing a variety of other forms of support, the effects of this low-keyed intervention was assessed. Parents evaluated the help they received and indicated whether they would be willing to pay for this service in the future if it were necessary to do so. Most indicated that they would do so within limits, evidence of their general enthusiasm for the program. The children who were the focus of the intervention received a battery of psychological tests of adjustment before the program began. A matched group with similar illnesses were also tested in an identical fashion. Both groups were reassessed at the end of the year of ''experimental counselling.'' The improvement in the test scores of the group that received the services of family counselor was statistically better than that of the controls, suggesting that this form of intervention is also effective in helping these children adjust to their illnesses. Although it was the children who were the main focus of this intervention, it was the parents, principally the mothers, who received most of the counselling time and attention. The fact that the benefits were in effect ''transferred to the child'' has simply added evidence that the family is a major intervening variable in the process of adjustment. It also provides a further example of the extent to which the illness affects the family and in particular places stress on the mother. By alleviating this stress in a nonspecific fashion child and family are benefited in ways that may have far-reaching consequences. Help of this nature should be a major ingredient of the management of these children, and the physician must ensure that it is provided when needed. It is of special importance that the help be provided before major problems emerge, not after. To do so, the physician must be helped to recognize situations that constitute a high risk for such problems because the physician obviously cannot provide intensive help of this kind for every family that has a child with a developmental disorder.

Setting and measuring goals

The objectives of care, both short-term and long-term, should be put in writing and reviewed against the listing of goals at regular intervals. There should be a list of services needed to accomplish these goals and a time by which they will be achieved. Goals and services must be reviewed, updated, and refined at regular interviews.

The initial and periodical reassessment of the child's needs in the form of such a treatment plan is an essential element in assisting the physician and providing management for children with developmental disorders. These needs must not only be comprehensive but should also include some indication of the manner in which their achievement will be assessed. The development of the goal-oriented plan is extensively discussed in Chapter 8 and applies to the care of all chronically ill or developmentally disabled children.

Parent participation in decision making

You want to be able to take part in the discussions that lead to decisions about your child.[11]

For the most part, parents do want to play this role, yet it is surprising how rarely they are given a truly effective voice. It is not easy for physicians to share with parents many key decisions, especially if they are predominantly "medical." But sometimes the distinction is not as clear as it seems at first; for example, the physician might assume that increasing the dosage of anticonvulsants to more effectively control seizures is a purely medical decision. But for some parents associated problems with behavior or decline in school performance, which may be a consequence of the higher

dosage, may be more important than good control.

To ensure that the outcome of care is as favorable as possible, particularly when compliance is involved, it is essential that parents agree with the management goals established from the outset. These goals emerge from a process of exploration, one in which the physician helps parents examine their priorities, their assets, and those of the child. Inevitably, value judgments enter into the picture, but the fact that this is so should deter neither party from making such judgments as explicit as possible.

Nor should it be assumed that these goals are immutable; as time passes and events occur, different sets of values may emerge. Opportunity is needed to reexamine these goals on a regular basis along with the assumptions on which they are based. Whenever preferences as to treatment, for example, are expressed, values and judgments are implied—on the part of the parents, physician, or society. What is unusual is to suggest that values be made as explicit as possible. Parents may be more concerned about a child's emotional well-being than they are about his locomotor development. In such cases they may, in the view of the physician, be wrong or misguided. The physician is free to say why, but in the end some common ground must be reached.

Although the principle of parent participation in the establishment of treatment objectives may seem unrealistic in the context of present-day physician-patient relationships, the principle is of potentially great importance to the success of care. Parents often imply that they want physicians to make decisions for them—especially the tough ones. Indeed, in many instances physicians *must* be prepared to make many difficult decisions on their own. In such cases it is just as wrong to abdicate all responsibility as it is to deny parents the opportunity to share in decision making. For example, even well-informed parents cannot be expected to make the final choice between radiotherapy alone or radiotherapy along with chemotherapy in the treatment of a child with a malignant tumor. But parents are entitled to enough information to enable them to express opinions about how much they think various side effects or the additional illness may outweigh the uncertain benefits of the more aggressive regimen. Invariably such decisions will be wiser, kinder, more appropriate, and more likely to lead to the desired end if they are based on a sound understanding of the parents' values and priorities.

Assessing the family

As has been emphasized throughout the preceding sections, the family is the focal point of the care of a child with a chronic illness. The need for involvement by parents in setting realistic goals should also be clear. However, to do this effectively physicians need to know a great deal about the family and to make good use of this knowledge. Some recent work has demonstrated that of all the factors that enable one child with a chronic illness to "adjust well" while another does not, few are more important than the nature of the family unit.[25]

Accordingly, the physician who wishes to use energies and resources most efficiently must constantly try to distinguish between "high-risk" and "low-risk" families, that is, children who will do well without extra help as opposed to those who need it. To help make this distinction, in addition to the attributes of the child and his illness, there remains the paramount factor of the family itself—its strengths and weaknesses. As with the comprehensive assessment of the child, much of this knowledge may come simply from accumulated experience with the family. If this knowledge does not already exist, however, the physician must spend the time needed to interview the family at length, or must find someone else, such as a social worker, to do so.

The dynamics of the marital relationship are of special importance for, as Travis[34] points out, the chronically ill child usually needs two parents.

It takes two to cope when a child is sick at home over a long period of time. One needs to earn while the other stays home and takes care of the sick child: one may need to take time off from work and care for siblings while the other parent takes the sick child to the doctor or attends to the chores of living. Two may be needed to lift a child in a cast or lift an older child who has become obese from inactivity.

It often takes two to "spell" each other during long drawn out and physically wearing home care and treatment. When children are ill for weeks on end, needing to be turned or sat with, medicated and comforted, exhaustion sets in if only one adult has the entire burden. And these things say nothing of the mutual support that parents need when fearful things are happening to a loved child, when worries mount, or when disaster strikes.

Obviously the disabled child in a single-parent household is almost certain to require extra help and attention. As an aid to making an assessment of the family, the Family Functioning Index (Appendix) is a guide that may identify potential problems. It can be used as a screen to help busy professionals.[24]

Education about the child's disorder

The trouble with his condition is that people don't know enough about it.[11]

These words, spoken by one parent with reference to autism, apply equally to many other developmental disorders and convey a deep-seated concern that is not often expressed openly to the physician. Lack of knowledge by health scientists and lack of understanding by parents (and patients) are two obstacles that underlie many of the most easily preventable problems in the care of disabled children. It is certainly true that there are many diseases about which health professionals know remarkably little. Many of the questions that are of greatest importance to parents are those about which we are frequently the most ignorant. We cannot, for example, say with certainty what the best approach to day-to-day management should be when it comes to such questions as whether to err on the side of protectiveness or independence. Nor can we say for certain which circumstances are most likely to produce secondary psychosocial maladjustment. For the most part we do not know what the impact of the disease will be on the child's scholastic performance. What physicians know about such issues is confined to generalities; it is far from the degree of precise knowledge that has been acquired about many of the more biological or technical aspects of disease. Yet even in the domain where physicians are best informed there are many gaps in our knowledge.

At the same time, however, it must be recognized that parents are often denied the full benefits of this knowledge. Study after study[15] has shown that many parents of children with developmental disorders are remarkably ignorant of even the most basic factors regarding their child's condition. In very few instances can this ignorance be laid entirely at the feet of the parents. Some physicians simply do not take sufficient time or trouble to pass on the information; others believe that they can do so by simply recommending pamphlets or books, not understanding that many parents cannot comprehend material in this form. Most often, however, physicians do attempt to convey the information parents so badly need to make intelligent decisions about their child's care. Unfortunately, as Korsch[5,16] and others have shown, many physicians have great difficulty conveying this information so it is easily understood. It is not only what parents are told (or not told) that is at fault, but also how and when they are told.

Whenever uncertainty about genetic components of the disease exist, the possibility of having a second (or third) child with the same disorder looms large. With improvements in genetic counselling, increasing opportunities for prenatal diagnosis through, for example, amniocentesis, along with more liberal criteria for therapeutic abortion, some of this stress may be alleviated. Several recent studies suggest, however, that the impact of these advances is extremely limited; for example, it has been estimated that less than 2% of pregnant women over 40 years of age, among whom the risk of having a child with Down's syndrome is three to four times greater than it is among younger mothers, have amniocentesis for prenatal diagnosis—despite its widespread availability. In general, genetic counselling is provided much less often that it should be. In our own studies[26] of children with spina bifida and rheumatoid arthritis, 38% and 77% of parents respectively reported that they had *not* received such advice. Although the physician may know that the genetic component of juvenile rheumatoid arthritis is small or perhaps nonexistent, few parents know this and most need to be told.

Another component of the genetic issue is the feeling of guilt, which it is commonly assumed many parents with a disabled child experience long after the birth of the affected child. Whether a spouse believes his or her genes or those of the other spouse are "responsible" is relatively unimportant. What is crucial is that physicians acknowledge the frequency with which misperceptions of this nature exist. Some evidence suggests that lack of understanding of the real cause of the illness is related to assumptions, often quite false, about the extent to which the condition could have been prevented. In simple, practical terms these findings suggest that the physician must be sure that parents receive as much accurate information as they can handle about the cause of a child's illness.

Planning for the future

For most parents a decision about residential care poses a terrible dilemma. The needs of the severely disabled child must be weighed against the effects of the continued presence of the child in the family unit. From the point of view of the family physician, the first problem is to recognize the enormity of this issue and to avoid simplistic solutions. The physician must first acquire information about all forms of residential care available.

Having identified the available possibilities, the next step for the physician is to be sure about the policies for admission and discharge, particularly with respect to permitting temporary returns to the home. Parents find it easier to make a final decision in such matters when they can be assured that admission policies are flexible. The physician may help most by encouraging hesitant parents to take advantage of arrangements whereby children receive residential care initially only on a "respite" basis.

When a decision about residential care must be seen as a "final" one, the physician has a key supportive role to play. It must be recognized that this decision is primarily one that the family alone can make; the physician's task is to help them examine the pros and cons as dispassionately as possible. It is important that the physician not have a clear bias toward either alternative; the physician should neither be convinced that *all* retarded children should be institutionalized, nor that it is *always* wrong to do so. These decisions must be tailored to individual families and must take into account the circumstances and resources of the community. As Hewett[10] states, "The main conclusion from this limited study must be that over-simplified approaches to the unravelling of parental attitudes to subnormal children and the means of institutionalization of such children, should be abandoned."

The film *Stress*[11] shows a 20-year-old person with athetoid cerebral palsy, the only child of middle-aged parents. It is clear that their lives revolve entirely around the care of this "child." Her simple skills in cutting, sewing, and pasting and her rudimentary speech appear to give them much pleasure and satisfaction. Many viewers find it difficult to accept that the parents' statement that their daughter has provided them with a "purpose in life" is anything but a rationalization. Medical students in particular often feel strongly that parents should be advised that a sacrifice of this kind is inappropriate in the context of present-day society. Certainly it is inconsistent with many widely held values.

As with most other problems in which difficult decisions must be made and in which the physician's role is ambiguous, the only means available for ensuring that the best possible advice is given is to invest the time needed to get to know the family well. An awareness of the family's structure and functioning and its values and resources (e.g., the availability of grandparents, uncles, and aunts) are each important factors. Likewise, as has been suggested, the availability and array of community resources must also be considered in helping parents reach important decisions. Perhaps the most important factor of all is the ability to reassure parents that most decisions are not irrevocable. In some instances the decision is more difficult the longer the child has been at home. This last concern should, however, be qualified. Although in theory it is undoubtedly true for some families, it is also true that for many others such a decision is easier when they know they have done the best they can and given the child as much of themselves as can reasonably be expected. Here again the physician's role is important in helping ensure that guilt feelings are minimized or at least that their effects are kept within reasonable limits.

SUMMARY

As has been implied throughout, perhaps because of their apparent simplicity, the two central components of care, education and counselling, are often neglected entirely or delivered too casually to be effective. Parents need as much information about the child's illness as they are able to comprehend, especially when they are expected to provide day-to-day care alongside the physician. Aside from understanding the disease, however, most parents also need much in the way of advice, instruction, helpful hints, and various kinds of psychological and social support, all of which comes under the broad heading of "counselling."

The successful management of children with chronic potentially handicapping conditions hinges as much on the physician's understanding of the psychosocial dimension of care as it does on appreciation of the technical dimensions. To provide such demanding care the physician must understand personal feelings and attitudes toward chronic illness and handicap. The physician needs to understand the parents' phases of adaptation and be able to cope without anger or frustration with the parents' frequent use of denial, feelings of guilt, projection of feelings, or tendency to become overly dependent on the physician. The counterparts of these phenomena in the child must also be understood so that the physician can assist in interpreting these feelings and reactions, help discover strengths as well as weaknesses, and enable both parents and children to ventilate their anxieties and other feelings. If the physician fails to understand personal feelings toward these children and their families there is little chance of success. Characteristically, these patients rarely show improvements related to the physician's actions and as a consequence there is an understandable tendency to reject them or accord them a low priority. The physician's own anxiety, sympathy, or identification may lead initially to trying too hard and later to disappointment and resentment. Truly professional health care workers must understand these feelings and learn to cope with them. The physician who is confronted with the care of a child with a permanent or lengthy illness faces a monumental challenge. If it is overcome successfully it may be one of the most satisfying experiences of one's professional career. If approached reluctantly or indifferently, it must inevitably bring frustration and disappointment—for the physician, the parents, and, above all, the sick child.

REFERENCES

1. Ashley, J.: Journey into silence, London, 1973, The Bodley Head, Ltd.
2. Carnegie United Kingdom Trust: Handicapped children and their families, London, 1964, Constable & Co., Ltd.
3. Cooke, R. E.: Foreword. In Debuskey, M. editor: The chronically ill child and his family, Springfield, Ill., 1970, Charles C Thomas, Publisher.
4. Foltz, A. M.: Uncertainties of federal child health policies: impact in two states, DHEW publ. no. (PHS) 78-3190, Washington D.C., 1978, National Center for Health Services Research.
5. Francis, V., Korsch, B. M., and Morris, M. J.: Gaps in doctor-patient communications: patients' response to medical advice, N. Engl. J. Med. **280:**535, 1969.
6. Gayton, W., et al.: Children with cystic fibrosis. I. Psychological test findings of patients, siblings and parents, Pediatrics **59:**888, 1977.
7. Gnagy, L., Satterwhite, B., and Pless, I. B.: The role of clergy in counseling the families of handicapped children, J. Religion Health **16:**15, 1977.
8. Haggerty, R. J. Roghmann, K. J., and Pless, I. B.: Child health and the community, New York, 1975, John Wiley & Sons, Inc.
9. Hewett, S.: The need for long-term care in mental retardation. In Holt, K. S., Hewett, S., and Robertson J., editors: Occasional papers nos. 2, 3, and 4, London, 1972, Butterworth & Co. (Publishers), Ltd.
10. Hewett, S., Newson, J., and Newson, E.: The family and the handicapped child, Chicago, 1970, Aldine Publishing Co.
11. Hill, D. producer: Stress: parents with a handicapped child, London, Short Film Service.
12. Jørgensen, I. S.: Special education in Denmark, Copenhagen, 1970, Det Danske Selskab.
13. Kanof, A., Kutner, B., and Gordon, N. B.: The impact of infantile amaurotic familial idiocy (Tay-Sachs disease) on the family, Pediatrics **29:**37, 1962.
14. Kanthor, H., et al.: Areas of responsibility in the health care of multiply handicapped children, Pediatrics **54:**779, 1974.
15. Kennell, J. H., et al.: What parents of rheumatic fever patients don't understand about the disease and its prophylactic management, Pediatrics **43:**160, 1969.
16. Korsch, B. M., et al.: Gaps in doctor-patient communication. I. Doctor-patient interaction and patient satisfaction, Pediatrics **42:**855, 1968.
17. Kushlick, A.: Residential care for the mentally subnormal, R. Soc. Health J. **90:**255, 1970.
18. Lippman-Hand, A.: Genetic counseling: parents' responses to uncertainty, unpublished doctoral dissertation, Montreal, 1977, McGill University.
18a. McInerny, T.: The role of the primary pediatrician in group practice. In Moore, T. D., editor: The care of children with chronic illness. Report of the Sixty-Seventh Ross Conference on Pediatric Research, 1975, Columbus, Ohio, Ross Laboratories, pp. 72-74.
19. Meyers, R. D., et al.: The social and economic impact of hemophilia—a survey of 70 cases in Vermont and New Hampshire, Am. J. Public Health **62:**530, 1972.
20. Miller, E. J., and Gwynne, G. V.: A life apart, London, 1972, Tavistock Publications, Ltd.
21. Pless, I. B.: Communities of the handicapped. In Apley J., editor: A Festschrift for Ronald MacKeith, Philadelphia, 1978, J. B. Lippincott Co.
22. Pless, I. B., and Pinkerton, P.: Chronic childhood disorder—promoting patterns of adjustment, London, 1975, Henry Kimpton Publishers.
23. Pless, I. B., and Satterwhite, B.: Chronic illness in childhood: selection, activities and evaluation of nonprofessional family counselors, Clin. Pediatr. **11:**403, 1972.
24. Pless, I. B., and Satterwhite, B.: A measure of family functioning and its application, Soc. Sci. Med. **7:**163, 1973.
25. Pless, I. B., Roghmann, K., and Haggerty, R. J.: Chronic illness, family functioning, and psychological adjustment: a model for the allocation of preventive mental health services, Int. J. Epidemiol. **1:**271, 1972.
26. Pless, I. B., Satterwhite, B., and VanVechten, D.: Division, duplication and neglect: patterns of care for children with chronic disorders, Child Care Health Dev. **4:**55, 1978.
27. Richardson, S. A.: Handicap, appearance and stigma, Soc. Sci. Med. **5:**621, 1971.
28. Richardson, S. A.: People with cerebral palsy talk for themselves, Dev. Med. Child Neurol. **14:**524, 1972.
29. Richardson, S. A., Hastorf, A. H., and Dornbusch, S. M.: Cultural uniformity in reactions to physical disabilities, Am. Sociol. Rev. **26:**241, 1961.
30. Rutter, M., Tizard, J., and Whitmore, K.: Education, health and behavior, London, 1970, Longman Group, Ltd.
31. Satterwhite, B. B.: Impact of chronic illness on child and family: an overview based on five surveys with implications for management, Int. J. Rehab. Res. **1:**7, 1978.
32. Tew, B. K., and Laurence, K. M.: Mothers, brothers, and sisters of patients with spina bifida, Dev. Med. Child Neurol. **15:**69, 1973.
33. Tizard, J., and Grad, J. C.: The mentally handicapped and their families—a social survey, London, 1961, Oxford University Press.

34. Travis, G.: Chronic illness in children: its impact on child and family, Stanford, Calif., 1976, Stanford University Press.
35. Turk, J.: Impact of cystic fibrosis on family functioning, Pediatrics **34:**67, 1964.
36. Vance, V. J., and Taylor, W. F.: The financial cost of chronic childhood asthma, Ann. Allergy **29:**455, 1971.
37. Vance, J. C., et al.: Effects of nephrotic syndrome on the family: a controlled study, Pediatrics (in press).
38. Van Vechten, D., and Pless, I. B.: Housing and transportation: twin barriers to independence, Rehabil. Lit. **37:**202, 1976.
39. Wright, B. A.: Physical disability—a psychological approach, New York, 1960, Harper & Row, Publishers.

Appendix*

<table>
<tr>
<td colspan="4" align="center">FAMILY LIFE QUESTIONNAIRE—WIFE</td>
<td align="center">Office
use
only</td>
<td>NF   OF
I DX TR</td>
</tr>
</table>

Following is a list of questions to be answered by you and your husband separately. They will help us to gain a better understanding of family life. Please do not discuss the questions until after you have completed the questionnaire and returned it to the secretary. Omit questions regarding children if there are none under 18 living at home. Your answers will be confidential. Do *not* sign your name at the end.

MEMBERS OF FAMILY

Relation	Age	Sex	Highest grade completed
Father			
Mother			
Oldest child			
Next			
Others in Household			

1. What sorts of things do you do as a family?
   a. In the evenings:_____

   _____

   b. On the weekends:_____

   _____

*A questionnaire that can be used to open discussion regarding family roles and function.

FAMILY LIFE QUESTIONNAIRE—WIFE—CONT'D

1. What sorts of things do you do as a family?—cont'd
   c. On vacations: _____

   _____

➤ Put a check in the box corresponding to your choice.

	Better	Same	Worse
2. How do you think the children get along together compared with other families? (Disregard if only one child.)	☐	☐	☐

	Yes	Sometimes	No
3. Do the children find it easy to talk to you about their problems?	☐	☐	☐
4. Do the children find it easy to talk to their father about their problems?	☐	☐	☐
5. Do you find your husband an easy person to talk to when something is troubling you?	☐	☐	☐
6. Is your husband able to spend a lot of time with the children in the evening?	☐	☐	☐
7. Is your husband able to spend a lot of time with the children on the weekend?	☐	☐	☐
8. Are you able to spend a lot of time with the children in the evening?	☐	☐	☐
9. Are you able to spend a lot of time with the children on the weekend?	☐	☐	☐

	Happier	Same	Less happy
10. Would you say, all in all, that your family is happier than most others you know, about the same, or less happy?	☐	☐	☐

11. What would you say was the most important problem you as a family had to deal with this last year?

   _____

	Yes	No
a. Was a solution arrived at?	☐	☐
b. Did you discuss the problem with your husband?	☐	☐
c. Was everyone satisfied with the solution?	☐	☐

12. In every family someone has to decide such things as where the family will live and so on. Many couples talk about such things with the family first, but the final decision often has to be made by the husband or the wife. If these are situations you have not decided on recently, how would they be decided on should they occur? (Write in the number corresponding to your choice.)

   1 = Husband always
   2 = Husband more than wife
   3 = Husband and wife exactly the same
   4 = Wife more than husband
   5 = Wife always

   a. Who usually makes the final decision about what kind of car to get? ☐
   b. Who usually makes the final decision about whether or not to buy some life insurance? ☐
   c. Who usually makes the final decision about what house or apartment to take? ☐
   d. Who usually makes the final decision about what job your husband should take? ☐
   e. Who usually makes the final decision about whether or not you should go to work or quit work? ☐

FAMILY LIFE QUESTIONNAIRE—WIFE—CONT'D

    f. Who usually makes the final decision about how much your family   ☐
       can afford to spend per week on food?

    g. Who usually makes the final decision about what physician to have   ☐
       when someone is sick?

    h. Who usually makes the final decision about where to go on a vaca-   ☐
       tion?

13. Thinking of marriage in general, which one of these five things would you say is the most valuable part of marriage? (Write in the number corresponding to your choice, *using each number only once.*)

       1 = The chance to have children
       2 = The standard of living—the kind of house, clothes, car, and so forth
       3 = The husband's understanding of the wife's problems and feelings
       4 = The husband's expression of love and affection for the wife
       5 = Companionship in doing things together with the husband

    a. What is the most valuable part of marriage?   ☐
    b. What is the next most valuable?   ☐
    c. What is third most valuable?   ☐
    d. What is fourth most valuable?   ☐
    e. What is fifth most valuable?   ☐

14. Of course, most couples differ sometimes over things. When you and your husband differ about something, do you usually give in and do it your husband's way or does he usually come around to your point of view?

☐	☐	☐
Husband's way	50/50	Wife's way

15. Would you say disagreements in your household come up more often, about the same, or less often than in other families you know?

☐	☐	☐
More often	Same	Less often

16. Would you say that, compared to most families you know, you feel less close to each other, about the same, or closer than other families do?

☐	☐	☐
Less close	Same	Closer

17. Following are some feelings you might have about certain aspects of marriage. (Write in the number corresponding to your choice.)

       1 = Pretty disappointed. I'm really missing out on that.
       2 = It would be nice to have more.
       3 = It's all right, I guess—I can't complain.
       4 = Quite satisfied—I'm lucky the way it is.
       5 = Enthusiastic—it couldn't be better.

    a. How do you feel about your standard of living, the kind of house,   ☐
       clothes, car, and so forth?

    b. How do you feel about the understanding of your problems and   ☐
       feelings you get?

    c. How do you feel about the love and affection you receive?   ☐
    d. How do you feel about the companionship of doing things together?   ☐

18. When your husband comes home from work, how often does he talk about things that happened there?

☐	☐	☐
Very often	Sometimes	Never

Index

Lead exposure and mental retardation, 195
Learning disabilities, 156, 312-339
  in child with myelodysplasia, 124
  in child, older, or adolescent, 331-333
  standardized tests for, 342
Learning disabled child
  care of, and primary care physician, 313
  model of, 312-313
Learning disorders, potential, screening for, 341
Learning process, 316
Legislative history of developmental disability, 7
Legislative issues and mental retardation, 217-218
Lennox-Gastaut syndrome, 170
Lens, 275
  dislocated, 276
Lesions
  lacunar, 274
  myelodysplasia, 118
Letter reversals, 322
Lexicon, 291
  first, 83
Life maintenance stress, 421-425
Limb malformation, 244
Linear hypoplasia, 392
Lingual frenum, prominent, 399-400
Lingual functions, 298
Lip(s), 397-398
  cleft, 254
  competency, 397-398
Lipid metabolism disorder, 236
Lipidoses, cerebral, 277
Localization response in infant, development of, 257
Locomotor prognosis and significant developmental motor disability, 158
Locus, 232
Long-term memory, 326, 327
Loss of hearing; *see* Hearing loss
Loudness, 295
Low birth weight infant, 33, 253
  appropriate for gestational age, 33-35
  disposition of, 147
  and significant developmental motor disability, 146-147
Low expressivity, 233
L/S ratio, 32
Lückerschädl, 119

M

Macrodontia, 405
Macroglossia, 395-396, 399
Mainstreaming, 190, 212
Malformations
  chest, 244-245
  congenital, 254
    and mental retardation, 209
  ear, 242, 243
  eye, 242
  face, 240-242
  genital, 244
  head, 239-240
  limb, 244

Malformations—cont'd
  nipple, 246
  nose, 242
  oral area, 242-244
  syndromes, 239-248
    diagnosis of, 239
    and environmental agents, 239
    and morphological abnormalities, 239-248
Malleus, 258
  short process of, 258
Malocclusion, 406
Management
  of autism, 372-373
  of adolescent with learning disability, 332
  of chronically ill child, 366
  of emotional problems, 375
  of hearing loss by primary care physician, 250-252
  of learning disorders, 333-336
  of practical problems, 412-436
  psychiatric, of schizophrenia, 374-375
  of resonance disorder, 294
    conservative, 294
    prosthetic, 294
  of seizures, 167-168, 176-178
  of significant developmental motor disability, 157-158
  skills, physician's, 16
  of voice disorders, 295-296
Maneuver, Credé, 121, 122
Manifestations of inborn errors of metabolism in infancy, 204
Mannerisms
  of blind child, 383
  of deaf child, 382
Manual communication, 266, 306
Marfan syndrome, 276
Marital relations of parents of handicapped child, 421, 432
Maroteaux-Lamy syndrome, 236
Masking, 262
Maternal age and perinatal risk, 28
Maternal attachment, 42
Maternal Behavior Progression, 42
Maternal diabetes, 29-30
Maternal weight gain and infant mortality, 28
Maternal-child health index, 23
Maturation, 62-64
  cognitive, 53-63
  motor, 54-56
  neurological, 53-63
  reflexive, 54-56, 63
  visual, 62
Measurement of height, weight, and head circumference, 108
Medical aspects
  of hearing loss, 250-267
  of significant developmental motor disability, 145-159
Medical interventions with preschool child, 356
Medical knowledge, core, for child development and rehabilitation, 12-13
Medical and obstetrical conditions, coexisting, 29-31
Medical records of chronically ill children, 361